Productivity Dynamics in Emerging and Industrialized Countries

The world, of late, has seen a productivity slowdown. Many countries continue to recover from various shocks in the macro business environment, along with structural changes and inward looking policies. In contemporary times of growth slumps, various exits and protectionist regimes, this book engages with the study of productivity dynamics in the emerging and industrialized economies. The essays address the crucial aspects, such as the roles of human capital, investment accounting and datasets, that help understanding of productivity performance of global economy and its several regions.

This book will be of interest to academics, practitioners and professionals in the field of economic growth, productivity and development studies. This will also be an important reference on empirical industrial economics in both India and the world.

Deb Kusum Das teaches at Ramjas College, University of Delhi. His research fields are productivity and growth in India, jobs and labor market, and empirical international trade. He received the EXIM Bank IEDRA Award 2004 for his doctoral dissertation, "Some Aspects of Productivity and Trade in Indian Industry". He holds a PhD from Delhi School of Economics and has studied at Delhi School of Economics and St Xavier's College, Kolkata. He is the co-founder of South Asia Economics Students Meet – a platform for undergraduate economics students of South Asia. He is also associated with ICRIER (Delhi) as an external researcher.

"This book represents a major contribution in enhancing our understanding of productivity trends across the globe. It combines general methodology and trends in aggregate growth worldwide with detailed analysis for specific regions and countries. Therefore, readers can trace the reasons for differential productivity growth and can contrast areas that witnessed rapid growth with those where the trends were more muted. This is a must-read for anyone interested in understanding growth and productivity in both emerging and industrialized economies."
—*Mary O'Mahony, King's College London, UK*

"More than ever, productivity is a leading topic on the analytical and policy agenda. The reason is simple: productivity growth and innovation shape the material well-being of economies and people. This book, with contributions from leading scholars, draws a broad picture of productivity dynamics and their determinants across the continents. An excellent reference for academics and practitioners alike!"
—*Paul Schreyer, OECD Paris, France*

"The papers collected in this volume are in honor of Professor K. L. Krishna, one of India's leading scholars in the field of development. Together they provide a broad outlook on economic growth and its determinants using state-of-the-art measurement frameworks. They cover a wide set of regions across the globe allowing for deep comparative analysis, with a special emphasis on India. The studies provide a valuable reference for practitioners and scholars interested in the sources of growth."
—*Marcel P. Timmer, Groningen University, Netherlands*

Productivity Dynamics in Emerging and Industrialized Countries

Edited by Deb Kusum Das

LONDON AND NEW YORK

First published 2018
by Routledge
2 Park Square, Milton Park, Abingdon, Oxon OX14 4RN

and by Routledge
711 Third Avenue, New York, NY 10017

Routledge is an imprint of the Taylor & Francis Group, an informa business

© 2018 selection and editorial matter, Deb Kusum Das; individual chapters, the contributors

The right of Deb Kusum Das to be identified as the author of the editorial material, and of the authors for their individual chapters, has been asserted in accordance with sections 77 and 78 of the Copyright, Designs and Patents Act 1988.

All rights reserved. No part of this book may be reprinted or reproduced or utilised in any form or by any electronic, mechanical, or other means, now known or hereafter invented, including photocopying and recording, or in any information storage or retrieval system, without permission in writing from the publishers.

Trademark notice: Product or corporate names may be trademarks or registered trademarks, and are used only for identification and explanation without intent to infringe.

British Library Cataloguing-in-Publication Data
A catalogue record for this book is available from the British Library

Library of Congress Cataloging-in-Publication Data
A catalog record has been requested for this book

ISBN: 978-1-138-74550-6 (hbk)
ISBN: 978-1-351-00254-7 (ebk)

Typeset in Sabon
by Apex CoVantage, LLC

Essays for Professor K. L. Krishna

Professor K. L. Krishna, addressed often by friends and students as "KLK", studied at the University of Chicago and pursued his doctoral dissertation on "Production Relations in Manufacturing" under Professor Zvi Grilliches. He taught at the Delhi School of Economics for over four decades and many generations of students have benefitted from his classes on applied research and econometrics. The list of his meritorious students include many of India's economists and policymakers. He supervised close to 40 research scholars for PhD and MPhil on many aspects of Indian economy, particularly economics of productivity, empirics of trade and industrial economics. In addition, he has guided students from different institutions from various corners of India by reading and commenting on their dissertations. Research scholars have gained from his inputs particularly in the areas of applied econometrics.

His expertise has been utilized by the Government of India in many committees which he chaired: Steering Committee for Annual Survey of Industries, 1998–99, 1999–2000; National Advisory Board on Statistics, 1990–94; Standing Committee on Industrial Statistics and as chairman of NSS 81st round. He also served as the President of the Indian Econometric Society in 1991. He has been a guiding spirit in development and growth of many prestigious research institutes in India like the Madras Institute of Development Studies (MIDS), Indira Gandhi Institute of Development Research (IGIDR), Institute of Economic Growth (IEG) and Centre for Economic and Social Studies (CESS).

After retirement from Delhi School of Economics, with zeal akin to that of a young scholar, Professor Krishna has been providing leadership to the INDIA KLEMS research project which aims to create a productivity database by industry and can be used to analyze India's industrial competitiveness in global markets. This book was conceived to celebrate his 80th birthday in 2015 as well as his leadership in creating the INDIA KLEMS database. At 83, when most prefer to walk into the sunset of their careers, he still remains young and enthusiastic to the challenges of research.

Contents

Lists of figures — xi
Lists of tables — xviii
Lists of contributors — xxiii
Preface — xxvi
Acknowledgements — xxviii
Abbreviations — xxix

Introduction — 1

PART I
Productivity and world economy: new insights — 35

1. The growth of the world economy — 37
   DALE W. JORGENSON

2. Productivity in the global economy — 58
   ABDUL A. ERUMBAN AND BART VAN ARK

3. Productivity growth in Asia and its country origins — 81
   KOJI NOMURA

4. Latin America: economic growth and productivity since the 1990s — 113
   ANDRE HOFMAN AND CLAUDIO ARAVENA

5. Human capital productivity — 140
   BARBARA M. FRAUMENI

6 Global growth accounting: the role of shifting
   investment patterns   154
   ABDUL A. ERUMBAN, ROBERT INKLAAR AND
   KLAAS DE VRIES

PART II
Productivity and growth – country experiences   175

7 Labor productivity and a test of the
   Kaldor-Verdoorn law in East Asia   177
   HAK K. PYO

8 Declining rate of return on capital and the role
   of intangibles in Japan: an empirical study
   using Japanese KLEMS (JIP) database   200
   TSUTOMU MIYAGAWA, MIHO TAKIZAWA, KONOMI
   TONOGI AND KYOJI FUKAO

9 The industry-level productivity of Taiwan
   in 1981–2010: evidence from Taiwan
   KLEMS database   230
   YIH-MING LIN, TSU-TAN FU, HSING-CHUN LIN,
   AND WEI-HSIN KONG

10 Total factor productivity and the sources of
   Singapore's economic growth: measurement,
   insights, and projection   275
   DALE W. JORGENSON AND KHUONG M. VU

11 Russia since 1995: natural gas, catching up
   and informality   313
   ILYA B. VOSKOBOYNIKOV

12 Accounting for the role of information and
   communication technology in China's
   productivity growth   331
   HARRY X. WU AND DAVID T. LIANG

13 Source of growth and structural changes
    in the Indian economy since 1980 363
    BISHWANATH GOLDAR

14 Productivity slowdown in Brazil 2000–13: general
    performance and sectoral contributions 398
    DAVID KUPFER AND THIAGO MIGUEZ

15 Argentina growth failure: an overview from
    ARKLEMS+LAND growth and productivity accounts 435
    ARIEL COREMBERG

16 Determinants of total factor productivity
    in Mexico: 1991–2014 467
    FRANCISCO GUILLÉN MARTÍN AND ALFREDO
    HENESTROSA OROZCO

17 What do we know about productivity in Arab
    economies: the challenges of generating multifactor
    productivity (MFP) estimates at industry level 487
    HOMAGNI CHOUDHURY AND DEB KUSUM DAS

PART III
India in the new global order: a productivity perspective 533

18 Dynamics of labor productivity in Indian industry:
    1980–2011 535
    SURESH CHAND AGGARWAL

19 Total factor productivity in Indian organized
    manufacturing: the story of the noughties 555
    PILU CHANDRA DAS

20 A state-level perspective of productivity growth
    of the Indian organized manufacturing sector 583
    PUSHPA TRIVEDI

21 Size and productivity in Indian manufacturing
 sector   605
 ARUP MITRA AND CHANDAN SHARMA

22 The challenges of "Make in India": does the
 investment climate matter for firm performance?   627
 RAJESH RAJ S.N. AND KUNAL SEN

Index   648

Figures

1.1	Contributions of industry groups to value-added growth, 1947–2012	45
1.2	Contributions of industry groups to value-added growth, 1995–2012	46
1.3	Contributions of individual industries to value-added growth, 1947–2012	47
1.4	Contributions of industry groups to productivity growth, 1947–2012	48
1.5	Contributions of industry groups to productivity growth, 1995–2012	49
1.6	Contributions of individual industries to productivity growth, 1947–2012	50
1.7	Sources of US economic growth, 1947–2012	52
1.8	Sources of US economic growth, 1995–2012	52
2.1	Growth rates of GDP, population, per capita GDP and labor productivity	59
2.2	Defining labor productivity and total factor productivity under growth accounting framework	61
2.3	Trend in labor productivity growth, 1970–2016	64
2.4	Sources of the global labor productivity growth – accumulation or assimilation	66
2.5	Contribution of individual countries to aggregate the global TFPG: Harberger diagram	71
3.1	PPP for capital and labor inputs relative to PPP for output in 2011	91
3.2	Impacts of price differential factors of capital and labor	95
3.3	Country origins of TFPG in entire Asia	102

4.1	Latin America and the Caribbean: evolution of the determinants of GDP growth measured with the modified growth accounting method, by subregion and period, 1990–2013	124
4.2	Latin America: relationship between the change in the contribution of capital to the growth of GDP and TFP, 2000–2013	126
5.1	Contributions to full gross private domestic product and economic growth with HC productivity and "deepening" components	149
6.1	ICT investment as a percentage of total ICT spending in select countries – communication equipment, 1992–2013	161
6.2	Non-ICT investment/GDP ratio (%) – advanced economies, emerging economies and world, 1990–2015	165
6.3	ICT investment/GDP ratio (%) – advanced economies, emerging economies and world, 1990–2015	167
6.4	Contribution of ICT capital services to GDP growth – advanced economies, emerging economies and world, 1990–2015	168
7.1	Effect of increase in the wage share in the post-Kaleckian model	182
8.1	Annual growth rate in capital formation in the recovery periods in Japan	201
8.2a	Growth accounting in Japan	202
8.2b	Growth accounting in the United States	203
8.2c	Growth accounting in Korea	204
8.2d	Growth accounting in the Republic of China	205
8.3	Movements in rate of return on capital	208
8.4	Capital/output ratio in Japan	209
8.5	Capital share in Japan	210
8.6a	Marginal rate of return on capital by industry (1980)	212
8.6b	Marginal rate of return on capital by industry (2012)	213
8.7a	Rates of return on capital in the chemical industry	214
8.7b	Rates of return on capital in the transportation equipment industry	215
8.7c	Rates of return on capital in the retail industry	215

8.7d	Rates of return on capital in the information service industry	216
8.8	Share of the service sector in intangible investment	221
8.9	Investments in human resources, 1980–2012	222
9.1	Overview of Taiwan's industrial development	233
9.2	Taiwan industrial structure, 1981–2010	241
10.1	GDP growth, 1965–2009	282
10.2	Price index: machinery and transport equipment	290
10.3	Price index: chemicals & chemical products	290
10.4	TFP growth	291
10.5	Manufacturing, value-added (% of GDP): Singapore vs. Hong Kong	294
10.6	Openness: Singapore vs. Hong Kong	295
11.1	Long run growth of the Russian economy (1990 = 100)	315
11.2	Inter-sectoral productivity variation and aggregate labor productivity levels in 1995	320
11.3	Labor reallocation in CEE and Russia (1995–2007)	321
11.4	The change of the number of workers in total economy and major sectors in 2000–13	322
11.5	Informal split, labor reallocation and aggregate labor productivity growth contributions to yearly average growth rates	324
12.1	China's production of ICT products vis-à-vis gross output of manufacturing	332
12.2	Total factor productivity index by ICT-specified group	344
12.3	Sources of gross output growth in China by ICT-specific industry group	344
12.4	An index of China's aggregate total factor productivity	349
12.5	Domar and non-Domar weighted factor input indices and reallocation effects	353
13.1	Growth rate in real GDP, India, 1981–82 to 2014–15	369
13.2	Share of broad sectors in aggregate GDP (at 2004–05 prices), India, 1980–2014	372
13.3	Relative share of different industries in Total GVA of the market services sector (at 2004–05 prices)	373

13.4	Relative shares of different industries in GVA of manufacturing sector (at 2004–05 prices)	375
13.5	TFP growth rate (percent per annum), Indian economy, by sub-period	381
13.6	Growth rate in real GVA (percent per annum), by sub-period	382
13.7	Double deflated GVA, aggregate economy and manufacturing, and share of manufacturing	383
13.8	Contribution of different industries to GVA growth acceleration in the period since 2003–04 (2003–11 minus 1980–2002) (percent per annum)	384
13.9	Contribution of different industries to aggregate level TFP growth acceleration in the period since 2003–04 (2003–11 minus 1980–2002) (percent per annum)	385
13.10	TFP growth rate, 1980–2002 and 2003–11, select KLEMS industries (percent per annum)	387
13.11	Changes in GDP growth rate and TFP growth rate (2008–14 vs. 2003–07), emerging economies, cross-country plot (percent per annum)	390
14.1	GDP annual growth rate – demand elements contributions (2001–13)	402
14.2	Productivity and GDP growth rates (2001–13)	404
14.3	Correlation between productivity and GFCF growth (2001–13)	405
14.4	Productivity evolution in selected countries (2000 = 100)	407
14.5	Sectoral labor productivity 2000–13 (2000 = 100)	408
14.6	Brazilian activities labor productivity shift-share 2000–13	415
14.7	Brazilian activities labor productivity shift-share 2000–04	416
14.8	Brazilian activities labor productivity shift-share 2004–10	417
14.9	Brazilian activities labor productivity shift-share 2010–13	418
15.1	GDP growth of Latin America, 1998–12	445
15.2	Source of Argentina economic growth	447

15.3	Source of Argentina capital service input contribution	448
15.4	Argentina labor input contribution by component	449
15.5	Source of Argentina economic growth	451
15.6	TFP of Argentina	453
15.7	Labor productivity in Argentina	454
15.8	Sources of Argentina's labor productivity growth	455
15.9	Industry origins of productivity slowdown, 1998–2010	456
16.1	Total factor productivity, 1991–2014 series (percentage annual growth rates)	469
16.2	Total factor productivity, the total factor contribution and gross output (percentage annual growth rates)	470
16.3	Contribution total factor (percentage annual growth rates)	470
16.4	Service cost of capital, 1991–2014 series (dollars)	473
16.5	Capital productivity, 1991–2014 series (dollars)	474
16.6	Capital income unit, 1991–2014 series (dollars)	475
16.7	Analytical indicators related to capital factor, series 1991–2014 (dollars)	476
16.8	Price of labor service, 1991–2014 series (dollars)	477
16.9	Labor productivity, 1991–2014 series (dollars)	478
16.10	Unit labor cost, 1991–2014 series (dollars)	479
16.11	Analytical indicators related to the labor factor, 1991–2014 series (dollars)	480
16.12	Primary sector: analytical indicators of the capital factor (dollars)	481
16.13	Primary sector: analytical indicators of the labor factor (dollars)	481
16.14	Secondary sector: analytical indicators of the capital factor (dollars)	482
16.15	Secondary sector: analytical indicators of the labor factor (dollars)	483
16.16	Tertiary sector: analytical indicators of the capital factor (dollars)	484
16.17	Tertiary sector: analytical indicators of the labor factor (dollars)	484
17.1	Arab countries had a low GDP per capita growth in the 1980s and 1990s	493

17.2	GDP growth in the Arab states (and three subregions) in the 2000s relative to the rest of the world	494
17.3	Employment elasticity with respect to output in the Arab World and Asia, 2000–10	495
17.4	Productivity gains in the Arab region in the 2000s in comparison to the rest of the world	495
17.5	Growth in GDP for Arab, MENA and other developing regions, 2010–14	497
17.6	Decade wise labor productivity growth for Egypt, Morocco, Tunisia and Middle East and North Africa, 1990–2014	514
17.7	Decade-wise MFP growth for Egypt, Morocco, Tunisia and Middle East and North Africa, 1990–2014	515
17.8	MFP growth and input growth for Egypt, Morocco and Tunisia, 1990–2014	516
17.9	MFP growth for Egypt, Morocco and Tunisia, 1960–2000	519
17.10	Decade-wise MFP growth for Egypt, Morocco and Tunisia, 1960–2000	520
18.1	Growth rate of labor productivity, 1980 to 2011 (% per annum)	543
18.2	Sources of labor productivity growth, 1980 to 2011 (% per annum)	547
18.3	Decomposition of labor productivity growth for the total economy based on gross output – 1980–2011 and subperiods	549
18.4	Labor reallocation effects in labor productivity decomposition	550
19.1	Sectoral share in aggregate registered manufacturing value added	569
19.2	Sectoral share in aggregate registered manufacturing employment	570
19.3	Ranges of TFP growth (2000–01 to 2008–09)	573
19.4	Average annual total factor productivity growth (2000–01 to 2008–09)	574
20.1	Contribution of states' MFG sector to India's MFG sector (2000–13)	586
20.2	Contribution of manufacturing sector in real SDP/GDP (2000–13)	586

21.1	Distributions of average log TFP levels for large firms vis-à-vis others	612
21.2	Distributions of average log TFP levels for small firms vis-à-vis others	613
22.A.1	Median labor productivity: firms with 10–49 workers	642
22.A.2	Median labor productivity: all firms	643

Tables

2.1	Sources of labor productivity growth, 2000–07 and 2008–15	68
3.1	PPPs for capital and labor inputs in 2011	88
3.2	Output, capital and labor inputs, and TFP of entire Asia	92
3.3	Sources of economic growth in entire Asia	94
3.4	Country origins of TFP growth in entire Asia	96
3.5	Country origins of output growth in entire Asia	99
3.6	Country origins of capital input growth in entire Asia	100
3.7	Country origins of labor input growth in entire Asia	101
3.8	TFP growth in entire Asia and country contributions	106
4.1	Latin America and developed countries (selected countries): labor productivity indicators, 1995–2007	116
4.2	Latin America and the Caribbean: contributions to GDP growth measured with the traditional growth accounting method, 1990–2013	120
4.3	Latin America: contributions to GDP growth measured with the modified growth accounting method, 1990–2013	122
4.4	Latin America (5 countries): disaggregation of gross fixed capital formation, selected years between 1995 and 2010	128
4.5	Latin America (5 countries): disaggregation of gross fixed capital formation by type of non-ICT asset, selected years between 1995 and 2010	129

4.6	Latin America (5 countries): determinants of growth in value added, by economic sector, 1990–2009	130
5.1	Comparison of human capital productivity change measures	144
5.2	International Standard Classification of Education (ISCED) definitions	146
5.3	Ratio of ISCED higher level to ISCED 2 in the United States J-F market lifetime income	147
5.4	Rates of growth of selected components	150
6.1	Asset breakdown of source data	156
6.2	Sources of ICT investment data	159
6.3	Depreciation rates (percent) by assets	162
6.4	Regression – Asset composition of investment and per capita income	170
7.1	Causality test between value added and labor productivity in EU	189
7.2	Causality test between income and labor productivity in East Asia	190
7.3	Unit root tests for real wages and labor productivity in East Asia (1970–2014)	191
7.4	Granger causality tests between real wages and labor productivity for Korea, Japan and China (1970–2014)	192
7.A.1	Empirical test results of the Kaldor-Verdoorn Law	194
7.A.2	Summary of the multiplier effects at the national and global level	195
7.A.3	Empirical tests on the effect of real wage on productivity growth	195
8.1	Variances and relative standard deviations in the average rate of return on capital	214
8.2	Summary statistics: market economy 1985–2012	218
8.3	Basic estimation results in the market economy	219
8.4	Estimation results by industry	220
8.A.1	Data definition	225
9.1	Industry value-added weights of primary, secondary, tertiary, and manufacturing industries by subperiod	240
9.2	Industry value added weights by selected year	242
9.3	Growth of industry value added by period	245
9.4	Growth of industry gross output by period	248

9.5	Growth of industry TFP by subperiod	250
9.6	Sources of industry output growth (in growth rate): 1981–2010	253
9.7	Sources of industry output growth (in % share): 1981–2010	255
9.8a	Sources of industry output growth (in growth rate): 1981–90	258
9.8b	Sources of industry output growth (in % share): 1981–90	260
9.9a	Sources of industry output growth (in growth rate): 1991–2000	262
9.9b	Sources of industry output growth (in % share): 1991–2000	264
9.10a	Sources of industry output growth (in growth rate): 2001–10	266
9.10b	Sources of industry output growth (in % share): 2001–10	268
9.11	Sources of GO growth for the electrical and optical equipment industry	270
9.12	Sources of GO growth for the wholesale and commission trade industry	270
9.13	Sources of GO growth for the post and telecommunications industry	271
10.1	Output and TFP growth in NICs from selected previous studies	276
10.2	Sources of GDP growth, 1965–2008	284
10.3	Sources of labor productivity growth, 1965–2008	285
10.4	TFPG estimated by Hsieh (2002) for the NICs	296
10.5	Selected indicators of economic development: Singapore vs. the United States	297
10.6	Projected productivity and output growth, 2009–19	299
11.1	Sources of economic growth of the Russian economy in 1995–2012 (contributions in p.p.)	317
11.2	Aggregate GDP growth and structural change in 1995–2012	319
11.3	Labor, capital services and MFP in 1995–2012, sectoral contribution	325
12.1	Sources of gross output growth in China by ICT-specific industry group	343

12.2	Sources of aggregate value-added growth in China, 1981–2012	348
12.3	Decomposition of aggregate labor productivity growth in China	350
12.4	Decomposition of China's aggregate total factor productivity growth: Domar-aggregation vis-à-vis factor reallocation effects	351
12.A.1	CIP/China KLEMS industrial classification and ICT-specific grouping	357
12.A.2	Industry contributions to value added and total factor productivity growth: 1981–2012	358
13.1	Trend growth rates in real GVA in various subperiods, aggregate Indian economy and broad sectors	371
13.2	Sources of growth, Indian economy, 1980–81 to 2011–12, by subperiod	379
13.A.1	List of KLEMS industries in India KLEMS database, 2015	393
14.1	Effects contributions to the Brazilian labor productivity growth rate (accumulated growth)	413
14.A.1	Activities labor share (% total)	423
14.A.2	Shift-share results for accumulated labor productivity growth rate, 2000–13	424
14.A.3	Shift-share results for accumulated labor productivity growth rate, 2000–04	426
14.A.4	Shift-share results for accumulated labor productivity growth rate, 2004–10	428
14.A.5	Shift-share results for accumulated labor productivity growth rate, 2010–13	429
16.1	Total factor productivity (percentage annual growth rates)	471
17.1	Selected macroeconomic indicators for Egypt, Morocco, Tunisia and MENA	491
17.2	GDP per capita growth and Inflation for Arab, MENA and other developing regions, 2010–14	492
18.1	Growth rate of labor productivity, 1980–2011	542
18.2	Sources of labor productivity growth, 1980–2011	545
18.3	Decomposition of labor productivity growth for the total economy based on gross output, 1980–2011 and subperiods	548

19.1	Selective productivity studies in India – a brief review	561
19.2	Industry contributions to aggregate GVA and LP growth	571
19.3	Average annual TFP growth, value-added share and industry contribution to aggregate GVA growth	575
19.4	Sources of output growth	577
20.1	Average share of nominal gross output of selected industries in total gross output of manufacturing output of the state/India (2000–01 to 2012–13)	588
20.2	Average share of employees in selected industries in total employees of the state (2000–01 to 2012–13)	589
20.3	Average annual growth rates of TFP (2000–01 to 2012–13)	592
20.4	Average annual growth rates of real gross output (2000–01 to 2012–13)	594
20.5	Ratio of annual average TFPG to annual average growth rate of real gross output (2000–01 to 2012–13)	595
20.6	Average annual growth rates of employment (2000–01 to 2012–13)	597
20.A.1	Selected states and their abbreviations used	600
20.A.2	Industry codes and description of selected industries	601
20.A.3	Codes of industries in various I-O matrices used for compiling input price index	602
21.1	Growth of output and TFP in broad sectors in 1960–2004 (% per annum)	606
21.2	Productivity growth at the aggregate level and across sectors (% per annum)	607
21.3	Data description	610
21.4	Production function estimation	611
21.5	Descriptive regression results	614
21.6	Determinants of TFP	615
21.7	Production function estimation	616
22.1	Construction of investment climate variables from the WBES	635
22.2	Regression results	638

Contributors

Suresh Chand Aggarwal is former Professor, Department of Business Economics, South Campus, University of Delhi, India.

Bart van Ark is Executive Vice President & Chief Economist, the Conference Board & Professor, University of Groningen, Netherlands.

Homagni Choudhury is Associate Professor in Economics, Head of the Department of Economics, Faculty of Arts and Social Sciences, Kingston University, London, UK.

Ariel Coremberg is Professor, Theory and Measurement of Economic Growth, University of Buenos Aires, Argentina.

Deb Kusum Das is Associate Professor, Ramjas College, University of Delhi, India.

Pilu Chandra Das is Assistant Professor, Kidderpore College, University of Calcutta, India.

Abdul A. Erumban is Senior Economist, the Conference Board & Assistant Professor, University of Groningen, Netherlands.

Claudio Aravena is affiliated with USACH and Economic Commission for Latin America and the Caribbean, ECLAC.

Barbara M. Fraumeni is affiliated with Central University for Finance and Economics, Beijing, China.

Tsu-tan Fu is Professor and the Dean of School of Business, Soochow University, Taiwan.

Kyoji Fukao is Professor, Institute of Economic Research, Hitotsubashi University, Japan.

Bishwanath Goldar is former Professor at Institute of Economic Growth, Delhi, India.

Francisco Gullen Martin is Economist, National Institute of Statistics and Geography, Mexico.

Alfredo Henestrosa Orozco is Economist, National Institute of Statistics and Geography, Mexico.

Andre Hofman is affiliated with University of Santiago, Chile, USACH.

Robert Inklaar is Professor of Economics, University of Groningen, Netherlands.

Dale W. Jorgenson is the Samuel W. Morris University Professor, Harvard University, USA.

Wei-hsin Kong is a research fellow, Agricultural Technology Research Institute, Taiwan.

David Kupfer is Associate Professor and Coordinator of Industry and Competitiveness Research Group, Federal University do Rio de Janeiro, Brazil.

David T. Liang is affiliated with Institute of Economic Research, Hitotsubashi University, Japan.

Hsing-chun Lin is Professor, Department of Applied Economics, National Chiayi University, Taiwan.

Yih-ming Lin is Professor, Department of Applied Economics, National Chiayi University, Taiwan.

Thiago Miguez is Economist, Brazilian Development Bank (BNDES) and the Industry and Competitiveness Research Group (GIC/IE/UFRJ).

Arup Mitra is Professor, Institute of Economic Growth, Delhi, India.

Tsutomu Miyagawa is Professor of Economics, Gakushuin University, Tokyo, Japan.

Koji Nomura is Professor, Keio University, Japan.

Hak K. Pyo is Professor of Economics Emeritus, Seoul National University, Seoul, South Korea.

Rajesh Raj S. N. is Associate Professor, Department of Economics, Sikkim University, Gangtok, Sikkim, India.

Kunal Sen is Professor, Institute for Development Policy and Management (IDPM), University of Manchester, UK.

Chandan Sharma is Associate Professor, Indian Institute of Management, Lucknow, India.

Miho Takizawa is Professor, Department of Economics, Toyo University, Tokyo.

Konomi Tonogi is Assistant Professor, Faculty of Economics, Rissho University, Japan.

Pushpa Trivedi is Professor and Institute Chair Professor, Department of Humanities and Social Sciences, Indian Institute of Technology Bombay, Mumbai, India.

Ilya B. Voskoboynikov is Senior Research Fellow, Higher School of Economics, National Research University, Moscow

Klaas de Vries is Associate Economist, The Conference Board.

Khuong M. Vu is Associate Professor, Lee Kuan Yew School of Public Policy, National University of Singapore.

Harry X. Wu is affiliated with Institute of Economic Research, Hitotsubashi University, Japan.

Preface

The world economy continues to recover from various shocks in the macro business environment alongside structural changes in the form of digitalization, globalization and tacit knowledge assuming importance and co-existing with inward looking populist changes in many economies of the world. The world of late has seen a productivity slowdown beginning from a period earlier than the global financial crisis; however, the rise of China and India in this new economic–political global world order continues to attract world attention. In the background of such a prevailing global world order, this book engages with the study of productivity dynamics in the emerging and industrialized economies. The empirics of understanding productivity improvements as a source of economic growth has a long legacy, and with the development of better and sophisticated methodologies and comparable datasets in recent past, the subject assumes importance and more so in difficult times of growth slumps, various exits and inward looking trade protectionist regimes.

The EU KLEMS project which tried to address why in the 1990s Europe lagged behind the United States in terms of productivity performance was the biggest attempt at understanding why productivity differs across nations. It was a collective effort of academics, statisticians and policymakers to provide fundamental policy insights into the changes which have occurred at the industry level in Europe, the United States and Japan over recent decades. Later the World KLEMS *initiative* of Professor Dale Jorgenson in allowing researchers in over 40 countries to develop a rich and detailed dataset called the KLEMS (K-capital, L-labor, E-energy, M-materials and S-purchased services) dataset gave a new direction to measurement of productivity and ensuing analysis of sources of economic growth. With several conferences (Harvard 2010, 2012, Tokyo 2014, Madrid 2016) and formation of regional forums – Asia KLEMS and Latin America KLEMS gave opportunity to regional scholars and academia to understand productivity dynamics at the industry level for individual countries. My involvement as a researcher in the India KLEMS research project provided me an opportunity to interact with leading scholars of *productivity* discipline all around the globe, and to learn from their papers about the country experiences and educate myself from various insights that their research offered. The book is a celebration of the knowledge sharing platform the WORLD KLEMS initiative has created.

The book showcases the analysis of growth and productivity patterns around the emerging and industrialized world, based on a growth accounting framework using the KLEMS dataset which provides databases on output, inputs and productivity at a detailed industry level, which is the new framework of productivity measurement. The essays in the book address some of the crucial aspects in productivity measurements – the roles of human capital and investment accounting that helps our understanding of productivity as a tool of economic performance in clearer and sharper terms. The performance of the global economy and its several regions – Asia as well as Latin America – continues to capture the contrasts in productivity and growth. The empirics of growth and the underlying causes are best explained by looking at various country studies. The essays on emerging markets, like China, India, Brazil, Argentina and Russia, are juxtaposed against industrialized countries of Asia, including Japan and Singapore, provide rich evidence on understanding the nature of growth observed by these economies. The case of India as the fastest of the emerging countries is a subject of intense study, especially after the major changes in economic policies were brought in 1980 and 1991, as a result of which interest in India as against China as the world's growth center assumes importance.

Acknowledgements

My first and foremost gratitude is to Professor K. L. Krishna, for his mentoring and leadership of the India KLEMS research initiative. On a personal level, I have benefitted immensely from his scholarship in his role as Advisor for my PhD and MPhil thesis and as a teacher at the Delhi School of Economics. These essays in this volume are dedicated to him and are a celebration of his scholarship that he continues to exhibit in his youthful age of 80-plus, when many prefer to retire to a quieter life. I also owe a debt of gratitude to Professor Dale Jorgenson, who with his World KLEMS initiative has given scholars of productivity research across the globe a platform to examine the dynamics of growth and undertake an in-depth analysis of sources of economic growth. I thank all authors for accepting my invitation to be part of this volume and providing original research papers. To Shoma Choudhury and the editorial office of Routledge, Taylor & Francis for making this volume a reality, a deeply felt note of thank you. To Kate Fornadel, your cooperation in helping me with last minute adjustments in the book is deeply appreciated. To Kumar Abhishek for assistance in coordinating as well as preparing the manuscripts till the final stage with inputs from Purushottam, Prashant Kumar and Anil. A warm thank you.

I am thankful to my wife, Soma, for the support she provided especially looking after the children while I spent time on this book. My children-twins Divit and Deetya, who will one-day, understand through this volume what it means to be blessed with a teacher who inspires, motivates, mentors and guides you like a parent.

Abbreviations

Abbreviation	Full Form
A&T	Andhra Pradesh & Telangana
AHVY	Baba Saheb Ambedkar Hastshilp Vikas Yojana
ALC	Average Labor Compensation
ALP	Average Labor Productivity
AMECO	Annual Macro-Economic Database
APF	Aggregate Production Function
APO	Asian Productivity Organization
APPF	Aggregate Production Possibility Frontier
ARKLEMS	Argentina K-capital, L-Labor, E-Energy, M-Materials and S-Services
ASI	Annual Survey of Industries
BEA	Bureau of Economic Analysis (USA)
BLS	Bureau of Labor Statistics (USA)
BRIC	Brazil, Russia, India and China (now BRICS)
BRICS	Brazil, Russia, India, China and South Africa
C&M	Commodities and Input Materials
CAPMAS	Central Agency for Public Mobilization and Statistics (Egypt)
CEEs	Central and East European Economies
CEPALSTAT	Comisión Económica para América Latina y el Caribe STAT
CFM	Commodity Flow Method
CHEM	Chemicals and Chemical Products
CIP	China Industrial Productivity
CMOS	Complementary Metal Oxide on Silicon
ConM	Contribution Share from Materials
ConS	Contribution Share from Services

CPI	Consumer Price Index
CSLS	Centre for the Study of Living Standards (Canada)
CSO	Central Statistics Office
DD	Double Deflation
DEA	Data Envelopment Analysis
EBO	Gross Operating Surplus
ECLAC	Economic Commission for Latin America and the Caribbean
EKS	Èltetö-Köves-Szulc method
ERS	Economic Research Service
ESA	European System of Accounts
EU	European Union
EU KLEMS	European Union K-capital, L-Labor, E-Energy, M-Materials and S-Services
EUS	Employment and Unemployment Surveys
FBT	Food, Beverages and Tobacco
FDI	Foreign Direct Investment
FPF	Factor Price Frontier
GA	Growth Accounting
GAA	Growth Accounting Approach
GDP	Gross Domestic Product
GEAD	Generalized Exactly Additive Decomposition
GFCF	Gross Fixed Capital Formation
GGDC	Groningen Growth and Development Center
GNI	Gross National Income
GO	Gross Output
GSDP	Gross State Domestic Product
GVA	Gross Value Added
GVO	Gross Value of Output
HP	Hodrick-Prescott Filter
HR	Human Resource
HSIP	Hsinchu Science-Based Industrial Park
I-O	Input-Output
ibid	in the same place
ICP	International Comparison Programme
ICRIER	Indian Council for Research on International Economic Relations
ICT	Information and Communication Technology
IDA	Infocomm Development Authority (Singapore)
IHDP	International Human Dimensions Program

ILO	International Labor Organization
IMF	International Monetary Fund
INDEC	National Statistics and Censuses Institute (Argentina)
INDSTAT	Industrial Statistics Database
INEGI	National Institute of Statistics and Geography (Mexico)
INS	Institute National De la Statistique (Tunisia)
IOTT	Input-Output Tables
IPEA	Institute of Applied Economic Research (Brazil)
ISCED	International Standard Classification of Education
ISI	Import Substitution Industries
ISIC	International Standard Industrial Classification
IT	Information Technology
ITAM	Mexico Autonomous Institute of Technology
ITC	International Trade Center
ITRI	Industrial Technology Research Institute
IVIE	Instituto Valenciano de Investigaciones Económicas
IWR	Inclusive Wealth Report
J-F	Jorgenson-Fraumeni
JGF	Jorgenson, Gallop and Fraumeni
JHS	Jorgenson, Ho and Stiroh
JIP	Japan Industrial Productivity
KIP	Korea Industrial Productivity
KLEMS	K-capital, L-Labor, E-Energy, M-Materials and S-Services
LA KLEMS	Latin America K-capital, L-Labor, E-Energy, M-Materials and S-Services
LCU	Local Currency Unit
LP	Labor Productivity
MENA	Middle East and North African Economies
METAL	Metal and Metal Products
MFG	Manufacturing
MFN	Most Favored Nation
MFP	Multifactor Productivity
MFPG	Multifactor Productivity Growth
MNCs	Multinational Corporations

MPIC	Ministry of Planning and International Co-Operation (Egypt)
MSMEs	Micro, Small and Medium Enterprises
MTE	Machinery and Transport Equipments
NAICS	North American Industry Classification System
NAS	National Accounts Statistics
NEC	Not Elsewhere Classified
NIC	National Industrial Classification
NICs	Newly Industrialized Countries
NIMZs	National Manufacturing Investment Zones
NIPAs	National Income and Product Accounts
NMP	National Manufacturing Policy
NOE	Non-Observed Economy
NSI	National Statistics Institute
NSIP	National Science and Technology Project
NSSO	National Sample Survey Office
NTBs	Non-Tariff Barriers
OECD	Organization for Economic Co-operation and Development
OMC	Organisation Mondiale Du Commerce (or WTO)
pcpa	percent per annum
PFA	Production Function Approach
PIAAC	Program for International Assessment of Adult Competencies
PIM	Perpetual Inventory Method
PISA	Program for International Student Assessment
PPF	Production Possibility Frontier
PPI	Producer Price Index
PPP	Purchasing Power Parity
PT	Refined Petroleum Products
PWT	Penn World Table
QR	Quantitative Restriction
R&D	Research and Development
RCA	Radio Corporation of America
RIETI	Research Institute of Economy, Trade and Industry
SD	Single Deflation
SDP	State Domestic Product
SF&F	Semi-finished and Finished manufactures
SFA	Stochastic Frontier Approach

SMEs	Small and Medium Enterprises
SNA	System of National Accounts
SOEs	State Owned Enterprises
STD	Statistics Directorate (OECD)
SUT	Supply-Use Tables
TCB	The Conference Board
TCF	Total Contribution Factor
TED	Total Economy Database
TFC	Total Factor Contribution
TFP	Total Factor Productivity
TFPG	Total Factor Productivity Growth
TLI	Translog Index
TRAD	Traditional Shift-Share Method
TSMC	Taiwan Semiconductor Manufacturing Company Limited
UK	United Kingdom
ULC	Unit Labor Cost
UMC	United Microelectronics Corporation
UN	United Nations
UNCTAD	United Nations Conference on Trade and Development
UNDESA	United Nations Department of Economic and Social Affairs
UNEP	United Nations Environment Program
UNIDO	United Nations Industrial Development Organization
UNU	United Nations University
UPSS	Usual Principal and Subsidiary Status
USA	United States of America
USDA	United States Department of Agriculture
VA	Value Added
WBES	World Bank Enterprise Survey
WIOD	World Input-Output Database
WITSA	World Information Technology and Services Alliance
WPI	Wholesale Price Index
WTO	World Trade Organization

Introduction

"Productivity isn't everything, but in the long run it is almost everything. . . ."

Paul Krugman (1994)

Background

The world economy today is still recovering from various shocks of the global financial crisis in 2008–09 and its aftermath – the collapse of the Lehman Brothers, the Greek debt problem and its development into the European debt crisis, and Brexit. Following on, both the world GDP growth rate and world trade volume have remained sluggish, with the result that unemployment rates have increased in advanced economies. In recent times, a slowdown stood out among emerging economies, especially in 2013; however, the two countries which have come most strongly through the financial crisis are China and India. The Latin American countries performed better than during the phase of Asian financial crisis – the policy responses during the recent global slowdown were different in terms of monetary and fiscal expansion (Alvarez and De Gregorio 2014). The Asian economies, which have become increasingly autonomous from the Western economies and even contributed to stabilizing the global economy at the time of the global financial crisis, have been maintaining a stable economic growth rate of 5.3 percent per annum on average during 2010–14 (Nomura 2017).

The World Economic Outlook (October 2016) projects global growth to recover to 3.4 percent in 2017. As regards the advanced countries, we find damage control policy measures at place since the subprime crisis in the United States. These economies, however, still continue to struggle with low growth, investment and productivity in part based on uncertainty on policy fronts. Further, with the exit of Britain from the EU, world economies are in for another adjustment subsequent to global financial crisis. The climb to periods of high and sustainable growth prospects differ sharply across countries and regions, with emerging Asia in general and India in particular showing robust growth. The new world order seems to indicate the rise of Asia. The new world order will look very different in 2020. Asia will boast three of the four biggest economies in the world and the largest economies in descending order would be China, the United States, India, Japan, Russia, Germany, Brazil and the United Kingdom, based on shares of world GDP expressed in current purchasing power parity (PPP; Jorgenson 2005).

In the years following the Great Recession, productivity has been on the slowdown in developed countries, especially the United States and Europe.[1] Cette et al. (2016) argue that factors which helped advance productivity in the United States were a burst of innovation and reallocation related to the production and use of information technology in the second-half of the 1990s and the early 2000s.[2] For Europe, the authors contended that both shocks and institutions were equally responsible for slowdown in productivity. In particular, the ICT revolution, where Europe generally struggled to keep up pace and convergence process in terms of interest rates within the euro zone required more flexibility in labor- and product-market institutions, which were missing. The emerging Asia, on the other hand, contributed to stabilizing the global economy at the time of the Global Crisis but the two giants suffered productivity decline of different magnitudes.[3] In major Organisation for Economic Co-operation and Development (OECD) countries, productivity levels had begun declining even prior to the global slowdown. Some key aspects of the productivity decline according to OECD (2015) are a decline in the contribution of human capital accumulation to GDP growth, and contribution of capital deepening slowed after 2000 in the United States, Europe, Korea and Japan, and this pattern was accentuated during the post-2007 crisis period. Capital accumulation remained robust in Australia and Canada, partly reflecting the significant ramp-up in mining sector investment to fuel the capital-intensive boom in China and India.

The book: objective and structure

Against this background, the collection of chapters which attempts to understand the economics of growth across the world economy specifically focusing on the productivity dynamics in emerging and industrialized economy offers fresh insights into the new global order and its associated dynamics in improving our understanding of the productivity potentials of the countries which form the core of the new world order. The volume is structured in three different sections and allows diverse research ideas to bind into an overall theme to explore *How is the productivity challenge being faced to understand the growth dynamics across the world?*

The first section provides an account of the datasets, including human capital and investment in shaping our perceptions of productivity changes in the world order. In addition, global productivity trends, together with regional trends especially in Asia and Latin America, give us insights into productivity dynamics in the global world. Beginning in 2009, on one hand, countries in the south American region are witnessing sharp economic downturn and economic problems are pressing for political change and, on the other hand, Asia's march to prosperity is being led by China and India. The country studies form the second section of the volume and cover both advanced economies like Japan, Korea, Singapore and Taiwan as well as major emerging economies like India, China, Brazil, Mexico, Russia and Argentina. The country chapters provide a rich array of issues that form the core of productivity dynamics in these economies – Kaldor-Verdoorn Law, tangibles and rate of return, informality and catch up, structural change, natural capital, capital services, measurement challenges and manufacturing growth. The final section is an effort to understand the productivity dynamics from an Indian perspective. The emphasis here is on labor quality, manufacturing productivity and state-level perspective on manufacturing productivity, size-productivity relationship and investment climate for "Make in India". All of these together attempt to unearth why India is considered to lead the emerging nations growth prospects in the next 20 years.

The different sections of the book are, however, bound together by two important aspects of modern productivity analysis – Disaggregated Industry Analysis using KLEMS dataset, and Comparative Country Studies that holds promise as a research agenda for both scholars and policymakers. The book highlight three important issues which underlie the chapters of this book: (1) the availability of detailed data sets, which allows in-depth analysis of crucial research questions/hypotheses; (2) country perspectives on sources of growth so as to enable an understanding of how the productivity dynamics evolves in different economic systems; and (3) the crucial economic features which explore why India is considered to be a major emerging economy of the world. To understand these aspects, we have structured this introduction in terms of three themes which form the core of the book: (1) Productivity measurement using comprehensive industry-level country datasets: The KLEMS approach; (2) Country perspectives on sources of growth; and (3) India in the new economic order. The final section provides a summary of the chapters and conclusions of the volume.

Fresh insights into productivity measurement using comprehensive industry-level country datasets: the KLEMS approach

Productivity measurement has been an important research agenda for both scholars and policymakers beginning with the seminal paper by Tinbergen (1942). However, over the last 60 years, several significant research in the field of productivity measurement and sources of growth analytics have shaped the modern research agenda of productivity measurement and analysis. Two pioneering papers – first by Robert Solow (1957), *Technical Change and Aggregate Production function*, and second by Dale Jorgenson et al. (1987), *Productivity and US Economic Growth* – showcased in-depth industry-level measurement and analysis of multifactor productivity. These groundbreaking advances in the domain of productivity research were to shape the understanding of postwar economic growth in the United States, the slowing of growth in Europe and the advances of emerging economies in a globalized world. Further, a satisfactory explanation of the sources of economic growth required a detailed sectoral analysis of the sources of TFP growth.[4]

The publication of the OECD manual on productivity (2001) constituted another landmark in the evolution of productivity measurement. It was the first comprehensive guide aimed at statisticians, researchers and policymakers to understand the nuances of constructing productivity indicators. The manual provided theoretical foundations of productivity measurement and alongside with it, detailed specifications of output and input measures.[5] The resurgence of the American economy post 1995 was against all expectations and raised serious questions about the sustainability of American economic performance. The research of Jorgenson et al. (2005) established that in the postwar period, America's economic growth was driven by investment. The investment in information technology accounted for a significant portion of America's growth and within information technology it was the role of computers that allowed America to have faster growth. The late 1990s witnessed differences in comparative growth performance between the United States and Europe. The slowing down of growth in Europe led to an action program of the European Commission called the "Lisbon Agenda" which aimed at restoring European competitiveness and productivity through innovation. Against this background, a research project called EU KLEMS was initiated to the study of productivity in the European Union. The EU KLEMS project aimed at creating a database on measures of economic growth, productivity, employment creation, capital formation and technological change at the industry level for all European Union member states from 1970 onward. The database will provide an important input to policy evaluation, in particular for the assessment of the goals concerning competitiveness and economic growth potential as established by the Lisbon and Barcelona Summit goal. A significant outcome of the project was the attempt to explain the distinctive reasons for European productivity slowdown and US acceleration since 1990s. Timmer et al. (2010)[6] base their explanations in accounting for slowdown in Europe vis-à-vis the United States on three different aspects – structural change and slowdown, market services and EU–US gap, and European diversity.

The shift of the balance in world economy from the industrialized countries to the emerging economies of Asia constitutes the new world order. The reforms undertaken in the last three decades in China and India have made the two Asian giants the front runners to the world's fastest-growing economy. There is today renewed emphasis on understanding the sources of growth all over again in order to examine the productivity dynamics in the Asian century. Jorgenson and Vu (2011) show that the world economy is undergoing a transformation where the new economic order is shifting toward the emerging economies of Asia, particularly China and India, and provides evidence of a new world economic order.[7]

Finally, underlying the modern research agenda outlined above is the development of KLEMS datasets – an international initiative to understand the growth empirics in the current economic scenario at a disaggregated level.[8] The construction of country datasets in association with national statistical agencies started as a research project to understand why Europe lagged behind the United States in terms of its economic growth and has now become the research agenda of explaining the dynamics of the emerging countries' high rates of economic growth despite global recession and other factors. The purpose of the World KLEMS dataset is to generate industry-level datasets, which allow measurement of multifactor productivity at the disaggregate industry level. The empirics of productivity measurement use the growth accounting framework, which in turn is rooted in the economic theory of production. The KLEMS production function uses a measure of output – gross output relative to a broad range of inputs, capital (K), labor (L), energy (E), materials (M) and service inputs (S).

The data on output, inputs and productivity at the industry level is crucial for understanding the sources of economic growth and the nature of structural change in the economy. The dataset with special focus on types of inputs – labor, capital, energy, material and services – provide a detailed examination of the contribution of each of these inputs into our understanding of the sources of growth. Further, the database can be used for analytical and policy-related purposes, in particular by studying the relationship between skill formation, technological progress and innovation on the one hand, and productivity on the other. The databases are now available for more than 40 countries worldwide, including China and India, the two largest emerging economies along with Russia and Brazil of the BRIC consortium.

Country perspectives on sources of growth

The world witnessed a growth slowdown in the post-global financial crisis period. The World Economic Outlook (WEO, April 2017) projects some recovery in 2018. The developments in the United States and China still remain crucial to reviving the world's growth. It is now also well known that the emergence of Asia is changing the world economic order, and the experience of Japan and the four Asian Tigers have pointed out that the growth centers can emerge outside of Europe and North America. An important challenge in analyzing growth across diverse countries in terms of economic maturity is the availability of comparable datasets.[9]

It is important to examine today – what is holding back the climb back to high growth in most parts of the globe? We have seen in the past few years that investment growth has slowed down in both developed and developing countries, and there has been sharp contraction across industries in these economies. Further, we have seen that investment has direct bearing on innovation, skills and infrastructure, and through these impacts on labor productivity. In addition to investment, world trade has also slowed down considerably since the global recession.[10] Some of the explanation for the slowdown lies in structural change, cyclical factors and also slow progress of trade liberalization. Other factors could be in regional aspects of growth.

Against this background, there seems much to explore and understand from the diverse growth experiences across the emerging and industrialized countries – East Asia, Japan, China, Taiwan, India and Singapore. In addition, some of the emerging market economies – Brazil and Russia – are expected to contribute to the new growth discourse following the recovery process from the global recession of 2007–09. Latin American countries also show promise in terms of improvements in growth in the 2000s and examination of the growth story in some of the large emerging markets – Mexico, Argentina and Brazil – would provide deeper insights into the world economy in the period of post-global recession. Therefore, the search for the main drivers of growth in these countries across the world economy forms a significant challenge in identifying the growth dynamics in these nations. It is expected that growth in emerging and developing economies will lead the return to high and sustainable rates of growth, but weak investments and productivity growth are the challenges that must be overcome if emerging economies are to lead this growth. The next section addresses the substantive issues in understanding the country perspectives of economic growth – the role of total factor productivity in explaining the growth performances. In addition, issues like tangible versus intangible capital in growth dynamics, labor productivity, informality, catching up and the role of land in understanding growth are examined.

India in the new global economic order

India's growth story

Today, India and China are considered to be the leading emerging economies of the world. After surpassing the growth rate of China, India has emerged as one of the major growing economies in the world. A comparison among BRICS countries shows India's economic growth rate was well above those of Brazil, Russia and South Africa. In addition, India's economic growth has not been much impacted by global recession – during 2003–07, the high-growth phase, the average growth rate in India's GDP was 8.2 percent and during 2008–15, it was 6.9 percent, lower by about 1.3 percentage points. The economic policy reforms undertaken since 1991 have encompassed sectors of the Indian economy – trade, industry, agriculture and finance. The objective of the reforms was to enhance India's global competitiveness. Overall, the economy registered a moderate TFP growth of 1 percent per annum during the period 1980–2011 without much fluctuation for the last three decades. Services seemed to be the main driver of this growth engine during 1990s and 2000s; however, the manufacturing sector witnessed a productivity growth of more than 2 percent during the 2000s. This is due in large part to the lagged effect of policy reforms initiated in 1991–92 in industry and trade and consolidation by successive governments. There is mixed evidence that points to policy reforms such as industrial de-licensing, tariff reductions, FDI liberalization or lifting of small-scale industry reservations and their resulting impact on manufacturing productivity. Therefore, an understanding of the barriers that inhibit manufacturing productivity growth becomes crucial if the government's policy initiative of "Make in India"[11] is to be successful.

Making India globally competitive

The emphasis of the present government as part of the "Make in India" policy initiative is to create a manufacturing hub in India. Barriers still remain in making India a functional manufacturing hub, especially in the form of poor core infrastructure, including power, ports and roads, land acquisition and labor market flexibility, which continue to challenge manufacturing performance, and manufacturing still accounts for only 16 percent of GDP, comparing weakly to other Asian countries of similar economic maturity. The need to raise the global competitiveness of the Indian manufacturing sector remains a significant policy agenda. One of the channels to improve global competitiveness is to improve the productivity performance of the Indian economy, especially the manufacturing sector. The India KLEMS research initiative supported by the Reserve Bank of India attempts to create a database of variables crucial for productivity measurement at the industry level. The core of the project includes – (1) The creation of database from 1980–81 onward for estimating productivity at the disaggregated industry level for the Indian economy and (2) Estimation of labor productivity and multifactor productivity for 26 industries as well as for broad sectors of the Indian economy, including manufacturing and services. The estimates of productivity – both labor as well as multifactor at the industry level – is expected to provide fundamental policy insights into the changes which have occurred at the industry level for Indian economy. In addition, the database will support empirical research on various aspects of economic growth in India, particularly job creation and productivity as well as investment, technological progress and innovation, and its impact on productivity. This will facilitate the formulation of policies aimed at encouraging economic growth and, in turn, global competiveness.

The way forward

In the two decades since reforms, we have observed large-scale progress in enhancing economic growth, reducing poverty and diversifying exports from textiles and leather to services exports, notably IT software. The road ahead for the Indian economy has many challenges which need to be overcome if India is to continue its march for the fastest growing economy. India is a classic case of growth without employment – *"Jobless growth"*. There are several issues that need examination in order to answer this – the reforms in the labor market still remain an unfinished agenda. The employment of contract workers in large numbers across most manufacturing factories seems to reflect the prevailing stringency of chapter VB of the Industrial Disputes Act. The rapid decline in labor intensity across labor-intensive manufacturing remains another issue that needs attention for India's concern of labor-intensive exports. The lack of quality employment also assumes significance, given that employers are unable to find skills commensurate with the jobs in place. Several other issues remain – land markets, need for good roads, ports, etc., along with electricity generation and business not out of captive power plants, which seems to be the norm in manufacturing plants. The last two years – 2015 as well as 2016 – also witnessed several reforms in the economy in areas of foreign direct investment, for enterprises in the category of micro, medium and small, e-biz portals for industrial sectors, infrastructures and also textiles and other export sectors. These, together with the goods and services tax (GST), by creating a national market will set India on the path to "Make in India" thereby allowing continuation of growth ahead of other competitor countries, and sustaining the high growth rate achieved.

Book summary and contribution

The book presents diverse range of issues to explain the productivity dynamics across the world economy, covering selectively both emerging and industrialized countries. The first section of the book presents fresh insights into productivity performance from both a global and regional perspective. The chapters in this section highlight the establishment of the KLEMS framework for productivity measurement at disaggregated industry level allowing comparisons of growth performance within and between world regions. The country studies form the core of the second section of the book – countries from all world regions have been included to portray the nuances of growth and productivity analysis specific to the needs and data availability in individual countries. The list of Asian countries includes the major economies of China, India and Japan, as well as countries from East Asia, including Korea, Taiwan and Hong Kong. The Latin American countries are well represented in terms of growth experiences of Argentina, Brazil and Mexico. The European zone from where bulk of the EU KLEMS studies originates find presence in the form of Russia. Finally, we observed that there is hardly any rigorous study that explains the African source of growth and we document this via sharing the growth patterns of Morocco, Egypt and Tunisia. The final section attempts to understand the growth dynamics in India and also why the Indian economy is poised to be the leading economy in the future. The range of essays covered here includes dynamics of labor productivity across industrial sectors, state-level perspective on manufacturing TFP, and size productivity and investment behavior in firms across India.

Fresh insights in measuring productivity

Chapter 1 (Growth of the world economy) by Dale Jorgenson outlines that the new framework for productivity measurement reveals that replication of established technologies explains by far the largest proportion of US economic growth. Replication takes place through the augmentation of the labor force and the accumulation of capital. Further, international productivity comparisons reveal similar patterns for the world economy; its major regions; and leading industrialized, developing and emerging economies. The World KLEMS Initiative has made it possible to extend these comparisons to countries around the world, including important emerging and transition economies. Industry-level production accounts are now prepared on a regular basis by national statistical agencies in Australia, Canada, Denmark, Finland, Italy, Mexico, the Netherlands, Sweden and the United Kingdom, as well as the United States. These accounts provide current information about the growth of outputs, inputs and productivity at the industry level and can be used in international comparisons of patterns of structural change like those presented by Jorgenson and Timmer (2011).

During the last three decades, the global economy has undergone significant transformation due to a number of dynamics, including the emergence of China and India as major growth contributors, the higher degree of globalization and the increased penetration of information and communication technology (ICT). During the 1993–2000 period, when the global economy grew at 3.2 percent, the emerging markets overtook the advanced economies. This trend continued during the 2000–07 period, with advanced economies seeing a growth rate of 2.6 percent – more than half a percentage lower than the previous period and the emerging markets increasing their growth rate by nearly 2.5 percentage points to 6.1 percent, resulting in a global growth of 4.2 percent. During the post financial crisis period from 2008 to 2015, growth in the global economy has slowed to 2.7 percent, with the emerging markets growing at 4.5 percent on average, and advanced economies by less than 1 percent. Against this background, Abdul Azeez Erumban and Bart Van Ark in Chapter 2 (Productivity in global economy) examine the global trends in total factor productivity (TFP). The objective of this paper is twofold. The first is to identify which proximate sources account for the slowdown in global labor productivity growth. For this purpose, they use The Conference Board's Total Economy Database™ (TED), which is specifically designed for international comparison of output and productivity, and which provides a unique opportunity to apply a growth accounting methodology at a global level. The paper identifies the sources of labor productivity growth in terms of factor accumulation and total factor productivity in about 125 individual countries for the period 1980–2016. Subsequently, the paper discusses various explanations, including the ones already available in the literature, for the ongoing declines in the global productivity, and provides insights on potential strategies that can change the gear toward improving productivity growth.

The Asian economy, which has become increasingly autonomous from the Western economies and even contributed to stabilizing the global economy at the time of the global financial crisis, has been maintaining a stable economic growth of 5.3 percent per annum on average during 2010–14. Yet, this represents a slowdown of one percentage point from the level recorded in the pre-crisis period; the study by Koji Nomura (Chapter 3: Productivity growth in Asia and its country origins) indicates that it is mainly due to the reduction in the growth of TFP of the Asian economy using a productivity index for "Entire Asia", which is defined as a group of 21 Asian countries, for the period of 1970–2014 and decomposing it to its country origins. The study showcases notable measurement improvement in the form of the development of the purchasing power parities (PPPs) for capital and labor inputs for Asian countries. Diewert and Fox (2014) recommend using the annual PPP information to adjust the country value shares in aggregating outputs across countries, taking price differentials in outputs across countries into consideration. A similar framework is applied for aggregating capital and labor inputs across countries in this paper. In developing the growth accounting framework for entire Asia, output and capital and labor inputs growths by country are aggregated, taking into account the price differentials not only in outputs, but also in capital and labor inputs across countries.

Chapter 4 (Latin America – economic growth and prosperity since 1990s) by Andre Hofman and Claudio Aravena attempts to explore the growth path of Latin America and Caribbean countries. The nature of economic growth since 1990 has been very different in Latin America and India – low and volatile growth in Latin America and the Caribbean, and sustained high growth in India. The analysis presented in this chapter helps explain the factors behind these different performances, and discusses the challenges Latin America and India face in achieving long-term growth, taking the most immediate determinants into account. A number of exercises, designed to quantify the factors that have driven growth, were therefore carried out on the basis of a "growth accounting" approach. The aim of this analysis is to identify elements that can help gear public policies toward raising growth rates sustainably for the economies of Latin America and the Caribbean. In all countries, the labor input that contributed most to value added was the number of hours worked, with the quality of labor much less influential. This contribution of labor was concentrated in the non-tradable services sectors, mainly commerce, financial and business services, and construction. The number of hours worked in the manufacturing sector rose very slightly in all countries except Mexico, where it fell. Labor quality improved in all sectors in four countries, although in Colombia this indicator decreased in some activities. In the primary sector, in keeping with the usual patterns of structural change observed elsewhere, the number of hours worked generally rose very slightly or decreased, while the quality of labor registered some improvement. The more disaggregated exercise reported above, covering nine sectors in five countries, found that TFP was generally negative during the study period. The main exception was Argentina, in which TFP was positive in five of the nine sectors considered, although it was negative for the economy as a whole. In four of the five countries studied, the sectors with the lowest levels of TFP were those in which capital made a greater contribution to growth in value added: the mining sector in Argentina and Brazil; electricity, gas and water in Chile; and transport and communications in Colombia. This could be a sign that weaker value-added growth in the region might be due not only to a low level of investment, but also to its sectoral allocation and management, two areas in which further study is required.

Human capital has long been recognized as an important contributor to economic growth. The human capital literature is extensive. Barbara Fraumeni (Chapter 5: Human capital productivity) addresses two questions: (1) how is human capital measured? and (2) how should the contribution of human capital to economic growth be measured? The answer to the first question provides a framework for the answer to the second question. In addition, the chapter provides estimates of human capital productivity change and the relationship between human capital productivity change and multifactor productivity change. The author tries to drive the point that much attention has been paid to labor productivity, but little to human capital productivity. As human capital productivity tells us about the future potential of a country and its sustainability, it is important that more attention is paid to this subject. As the chapter demonstrates, estimates of human capital productivity change can vary widely depending upon what measure of human capital is used. Also, economists should think carefully about how to formulate production functions if human capital is to be included and consider the relationship between human capital productivity change and present and future multifactor productivity change. The opportunities for further research are substantial.

Chapter 6 (Global growth accounting: the role of shifting investment patterns) of the first segment by Abdul Azeez Erumban, Robert Inklaar and Klaas de Vires argues that accounting for the sources of economic growth on a global scale has long been held back by missing or inadequate information about the asset composition of investment for many countries. This chapter details the construction of a new, comprehensive dataset on investment by asset across nearly all countries in the world. This dataset fills an important gap in cross-country data, as such data are not compiled in a comprehensive fashion by organizations such as the World Bank or United Nations, and researchers also commonly rely on shortcuts, such as assuming there is only a single, homogenous asset type. The authors combine data from a large range of national and international sources and supplement official, national accounts data by estimates from outside data compilers (WITSA) and estimates using the Commodity-Flow Method. The chapter confirms earlier studies, which found that advanced economies tend to investment in high-cost (and thus high-return) assets like machinery at a greater rate than do emerging economies. Further, it shows that this result extends to investment in ICT assets as well. This raises the question of why emerging economies are not investing at a higher rate, as this would (presumably) allow them to achieve faster economic growth.

Understanding growth and productivity: country perspectives

The second section of the book attempts to explore and understand the sources of growth and productivity in different countries – some emerging and some industrialized. The selection of countries is guided by the usage of KLEMS database in addressing the important question of "Growth". Our coverage of European Union is limited to Russia – one of the BRIC countries that underwent a transformation from planned to market economy in the 1980s, though the creation of KLEMS dataset began around mid-1990s in almost all major EU economies.[12] The contribution in these sections raises several interesting hypotheses regarding the growth patterns in these countries.

Chapter 7 (Labor productivity and a test of Kaldor-Verdoorn Law in East Asia) by Hak K. Pyo attempts to investigate the causality between aggregate demand and labor productivity, and examine the implication of the Kaldor-Verdoorn Law in East Asia using databases for three East Asian countries (China, Japan and Korea). He finds that the Kaldor-Verdoorn Law is partly accepted from the data set of China and Korea, and also the causality of real wages on labor productivity growth from the dataset of China and Korea, but not from the data set of Japan. The causality test was carried out with the data set of four East Asian countries. The Kaldor-Verdoorn Law is accepted with the causality running from aggregate income (demand) growth to labor productivity growth in Korea (both annual and quarterly data), Japan (quarterly data) and China (annual data). It is not accepted in Japan (annual data) or Taiwan (annual data). The reverse causality is accepted only in Korea (both annual and quarterly data) and Japan (annual data). Therefore, one can conclude that the Kaldor-Verdoorn Law is partly accepted in East Asia and has mixed evidence. Further, the causality test results accept the existence of causality from real wages to labor productivity in Korea and China but not in Japan. The reverse causality from labor productivity growth to real wage increase seems non-existent in all East Asian countries.

Chapter 8 (Declining rate of return on capital and role of intangibles in Japan: an empirical study using the Japanese KLEMS (JIP) database) examines Japan's slowing down of economic growth. Since the collapse of the bubble economy, economic growth rates in Japan have slowed down as a result of low capital accumulation. The study by Miyagawa et al. focuses on the low rate of return on capital, which led to this slow capital accumulation. Using Japanese KLEMS (JIP) database, one finds that the increase in the capital/output ratio and low capital share led to the low rate of return on capital. Not only has the rate of return on capital declined, but also its variance has grown and the number of industries with negative rates of return has increased. Then, estimation is done using a modified factor price frontier model using industry-level data. In the estimations, the profit rate is explained not only by the real wage but also by intangible investments. Estimation results show that investment in IT and human resources leads to an increase in the profit rate. The study implies that the government should implement a comprehensive innovation policy, including improvements in IT and human resources and organizational structure, as well as R&D investments to revitalize capital formation in Japan.

Taiwan's economic growth slowed down in the late 1990s and became sluggish in the 2000s as a result of a sequence of severe negative impacts from the Asian financial crisis, the worldwide economic recession after the dot-com bubble, the recent global financial crisis and Europe's latest financial debt crisis. In addition, strong competition from newly industrialized and emerging economies also cut into the profit margins of Taiwan's information and communications technology industries. Chapter 9 (The industry-level productivity of Taiwan in 1981–2010: evidence from the Taiwan KLEMS database) by Lin et al. aims to improve our understanding of this country's economic growth performance at the industry level during the past three decades (1981–2010) based on the Taiwan KLEMS database. The empirical results show that the output growth rate for the 31 industries ranged from 11.92 percent to −2.97 percent in 1981–2010 and varied by subperiod. The results also present that the structure of the factor contribution share differed by industry. However, in general, the contribution share from intermediate inputs dominates that from other inputs (capital and labor) for most sectors in secondary industries. In several industries, such as food products and textile, and rubber and plastics, the growth rates of labor input are negative. The TFP growth rate of electrical and optical equipment is the highest among secondary industries, while the TFP growth rate of "post and telecommunications" is the largest among tertiary industries. The authors conclude that the industrial policy not only impacts structural change, but also influences the TFP growth rate.

Singapore has been a focal point in the debate on the East Asian growth model, in which total factor productivity growth (TFPG) is unusually low relative to remarkable output growth. Chapter 10 (Total factor productivity and sources of Singapore's economic growth) by Dale Jorgenson and Khong Vu uses a rigorous growth accounting framework to decompose the sources of Singapore's growth, including information technology and labor quality. The results show that TFPG in Singapore for long periods was as low as 0.5–0.6 percent, which verifies Singapore's low TFPG. However, it was found that Singapore's low TFPG was caused not by a steady low TFPG pattern, but rather by its acute vulnerability to external shocks, which cause TFPG to plummet in periods of turmoil. Singapore's vulnerability to external shocks is due to its large export-reliant manufacturing sector and small domestic market. The results help to further advance our understanding of

Singapore's growth model from previous studies. We predict that, based on our base-case projection results, Singapore's growth over the next decade will be at 2.35 percent for labor productivity and 3.10 percent for GDP relative to the respective rates of 2.52 percent and 5.45 percent, for the period of 1998–2008.

Despite a large number of countries present from different parts of the world, representation from Europe remains confined to Russia. This is for two major reasons – Russia is a major emerging economy and it has already a well-developed KLEMS dataset, and in Europe, recent decades were turbulent for the Russian economy and include the transformational output fall until 1998, recovery in 1999–2008 and stagnation after the global crisis of 2008. What were main drivers of performance of the Russian economy in these years? Using the conventional industry growth and level accounting, as well as the shift share analysis within the World KLEMS framework, Chapter 11 (Russia since 1995: natural gas, catching up and informality) by Ilya B. Voskoboynikov highlights three main sources of growth, which are windfall profits from energy export; technology catching up in manufacturing, finance and business services; and the negative influence of expanding informal economy to aggregate labor productivity growth. The present study reports that oil and gas money fueled Russian growth in the form of capital services in extended mining and market services. The contribution of capital input was higher in years of soaring oil prices. One more factor of growth was catching up, which is rooted in the fact that Russia, as well as other Central and East European socialist economies (CEEs) on the eve of transition from plan to market, were backward in technologies in comparison with advanced economies. Similar to CEEs, in years after transition Russian manufacturing over-performed the West in productivity growth. This provided a remarkable contribution to aggregate productivity. Before 2008, Russia also gained from MFP growth in financial and business services, because the initial level of these sectors was low even in comparison with CEEs. Finally, the remarkable peculiarity of the Russian economy is the expanding share of informal labor, especially in years of outstanding growth before 2008. This makes Russia, to a certain extent, similar to India. Splitting industries into formal and informal segments and estimating the contribution of labor reallocation, we report that expanding informality slows down labor productivity growth.

Recent authoritative assessments show that the balance of the world economy has shifted from the industrialized economies to the emerging economies of Asia, especially China and India.[13] Both giant economies, China and India, will continue to grow faster than the world economy as per Jorgenson's (2016) projection for the period 2012–22. China with about 19 percent of the world's population of about 7 billion, and India with about 17 percent, together account for about 44 percent of the population of the low- and middle-income economies. Over the past three decades, China has experienced one of the highest economic growth rates in the world. For the period 1990–2000, the average annual growth rate in per capita GDP was 9.5 percent for China and over the decade 2000–2010, even in spite of the global recession toward the end of decade, China's growth rates accelerated to 10.5 percent. Further, since 1990s, two important aspects have shaped the world economy: globalization through trade and investment brought about by market reforms, and the role of information and technology (ICT). The non-availability of industry-level information on ICT has hampered the examination of the impact of ICT on growth in emerging nations. Against this context, Chapter 12 (Accounting for the role of information and communication technology (ICT) in China's productivity growth) by Harry X. Wu and David T. Liang adopts Jorgenson's aggregate production possibility frontier (APPF) to examine the role of ICT industries in Chinese growth during the post-reform period. This approach is applied to a newly constructed industry-level data set for Chinese industry for the period 1980–2012. The results show that Chinese ICT-producing and ICT-using manufacturing industries appear to be the most important driver of China's productivity growth over the entire period in question. While sharing 29 percent of China's 9.38 percent annual value-added growth, these industries contributed 149 percent to China's 0.83 percent annual aggregate TFP growth. This, together with a strong gain from the labor reallocation effect across industries, has enabled the economy to compensate for its heavy productivity losses by non-ICT services and the economy-wide misallocation of capital resources.

Several studies have noted that a significant acceleration in the pace of economic growth in India took place from around 1980 or from the late 1970s. In the 1980s, there was a marked step-up in rate of growth in real GDP; the average annual growth rate rose to about 5.5 percent per annum.[14] In the next decade, i.e. the 1990s, the average annual growth rate in real GDP of the Indian economy was slightly higher than 5.5 percent per annum, which accelerated further in the 2000s to reach more than seven percent per annum. The objective of Chapter 13 (Sources of growth and structural change in the Indian economy since 1980) by B. N. Goldar is to study the sources of growth and changes in the structure of the Indian economy since 1980. For the core part of the analysis presented in the paper, the period covered is 1980–81 to 2011–12. This paper examined the sources of growth and changes in structure of the Indian economy in the period 1980–81 to 2014–15. It was observed that there was a marked acceleration in GDP growth in the period since 2003–04 which was accompanied by an accelerated growth in TFP. The trend growth rates in real GDP in the periods 1980–81 to 1993–94 and 1993–94 to 2002–03 were 5.1 and 5.8 percent per annum, respectively, while that in the period 2002–03 to 2014–15 was higher at 8.0 percent per annum. Similarly, the average annual growth rate in TFP in the Indian economy increased from 0.7 percent per annum during 1980–81 to 2002–03 to 1.5 percent per annum during 2003–04 to 2011–12. Looking into the industry origins of TFP growth acceleration in the period 2003–04 to 2011–12, it was found that the main contributors to the acceleration in TFP growth at the aggregate economy level are petroleum refining; agriculture and allied activities; financial services; post and telecommunication; transport and storage; chemicals and chemical products; public administration and defense; textiles, textile products, leather and leather products; and construction. The analysis of sources of growth revealed that GDP growth in India is mainly attributable to increases in fixed capital stock and number of persons working, and the contribution of improvements in quality of labor and capital inputs, and reallocation of labor and capital across industries is relatively minor. Also, the marked acceleration in economic growth that took place in India in the period since 2003 is found to be mostly traceable to an increased rate of accumulation of fixed capital, a reallocation of labor to more productive industries, and a faster growth rate in TFP.

The next three chapter focus on Latin American economies – Brazil, Argentina and Mexico, which are the largest economies in the region. Latin American economies have enjoyed strong growth in recent years, but slowed down since 2014. The overall sluggish growth in the region resulted from slow or negative growth in some of its largest economies: Argentina (–0.2 percent), Brazil

(0.2 percent) and Mexico (2.1 percent). In Brazil, both the perspective of macro-micro changes and the one related to the international integration of the economy have remained kind of frozen in the last few decades. For that reason, increase in productivity is currently a major concern in the Brazilian economy. Even though during the 2000s Brazil experienced small, but positive, GDP growth rates, the low levels of productivity growth displayed during these years are a sign that something is not working well. With a view to addressing this issue, the newly adopted Brazilian industrial policy, called "*Brasil Mais Produtivo*" ("More Productive Brazil"), focuses on helping micro, small and medium enterprises (MSMEs) to increase their productivity levels. The aim of this study by David Kupfer and Thiago Miguez in Chapter 14 (Productivity slowdown in Brazil 2000–2013: general performance and sectoral contributions) is about Brazilian labor productivity in the 2000–2013 period. They find that during 2000–2013, Brazil had fared well, especially during the years 2004–10 when the gross domestic product (GDP) and the gross fixed capital formation (GFCF) achieved expressive growth rates and a general positive effect spread throughout the economy. Low unemployment rates, better income distribution and a strong poverty reduction were the main characteristics of these years. In contrast, the labor productivity has not achieved such good results. The cumulative progress in labor productivity during the entire period was only 18.3 percent, a worst result than developed and other BRIC economies. These results put productivity as a major concern in Brazil. The "shift-share" analysis have shown that the structural change, the between effect, still has an important role in the labor productivity growth. It certainly could soften any (improbable) effect from an end in the "demographical bonus". In fact, with the current depression in Brazil, as long as the unemployment rate continuously to rise, or keep its high levels, any source of problems from labor restriction is unlikely to happen. Another result from the shift-share analysis was that the main explanation for the low evolution of the labor productivity was the low performance of the within effect. In a sectoral perspective, apart from the good contribution from the agriculture activities, we could see that the mining and quarrying and manufacturing activities were the main responsible for this low productivity.

The failure of economic development in Argentina is well known by academics and policymakers, qualifying this as a resource curse and Dutch disease case. Using the ARKLEMS+LAND productivity and growth accounts, as counterpart of the World KLEMS initiative, allows an expansion of KLEMS methodology to key characteristics of developing economies as GDP volatility, natural capital and informal employment. Chapter 15 (Argentina growth failure: an overview from ARKLEMS+Land growth and productivity accounts) by Ariel Coremberg analyses the Argentina growth profile and productivity using the Argentina KLEMS+LAND database, which takes into account the effect of natural resource and short-run recovery effects. The study overviews the ARKLEMS methodology and analyses main stylized facts of the last two decades during very different macroeconomic regimes. The Argentinean economy could not take advantage in the long run from supposed positive spillovers and complementarities from special inputs and dynamic sectors. Multifactor productivity (MFP) slowdown ratifies that Argentina didn't take advantage of the recent commodities price boom and was unable to evade failure destiny since the last century.

In Chapter 16 (Determinants of total factor productivity in Mexico), the main objective of the Mexican study by Francisco Martin Guillen and Alfredo Orozco Henestrosa is to identify determinants of TFP in the Mexican economy. The study uses the Mexico KLEMS dataset of the National Institute of Statistics and Geography (INEGI), and six analytical indicators are identified as determinants of productivity growth. These six determinants of productivity allow the analysis of the factors that influence the behavior of TFP. The results of labor productivity and capital show that prices of capital and labor have a material impact on unit costs of capital and labor services. With regard to the productivity of capital, it is found that the price of capital service is who causes an increase in production costs; this is probably due to increased borrowing costs to finance productive activities, applied mainly in the acquisition of non-financial assets. With respect to labor productivity, it draws attention to the rising cost per labor unit, even though the price of labor service is stable, so the arguments can be diverse as the effect of the informal sector in the economy; but what is technically verifiable is that due to a decline in labor productivity, influenced by an increase in hours worked ineffective. Similarly, the fall in labor productivity in 1995 was caused by the crisis of drop in production resulting in workers lay off and thereby impacting the growth of unit labor costs during 1995–2014.

Chapter 17 (What do we know about productivity in Arab economies – the challenges of generating multifactor productivity (MFP) estimates at the industry level) covers a geographical area which witnessed significant economic–political upheaval in recent times. The Arab world has witnessed major economic, political and social changes since the onset of the Arab Spring in 2011. Despite the rapidly spreading and worsening political turmoil, as well as, in many cases, an unstable internal socio-political environment, many of the Arab countries in transition – which include Egypt, Jordan, Libya, Morocco, Tunisia and Yemen – have more or less maintained macroeconomic stability. However, these countries have not been able to generate the kind of growth rates required for a meaningful reduction in poverty and creation of jobs. Notwithstanding diversity of conditions, there is need to advance structural reforms to foster higher and more-inclusive growth. It is well known that Arab countries do not rank very high in terms of global competitiveness. Further, in some of the Arab countries, there has been uneven implementation of structural reforms carried out in the mid-1980s. The important question to pose is – *Has growth delivered following such reforms in the Arab world?* Given this backdrop, this chapter by Homagni Choudhury and Deb Kusum Das aims to explore aspects of productivity dynamics in the Arab world and assess the challenges in estimating multifactor productivity for the North African countries of Egypt, Morocco and Tunisia, as particular cases. Estimation of MFP is at the heart of understanding growth paradigm and the effects of economic reforms on growth and development. However, the problem is lack of appropriate datasets that will allow comparison of growth performance between the Arab countries themselves as well as between the Arab region as whole and other regions of the world. As such, the authors attempt to explore the possibility of empirically estimating MFP using a KLEMS framework for the North African countries of Egypt, Morocco and Tunisia. This, in turn, will set the context for estimation of multifactor productivity for the Arab world and allow us to identify the challenges and lay a roadmap for an Arab KLEMS database.

India in the new global order – insights from productivity performances

It is well known that that a sharp acceleration in investment is the predominant source of growth in the world economy (Jorgenson

2016) and this was led by China and India, two of the emerging growing economies. Therefore, in the last section of the book, we seek to explore whether the growing concerns about Indian economy to lead the rest of the world in terms of growth rate is attainable as well as sustainable. The dynamics of economic growth in India continues to engage economists and remains an enigma. The trends and patterns of growth observed in India have seen acceleration in growth in the Indian economy in the period following macroeconomic reforms and policy changes in investment and trade regimes. However, when and how, India transformation from the Hindu rate of growth to the present growth regime continues to be debated. In addition, how did India fare in comparison to China in the period following global financial crisis is also now an important research agenda. The ideas presented in this section accordingly covers the dynamics which center around growth performance of the Indian economy – labor productivity, manufacturing productivity including state-level perspective on productivity, size distribution of productivity and investment climate for firm performance – in short, all these aspects clearly sum up to the "Make in India" policy program of the government of India.[15]

Many studies show that growth rate of GDP in India has been quite remarkable during the period 2001 to 2010 (7.9 percent) as compared to the earlier decade of 1991–2000 (5.6 percent). At the level of broad sectors, we find that alongside, the GDP growth of 7.9 percent, industry grew at 7.8 percent and services at 9.4 percent. After a brief period of slowdown (2011–2013), the cconomy registered a growth of 7.6 percent in 2015–16. The economy exhibits some structural transformation whereby it is seen that the share of agriculture sector has reduced to just 15.4 percent in 2015–16 and the share of services has increased to 53.4 percent and the share of manufacturing is 17.5 percent. Further, it is noticed that the structural change in GDP has not happened in employment as agriculture and mining still absorbs around fifty percent of the labor force in 2013–14 and the secondary and service sector employs 22.4 percent and 29.3 percent, respectively of the labor force. Thus the observed structural transformation in economy has consequences for employment growth in the economy and in turn for generating jobs beyond the non farm sector. In view of the poor growth in employment during the period of 2001–02 to 2011–12 (1.3 percent), it is essential to understand the dynamics of labor productivity in Indian economy keeping the overall structural changes in labour market in mind. This has implications for worker productivity across different sectors of the economy especially the formal manufacturing industries and market based services.

Chapter 18 (Dynamics of labor productivity in Indian industry 1980–2011) by Suresh Aggarwal is an attempt to understand the dynamics of labor productivity in India during 1980–81 to 2011–12 at the disaggregate level of 27 industries/sectors of the economy. It finds that growth of labor productivity varies across different industries. The status of labor productivity becomes more adverse when we analyze the sources of growth of labor productivity – the sources of growth of labor productivity are not only different for different industries but in most of them it is either the growth in intermediate inputs or growth in capital intensity, which basically means it is factor accumulation that is leading to a growth in labor productivity. The contribution of both growth in labor composition as well as of TFP growth in growth of labor productivity is marginal. So more than the quality of factors, it is the quantity which is the main source of labor productivity growth. From long-term perspective of growth of the economy, it is growth in TFP and growth in labor composition which are desirable and sustainable and not the growth in factor accumulation.

Several studies have attempted to analyze the productivity performance of the organized Indian manufacturing sector during the 1990s at both aggregated as well as at the disaggregated levels. Most of these studies observed that there has been a fall in total factor productivity (TFP) growth rate in the 1990s compared to 1980s. Chapter 19 (Total factor productivity in Indian organized manufacturing – the story of the noughties) by Pilu Chandra Das aims to estimate and analyze the Indian organized manufacturing sector's growth and productivity performance during 2000–01 to 2009–10. The study undertakes a comparison of TFP growth for selected three-digit industries to evaluate the Indian manufacturing sector's productivity performance in 2000s. In addition, estimates the relative contribution of TFP growth to output growth in order to examine whether the growth of output of the Indian manufacturing sector has been driven by productivity growth or by input expansion. The majority of the earlier studies usually applied the value-added function or the KLEM (capital-labor-energy-materials) production function as the basic framework. This study analyzes the productivity performance and sources of output growth in Indian organized manufacturing, using the KLEMS production function as an underlying production function framework. Comparing findings of this research with the earlier findings for the 1990s, Das has found that total factor productivity growth rate has to some extent improved in the 2000s, but TFP contribution to output growth has been insignificant. Our results have also indicated that there exist sharp inter-industry differences in productivity performance. Even now, the Indian manufacturing sector output growth has been driven by input accumulation. The TFP contribution has also varied across different ranges of output growth. Findings of the study have also indicated that the intermediate inputs contributed most of the output growth than the traditional inputs (labor and capital). Material input alone has been contributed more than half of the output growth followed by services input. Use of services in manufacturing has grown at an accelerated pace in the 2000s compared to the earlier period. The contribution of services to output growth has also increased.

The National Manufacturing Policy (NMP) 2011[16] of India aims at increasing the share of manufacturing sector in GDP to about 25 percent by 2022, i.e. within a decade of its announcement, and creating about 100 million additional jobs during 2011 to 2022. The strategy embedded in NMP is said to be neutral with respect to sectors, location and technology. It may not be out of place to mention here that the two major states of India, viz. Maharashtra and Gujarat account for almost one-third of India's GDP originating from the manufacturing sector, whereas, the corresponding figure for Bihar, the third most-populous state of India, is merely 1 percent. Given this context, Chapter 20 (A state-level perspective of productivity growth of India's registered manufacturing sector) by Pushpa Trivedi aims to study the growth path of the registered manufacturing sector of the selected states of the Indian economy. The growth performance of the period 2000–01 to 2012–13 was impressive in spite of the global financial crisis and greater trade openness. Real output of the MFG sector in many states witnessed double-digit growth. The floor for this variable across the states was about 8 percent. TFPG performance was not all that impressive if we judge its role in explaining the growth of real output. TFPG explained just about 14 percent of growth of the sector. The highest contribution of TFPG to growth was witnessed by West Bengal, which recorded very low growth rate of employment (0.7 percent per annum (pcpa)) as compared to the national average (3.4 pcpa). However, if compare the performance of TFPG in absolute terms then as indicated by the previous studies, such as

Das et al. (2016), Trivedi (2004), and Trivedi et al. (2010), the TFPG for MFG was merely 1.0 pcpa for the period 1980–81 to 2009–10, 1980–81 to 2000–01 and 1980–81 to 2003–04, respectively. The growth performance has improved during the subsequent periods, and the TFPG has almost doubled. Hence, the contribution of TFPG to growth seems to be more or less stagnant. Following Krugman (1994), this seems to be the result of perspiration rather than inspiration and, hence, sustainability of the resource intensive growth process must be guarded by the policymakers.

It is a well-known fact that several factors cause differentials in productivity across firms within the same industry. Chapter 20 (Size and productivity in Indian manufacturing) by Arup Mitra and Chandan Sharma, using a recent firm-level survey data, estimates TFP of the Indian manufacturing firms and attempts to analyze the productivity differential among firms of different sizes. On the whole, the findings confirm the results of kernel distribution and endorse that large firms are more productive, and the small firms comprise the least-productive group. The productivity dynamics in different categories of firms indicates that the growth in small firms is mainly driven by growth in inputs, but output growth of large firms is comparatively driven by technology and productivity enhancement. However, the findings in this study indicate that firm size is an important factor determining its productivity performance. Large firms are robustly found to have 9–11 percent more productivity than small firms. Also, smaller firms are significantly lower in terms of productivity performance in comparison to other firms. The rate of return of inputs is also found to be higher among large firms. More importantly, these results are robust across the alternative analyses. The findings raise questions on existing industrial policies in the country that aim at encouraging small firms. For example, small- and medium-scale firms enjoy several benefits, such as easy and subsidized credit, support for R&D and technology transfer, infrastructure building and support in selling output in domestic and international markets. However, they do not argue for abolition of these incentives but recommend a better designed and efficient policy to help the small- and medium-scale firms in enhancing their use of technology and augmenting the productivity level. Furthermore, large firms have productivity advantages which also help other firms through several spillover channels. The policymakers need to keep in mind these issues.

Chapter 22 (The challenges of "Make in India": does investment climate matter for firm performance?) by Rajesh Raj and Kunal Sen seeks to examine in the Indian context, how the issue of investment climate reform has taken on particular relevance with the Indian government's "Make in India" initiative. This chapter uses a very recent rich firm-level database to look at the effect of the investment climate on firm performance in India. The data is the World Bank Enterprise Survey, which is an all India firm-level dataset covering a broad range of business environment topics, such as access to finance, corruption, infrastructure, crime, competition and performance measures. These surveys intend to provide information pertaining to measures of firm performance, firm structure as well as business perceptions on the major impediments to firm growth, and the business environment in general. The data has several measures of the investment climate which allows assessing which specific feature of the investment climate matters for firm performance. Surprisingly, the finding is that conventional measures of ease of doing business such as the amount of time firm management spends with government officials and the frequency of visits of tax inspectors are not important in explaining firm productivity. Instead, finds that corruption has a clear and discernible negative effect on firm productivity. This suggests that the focus of Indian policy makers should be on reducing corruption rather than in improving the conventional measures of doing business.

Summary and conclusion

The chapters in this volume have addressed topical and contemporary issues underlying our understanding of productivity dynamics in the world economy today. The importance of KLEMS datasets, so crucial to understanding the global as well as the regional trends in productivity, has brought to the fore the usefulness of detailed industry-level analysis of growth using measures of outputs, labor and capital inputs and derived measures of labor, as well as multifactor productivity. In addition, various concepts of human capital and its relationship with productivity are explored and examined. The role of investment in enhancing productivity growth is widely known, however lack of information on investment by asset types raises the question about why emerging economies are not investing at a higher rate, and availability of data on investment by asset types adds another dimension to research on productivity–investment nexus.

The studies presented in different chapters offers several important findings. At the outset, the new framework for productivity measurement reveals that replication of established technologies explains by far the largest proportion of US economic growth. International productivity comparisons reveal similar patterns for the world economy, its major regions, and leading industrialized, developing and emerging economies. The pace of the global labor productivity growth has slowed drastically since the beginning of the current decade, and the decline in labor productivity is primarily due to continuous decline in TFPG. At the regional level, the current pace of TFP growth in Asia in the post-crisis period with an average annual growth rate of 1.6 percent is still to revert to the pace in the pre-crisis period; however, it is not very far behind its long-term achievement of 2.0 percent for the past three decades from 1985 to 2014. Latin American countries have considerably lower productivity than do developed countries and, with rare exceptions, these gaps are widening. The papers in this section also offer insights into measuring human capital productivity and role of shifting investment patterns.

The availability of the KLEMS dataset allows examination of country's growth from the perspective of disaggregated industry dynamics and brings rich insights from country experiences. The chapters present several interesting features of the productivity dynamics in these countries and therefore provide valuable insights into comparative growth dynamics. The causality between aggregate demand and labor productivity and the implication of the Kaldor-Verdoorn Law were examined for Korea and were found valid. Since the collapse of the bubble economy, economic growth rates in Japan have slowed down as a result of low capital accumulation and the government needs comprehensive innovation policy to revitalize capital formation in Japan. Taiwan also posted its best economic growth in 1981–90, but this performance decreased over time after 1990. Singapore has been a focal point in the debate on the East Asian growth model, in which total factor productivity growth (TFPG) is unusually low relative to remarkable output growth. However, it was found that Singapore's low TFPG was caused not by a steady low TFPG pattern but by its acute vulnerability to external shocks, which cause TFPG to plummet in periods of turmoil. In the case of Russia, oil and gas money fueled Russian growth in the form of capital services in extended mining and market services. Further, 'catching up' was also instrumental in driving growth. China's industrial TFP performance was fairly sensitive to external shocks, but both institutional and market-wise industries that are less prone to government interventions tended to have a much faster TFP growth than those subject to more government controls. Marked acceleration in economic growth that took place in India in the period since 2003 is found to be mostly traceable to an increased rate of accumulation of fixed capital, a reallocation of labor to more productive industries and a faster growth rate in TFP. In the Southern Hemisphere, Brazil had faced a good moment in its economy, especially during the years 2004–10 when the GDP and the GFCF achieved expressive growth rates and a general positive effect spread throughout the economy, whereas the neighboring Argentina economy could not take advantage in the long run from supposed positive spillovers and complementarities from special inputs and dynamic sectors. Multifactor productivity slowdown ratifies that Argentina didn't take advantage from recent commodities prices boom and could not evade failure destiny since the last century. Mexico had wide fluctuations in TFP, with sharp falls in 1995 and 2009.

Given that India is expected to be a significant player in the "New World Economic Order", perspectives on productivity challenges which include both industry as well as firm dynamics and also capture the state perspectives in Indian federal structure offers several interesting findings. Despite structural changes since 1980s, labor productivity in the economy remained low and plausible reason could be the very low proportion of labor in regular job employment and the pre-dominance of self-employed and casual labor. Further, TFP for the organized manufacturing sector ranged between –4 percent to +7 percent per annum with negligible contribution to output growth. At the state level, Karnataka, UP, MP Gujarat and Tamil Nadu performed better as compared to the all-India average. Understanding the relationship between productivity and size is of special interest for India, given the fact that most firms are small and enjoy several exemptions and subsidies. We conclude that firm size is an important determinant of its productivity performance. Large firms are robustly found to have 9–11 percent more productivity than other firms. Finally, ease of doing business and greater awareness about opportunities in India in manufacturing sector are expected to lead to growth in the manufacturing sector.

Instead, we find that corruption has a clear and discernible negative effect on firm productivity.

In conclusion, economists have long been worried about why some countries grow faster than others and what accounts for source of growth. The chapters in this volume, by concentrating on some of the major economies of the world including both industrialized and emerging countries, provide an insight into the country growth dynamics. The non-availability of KLEMS-type datasets in African countries acts as a barrier to understanding the African growth dynamics. The focus of the chapters in the last section underlies the productivity insights into one of the major growing economies of the world. Important insights from both industry and state perspectives offer powerful insights into how important has been productivity enhancement for India's growth.

Finally, we hope that the underlying subject matter of the book will make an important contribution to our understanding of the global economy in the times of weak investment, stagnant trade, and era of regional perspective to both scholars and policy practitioners.

Notes

1 See, Dervis, Kemal, and Zia Qureshi. 2016. "The Productivity Slump – Fact or Fiction the Measurement Debate." *Journal of Economic Literature 2011.*
2 Refer to Gordon, Robert. 2012. "Is U.S. Economic Growth Over? Faltering Innovation Confronts the Six Headwinds." *NBER Working Paper* #18315. Further, Robert Gordon and Erik Brynjolfsson debate the role of technology in growth, particularly in the context of US economic growth, whether the digital revolution of the 1980s and 1990s has delivered a productivity payoff. www.bloomberg.com/news/articles/2016-09-12/the-great-debate-can-technology-transform-the-economy-again
3 Refer Harry X. Wu (2016) and Deb Kusum Das et al. (2016) papers on China and India, respectively, where the authors have provided detailed examination of productivity growth during the crisis periods of 2000s.
4 Jorgenson has been a strong advocate of discarding the aggregate production function models used in analyzing long-term growth and instead use of disaggregate industry-level analysis for understanding growth trends.
5 Refer for construction of capital stock as well as services as part of productivity measurement in OECD (2001) and revised version OECD (2009) – Measuring Capital.
6 The EU KLEMS project enabled building a country datasets for around 25 member states of the European Union and, in turn, these datasets allowed examining the EU–US growth differential.

7 The New World Economic Order will consist of China, the United States, India, Japan, Russia, Germany and Brazil. Refer to Jorgenson and Vu (2011).
8 The World KLEMS initiative pioneered by Dale Jorgenson's KLEMS approach to productivity measurement was launched at the First World KLEMS Conference in Harvard University in 2010, with more than 40 countries constructing the KLEMS datasets and, in turn, using the datasets to understand the sources of economic growth at the industry level. Following the World KLEMS Initiative, similar initiatives were also launched in Asia (Asia KLEMS) as well as Latin American countries (LA KLEMS), and regular conferences and workshops have been held to examine growth empirics using the datasets created. For details, refer to change being undertaken at www.worldklems.net
9 The primary aim of the EU KLEMS project was to arrive at an internationally comparable dataset, which can be used to undertake the analysis of economic growth in different economies – both developed and emerging. The EU dataset was linked with Canada-Japan-USA databases to allow for international comparisons. Also a consortium coordinated by RIETI in Japan developed an Asian database, called the ICPA database (International Comparison of Productivity among Asian countries; see www.rieti.go.jp/en/database/data/icpa-description.pdf) along the same lines as the EU KLEMS, for China, Japan, Korea and Taiwan. The advent of these through the EU KLEMS project gave rise to the international comparability of growth in various countries.
10 Refer to IMF world Economic Outlook April 2016, chapter 2.
11 "Make in India" is an initiative launched by the Government of India under the leadership of Prime Minister Narendra Modi to encourage production of "goods" by national and overseas companies in India.
12 The EU KELMS project covered all member states of the EU as of 1 May 2004, but excluding Bulgaria and Romania, which joined only in 2007. Due to data limitations, the coverage differs across countries, industries and variables. The first release of the EU KLEMS database confirmed the view that European countries showed a significant slowdown in productivity growth since 1995, which is shown to be widespread across countries and industries, but with notable differences.
13 Refer Jorgenson (2016) "The New World Order." In Jorgenson et al. (2016), *The World Economy Growth or Stagnation?* Cambridge: Cambridge University Press.
14 Even though the average growth rate of the Indian economy in the 1980s was higher than that during the previous three decades, doubts have been raised on whether the hike in growth rate was statistically significant, or whether it is right to date the growth turnaround to the late 1970s. Ghate and Wright (2012), for instance, take the position that the turnaround in India's economic growth took place in 1987.
15 The "Make in India" policy initiative of the Modi government is an attempt to make Indian manufacturing globally competitive. Improving productivity across all categories of manufacturing remains the key but other factors, such as skilled competence, quality control, infrastructural bottlenecks including land acquisition and labor market

reforms remain major hindrances to enhancing productivity as well as efficiency of production.

16 The Department of Industrial Policy and Promotion, Ministry of Commerce and Industries, Government of India, notified the National Manufacturing Policy (NMP) through a Press Note dated 4 November 2011 with the objective of enhancing the share of manufacturing and creating jobs. The policy is based on the principle of industrial growth in partnership with the states. The Central Government will create the enabling policy framework and provide incentives for infrastructure development on a Public Private Partnership (PPP) basis through appropriate financing instruments, and state governments will be encouraged to adopt the instrumentalities provided in the policy.

Bibliography

Alvarez, Roberto, and José De Gregorio. 2014. "Understanding Differences in Growth Performance in Latin America and Developing Countries Between the Asian and Global Financial Crises."

Cette, Gilbert, John Fernald, and Benoit Mojon. 2016. "The Pre-Great Recession Slowdown in Productivity." *European Economic Review* 88: 3–20.

Das, D. K., A. A. Erumban, S. Agarwal, and S. Sengupta. 2016. "Productivity Growth in India Under Different Policy Regimes." In D. W. Jorgenson, K. Fukao, and M. P. Timmer (eds.), *The World Economy Growth or Stagnation?* Cambridge: Cambridge University Press.

Derviş, Kemal, and Zia Qureshi. 2016. "The Productivity Slump – Fact or Fiction: The Measurement Debate." *Brookings Global Economy and Development Working Paper*.

Diewert, W. Erwin, and Kevin J. Fox. 2014. "Reference Technology Sets, Free Disposal Hulls and Productivity Decompositions." *Economics Letters* 122(2): 238–242.

Fraumeni, Barbara M., and Frank M. Gollop. 1987. *Productivity and US Economic Growth*. Cambridge, MA: Harvard University Press.

Ghate, C., and S. Wright. 2012. "The V-factor: Distribution, timing and correlates of the great Indian growth turnaround", *Journal of Development Economics*, 99(1): 58–67.

Gordon, Robert J. 2012. "Is US Economic Growth Over? Faltering Innovation Confronts the Six Headwinds." *National Bureau of Economic Research*, No. w18315.

International Monetary Fund. 2016a. *World Economic Outlook: Too Slow for Too Long*. Washington, DC: International Monetary Fund, April.

International Monetary Fund. 2016b. *World Economic Outlook: Subdued Demand: Symptoms and Remedies*. Washington, DC: International Monetary Fund, October.

International Monetary Fund. 2017. *World Economic Outlook: Gaining Momentum?* Washington, DC: International Monetary Fund, April.

Jorgenson, D.W. et. al. 1987. Productivity and U.S. *Economic Growth*. Harvard University Press.

Jorgenson, Dale W. 2016. "The New World Order." In D. W. Jorgenson, K. Fukao, and M. P. Timmer (eds.), *The World Economy Growth or Stagnation?* Cambridge: Cambridge University Press.

Jorgenson, Dale W., Mun S. Ho, and Kevin J. Stiroh. 2005. "Productivity, Volume 3: Information Technology and the American Growth Resurgence." *MIT Press Books* 3.

Jorgenson, Dale W., and Marcel P. Timmer. 2011. "Structural Change in Advanced Nations: A New Set of Stylised Facts." *The Scandinavian Journal of Economics* 113(1): 1–29.

Jorgenson, Dale W., and Khuong M. Vu. 2011. "The Rise of Developing Asia and the New Economic Order." *Journal of Policy Modeling* 33(5): 698–716.

Krugman, Paul. 1990, 1994. *The Age of Diminished Expectation- U.S. Economic Policy in the 1990s*. Cambrige, MA: MIT Press.

Nomura, K. Forthcoming. "Productivity Growth in Asia and Its Country Origins." In Deb Kusum Das (ed.), *Productivity Dynamics in Emerging and Industrialized Countries*. Routledge, Taylor and Francis.

Organisation for Economic Co-Operation and Development. 2001. *Measuring Productivity: Measurement of Aggregate and Industry-Level Productivity Growth: OECD Manual*. Paris: Organisation for Economic Co-Operation and Development.

Organisation for Economic Co-Operation and Development. 2009. *Measuring Capital: OECD Manual*. Paris: Organisation for Economic Co-operation and Development.

Organisation for Economic Co-Operation and Development. 2015. *The Future of Productivity*. Paris: Organisation for Economic Co-operation and Development.

Solow, Robert M. 1957. "Technical Change and the Aggregate Production Function." *The Review of Economics and Statistics* 1957: 312–320.

Tinbergen, J. 1942. 'On the Theory of Trend Movements', in Klassen, L.H., Koych, L.M. and Witteveen, H.J. (eds), *Jan Tinbergen Selected Papers, Amsterdam*, North Holland: 82–221.

Timmer, Marcel P., R. Inklaar, Mary O. Mahony, and Bart Van Ark, eds. 2010. *Economic Growth in Europe*. Cambridge: Cambridge University Press.

Trivedi, Pushpa. 2004. "An Inter-State Perspective on Manufacturing Productivity in India: 1980–81 to 2000–01." *Indian Economic Review*, New Series 39(1): 203–237.

Wu, Harry X. 2016. "On China's Strategic Move for a New Stage of Development-a Productivity Perspective." In D. W. Jorgenson, K. Fukao, and M. P. Timmer (eds.), *The World Economy Growth or Stagnation?* Cambridge: Cambridge University Press.

Part I

Productivity and world economy

New insights

Chapter 1
The growth of the world economy

Dale W. Jorgenson

Introduction

The World KLEMS Initiative was established at the First World KLEMS Conference, held at Harvard University in August 2010.[1] The purpose of the initiative is to generate industry-level datasets, consisting of outputs and inputs of capital (K) and labor (L), together with inputs of energy (E), materials (M), and services (S). Productivity for each industry is defined as output per unit of all inputs. These datasets provide a new framework for analyzing the sources of economic growth at the industry and aggregate levels for countries around the world. This framework has closed a critical gap in systems of national accounts.

Growth of output, inputs, and productivity at the industry level is important for understanding changes in the structure of an economy and the contributions of different industries to economic growth. International comparisons of differences in productivity levels based on purchasing power parities of outputs and inputs at the industry level provide a second focus for industry-level productivity research. These comparisons are essential in assessing changes in comparative advantage and formulating strategies for economic growth.

The EU (European Union) KLEMS study provides industry-level datasets on the sources of growth for 25 of the 27 EU member countries.[2] These datasets are essential for analyzing the slowdown in European economic growth that preceded the current financial and fiscal crisis. The datasets and results were presented at the Final EU KLEMS Conference in Groningen, the Netherlands, in June 2008.[3] Marcel P. Timmer et al. (2010) describe the datasets and analyze the sources of economic growth in Europe at the industry level.

The EU KLEMS project also included datasets for Australia, Canada, Japan, Korea, and the United States. Matilde Mas and Robert Stehrer (2012) present international comparisons within Europe, and between Europe and the advanced economies in Asia and North America. As European policymakers focus on removing barriers to the revival of economic growth, international differences in the sources of growth have become central in understanding the impacts of changes in economic policy.

The EU KLEMS project identified the failure to develop a knowledge economy as the most important source of the slowdown in European economic growth. Development of a knowledge economy will require investments in human capital, information technology, and intellectual property. An important policy implication is that extension of the single market to the services industries, which are particularly intensive in the use of information technology, will be essential for the removal of barriers to the knowledge economy.

The Second World KLEMS Conference was held at Harvard University in August 2012.[4] The conference included reports on recent progress in the development of industry-level datasets, as well as extensions and applications.[5] Regional organizations in Asia and Latin America have now joined the European Union in supporting research on industry-level datasets. Due to the growing recognition of the importance of these datasets, an effort is underway to extend the new framework to emerging and transition economies, such as Brazil, China, India, and Russia.

LA KLEMS, the Latin American chapter of the World KLEMS Initiative, was established in December 2009 at a conference at ECLAC, the Economic Commission for Latin America and the Caribbean, in Santiago, Chile.[6] This chapter is coordinated by ECLAC and includes seven research organizations in four leading Latin American countries – Argentina, Brazil, Chile, and Mexico.[7] Mario Cimoli et al. (2010) have summarized the results of the initial phase of the LA KLEMS project.

A detailed report on Mexico KLEMS was published in 2013 by INEGI (National Institute of Statistics and Geography).[8] This was presented at an international seminar at the Instituto Tecnologico Autonomo de Mexico (ITAM) in Mexico City in October 2013.[9] Mexico KLEMS includes a complete industry-level productivity database for 1990–2011 that is integrated with the Mexican national accounts. This database will be updated annually. An important finding is that productivity has not grown in Mexico since 1990. Periods of positive economic growth have been offset by the negative impacts of the Mexican sovereign debt crisis of 1995, the US dot-com crash in 2000, and the US financial and economic crisis of 2007–09.

Asia KLEMS, the Asian chapter of the World KLEMS Initiative, was founded in December 2010 and the First Asia KLEMS Conference was held at the Asian Development Bank Institute in Tokyo in July 2011.[10] Asia KLEMS includes the Japan Industrial Productivity (JIP) database,[11] the Korean Industrial Productivity database,[12] and the China Industrial Productivity database.[13] Industry-level databases have been constructed for Taiwan and work is underway to develop a similar database for Malaysia. These databases were discussed at the Second Asia KLEMS Conference, held at the Bank of Korea in Seoul in August 2013.[14]

Kyoji Fukao (2012, 2013) has employed the JIP data base in analyzing the slowdown in productivity growth in Japan after 1991, now extending into the Two Lost Decades. The initial downturn in productivity growth followed the collapse of the "bubble" in Japanese real estate prices in 1991. A brief revival of productivity growth after 2000 ended with the sharp decline in Japanese exports in 2008–09. This followed the rapid appreciation of the Japanese yen, relative to the US dollar, after the adoption of a monetary policy of quantitative easing by the US Federal Reserve, the US central bank. When the Bank of Japan failed to respond, Japan experienced a much more severe downturn in productivity growth and a larger decline in output than the United States in the aftermath of the financial and economic crisis of 2007–09.

The Third World KLEMS Conference was held in Tokyo in May 2014.[15] This conference discussed industry-level datasets for more than 40 countries, including those that participate in the three regional organizations that make up the World KLEMS Initiative – EU KLEMS in Europe, LA KLEMS in Latin America, and Asia KLEMS in Asia. In addition, the conference considered research on linking datasets for the 40 countries through the World Input-Output Database (WIOD).[16] Another important theme of the conference was the extension of the measurement of capital inputs to include intangibles, such as human capital and intellectual property, as well as the familiar tangible assets – plant, equipment, and inventories.

Linked data sets are especially valuable in analyzing the development of global value chains in Asia, North America, and Europe.

For this purpose, international trade can be decomposed by tasks performed at each link of the value chain. Trade in tasks can be compared with trade in commodities, which involves "double-counting" of intermediate goods as products pass through the value chain. A central finding is that regional value chains are now merging into global value chains involving all the major countries in the world. The WOID is now undergoing a substantial expansion at the OECD, with support from the World Trade Organization (WTO).[17]

The Third World KLEMS Conference included reports on new industry-level datasets for India and Russia. Russia KLEMS was released in July 2013 by the Laboratory for Research in Inflation and Growth at the Higher School of Economics in Moscow.[18] Russia's recovery from the sharp economic downturn that followed the dissolution of the Soviet Union and the transition to a market economy has been very impressive. Surprisingly, increases in productivity growth widely anticipated by observers inside and outside of Russia have characterized only the service industries, which were underdeveloped under central planning. Mining industries have attracted large investments, but these have not been accompanied by gains in efficiency. The recent collapse in world oil prices poses an important challenge for the future growth of the Russian economy.

The India KLEMS database was released in July 2014 by the Reserve Bank of India,[19] shortly after the Third World KLEMS Conference in Tokyo. This database covers 26 industries for the period 1980–2011. Beginning in the 1980s, liberalization of the Indian economy has resulted in a gradual and sustained acceleration in economic growth, and a transfer of resources from agriculture and manufacturing to the service industries. The most surprising feature of the acceleration in Indian economic growth has been the stagnant share of manufacturing and the rapid growth in the share of services. Given the shrinking share of agriculture and the size of the Indian agricultural labor force, another surprise is that growth of capital input has been the most important source of growth in manufacturing and services, as well as more recently in agriculture.

The new framework for productivity measurement

Jorgenson et al. (1987) construct the first dataset containing annual time series data on output, inputs of capital, labor, and intermediate goods, and productivity for all the industries in the US economy. This study has provided the model for the methods of economy-wide and industry-level productivity measurement presented in Paul Schreyer's (2001) OECD *Productivity Manual*. The hallmarks of the new framework for productivity measurement are constant quality indexes of capital and labor services at the industry level, and indexes of energy, materials, and services inputs constructed from a time series of input-output tables.

Jorgenson et al. (2005) update the US dataset and revise it to include investment in information technology (IT). This required developing new data on the production of hardware, telecommunications equipment, and software, as well as inputs of IT capital services. The new dataset has demonstrated the importance of industry-level productivity growth in understanding the US investment boom of the 1990s. Jorgenson et al. (2005) provide the framework for the new datasets and international comparisons for Europe, Japan, and the United States presented by Jorgenson (2009).

The key idea underlying a *constant quality index of labor input* is to capture the heterogeneity of different types of labor inputs. Hours worked for each type of labor input are combined into a constant quality index of labor input, using labor compensation per hour as weights. Constant quality indexes of labor input for the United States at the industry level are discussed in detail by Jorgenson et al. (2005: 201–290, Chapter 6).

Similarly, a *constant quality index of capital input* deals with the heterogeneity among different types of capital inputs. These capital inputs are combined into a constant quality index, using rental prices of the inputs as weights, rather than the asset prices used in measuring capital stocks. This makes it possible to incorporate differences among asset-specific inflation rates that are particularly important in analyzing the impact of investments in information technology, as well as differences in depreciation rates and tax treatments for different assets. Constant quality indexes of capital input for the United States at the industry level are presented by Jorgenson et al. (2005: 147–200, Chapter 5).

The new framework for productivity measurement incorporates a time series of input-output tables in current and constant prices. Estimates of intermediate inputs of energy, materials, and services are generated from these tables. Details on the construction of the time series of input-output tables and estimates of intermediate inputs are presented by Jorgenson et al. (2005: 87–146, Chapter 4).

Jorgenson and Steven Landefeld (2006) develop a new architecture for the US national income and product accounts (NIPAs) that include prices and quantities of capital services for all productive assets in the US economy. This is published in a volume on the new architecture by Jorgenson et al. (2006). The incorporation of the price and quantity of capital services into the United Nations' *System of National Accounts 2008* (2009) was approved by the United Nations Statistical Commission at its February-March 2007 meeting. Schreyer, then head of national accounts at the OECD, prepared an OECD Manual, *Measuring Capital*, published in 2009. This provides detailed recommendations on methods for the construction of prices and quantities of capital services.

In Chapter 20 of *SNA 2008* (page 415), estimates of capital services are described as follows: "By associating these estimates with the standard breakdown of value added, the contribution of labor and capital to production can be portrayed in a form ready for use in the analysis of productivity in a way entirely consistent with the accounts of the System." The measures of capital and labor inputs in the prototype system of US national accounts presented by Jorgenson and Landefeld (2006) are consistent with the *OECD Productivity Manual*, *SNA 2008*, and the OECD Manual, *Measuring Capital*.

The new architecture for the US national accounts was endorsed by the Advisory Committee on Measuring Innovation in the 21st Century Economy to the US Secretary of Commerce:[20]

> The proposed new 'architecture' for the NIPAs would consist of a set of income statements, balance sheets, flow of funds statements, and productivity estimates for the entire economy and by sector that are more accurate and internally consistent. The new architecture will make the NIPAs much more relevant to today's technology-driven and globalizing economy and will facilitate the publication of much more detailed and reliable estimates of innovation's contribution to productivity growth.

In response to the Advisory Committee's recommendations, the US Bureau of Economic Analysis (BEA) and Bureau of Labor Statistics (BLS) produced an initial set of multifactor productivity estimates integrated with the NIPAs. Data on capital and labor inputs are provided by the BLS. The results are reported by Michael Harper et al. (2009) and will be updated annually.[21] This is a critical step in implementing the new architecture. The omission of productivity statistics from the NIPAs and *SNA 1993* has been a serious barrier to assessing potential growth.

Reflecting the international consensus on productivity measurement at the industry level, the Advisory Committee on Measuring Innovation in the 21st Century Economy to the US Secretary of Commerce (2008: 7) recommended that the BEA should:

> Develop annual, industry-level measures of total factor productivity by restructuring the NIPAs to create a more complete and consistent set of accounts integrated with data from other statistical agencies to allow for the consistent estimation of the contribution of innovation to economic growth.

In December 2011, the BEA released a new industry-level data set. This integrated three separate industry programs – benchmark input-output tables released every five years, annual input-output tables, and gross domestic product by industry, also released annually. The input-output tables provide data on the output side of the national accounts along with intermediate inputs in current and constant prices. The BEA's industry-level dataset is described in more detail by Nicole M. Mayerhauser and Erich H. Strassner (2010).

The BEA's annual input-output data are employed in the industry-level production accounts presented by Susan Fleck et al. (2014) in their paper for the Second World KLEMS Conference, "A Prototype BEA/BLS Industry-Level Production Account for the United States." The paper covers the period 1998–2009 for the 65 industrial sectors used in the NIPAs. The capital and labor input are provided by the BLS, while the data on output and intermediate inputs are generated by the BEA. This paper was published in a second volume on the new architecture for the US national accounts by Jorgenson et al. (2014).

Stefanie H. McCulla et al. (2013) summarize the 2013 benchmark revision of the NIPAs. A particularly significant innovation is the addition of intellectual property products, such as research and development and entertainment, artistic, and literary originals. Investment in intellectual property is treated symmetrically with other types of capital expenditures. Intellectual property products are included in the national product, and the capital services generated by these products are included in the national income.

Donald D. Kim et al. (2014) discuss the 2014 benchmark revision of the industry accounts, including the incorporation of intellectual property.

The 2014 benchmark revision of the US industry accounts is incorporated into the paper by Steven Rosenthal et al. (2015), "Integrated Industry-Level Production Account for the United States: Intellectual Property Products and the 2007 NAICS." The paper covers the period 1997–2012 for the 65 industrial sectors used in the NIPAs. The capital and labor inputs are provided by the BLS, while output and intermediate inputs are generated by the BEA.[22] This paper was presented at the Third World KLEMS Conference and published in a new volume by Jorgenson et al. (2015) that contains papers presented at the conference.

A prototype industry-level production account for the United States, 1947–2012

Jorgenson and Schreyer (2013) show how to integrate a complete system of production accounts at the industry level into the *2008 System of National Accounts*. To illustrate the application of these production accounts, I will summarize the prototype production account for the United States for 1947–2012 constructed by Jorgenson, Ho, and Jon Samuels (2015) in a paper presented at the Third World KLEMS Conference. The lengthy time series is especially valuable in comparing recent changes in the sources of economic growth with longer-term trends.

Jorgenson et al. (2015) illustrate the application of the prototype industry-level production account by analyzing postwar US economic history for three broad periods. These are the Postwar Recovery, 1947–73; the Long Slump following the energy crisis of 1973, 1973–95; and the period of Growth and Recession, 1995–2012. To provide more detail on the period of Growth and Recession, they consider the subperiods 1995–2000, 2000–2007, and 2007–10 – the Investment Boom, the Jobless Recovery, and the Great Recession.

The North American Industry Classification System (NAICS) includes the industries identified by Jorgenson et al. (2015) as IT-producing industries, namely computers and electronic products, and two IT-services industries, information and data processing and computer systems design. Jorgenson et al. (2015) classify industries as IT-using if the intensity of IT capital input is greater than the median for all US industries that do not produce IT equipment, software, and services. All other industries are classified as Non-IT.

Value added in the IT-producing industries during 1947–2012 is only 2.5 percent of the US economy, in the IT-using industries about 47.5 percent, and the Non-IT industries the remaining fifty percent. The IT-using industries are mainly in trade and services and most manufacturing industries are in the Non-IT sector. The NAICS provides much more detail on services and trade, especially the industries that are intensive users of IT. I begin by discussing the results for the IT-producing sectors, now defined to include the two IT-service sectors.

Figure 1.1 reveals a steady increase in the share of IT-producing industries in the growth of value added since 1947. This is paralleled by a decline in the contribution of the Non-IT industries, while the share of IT-using industries has remained relatively constant through 1995. Figure 1.2 decomposes the growth of value added for the period 1995–2012. The contributions of the IT-producing and IT-using industries peaked during the Investment Boom of 1995–2000 and have declined since then. The contribution of the Non-IT industries also declined substantially. Figure 1.3 gives the

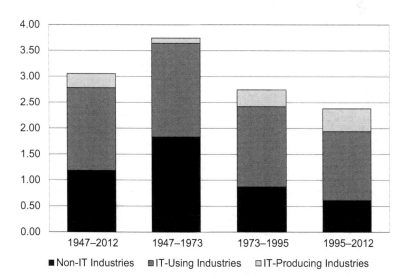

Figure 1.1 Contributions of industry groups to value-added growth, 1947–2012

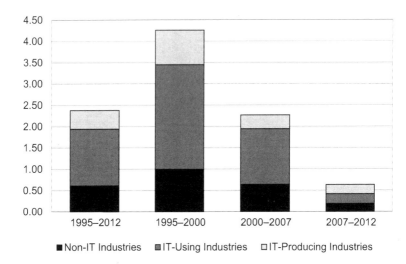

Figure 1.2 Contributions of industry groups to value-added growth, 1995–2012

contributions to value added for the 65 individual industries over the period 1947–2012.

The growth rate of aggregate productivity includes a weighted average of industry productivity growth rates, using an ingenious weighting scheme originated by Domar (1961). In the Domar weighting scheme, the productivity growth rate of each industry is weighted by the ratio of the industry's gross output to aggregate value added. A distinctive feature of Domar weights is that they sum to more than one, reflecting the fact that an increase in the rate of growth of the industry's productivity has two effects. The first is a direct effect on the industry's output, and the second an indirect effect via the output delivered to other industries as intermediate inputs.

The rate of growth of aggregate productivity also depends on the reallocations of capital and labor inputs among industries. The rate of aggregate productivity growth exceeds the weighted sum of industry productivity growth rates when these reallocations are positive. This occurs when capital and labor inputs are paid different prices in different industries and industries with higher prices have more rapid input growth rates. Aggregate capital and labor

The growth of the world economy   47

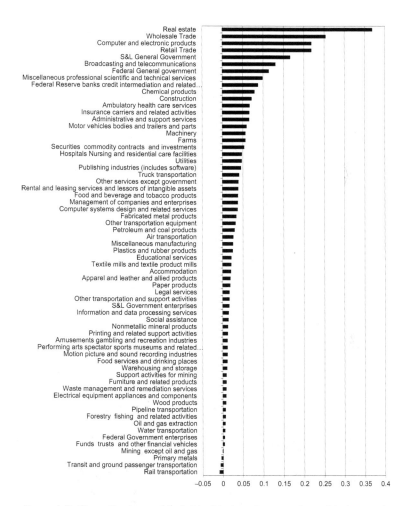

Figure 1.3 Contributions of individual industries to value-added growth, 1947–2012

inputs then grow more rapidly than weighted averages of industry capital and labor input growth rates, so that the reallocations are positive. When industries with lower prices for inputs grow more rapidly, the reallocations are negative.

Figure 1.4 shows that the contributions of IT-producing, IT-using, and Non-IT industries to aggregate productivity growth

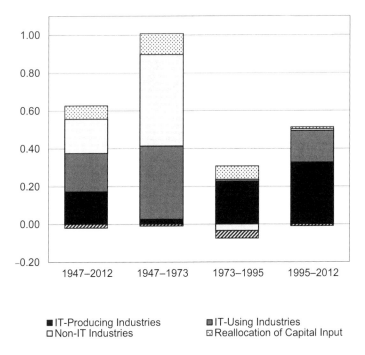

- IT-Producing Industries   - IT-Using Industries
- Non-IT Industries   - Reallocation of Capital Input

Figure 1.4 Contributions of industry groups to productivity growth, 1947–2012

are similar in magnitude for the period 1947–2012. The Non-IT industries greatly predominated in the growth of value added during the Postwar Recovery, 1947–73, but this contribution became negative after 1973. The contribution of IT-producing industries was relatively small during this Postwar Recovery, but became the predominant source of growth during the Long Slump, 1973–95, and increased considerably during the period of Growth and Recession of 1995–2012.

The IT-using industries contributed substantially to US economic growth during Postwar Recovery, but this contribution disappeared during the Long Slump, 1973–95, before reviving after 1995. The reallocation of capital input made a small but positive contribution to growth of the US economy for the period 1947–2012 and for each of the subperiods. The contribution of reallocation of labor input was negligible for the period as a whole. During the Long

Slump and the period of Growth and Recession, the contribution of the reallocation of labor input was slightly negative.

Considering the period 1995–2012 in more detail in Figure 1.5, the IT-producing industries predominated as a source of productivity growth during the period as a whole. The contribution of these industries remained substantial during each of sub-periods – 1995–2000, 2000–07, and 2007–12 – despite the strong contraction of economic activity during the Great Recession of 2007–09. The contribution of the IT-using industries was slightly greater than that of the IT-producing industries during the period of Jobless Growth, but dropped to nearly zero during the Great Recession. The Non-IT industries contributed positively to productivity growth during the Investment Boom of 1995–2000, but these contributions were

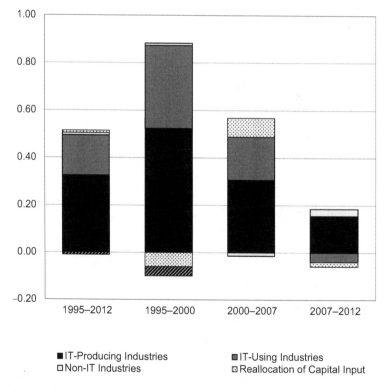

Figure 1.5 Contributions of industry groups to productivity growth, 1995–2012

50 Dale W. Jorgenson

almost negligible during the Jobless Recovery and became substantially negative during the Great Recession. The contributions of reallocations of capital and labor inputs were not markedly different from historical averages.

Figure 1.6 gives the contributions of each of the 65 industries to productivity growth for the period as a whole. Wholesale and retail trade, farms, computer and peripheral equipment, and semiconductors and other electronic components were among the

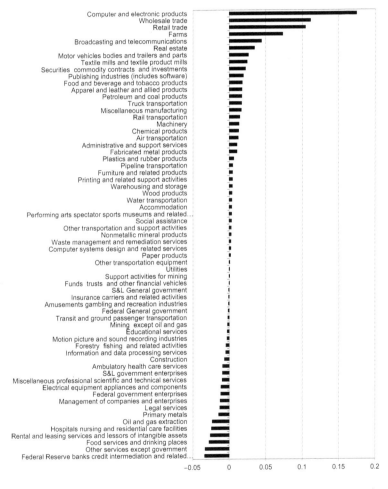

Figure 1.6 Contributions of individual industries to productivity growth, 1947–2012

leading contributors to US productivity growth during the postwar period. About half the 65 industries made negative contributions to aggregate productivity for the period 1947–2012 as a whole. These include non-market services, such as health, education, and general government, as well as resource industries, such as oil and gas extraction and mining, affected by resource depletion. Other negative contributions reflect the growth of barriers to resource mobility in product and factor markets due, in some cases, to more stringent government regulations.

The price of an asset is transformed into the price of the corresponding capital input by the *cost of capital*, introduced by Jorgenson (1963). The cost of capital includes the nominal rate of return, the rate of depreciation, and the rate of capital loss due to declining prices. The distinctive characteristics of IT prices – high rates of price decline and rates of depreciation – imply that cost of capital for the price of IT capital input is very large relative to the cost of capital for the price of Non-IT capital input.

The contributions of college-educated and non-college-educated workers to US economic growth are given by the relative shares of these workers in the value of output, multiplied by the growth rates of their labor input. Personnel with a college degree or higher level of education correspond closely with "knowledge workers" who deal with information. Of course, not every knowledge worker is college educated and not every college graduate is a knowledge worker.

Figure 1.8 reveals that all of the sources of economic growth contributed to the US growth resurgence during the 1995–2000 boom, relative to the Long Slump of 1973–95 represented in Figure 1.7. Jorgenson et al. (2005) analyze the sources of the US growth resurgence in greater detail. After the dot-com crash in 2000, the overall growth rate of the US economy dropped to well below the long-term average of 1947–2012. The contribution of investment also declined below the long-term average, but the shift from Non-IT to IT capital input continued. Jorgenson et al. (2008) argue that the rapid pace of US economic growth after 1995 was not sustainable.

The contribution of labor input dropped precipitously during the period of Growth and Recession, accounting for most of the decline in the rate of US economic growth during the Jobless Recovery. The contribution to growth by college-educated workers continued at a reduced rate, but that of non-college workers was negative. The most remarkable feature of the Jobless Recovery was the continued growth in productivity, indicating a continuing surge of innovation.

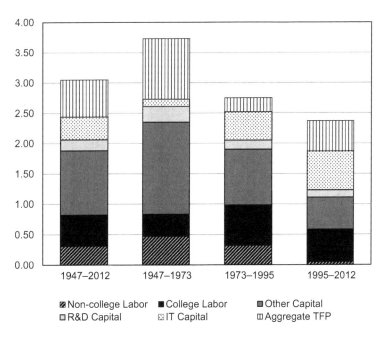

Figure 1.7 Sources of US economic growth, 1947–2012

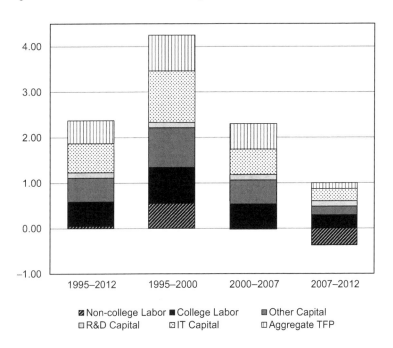

Figure 1.8 Sources of US economic growth, 1995–2012

Both IT and non-IT investment continued to contribute substantially to US economic growth during the Great Recession period after 2007. Productivity growth became negative, reflecting a widening gap between actual and potential growth of output. The contribution of college-educated workers remained positive and substantial, while the contribution of non-college workers became strongly negative. These trends represent increased rates of substitution of capital for labor and college-educated workers for non-college workers.

Conclusions

The new framework for productivity measurement reveals that replication of established technologies explains by far the largest proportion of US economic growth. Replication takes place through the augmentation of the labor force and the accumulation of capital. International productivity comparisons reveal similar patterns for the world economy; its major regions; and leading industrialized, developing, and emerging economies.[23] Studies are now underway to extend these comparisons to the countries included in the World KLEMS Initiative.

Innovation is indicated by productivity growth and accounts for a relatively modest portion of US economic growth. Innovation is far more challenging than replication of established technologies and subject to much greater risk. The diffusion of successful innovation requires substantial financial commitments. These fund the investments that replace outdated products and processes and establish new organization structures, systems, and business models. Although innovation accounts for a modest portion of economic growth, this is vital for maintaining gains in the US standard of living in the long run.

Industry-level production accounts are now prepared on a regular basis by national statistical agencies in Australia, Canada, Denmark, Finland, Italy, Mexico, the Netherlands, Sweden, and the United Kingdom, as well as the United States. These accounts provide current information about the growth of outputs, inputs, and productivity at the industry level and can be used in international comparisons of patterns of structural change like those presented by Jorgenson and Timmer (2011). The World KLEMS Initiative has made it possible to extend these comparisons to countries around the world, including important emerging and transition economies.

Notes

1. For the program and participants see: www.worldklems.net/conference1.htm, accessed 3 March 2016.
2. Updated data are available for the EU countries are posted on the EU KLEMS website: www.euklems.net/eukNACE2.shtml, accessed 3 March 2016.
3. For the program and participants see: www.euklems.net/conference.html, accessed 3 March 2016.
4. For the program and participants see: www.worldklems.net/conference2.htm, accessed 3 March 2016.
5. The conference program and presentations are available at: www.worldklems.net/conference2.htm, accessed 3 March 2016.
6. For the program and participants see: www.cepal.org/de/agenda/8/38158/Agenda.pdf, accessed 3 March 2016.
7. Additional information about LA-KLEMS is available on the project website: www.cepal.org/cgi-bin/getprod.asp?xml=/la-klems/noticias/paginas/4/40294/P40294.xml&xsl=/la-klems/tpl-i/p18f-st.xsl&base=/la-klems/tpl-i/top-bottom.xsl, accessed 3 March 2016.
8. www.inegi.org.mx/inegi/contenidos/espanol/prensa/Boletines/Boletin/Comunicados/Especiales/2013/agosto/comunica9.pdf, accessed 3 March 2016.
9. For the program and participants see: www.inegi.org.mx/eventos/2013/contabilidad_mexico/presentacion.aspx, accessed 3 March 2016.
10. For the program and participants see: http://asiaklems.net/conferences/conferences.asp. Asia KLEMS was preceded by International Comparison of Productivity among Asian Countries (ICPAC). The results were reported by Jorgenson et al. (2007).
11. www.rieti.go.jp/en/database/JIP2014/index.html, Data are available for 108 industries covering the period 1070–2011.
12. www.kpc.or.kr/eng/state/2011_kip.asp?c_menu=5&s_menu=5_4, accessed 3 March 2016.
13. www.rieti.go.jp/en/database/CIP2011/index.html, accessed 3 March 2016.
14. For the program and participants see: http://asiaklems.net/conferences/conferences.asp, accessed 3 March 2016.
15. http://scholar.harvard.edu/jorgenson/world-klems, accessed 3 March 2016.
16. www.wiod.org/new_site/home.htm, accessed 3 March 2016.
17. See: www.oecd.org/sti/ind/measuringtradeinvalue-addedanoecd-wtojointinitiative.htm, accessed 3 March 2016.
18. See: www.hse.ru/en/org/hse/expert/lipier/ruklems, accessed 3 March 2016.
19. www.rbi.org.in/scripts/PublicationReportDetails.aspx?UrlPage=&ID=785, accessed 3 March 2016.
20. The Advisory Committee was established on 6 December 2007, with ten members from the business community, including Carl Schramm, President and CEO of the Kauffman Foundation and chair of the

Committee. The Committee also had five academic members, including myself. The Advisory Committee met on 22 February and 12 September 2007, to discuss its recommendations. The final report was released on 18 January 2008.
21 The most recent data set is available at: www.bea.gov/national/inte grated_prod.htm, accessed 3 March 2016.
22 For current data, see: www.bea.gov/industry/index.htm#integrated, accessed 3 March 2016.
23 See Jorgenson and Vu (2013).

Bibliography

Advisory Committee on Measuring Innovation in the 21st Century Economy. 2008. *Innovation Measurement: Tracking the State of Innovation in the American Economy*. Washington, DC: U.S. Department of Commerce, January.

Cimoli, Mario, Andre Hofman, and Nanno Mulder, eds. 2010. *Innovation and Economic Development*. Northampton, MA: Edward Elgar.

Domar, Evsey. 1961. "On the Measurement of Technological Change." *Economic Journal* 71(284): 709–729.

Fleck, Susan, Steven Rosenthal, Matthew Russell, Erich Strassner, and Lisa Usher. 2014. "A Prototype BEA/BLS Industry-Level Production Account for the United States." In *Jorgenson, Landefeld, and Schreyer*, 323–372.

Fukao, Kyoji. 2012. *Japan's Economy and the Lost Two Decades*. Tokyo: Nikkei Publishing (in Japanese).

Fukao, Kyoji. 2013. "Explaining Japan's Unproductivity Two Decades." *Asian Economic Policy Review* 8(2): 193–213.

Harper, Michael, Brent Moulton, Steven Rosenthal, and David Wasshausen. 2009. "Integrated GDP-Productivity Accounts." *American Economic Review* 99(2): 74–79.

Jorgenson, Dale W. 1963. "Capital Theory and Investment Behavior." *American Economic Review* 53(2): 247–259.

Jorgenson, Dale W., ed. 2009. *The Economics of Productivity*. Northampton, MA: Edward Elgar.

Jorgenson, Dale W., Kyoji Fukao, and Marcel P. Timmer, eds. 2015. *Crisis and Stagnation in the World Economy*. Cambridge, UK: Cambridge University Press.

Jorgenson, Dale W., Frank M. Gollop, and Barbara M. Fraumeni. 1987. *Productivity and U.S. Economic Growth*. Cambridge, MA: Harvard University Press.

Jorgenson, Dale W., Mun S. Ho, and Jon D. Samuels. 2015. "U.S. Economic Growth – Retrospect and Prospect: Lessons from a Prototype Industry-Level Productivity Account for the United States, 1947–2012." In *Jorgenson, Fukao, and Timmer*.

Jorgenson, Dale W., Mun S. Ho, and Kevin J. Stiroh. 2005. *Information Technology and the American Growth Resurgence.* Cambridge, MA: The MIT Press.

Jorgenson, Dale W., Masahiro Kuroda, and Kazuyuki Motohashi, eds. 2007. *Productivity in Asia.* Northampton, MA: Edward Elgar.

Jorgenson, Dale W., and J. Steven Landefeld. 2006. "Blueprint for an Expanded and Integrated U.S. National Accounts: Review, Assessment, and Next Steps." In *Jorgenson, Landefeld and Nordhaus*, 13–112.

Jorgenson, Dale W., J. Steven Landefeld, and William D. Nordhaus, eds. 2006. *A New Architecture for the U.S. National Accounts.* Chicago: University of Chicago Press.

Jorgenson, Dale, W., Mun S. Ho, and Kevin J. Stiroh. 2008. "A Retrospective Look at the U.S. Productivity Growth Resurgence." *Journal of Economic Perspectives*, 22(1): 3–24.

Jorgenson, Dale W., J. Steven Landefeld, and Paul Schreyer, eds. 2014. *Measuring Economic Stability and Progress.* Chicago: University of Chicago Press.

Jorgenson, Dale W. and Schreyer, Paul, Industry-Level Productivity Measurement and the 2008 System of National Accounts (June 2013). *Review of Income and Wealth*, Vol. 59, Issue 2, pp. 185–211, 2013.

Jorgenson, Dale W., and Paul Schreyer. 2013. "Industry-Level Productivity Measurement and the 2008 System of National Accounts." *Review of Income and Wealth* 58(4): 185–211.

Jorgenson, Dale W., and Marcel P. Timmer. 2011. "Structural Change in Advanced Nations: A New Set of Stylized Facts." *Scandinavian Economic Journal* 113(1): 1–29.

Jorgenson, Dale W., and Khuong M. Vu. 2013. "Emergence of the New Economic Order: Economic Growth in the G7 and the G20." *Journal of Policy Modeling* 35(3): 389–399.

Kim, Donald D., Erich H. Strassner, and David B. Wasshausen. 2014. "Industry Economic Accounts: Results of the Comprehensive Revision Revised Statistics for 1997–2012." *Survey of Current Business* 94(2): 1–18.

Mas, Matilde, and Robert Stehrer, eds. 2012. *Industrial Productivity in Europe.* Northampton, MA: Edward Elgar.

Mayerhauser, Nicole M., and Erich H Strassner. 2010. "Preview of the Comprehensive Revision of the Annual Industry Accounts: Changes in Definitions, Classification, and Statistical Methods." *Survey of Current Business* 90(3): 21–34.

McCulla, Stephanie H., Alyssa E. Holdren, and Shelly Smith. 2013. "Improved Estimates of the National Income and Product Accounts: Results of the 2013 Comprehensive Revision." *Survey of Current Business* 93(9): 14–45.

National Institute of Statistics and Geography (INEGI). 2013. *Sistema de Cuentas Nacionales de Mexico: Productividad Total de los Factores, 1990–2011.* Aguascalientes, Mexico: INEGI (in Spanish).

Reserve Bank of India. 2014. *Estimates of Productivity Growth for the Indian Economy*. Mumbai, India: Reserve Bank of India.

Rosenthal, Steven, Matthew Russell, Jon D. Samuels, Erich H. Strassner, and Lisa Usher. 2015. "Integrated Industry-Level Production Account for the United States: Intellectual Property Products and the 2007 NAICS." In *Jorgenson, Fukao, and Timmer*.

Schreyer, Paul. 2001. *OECD Manual: Measuring Productivity: Measurement of Aggregate and Industry-Level Productivity Growth*. Paris: Organisation for Economic Development and Cooperation.

Schreyer, Paul. 2009. *OECD Manual: Measuring Capital*. Paris: Organisation for Economic Development and Cooperation.

Timmer, Marcel P., Robert Inklaar, Mary O'Mahony, and Bart van Ark. 2010. *Economic Growth in Europe: A Comparative Industry Perspective*. Cambridge, UK: Cambridge University Press, 2010.

Timmer, Marcel P., and Ilya Voskoboynikov. 2015. "Is Mining Fueling Long-Run Growth in Russia: Industry Productivity Trends Since 1995." In *Jorgenson, Fukao, and Timmer*.

United Nations, Commission of the European Communities, International Monetary Fund, Organisation for Economic Co-Operation and Development, and World Bank. 1993. *System of National Accounts 1993*. New York: United Nations.

United Nations, Commission of the European Communities, International Monetary Fund, Organisation for Economic Co-Operation and Development, and World Bank. 2009. *System of National Accounts 2008*. New York: United Nations.

Chapter 2

Productivity in the global economy[1]

Abdul A. Erumban and Bart van Ark

Introduction

During the last three decades, the global economy has undergone significant transformation due to a number of dynamics, including the emergence of China and India as major growth contributors, the higher degree of globalization and the increased penetration of information and communication technology (ICT). These developments have helped to greatly improve the well-being of population beyond advanced economies where many of the benefits of post-industrial revolution development process had been concentrated so far. For example, during the 1985–92 period, the global economy grew at an average rate of 2.5 percent, with the advanced economies growing faster than emerging markets (Figure 2.1). During the 1993–2000 period, when the global economy grew at 3.2 percent, the emerging markets overtook the advanced economies. This trend continued during the 2000–07 period, with the advanced economies seeing a growth of 2.6 percent – more than half a percentage point lower than the previous period, and the emerging markets increasing their growth rate by nearly 2.5 percentage points to 6.1 percent, resulting in a global growth of 4.2 percent.

During the post-financial crisis period from 2008 to 2015, growth in the global economy has slowed to 2.7 percent, with the emerging markets growing at 4.5 percent and the advanced economies by less than 1 percent.[2] This slowdown in global growth is worrying, as it affects the ability of the advanced economies to maintain the higher levels of well-being they achieved and the ability of the emerging and developing economies to further improve their income and welfare. Per capita income in the global economy grew at an impressive 3.3 percent during the 2000–07 period, with the emerging markets

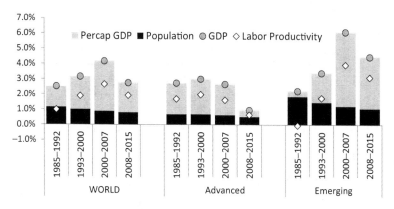

Figure 2.1 Growth rates of GDP, population, per capita GDP and labor productivity

Note: All growth rates are expressed in log changes. Population growth and per capita GDP growth adds up to GDP growth.

Source: The Conference Board Total Economy Database, November 2016

improving their income levels much faster, at nearly 5 percent. The global per capita income growth has declined to 2 percent, with both the advanced and the emerging markets seeing notable drop, respectively, from 2 percent to a mere 0.4 percent in the advanced economies and from 5 percent to 2.4 percent in the emerging economies (Figure 2.1).

This decline in GDP and per capita GDP growth has been proportionately reflected in slower labor productivity growth. The global labor productivity growth declined from 2.7 percent during 2000–07 to 1.9 percent during the last 7 years, posing major threats to competitiveness, profitability, wages and living standards.

The objective of this chapter is twofold. The first is to identify which proximate sources account for the slowdown in global labor productivity growth. For this purpose, we use The Conference Board's Total Economy Database (TED), which is specifically designed for international comparison of output and productivity, and which provides us with a unique opportunity to apply a growth accounting methodology at a global level. We identify the sources of labor productivity growth in terms of factor accumulation and total factor productivity in about 125 individual countries for the period 1980–2016. Subsequently, the chapter discusses various explanations, including the ones already available in the literature, for the ongoing declines in the global productivity, and provides insights on potential strategies that can change the gear toward improving productivity growth.

The remainder of the chapter is organized in six sections. In the first section (Understanding productivity using growth accounting), we discuss the importance of looking at productivity, preceded by a discussion on the growth accounting framework to analyze the proximate sources of GDP and labor productivity growth. The next section discusses the trends in the global labor productivity and its sources are analyzed. We then provide important general explanations for the productivity trend observed in the data, next discussing some potential strategies that could help regain productivity growth, and in the final section, we conclude.

Understanding productivity using growth accounting

Figure 2.2 provides a graphical presentation of how economic growth can be achieved by activating proximate sources of growth.[3] Firms, industries or countries can increase their output either by employing more workers (or increasing working hours) or by increasing the amount of output produced by each worker per working hour, i.e. labor productivity, or both. Increases in labor productivity can be achieved by increasing capital deepening – i.e. by increasing the amount of capital equipment such as machines, computers, trucks with which workers work; by improving the worker skills and competencies (for instance by changing the composition of work force towards higher skill levels); or by improving the overall efficiency by which labor and capital is combined to production process. While the contributions of labor quality and capital deepening to labor productivity growth can be quantified using data on worker skills and investment in capital assets, the contribution of overall efficiency is unobservable. The growth accounting framework allows for a quantification of this efficiency change – referred to as total factor productivity growth (TFPG) – as a residual after accounting for contributions from capital accumulation and labor quality. Under strict assumptions of perfect competition and constant returns to scale, this residual – also called the Solow residual following the seminal works of Solow (1957) – measures disembodied technological change. However, when these assumptions are

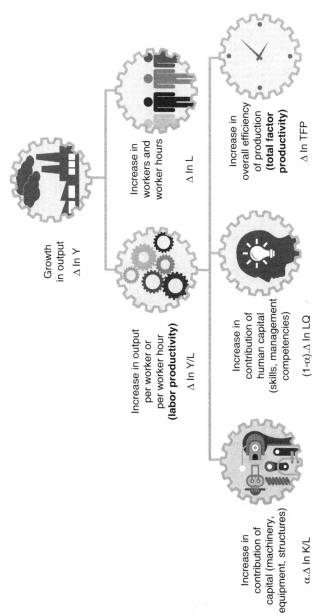

Figure 2.2 Defining labor productivity and total factor productivity under growth accounting framework

Note: The standard growth accounting equation is: $\Delta \ln Y/L = \alpha \cdot \Delta \ln K/L + (1 - \alpha) \cdot \Delta \ln LQ + \Delta \ln TFP$, where Y/L is labor productivity (output per workers or worker hour), K/L is capital services per worker, LQ is labor quality and TFP is total factor productivity. $\Delta \ln$ indicates growth rates (i.e. changes in the log values of each indicator).

Source: van Ark et al. (2016)

violated – which is often the case in the real world – the measure of TFPG might also reflect several other things beyond technological change, such as market power, returns to scale and institutional and policy effectiveness.

Regardless of these caveats, aggregate total factor productivity – as measured by the Solow residual – has clear welfare implications, as it is directly related to GDP and per capita income: TFPG implies an increase in output per unit of inputs. Since the growth of aggregate output measures a country's consumption potential, subtracting the opportunity cost of factor inputs used to produce the output from it provides a measure of welfare change (Basu and Fernald 2002). Basu et al. (2014) provide a consumer perspective on TFP by measuring it from domestic absorption rather than domestic production, so that the marginal costs are prices faced by consumers rather than producers. They show that this 'household centric Solow residual' is a good representative of welfare, even when it does not measure technical change.

Viewed from either angle – technological change or welfare – productivity, in particular aggregate productivity, becomes an important aspect of policy making. Indeed, the capital accumulation is essential in fueling output and labor productivity growth, but the growth achieved through factor accumulation is not sustainable in the longer run, due to diminishing returns. In this framework, TFPG is the only sustainable source of growth, as it ensures improved welfare at no cost from a societal perspective, and improved efficiency, competitiveness and profits from the producers' perspective. Past studies indicate the role of TFPG differences across countries in explaining cross-country growth differences (Hall and Jones 1999; Easterly and Levine 2001; Caselli 2004; Jones and Olken 2008).[4] Basu et al. (2014) suggests that TFPG and capital accumulation explain most of the welfare differences across countries. In going forward, the importance of productivity – both from a technology perspective and from a welfare perspective – will further increase, as several countries are likely to see a decline in either absolute number or growth rates of working-age population (Levanon et al. 2016).

This paper use the growth accounting framework to examine the sources of labor productivity growth in the global economy and major regions. For this, we use The Conference Board Total Economy Database™ (TED), which provides comprehensive annual data covering GDP, population, employment, hours, labor quality, capital services, labor productivity and total factor productivity for more than 120 countries in the world.[5] Capital input in the

TED is calculated as capital services, using real investment, depreciation rate, rates of return and asset prices for six different asset types – transport equipment, non-ICT machinery, structures, hardware, software and communication. They are finally combined into two main categories, ICT and non-ICT capital.[6] Labor quantity is defined as total employee hours worked. However, when such data is not available, we assume a proportionality between growth rate of employment and hours, and hence we use the growth rate of employment to proxy growth rate of hours. Labor quality is measured using a Törnqvist index of three worker categories – low-skilled, medium-skilled and high-skilled.

In general, the TED is consistent with official GDP data published by national statistical offices. One major exception to this is China, where several earlier studies have observed that the official data is less reliable. Following earlier works of Angus Maddison and Harry Wu, The Conference Board China Center for Economics and Business have systematically revised and updated the Maddison-Wu alternative estimates of China's GDP growth since 1950 by resolving some earlier empirical and data problems.[7] We use this alternative series for China in all our analysis in this paper. A second adjustment that makes the TED differ from the official data is an adjustment for the prices of ICT goods (see Erumban and de Vries (2016) for more details). Byrne and Corrado (2016) shows that the official price deflators for ICT assets in the United States understates the true declines in ICT prices significantly, leading to a downward bias in the real investment in ICT assets and, consequently, the real GDP. We correct for this downward bias in investment and GDP by deflating ICT assets by an alternative ICT deflators developed by Byrne and Corrado (2016). Since these deflators are available only for the United States, we use harmonized ICT price deflators for all other countries following the approach suggested by Schreyer (2002). A corresponding correction (i.e. an upward revision) is made to the GDP as well, but only for countries with significant ICT production and export (Canada, China, Ireland, Japan, Malaysia, Philippines, Singapore, South Korea, Taiwan and the United States).

Trends in and sources of the global labor productivity growth

Figure 2.3 shows the growth trend of labor productivity since 1970 for the emerging markets, the advanced economies, the United States and the global economy. The annual productivity growth

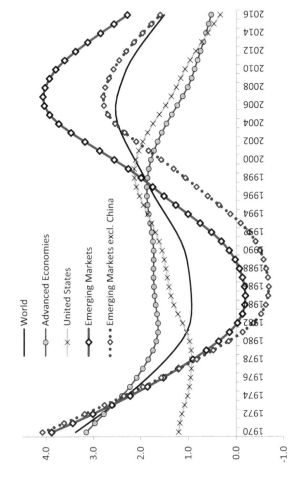

Figure 2.3 Trend in labor productivity growth, 1970–2016

Note: Trend growth rates are obtained using HP filter, assuming a $\lambda = 100$.
Source: The Conference Board Total Economy Database, November 2016

series have been smoothed using a Hodrick-Prescott (HP) filter.[8] The figure shows that during the period 1985–2007, labor productivity growth increased rapidly in the emerging markets, and moderately in the advanced economies. While China has been an important contributor to this labor productivity surge among the emerging market economies, this was not only due to China. Indeed, the emerging market group showed a significant acceleration in productivity growth, even with China being excluded. However, labor productivity growth rates in the advanced economies started falling rapidly in the beginning of this decade. This decline therefore started well before the global financial crisis in 2008/09, while the decline in the emerging markets only started around 2010. This slowing productivity trend has continued until today. Just as with the acceleration, a large part of the emerging market decline in productivity is due to substantial slowdown in Chinese labor productivity growth, but the emerging markets group shows massive productivity declines, even when China is excluded.

An obvious question is which proximate factors drive these productivity trends we observe. In Figure 2.4, we replicate the HP filtered labor productivity trend, along with HP filtered TFPG. We also superimpose the contribution of factor deepening and TFPG averaged over 5 time periods since 1992. The figure allows to make some important observations on the dynamics of productivity. Firstly, there is a strong correlation between the trend in labor productivity and TFPG. The simple correlation between TFPG and labor productivity growth for the entire period 1970–2015 is 0.90, whereas it is only 0.3 for capital deepening. Indeed, factor input (capital and labor) growth is a more constant growth factor than the variety of drivers of total factor productivity. The period 1992–2007 was clearly a period of ICT deepening, and especially during 2000–07 – a period of significant increase in global trade, and the widespread use of information and communication technology – the global economy witnessed massive TFPG gains. The decline in labor productivity growth since 2007 is primarily driven by a decline in TFP growth, as the weakness in demand in the advanced economies and the more slowdown global trade have been important brakes on TFPG. The global labor productivity growth has declined by almost 1 percentage point, from 3.2 percent to 2.3 percent, whereas the TFPG has decelerated from 1.1 percent to −0.1 percent (Table 2.1). Meanwhile the contribution of non-ICT capital deepening has in fact increased from 1.3 percent to 1.9 percent, especially

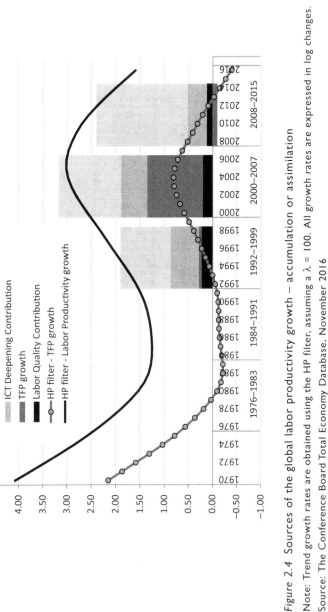

Figure 2.4 Sources of the global labor productivity growth – accumulation or assimilation

Note: Trend growth rates are obtained using the HP filter, assuming a λ = 100. All growth rates are expressed in log changes.

Source: The Conference Board Total Economy Database, November 2016

because of investment in the emerging markets. The contribution of ICT capital, which is characterized by higher returns, however, has declined marginally from 0.5 percent to 0.4 percent, thus suggesting a lesser impact of technological change on labor productivity. In fact, TFPG has weakened much more than labor productivity growth during this period.

Table 2.1 further provides the sources of labor productivity growth for the 2000–07 and 2008–15 periods for major regions and countries of the global economy. The United States and Japan, two technologically leading advanced economies, have witnessed a significant drop in their labor productivity growth rates, from 2.5 percent to 1.2 percent in the United States and from 2 percent to 0.9 percent in Japan. In both countries, this decline has been driven by declines in capital deepening – both ICT and non-ICT, though non-ICT decline was much larger – and TFPG. TFPG has entered negative territory in both countries. European countries, especially Euro Area countries also did see substantial losses in TFPG – again moving into negative territory – bringing their labor productivity growth to less than half of the rate at which they were growing in the pre-2007 period. While the contributions from capital deepening – both ICT and non-ICT – declined marginally or stayed the same, the TFPG decline was substantial, and dominant in driving the labor productivity growth decline in Europe.

The emerging market economies also witnessed huge declines in TFPG, while the factor inputs contributions remained relatively strong. TFPG declined by 2 percentage points to zero, whereas the contribution from ICT capital in these economies remained, by and large, the same in absolute terms and the non-ICT capital contribution increased by more than 1 percentage point. The only country among the regions and countries in the table that has registered an improvement in labor productivity growth is India, since 2008. India's labor productivity growth increased by almost 2.5 percentage points from 4 percent to 6.5 percent, with most of it coming from capital deepening – both ICT and non-ICT, but also with notable improvement in TFPG. It has been observed that India's aggregate growth is primarily spurred by the services sector, for which TFPG has been crucial (Verma 2012; Das et al. 2016). Much of the ICT gain in India was also concentrated in the service sector, whereas its manufacturing sector did not gain much (Erumban and Das 2016). China, the other major player in driving global labor productivity growth, experienced a TFPG of nearly

Table 2.1 Sources of labor productivity growth, 2000–07 and 2008–15

	2000–07					2008–15				
	Labor Pro-ductivity Growth*	Contributions from:				Labor Pro-ductivity Growth*	Contributions from:			
		ICT capital deepening	Non-ICT capital deepening	Labor quality	TFPG		ICT capital deepening	Non-ICT capital deepening	Labor quality	TFPG
World**	**3.2**	0.5	1.3	0.2	1.1	**2.3**	0.4	1.9	0.1	–0.1
Advanced Economies	**2.3**	0.6	1.0	0.3	0.4	**1.1**	0.4	0.7	0.1	–0.2
United States	**2.5**	0.7	1.2	0.3	0.3	**1.2**	0.4	0.6	0.1	–0.1
Japan	**2.0**	0.7	0.8	0.4	0.2	**0.9**	0.4	0.5	0.1	–0.1
Europe	**1.8**	0.4	0.8	0.2	0.4	**0.6**	0.3	0.7	0.1	–0.5
of which: Euro Area	**1.4**	0.4	0.7	0.2	0.1	**0.5**	0.3	0.7	0.1	–0.6
Other Advanced Economies	**3.7**	0.9	1.5	0.3	1.0	**2.3**	0.6	1.4	0.2	0.2
Emerging & Developing Economies**	**4.2**	0.4	1.7	0.1	2.0	**3.4**	0.4	3.0	0.1	0.0
China	**8.5**	0.7	4.7	0.2	2.9	**6.6**	0.3	5.8	0.1	0.4
China (official data)	**9.7**	0.9	5.2	0.2	3.4	**8.4**	0.4	6.5	0.1	1.4
India	**4.0**	0.8	2.8	0.1	0.3	**6.5**	1.3	4.2	0.1	0.9
Other Developing Asia	**3.4**	0.4	0.8	0.2	2.0	**3.2**	0.3	2.0	0.2	0.7
Latin America	**1.4**	0.2	0.6	0.1	0.6	**0.9**	0.1	1.4	0.1	–0.8
Brazil	**1.4**	0.1	0.2	0.1	1.0	**1.1**	0.1	1.3	0.2	–0.5
Mexico	**1.8**	0.3	1.8	0.1	–0.4	**–0.2**	0.2	0.8	0.1	–1.3
Other Latin America	**1.2**	0.1	0.2	0.2	0.8	**1.3**	0.2	1.8	0.1	–0.8

Middle East & North Africa	**1.2**	0.2	0.5	0.1	0.3	**0.2**	0.3	1.6	0.0	-1.7
Sub-Saharan Africa	**3.4**	0.2	0.5	0.1	2.7	**3.1**	0.3	2.0	0.1	0.8
Southeast Europe, Russia & Central Asia	**5.5**	0.3	0.2	0.0	5.0	**1.1**	0.2	0.7	0.0	0.2

Note: All growth rates are expressed in log changes. * Labor productivity is defined as GDP per hour. If hours data is not available, it is measured as GDP per worker. ** World and Emerging & Developing Economies aggregates are with alternative estimates for China, and therefore, will not reflect the official Chinese data.

Source: The Conference Board Total Economy Database (November 2016)

3 percent in the pre-crisis period, which has declined to just 0.4 percent since 2008 while capital deepening, in fact, increased. This trend remains unchanged even if we use official national accounts data for China, even though the rate of growth is then, of course, higher. China's economy, which has become increasingly dependent on capital deepening, is now experiencing a "soft fall", as it is moving to a service sector – domestic-oriented economy, and witnessing diminishing returns on capital (Hoffman and Polk 2014). Both capital and TFP contributions declined in other developing Asian economies, and in Latin America, Middle East and North Africa regions, productivity has declined substantially toward even negative territory.

Explaining productivity slowdown

The slowing trend in total factor productivity growth since the mid-2000s is quite substantial, long-lasting and across the board. Figure 2.5 provides a Harberger diagram which depicts the cumulative share of individual countries in the global GDP on the X-axis vis-à-vis the cumulative contribution of these countries into the global TFPG on the Y-axis. The upper plot is for 2000–07, and the lower one is for 2008–15. The two horizontal lines represent the global TFPG in each period. The decline in the global TFPG from 1.1 percent to –0.1 percent between the two periods was caused by a deceleration in TFPG in more than 60 percent of the countries included in the chart, and lower TFPG in 85 percent of countries compared to the previous period. The decline in TFPG is evident across the board, even though exactly when the slowdown began varies by country and region, notably with the decline starting earlier in the advanced economies compared to the emerging markets.

It is hard to attribute the slowdown in productivity growth to a single factor, but given the fact that the decline has been a global phenomenon, some important general explanations can be made.

The recession effect: Productivity growth – both labor productivity and TFP – is known to be pro-cyclical. During recessions, when output drops productivity growth mostly declines as well because firms hold on to their people and other assets, awaiting the recovery. This was clearly the case in several advanced economies, where productivity declined even when unemployment remained relatively slow in the post-crisis period.[9] Some other countries, for example Spain and the United States, showed a different picture, with

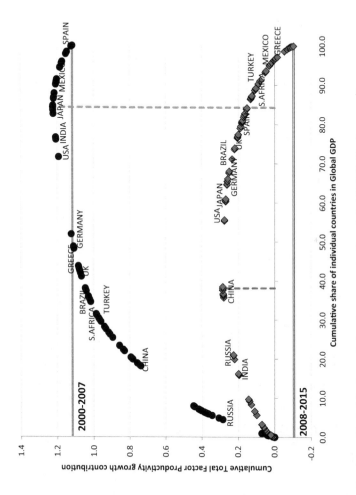

Figure 2.5 Contribution of individual countries to aggregate the global TFPG: Harberger diagram

Note: Each point represents a country's contribution to aggregate TFP growth (Y-axis) against its share in global GDP. All growth rates are expressed in log changes.

Source: The Conference Board Total Economy Database, November 2016

massive layoffs during the crisis.[10] Yet their TFPG has declined, on average, in the post-crisis period (see Figure 2.5). It is undoubtedly true that the financial crisis has played a crucial role in nurturing the rapid slowdown in the global productivity growth. The loss of output was much larger than the loss of employment and investment, thus suggesting a larger impact of crisis on TFPG. In addition to the direct impact of recession on output and productivity, tighter credit conditions in the post-crisis period might have weakened the entry of new firms into the market, limiting increased competitiveness and TFP, particularly in the advanced countries.

The pace of technology translating into productivity growth: As is evident from Figure 2.4, the global decline in productivity growth started earlier than the 2008/2009 crisis and has continued throughout its aftermath. Despite ongoing technological advances in many areas, the speed by which innovation translated into faster productivity growth has been disappointing since around 2005. Technology pessimists hold the view that the boom in ICT during the late-1990s and early-2000s was short-lived and that the current pace of technology has moved back to its natural slow path, as it was before the mid-1990s (Gordon 2016). For example, since the mid-2000s, the emerging technologies related to ICT have had less of an impact on productivity than on the value of new devices and applications to consumers.[11] Moreover, the newly available technologies are highly skill-biased, and therefore, the adoption of technology gets delayed due to the mismatch between skill availability and skill requirement.

Optimists argue that the current slowdown is just a timing issue because new technologies need time to diffuse within firms before showing a productivity payoff. In this line of thinking, technology use will expand even more rapidly in the coming years, even challenging the creation of future jobs (Brynjolfsson and McAfee 2011). The impact of new digital technologies and applications – including big data analytics, artificial intelligence and the Internet of Things – may help strengthen productivity growth, but that has yet to come to fruition (van Ark et al. 2016).

The secular stagnation hypothesis: A third explanation refers to an even bigger problem than just the pace of technology diffusion and adoption. It relates to an ongoing slowdown in demand and weak investment in physical and human capital, as well as other intangible assets. This view sees the advanced economies going into long-term stagnation, exacerbated by slow growth in labor supply and low inflation, which is at the heart of the so-called "secular stagnation" hypothesis, reducing firms' incentive to invest in new capital goods that could accelerate productivity (Summers 2014).

The role of the emerging markets: As we observed above, much of the slowdown in the global TFP growth stems from several emerging market economies. To a large extent, the productivity slowdown in these economies is a result of their success in previous decades. During the 1990s and early 2000s several large emerging markets benefited from a productivity catch-up; often as the result of major public policy shifts, such as greater access to the global markets, the quick adoption of technologies from the advanced economies, and social and economic reforms that created more domestic demand.

China, for example, generated a huge productivity boost after it became a member of the World Trade Organization in 2001, unleashing its potential to develop into the world's largest manufacturing hub, benefiting from low labor cost and high infrastructure investment. Other emerging markets, including Brazil, Mexico, India, South Africa and Turkey, also went through period of rapid catch-up growth.

Today, however, emerging markets like China are in the process of transitioning from a dependency on large investment and manufacturing exports as growth drivers to greater domestic consumption of goods and especially services, even if most of those economies are still at middle-income level. As a result, there is a gradual shift underway in these economies from high-productivity manufacturing industries to low-productivity consumer services. For instance, the share of service sector in Chinese GDP has increased from about 25 percent in 1980 to above 40 percent in 2010 (China Industry Productivity Database 2015). Also, as labor costs begin to rise, workers need to be equipped with new skills and competencies to move their production activities higher up in the value chain. Innovation and new technologies can no longer be simply borrowed from foreign firms. Many of these economies are also currently under severe skill challenges (Levanon et al. 2016). Organizational investments will become much more important as production processes become more complex, and optimizing the mix of labor, capital and access to shared services becomes harder and requires deeper collaboration with partners in the supply chain. Several emerging economies, including China, India, Brazil and Mexico, have been struggling recently to make appropriate policy reforms that would ease supply-side bottlenecks and strengthen the performance of markets so that faster productivity growth can be achieved.[12]

Policy and regulatory environment: Several factors that have an impact on productivity are beyond the purview of firms, such as a non-conducive regulatory and policy environment. During the past decade, several of those external factors have added to the productivity slowdown. For example, new financial sector reforms in the United States, while necessary to avoid the negative effects from unregulated financial innovations that were some of the important causes of the financial crisis, have stifled the ability of banks to provide ample lending for new investment by firms, especially for small and medium enterprises. Access to venture capital and other types of lending for high-risk projects, which are often the source of bringing new technology and innovations to the fore, has become more difficult. In Europe, the failure to complete a single market for goods and services across the member states of the European Union has seriously reduced the region's ability to scale economic activity and achieve higher productivity. In particular, new applications in the area of ICT have been hampered by the lack of a single digital market, with fragmented regulations related to several ICT-related services. Europe has been lagging behind the United States in terms of ICT adoption for quite a long time now. Regulations to protect privacy and increased cybersecurity, while necessary to sustain the technology, can have sharply negative effects on productivity. Weak policy environments and poor institutional quality have also been major impediments to attain higher productivity growth in several emerging market economies. For instance, rigid labor market policies play an important role in fostering expansion of informal economy in India, which reduces aggregate productivity growth (Das et al. 2016).

Measurement issues: For better understanding of productivity dynamics, it is essential to have well-measured inputs (capital and labor) and output. The nature of production and consumption has changed drastically in the recent years – be it in the form of increased fragmentation of global production and consequent increases in trade in intermediate goods (see Timmer et al. 2014), or increasing role of digital and shared economy and cashless payments. In an increasingly "weightless" economy, with increasing role of services than manufacturing and increasing role of digital than physical output, conventional macroeconomic statistics, such as GDP, might not be appropriate for capturing productivity and welfare. While measurement issues are a great challenge for statisticians and academics, one cannot be nihilistic about what the major biases are, and how to correct for them.

In our analysis in this Chapter, we have deviated from official government statistics on investment in information and technology, which are notoriously understating the quality gains and price declines embodied in these new technologies. We make a partial correction for the faster declines in ICT investment prices by deflating ICT investment by alternative quality-adjusted prices developed by Byrne and Corrado (2016). The faster declines in ICT goods and services prices, and the increased role of shared services, should ideally also increase real output – both in terms of increased availability of real output and increased consumer surplus. In our results so far, we only made an adjustment to GDP in select countries with relatively larger production and export of ICT goods. This correction, however, does not help eliminate the large declines in productivity growth, observed in this chapter.[13]

Concluding remarks

The pace of the global labor productivity growth has slowed drastically since the beginning of the current decade. This chapter has documented that the decline in labor productivity is primarily due to continuous decline in TFPG. A multitude of factors have shown to be important in explaining the decline of TFP growth in the global economy.

The question is what is needed to counter the downward trend. This challenge is especially large as the growth of the working-age population is expected to decline (in the advanced economies) or at least moderate (in the emerging markets) in the coming decade. The direct implication of this demographic change will be a shortage of workers for several jobs in the advanced economies. In several emerging market economies, an acceleration in already existing skill-shortage problem may occur as the competition for skilled workers will intensify. Peri et al. (2015) suggest that the role of foreign STEM workers in raising aggregate total factor productivity growth in the United States was pivotal, as they explained 30–50 percent of aggregate TFPG between 1990 and 2010. For the advanced economies, increasing participation of female and retired workers, creating and securing workforce skills (such as those of millennial and digital workers), opening up boarders for immigrants, and even off-shoring or teleworking will therefore remain important human capital strategies (Levanon et al. 2016). New approaches to investing in knowledge-based assets (such as research and development, design, training, brand and organizational improvements); strengthening better management competencies within firms; and embracing reforms in product, labor and capital markets will all help firms reallocate labor and capital to more productive uses. Finally, the fruits of the transition towards new digital technologies and applications also critically depend on companies' ability to access digital services and create digital skills, strengthening inter and intra-firm collaboration.

For many emerging market economies, there is still catch-up potential, as most are far below the productivity level of the advanced economies. For instance, even today China and India, two of the fastest-growing economies in Asia during the last decade, are still at 19 percent and 14 percent of the United States labor productivity level, respectively (The Conference Board Total Economy Database 2016). The potential for catch-up growth from low levels of development is still available to many smaller emerging and developing markets. Productivity levels of many economies in sub-Saharan Africa, Asia and Latin America are still well below those of the BRICS (Brazil, Russia, India, China, South Africa) economies, and many of them have large consumer populations and an ample supply of low-wage labor. Policies that enhance structural change, by which resources can be relocated from low productive use to high productive sectors, is an essential aspect of the growth process of several of these emerging market economies. Most emerging markets also need to increase their focus on improving human capital to regain growth and productivity.

Several uncertainties surrounding the global economy – for instance, the scale of creative destruction that the new technologies could bring – limit our ability to foresee which direction we are heading. Whether the digital revolutions will boost productivity growth sufficiently to offset the slowdown in labor supply due to aging, but also because of the technology bias against jobs is still unclear. The fact that TFPG has weakened much more than has labor productivity indicates that the productivity decline is not primarily a matter of inefficient workers, but of ineffective investment in other inputs that help firms combine factors efficiently such as knowledge-based assets (intangibles, ICT, R&D and competencies). It is also clear that the ultimate sources of growth, which includes institutional and policy changes, are crucial both in the emerging and the advanced economies to fuel their future productivity growth.

Notes

1 This chapter draws heavily on several past researches undertaken at the Conference Board. The authors are thankful to Ataman Ozyildirim and Klaas de Vries. The views expressed in the chapter are those of the authors and not necessarily reflect the views of the Conference Board.
2 According to The Conference Board Total Economy Database, almost 80 percent of countries in the global economy had a slower growth rate during the 2008–2015 period compared to the 2000–2007 period.
3 See Maddison (1991) for discussions on the distinction between ultimate and proximate sources of growth. Ultimate sources of growth, which can in fact influence proximate sources, include institutions, historic incidents and policy changes.
4 The importance of capital deepening in driving growth has also been evident in several regional and global studies (World Bank 1993; Krugman 1994; Young 1995; Jorgenson and Vu 2005).
5 The TED was developed by the Groningen Growth and Development Centre (University of Groningen, The Netherlands) in the early 1990s, and starting in the late 1990s, it was produced in partnership with The Conference Board. As of 2007, the database was transferred from the University of Groningen to The Conference Board, which has maintained and extended the database since then. In January 2010, the database was extended with a module on sources of growth, including labor quantity and quality, capital services (non-ICT and ICT) and total factor productivity. For detailed discussion on the sources and methods used in the TED, see www.conference-board.org/data/economydatabase/, accessed 29 November 2016.
6 The ICT investment were originally developed by Jorgenson and Vu (2005) using data from WITSA (also see Jorgenson and Vu 2013). The current version of the TED has built further upon this data to measure ICT investments more accurately.
7 The spirit of the Maddison-Wu adjustment is by no means to treat official data as totally devoid of credibility. Rather, it aims to systematically dig out the most useful, least-biased information from all available official sources. The Conference Board estimate that the over-reporting of the official estimates over the past 10 years is about two-thirds attributable to a "misreport effect", including data fabrications at any level of the data-generating process from localities to the central authorities (often to meet official high targets, at any cost); and the remaining one-third to a "price effect", i.e., an underestimation of price changes (or inflation). See Wu (2014a, 2014b) and The Conference Board (2015) for detailed discussions on the methodology of the alternative estimates, and analysis of the results.
8 The HP filter helps decompose a time series into trend and cyclical components (see Hodrick and Prescott 1997). It requires a smoothing

parameter λ, the value of which determines the smoothness of the trend line. The larger the value of λ, the smoother the resulting trend will be. For instance, a λ = 0 would imply the trend is the same as the original series and as λ gets larger, the trend gets closer to a linear OLS regression line. We assume a λ = 100, which is most commonly used in the literature to smooth annual time series data. A major drawback of HP filter is endpoint bias, but that does not affect our observation that productivity growth has been declining for a longer period of time.
9 For instance, in countries such as Germany, Japan and the United Kingdom, unemployment rates remained relatively low since the 2008–2009 global economic and financial crisis but productivity growth weakened.
10 For instance, at the end of 2007, the US unemployment rate was 5 percent, which increased to 10 percent by the end of 2009 (BLS 2012).
11 For instance, Byrne et al. (2016) show that consumer well-being increases more due to several 'new economy' technologies without necessarily shifting the market economy production functions.
12 For a more detailed analysis of productivity challenges in China, see Hoffman and Polk (2014) and Wu (2014a). And for analysis on India's productivity trends and challenges see Das et al. (2016).
13 The findings of Syverson (2016) and Byrne et al. (2016) for the United States also indicate that the productivity decline is a larger problem and is not related to mismeasurement of ICT only.

Bibliography

Basu, S., and J. G. Fernald. 2002. "Aggregate Productivity and Aggregate Technology." *European Economic Review* 46: 963–991.

Basu, S., L. Pascali, F. Schiantarelli, and L. Serven. 2014. "Productivity and the Welfare of Nations." *NBER Working Paper* #17971. www.nber.org/papers/w17971, accessed May 2016.

BLS. 2012. *The Recession of 2007–2009*. United States Bureau of Labor Statistics. www.bls.gov/spotlight/2012/recession/pdf/recession_bls_spot light. pdf, accessed May 2016.

Brynjolfsson, E., and A. McAfee. 2011. *Race Against the Machine – How the Digital Revolution Is Accelerating Innovation, Driving Productivity, and Irreversibly Transforming Employment and the Economy*. Lexington, MA: Digital Frontier Press.

Byrne, D., and C. Corrado. 2016. "ICT Prices and ICT Services: What Do They Tell Us About Productivity and Technology." *The Conference Board Working Paper* EPWP#16-05.

Byrne, D., J. Fernald, and M. Reinsdorf. 2016. "Does the United States Have a Productivity Slowdown or a Measurement Problem?" *Brooking Papers on Economic Activity*, Spring: 109–157.

Caselli, F. 2004. "Accounting for Cross-Country Income Differences." In *Handbook of Economic Growth*, vol. 1A. North Holland: Elsevier.

China Industry Productivity Database. 2015. Tokyo: RIETI. www.rieti.go.jp/en/database/CIP2015/, accessed May 2016.

The Conference Board. 2015. *Frequently Asked Questions on The Conference Board's Alternative China GDP Series*, November. http://bit.ly/2fPBgqT, accessed May 2016.

The Conference Board. 2016. *The Conference Board Total Economy Database*, November.

Das, D. K., A. A. Erumban, S. Aggarwal, and S. Sengupta. 2016. "Productivity Growth in India Under Different Policy Regimes." In D. Jorgenson, M. P. Timmer, and K. Fukao (eds.), *The World Economy: Growth or Stagnation?* Cambridge: Cambridge University Press.

Easterly, W., and R. Levine. 2001. "It's Not Factor Accumulation: Stylized Facts and Growth Models." *The World Bank Economic Review* 15(2): 177–219.

Erumban, A. A., and D. K. Das. 2016. "Information and Communication Technology and Economic Growth in India." *Telecommunications Policy* 40(5): 412–431. DOI: 10.1016/j.telpol.2015.08.006

Erumban, A. A., and G. J. de Vries. 2016. *The Conference Board Total Economy Database, Sources and Methods*. The Conference Board.

Gordon, R. J. 2016. *The Rise and Fall of American Growth*. Princeton, NJ: Princeton University Press.

Hall, R., and C. Jones. 1999. "Why Do Some Countries Produce So Much More Output Per Worker Than Others?" *Quarterly of Economics* 114(1): 84–116.

Hodrick, R., and E. C. Prescott. 1997. "Postwar Business Cycles: An Empirical Investigation." *Journal of Money, Credit, and Banking* 29: 1–16.

Hoffman, D., and A. Polk. 2014. *The Long Soft Fall in Chinese Growth: Business Realities, Risks, and Opportunities*. The Conference Board. www.conference-board.org/china-growth/, accessed May 2016.

Jones, B. F., and B. A. Olken. 2008. "The Anatomy of Start-Stop Growth." *Review of Economics and Statistics* 90(3): 582–587.

Jorgenson, D. W., and K. Vu. 2005. "Information Technology and the World Economy." *Scandinavian Journal of Economics* 107(4): 631–650.

Jorgenson, D. W., and K. Vu. 2013. "The Emergence of the New Economic Order: Growth in the G7 and the G20." *Journal of Policy Modeling* 35(3): 389–399.

Krugman, P. 1994. "The Myth of Asia's Miracle." *Foreign Affairs* 73(6): 62–78.

Levanon, G., A. A. Erumban, B. Cheng, E. Hayek, B. Schaitkin, F. Steemers, and E. Winger. 2016. *Help Wanted: What Looming Labor Shortages Mean for Business – CHRO Implications*. The Conference Board.

Maddison, A. 1991. *Dynamic Forces in Capitalist Development*. Oxford, UK: Oxford University Press.

Peri, G., K. Y. Shih, and C. Sparber. 2015. "STEM Workers, H-1B Visas, and Productivity in US Cities." *Journal of Labor Economics* 33(3): S225–S255.

Schreyer, P. 2002. "Computer Price Indices and International Growth and Productivity Comparisons." *Review of Income and Wealth* 48(1): 15–31.

Solow, R. M. 1957. "Technical Change and the Aggregate Production Function." *Review of Economics and Statistics* 39: 312–320.

Summers, L. H. 2014. "US Economic Perspectives: Secular Stagnation, Hysteresis, and the Zero Lower Bound." *Business Economics* 49(2).

Syverson, C. 2016. "Challenges to Mismeasurement Explanations for the U.S. Productivity Slowdown." *NBER Working Paper Series*, Working Paper 21974, National Bureau of Economic Research, Cambridge, MA.

Timmer, M. P., A. A. Erumban, B. Los, R. Stehrer, and G. J. de Vries. 2014. "Slicing Up Global Value Chains." *Journal of Economic Perspectives* 28(2): 99–118.

van Ark, B., A. A. Erumban, C. Corrado, and G. Levanon. 2016. *Navigating the Digital Economy: Driving Digital Growth and Productivity From Installation to Deployment*. The Conference Board.

Verma, R. 2012. "Can Total Factor Productivity Explain Value Added Growth in Services?" *Journal of Development Economics* 99(1): 163–177.

World Bank. 1993. *The East Asian Miracle: Economic Growth and Public Policy*. Oxford and New York: Oxford University Press.

Wu, Harry X. 2014a. "Re-Estimating Chinese Growth: How Fast Has China's Economy Really Grown?" *Special Briefing Paper*, The Conference Board China Center for Economics and Business, June. www.conference-board.org/publications/publicationdetail.cfm?publicationid=2780, accessed May 2016.

Wu, Harry X. 2014b. "China's Growth and Productivity Performance Debate Revisited." *The Conference Board Economics Working Papers*, February. www.conference-board.org/publications/publicationdetail.cfm?publicationid=2690, accessed May 2016.

Young, A. 1995. "The Tyranny of Numbers: Confronting the Statistical Realities of the East Asian Growth Experience." *Quarterly Journal of Economics* 110(3): 641–680.

Chapter 3

Productivity growth in Asia and its country origins

Koji Nomura

Introduction

Recovery from the global financial crisis of 2008–09 has been notably slow in the European economy, with its growth rate for 2010–14 steady at 0.5 percent per annum on average, relative to 2.1 percent growth in the pre-crisis period of 2000–07 (as represented by 15 member countries of EU prior to enlargement). In contrast, the United States has managed to raise its growth rate to 1.9 percent for 2010–14, and is beginning to return to its long-term growth track. The Asian economy, which has become increasingly autonomous from the Western economies and even contributed to stabilizing the global economy at the time of the global financial crisis, has been maintaining a stable economic growth of 5.3 percent per annum on average during 2010–14. Yet, this represents a slowdown of 1 percentage point from the level recorded in the pre-crisis period. Our study indicates that it is mainly due to the reduction in the growth of total factor productivity (TFP) of the Asian economy.

The purpose of this study is to develop a productivity index for "Entire Asia", which is defined as a group of 21 Asian countries, for the period of 1970–2014 and to decompose it to its country origins. The notable improvement made to our measurement is the development of the purchasing power parities (PPPs) for capital and labor inputs for Asian countries. Diewert and Fox (2015) recommend using the annual PPP information to adjust the country value shares in aggregating outputs across countries. In the development of the growth accounting framework for Entire Asia in this study, a similar framework is applied for aggregating capital and labor inputs by country, taking into account the price differentials in capital and labor inputs across countries.

This chapter is organized as follows. The next section presents the methodological framework to measure the real output and capital and labor inputs, which are comparable across countries. The country-level productivity data used in this paper is mainly based on the APO Productivity Database 2016, which is developed at our joint research with Asian Productivity Organization (APO 2016). The estimates of PPPs for outputs for 21 Asian countries are based on the International Comparison Program 2011 round, coordinated jointly by the World Bank, OECD and Eurostat (World Bank 2014). In the following section, we develop the new measures of PPPs for capital and labor inputs for 21 Asian countries in the base period of 2011. The estimated results on the growth accounting for Entire Asia are presented next, and the last section concludes.

Framework

Productivity by country

We begin with the definitions of price and volume for output (Y) and capital (K) and labor (L) at the aggregate level in each country. The nominal output value $P_{Y,c}Y_c$ ($=V_{Y,c}$) evaluated at the basic prices in the local currency unit (LCU) in country c is defined as:

$$P_{Y,c}Y_c = P_{K,c}K_c + P_{L,c}L_c \quad (3.1)$$

where $P_{Y,c}$, $P_{K,c}$ and $P_{L,c}$ are the respective prices of the volumes of output Y_c and inputs of capital K_c and labor L_c. The capital and labor costs are denoted as $P_{K,c}K_c$ ($=V_{k,c}$) and $P_{L,c}L_c$ ($=V_{L,c}$). Under the assumptions of constant returns to scale and competitive markets, a translog index of total factor productivity (TFP) growth is defined as:

$$v_{T,c} = \Delta \ln Y_c - \bar{v}_{K,c}\Delta \ln K_c - \bar{v}_{L,c}\Delta \ln L_c \quad (3.2)$$

where $\bar{v}_{K,c}$ and $\bar{v}_{L,c}$ are the two-period average shares of the capital and labor inputs in the value of output, respectively. For measuring the country-level productivity, we use data on output and inputs in Equation (3.1) from the APO Productivity Database 2016, in which country data are harmonized for better comparability across the Asian countries based on the 2008 SNA (APO 2016). The capital input is measured as capital services by aggregating 11 types of capital input and labor input is measured as total hours worked.[1] This data covers the entire country group of the Asian economy except Bhutan, for which we use the productivity data developed in the UNDESA research project (UNDESA 2016).[2] Although the accuracy of our estimates for Entire Asia depends on the data quality in country-level productivity, this study does not examine the issues involved in the country data, in which a number of data uncertainties remain.

Country aggregation

Next, we measure the output and capital and labor inputs growths for a group of countries. The values evaluated at LCU in Equation (3.1) are converted to that at the US dollar in two ways: the market exchange rates and the PPPs. Taking the price differentials in outputs across countries into consideration, Diewert and Fox (2015) recommend using the annual PPP information to adjust the country value shares in aggregating outputs across countries. The PPP-adjusted output value in each country is defined as:

$$V_{Y^*,c} = V_{Y,c} / PPP_{Y,c} \qquad (3.3)$$

where $PPP_{Y,c}$ is the annual PPP, which measures the prices in LCU of country c, required to purchase the same amount of output as purchased by one dollar in the United States in each period of t. The measures $V_{Y^*,c}$ are comparable across countries and are called as "real" GDP in the context of spatial (as opposed to intertemporal) international comparison research as the Penn World Table (Feenstra et al. 2015). The aggregate of real output for a group of countries is measured by a simple sum of real outputs by country ($V_{Y^*} = \sum_c V_{Y^*,c}$). We define the output growth for the country group as a translog index:

$$\Delta \ln Y = \sum_c \bar{s}_{Y,c} \Delta \ln Y_c \qquad (3.4)$$

where $\bar{s}_{Y,c}$ is the two-period average share of the country output ($V_{Y^*,c}$) in the country-group output value (V_{Y^*}).

In aggregating capital and labor inputs across countries, the same weights ($\bar{s}_{Y,c}$) that are measured based on PPPs for GDP have been used in the exercises as the Total Economy Database (TED) by the Conference Board (De Vries and Erumban 2015). Using $\bar{s}_{Y,c}$ as the country weights, the growths of capital and labor inputs for the country group are measured as a translog index:

$$\Delta \ln \hat{K} = \sum_c \bar{s}_{Y,c} \Delta \ln K_c \text{ and } \Delta \ln \hat{L} = \sum_c \bar{s}_{Y,c} \Delta \ln L_c \quad (3.5)$$

respectively. If we take into account the price differentials of capital and labor inputs across countries in country aggregation, the "real" inputs of capital and labor for the country group are measured as:

$$V_{K^*,c} = V_{K,c} / PPP_{K,c} \text{ and } V_{L^*,c} = V_{L,c} / PPP_{L,c} \quad (3.6)$$

respectively. Using these real factor inputs that are comparable across countries, the aggregate inputs of capital and labor for a country group by a simple sum of real inputs by country as $V_{K^*} = \sum_c V_{K^*,c}$ and $V_{L^*} = \sum_c V_{L^*,c}$, respectively. We define the growths of capital and labor inputs for a country group as translog indices:

$$\Delta \ln K = \sum_c \bar{s}_{K,c} \Delta \ln K_c \text{ and } \Delta \ln L = \sum_c \bar{s}_{L,c} \Delta \ln L_c \quad (3.7)$$

respectively, where $\bar{s}_{K,c}$ and $\bar{s}_{L,c}$ are the two-period average shares of the country inputs in the country-group real inputs of capital and labor, respectively, defined in Equation (3.6).

For our measurement, the PPPs for GDP in the base period of 2011 for 21 Asian countries are based on the estimates in the International Comparison Program (ICP) 2011 round, coordinated jointly by the World Bank, OECD and Eurostat (World Bank 2014). PPPs for capital and labor inputs are estimated in the third section. Our estimates indicate that there are considerable differences between the PPPs for GDP and the PPPs for factor inputs, especially in emerging Asian countries. Using the single base-year estimates of the 2011 PPPs for output and factor inputs, annual PPPs are extrapolated using prices for output and factor inputs, which are measured in our productivity data for each country.

Productivity in a country group

In the TED (De Vries and Erumban 2015), TFP growth in a country group is measured using the aggregated measures of output and capital and labor inputs, which are measured in Equations (3.4) and (3.5), respectively, as:

$$\hat{v}_T = \Delta \ln Y - \overline{v}_K \Delta \ln \hat{K} - \overline{v}_L \Delta \ln \hat{L} \tag{3.8}$$

where $\overline{v}_K$ and $\overline{v}_L$ are the two-period average shares of capital and labor inputs in the output value, which are defined using PPPs for output in each year as

$$v_K = \sum_c \left(V_{K,c} / PPP_{Y,c} \right) / V_Y \quad \text{and} \quad v_L = \sum_c \left(V_{L,c} / PPP_{Y,c} \right) / V_Y. \tag{3.9}$$

respectively. The sum of v_K and v_L is 1.0 in each year. Alternatively, we define a translog index of TFP growth in a country group based on the real inputs of capital and labor defined in Equation (3.7):

$$v_T = \Delta \ln Y - \overline{v}_K \Delta \ln K - \overline{v}_L \Delta \ln L \tag{3.10}$$

Our measure on the aggregated growth of TFP in Equation (3.10) can be decomposed to the country origins of TFP growths and the price-differential factors of capital and labor:

$$v_T = \sum_c \overline{s}_{Y,c} v_{T,c} + \gamma_K + \gamma_L \tag{3.11}$$

where γ_K and γ_L are defined as:

$$\gamma_K = \sum_c \left(\overline{s}_{Y,c} \overline{v}_{K,c} - \overline{v}_K \overline{s}_{K,c} \right) \Delta \ln K_c \quad \text{and}$$
$$\gamma_L = \sum_c \left(\overline{s}_{Y,c} \overline{v}_{L,c} - \overline{v}_L \overline{s}_{L,c} \right) \Delta \ln L_c \tag{3.12}$$

These factors are originated to the differences between the PPP for output and the PPPs for factor inputs. If the PPPs for output and PPPs for capital and labor inputs are identical, γ_K and γ_L are measured as 0 and $\hat{v}_T$ is not biased ($v_T = \hat{v}_T$). However, in the case that the relative prices for labor input are lower than the relative prices for output ($PPP_{L,c} < PPP_{Y,c}$) in the countries with larger increases of labor inputs, γ_L is to be negative. Then, as a measure of the country-group TFP growth, $\hat{v}_T$ carries an upward bias due to an underestimation of its labor input growth $\hat{L}$ measured in Equation (3.5). Our alternative measure v_T improves the measurement of country-group

TFP growth, since the labor input L measured in Equation (3.7) evaluates labor inputs in the country group appropriately.

Factor price PPPs

PPP for capital

The growth of capital input price, $P_{K,c}$ in Equation (3.1), is measured as a translog index of the growths of capital input prices by k-type of assets in each country, $P_{K,k,c}$. The first step in measuring PPP for capital inputs is to construct a common asset classification across the Asian countries and the United States as a reference country. Our asset classification employs 11 types of assets, including two intellectual property products, research and development (R&D) and computer software.[3] The price of a capital input is the product of the price of acquisition of the corresponding asset and the annualization factor that converts the capital stock into a flow of capital services as:

$$P_{K,k,c} = \varphi_{k,c} P_{A,k,c} \qquad (3.13)$$

where $P_{A,k,c}$ represents the acquisition price for one dollar's worth of assets in country c and the coefficient $\varphi_{k,c}$ is the annualization factor that transforms the acquisition price into the price of capital services by type of assets. The annualization factors by assets are assumed to be constant over periods in each country.

We define PPP for capital input by type of assets in the base year as the ratio between country c and the United States as follows:

$$PPP_{K,k,c/U} = \left(\varphi_{k,c} / \varphi_{k,U}\right) PPP_{A,k,c/U} \qquad (3.14)$$

The key to measuring PPP for capital input is the relative value of the annualization factor $\varphi_{k,c}/\varphi_{k,U}$ and the PPP for capital acquisition $PPP_{A,k,c/U}$. Data on PPPs for capital acquisition of eleven types of assets are based on the ICP 2011 Round (World Bank 2014).[4] In measuring the annualization factor, we apply the ex-post approach for measuring user cost of capital, originated in Jorgenson and Griliches (1967). Assuming constant returns to scale and competitive markets, capital compensation can be derived from the summation of the capital input cost for each asset, which is defined as the product of the user cost of capital and the productive capital stock.[5] Based on this identity, the equations of user costs of capital by asset and the ex-post rate of returns are simultaneously determined. The estimated PPPs for capital input by asset are aggregated to the country-level estimates, based on the EKS method across 21 Asian countries and the United States in the base year 2011. Finally, annual PPP for capital input $PPP_{K,c}$ is extrapolated using the price indices of capital input in each country relative to that in the United States.

PPP for labor

The elementary level PPPs for labor input across the Asian countries are measured as average hourly labor compensation in each labor group, taking one dollar's worth as the unit at the elementary level. We use the harmonized data on hours worked, which are cross-classified by gender, age, education, and employment status, based on the common classification systems for 21 Asian countries and the United States as a reference country.[6] We choose a common classification of six age groups – under 14 years old, 15–24, 25–34, 35–44, 45–54 and over 55 years of age. As a common education classification, we choose four education categories – less than primary school, secondary school, tertiary school and other category (e.g. religious professionals). Workers are classified as employees, self-employed and unpaid family workers. After cross-classifying the data by all the demographic characteristics, we have 144 groups in total. Only employees are considered when measuring the elementary level PPP for labor input. The estimated PPPs for labor input in elementary level are aggregated to the country-level estimates, based on the EKS method across 21 Asian countries and the United States in the base year. Finally, annual PPP for labor input $PPP_{L,c}$ is extrapolated using the price indices of labor input in country c relative to those in the United States.

Factor price differentials

Table 3.1 presents our estimates of the factor-price PPPs, in comparison with PPPs for output and the average exchange rates in 2011. Our first observation is that the exchange rates systematically underrepresent the relative purchasing power in all the countries, with the exception of Japan. Especially in the South Asian countries, the price level indices for output, which is defined as PPP for

Table 3.1 PPPs for capital and labor inputs in 2011

	(a) PPP for Output		(b) PPP for Capital Input			(c) PPP for Labor Input				(d) Exchange rate
		(a/d)		(b/d)	(b/a)		(c/d)	(c/a)	(b/c)	
East Asia										
China	3.51	(0.54)	3.81	(0.59)	(1.09)	0.71	(0.11)	(0.20)	(5.4)	6.46
Hong Kong	5.46	(0.70)	5.55	(0.71)	(1.02)	4.89	(0.63)	(0.90)	(1.1)	7.78
Japan	107.5	(1.35)	70.6	(0.88)	(0.66)	77.4	(0.97)	(0.72)	(0.9)	79.8
Korea	855	(0.77)	721	(0.65)	(0.84)	420	(0.38)	(0.49)	(1.7)	1108
Mongolia	537	(0.42)	833	(0.66)	(1.55)	111	(0.09)	(0.21)	(7.5)	1266
ROC (Taiwan)	15.1	(0.51)	16.6	(0.56)	(1.10)	12.0	(0.41)	(0.79)	(1.4)	29.5
Southeast Asia										
Cambodia	1347	(0.33)	4734	(1.17)	(3.51)	170	(0.04)	(0.13)	(27.9)	4059
Indonesia	3607	(0.41)	4606	(0.53)	(1.28)	1364	(0.16)	(0.38)	(3.4)	8770
Malaysia	1.46	(0.48)	2.92	(0.95)	(2.00)	0.56	(0.18)	(0.38)	(5.2)	3.06
Philippines	17.9	(0.41)	33.0	(0.76)	(1.85)	2.9	(0.07)	(0.16)	(11.3)	43.3
Singapore	0.89	(0.71)	1.17	(0.93)	(1.31)	0.72	(0.57)	(0.81)	(1.6)	1.26
Thailand	12.4	(0.41)	14.9	(0.49)	(1.21)	4.0	(0.13)	(0.33)	(3.7)	30.5
Vietnam	6709	(0.33)	14485	(0.71)	(2.16)	703	(0.03)	(0.10)	(20.6)	20510

South Asia								
Bangladesh	23.1	(0.31)	52.4	(0.71)	(2.26)	3.2	(0.04)	(0.14)	74.2
Bhutan	16.9	(0.36)	25.0	(0.53)	(1.48)	4.8	(0.10)	(0.29)	46.7
India	15.1	(0.32)	23.5	(0.50)	(1.56)	4.7	(0.10)	(0.31)	46.7
Nepal	24.6	(0.33)	39.7	(0.54)	(1.61)	3.4	(0.05)	(0.14)	74.0
Pakistan	24.3	(0.28)	73.3	(0.85)	(3.01)	6.4	(0.07)	(0.26)	86.3
Sri Lanka	38.7	(0.35)	66.5	(0.60)	(1.72)	10.1	(0.09)	(0.26)	110.6
Other Asia								
Fiji	1.04	(0.58)	0.50	(0.28)	(0.48)	0.36	(0.20)	(0.35)	1.79
Iran	4657	(0.44)	14423	(1.36)	(3.10)	1763	(0.17)	(0.38)	10616

Note: The PPPs and exchange rates are defined by the local currency unit per US dollar.

Source: PPPs for output are the ICP 2011 Round estimates (World Bank 2014). The exchange rates are the adjusted rates, which are called the Analysis of Main Aggregate rates in the UN Statistics Division's National Accounts Main Aggregate Database. PPPs for capital and labor inputs are our estimates.

output over the exchange rate, are about 0.3 in 2011. Second, PPP for output still overestimates PPP for labor input in all countries.[7] In particular, the price level indices for labor inputs are less than 0.1 in the South Asian countries and 0.2 in the Southeast Asian countries (except Singapore) in 2011. In other words, the labor input prices are 62–90 percent lower than the output prices in those countries. This implies that, in aggregating country growths of labor input, the use of PPPs for labor is expected to improve the estimates of country-group growth by appropriately evaluating the growths in the countries with a generally lower price of labor input.

Third, in contrast to the above, our estimates of PPPs for capital input are considerably higher than the PPPs for output (except Japan, Korea and Fiji). Higher costs of capital in the Southeast and South Asian countries originate from higher required rates of return and higher acquisition price of assets. In emerging countries, although the price of construction tends to have a larger share in GFCF and the price of construction tends to be lower due to lower labor costs, the often-observed undervaluation in the market exchange rates relative to their PPPs is translated into higher import prices of machinery and equipment in local currency unit. If emerging countries with higher costs of capital have larger growths in capital input, the use of PPPs for capital, in place of PPPs for output, in aggregating country growths of capital input will appropriately shave off the estimates of country-group growth of capital input. Figure 3.1 plots the PPPs for capital and labor inputs relative to PPPs for output in 2011. This chart shows that the countries with lower labor prices tend to have higher capital prices, such as Cambodia, Pakistan, Vietnam, Bangladesh and Iran,[8] which have capital input prices more than two times higher than output prices.

Estimated results

Estimated indices of output, capital and labor inputs, and TFP for Entire Asia, which consists of 21 economies, are presented in Table 3.2, covering the period of 1970–2014. Table 3.3 examines the sources of the regional economic growth in five-year intervals of our observation period. Our estimates on the TFP growth of Entire Asia (v_T), which are measured taking into account the price differentials of output and capital and labor inputs across countries in country aggregation, emphasize the deterioration in the 1970s and the improvement in the 2000s of regional TFP growth, compared

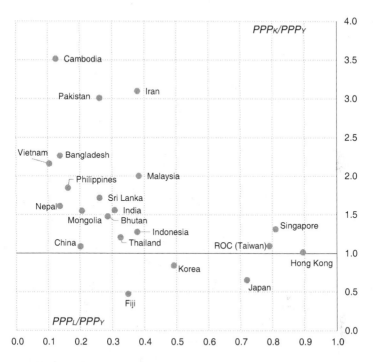

Figure 3.1 PPP for capital and labor inputs relative to PPP for output in 2011

Source: PPPs for output are the ICP 2011 Round estimates and PPPs for capital and labor inputs are our estimates.

to the measures without considering the factor price differentials across countries (v_T).

In the 1970s, our estimates indicate that TFP of Entire Asia has deteriorated by 0.13 percent per year on average in the first half of the 1970s and by 0.18 percent in the latter half. In particular, as shown in the far-right chart of Figure 3.2, the oil crises in 1973 and 1979 adversely affected regional TFP growth. The country origins of the TFP growth of Entire Asia are presented in Table 3.4. In the first half of the 1970s, the hikes in oil price proved a drag, especially on Japan's TFP growth, with the deepening of the use of crude oil as an energy input in the 1950s and 1960s contributing to

Table 3.2 Output, capital and labor inputs, and TFP of Entire Asia

	P_Y	P_K	P_L	Y	K	L	TFP	v_K	v_L	gr(Y)	gr(K)	gr(L)	gr(TFP)
1970	1.000	1.000	1.000	1.000	1.000	1.000	1.000	0.407	0.593	—	—	—	—
1971	1.039	0.991	1.058	1.051	1.104	1.032	0.991	0.407	0.593	0.050	0.099	0.031	−0.009
1972	1.079	1.003	1.147	1.119	1.213	1.047	1.007	0.410	0.590	0.063	0.094	0.014	0.016
1973	1.126	1.040	1.243	1.205	1.330	1.077	1.026	0.415	0.585	0.073	0.092	0.028	0.019
1974	1.212	1.021	1.344	1.226	1.462	1.103	0.991	0.409	0.591	0.018	0.095	0.024	−0.035
1975	1.287	1.048	1.467	1.290	1.590	1.129	0.993	0.409	0.591	0.051	0.084	0.023	0.003
1976	1.357	1.088	1.583	1.363	1.722	1.158	1.000	0.412	0.588	0.055	0.079	0.026	0.007
1977	1.437	1.116	1.734	1.437	1.863	1.185	1.007	0.410	0.590	0.053	0.079	0.023	0.007
1978	1.545	1.182	1.898	1.514	2.007	1.220	1.012	0.413	0.587	0.052	0.074	0.029	0.005
1979	1.675	1.222	2.073	1.563	2.167	1.253	0.996	0.412	0.588	0.031	0.077	0.027	−0.016
1980	1.791	1.248	2.241	1.618	2.327	1.291	0.984	0.408	0.592	0.035	0.071	0.030	−0.012
1981	1.936	1.333	2.445	1.694	2.490	1.330	0.985	0.412	0.588	0.046	0.068	0.030	0.000
1982	1.984	1.326	2.570	1.779	2.655	1.375	0.988	0.406	0.594	0.049	0.064	0.033	0.003
1983	2.048	1.390	2.721	1.889	2.824	1.409	1.008	0.413	0.587	0.060	0.062	0.024	0.021
1984	2.136	1.455	2.899	1.999	3.002	1.450	1.023	0.416	0.584	0.057	0.061	0.029	0.014
1985	2.186	1.501	3.038	2.119	3.188	1.490	1.041	0.420	0.580	0.058	0.060	0.027	0.017
1986	2.219	1.490	3.154	2.215	3.386	1.529	1.045	0.418	0.582	0.044	0.060	0.026	0.004
1987	2.247	1.502	3.312	2.349	3.593	1.569	1.065	0.416	0.584	0.059	0.059	0.026	0.019
1988	2.286	1.555	3.537	2.535	3.821	1.609	1.104	0.417	0.583	0.076	0.061	0.025	0.036
1989	2.346	1.605	3.751	2.691	4.082	1.640	1.127	0.422	0.578	0.060	0.066	0.019	0.021
1990	2.382	1.627	3.956	2.863	4.362	1.676	1.151	0.423	0.577	0.062	0.066	0.022	0.021
1991	2.400	1.597	4.163	3.013	4.671	1.699	1.168	0.420	0.580	0.051	0.068	0.014	0.015
1992	2.431	1.564	4.476	3.187	4.995	1.721	1.192	0.410	0.590	0.056	0.067	0.013	0.020
1993	2.465	1.607	4.642	3.361	5.335	1.741	1.215	0.421	0.579	0.053	0.066	0.011	0.019
1994	2.495	1.623	4.894	3.564	5.686	1.769	1.243	0.422	0.578	0.059	0.064	0.016	0.023

1995	2.511	1.627	5.164	3.788	6.062	1.796	1.275	0.422	0.578	0.061	0.064	0.015	0.025
1996	2.530	1.650	5.397	4.032	6.471	1.830	1.306	0.426	0.574	0.062	0.065	0.019	0.024
1997	2.574	1.623	5.681	4.212	6.921	1.861	1.313	0.422	0.578	0.044	0.067	0.017	0.005
1998	2.644	1.546	5.877	4.244	7.381	1.887	1.277	0.414	0.586	0.007	0.064	0.014	−0.027
1999	2.689	1.574	6.090	4.433	7.776	1.921	1.292	0.418	0.582	0.044	0.052	0.018	0.012
2000	2.734	1.610	6.432	4.681	8.167	1.952	1.325	0.418	0.582	0.054	0.049	0.016	0.025
2001	2.760	1.616	6.629	4.869	8.602	1.980	1.337	0.421	0.579	0.039	0.052	0.014	0.009
2002	2.760	1.639	6.792	5.118	9.050	2.008	1.364	0.427	0.573	0.050	0.051	0.014	0.020
2003	2.776	1.695	7.055	5.435	9.518	2.038	1.406	0.435	0.565	0.060	0.050	0.015	0.030
2004	2.818	1.798	7.307	5.804	10.037	2.080	1.450	0.449	0.551	0.066	0.053	0.020	0.031
2005	2.867	1.900	7.689	6.220	10.622	2.109	1.503	0.461	0.539	0.069	0.057	0.014	0.036
2006	2.898	1.978	8.214	6.701	11.278	2.123	1.569	0.467	0.533	0.075	0.060	0.007	0.043
2007	2.902	2.056	8.773	7.281	11.996	2.132	1.652	0.475	0.525	0.083	0.062	0.004	0.052
2008	2.906	1.942	9.508	7.622	12.806	2.134	1.677	0.457	0.543	0.046	0.065	0.001	0.015
2009	2.856	1.811	9.895	7.945	13.669	2.149	1.691	0.444	0.556	0.041	0.065	0.007	0.008
2010	2.838	1.874	10.307	8.630	14.636	2.181	1.766	0.456	0.544	0.083	0.068	0.015	0.044
2011	2.865	1.827	11.010	9.087	15.721	2.197	1.793	0.449	0.551	0.052	0.072	0.007	0.015
2012	2.893	1.787	11.686	9.566	16.900	2.220	1.818	0.444	0.556	0.051	0.072	0.010	0.013
2013	2.905	1.738	12.453	10.109	18.218	2.232	1.853	0.439	0.561	0.055	0.075	0.005	0.019
2014	2.929	1.707	13.188	10.660	19.642	2.248	1.883	0.437	0.563	0.053	0.075	0.007	0.016

Source: Authors' estimates.

Table 3.3 Sources of economic growth in entire Asia

	1970–75	1975–80	1980–85	1985–90	1990–95	95–2000	2000–05	2005–10	2010–14	2000–07	2000–14
a) Output	5.10	4.53	5.39	6.02	5.60	4.23	5.68	6.55	5.28	6.31	5.88
b) Capital Input (growth)	3.80 (9.28)	3.13 (7.61)	2.59 (6.29)	2.63 (6.27)	2.76 (6.58)	2.51 (5.96)	2.29 (5.26)	2.95 (6.41)	3.27 (7.35)	2.45 (5.49)	2.80 (6.27)
c) Labor Input (growth)	1.43 (2.42)	1.58 (2.68)	1.69 (2.87)	1.37 (2.36)	0.80 (1.38)	0.96 (1.66)	0.88 (1.55)	0.37 (0.67)	0.42 (0.75)	0.71 (1.26)	0.56 (1.01)
d) TFP	−0.13	−0.18	1.11	2.02	2.04	0.76	2.52	3.24	1.59	3.16	2.51
Reference: estimates without considering factor price differentials across countries											
e) Capital Input (growth) (b−e)	3.72 (9.07) (0.08)	3.34 (8.13) (−0.21)	2.72 (6.61) (−0.13)	2.69 (6.42) (−0.06)	2.87 (6.85) (−0.11)	2.75 (6.54) (−0.24)	2.61 (6.00) (−0.33)	3.40 (7.39) (−0.45)	3.37 (7.58) (−0.10)	2.83 (6.34) (−0.38)	3.11 (6.95) (−0.31)
f) Labor Input (growth) (c−f)	0.76 (1.29) (0.67)	1.24 (2.11) (0.34)	1.02 (1.73) (0.67)	1.06 (1.82) (0.31)	0.56 (0.97) (0.24)	0.52 (0.91) (0.44)	0.64 (1.14) (0.23)	0.36 (0.66) (0.01)	0.40 (0.73) (0.02)	0.61 (1.10) (0.10)	0.47 (0.85) (0.09)
g) TFP (d−g)	0.62 (−0.75)	−0.06 (−0.12)	1.65 (−0.54)	2.27 (−0.25)	2.17 (−0.13)	0.96 (−0.20)	2.43 (0.09)	2.80 (0.44)	1.51 (0.09)	2.88 (0.28)	2.30 (0.22)

Unit: Average annual growth rate (percentage) in each period.

Source: Authors' estimates.

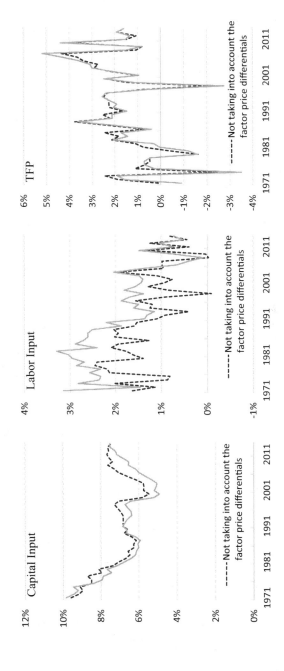

Figure 3.2 Impacts of price differential factors of capital and labor
Source: Authors' estimates.

Table 3.4 Country origins of TFP growth in Entire Asia

	1970–75	1975–80	1980–85	1985–90	1990–95	95–2000	2000–05	2005–10	2010–14	2000–07	2000–14
Entire Asia	−0.13	−0.18	1.11	2.02	2.04	0.76	2.52	3.24	1.59	3.16	2.51
East Asia	−0.16	0.50	1.45	1.31	1.31	0.82	1.23	1.75	1.06	1.61	1.37
China	0.01	0.09	0.60	0.27	1.27	0.65	0.97	1.46	0.88	1.28	1.12
Hong Kong	0.01	0.06	0.01	0.06	0.01	−0.03	0.02	0.02	0.02	0.03	0.02
Japan	−0.19	0.37	0.72	0.76	−0.12	0.08	0.12	0.08	0.11	0.15	0.10
Korea	0.01	−0.08	0.09	0.11	0.08	0.06	0.08	0.11	0.03	0.10	0.07
Mongolia	0.00	0.00	0.00	0.00	0.00	0.00	0.00	0.00	0.00	0.00	0.00
ROC (Taiwan)	0.00	0.06	0.04	0.12	0.08	0.05	0.03	0.07	0.03	0.05	0.04
Southeast Asia	0.19	0.11	−0.36	0.38	0.29	−0.46	0.34	0.19	0.26	0.32	0.26
Cambodia	0.00	0.00	0.00	0.00	0.00	0.00	0.00	0.00	0.00	0.00	0.00
Indonesia	0.16	0.06	−0.17	0.11	0.18	−0.33	0.12	0.09	0.13	0.10	0.11
Malaysia	0.01	0.02	−0.06	0.03	0.03	−0.05	0.03	0.02	0.02	0.03	0.02
Philippines	0.01	0.00	−0.18	0.08	−0.01	0.00	0.02	0.03	0.05	0.03	0.03
Singapore	−0.01	0.00	−0.01	0.02	0.02	0.00	0.02	0.02	0.00	0.02	0.01
Thailand	0.02	0.02	0.03	0.14	0.04	−0.08	0.14	0.04	0.05	0.12	0.08
Vietnam	0.00	0.01	0.03	0.00	0.02	0.00	0.02	−0.02	0.01	0.01	0.00
South Asia	−0.11	0.05	0.41	0.45	0.31	0.39	0.56	0.58	0.19	0.64	0.46
Bangladesh	−0.04	0.01	0.01	0.00	0.00	−0.01	−0.01	0.00	0.00	0.00	0.00
Bhutan	0.00	0.00	0.00	0.00	0.00	0.00	0.00	0.00	0.00	0.00	0.00
India	−0.05	−0.03	0.31	0.41	0.26	0.38	0.49	0.56	0.13	0.55	0.41
Nepal	0.00	−0.01	0.00	0.00	0.00	0.00	0.00	0.00	0.00	0.00	0.00
Pakistan	0.00	0.06	0.08	0.04	0.03	0.02	0.08	0.01	0.05	0.08	0.05
Sri Lanka	0.00	0.01	0.01	0.00	0.02	0.01	0.00	0.01	0.01	0.01	0.01

Other Asia	0.25	−0.94	0.01	−0.03	0.10	0.09	0.14	0.06	−0.08	0.13	0.05
Fiji	0.00	0.00	0.00	0.00	0.00	0.00	0.00	0.00	0.00	0.00	0.00
Iran	0.25	−0.94	0.01	−0.03	0.10	0.09	0.14	0.06	−0.08	0.13	0.05
Price differential factors	−0.30	0.10	−0.39	−0.10	0.04	−0.07	0.25	0.66	0.17	0.46	0.37
Capital	0.44	0.51	0.33	0.27	0.31	0.39	0.52	0.69	0.19	0.60	0.49
Labor	−0.74	−0.41	−0.72	−0.37	−0.27	−0.46	−0.27	−0.03	−0.02	−0.14	−0.11

Note: All figures present the average annual growth rates in each period.

Source: Authors' estimates.

the slowdown in regional TFP growth by 0.19 percent per year on average. This was counterbalanced by the positive impact of the oil price rise on the Indonesia's TFP growth, which contributed to an increase in regional TFP by 0.16 percent, regardless of the smaller scale of its economy.[9]

Another factor of the deterioration in regional TFP in the 1970s is the negative impact of the price differential factor of labor in Table 3.4. Based on the labor input measure without considering factor price differentials ($\hat{L}$ in Equation (3.5)), the labor input in Entire Asia increased by 1.29 percent per year on average in the first half of the 1970s, as presented in the lower panel of Table 3.3. Our estimates (L in Equation (3.7)) revise it upwardly to 2.42 percent in the same period. Table 3.7 presents the country origins of labor input growth in Entire Asia. In the first half of the 1970s, 64 percent of the reevaluated regional growth of labor input is accounted by China, 17 percent by India and 13 percent by Southeast Asia. If price differentials for labor input are not properly accounted for, the measure of $\hat{L}$ will underestimate the contributions of countries with lower labor price to the regional growth of labor input. This bias is appropriately corrected, in the measure of L. By our calculations, the price differential factor of labor input (γ_L in Equation (3.11)) is negative (−0.74 percent per year) in the first half of the 1970s in Table 3.4. On the other hand, in the same period, 35 percent of the reevaluated regional growth of capital input was accounted by Japan, 16 percent by Iran, 11 percent by China and 9 percent by Indonesia and India in Table 3.6. If the price differentials of capital are not properly accounted for, the measure of $\hat{K}$ will overestimate the contributions of countries with higher capital price to the regional growth of capital input. Our findings suggest the price differential factor of capital input (γ_K in Equation (3.11)) has the impact of raising regional TFP by 0.44 percent per year on average in the same period, as presented in Table 3.4. Even so, this is not enough to fully offset the negative reevaluation effect from labor input, resulting in a downward revision of 0.30 percent on average per annum in TFP of Entire Asia by our measure in this period.

Since the early 1980s, TFP growth of Entire Asia has recovered. Regional TFP growth reached about 2 percent in the late 1980s and this sustained until the middle of the 1990s, except the period of the Asian financial crisis of 1997–98, as shown in the far-right chart of Figure 3.2. Figure 3.3 illustrates the country origins of the TFP growth of Entire Asia in each decade of our observation period.

Table 3.5 Country origins of output growth in Entire Asia

	1970–75	1975–80	1980–85	1985–90	1990–95	95–2000	2000–05	2005–10	2010–14	2000–07	2000–14
Entire Asia	5.10	4.53	5.39	6.02	5.60	4.23	5.68	6.55	5.28	6.31	5.88
East Asia	2.82	2.90	3.46	3.71	3.22	2.62	3.29	4.03	3.38	3.74	3.58
China	0.57	0.64	1.24	1.15	2.06	1.88	2.60	3.59	3.05	2.99	3.08
Hong Kong	0.06	0.13	0.08	0.11	0.08	0.04	0.05	0.05	0.03	0.06	0.04
Japan	1.81	1.68	1.66	1.78	0.47	0.24	0.26	0.06	0.09	0.29	0.14
Korea	0.22	0.22	0.30	0.40	0.38	0.27	0.25	0.20	0.13	0.25	0.20
Mongolia	0.01	0.01	0.01	0.00	0.00	0.00	0.00	0.00	0.01	0.00	0.01
ROC (Taiwan)	0.15	0.22	0.18	0.26	0.23	0.20	0.13	0.13	0.08	0.15	0.12
Southeast Asia	0.93	1.10	0.66	1.18	1.27	0.40	0.84	0.84	0.76	0.87	0.82
Cambodia	0.00	0.00	0.00	0.00	0.00	0.01	0.01	0.01	0.01	0.01	0.01
Indonesia	0.47	0.51	0.34	0.54	0.60	0.06	0.33	0.41	0.37	0.35	0.37
Malaysia	0.10	0.12	0.08	0.11	0.17	0.10	0.10	0.10	0.10	0.11	0.10
Philippines	0.16	0.18	–0.03	0.12	0.05	0.07	0.08	0.08	0.09	0.09	0.08
Singapore	0.06	0.06	0.06	0.07	0.09	0.06	0.05	0.07	0.05	0.07	0.06
Thailand	0.13	0.19	0.15	0.30	0.29	0.03	0.17	0.11	0.08	0.16	0.12
Vietnam	0.02	0.03	0.05	0.04	0.07	0.07	0.09	0.07	0.07	0.09	0.08
South Asia	0.52	0.70	1.02	1.10	0.94	1.02	1.23	1.46	1.14	1.38	1.29
Bangladesh	–0.04	0.05	0.05	0.05	0.06	0.06	0.06	0.07	0.07	0.06	0.06
Bhutan	0.00	0.00	0.00	0.00	0.00	0.00	0.00	0.00	0.00	0.00	0.00
India	0.45	0.47	0.75	0.84	0.69	0.82	0.99	1.25	0.94	1.12	1.07
Nepal	0.01	0.01	0.01	0.01	0.01	0.01	0.01	0.01	0.01	0.01	0.01
Pakistan	0.08	0.13	0.19	0.18	0.15	0.11	0.16	0.10	0.08	0.16	0.11
Sri Lanka	0.02	0.03	0.03	0.02	0.03	0.03	0.02	0.03	0.03	0.02	0.03
Other Asia	0.83	–0.17	0.25	0.04	0.18	0.18	0.32	0.23	0.00	0.32	0.19
Fiji	0.00	0.00	0.00	0.00	0.00	0.00	0.00	0.00	0.00	0.00	0.00
Iran	0.83	–0.17	0.25	0.04	0.18	0.18	0.32	0.22	0.00	0.32	0.19

Note: All figures present the average annual growth rates in each period.

Source: Authors' estimates.

Table 3.6 Country origins of capital input growth in Entire Asia

	1970–75	1975–80	1980–85	1985–90	1990–95	95–2000	2000–05	2005–10	2010–14	2000–07	2000–14
Entire Asia	9.28	7.61	6.29	6.27	6.58	5.96	5.26	6.41	7.35	5.49	6.27
East Asia	7.14	5.22	4.24	4.67	4.52	4.02	3.83	4.53	5.30	3.95	4.50
China	0.82	0.80	0.77	1.10	1.18	1.75	2.47	3.82	5.02	2.72	3.68
Hong Kong	0.09	0.09	0.11	0.10	0.11	0.11	0.06	0.04	0.03	0.06	0.05
Japan	5.84	3.77	2.80	2.83	2.35	1.28	0.63	0.20	−0.06	0.54	0.28
Korea	0.18	0.33	0.32	0.42	0.60	0.57	0.44	0.32	0.24	0.41	0.34
Mongolia	0.01	0.01	0.01	0.01	0.00	0.00	0.00	0.00	0.01	0.00	0.00
ROC (Taiwan)	0.20	0.22	0.23	0.21	0.28	0.31	0.23	0.13	0.07	0.21	0.15
Southeast Asia	0.83	0.95	1.09	0.87	1.34	1.23	0.67	0.74	0.76	0.69	0.72
Cambodia	0.00	0.00	0.00	0.00	0.00	0.00	0.00	0.00	0.00	0.00	0.00
Indonesia	0.29	0.39	0.47	0.43	0.57	0.54	0.33	0.39	0.42	0.34	0.37
Malaysia	0.08	0.08	0.12	0.07	0.14	0.15	0.08	0.07	0.07	0.08	0.08
Philippines	0.14	0.19	0.15	0.04	0.07	0.08	0.06	0.04	0.04	0.06	0.05
Singapore	0.10	0.08	0.11	0.08	0.09	0.11	0.07	0.06	0.06	0.07	0.06
Thailand	0.21	0.19	0.22	0.23	0.45	0.29	0.07	0.10	0.09	0.08	0.09
Vietnam	0.01	0.02	0.01	0.02	0.03	0.05	0.06	0.07	0.07	0.06	0.07
South Asia	0.78	0.72	0.68	0.70	0.65	0.66	0.64	1.02	1.23	0.72	0.94
Bangladesh	0.01	0.01	0.02	0.03	0.03	0.04	0.05	0.06	0.06	0.05	0.06
Bhutan	0.00	0.00	0.00	0.00	0.00	0.00	0.00	0.00	0.00	0.00	0.00
India	0.64	0.57	0.50	0.53	0.50	0.53	0.52	0.88	1.12	0.60	0.82
Nepal	0.01	0.01	0.01	0.01	0.01	0.01	0.01	0.01	0.01	0.01	0.01
Pakistan	0.09	0.09	0.09	0.11	0.10	0.07	0.04	0.04	0.03	0.04	0.03
Sri Lanka	0.04	0.04	0.05	0.02	0.01	0.01	0.02	0.02	0.03	0.02	0.02
Other Asia	0.52	0.73	0.29	0.04	0.07	0.06	0.12	0.13	0.07	0.13	0.11
Fiji	0.01	0.01	0.00	0.00	0.00	0.00	0.00	0.00	0.00	0.00	0.00
Iran	0.52	0.73	0.28	0.04	0.06	0.06	0.12	0.13	0.07	0.12	0.11

Note: All figures present the average annual growth rates in each period.

Source: Authors' estimates.

Table 3.7 Country origins of labor input growth in Entire Asia

	1970–75	1975–80	1980–85	1985–90	1990–95	95–2000	2000–05	2005–10	2010–14	2000–07	2000–14
Entire Asia	2.42	2.68	2.87	2.36	1.38	1.66	1.55	0.67	0.75	1.26	1.01
East Asia	1.63	1.79	2.09	1.61	0.76	1.09	0.97	0.06	0.37	0.63	0.48
China	1.54	1.55	1.96	1.44	0.72	1.16	0.96	0.12	0.34	0.61	0.48
Hong Kong	0.01	0.01	0.00	0.00	0.00	0.01	0.00	0.00	0.00	0.00	0.00
Japan	−0.06	0.11	0.04	0.05	−0.04	−0.08	−0.01	−0.05	0.02	0.00	−0.02
Korea	0.10	0.09	0.06	0.09	0.05	0.00	0.01	−0.01	0.00	0.01	0.01
Mongolia	0.00	0.00	0.00	0.00	0.00	0.00	0.00	0.00	0.00	0.00	0.00
ROC (Taiwan)	0.04	0.04	0.02	0.02	0.02	0.01	0.00	0.00	0.01	0.01	0.01
Southeast Asia	0.31	0.36	0.34	0.34	0.21	0.18	0.16	0.36	0.08	0.22	0.21
Cambodia	0.00	0.00	0.00	0.00	0.00	0.01	0.01	0.01	0.00	0.01	0.01
Indonesia	0.12	0.12	0.13	0.15	0.05	0.07	0.05	0.16	0.04	0.10	0.09
Malaysia	0.02	0.02	0.02	0.02	0.02	0.03	0.05	0.02	0.03	0.02	0.02
Philippines	0.07	0.06	0.06	0.03	0.04	0.03	0.05	0.05	0.03	0.05	0.04
Singapore	0.01	0.01	0.01	0.01	0.01	0.01	0.00	0.02	0.01	0.01	0.01
Thailand	0.04	0.12	0.04	0.07	0.04	−0.01	0.00	0.02	0.00	0.01	0.00
Vietnam	0.05	0.04	0.08	0.05	0.05	0.05	0.03	0.08	−0.02	0.04	0.04
South Asia	0.47	0.49	0.40	0.38	0.38	0.34	0.38	0.26	0.28	0.36	0.31
Bangladesh	0.00	0.04	0.03	0.04	0.05	0.05	0.04	0.04	0.03	0.03	0.03
Bhutan	0.00	0.00	0.00	0.00	0.00	0.00	0.00	0.00	0.00	0.00	0.00
India	0.40	0.40	0.33	0.29	0.29	0.23	0.29	0.14	0.19	0.27	0.21
Nepal	0.01	0.01	0.00	0.00	0.01	0.01	0.01	0.01	0.01	0.01	0.01
Pakistan	0.05	0.03	0.03	0.04	0.03	0.03	0.04	0.06	0.03	0.05	0.05
Sri Lanka	0.01	0.01	0.00	0.01	0.00	0.01	0.01	0.01	0.01	0.01	0.01
Other Asia	0.02	0.04	0.03	0.03	0.03	0.05	0.05	0.00	0.01	0.05	0.02
Fiji	0.00	0.00	0.00	0.00	0.00	0.00	0.00	0.00	0.01	0.00	0.00
Iran	0.02	0.04	0.03	0.03	0.03	0.05	0.05	0.00	0.01	0.05	0.02

Note: All figures present the average annual growth rates in each period.

Source: Authors' estimates.

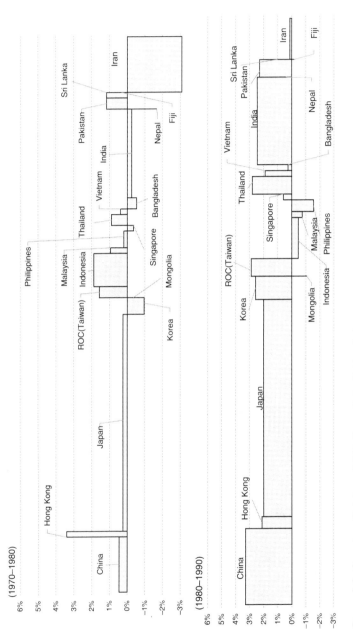

Figure 3.3 Country Origins of TFP Growth in Entire Asia

Note: The height, the width and the area of each country's box indicate the average annual growth rate of the country TFP, the country share of real output and the county contribution to the TFP growth of Entire Asia.

Source: Authors' estimates.

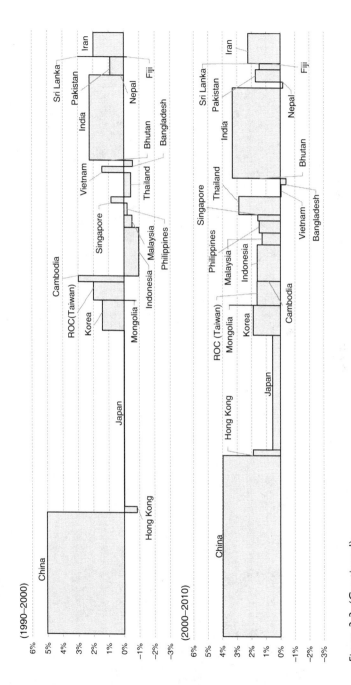

Figure 3.3 (Continued)

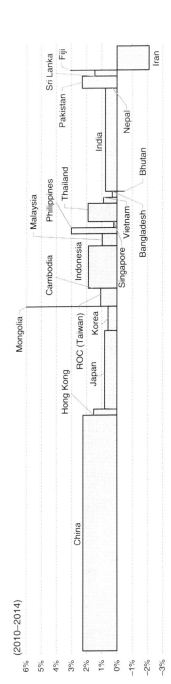

Figure 3.3 (Continued)

In this chart, the height and the width of each country's box indicate the average annual growth rate of country TFP and the country share of output, respectively, thus the area of the box represents the county contribution to the TFP growth of Entire Asia. The data used in Figure 3.3 are presented in Table 3.8. The main engine of regional TFP growth in the 1980s was a recovery of Japan's TFP, which explains 47 percent of the TFP growth of Entire Asia. In the 1990s, China emerged as the driving force propelling Asian TFP forward. China's TFP improvement of 5.0 percent per year on average contributes 68 percent of the TFP growth of Entire Asia. The properties of an overestimation of regional capital input growth in $\hat{K}$ and an underestimation of regional labor input growth in $\hat{L}$ are sustained throughout the whole observation period with minor exceptions, as shown in the far-left and middle charts of Figure 3.2, respectively. Thus, γ_K tends to be positive and γ_L negative. Until the late 1990s, the sums of γ_K and γ_K were negative, thus our measure revises regional TFP growth downward by about 0.2 percent per year on average from 1985 to 2000.

In the early 2000s, labor input growth slowed significantly. In East Asia, it slowed from 1.61 percent per year on average in 1985–90 to 0.48 percent in 2000–14 (Table 3.7), of which 1.44 percentage points and 0.48 percentage point were contributed by China, respectively. Similarly, in Southeast Asia, it decreased from 0.34 percent to 0.21 percent over the two periods. Reflecting these structural changes, the total of factor price differential factors ($\gamma_K + \gamma_K$) turns to be positive since the early 2000s and our measure of TFP of Entire Asia was higher than $\hat{v}_T$, which does not account for the factor price differential effect, as shown in the far-right chart of Figure 3.2. Regional TFP growth recovered strongly from the trough of 0.76 percent precipitated by the Asian financial crisis of 1997–98 and reached 2.52 percent in the first half of the 2000s. In the latter half, it accelerated to 3.24 percent. Although the main engine was the improvement in China's TFP with 4.0 percent on average per annum in the 2000s, its contribution share in regional TFP growth fell to 45 percent in the late 2000s from 86 percent in the late 1990s, reflecting recovery in TFP performance in other Asian countries. The contribution of Indian TFP has increased from 0.38 percent in the latter half of the 1990s to 0.56 percent in the latter half of the 2000s. In addition, TFP contribution by Southeast Asia recovered from −0.46 percent to 0.19 percent in the two periods. TFP

Table 3.8 TFP growth in Entire Asia and country contributions

	1970–1980			*1980–1990*			*1990–2000*			*2000–2010*			*2010–2014*		
			share			*share*			*share*			*share*			*share*
Entire Asia	–0.16		1.00	1.57		1.00	1.40		1.00	2.88		1.00	1.59		1.00
East Asia	0.3	(.17)	.547	2.4	(1.38)	.584	1.8	(1.06)	.585	2.5	(1.49)	.587	1.8	(1.06)	.605
China	0.5	(.05)	.105	3.3	(.43)	.132	5.0	(.96)	.190	4.0	(1.22)	.307	2.2	(.88)	.392
Hong Kong	3.4	(.04)	.011	2.1	(.03)	.015	–0.8	(–.01)	.013	1.9	(.02)	.012	1.5	(.02)	.010
Japan	0.2	(.09)	.375	2.0	(.74)	.370	0.0	(–.02)	.298	0.5	(.10)	.187	0.8	(.11)	.131
Korea	–1.0	(–.03)	.035	2.6	(.10)	.038	1.4	(.07)	.049	1.9	(.09)	.050	0.6	(.03)	.044
Mongolia	–0.3	(–.00)	.001	–1.1	(–.00)	.001	–0.8	(–.00)	.001	3.5	(.00)	.001	6.0	(.00)	.001
ROC (Taiwan)	1.6	(.03)	.020	2.9	(.08)	.028	2.0	(.07)	.033	1.6	(.05)	.031	1.1	(.03)	.027
Southeast Asia	1.1	(.15)	.140	0.1	(.01)	.168	–0.5	(–.09)	.181	1.6	(.27)	.166	1.7	(.26)	.152
Cambodia	–			–			3.0	(.00)	.001	0.8	(.00)	.001	1.6	(.00)	.001
Indonesia	1.9	(.11)	.057	–0.5	(–.03)	.070	–1.0	(–.07)	.077	1.6	(.11)	.067	1.9	(.13)	.066
Malaysia	0.9	(.01)	.013	–0.7	(–.01)	.017	–0.5	(–.01)	.024	1.3	(.03)	.020	1.0	(.02)	.019
Philippines	0.2	(.01)	.028	–1.5	(–.05)	.033	–0.2	(–.01)	.024	1.5	(.03)	.017	3.0	(.05)	.016
Singapore	–0.4	(–.00)	.006	0.6	(.01)	.010	0.8	(.01)	.010	1.6	(.02)	.011	0.2	(.00)	.012
Thailand	0.9	(.02)	.023	2.8	(.08)	.030	–0.4	(–.02)	.036	2.9	(.09)	.031	1.9	(.05)	.026
Vietnam	0.4	(.01)	.013	1.9	(.02)	.008	1.4	(.01)	.008	–0.1	(–.00)	.019	0.9	(.01)	.012
South Asia	–0.1	(–.03)	.229	2.2	(.43)	.193	1.9	(.35)	.188	2.8	(.57)	.203	0.9	(.19)	.207
Bangladesh	–0.5	(–.01)	.027	0.3	(.00)	.013	–0.6	(–.01)	.012	–0.4	(–.00)	.012	0.3	(.00)	.011
Bhutan	–			–			0.8	(.00)	.000	1.4	(.00)	.000	–0.5	(–.00)	.000
India	–0.3	(–.04)	.172	2.5	(.36)	.146	2.3	(.32)	.141	3.3	(.52)	.157	0.8	(.13)	.166
Nepal	–1.7	(–.00)	.003	0.4	(.00)	.002	0.2	(.00)	.002	–0.2	(–.00)	.003	0.3	(.00)	.002
Pakistan	1.2	(.03)	.022	2.3	(.06)	.026	0.9	(.02)	.027	1.7	(.05)	.027	2.3	(.05)	.022
Sri Lanka	1.2	(.01)	.006	1.0	(.01)	.006	3.0	(.02)	.005	1.5	(.01)	.005	1.5	(.01)	.005

	-4.0 (-.35)	.087 -0.2 (-.01)	.056 2.0 (.09)	.046 2.2 (.10)	.046 -2.1 (-.08)
Other Asia	-4.0 (-.35)	.087 -0.2 (-.01)	.056 2.0 (.09)	.046 2.2 (.10)	.046 -2.1 (-.08)
Fiji	0.3 (.00)	.001 -0.2 (-.00)	.001 -0.2 (-.00)	.000 0.5 (.00)	.000 3.1 (.00)
Iran	-4.0 (-.35)	.087 0.0 (-.01)	.055 2.0 (.09)	.046 2.2 (.10)	.046 -2.1 (-.08)
Price differential factors	(-.10)	(-.25)	(-.02)	(-.45)	(.17)
Capital	(.48)	(.30)	(.35)	(.60)	(.19)
Labor	(-.58)	(-.55)	(-.36)	(-.15)	(-.02)

Unit: Average annual growth rate (percentage), contribution in parentheses.

Source: Authors' estimates.

growth of Entire Asia in the 2000s was more broadly based with smaller variation across country TFP growths, compared to that in the 1990s, as shown in Figure 3.3.

After the global financial crisis of 2008–09, the Asian economy has been maintaining a stable economic growth of 5.3 percent per annum on average during 2010–14. Yet, it has slowed down by one percentage point from the level recorded in the pre-crisis period of 2000–07 (6.3 percent in Table 3.2). This is mainly due to a reduction in the TFP growth of Entire Asia with 1.6 percentage points as a difference between the two periods, as presented in Table 3.4. The first reason for the slowdown in regional TFP seems to be the end of the latecomer advantage that China has been enjoying with its economic growth model built around manufacturing expansion materialized in the past two decades in the form of 4.5 percent TFP growth per annum, which, in turn, contributed to around 40 percent of the nation's economic growth rate. In 2010–14, TFP growth has halved to 2.2 percent in Table 3.8, and approximately 70 percent of the country's growth depends on the expansion of capital input. The trend of losing high TFP growth and increasing the role of capital input while suffering a decline in its investment efficiency appears similar to the trend experienced by the Japanese economy during the 1960s and into the 1970s. As the Asian economy gets more integrated with and increasingly reliant on the Chinese economy, the slowdown in China has wider repercussion in the region, notably in Korea and Taiwan.[10] In the 2000s, Korea and Taiwan achieved annual TFP growth of 1.9 percent and 1.6 percent per annum, respectively. However, their rates of TFP growth slowed significantly to an average of 0.6 percent and 1.1 percent per annum in 2010–14, respectively.

Another reason is the decline in the contribution of the India's TFP from 0.55 percent in the pre-crisis period to 0.13 percent in the post-crisis period, regardless of the recoveries in TFP growths in other South Asian countries like Pakistan and Bangladesh. India surpassed Japan based on the output share in the late 2000s, as illustrated in Figure 3.3. However, its per-capita GDP does not even reach half of that of China at present. The manufacturing sector has been expanding, but its effect of boosting employment has been marginal since 2000. India faces a key policy task of creating employment even if that means sacrificing the increase of labor productivity to some extent. The government's "Make in India" initiative is aimed at expanding the manufacturing sector even further, poising itself to enjoy the latecomer advantage and to capitalize on the demographic dividend, which is promised for the 2030s.

The decline in TFP in Southeast Asia has a minor impact on the slowdown of regional TFP in the post-crisis period. In the two largest economies in Southeast Asia, Indonesia's TFP contributions improved by 0.03 percentage point and that of Thailand deteriorated by 0.07 percentage point per year on average between the pre-crisis and post-crisis periods. TFP in the Philippines grew strongly at 3.0 percent per annum, as presented in Table 3.8, contributing to an increase in TFP of Entire Asia by 0.02 percentage point per year on average between the two periods.[11]

Although the current pace of TFP growth of Entire Asia in the post-crisis period with an average annual growth rate of 1.6 percent does not fully recover the pace in the pre-crisis period, it is not largely behind the long-term achievement of 2.0 percent for the past three decades from 1985 to 2014. Two-thirds of this long-term pace in regional TFP improvement have been accounted for by the East Asian countries. Looking forward, they are unlikely to remain a front-runner of TFP growth in Asia. However, their larger share of real outputs in the region, which has expanded from 54.7 percent in the 1970s to 60.5 percent in the post-crisis period in Table 3.8, may enable them to sustain a sound contribution to improving regional TFP with about 1.2 percentage point, even if their TFP growth rate is moderate at around 2.0 percent. In order to return to the long-term pace, it is crucial that the Southeast and South Asian countries capitalize their productivity potential.

Conclusion

This study may be the first trial to measure PPPs for capital and labor inputs for Asian countries. Our estimates for the period of 2011 indicate that PPPs for output considerably overestimates PPPs for labor input and underestimates PPPs for capital in many Asian countries. Taking into account the factor price differentials across countries may improve the growth accounting framework for Entire Asia. Based on our measurement, although TFP growth in Entire Asia has deteriorated in the 1970s, it has achieved 2.0 percent per year on average for the past three decades from 1985 to 2014, and two-thirds of this sound pace in regional TFP improvement has been accounted for by the East Asian countries.

This chapter did not examine the issues involved in the country-level data. In particular, there is room for further revision in the estimates on the hours worked and compensations of employees, self-employed and contributing family workers in the countries with larger informal sector. Adjusting quality in labor inputs is our next challenge. For improving the productivity measures, further research is required on these data issues especially in the South and Southeast Asian countries.

Notes

1 Recent significant revisions based on the System of National Accounts in 2008 (2008 SNA) have resulted in updates for Bangladesh, the Republic of China (Taiwan), Indonesia, Korea, Mongolia and Singapore in 2014–15, and for Sri Lanka and Japan in 2016. While there are movements toward upgrading the SNA, some countries, such as Cambodia and Nepal, have yet to fully introduce the earlier version 1993 SNA. This project attempts to reconcile the national accounts variations across countries and to develop the harmonized data by following the 2008 SNA for comparative productivity analyses.
2 The UNDESA project on developing a growth accounting framework for Bhutan was led by the author and Dr. Hamid Rashid (Senior Advisor for Macroeconomic Policy in UNDESA), supported by Mr. Nyingtob Pema Norbu (Gross National Happiness Commission, Royal Government of Bhutan), Mr. Sonam Tshering (Bhutan Interdisciplinary Research & Development), Mr. Sonam Laendup (National Statistics Bureau), and Mr. Tandin Dorji and Ms. Dechen Dema (Ministry of Labor and Human Resources).
3 In this study, the inventories and land are not counted as capital input due to data limitation on land price. Nomura (2004) shows that Japan's acquisition price of land for commercial and industrial uses was 9.1 times higher than that in the United States in 1990. The price for capital acquisition in Japan was 2.9 times higher than that in the United States in 1990 if we include land in capital input, but only 24 percent higher if land is excluded. After then, the price of land in Japan fell sharply during the real estate price collapse of 1991 that ended the "bubble economy". Jorgenson et al. (2016) estimate that the average price of land in 2005 is only 56.5 percent of that in 1990. The US land price increased substantially from the beginning of the 2000s, so that the average price in 2005 is 3.7 times higher than that in 1990. Reflecting these changes in both countries, the price differential for land between Japan and the United States has decreased to 1.9 times in 2005, compared to 11 times in 1990. The price for acquisition of fixed assets, produced assets and land, in Japan is 1.39 times higher than that in the United States in 2005 if land is included in capital input, but would be almost identical if land were excluded.
4 The unpublished data at the most detailed level (basic heading) of the PPPs for GFCF by products are aggregated to those based on our common asset classification, using EKS (Éltetö-Köves-Szulc) method.

5 The estimates of the productive capital stock are available in the APO Productivity Database 2016 for 20 Asian countries (APO 2016) and UNDESA project for Bhutan (UNDESA 2016).
6 The author, with Hiroshi Shirane, Naoyuki Akashi and Shinyoung Oh at Keio University, has developed the comprehensive data on number of workers, average hours worked per worker, and hourly wages, cross-classified by gender, age, education and employment status for the Asian economies. In this study, we use the work-in-progress estimates on hours worked for all countries and the estimates on average hourly labor compensation for six countries (Japan, Korea, Pakistan, Taiwan, Singapore and Thailand). The averages of the elementary-level wage differentials observed in Japan, Korea and Taiwan are assumed to approximate the relative wages in other East Asian countries. The wage differentials observed in Pakistan and Thailand are applied to other South and Southeast Asian countries, respectively. The total of labor compensation of employees (COE) derived from this approach is adjusted to be consistent with the COE in the national accounts in each country. If COE is not available in the national accounts (i.e. Bangladesh, Pakistan and Vietnam), we used our estimates in the APO Productivity Database 2016.
7 Although our estimate on the price level of labor for Japan is almost equivalent to the US level (0.97) in Table 3.1, this is evaluated based on the exchange rate (79.8 yen per dollar) on average in 2011, which was overvalued considerably.
8 The higher capital price in Iran may reflect the strengthened sanctions since 2010.
9 In 1975, the share of the country output in Entire Asia is 37.5 percent and 5.7 percent for Japan and Indonesia, respectively.
10 In Mongolia, the two world-class large mines (coal and copper) started production in 2010, sparking a resource boom. The country's capital investment ratio jumped from 30 percent of GDP in 2009 to 58 percent in 2011, accelerating the rate of economic growth from 2010 to 2013 to 12.9 percent per annum, of which 6 percentage points are attributed to the TFP increase (Table 3.8). However, it is only a temporary surge resulting from resource development. The slowdown of the Chinese economy also applied a sudden brake to Mongolia, which is now working on rebuilding its economy under the new government formed in November 2014.
11 Since the early 1990s in the Philippines, income transfer from abroad (remittances from overseas Filipino workers to the country) has expanded to reach as much as one-third of GDP in 2014. While stable domestic demand continues to support growth, labor productivity has also improved mainly in the service industry.

Bibliography

APO. 2016. *APO Productivity Databook 2016*. Tokyo: Asian Productivity Organization, Keio University Press.
De Vries, Klaas, and Abdul Azeez Erumban. 2015. *Total Economy Database-Sources and Methods*. The Conference Board.

Diewert, W. Erwin, and Kevin J. Fox. 2015. "Output Growth and Inflation Across Space and Time." *UNSW Business School Working Paper*, No. 2015, ECON 4.

Feenstra, Robert C., Robert Inklaar, and Marcel Timmer. 2015. "The Next Generation of the Penn World Table." *American Economic Review* 105(10): 3150–3182.

Jorgenson, Dale W., and Zvi Griliches. 1967. "The Explanation of Productivity Change." *Review of Economic Studies* 34(3): 249–283.

Jorgenson, Dale W., Koji Nomura, and Jon D. Samuels. 2016. "A Half Century of Trans-Pacific Competition: Price Level Indices and Productivity Gaps for Japanese and U.S. Industries, 1955–2012." In D. W. Jorgenson et al. (eds.), *The World Economy – Growth or Stagnation?* Cambridge: Cambridge University Press.

Nomura, Koji. 2004. *Measurement of Capital and Productivity in Japan*. Tokyo: Keio University Press (in Japanese).

UNDESA. 2016. *A Growth Accounting Framework for the Kingdom of Bhutan, 1990–2014*. New York: Development Policy and Analysis Division United Nations Department of Economic and Social Affairs.

World Bank. 2014. *Purchasing Power Parities and Real Expenditures of World Economies: Summary of Results and Findings of the 2011 International Comparison Program*. Washington, DC: World Bank.

Chapter 4

Latin America
Economic growth and productivity since the 1990s

Andre Hofman and Claudio Aravena

Introduction

Economic growth since 1990 in Latin America and India has been very different, with low and volatile growth in Latin America and the Caribbean, and sustained high growth in India. The analysis presented in this chapter helps explain the factors behind these different performances, and discusses the challenges Latin America and India face in achieving long-term growth, taking the most immediate determinants into account. A number of exercises, designed to quantify the factors that have driven growth, were therefore carried out on the basis of a "growth accounting" approach. The aim of this analysis is to identify elements that can help gear public policies toward raising growth rates sustainably for the economies of Latin America and the Caribbean.

The international literature on growth accounting is generally structured around an approach which, according to Caselli (2004), might be expressed as: Output = F (factors, efficiency). In other words, output, usually measured in per capita terms, is a function of certain factor inputs, normally some measurement of capital and labor, and of total factor productivity (TFP) or the "efficiency" with which inputs are utilized. TFP, in turn, is a measure of the shift in the production function (of an economy, a production facility, or an economic sector), for a given level of capital and labor inputs. Intuitively, it also measures the shift in the production function that results in addition to the contributions of the capital and labor inputs. Many factors might cause this shift: technical innovation, organizational or institutional changes, changes in factor shares, scale effects, variations in work intensity, and measurement errors, among others (Hulten 2001).

As with many growth theories, this approach considers a long-term relationship and assumes the full employment of resources. Accordingly, the empirical studies are based on long statistical time series and, in some cases, use averages over several years, in order to obtain a quantitative approximation of growth trends that is unaffected by short-term cyclical fluctuations, insofar as is possible.

This approach intrinsically presents two major challenges. The first consists in attempting to determine the content of the inputs as best possible. The second, and the more difficult, is to determine what is explained by "efficiency". Maddison (1987: 651) states, "growth accounting of this kind cannot provide a full causal story. It deals with 'proximate' rather than 'ultimate' causality and registers the facts about growth components; it does not explain the elements of policy or circumstance, national or international, that underlie them, but it does identify which facts need more ultimate explanation".

In this context, the LA KLEMS project, in cooperation with the Groningen Growth and Development Center, the Valencian Institute of Economic Research and Harvard University, has developed a database that will help improve the identification of "proximate" causes of growth trends in the region.[1] The result is a homogeneous database, known as KLEMS, which allows the improved measurement and identification of capital (K), labor (L), energy (E), materials (M) and services (S) inputs.

The second section of this chapter contrasts the key growth-related dimensions in five Latin American countries and seven developed economies. This comparison illustrates some of the gaps that determine the region's lower productivity levels. The third section examines the evidence, based on detailed exercises, regarding the "proximate" causal factors of growth in Latin America and the Caribbean between 1990 and 2013. And the final section brings together the main findings and briefly discusses some policy guidelines for sustainable growth.

Productivity gaps between Latin America and developed countries

In line with the approach of Maddison (1987), an initial exercise was carried out to identify the factors that account for the region's low growth and require subsequent explanation. This took the form of a comparative analysis of the key dimensions of growth and shed some initial light on the challenges of devising policies to improve the long-term performance of Latin America and the Caribbean. The subsequent sections expand on this analysis.

Table 4.1 compares the values of variables that are key under different growth theories. They include labor productivity (the ratio between output and employment), capital intensity (the ratio between the capital stock and employment) and TFP. Capital is broken down into the components of ICT capital (associated with information and communications technologies) and non-ICT capital. The comparison includes seven developed countries (France, Germany, Italy, Japan, Spain, the United Kingdom and the United States) and five Latin American countries (Argentina, Brazil, Chile, Colombia and Mexico). The latter accounted for about 81 percent of Latin American and Caribbean GDP, in nominal dollars, between 2009 and 2013.

The first finding is the significant labor productivity gap (measured in purchasing power parity (PPP) at constant 1995 prices) between the Latin American and the developed countries, both in 1995 and in 2007. Moreover, labor productivity grew more slowly in the region's three largest economies (Argentina, Brazil and Mexico) than in the United States, so in practice the gap widened. Colombia maintained its relative position, while Chile narrowed the gap, having started from a low level.

These differences in labor productivity are in turn associated with wide gaps in the capital-labor ratio, with labor measured by the number of hours worked. Capital deepening is seen to be much greater in developed countries. Moreover, although Chile and Colombia have increased their capital-labor (K/L) ratio significantly, the other three Latin American countries have done so only very slowly, which has prevented them from closing the gap with the developed countries. Indeed, K/L ratios intensified in all the industrialized countries included, from an average of 52.4 in 1995 to 67.2 in 2007. The five Latin American economies also posted an increase in that period, from an average of 12.1 in 1995 to 20.8 in 2007. However, this capital deepening process was uneven, occurring most vigorously in Colombia and, to a lesser extent, in Chile. These lower levels of capital per worker, and their slowness to increase, help explain the region's growing labor productivity lag.

A disaggregation of capital enables an evaluation of the pace at which information and communications technologies (ICTs) have

Table 4.1 Latin America and developed countries (selected countries): labor productivity indicators, 1995–2007

(PPP dollars at constant 1995 prices)

	Germany	Spain	United States	France	Italy	Japan	United Kingdom	Argentina	Brazil	Chile	Colombia	Mexico
Total economy labor productivity												
1995	25.8	22.8	25.8	25.6	24.0	19.9	20.7	11.0	6.3	7.8	6.6	10.0
2007	31.0	24.5	33.3	30.8	25.4	25.7	26.7	13.5	6.7	10.9	8.4	11.7
Annual growth rate of total economy labor productivity												
1995–2007	1.6	0.7	2.0	1.5	0.5	2.1	2.1	1.7	0.6	2.6	2.0	1.2
Total economy capital-labor ratio												
1995	50.3	45.9	40.9	52.9	99.2	46.0	31.6	15.9	9.2	10.8	4.6	20.0
2007	66.3	57.4	60.0	62.2	113.5	65.4	46.0	18.0	10.6	21.8	29.9	23.8
Annual growth rate of total economy capital-labor ratio												
1995–2007	3.48	2.56	3.71	2.49	2.33	3.45	3.97	1.82	0.79	6.05	15.5	1.64
Total economy non-ITC capital-labor ratio[a]												
1995	47.9	43.7	37.8	50.9	96.9	43.9	29.5	15.2	8.0	10.7	4.2	19.4
2007	57.7	50.8	45.7	57.5	106.9	60.2	35.0	15.5	7.3	19.9	24.2	21.1
Annual growth rate of total economy non-ITC capital-labor ratio[a]												
	2.1	1.6	1.3	1.6	1.6	2.7	1.4	1.1	−1.0	5.2	15.7	0.8
Total economy ITC capital-labor ratio[a]												
1995	2.4	2.3	3.1	2.0	2.3	2.1	2.1	0.6	1.3	0.1	0.4	0.6
2007	8.6	6.6	14.4	4.7	6.6	5.2	11.0	2.5	3.3	1.9	2.4	2.7

Annual growth rate of total economy ITC capital-labor ratio

	10.8	8.9	12.8	7.7	8.8	8.2	13.9	8.9	8.0	27.2	14.0	11.9

Total economy total factor productivity

| 1995 | 95.9 | 86.3 | 100.0 | 94.4 | 75.6 | 75.4 | 86.3 | 61.5 | 37.4 | 46.0 | 43.4 | 49.6 |
| 2007 | 100.8 | 79.5 | 109.7 | 99.6 | 71.4 | 78.0 | 92.8 | 66.7 | 33.0 | 43.6 | 32.6 | 47.0 |

Annual growth rate of total economy total factor productivity

| 1995–2007 | 0.4 | −0.7 | 0.8 | 0.5 | −0.5 | 0.3 | 0.6 | 0.7 | −1.0 | −0.5 | −2.4 | −0.4 |

Source: LA KLEMS and EU KLEMS
[a] Information and communications technologies.

been integrated in Latin American economies, compared with the industrialized countries. Comparing the ICT-capital-to-hours-worked ratio (K-ICT/L) in the five Latin American countries with the average for the industrialized countries shows that the gap between them has narrowed slightly, from a multiple of 3.8 to a multiple of 3.2. Yet this convergence is due to the rapid rise of K-ICT/L in Chile and Colombia, while in the other countries the change is much slower.

In brief, the capital-labor ratio (measured in PPP dollars at 1995 constant prices) in these five Latin American countries is approximately one-third (31 percent) of the ratio in the developed countries used as a reference, and has remained fairly stable over the study period. However, if Chile and Colombia are excluded from the analysis, the region has lagged further behind the industrialized countries in respect of capital intensity. The productivity gaps between Latin America and the developed countries may, therefore, be expected to widen even further unless major additional efforts are made over a lengthy period of time.

Lastly, Table 4.1 includes an index of total factor productivity (TFP), taking the 1995 figure for the United States as the base value of 100. In comparative terms, TFP replicates the behavior of the other variables, being much lower in the five selected Latin American economies than in the developed countries and actually falling – meaning that productivity declined – in some cases.

Productivity and growth in Latin America and the Caribbean

This section discusses the findings obtained by applying the growth accounting method. As explained below, the analysis progresses from a "traditional" approach toward more refined applications and the inclusion of more disaggregated information. The exercises under the traditional methodology are presented in order to include the greatest possible number of countries using comparable data. As the methodology demands more rigorous and accurate measurements, the bar is raised regarding information requirements, leaving some countries out of the analysis.

Methodology

For the purposes of this analysis, data on 23 Latin American and Caribbean countries were collected for the period between 1990 and 2013. As in previous chapters, the study period was divided into four subperiods: 1990–1997, 1998–2003, 2004–2008 and 2009–2013. Depending on the availability of data, three types of exercise were performed. The first covers 23 countries of the region: 18 from Latin America (17 continental countries plus the Dominican Republic) and five from the Caribbean (the Bahamas, Barbados, Belize, Jamaica, and Trinidad and Tobago). The approach taken in this exercise could be termed "traditional" growth accounting. The capital stock was examined using series of gross capital formation at constant prices,[2] with labor corresponding to the total number of hours worked.

In the second exercise, performed for only 18 Latin American countries and termed "modified" growth accounting, the number of hours worked is structured by educational level (primary, secondary, and tertiary) and valued according to their respective rates of return. Capital is also broken down by various components,[3] whose estimation differs from the previous method in that measurement is based on the capital stocks available at the time, instead of the accumulation of investment flows. Once the components of the capital stock have been estimated, the respective user cost,[4] which varies depending on the nature of each component, is calculated. Different types of capital can thus be aggregated into an index of capital services.[5]

The third exercise, applied to just five Latin American countries, uses the LA KLEMS database[6] to obtain disaggregated information on nine economic sectors. In each of these sectors, a distinction is made between three characteristics of the labor factor (sex, age and education level) and eight types of capital asset. These disaggregated data are available only for Argentina, Brazil, Chile, Colombia and Mexico. The TFP series were estimated in all cases by deducting, from GDP growth, the sum of capital and labor inputs weighted by each input's share in the income recorded in national accounts.[7,8]

Findings of the traditional method of growth accounting

Table 4.2 presents the main findings resulting from the application of the traditional methodology. As can be seen, with the sole exception of Argentina, factor accumulation (capital and labor) accounted for most of the growth between 1990 and 2013. The situation in the Caribbean is similar, so that in most cases, TFP exerts very little influence, or even reduces growth. In almost half of

Table 4.2 Latin America and the Caribbean: contributions to GDP growth measured with the traditional growth accounting method, 1990–2013

(Percentages)

	Average annual GDP growth	Contributions to GDP growth		
		Capital stock	Hours worked	Total Factor Productivity
Argentina	3.9	1.0	1.0	2.0
Bolivia (Plurinational State of)	4.0	1.6	3.6	−1.2
Brazil	2.5	0.9	1.2	0.4
Chile	4.9	2.3	0.8	1.8
Colombia	3.6	1.2	1.4	1.0
Costa Rica	4.6	2.4	1.3	0.9
Dominican Republic	4.9	1.9	1.7	1.2
Ecuador	3.3	1.6	1.2	0.5
El Salvador	4.2	1.8	1.5	0.9
Guatemala	3.7	1.4	1.8	0.4
Honduras	3.5	1.6	2.2	−0.4
Mexico	2.8	1.6	0.8	0.4
Nicaragua	3.1	0.5	2.8	−0.2
Panama	6.0	2.9	1.6	1.6
Peru	4.4	1.4	1.9	1.1
Paraguay	3.1	1.4	1.9	−0.3
Uruguay	3.4	0.7	0.7	2.0
Venezuela (Bolivarian Republic of)	2.8	0.8	1.4	0.7
Latin America	**3.8**	**1.5**	**1.6**	**0.7**
Bahamas	1.5	1.1	1.0	−0.6
Barbados	0.9	0.1	0.5	0.3
Belize	4.1	1.6	2.0	0.5
Jamaica	0.7	1.0	0.6	−0.8
Trinidad and Tobago	4.5	0.0	1.3	3.2
The Caribbean (1990–2012)	**2.3**	**0.8**	**1.1**	**0.5**

Source: ECLAC on the basis of LA KLEMS

the countries, labor contributed more to growth than capital only slightly more often, so that on average both factors made virtually equal contributions to growth. In short, the main conclusion is that growth in Latin America and the Caribbean is driven more by factor accumulation than by productivity or efficiency gains, which in the past 23 years have had very little impact in the region.

Findings of the modified method of growth accounting

The modified method of growth accounting is better than the traditional method, for two main reasons. First, because it distinguishes capital components by their production capacity, it reveals how changes in the composition of capital over time potentially improve that capacity (for example, improvements in the school enrolment rate and in education levels, or the take-up of more modern technologies through a relative increase in the proportion of computing and telecommunications equipment compared with traditional capital). Second, valuing these capital components using parameters closer to the cost of their services give a more accurate value of the inputs utilized by an economy to generate a certain level of production.

The improvements in the calculation are expressed in the changes in the contributions made by the "proximate" factors of growth, as shown in Table 4.3.

The results shown in this table are significant, especially by comparison with the first exercise. First, Latin America has increased the use of capital services compared with those of human capital, which is consistent with findings of Table 4.1, which noted a rise in the capital-labor ratio. More rigorous application of the growth accounting methodology thus found that capital had a greater impact than labor on growth, since on average it contributed 68 percent of Latin America's growth in 1990–2013. Much of this has to do with the great shift in the structure of capital in recent decades, especially in relation to ICTs, whose rapid spread should be reflected by an increase in production capacity. Furthermore, the boom in certain commodities led to a surge in investment in extractive industries (such as metal mining and hydrocarbons), which are extremely capital intensive. Improving the measurement of capital services had an especially large impact in faster-growing countries (Chile, Colombia, El Salvador, Panama, the Plurinational State of Bolivia and, to a lesser extent, Costa Rica and Peru), which constitutes evidence that not only the amount, but also the quality of investment (as reflected by the adjustment to take into account its composition and especially the use of ICTs) has assumed greater importance as a source of growth.

Labor inputs also made a larger contribution to growth, owing to an increase in total hours worked and the progress achieved in the sphere of education during the study period.[9] These advances, captured by the measurement of labor skill level, also increase

Table 4.3 Latin America: contributions to GDP growth measured with the modified growth accounting method, 1990–2013

	Average annual GDP growth	Contributions to GDP growth		
		Capital services	Hours worked weighted by labor skill level	Total factor productivity
Argentina	3.9	1.7	0.9	1.4
Bolivia (Plurinational State of)	4.0	3.0	4.0	−3.0
Brazil	2.5	2.3	2.0	−1.8
Chile	4.9	3.6	1.2	0.0
Colombia	3.6	3.1	2.1	−1.6
Costa Rica	4.6	3.2	1.8	−0.5
Dominican Republic	4.9	3.8	2.1	−1.0
Ecuador	3.3	1.2	1.5	0.6
El Salvador	4.2	3.6	1.9	−1.2
Guatemala	3.7	2.5	2.4	−1.2
Honduras	3.5	4.0	2.8	−3.3
Mexico	2.8	2.4	1.2	−0.8
Nicaragua	3.1	1.6	3.5	−2.0
Panama	6.0	3.5	2.0	0.6
Peru	4.4	2.2	2.4	−0.3
Paraguay	3.1	2.5	2.3	−1.8
Uruguay	3.4	1.5	1.1	0.9
Venezuela (Bolivarian Republic of)	2.8	0.9	1.9	0.0
Latin America	**3.8**	**2.6**	**2.1**	**−0.8**

Source: ECLAC, on the basis of LA KLEMS

production potential, albeit less quickly than capital, given the inertia typical of demographic processes.

The progress of capital and labor inputs outperformed GDP growth (as documented in the first column of Tables 4.2 and 4.3), meaning that total factor productivity actually made a negligible or even negative contribution to regional growth in the last 23 years (see the final column of Table 4.3). In other words, the region has been unable to efficiently use the totality of its investment effort in physical and human capital. Following Maddison (1987), this is a stylized feature requiring explanation, which will be discussed later.

In summary, the improved application of the growth accounting approach yielded certain findings that help explain the region's poor long-term growth. Capital is largely responsible for growth, despite increasing only modestly owing to low levels of investment both as a proportion of GDP and in comparison with other regions. Other elements, in particular the quality of the labor force and total productivity, have made low or even negative contributions to growth. It follows that to boost the growth rate, countries will have to overcome lags in the areas of investment, workforce skills, and productivity.

Recent performance of the proximate determinants of growth: procyclical productivity

By examining contributions to growth over time, some explanations may be formulated regarding the region's slack productivity growth. For this analysis, growth components were calculated for shorter time periods than in the previous exercise, so that the calculation of TFP is influenced by cyclical factors, among others. For this reason, the basis for calculating TFP over shorter periods is conceptually different to that used in the preceding sections, which is more focused on long-term resource utilization efficiency. The calculation of TFP over shorter periods reflects instead the degree of capacity utilization, which is largely determined by cyclical fluctuations.

The following figures (Figure 4.1a, 4.1b, and 4.1c) illustrate the performance of contributions to growth, by subregion and period. They also reflect the procyclical nature of TFP during shorter periods: its contribution to growth is positive in countries and in periods with faster GDP growth, but turns negative where activity levels slump; in other words, when capacity utilization diminishes. The collapse and revival of TFP during downturns and booms give rise to the theory that these swings in estimated TFP reflect not technological factors, but financial constraints and macroeconomic shocks (Calvo et al. 2006). In the absence of countercyclical action, these shocks translate into changes in the utilization of factors. As growth slows (quickens) the number of hours worked falls (increases), and less (more) is produced with the same capital endowment. The consequence is that the economy's total productivity diminishes (or increases).

As is documented in ECLAC (2013b), in the past 30 years the region's economy has yielded only low and unstable growth,[10] with

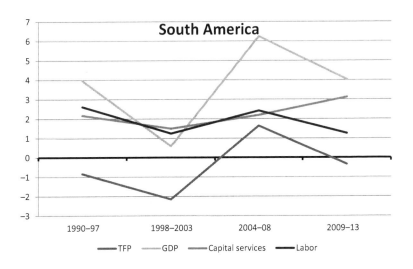

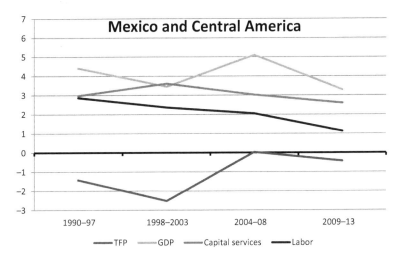

Figure 4.1 Latin America and the Caribbean: evolution of the determinants of GDP growth measured with the modified growth accounting method, by subregion and period, 1990–2013

Source: LA KLEMS database

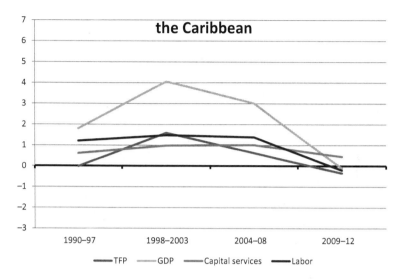

Figure 4.1 (Continued)

frequent external shocks and domestic crises resulting in economic contractions and setting back living standards and productivity. Productivity losses are, therefore, due partly to the vulnerabilities described in the previous chapter and the lack of countercyclical capacities to prevent or mitigate the consequences of external shocks and internal imbalances (i.e. the capacity to make the region more resilient).

However, as indicated in ECLAC (2013b), the structural heterogeneity of the region's economies, manifested in major differences in productivity between large corporations and SMEs (which are much more numerous), with the consequent segmentation of the labor market, has a further adverse impact on productivity, in addition to the aforementioned macroeconomic variability. Two different labor segments exist in Latin America and the Caribbean. One is dependent on the demand for formal employment from large and medium enterprises and some households, and the other comprises a surplus labor force that finds work in low-productivity sectors with fewer access barriers. This structure affects the way in which the region's labor markets adapt to different phases of the business cycle (Ocampo et al. 2009). Unlike in developed economies, labor supply patterns are such that adjustments in times of low economic growth and weak labor demand take the form of falling labor productivity more than falling employment (ECLAC/ILO 2012).

This trend is aggravated by the underdevelopment of unemployment insurance, in that unemployment does not increase as much during slowdowns as it would in industrialized countries. This is because people take up less productive activities and seek refuge in (often informal) microenterprises as a defensive strategy against falling labor demand, thereby reducing the total productivity of the economy in a procyclical manner.

In short, unless the effects of short-term shocks on the level of economic activity are offset or moderated through countercyclical policies, production capacity utilization, and productivity will fall. Moreover, these short-term effects influence long-term growth in two ways. First, the decline in growth (and the increase in idle capacity) usually has a negative impact on investment (Jiménez and Manuelito 2013), so that temporary shocks affect trend growth. Second, as can be seen in Figure 4.2, variations in the contribution of capital to growth are positively correlated with changes in TFP. In other words, as capacity utilization decreases during cyclical downturns, total factor productivity also diminishes, thus

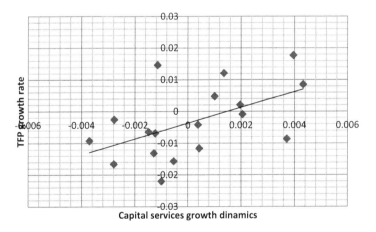

Figure 4.2 Latin America: relationship between the change in the contribution of capital to the growth of GDP and TFP, 2000–2013 (percentage points and percentages)

Source: ECLAC/ILO (2012). The employment situation in Latin America and the Caribbean. October 2012. Number 7.2012-848.

constituting a second channel for the deterioration of long-term growth.

Sectoral aspects of productivity determinants in five Latin American countries

Up to this point, the analysis of productivity trends has been conducted at the aggregate level. This section examines economic growth, productivity, and its determinants in nine economic sectors in five Latin American countries (Argentina, Brazil, Chile, Colombia, and Mexico) during the period 1990–2012.

Series on output by economic sector, as well as on employment and capital services, are taken from the LA KLEMS database. For employment, the analysis considers changes in the structure of the labor force, and for capital, it includes the effects of the rate at which investment has shifted in favor of ICT assets in recent years.

Investment by asset type

Gross fixed capital formation in ICTs covers three types of asset: office and computing equipment, telecommunications equipment, and software. The disaggregation of gross fixed capital formation by ICT and non-ICT assets, as presented in Table 4.4, shows that investment in ICTs makes a significant contribution to GDP in Brazil, which in relative terms is double that of Colombia, the country with the second highest rate of ICT investment. Chile, which in 1995 lagged behind the other countries in its percentage of ICT investment, achieved the fastest rise, overtaking Argentina and Mexico. On average during the period, about 7 percent of the investment effort was allocated to ICTs in Argentina, Chile, and Mexico, 12 percent in Colombia, and 19 percent in Brazil.

Table 4.5, in which data is disaggregated by type of non-ICT asset, shows the greater sustained investment effort made by Chile, Colombia, and Mexico in non-residential construction, as well as that of Argentina in residential construction. Brazil's investment is most concentrated in the "other machinery" category, closely followed by residential investment.

Considering that investment brings technical progress, the investment destination by type of asset is important. With regard to the size of non-ICT production investment (not including residential investment), Argentina allocates 60 percent of total investment to

Table 4.4 Latin America (5 countries): disaggregation of gross fixed capital formation, selected years between 1995 and 2010

(Percentages of GDP)

	Investment effort (gross fixed capital formation)					
	Total	ICT	No TIC	Total	ICT	No TIC
	1995			2000		
Argentina	19.1	1.2	17.9	17.2	1.8	15.4
Brazil	22.2	4.0	18.2	21.0	3.9	17.1
Chile	26.0	0.3	25.7	22.1	1.3	20.8
Colombia	19.3	2.0	17.3	12.7	1.6	11.0
Mexico	18.2	1.0	17.2	21.5	1.9	19.6
	2005			2010		
Argentina	23.2	1.6	21.6	25.4	1.4	24.0
Brazil	20.0	4.1	15.9	24.7	4.9	19.7
Chile	23.9	1.5	22.4	24.0	2.1	22.0
Colombia	18.3	2.6	15.7	20.2	2.0	18.1
Mexico	21.4	1.4	19.9	22.5	1.7	20.8

Note: The investment rates shown do not correspond to the official figures in the countries' national accounts, since ICT investment series are deflated by hedonic price indices. See Aravena and Hofman (2014) for further information.
Source: Economic Commission for Latin America and the Caribbean (ECLAC), on the basis of LA KLEMS.

production investment, Brazil and Mexico 70 percent, and Chile and Colombia 80 percent. Capital makes a greater contribution to GDP in the latter two countries, which have also made larger improvements in productivity.

Proximate determinants of growth by sector

The findings of the aggregate analysis reveal that in four of the five countries, investment (particularly in non-ICT assets) was the main driver behind the overall growth of value added, as well as growth in the best performing sector, transport and communications. An exception was noted in Brazil, where it was mainly the contributions of labor – especially hours worked – that fueled the rise in value added, including in the transport and communications sector (Table 4.6). By contrast, the quality of labor and TFP generally made only minor contributions.

Table 4.5 Latin America (5 countries): disaggregation of gross fixed capital formation by type of non-ICT asset, selected years between 1995 and 2010

(Percentages of GDP)

Investment effort (gross fixed capital formation)

	Total non-ICT	Residential structures	Other structures	Transport equipment	Other machinery	Total non-ICT	Residential structures	Other structures	Transport equipment	Other machinery
	1995					2000				
Argentina	17.9	7.2	4.9	2.0	5.0	17.2	6.3	4.5	1.8	4.6
Brazil	18.2	5.1	4.0	3.4	5.6	17.1	5.4	4.2	2.2	5.2
Chile	25.7	6.5	8.7	2.3	8.1	20.8	4.6	8.5	1.6	6.1
Colombia	17.3	2.1	11.4	1.0	2.8	11.0	1.9	5.6	1.0	2.6
Mexico	17.2	4.6	5.4	1.3	5.9	19.6	6.0	6.3	2.5	4.9
	2005					2010				
Argentina	21.6	7.2	4.9	2.0	5.0	17.2	6.3	4.5	1.8	4.6
Brazil	15.9	4.4	3.5	2.5	5.6	19.7	5.0	3.9	3.8	7.0
Chile	22.4	4.6	8.8	2.4	6.6	22.0	3.8	9.5	1.7	7.0
Colombia	15.7	3.7	7.2	1.7	3.0	18.1	4.0	8.8	2.1	3.1
Mexico	19.9	6.5	6.6	2.1	4.8	20.8	6.5	7.2	1.9	5.3

Source: Economic Commission for Latin America and the Caribbean (ECLAC), on the basis of LA KLEMS.

Table 4.6 Latin America (5 countries): determinants of growth in value added, by economic sector, 1990–2009[a]

	Value added	Hours worked	Quality of labor	ICT capital[b]	Non-ICT capital[b]	Total factor productivity
Argentina						
Total	3.9	0.8	0.2	0.6	2.6	-0.3
Agriculture, forestry and fishing	3.0	0.0	0.5	0.0	3.3	-0.9
Mining	3.0	2.2	-0.3	0.2	9.4	-8.5
Manufacturing	3.5	0.0	0.5	0.4	3.0	-0.3
Electricity, gas and water	5.3	-0.9	0.0	0.7	3.4	2.1
Construction	5.6	2.1	-0.2	0.1	0.9	2.7
Commerce, restaurants and hotels	4.0	2.1	0.0	0.6	2.1	-0.8
Transport and communications	6.9	0.5	0.4	0.3	3.5	2.2
Financial and business services	4.2	0.8	0.0	1.7	3.2	-1.5
Community, social and personal services	2.9	1.0	0.3	0.3	0.6	0.7
Brazil						
Total	2.6	1.8	1.0	0.8	0.4	-1.4
Agriculture, forestry and fishing	3.5	-0.8	1.0	0.3	0.6	2.4
Mining	3.9	1.1	0.8	2.7	1.6	-2.4
Manufacturing	1.1	1.3	0.7	1.1	0.2	-2.2
Electricity, gas and water	2.9	0.3	0.5	1.4	1.2	-0.6
Construction	2.0	2.0	0.8	0.2	0.8	-1.8
Commerce, restaurants and hotels	2.5	2.2	1.0	0.2	0.1	-1.1
Transport and communications	4.0	1.5	0.6	1.2	0.7	0.0
Financial and business services	3.5	4.0	0.5	0.6	0.0	-1.6
Community, social and personal services	2.6	1.3	1.6	0.9	0.6	-1.7

Chile
Total	4.3	1.6	0.9	0.3	2.0	-0.4
Agriculture, forestry and fishing	4.3	-0.6	0.9	0.1	-0.7	4.6
Mining	4.0	0.1	0.7	0.3	4.5	-1.6
Manufacturing	3.1	0.4	1.1	0.2	2.1	-0.7
Electricity, gas and water	4.6	0.4	0.1	0.4	6.2	-2.5
Construction	4.1	3.0	1.1	0.1	0.4	-0.4
Commerce, restaurants and hotels	6.0	2.1	1.1	0.3	1.1	1.4
Transport and communications	6.9	1.8	0.9	0.4	3.7	0.1
Financial and business services	5.9	4.3	0.6	0.5	2.0	-1.5
Community, social and personal services	3.3	1.5	1.5	0.3	1.2	-1.2

Colombia
Total	3.2	2.3	0.4	0.4	2.5	-2.5
Agriculture, forestry and fishing	1.8	0.0	-1.8	0.0	2.5	1.1
Mining	3.8	0.9	0.2	0.7	9.3	-7.3
Manufacturing	1.9	1.5	0.8	0.1	3.0	-3.5
Electricity, gas and water	3.0	-0.4	-0.9	0.0	10.3	-6.1
Construction	3.2	3.8	-0.9	0.0	1.3	-1.1
Commerce, restaurants and hotels	2.5	3.2	1.6	0.3	1.4	-4.0
Transport and communications	4.4	2.4	1.7	4.1	3.4	-7.1
Financial and business services	3.4	4.4	1.3	0.3	1.1	-3.7
Community, social and personal services	4.9	0.4	-1.0	0.1	1.7	3.8

Mexico
Total	1.8	1.2	0.5	0.4	1.2	-1.4
Agriculture, forestry and fishing	1.0	0.0	0.4	0.1	1.6	-1.0
Mining	0.4	-0.4	0.6	0.1	2.0	-1.9
Manufacturing	1.6	-0.1	0.4	0.2	1.1	0.0

(*Continued*)

Table 4.6 (Continued)

	Value added	Hours worked	Quality of labor	ICT capital[b]	Non-ICT capital[b]	Total factor productivity
Electricity, gas and water	2.9	0.3	0.1	0.5	1.0	1.1
Construction	1.6	2.3	1.0	0.4	1.3	−3.3
Commerce, restaurants and hotels	1.6	3.5	1.1	0.8	0.9	−4.7
Transport and communications	3.9	1.1	0.7	0.6	1.1	0.5
Financial and business services	2.9	1.2	0.0	0.4	1.8	−0.5
Community, social and personal services	0.5	1.1	0.1	0.4	0.5	−1.5

Source: Economic Commission for Latin America and the Caribbean (ECLAC), on the basis of KLEMS [online] www.worldklems.net/data.htm, accessed on 19 September 2016.

a Data for Argentina refer to 1993–2008, while those of Brazil refer to 1996–2009.
b ICT: Information and communications technologies.

In all countries, the labor input that contributed most to value added was the number of hours worked, with the quality of labor much less influential. This contribution of labor was concentrated in the non-tradable services sectors, mainly commerce, financial, and business services, and construction. The number of hours worked in the manufacturing sector rose very slightly in all countries except Mexico, where it fell. Labor quality improved in all sectors in four countries, although in Colombia this indicator decreased in some activities. In the primary sector, in keeping with the usual patterns of structural change observed elsewhere, the number of hours worked generally rose very slightly or decreased, while the quality of labor registered some improvement.

The more disaggregated exercise reported above, covering nine sectors in five countries, found that TFP was generally negative during the study period. The main exception was Argentina, in which TFP was positive in five of the nine sectors considered, although it was negative for the economy as a whole.

In four of the five countries studied, the sectors with the lowest levels of TFP were those in which capital made a greater contribution to growth in value added: the mining sector in Argentina and Brazil; electricity, gas, and water in Chile; and transport and communications in Colombia. This could be a sign that weaker value-added growth in the region might be due not only to a low level of investment, but also to its sectoral allocation and management, two areas in which further study is required.

Concluding remarks

This chapter has examined the available empirical evidence with respect to growth in Latin America and the Caribbean during the period 1990–2013. For these purposes, the "growth accounting" model was used, following the tradition of authors such as Solow (1956), Denison (1967), Jorgensen and Griliches (1967), and Maddison (1987). In keeping with the available information, four exercises were carried out in order to explain the "immediate causes" of the region's economic growth. The first exercise applied a traditional growth accounting method, using the cumulative value of investment and the number of hours worked as inputs. The second exercise introduced changes to account for the different types of asset which comprise capital, and the quality of the labor force by education level. The third exercise examined how the proximate factors of growth evolve over time, and the fourth exercise analyzed the sectoral dimensions of these factors, in greater depth and for a smaller group of countries. Analysis of the data enabled the deduction of a series of observations and stylized facts, giving deeper insights into the challenge faced by the region's countries in order to achieve long-term growth.

Latin American countries have considerably lower labor productivity than developed countries and, with rare exceptions, these gaps are widening.

One of the main reasons for this disparity is the much greater capital deepening in developed countries, which translates into considerably higher capital-labor ratios. Latin American and Caribbean countries are lagging further behind in this respect, which could lead to losses in competitiveness compared with developed countries, owing to lower relative growth in productivity.

In the projected external environment – described in Chapter 1 – in which global demand will be less buoyant than in 2003–2008, these trends will have to be reversed in order to sustain growth on the basis of competitiveness. This is a serious challenge.

The region has experienced low growth over the past 30 years. This is due partly to the small contribution of certain factors, especially labor-force quality and productivity. Although the region's investment levels are lower than those of countries that maintained high growth over a lengthy period, the increase in capital services on average accounted for 68 percent of Latin America's growth between 1990 and 2013, while the contribution of other factors was either very modest or negative.

Labor inputs made a positive contribution, although largely through the number of hours worked. Up until now, the quality of labor, measured by employee skill levels, has exerted a smaller influence.

This predominance of quantity over quality draws attention to one of the region's toughest challenges: the urgency of increasing skill levels and the contribution of the labor force to production, both by improving education at all levels, and by promoting employment in higher-productivity sectors. These are among the issues that are addressed in Chapter 4.

The largest capital contribution has been made by non-ICT capital. However, several countries have recently increased their ICT capital investment.

In the short and medium terms, total factor productivity behaves procyclically, increasing during economic booms and diminishing as growth slows. Productivity losses associated with low-growth periods in turn have an adverse impact on long-term growth, both because of disincentives to investment resulting from reduced capacity utilization, and because of the fall in TFP caused by the lower utilization of capital services.

In view of the policy challenges facing the region, the following guidelines are relevant for initiatives to promote sustainable growth.

Macroeconomic policies that maximize the utilization of production capacity, on a sustainable basis, are critical for long-term growth and for protecting labor productivity and income.

Macroeconomic policies need to place emphasis on promoting investment. As the exercises show, neither productivity nor income will increase without a significant investment effort. However, the near-universal prevalence of negative total factor productivity in the region over a period of 23 years is a symptom that the allocation and utilization of resources has not been as efficient as it should have been. While factor accumulation through investment and human capital gains are necessary for long-term growth, so too are microeconomic policies that use appropriate stimulus and public measures to help overcome the structural barriers that limit productivity and prevent the transformation of production patterns, as envisaged by ECLAC (2012).

Macroeconomic policies must also focus on safeguarding the competitiveness of tradable sectors, in order to raise productivity in the spheres in which competition and innovation stand a greater chance of becoming a reality. While some services (such as telecommunications) contribute to increasing productivity, this has proved difficult in other service-related spheres.

Microeconomic policies must aim to improve labor productivity and total factor productivity in key sectors. This may be achieved in a number of ways, for example by identifying barriers to production and competition, improving training to raise labor productivity per unit of capital invested, or supporting investment in key infrastructures for growth.

It should be recalled that the average productivity of the region's economies is less than one-third of that of the industrialized countries (see Table 4.1) and that until now, the main contribution of the labor factor has been through the rise in the number of hours worked, which has its limits. Boosting the region's growth therefore requires strengthening investment, productivity, and competitiveness, given that the external environment is expected to provide less impetus in the coming years.

None of the above suggests that there is a single recipe for achieving and maintaining high growth rates. The experience of other regions shows that policy mixes that have enabled a small group of countries to make rapid progress towards higher income levels entail much "sweat and sacrifice" (high rates of investment, which defer present consumption). The available evidence for Latin America and the Caribbean seems to support this hypothesis, while the current gaps in productivity and resource utilization efficiency also represent opportunities for boosting growth.

Notes

1 The LA KLEMS project currently includes 10 Latin American and Caribbean countries. The database is built on employment and national accounts statistics provided by the countries of Latin America and the Caribbean and generated by their respective national statistical institutes and central banks. The results of LA KLEMS are comparable with those of the World KLEMS database and support disaggregated analysis of a large group of developed and developing countries.
2 This is known as the "perpetual inventory" method.
3 Capital components include machinery and equipment (including transport equipment), buildings, telecommunications equipment, and computing equipment.
4 User cost includes the long-term real interest rate and the rate of depreciation, which differs for each capital component.
5 Capital measurement has long been a source of dispute between those who believe it is not possible to obtain an adequate measurement of something as heterogeneous as capital (along the lines of Robinson (1961) and Sraffa (1960)) and those who consider that the use of appropriate indexes yields useful measures (Jorgensen and Griliches 1967). This is not a case of Keynesian versus neoclassical, since not all the authors of growth accounting studies are neoclassical economists, nor do they adopt neoclassical approaches (for example, authors such as Denison (1967), and ECLAC). A capital measurement is used herein that helps better measure the "services" provided by this heterogeneous inventory of buildings, machinery, equipment and, more recently, information and communications technologies (ICTs), without entering into the substantive debate. See Harcourt and Laing (1971) for a description of the technical debate on capital.
6 See Aravena and Hofman (2014) and www.cepal.org/la-klems, accessed September 19, 2016.
7 Since mixed income cannot be distributed, it is allocated to remuneration of labor.

8 Data are from Aravena and Fuentes (2013).
9 Labor contributed 54 percent of growth and TFP made a negative contribution (-22 percent).
10 See part II of *Economic Survey 2013* (ECLAC 2013b).

Bibliography

Abramovitz, M. 1956. "Resource and Output Trends in the United States Since 1870." *American Economic Review* 46, Mayo: 5–23.
Aravena, C., J. A. Fernández, A. A. Hofman, and M. Más. 2014. :Structural Change in Four Latin American Countries. An International Perspective." *Serie Macroeconomía del Desarrollo*, No. 150, julio, LC/L.3852.
Aravena, C., and J. A. Fuentes. 2013. "El desempeño mediocre de la productividad laboral en América Latina: una interpretación neoclásica." *Serie Macroeconomía del Desarrollo*, No. 140, noviembre, LC/L.3725.
Aravena, C., and A. A. Hofman. 2014. "Crecimiento Económico y Productividad en América Latina. Una perspectiva por industrias-base de datos LA KLEMS." *Serie Macroeconomía del Desarrollo*, No.152, agosto, LC/L.3870.
Bosworth, B., and S. M. Collins. 2003. "Empirics of Growth: An Update." *Brookings Papers on Economic Activity* (2): 113–206.
Calvo, G. A., A. Izquierdo, and E. Talvi. 2006. "Sudden Stops and Phoenix Miracles in Emerging Markets." *American Economic Review*, American Economic Association 96(2): 405–410.
Caselli, F. 2004. "Accounting for Cross-Country Income Differences." *NBER Working Paper* 10828.
CEPAL. 2008. "La Transformación Productiva 20 años después. Viejos problemas, nuevas oportunidades." Trigésimo segundo período de sesiones.
CEPAL. 2012. "Cambio Estructural para la Igualdad. Una visión integrada del desarrollo." Trigésimo cuarto período de sesiones.
Cimoli, M., G. Dosi, and J. E. Stiglitz. 2009. *The Political Economy of Capabilities Accumulation: The Past and Future of Policies for Industrial Development*. Oxford: Oxford University Press. http://fds.oup.com/www.oup.com/pdf/13/9780199235278_chapter1.pdf, accessed September 19, 2016.
Denison, E. F. 1967. *Why Growth Rates Differ*. Washington, DC: The Brookings Institution.
Denison, E. F. 1985. *Trends in American Economic Growth, 1929–1982*. Washington, DC: The Brookings Institution.
Denison, E. F., and W. K. Chung. 1976. *How Japan's Economy Grew So Fast*. Washington, DC: The Brookings Institution. www.iberlibro.com/buscar-libro/autor/DENISON,-E-F-CHUNG,-W-K?cm_sp=brcr-_-bdp-_-author, accessed September 19, 2016.

Duarte, M., and D. Restuccia. 2010. "The Role of the Structural Transformation in Aggregate Productivity." *The Quarterly Journal of Economics*, MIT Press 125(1): 129–173. http://ideas.repec.org/a/tpr/qjecon/v125y2010i1p129-173.html, accessed September 19, 2016.

February, Easterly W., and R. Levine. 2001. "It's Not Factor Accumulation: Stylized Facts and Growth Models," *World Bank Economic Review*, Washington, DC.

Hall, R. J., and C. I. Jones. 1999. "Why Do Some Countries Produce So Much More Output Per Worker Than Others?" *The Quarterly Journal of Economics*, MIT Press 114(1): 83–116. http://ideas.repec.org/a/tpr/qjecon/v114y1999i1p83-116.html, accessed September 19, 2016.

Harcourt, G. C., and N. Laing. 1971. *Capital and Growth: Selected Readings*. Baltimore: EEUU, Penguin Books.

Hofman, A. A., M. Mas, C. Aravena, and J. Fernández. 2014. "Structural Change in Four Latin American Countries. An International Perspective." Presentado en la *Conferencia World KLEMS*, Mayo, Tokio, May 19.

Hsie, C-T., and P. J. Klenow. 2010. "Development Accounting." *American Economic Journal*, Macroeconomics 2(1): 207–223.

Hulten, C. 2001. "Total Factor Productivity: A Short Biography, Capítulo 1." In C. R. Hulten, E. R. Dean, and M. J. Harper (eds.), *New Developments in Productivity Analysis*. Chicago: University of Chicago Press.

Jorgensen, D. W., and Z. Griliches. 1967. "The Explanation of Productivity Change." *Review of Economic Studies* 34(3): 249–283.

Kendrick, J. W. 1977. "The Formation and Stocks of Total Capital." *NBER General Series* no. 100, Columbia University Press, New York.

King, R., and R. Levine. 1994. "Capital Fundamentalism, Economic Development and Economic Growth." *Carnegie-Mellon Series on Public Policy* 40, North Holland.

Klenow, P., and A. Rodriguez-Clare. 2008. "The Neoclassical Revival in Growth Economics: Has It Gone Too Far?" In Ben S. Bernanke and Julio J. Rotemberg (eds.), *NBER Macroeconomics Annual 1997*. Cambridge, MA: MIT Press.

Krugman, P. 1994. "The Myth of Asia's Miracle." *Foreign Affairs* 73(6), noviembre–diciembre.

Lucas (Jr.), R. E. 1988. "On the Mechanics of Economic Development." *Journal of Monetary Economics* 22.

Maddison, A. 1987. "Growth and Slowdown in Advanced Capitalist Economies: Techniques of Quantitive Assessment." *Journal of Economic Literature* 25(4): 649–698.

McMillan, M., and D. Rodrik. 2012. "Globalization, Structural Change and Productivity Growth." *IFPRI Discussion Paper* 01160.

Manuelito, Sandra y F. Jiménez, "La inversión y el ahorro en América Latina: nuevos rasgos estilizados, requerimientos para el crecimiento y elementos de una estrategia para fortalecer su financiamiento", serie Macroeconomía del Desarrollo, N° 129 (LC/L.3603), Santiago de Chile, CEPAL.

Ocampo, Jose. 2009. Latin America and the global financial crisis Cambridge *Journal of Economics*, 33(4): 703–724.

OECD. 2008. *Productivity Measurement and Analysis*. Paris: OECD and Swiss Federal Statistical Office.

Restuccia, D., and R. Rogerson. 2013. "Misallocation and Productivity." *Review of Economic Dynamics* 16(1): 1–10.

Robinson, J. 1961. *Exercises in Economic Analysis*. London: Macmillan & Co. Ltd.

Solow, R. 1956. "A Contribution to the Theory of Economic Growth." *The Quarterly Journal of Economics* 70(1): 65–94.

Solow, R. 1957. "Technical Change and the Aggregate Production Function." *The Review of Economics and Statistics* 39(3): 312–320.

Sraffa, Piero. 1960. *Production of commodities by means of commodities. Prelude to a critique of economic theory*. Vora and Co., Publishers Pvt. Ltd. 3, Round Building, Bombay 2.

Weller, J. 2012. "Crecimiento, empleo y distribución de ingresos en América Latina." *serie Macroeconomía del desarrollo*, no. 122, CEPAL, Santiago de Chile.

Young, A. 1994. "The Tyranny of the Numbers: Confronting the Numbers of the East-Asian Growth Experience." *NBER, Working Paper* No. 4680.

Chapter 5

Human capital productivity

Barbara M. Fraumeni

Human capital has long been recognized as an important contributor to economic growth. The human capital literature is extensive. In the sixties, two Nobel prize winners: Becker (1964) and Schultz (1961), concentrated on this topic. A very partial list of other well-known papers or books on human capital includes those by Lucas (1988), Romer (1990a, 1990b), and Barro and Sala-I-Martin (1995). The Stiglitz-Sen-Fitoussi Commission recognized measurement of human capital as a critical element of economic accounts innovation and sustainability indicators in its "Beyond GDP" theme (Stiglitz, Sen, and Fitoussi, 2009, chapter 1, para. 30, p. 29). Jorgenson and Fraumeni and their collaborators have emphasized human capital measurement, rather than theory or analysis (Jorgenson and Fraumeni, 1989, 1992a, 1992b; Fraumeni, Christian, and Samuels, forthcoming).

This chapter addresses two questions: (1) How is human capital measured? and (2) How should the contribution of human capital to economic growth be measured? The answer to the first question provides a framework for the answer to the second question. In addition, this chapter provides estimates of human capital productivity change and the relationship between human capital productivity change and multifactor productivity change.

There are a number of approaches to human capital measurement; however this chapter will briefly describe four approaches: Barro-Lee, World Bank, Inclusive Wealth Report, and Jorgenson-Fraumeni. Either an index number or an econometric approach can be used to measure the contribution of human capital to economic growth; this chapter focuses on estimates using an index number approach.[1]

Human capital measures

Barro-Lee

The Barro-Lee (2013a, 2013b, 2015) data set of average formal educational attainment by age categories is probably the most widely used human capital proxy or indicator dataset, at least in part because a large number of countries (146) are covered. The Barro-Lee series is one of many possible human capital indicators, such as knowledge or competencies tests. The Organisation for Economic Cooperation and Development's (OECD) Programme for International Student Assessment (PISA) or OECD's Programme for International Assessment of Adult Competencies (PIAAC) are the most well-known of this latter category.

The Barro-Lee dataset covers country average educational attainment, total and by subcategories, beginning at age 15, in five-year age increments, for the total population and by gender; data is available for every five years from 1950 to 2010. Population numbers are also available in the data set for each associated educational attainment estimate.

World Bank

The World Bank (2006, 2011) uses a residual approach to estimating human capital for more than 120 countries. Total wealth for the years 1995, 2000, and 2005 is measured as the net present value of an assumed future consumption stream. Intangible capital is equal to total wealth minus produced and natural capital. Intangible capital is an aggregate which includes human capital, the infrastructure of the country, social capital, and the returns from net foreign financial assets. The returns from net foreign financial assets are subtracted from the residually estimated intangible capital to create other intangible capital, which is for the majority of countries is primarily human capital.[2,3]

Inclusive Wealth Report

The Inclusive Wealth Report (IWR) (UNU-IHDP and UNEP 2014) uses a country representative person lifetime income approach to estimate human capital. It slightly modifies the methodology of Arrow et al. (2012) and Klenow and Rodríguez-Clare (1997, 2005). IWR 2014 country aggregates are estimated for 140 countries. Average educational attainment of a country's population and expected number of working years remaining is allowed to vary over time, but the real wage rate paid to a worker is held constant. The age of the adult population is defined by average educational attainment plus five. In the IWR steady state model, human capital rises exponentially with the number of years of education, and future lifetime income is discounted to the present.

Jorgenson-Fraumeni

Jorgenson-Fraumeni (J-F) is also a lifetime income approach, but one that uses information on annual income by gender, age, and education (Jorgenson and Fraumeni 1989, 1992a, 1992b; Fraumeni et al. forthcoming). Accordingly, it requires much more data than the IWR. Future annual labor income is hypothesized to grow at a specified real rate and is discounted to the present. Estimates of lifetime income are created recursively backward from the oldest individuals to the youngest. Information on future expected annual income is determined from contemporaneous relative wage rates, survival rates, and enrollment rates.

Labor productivity compared to human capital productivity

It is easier to measure labor productivity than human capital productivity. Labor productivity can be defined as the ratio of real output to real labor input, where, if at all possible, both the numerator and the denominator should be a flow variable. There is more than one possible choice of an output measure: typically either gross output, which includes intermediate inputs, or value-added output, sometimes called net output, which excludes intermediate inputs (OECD 2001). Frequently, GDP is the measure of output as it is readily available, although in nominal dollars it is larger than value added output as it is equal to gross national income (GNI), which includes taxes on production and imports and subsidies. In the US National Income and Product Accounts, it also differs from GDP by the statistical discrepancy. In addition, the price of GDP is typically different than the price of value added output. Labor input might be measured by hours, employees, or quality-adjusted hours (typically called labor input); at least one of these measures is usually available. Labor productivity is often measured as it is relatively easy to do so, yet it is still a complex measure. The rate of change in labor productivity can be related to multifactor productivity by the following equation:[4]

$$\ln(O(t)/L(t)) - \ln((O(t-1)/L(t-1)) = V_K(t)*[\ln(K(t)/L(t)) \\ - \ln(K(t-1)/L(t-1))] \\ + \ln(MFP(t)) - \ln(MFP(t-1)), \quad (5.1)$$

where O is value added output, L is labor input, V_K is the two-period average (t and t–1) nominal share of capital input in value added, K is capital input, MFP is multifactor productivity, and t is time. The first term to the right of the equal sign is the contribution of capital deepening. This equation demonstrates that labor productivity depends on other factors besides labor input.[5]

Human capital productivity can be defined in more than way, as is true with labor productivity. For both labor and human capital productivity, the numerator is a flow variable, e.g., real gross output or real value added output per year. The denominator of labor productivity preferably is a flow variable: e.g., hours per year or quality-adjusted hours per year, but could be a stock variable, e.g., the number of employees, which has to be counted as of a certain date, if no flow variable is available. For all but a measure of human capital based upon Jorgenson-Fraumeni in the estimates in Table 5.1, the denominator is a stock variable, e.g., educational attainment counted as of a certain date or intangible or human capital wealth. The denominator of the Barro-Lee measure of human capital productivity is the average educational attainment for the population either age 15 or above or those age 15 through 64 (Barro and Lee 2013b). The denominator of the World Bank measure is real intangible capital (World Bank 2011). The denominator of the Inclusive Wealth Report measure is real human capital (UNU-IHDP and UNEP 2014). The denominator of the Jorgenson-Fraumeni measure (Fraumeni et al. forthcoming) is real human capital labor outlay, which includes bearing children and time spent in school and studying. The former is measured by the expected lifetime income of a newborn; the latter is measured by the impact on a student's lifetime income of completing an additional year of school.[6] In Table 5.1 the numerator of all but the Jorgenson-Fraumeni measure is real GDP. As in the earlier paper (Jorgenson and Fraumeni 1989), Fraumeni et al. (forthcoming) include both market and nonmarket production in their formulation. Accordingly, the numerator in the Jorgenson-Fraumeni human capital productivity measure includes both market and nonmarket output in its real full gross private domestic product

Table 5.1 Comparison of human capital productivity change measures

United States	Barro-Lee 1995–2005 15–64	Barro-Lee 1995–2005 15+	World Bank 1995–2005	IWR 1995–2005	J-F (F-C-S) 1998–2005
Numerator Measure	Real GDP	Real GDP	Real GDP	Real GDP	Real Full GPDP
Numerator Avg. Annual ROG	3.36	3.36	3.36	3.36	0.89
Denominator Measure	Average Educational Attainment	Average Educational Attainment	Real Intangible Capital	Real Human Capital	Real Human Capital Labor Outlay[i]
Denominator Avg. Annual ROG	0.21	0.14	3.50	1.42	0.11
Human Capital Productivity Avg. Annual ROG	3.22	3.15	−0.15	1.94	1.31

Source: Barro and Lee 2013b; Table C1 in World Bank 2011; Annex 3 in UNU-IHDP and UNEP 2014; Data underlying Fraumeni, Christian, and Samuels (F-C-S) (forthcoming).

Abbreviations: ROG for rate of growth, GPDP for Gross Private Domestic Product, J-F for Jorgenson-Fraumeni.

i If Jorgenson-Fraumeni real nonmarket labor outlay is used instead of real human capital labor outlay, the productivity estimate is .78 percent. Time in household production and leisure is included in nonmarket labor outlay; it is excluded from human capital labor outlay.

measure. Nonmarket output includes the value of time spent in household production and leisure, and investment in education and births (see Table 5.1 of Fraumeni, Christian, and Samuels, forthcoming). In the examples in Table 5.1 for the United States which follow, estimates are calculated for 1995–2005, except in the case of Jorgenson-Fraumeni for which the estimates are calculated from 1998 to 2005, as the earlier three years are not available.

The estimates of human capital productivity change vary significantly, from a low of an average –.15 percent per year to a high of an average 3.22 percent per year. This significant variation clearly indicates the importance of the human capital measure choice.

Measurement of human capital's contribution to economic growth

In a typical econometric market sector model which measures the contribution of human capital's contribution to economic growth, a measure of human capital is a right-hand-side exogenous variable. GDP, or some other measure of market output, is the endogenous or left-hand-side variable. If a Barro-Lee educational attainment measure is the human capital measure, this variable is the current education-related quality of labor or labor composition. Many productivity models quality or composition adjust their labor input. If either an IWR or an intangible World Bank wealth measure is the human capital measure, as previously noted, this measure is a stock measure. Certainly, there should be a correlation or explanatory power with either educational attainment or wealth in such an econometric model, but conceptual elements are missing.

Human capital is expected to generate market economic growth in this and future periods if the individual human capital is employed any time in the future. The output being produced over the same time period as human capital is productive is greater than current market output or any current GDP-related measure. Accordingly, if the econometric model is conceived as a production model, the variables must be different from the typical variables. If the flow from human capital generates present and future output, then the flow from nonhuman stock should also include generation of present and future output. In addition, the output measure should include present and future output.

In addition, labor productivity and annual earnings can vary over time, and typically increase if a work force becomes more highly educated. In another paper, Fraumeni (2012) illustrates how Jorgenson-Fraumeni lifetime market income diverges when some individuals continue their education and others do not. The example uses J-F data from the OECD Human Capital Project (Liu 2011). In Table 5.3, ratios of lifetime market income higher levels of International Standard Classification of Education (ISCED) categories to ISCED 2 are given. Table 5.2 describes the ISCED categories.

In order to make comparisons between the market lifetime income of an individual who ends his formal education at the ISCED 2 level with someone who continues on, two assumptions are made in the

Table 5.2 International Standard Classification of Education (ISCED) definitions

Level 2, Lower secondary or second stage of basic education	Lower secondary education (ISCED 2) generally continues the basic programs of the primary level, although teaching is typically more subject-focused, often employing more specialized teachers who conduct classes in their field of specialization.
Level 3, Upper secondary education	Upper secondary education (ISCED 3) corresponds to the final stage of secondary education in most OECD countries. Instruction is often more organized along subject-matter lines than at ISCED level 2, and teachers typically need to have a higher level, or more subject-specific, qualifications than at ISCED 2. The entrance age to this level is typically 15 or 16 years. ISCED 3A: programs at Level 3 designed to provide direct access to ISCED 5A.
Level 5, First stage of tertiary education	Tertiary-type A programs (ISCED 5A) are largely theory based and are designed to provide sufficient qualifications for entry to advanced research programs and professions with high skill requirements, such as medicine, dentistry, or architecture. They have a minimum cumulative theoretical duration (at tertiary level) of three years full-time equivalent, although they typically last four or more years. Tertiary-type B programs (ISCED 5B) are typically shorter than those of tertiary-type A and focus on practical, technical or occupational skills for direct entry into the labor market, although some theoretical foundations may be covered in the respective programs. They have a minimum duration of two years full-time equivalent at the tertiary level.

Source: Organisation for Economic Cooperation and Development 2001.

Abbreviation: OECD for Organisation for Economic Cooperation and Development.

Table 5.3 Ratio of ISCED higher level to ISCED 2 in the United States J-F market lifetime income

	ISCED 3A	ISCED 5B	ISCED 5A
	Age 18 in 2000	Age 20 in 2002	Age 22 in 2004
Male	1.4	1.2	3.4
Female	1.6	1.5	1.9

Source: Table 2 in Fraumeni 2012; data from Liu 2011.
Abbreviation: ISCED for International Standard Classification of Education.

Table 5.3 example. First, it is assumed that individuals who continue their education will do so without a break and will not skip grades. Second, it is assumed that individuals begin ISCED 3 at age 15. If individuals take the normal three years to complete ISCED 3, they will be 18 in 2000 when they enter ISCED 5, 20 when they complete ISCED 5B in 2002, and 22 when they complete ISCED 5A in 2004. These assumptions have little impact on the nature of the comparative results.

Labor productivity for the 18 year olds is most likely the same or very similar, however labor productivity in future years should be significantly higher for those who continue their education compared to those who do not. A human capital productivity measure should ideally distinguish between those who are expected (with some probability) to continue, versus those who are not expected to continue. J-F market annual income is allowed to increase by a real rate of growth in labor income. The real rate of growth reflects among other things expected future increases in labor productivity.

The alternative to a typical market sector production model, which is conceptually different, is the previously briefly described production model which includes current market and nonmarket output and lifetime income components. Human capital is mainly produced in the nonmarket sector, as individuals normally are conceived and raised in the household/nonmarket sector and individual's time is a critical input to education. Jorgenson and Fraumeni (1989) outline such an accounting structure; this set of accounts is updated and revised in Fraumeni et al. (forthcoming). Equation (1) can be expanded by decomposing labor outlay into its three components parts: human capital, market, and time in household production and leisure labor outlay. In this expanded equation which now relates change in human capital productivity to change in multifactor productivity, there are now three "deepening" terms: market labor deepening (first right-hand-side term), time in household production and leisure labor deepening (second right-hand-side term), and capital deepening (third right-hand-side term):

$$\ln(FO(t)/L_{HC}(t)) - \ln((FO(t-1)/L_{HC}(t-1)) = V_{LM}(t)^*$$
$$\left[\ln(L_M(t)/L_{HC}(t)) - \ln(L_M(t-1)/L_{HC}(t-1))\right]$$
$$+ V_{LT}(t)^*\left[\ln(L_T(t)/L_{HC}(t)) - \ln(L_T(t-1)/L_{HC}(t-1))\right] \quad (5.2)$$
$$+ V_K(t)^*\left[\ln(K(t)/L_{HC}(t)) - \ln(K(t-1)/L_{HC}(t-1))\right]$$
$$+ \ln(MFP(t)) - \ln(MFP(t-1)),$$

where FO is full value added output, L_{HC} is human capital labor outlay, L_M is market labor outlay, and L_T is time in household production and leisure labor outlay.[7] The two-period average nominal shares are defined as before, with V_{LM} referring to the average share for market labor outlay, and V_{LT} referring to the average share for time in household production and leisure labor outlay.

Figure 5.1 shows the contribution of these terms to economic growth with data underlying Fraumeni, Christian, and Samuels (forthcoming).[8] The subperiod breakpoints reflect economic conditions; in the productivity literature, it has been clearly documented that productivity shifted downward post-1973; the period 1999–2000 corresponds to the end of the "IT Boom" period which began in 1995; and by 2006 the economy was headed toward the Great Recession (Jorgenson et al. 2014).

Abbreviations: HC for human capital, L for labor outlay, t for time in household production and leisure labor outlay, and K for capital outlay.

In the two subperiods, excluding the overall periods 1950–1984 and 1999–2009, in which multifactor productivity change is the greatest contributor to economic growth: 1950–1973 and 1999–2000, capital deepening is the second largest contributor. Both subperiods are well-known as periods of high rates in multifactor productivity growth. In the other subperiods, time in household production and leisure labor outlay deepening is the largest contributor to economic growth, followed by capital deepening. To understand why this is so, Table 5.4 shows the rate of growth in market labor outlay, human capital labor outlay, time in household production and leisure outlay, and capital outlay. In all subperiods, although total labor contribution is the largest single contributor to economic growth in five out of seven periods (Fraumeni et al. forthcoming: Figure 9), capital outlay has a higher rate of growth than

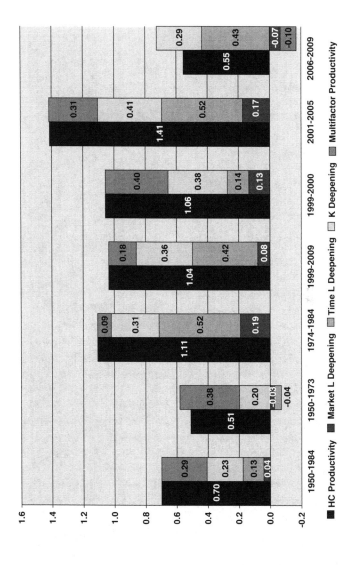

Figure 5.1 Contributions to full gross private domestic product and economic growth with HC productivity and "deepening" components

Source: Data underlying Fraumeni, Christian, and Samuels forthcoming.

Table 5.4 Rates of growth of selected components

	ROG of Human Capital	ROG of Market Labor	ROG of Time in HH Production & Leisure	ROG of Capital	Two Largest Contributors to Economic Growth
1950–1984	.0150	.0180	.0189	.0372	
1950–1973	.0193	.0177	.0179	.0387	MFP growth & K deepening
1974–1984	.0056	.0185	.0210	.0339	Time & K deepening
1999–2009	–.0022	.0037	.0173	.0345	
1999–2000	.0070	.0180	.0139	.0482	MFP growth & K deepening
2001–2005	–.0086	.0042	.0159	.0351	Time & K deepening
2006–2009	.0012	–.0041	.0206	.0268	Time & K deepening

Source: Data underlying Fraumeni, Christian, and Samuels forthcoming.

Abbreviations: ROG for rate of growth, HH for household, MFP for multifactor productivity, Time for time in household production and leisure, and K for capital.

any of the labor subcomponents (Table 5.4). Human capital growth is the next highest of the outlay subcomponents growth in 1950–1973, but the subperiod growth rates diminish except for a slight rebound in 1999–2000. Several social changes which impacted economic growth occurred during the covered period. The pace of increases in the average educational attainment of worker-aged individuals slowed in the United States in about 1980. Increases in female labor force participation continued until the mid-1990s.[9] Between 1965 and 2010, actual time spent in household production by women decreased by 35 percent and by men increased by 23 percent. The net effect was a 15 percent decrease in time spent in household production by all individuals.[10] The median gender pay gap decreased by 20 percentage points between mid- to late-1970s and mid-2000s.[11] Time in household production and leisure labor outlay growth is positive in all subperiods. As women, who on average spend more time in household production than do men, earn higher median salaries, offset to some extent by less time spent in household production, and men spend more time in household production, it is not surprising that this occurs. Not surprisingly, market labor outlay growth is negative in the last subperiod: 2006–2009, which includes the Great Recession time period, and slowed significantly after both 1950–1984 subperiods and the end of the New Economy boom economy: 1999–2000. Considering labor and capital outlay growth rates as impacted by the economy and social trends, the deepening equation results make sense.

Conclusion

Much attention has been paid to labor productivity, but little to human capital productivity. As human capital productivity tells us about the future potential of a country and its sustainability, it is important to pay more attention to this subject. As this chapter demonstrates, estimates of human capital productivity change can vary widely, depending upon what measure of human capital is used. Also, economists should think carefully about how to formulate production functions if human capital is to be included and consider the relationship between human capital productivity change and present and future multifactor productivity change. The opportunities for further research are substantial.

Notes

1. An index number approach is a numerical approach which typically uses survey data to compile nominal values and some sort of an index (e.g., Paasche, Laspeyres, Fisher, or Divisia/Thornqvist) to measure what is called volumes by the System of National Accounts (European Commission, et al., 2009).
2. The 1997 World Bank report estimated that in over 60 percent of the countries included, human capital accounted for more than 60 percent of the nation's wealth.
3. A proposed World Bank project will create a direct estimate of human capital wealth.
4. Oliner and Sichel (2000) use this equation in their analysis of the resurgence in post-1990 US economic growth.
5. To show the simplest case, changes in the composition or quality of capital and labor are ignored in this equation.
6. In Jorgenson and Fraumeni (1989) and Fraumeni, Christian, and Samuels (forthcoming) the concept used is factor outlay.
7. Output is called full output as output in Jorgenson and Fraumeni (1989) and Fraumeni, Christian, and Samuels (forthcoming) is increased due to future nonmarket labor as this labor is the present value of adjusted lifetime income. Nonmarket labor includes human capital and time in household production and leisure labor. However, there is no impact of future capital input on output.
8. The data for the latest subperiod, 2006–2009, has been slightly revised since the Fraumeni, Christian, and Samuels paper was written. In that forthcoming paper, quantity components are constructed using Törnqvist indexes. This forthcoming paper demonstrates the importance of including human capital in an analysis of economic growth. Human capital, which is a major source of growth in the 1949–1984 period, becomes a minor source of growth during the 1998–2009 period. Accordingly, the paper concludes that excluding human capital will lead

to an overestimation of economic growth, including multifactor productivity growth, in the United States going beyond the present period.
9 See Figures 5.1 and 4 of Fraumeni et al. (forthcoming).
10 Bridgman et al. 2012: Table 5.1.
11 See Figure 5.1 of the American Association of University Women 2016; and Table 5.1 of U.S. Bureau of Labor Statistics 2014.

Bibliography

American Association of University Women. 2016. "The Simple Truth About the Gender Pay Gap." Spring.
Arrow, K. J., P. Dasgupta, L. H. Goulder, K. J. Mumford, and K. Oleson. 2012. "Sustainability and the Measurement of Wealth." *Environment and Development Economics* 17: 317–353.
Barro, R. J., and J. Lee. 2013a. "A New Data Set of Educational Attainment in the World, 1950–2010." *Journal of Development Economics* 104(C): 184–198.
Barro, R. J., and J. Lee. 2013b. *Barro-Lee Educational Attainment Data Set.* Last updated April 9, 2013. www.barrolee.com, accessed October 2013.
Barro, R. J., and J. Lee. 2015. *Education Matters, Global Schooling Gains From the 19th to the 21st Century.* New York: Oxford University Press.
Barro, R. J., and X. Sala-i-Martin. 1995. *Economic Growth.* New York: McGraw-Hill.
Becker, G. 1964. *Human Capital.* 2nd edition. New York: Columbia University Press.
Bridgman, B., A. Dugan, M. Lal, M. Osborne, and S. Villones. 2012. "Accounting for Household Production in the National Accounts, 1965–2010." *Survey of Current Business*, Bureau of Economic Analysis, U.S. Department of Commerce, Washington, DC, May.
European Commission, International Monetary Fund, Organization for Economic Co-Operation and Development, and World Bank. 2009. *System of National Accounts 2008.* New York: United Nations, ST/ESA/STAT/SER.F/2/Rev.5.
Fraumeni, B. M. 2012. "Human Capital Productivity: A New Concept for Productivity Analysis." *International Productivity Monitor* 24, Fall: 20–26.
Fraumeni, B. M., M. S. Christian, and J. D. Samuels. Forthcoming. "The Accumulation of Human and Non-Human Capital, Revisited." *Review of Income and Wealth*, an earlier version paper available as a National Bureau of Economic Research, *Working Paper 21284*, June 2015. www.nber.org/papers/w212834, accessed March 24, 2016.
Jorgenson, Dale W., and Barbara M. Fraumeni. 1989. "The Accumulation of Human and Non-Human Capital, 1948–1984." In R. Lipsey and H. Tice (eds.), *The Measurement of Saving, Investment and Wealth.* Chicago: University of Chicago Press, NBER, pp. 227–282.
Jorgenson, Dale W., and Barbara M. Fraumeni. 1992a. "Investment in Education and U.S. Economic Growth." *Scandinavian Journal of Economics* 94(supplement): S51–S70.

Jorgenson, Dale W., and Barbara M. Fraumeni. 1992b. "The Output of the Education Sector." In Z. Griliches, T. Breshnahan, M. Manser, and E. Berndt (eds.), *The Output of the Service Sector*. Chicago: University of Chicago Press, NBER, pp. 303–341.

Jorgenson, D. W., M. S. Ho, and J. D. Samuels. 2014. "What Will Revive U.S. Economic Growth? Lessons From a Prototype Industry-Level Production Account for the United States." *Journal of Policy Modeling* 34(4), July–August: 674–691.

Klenow, P. J., and A. Rodriguez-Clare. 1997. "The Neoclassical Revival in Growth Economics: Has It Gone Too Far?" *NBER Macroeconomics Annual* 1: 73–103.

Klenow, P. J., and A. Rodríguez-Clare. 2005. "Externalities and Growth." In P. Aghion and S. Durlauf (eds.), *Handbook of Economic Growth*. Amsterdam: North Holland, pp. 817–886.

Liu, G. 2011. "Measuring the Stock of Human Capital for Comparative Analysis: An Application of the Lifetime Income Approach to Selected Countries." OECD Statistics Directorate, *Working Paper* #41, STD/DOC(2011)6, October 10.

Lucas, R. E. Jr. 1988. "On the Mechanics of Economic Development." *Journal of Monetary Economics* 22(1): 3–42.

Oliner, S. D., and D. E. Sichel. 2000. "The Resurgence of Growth in the Late 1990s: Is Information Technology the Story?" *Journal of Economic Perspectives* 14(4): 3–22.

Organisation for Economic Cooperation and Development. 2001. *Measuring Productivity, OECD Manual, Measurement of Aggregate and Industry-Level Productivity Growth*. www.oecd.org/std/productivity-stats/2352458.pdf, accessed March 27, 2016.

Romer, P. M. 1990a. "Endogenous Technological Change." *Journal of Political Economy* 98(5), Part 2: 71–102.

Romer, P. M. 1990b. "Human Capital and Growth: Theory and Evidence." *Carnegie-Rochester Conference Series on Public Policy* 32: 251–286.

Schultz, T. 1961. "Investment in Human Capital." *American Economic Review* 51(1): 1–17.

Stiglitz, J. E., A. Sen, and J.-P. Fitoussi. 2009. *Report by the Commission on the Measurement of Economic Performance and Social Progress*. www.stiglitz-sen-fitoussi.fr/documents/rapport_anglais.pdf, accessed March 24, 2016.

U.S. Bureau of Labor Statistics. 2014. "Women in the Labor Force: A Databook." *BLS Reports*, Report 1052, U.S. Department of Labor, Washington, DC, December.

UNU-IHDP, and UNEP. 2014. *Inclusive Wealth Report 2014: Measuring Progress Toward Sustainability*. Cambridge: Cambridge University Press.

World Bank. 2006. *Where Is the Wealth of Nations: Measuring Capital for the 21st Century*. Washington, DC: World Bank.

World Bank. 2011. *The Changing Wealth of Nations: Measuring Sustainable Development in the New Millennium*. Washington, DC: World Bank.

Chapter 6

Global growth accounting
The role of shifting investment patterns

Abdul A. Erumban, Robert Inklaar and Klaas de Vries

Introduction

Investment in new capital assets, be it in the form of buildings, machinery or intangible assets like software or research development (R&D), is long identified as a major engine of economic growth (e.g. Solow 1957; Jorgenson and Griliches 1967).[1] In the more recent period, the growth potential of information and communication technologies (ICT) has drawn considerable attention, starting with the analysis of growth in the United States in Jorgenson (2001) and more recently covered in Jorgenson and Vu (2016) with global coverage. Yet at the same time, our understanding of the sources of global growth have been hampered by relatively fragmented, and often inadequate, data on the composition of investment outside advanced economies, see e.g. Caselli and Wilson (2004) and Bems (2008) on the sparseness of cross-country data. In this chapter, we take a major step forward by developing a more reliable and useful dataset of cross-country investment by asset than previously available.[2] In contrast to most earlier works, we carefully integrate information from a range of data sources within the framework of the System of National Accounts (SNA) – the global benchmark used to compile national accounts. We construct a comprehensive dataset of investment by asset – both Information and Communication Technology (ICT) and non-ICT capital assets – that is fully consistent with aggregate investment levels obtained from national accounts.[3] Compared to our more recent data construction efforts, this new database is superior by relying more on country National Accounts data and less on other estimations; by distinguishing a broader range of assets, consistent with the latest version of the SNA, for 2008; and by its comprehensive coverage in terms of countries and time period.

This new data serves as the main source for capital stock and capital service estimates used in the global growth accounting analysis in two widely used cross-country databases – the Penn World Table (PWT) and the Conference Board Total Economy Database (TED).[4] The main contribution of this chapter is to document this new dataset, in terms of sources, methods and main features, and to highlight the implications for our understanding of global economic growth. The chapter also provides an overview of the changes in global investment rates and the contribution of capital to growth. In the next section, we present the measurement approach and data sources of our new investment and capital estimates. Next, the results on cross-country trends in investment shares in GDP and the contribution of ICT capital to GDP growth are presented, and finally we conclude.

Measurement approach and data sources

Gross fixed capital formation by assets

Investment or gross fixed capital formation (GFCF) in the National Accounts is defined as the net acquisition of produced fixed assets, i.e. assets intended for use in the production of other goods and services for a period of more than one year (SNA 2008). International guidelines distinguish a wide range of assets, such as machinery, vehicles, computer software, computer hardware, research and development spending (R&D), office buildings and other industrial buildings, etc. However, individual countries differ in their practices of defining and collecting these data. In general, advanced countries report detailed asset-wise investment data, while many developing countries only report higher-level aggregates, such as aggregates of all machinery and all buildings, or in some cases even only aggregate investment data. Furthermore, definitions of investment and asset structure also differ across various editions of the system of national accounts. For example, intangibles such as computer software and R&D were only recognized as investments, respectively, in the SNA 1993 and 2008 versions. Earlier, these assets were considered as intermediate inputs. Such differences in definitions over time also create additional problems in constructing a consistent time-series of investment data.

Our approach is to maintain consistency with national accounts, and therefore, we use the reported national accounts data whenever available. This consistency is important for productivity analysis, as these estimates are used in conjunction with official GDP and employment data. In order to fill the missing asset details, we construct our own series using the commodity flow method (see next subsection).[5] We first distinguish three relatively broad asset categories in the source data (see Table 6.1), in order to ensure consistency over time and across countries.

National Accounts investment data on aggregate GFCF, the 3 broad asset groups, and their sub-groups as listed in Table 6.1 are collected from various sources whenever available. These include national statistics institutes (NSI) and national and international databases such as Eurostat, AMECO,[6] United Nations (UN), CEPALSTAT,[7] OECD and various KLEMS[8] projects. Investment levels from the most recent benchmark revision for each country is considered as benchmarks levels (in most cases, these are based on 2008 SNA), using data from earlier vintages to extrapolate trends in investment. We were able to obtain actual national accounts investment data by assets for at least 106 countries (out of 182), and for at least one or more years. In addition, the benchmark expenditure data from the International Comparison Program (World Bank 2014) for one or more years also allow for a distinction of investment by asset, though there too the level of detail – in terms of country and asset coverage – differs across the benchmark years. Detailed information on country specific sources and methods can be found on the Conference Board Total Economy Database website.[9] For all other countries, and for missing years, we obtain asset distribution using a commodity flow method, which is discussed below.

Table 6.1 Asset breakdown of source data

1- Machinery and Equipment	2- Construction	3- Other Products
Transport equipment	Residential construction	Cultivated Assets
Machinery	Non-residential construction	Intangible Assets
Computer Hardware		Software
Communication equipment		Intellectual Property products (IPP)
Other machinery		

Source: Authors' compilation

The commodity flow approach as a proxy for investment

To allow for a more comprehensive coverage of investment by asset data than possible based purely on national accounts data, we rely on the commodity flow method (CFM). This approach is commonly used to incorporate a greater level of asset detail in investment. It is used, for instance, in some early studies on the role of information and communication technologies (ICT) for economic growth in Europe (Timmer and van Ark 2005) or in broader international comparisons (Caselli and Wilson 2004). The CFM method relies on information on the supply (S) of investment goods:

$$S_i = M_i - X_i + Y_i \qquad (6.1)$$

where supply of asset i is computed as imports M minus exports X plus production Y. Note that for construction projects, only production will be relevant as these are non-traded products. Economy-wide supply equals the total use of these goods, which includes investment in fixed assets by firms but also consumer purchases, and the ratio of investment-to-total use varies. This means that it is important to have at least one benchmark observation on the asset composition of investment to serve as an anchor for the investment-to-total use ratio. We follow the approach also applied in Feenstra et al. (2015) for estimating investment by asset for the Penn World Table, versions 8.0 and 8.1. In this approach, national accounts data are used first, and only when these are unavailable do we use CFM series to extrapolate growth in each asset. In the final step, investment is normalized to add up to total investment from the national accounts. Data on imports and exports are drawn from the UN Comtrade database, industrial production is from the UNIDO INDSTAT database and value added in construction is from the UN National Accounts Main Aggregates Database.[10]

Investment in information, technology and communication assets

It is widely acknowledged that investment in ICT is an important contributor to overall economic growth (e.g. Jorgenson and Vu 2013, 2016). Nevertheless, actual data on ICT investment is sparsely available due to difficulties in obtaining such information for the entire economy. Even though the National Accounts guidelines distinguish three ICT assets – computer hardware and communication equipment as part of machinery, and software as part of intangible assets – only around 50 countries produce official data on one or more of the above-mentioned ICT assets for at least one year. Whenever available, we obtain these data either from National Statistical Institutes or from cross-country sources that rely primarily on detailed official data, such as Eurostat or OECD. In order to extent these official series back and forth to fill the missing years, and also for countries for which the official data is not available, we rely on a range of alternative sources and methods.

To complement the National Accounts-based estimates, we first consider the sources which are most closely in line with National Accounts data. Examples are research initiatives such as KLEMS, in which there is close collaboration with national statistical agencies or national policy institutes and thus have access to detailed and often unpublished official data. Therefore, KLEMS-type data has been used whenever available. For instance, we use the underlying investment series from the Japan JIP database, Russia and India KLEMS, while for several European countries we use EU KLEMS data to extend the series back in time. To further complement these series, we used historical trends for some European countries from older vintages of the Total Economy Growth Accounting database (GGDC TED), originally set up by the Groningen Growth and Development Center. For a number of Latin American countries, we relied on data originally compiled by de Vries et al. (2010). Table 6.2 provides an overview of various sources we used to compile the ICT data.

The above-mentioned official and semi-official sources provide a reasonably good coverage in terms of countries and years, but not complete. To increase the country coverage further, we use ICT expenditure data, made available by the World Information Technology and Services Alliance (WITSA). WITSA's main publication, the *Digital Planet Report on Global ICT spending*, provide detailed data on total national spending on ICT goods (computer hardware, communication equipment and software) across 73 countries since 1992 until 2013, of which 2010 to 2013 are forecasts. This data has been used by Jorgenson and Vu (2013, 2016) in their global growth accounting analysis, in order to quantify the contribution of ICT to global growth. The database developed by Jorgenson and

Table 6.2 Sources of ICT investment data

Country	Source	Coverage
Official sources		
European countries	Eurostat	1995–2014*
Other advanced economies	OECD	1995–2014*
Remaining advanced and emerging economies	National Statistical Institutes	**
Semi-official sources		
Austria, Denmark, Finland, France, Germany, Italy, Netherlands, UK	EU-KLEMS	1970–2007*
India	Erumban and Das (2016)	1973–2012
Russia	Russia KLEMS	1995–2014
Mexico	KLEMS	1990–2014
Japan	JIP2015	1970–2012
China	Underlying WIOD data	1995–2009
Belgium, Greece, Ireland, Portugal, Sweden	GGDC TED	1980–2004*
Argentina, Brazil, Chile, Costa Rica, Uruguay, Venezuela	De Vries et al. (2010)	1994–2004*

Notes: *Coverage varies across countries, but this is the most common period for which data is available; **Variation across countries is too large to provide a common period for which data is available;

Source: Authors' compilation

Vu (2013, 2016) has also been the primary source of ICT capital data in the previous versions of the TED for all countries except those covered by the EU KLEMS. As mentioned earlier, we use national accounts data as much as possible, and rely on the WITSA only in cases where there is no data available from the sources listed in Table 6.2.

Approach to derive investment from WITSA spending data

Since WITSA provides data on total ICT spending – both consumer spending and investment spending – it is necessary to disentangle business investment from consumer spending. To construct a consistent series of investment from total spending data, Jorgenson and Vu (2013) apply the average investment-to-spending ratio from the United States – a country for which both official national accounts data on ICT investment, and WITSA ICT spending data are available – to all other countries, i.e.:

$$I_{i,t}^j = \phi_i^{US} S_{i,t}^{j,w} \qquad (6.2)$$

where $I_{i,t}^j$ is the current price investment in asset i (with $i = 1, \ldots, 3$; hardware, software and communication equipment) and $S_{i,t}^{j,w}$ is WITSA ICT spending data – both for year t and country j. ϕ_i^{US} is the average investment-to-spending ratio for ICT good i across all years: $\phi_i^{US} = \sum_{t=1}^{T} \left(\frac{I_{i,t}^{US,na}}{S_{i,t}^{US,w}} \right) / T$ where $I_{i,t}^{US,na}$ and, $S_{i,t}^{US,w}$ are respectively US ICT investment from the national accounts and US ICT spending from WITSA. The approach of Jorgenson and Vu (2013) is criticized by de Vries et al. (2010) and Erumban and Das (2016) as it will lead to biased estimates of investment if the true ratio ϕ_i differs across countries and over time.

We build on Jorgenson and Vu (2013, 2016), but seek to improve it by relaxing some of the underlying assumptions. Using the rich base of official and semi-official data, as described, it is now possible to compare official data with WITSA total spending data for more countries than just the United States. Figure 6.1 compares the US investment to spending ratio with that of several developing and developed economies for communication equipment. We find that the investment-to-spending ratios differ widely over time and across countries.[11] For instance, it is clear that consumer expenditure on telecommunication equipment gradually outpaced business investment over the course of the last decade, coinciding with the increased consumer adoption of mobile phones and smartphones. This is the case in Germany and Czech Republic, and is even more pronounced in the Philippines. In contrast, the US data suggest a relatively stable rate throughout, apart from a surge around the turn of the century at the time of the dotcom bubble when business investment temporarily increased relative to consumer spending before settling at the pre-bubble rate.

The investment-to-spending ratio is not constant across countries and over time, but assumptions about this ratio are still required to estimate ICT investment for the full set of countries and years. We suggest using a regional moving average of investment to total spending ratio. In terms of equation (2), we replace ϕ_i^{US} by $\phi_{i,T}^J$, defined as:

Global growth accounting 161

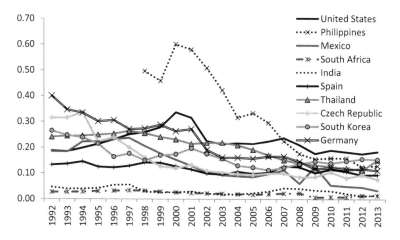

Figure 6.1 ICT investment as a percentage of total ICT spending in select countries – communication equipment, 1992–2013

Source: Bureau of Economic Analysis (United States), Eurostat (Czech Republic, Spain), EU KLEMS, and DESTATIS (Germany), National Economic and Social Development Board (Thailand), Philippine Statistics Authority (Philippines), OECD National Accounts at a Glance, and Mexico KLEMS (Mexico), World-KLEMS (South Korea), Erumban and Das 2016 (India) and WITSA (Total ICT spending for all countries).

$$\phi_{i,T}^{J} = \sum_{T=t-4}^{t} \left(\frac{I_{i,t}^{na}}{S_{i,t}^{w}} \right)^{J} \Big/ 5, \text{ for } j \in J \qquad (6.3)$$

where J denotes the region. As official (or semi-official) data on ICT investment is missing for nearly all Middle Eastern and African countries we apply a global moving average investment-to-spending ratio for these countries.

By combining official, semi-official and WITSA-based data, we construct ICT investment series for as many as 85 countries. CFM-based data – as discussed– is used for remaining countries, and also for years and or assets for which we could not obtain data according to the abovementioned sources and methods. The resulting dataset on investment on ICT assets is unique in its quality and coverage, and provides a good basis to understand the dynamics of ICT investments and its impact on growth across countries and time.

Constructing capital stocks and capital services using the new investment series

Data on investment is ultimately used to generate measures of capital stock and capital services. We construct capital stocks for each asset category listed in Table 6.1, except that in the TED, we combine R&D and other intellectual property products into one single asset. The final estimates of capital stock and capital services are aggregated to ICT assets, which consist of hardware, software and communication equipment, and non-ICT assets, which consist of residential and non-residential structures (if the distinction of residential and non-residential is not available, we treat them as a single asset), transport equipment and all other non-ICT machinery categories.

Capital stocks are calculated using the perpetual inventory method (PIM), which requires depreciation rates and asset price deflators. We assume geometric depreciation rates that are common across countries and constant over time (see Table 6.3). It is debatable whether this assumption is appropriate (see Bu 2006), but we follow this approach in order to ensure international comparability in assumptions in our database. Investment price deflators of individual assets are obtained from national accounts (as described) and, when not available, we use the aggregate investment deflator. If a benchmark estimate is available, we use it as the base estimate,

Table 6.3 Depreciation rates (percent) by assets

Asset	Depreciation rate(%)
1. Machinery and Equipment	
Transport equipment	18.9
Machinery	31.5
Computer Hardware	11.5
Communication equipment	12.6
Other machinery	
2. Construction	
Residential construction	1.1
Non-residential construction	3.1
3. Other Products	
Cultivated Assets	12.6
Intangible Assets	31.5
Software	15.0
Intellectual Property products (IPP)	

Source: Authors' calculations

and extrapolate backward and forward using the trend in aggregate investment deflator. For ICT assets, we use constant-quality price deflators from the United States, corrected for domestic inflation rates, following Schreyer (2002).[12] Since there is large debate on the overstatement of official hedonic prices in the United States (See Byrne and Corrado 2016), we generate two sets of ICT capital – one using official US price deflators obtained from the Bureau of Economic Analysis (BEA) and the other using alternate ICT price estimates developed by Byrne and Corrado (2016), which show much faster declines in ICT prices in the United States. The results discussed in this chapter are based on the alternative set of ICT prices, as they are argued to better capture ICT price decline.

Given investment at current prices, investment deflators and depreciation rates, the capital stock of each asset is computed as:

$$A_{i,t} = A_{i,t-1}(1-\partial_t) + I_{i,t} \tag{6.4}$$

where $A_{i,t}$ is the capital stock in asset i in year t, ∂ is the geometric depreciation rate and I is investment at constant prices. The implementation of this equation requires an initial stock estimate, as the annual stream of investment is added to existing stock after allowing for depreciation. The typical approach in choosing an initial is to assume the economy was in a steady-state, which allows the capital stock to be derived from initial investment and assumed growth of investment in the preceding period (Harberger 1978). However, this assumption can lead to problematic outcomes when an economy is not in a steady state, such as the formerly communist countries in the early 1990s. An alternative is to assume an initial capital-output ratio. Following the analysis and argumentation in Feenstra et al. (2015), we set the economy-wide capital-output ratio in the initial year equal to 2.6, divided between residential structures (1.1), non-residential structures (1.1), other machinery (0.3) and transport equipment (0.1). For ICT and other assets, the initial capital stock is assumed to be zero.[13]

Capital stock is in itself a useful indicator for several policy analysis and research purposes. However, the amount of capital used in the production process in any given year, also referred to as capital services, is more relevant for the analysis of the contribution of capital to economic growth. While it is hard to precisely measure the amount of services provided by each capital asset, following Jorgenson and Griliches (1967), we assume a proportionality between capital stock and capital service growth rates at the individual asset level, but allow for differences in capital services growth rates across assets. Estimates of aggregate capital services are obtained as weighted growth rates of individual asset wise capital stock, where the weights are derived as the rental share of individual assets in total capital compensation.[14] More specifically, we measure capital service growth as:

$$\Delta \ln K_t = \sum_{i=1}^{k} \bar{v}_{i,t} \Delta \ln A_{i,t} \qquad (6.5)$$

where $\bar{v}_{i,t}$ is the two-year average share of each individual asset in total capital compensation and where total capital compensation (M) is defined as value added net of labor compensation. Individual asset-wise capital compensations are obtained as products of individual capital stock, and the rental price of each asset, where rental prices are defined as:

$$c_{i,t} = r_t P_{i,t-1} + \partial_t P_{i,t} - \left(P_{i,t} - P_{i,t-1} \right) \qquad (6.6)$$

where r is the internal rate of return, measured as:

$$r_t = M_t - \sum_{i=1}^{k} \left[\partial_t P_{i,t} A_{i,t} - A_{i,t} \left(P_{i,t} - P_{i,t-1} \right) \right] \qquad (6.7)$$

where P is the investment price deflator. The difference between growth rates of capital services (equation 5) and growth rates of aggregate capital stock obtained by adding asset wise capital stock measured using equation 4 is the so-called capital composition effect (Erumban 2008; Inklaar 2010). This is a proxy measure of how fast a country is upgrading its capital by increasing the share of assets of high marginal productivity.

Results

In this section, we examine the pattern of investment to GDP ratios in the three asset types – non-ICT machinery, ICT and structures – across different regions of the world. We group countries into advanced economies and emerging markets, for expositional clarity. Figure 6.2 depicts the trends in the share of non-ICT equipment

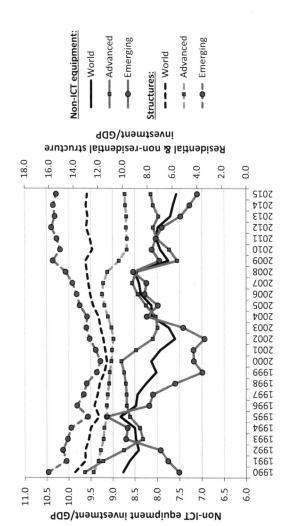

Figure 6.2 Non-ICT investment/GDP ratio (%) – advanced economies, emerging economies and world, 1990–2015

Note: The solid lines are investment to GDP ratios for non-ICT machinery, which consists of transport equipment and other machinery (left axis), while the dotted lines denote the investment to GDP ratios for residential and non-residential structures (right axis).

Source: The Conference Board Total Economy Database, November 2016[i]

i Note that these numbers may not match with the PWT data published at www.ggdc.net/pwt. This is because The Conference Board Total Economy Database uses GDP PPPs rather than investment PPPs to convert national currency values to a common currency.

investment – which includes non-ICT machinery and transport equipment – and residential and non-residential buildings in GDP for the global economy and for advanced and emerging economies. The dotted lines in the chart are investment share of structures and the solid lines are investment shares of non-ICT machinery.

Globally, investment in non-ICT equipment as a share of GDP has declined over the last 25 years from approximately 9 percent to 7.5 percent, primarily driven by substantive declines since the Great Recession of 2008/2009 in both emerging markets and advanced economies. The recent decline in the investment shares for emerging markets is primarily driven by declines in Chinese investment in machinery and equipment.[15] A different trend is observed with regard to investment in construction as a share of GDP, with emerging markets seeing a stabilization in recent years after a continuous increase since the late 1990s. In the advanced economies, the construction to GDP ratio started declining since the mid-2000s, and has also stabilized in the recent years, but at a relatively lower level compared to the emerging economies. As of 2015, advanced economies spent almost 18 percent of their GDP on non-ICT investment (structures and machinery combined), which is lower than the 23 percent spent in emerging markets. This difference stems primarily from investment in construction, which is at 15 percent of GDP in emerging markets and 10 percent in advanced economies. The difference in non-ICT equipment spending is considerably smaller, though with a slightly higher spending share in advanced economies (8 percent) than in emerging economies (7 percent).

Figure 6.3 provides the trend in ICT investment to GDP ratios for major regions. Globally, ICT investment relative to GDP increased markedly from 1990 onward, but after reaching its peak in 2000 the trend reversed and it slowly declined until it settled at around 2 percent in 2011 and has remained fairly unchanged since then. While these trends are more pronounced for advanced economies, they also hold for the emerging markets in our sample, which reflects the globalized nature of ICT technologies. Indeed, rather than catching up to advanced economies, ICT investment levels relative to GDP in emerging markets remain far below those in advanced economies, and seem to have peaked simultaneously with advanced economies.

In Figure 6.4, we further provide the contribution of ICT capital services to GDP growth, obtained using the standard growth accounting equation as $\alpha^{ICT} \Delta \ln K_t^{ICT}$, where α^{ICT} is the share of ICT capital compensation in nominal GDP and K_t^{ICT} is the capital

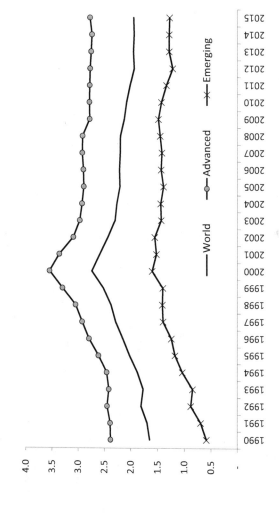

Figure 6.3 ICT investment/GDP ratio (%) – advanced economies, emerging economies and world, 1990–2015

Note: ICT includes computer hardware, software and communication equipment.

Source: The Conference Board Total Economy Database, November 2016

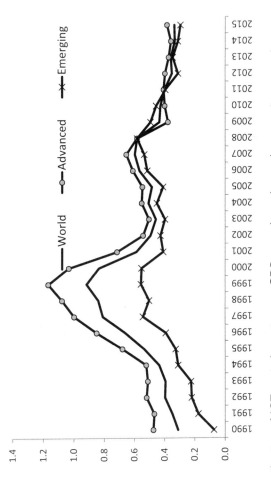

Figure 6.4 Contribution of ICT capital services to GDP growth – advanced economies, emerging economies and world, 1990–2015

Note: ICT includes computer hardware, software and communication equipment. ICT Capital service growth rates are calculated as weighted growth rate of these three ICT assets, with weights being their respective compensation share in GDP (see equation 5).

Source: The Conference Board Total Economy Database, November 2016

services in ICT (see equation 5). The figure shows that advanced economies have tapped the benefits of investment in ICT, as it lifted their GDP growth during the first wave of the ICT revolution that occurred in the second half of the 1990s. However, the contribution of ICT capital to GDP growth declined ever since. Even though it picked up somewhat between 2004 and 2007, it has continuously declined since the financial crisis. As one would expect, emerging market economies were initially slow in adopting ICT, and consequently, their ICT contribution to GDP growth was also lower in the 1990s. However, since the early 2000s, they started converging to advanced economies in terms of absolute contribution of ICT investment. Of course, these emerging market economies are growing much faster than most advanced economies, and the relative contribution of ICT is still much lower. Given the fact that these economies are still far below their advanced counter parts in terms of productivity levels and investment ratios, it is imperative for them to improve the quality of their capital assets. However, they do not seem to be moving in that direction, as we see a continuing decline in the contribution of ICT capital in these economies as well.

So far, we have discussed the pattern of investment and contribution of capital in global economy and the two major subgroups – emerging and advanced economies. Table 6.4 further presents a regression analysis which describes the correlation between a country's level of development (measured as per capita GDP) and the asset composition of its investment (ICT, non-ICT machinery and structures), aiming to summarize the patterns we observe at the aggregate level. Note that this table aims to provide a descriptive overview and does not attempt to explain any causal relationship. The results show that richer countries are investing relatively more in equipment and ICT and less in structures, whereas poorer countries tend to invest more in structures. The per capita GDP elasticity of equipment investment is 0.026, implying that an increase in per capita income of one percent increases the equipment-to-GDP ratio by 0.026 percentage point. The elasticity is slightly lower for the ICT to GDP ratio at 0.016 percentage point, though it underscores the fact that high-income countries tend to invest more in machinery and equipment. Since the equipment and structure shares in total investment adds to unity, the results for structures is just the reciprocal of equipment, where we see that richer countries tend to invest less in structures.[16]

Table 6.4 Regression – Asset composition of investment and per capita income

	Asset share in total investment			Capital composition effect[a]
	Equipment	ICT	Structures	
Constant	0.329 ***	0.001 *	0.671 ***	−0.383 ***
	0.011	0.004	0.011	0.092
log of GDP per capita	0.026 ***	0.016 ***	−0.026 ***	0.224 ***
	0.002	0.001	0.002	0.019
Adjusted R^2	0.050	0.154	0.050	0.051
Observations	2,604	2,189	2,604	2,604

Note: [a] Capital composition effect is the impact of changing composition of capital. Typically, it will be larger when the share of high-quality, fast-depreciating capital equipment increases in overall capital stock. It is measured as the difference between growth rate of capital stock and growth rate of capital services (see Erumban 2008).

* indicates significance at 10 percent level, *** indicates significance at 1 percent level.

Source: Authors' calculations

In the last column of Table 6.4, we provide the results of the so-called capital composition effect. The capital composition effect is measured as the difference between capital service growth rate (equation 5) and capital stock growth rate (i.e. the growth rate of capital stock in equation 4, aggregated across assets). This reflects the changing composition of a country's capital stock, i.e. the degree to which investment is shifting towards higher marginal-cost assets, such as ICT. A one percent higher per capita income is associated with a 0.224 percent higher capital composition effect, implying that a standard capital stock measure will understate the contribution of capital growth to GDP growth by a greater extent in higher-income countries.

Conclusion

This chapter has detailed the construction of a new, comprehensive dataset on investment by asset across nearly all countries in the world. This dataset fills an important hole in cross-country data as such data are not compiled in a comprehensive fashion by organizations such as the World Bank or United Nations and researchers also commonly rely on shortcuts, such as assuming there is only a single, homogenous asset type. We combine data from a large range of national and international sources and supplement official, National Accounts data by estimates from outside data compilers (WITSA) and estimates using the commodity flow method.

The remainder of the chapter describes the main features of the resulting data. We confirm earlier studies, who found that advanced economies tend to investment in high-cost (and thus high-return) assets like machinery at a greater rate than emerging economies. We show that this result extends to investment in ICT assets as well. This raises the question why emerging economies are not investing at a higher rate, as this would (presumably) allow them to achieve faster economic growth.

Notes

1 The role of investment in physical capital has been a dominant subject in the field of economics since the early growth theories of Harrod (1939) and Domar (1946), with it being more formalized by the seminar works of Robert Solow in the late 1950s (Solow 1957).
2 The approach is built on de Vries and Erumban (2015) and Feenstra et al. (2015).
3 Caselli and Wilson (2004) also make a similar attempt, but their asset wise investment levels are not fully consistent with the published aggregate investment levels and do not cover investment in structures.
4 The Penn World Table covers 182 countries and the Conference Board Total Economy Database covers 124 countries – both since 1950. In the analysis presented in this chapter, we use the data for 124 common countries in both datasets.
5 Note that some countries report national accounts investment data based on the commodity flow approach. See, for instance, AFDB (2014) for a list of African economies using CFM.
6 Annual macro-economic database, maintained by the European Commission.
7 CEPALSTAT – Databases and statistical publications, maintained by UN's Economic Commission for Latin America and the Caribbean.
8 The KLEMS stand for capital, labor, energy, material and services data bases, which started originally with the EU KLEMS initiative (www.euklems.net, accessed 21 November 2016), and later extended to a global scale to construct a globally comparable industrial productivity database (www.worldklems.net, accessed 21 November 2016). The project has been extended to several individual countries and regions such as Asia KLEMS and India KLEMS. The KLEMS data used in this study are accessed in November 2016.
9 www.conference-board.org/data/economydatabase/, accessed 21 November 2016.

10 Practical complications arise from imperfect coverage of trade and production data, which requires the use of long-run trends and smoothing to avoid unrealistic swings in asset shares.
11 A similar picture is observed in the case of software and hardware.
12 Since software investment is typically also done by software engineers in individual countries, the assumption that US deflators are appropriate may be less suited to this asset. We leave this issue for future work.
13 The TED database continues to use a steady state assumption, where initial capital stock is obtained as $A_{i,0} = I_{i,0}/(gI_i + \partial_i)$, where $A_{i,0}$ is the initial capital stock, $I_{i,0}$ is the real investment in the first year, gI_i is the growth rate of real investment during the first ten years, and ∂_i is the depreciation rate – all for asset i. The empirical impact of this choice on capital stock in the recent years is very trivial, due to depreciation of assets.
14 See Erumban (2008) for a detailed discussion.
15 Note that The Conference Board Total Economy provides alternative estimates of GDP, investment and employment for China, as there have been substantial debates over the quality of Chinese official data. The discussions in this paper are based on these alternative estimates. Data based on official data can be obtained at the Conference Board website. For a detailed discussion on the construction of the new alternative series of Chinese statistics, see Wu (2014).
16 We replicated the same regression using the investment to GDP ratio on the lefthand side, and the results suggest a similar relationship.

Bibliography

AFDB. 2014. *In-Depth Situational Analysis of the Reliability of Economic Statistics in Africa: With a Special Focus on GDP Measurement and Methodological Requirements*. Arica Development Bank. www.afdb.org/en/documents/document/economic-brief-in-depth-situational-analysis-of-the-reliability-of-economic-statistics-in-africa-with-a-special-focus-on-gdp-measurement-methodological-requirements-48818/, accessed November 21, 2016.

Bems, Rudolfs. 2008. "Aggregate Investment Expenditures on Tradable and Nontradable Goods." *Review of Economic Dynamics* 11(4): 852–883.

Bu, Yisheng. 2006. "Fixed Capital Stock Depreciation in Developing Countries: Some Evidence From Firm Level Data." *Journal of Development Studies* 42(5): 881–901.

Byrne, D., and C. Corrado. 2016. "ICT Prices and ICT Services: What Do They Tell Us About Productivity and Technology." *The Conference Board Working Paper* EPWP#16-05.

Caselli, Francesco, and Daniel J. Wilson. 2004. "Importing Technology." *Journal of Monetary Economics* 51(1): 1–32.

De Vries, K., and A. A. Erumban. 2015. *Total Economy Database: Sources & Methods*. The Conference Board. www.conference-board.org/data/economydatabase/index.cfm?id=27770, accessed November 21, 2016.

De Vries, G. J., N. Mulder, M. Dal Borgo, and A. A. Hofman. 2010. "ICT Investment in Latin America: Does IT Matter for Economic Growth?" In M. Cimoli, A. A. Hofman, and N. Mulder (eds.), *Innovation and Economic Development: The Impact of Information and Communication Technologies in Latin America*. Cheltenham, UK and Northampton: Edward Elgar.

Domar, Evsey D. 1946. "Capital Expansion, Rate of Growth, and Employment." *Econometrica, Journal of the Econometric Society*: 137–147.

Erumban, Abdul Azeez. 2008. "Rental Prices, Rates of Return, Capital Aggregation and Productivity: Evidence From EU and US." *CESifo Economic Studies* 54(3): 499–533.

Erumban, Abdul Azeez, and D. K. Das. 2016. "Information and Communication Technology and Economic Growth in India." *Telecommunications Policy* 40(5): 412–431. DOI: 10.1016/j.telpol.2015.08.006, accessed November 21, 2016.

Feenstra, Robert C., Robert Inklaar, and Marcel P. Timmer. 2015. "The Next Generation of the Penn World Table." *The American Economic Review* 105(10): 3150–3182.

Harberger, A. 1978. "Perspectives on Capital and Technology in Less Developed Countries." In M. J. Artis and A. R. Nobay (eds.), *Contemporary Economic Analysis*. London: Croom Helm.

Harrod, Roy F. 1939. "An Essay in Dynamic Theory." *The Economic Journal* 49(193): 14–33.

Inklaar, Robert. 2010. "The Sensitivity of Capital Services Measurement: Measure All Assets and the Cost of Capital." *Review of Income and Wealth* 56(2): 389–412.

ISWGNA. 2009. *System of National Accounts 2008*. Brussels, Luxembourg, New York, Paris, Washington, DC: Commission of the European Communities-Eurostat, International Monetary Fund, OECD, United Nations.

Jorgenson, Dale W. 2001. "Information Technology and the U.S. Economy." *American Economic Review* 91(1): 1–32.

Jorgenson, Dale W., and Zvi Griliches. 1967. "The Explanation of Productivity Change." *The Review of Economic Studies* 34(3): 249–283.

Jorgenson, Dale W., and Khuong Minh Vu. 2013. "The Emergence of the New Economic Order: Growth in the G7 and the G20." *Journal of Policy Modeling* 35(3): 389–399.

Jorgenson, Dale W., and Khuong Minh Vu. 2016. "The ICT Revolution, World Economic Growth, and Policy Issues." *Telecommunication Policy* 40: 383–397.

Schreyer, Paul. 2002. "Computer Price Indices and International Growth and Productivity Comparisons." *Review of Income and Wealth* 48(1): 15–31.

Solow, Robert M. 1957. "Technical Change and the Aggregate Production Function." *The Review of Economics and Statistics* 1957: 312–320.

Timmer, Marcel P., and Bart Van Ark. 2005. "Does Information and Communication Technology Drive EU-US Productivity Growth Differentials?" *Oxford Economic Papers* 57(4): 693–716.

WITSA. Various issues. *Digital Planet: The Global Information Economy*. Vienna: World Information Technology and Services Alliance.

Wu, Harry X. 2014. "China's Growth and Productivity Performance Debate Revisited – Accounting for China's Sources of Growth with a New Data Set." *The Conference Board Working Paper Series*, EPWP #14-01, January.

Part II

Productivity and growth – country experiences

Chapter 7

Labor productivity and a test of the Kaldor-Verdoorn law in East Asia

Hak K. Pyo

Introduction

There have been two stylized facts in the global economy after the global financial crisis in 2007–08. The first one is the decline of labor income share in both advanced and emerging nations and the second one is the continuation of slow recovery and stagnation despite massive monetary and fiscal expansion measures by the United States, Euro area and Japan. Onaran and Galanis (2013) reports that there is a clear secular decline in the wage share in both developed and emerging developing countries (Turkey, Mexico, South Korea (henceforth Korea), Argentina, China, India and South Africa) from the late 1970s or early 1980s onwards. In the Euro area and in Japan, the decline in the unadjusted wage share (not adjusted by the wage income by self-employed) exceeded 15 percent points and 20 points respectively in the index value. The fall is lower, but still strong, in the United States and UK, with a decline of 8.9 percent and 11.1 percent respectively. They note that a correction of the wage share by excluding the high managerial wages, which have increased very sharply in these developed countries, would have provided a more realistic picture about the loss in labor's income share. They also note that in the developing world, Turkey and Mexico have experienced the strongest decline in the wage share (–31.8 percent and –37.9 percent, respectively) followed by South Africa (–17 percent), Argentina (–12 percent) and India (–17.6 percent) from the base year of 1980. In China, the improvement in the wage share in the 1980s was reversed in 1990 culminating in a cumulative decline of 12.8 percent in the index value. In Korea, the increase in the wage share from the mid-1980s onwards was reversed by the crisis in 1997. Pyo (2015) estimates the unadjusted wage share (year) in Korea as: 0.45 (1970), 0.55 (1997) and 0.5 (2012) and Cho et al. (2015) estimate the adjusted wage share (adjusted by assuming the wage level of self-employed and unpaid workers as 80 percent of wage earners' average wage rate) as: 0.82 (1970), 0.78 (1997) and 0.67 (2012). Onaran and Galanis (2013) report the mean values of the wage share from the sample as: Euro area-12 (0.693), UK (0.727), the United States (0.684), Japan (0.721), China (0.581) and Korea (0.845) (adjusted wage share assuming the average wage level of self-employed would be equal to 100 percent of average wage level of workers in the aggregate economy).

The empirical finding of the declining wage share in both developed and major developing economies is equivalent to and consistent with the empirical finding of the increasing capital share as reported in Piketty (2014). Piketty (2014: 211–212) notes that capital income share was around 15–25 percent of national income in rich countries in 1970 but reached the 25–30 percent level in 2000–10. He further notes that the upward trend in capital's share of income is consistent not only with an elasticity of substitution of capital for labor greater than one but also with an increase in capital's bargaining power vis-à-vis labor over the past few decades, which have seen increased mobility of capital and heightened competition between states eager to attract investments. He argues that over a very long period of time, the elasticity of substitution between capital and labor seems to have been greater than one: an increase in the capital/income ratio seems to have led to a slight increase in capital's share of national income, and vice versa. While he does not estimate capital's share of income in developing countries, he notes that the uppercentile's share of national income in poor and emerging economies is roughly the same as in the rich economies: the top centile's share of national income moved from around 20 percent in four countries – India, South Africa, Indonesia and Argentina – then fell to the 6–12 percent level during 1950–80 but rebounded in the 1980s to reach 15 percent of national income.

While there is a secular decline in the labor share of national income and correspondingly an increase in the capital share, two stylized facts seem to have emerged: polarization of personal income distribution and weaker growth performance in most countries except China and India. The polarization of personal income and its rising inequality has been observed by Atkinson et al. (2009) and Piketty (2014). Piketty (2014) relies on the historical trend of capital/income ratio (β) and has observed its U-shaped curve implying that the income inequality in recent years is getting worse going back toward the level observed at the end of 19th century and early 20th century in both developed countries and emerging developing countries. He estimates the capital/income ratio in Italy and Japan reaching above 6, France around 5.8 and the United States and Germany slightly less than 5. He also observes a similar U-shaped pattern from the historical data of India, South Africa, Indonesia, Argentina, China and Colombia and concludes that the share of income held by the richest 10 percent income group in these emerging economies is as large as the level observed in developed countries. But he notes that the income inequality measured by household survey in developing economies tends to underestimate the degree of inequality. For example, in case of Colombia and Argentina, the richest 10 percent income group is estimated to hold more than 20 percent of national income according to tax records, while it is estimated to hold 5 percent of national income according to household survey. Kim and Kim (2013) estimate the income concentration ratio by top 1 percent income group from tax records in Korea and observe that the ratio increased from 7 percent in 1996 to 12 percent in 2010. They also observe that the top 1 percent's income share in the United States, Japan and Korea in the mid-1970s was similar at the level of around 5 percent but it reached in the United States the level of 12 percent in 2008 and in Japan the level of 5.5 percent.

While the income inequality is rising, the growth performance in both developed economies and most developing economies has been stagnant after the global financial crisis in 2007. Onaran and Galanis (2013) report the average growth rates of GDP between two sub-periods (1970–79 and 2000–07) in Euro area-12 (3.78 percent and 2.13 percent), the United States (3.32 percent and 2.61 percent), Japan (5.21 percent and 1.73 percent), Korea (10.27 percent and 5.20 percent), China (6.11 percent and 10.51 percent) and India (2.68 percent and 7.26 percent).

With these stylized facts observed from the recent economic trend in the global economy, there has been debate on wage-led growth vs. profit-led growth. Wage-led growth is often called income-led growth or demand-led growth while profit-led growth is also called supply-led growth. The purpose of this paper is to reexamine the theoretical background of two contesting economic policy platforms and derive implications for the East Asian countries of

China, Japan and Korea who have a diverse historical background and economic regimes.

The paper is organized as follows. Section 2 reviews the theoretical backgrounds of two contesting economic regimes: wage-led growth and profit-led growth. In Section 3, we examine the result of empirical studies and conduct the Granger causality tests from the countries' dataset. The last section concludes the paper.

Wage-led growth and profit-led growth: two contesting economic regimes

Kaldor-Verdoorn Law and wage-led growth

According to Bleaney (1976) and Lavoie and Stockhammer (2012), a wage-led economic strategy has a long history and was advocated in the form of 'under-consumption theory' in the 19th century by classical economists including Malthus, Sismondi and Hobson. It was Keynes (1936) who endorsed it in his theory of effective demand arguing that excessive savings rates relative to deficient investment rates were at the core of depressed economies. Under-consumption theories have two groups of followers. One group is Marx (1979) and subsequent Marxist theorists such as Baran and Sweezy (1966) who related under-consumption theories to the principle of infinite accumulation and the problems of the realization of the profit and the other group is Kalecki (1971) and post-Kaleckian authors such as Steindl (1952) and Bhaduri (1986) who have brought together the theory of effective demand and the problem of realization of profit.

As reviewed and revisited recently by Piketty (2014: 227–230), Marx (1979) predicted that capitalists would accumulate ever increasing quantities of capital, which ultimately would lead inexorably to a falling rate of profit (i.e., return on capital) and eventually to their own downfall. The under-consumption theory is related to the problem of the realization of profit. It was Kaleckian and post-Keynesian authors such as Rawthorn (1981), Taylor (1988) and Dutt (1987) who have revisited the relationship between the under-consumption theories and the problem of realization of profit. In the context of the present paper, we should pay attention to Taylor (1988), who showed early on that when emerging countries had enough capacity to adjust, a wage-led growth strategy is preferred to profit-led growth strategy.

Kaldor (1957) had defined the technical progress function and had initiated a debate on what he called the Verdoorn Law in Kaldor (1967) which claims that there is a positive causal relationship going from the demand-led growth of GDP to the growth rate of labor productivity which is the supply components of growth. It was later called the Kaldor-Verdoorn Law by Kaldorians such as Boyer (1988), Setterfield and Cornwall (2002) and Naastepad and Storm (2010) who argued for a long time that supply-side growth is endogenous which predates neoclassical theory of endogenous growth. The Kaldor-Verdoorn Law has now a series of empirical evidence such as McCombie and Thirwall (1994), McCombie (2002), Leon-Ledesma and Thirlwall (2002) and Dray and Thirlwall (2011).

Mainstream neoclassical economists such as Hicks (1932: 124–125) and Samuelson (1965: 354) have argued that rising real wages would induce firms to invest in more capital-intensive methods which would lead to higher labor productivity. Kaldor (1961) called the constancy of the wage share in total national income a stylized fact of economic growth implying that there a long-run relationship between real wages and labor productivity. Dumenil and Levy (1993) introduced a stochastic model of induced technical change where the selection of new technologies is based on the profitability criterion, with only techniques yielding a profit rate higher than the present being adopted. The model suggests that if the labor share is larger than the capital share, then the savings in labor will tend to be larger than in capital and that a rise in real wages also increases the labor share and the probability of the selected new technology being labor-saving and capital-using. It also suggests that real wages affect the trajectory of technical change through the profit rate such that an increase in real wages reduces profitability, driving profit-seeking capitalists to implement labor-saving technologies in order to reduce labor costs. Marquetti (2004) has carried out Granger (1969) causality tests on the causal relationship between real wages and labor productivity for the United States over the period 1869–1999 and supported a unidirectional Granger causality from real wages to labor productivity. Piketty (2014: 220–221) argues that over a very long period of time Kaldor's constancy of the wage share has been rejected by the rising capital's share of national income which is consistent with an elasticity of substitution between labor and capital greater than one confirming the inadequacy of the Cobb-Douglas model for studying evolutions over the very long run.

In order to highlight the effects of an increase in the wage share on profitability and aggregate demand, we may revisit the post-Kaleckian model as illustrated in Figure 7.1 following Lovoie and Stockhammer (2012: 9–12). We start with a closed economy without government in which a short-run equilibrium level of GDP is established by the intersection of the saving and investment functions. Following standard Keynesian and Kaleckian models, we assume that saving (S) and investment (I) are positive functions of income (Y). We further assume both investment multiplier effect and acceleration effect which is reflected in the steeper savings function than the investment slope.

Suppose there is an exogenous increase in real wages or in the wage share. The effect on the saving function depends on the saving propensities. If the propensities to save out of profits and out of wages are the same, which is the standard assumption in the neoclassical model, then the change in real wages will have no impact on saving and consumption. However, if the propensity to save out of wages is lower than that out of profits, which is the standard assumption in Kaldorian models, then the saving function

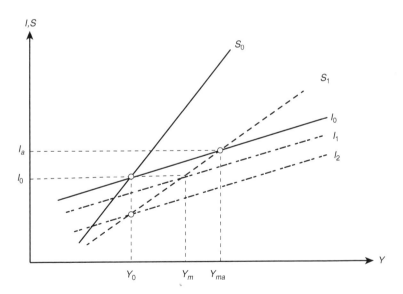

Figure 7.1 Effect of increase in the wage share in the post-Kaleckian model
Source: Lavoie and Stockhammer (2012), Figure 3.

of Figure 7.1 will rotate downwards, to S1, meaning that less saving and hence more consumption will occur at the same GDP level. Saving will drop from S00 to S 01 at the given GDP level (Y0). When real wages and the wage share increase, the equilibrium GDP will move from Y0 to Y ma due to the acceleration effect as underlined by the canonical Kaleckian models of Rowthorn (1981), Taylor (1988) and Dutt (1987). Seemingly an increase in the wage share has a positive impact on the increase in both consumption and investment. However the post-Kaleckian models of growth and distribution including Bhaduri and Marglin (1990), Kurz (1990), Taylor (1991) and Blecker (2010) argue that investment depends on not only sales but also expected profitability, which would depend on the share of profits in national income, that is the profit margin of firms or, more precisely, on the profit rate that firms expect to achieve on their capital when the capacity is utilized at its normal rate (see Lovie 1995: 795–800; Lavoie and Stockhammer 2012: 10–11). A higher real wage increases consumption but reduces investment, in so far as investment depends on the profit margin (Bhaduri and Marglin 1990: 378). Therefore, the final outcome of a higher real wage increase depends on the magnitude of investment reduction.

There are three possible cases that may arise when profitability and the impact on net exports are considered. The first case is when the profitability is weak relative to consumption and the accelerator effect and therefore the new equilibrium level of GDP is set at Ym level. The second case is the intermediate case when the profitability effect reduces investment and settles at a level between I1 and I2 curves: higher real wage generates higher GDP level but investment will be lower. Lavoie and Stockhammer (2012: 11–12) define it as a wage-led demand regime and a profit-led investment regime. The third case is illustrated by a shift of the investment curve below the I2 curve implying that the increase in real wages induces a reduction in real output and investment expenditure resulting in a profit-led demand regime and a profit-led investment regime. In addition, as Blecker (1989, 2010) and Bhaduri and Marglin (1990) have pointed out, the effects of an increase in wages and the resulting change in income distribution between workers and capitalists can have negative impacts on net exports because the exporter's profit margin can be squeezed between domestic costs and foreign competition. They note that the negative effects of a higher wage share are likely to be bigger in small open economies. This negative effect on net exports is represented by a backward shift of the saving function from S1 towards S0 reducing the level of GDP further down to the level of Yu. Therefore, we conclude that the net effect of an increase in the wage share on GDP depends on the relative size of the effects on the three components of aggregate demand – consumption, investment and net exports. Onaran and Galanis (2013) have reflected the post-Kaleckian views in deriving their empirical model, as we review in section 3.

Profit-led growth and innovation

While the effects of profit-led growth are implicit in the theories of under-consumption and post-Kaleckian theories of income distribution and growth, it is a passive treatment of the effects of profit-led growth in the sense that they regarded a profit squeeze and contraction of aggregate demand through reduced consumption, investment and net exports as an exception which usually applies to only small open economies. The wage-led growth theories have not considered much on the effects of profits on not only on labor productivity but also total factor productivity and neglected the effects of profitability on innovation and the growth rate of population and human capital.

The falling rate of profit in the capitalist system was well predicted by Marx, who wrote that 'the bourgeoisie digs its own grave', implying that capitalists accumulate ever-increasing capital and it will ultimately lead to a falling rate of profit (i.e., return on capital) and eventually to their own downfall. Piketty (2014: 227–228) defines it as 'the principle of infinite accumulation' with what he calls the second law of capitalism as follows:

$$\alpha = r \times \frac{s}{g} \tag{7.1}$$

where α is the share of profit income in national income, r is the rate of return to capital, s is savings rate and g is growth rate of real GDP. Piketty (2014) also derives the following equation as a long run equilibrium path of a capitalist economy from the wealth accumulation identity in his Technical Appendix, which is available online on his website:

$$\alpha = r \times \frac{s}{g} = r \times \beta \tag{7.2}$$

where $\beta = \frac{s}{g}$ β is the ratio of capital (K) to income(Y). In Pyo (2015, forthcoming), I have derived alternatively the Equation 7.2 based on the neoclassical growth models of Solow (1956), Barro and Sala-i-Martin (2004) and Acemoglu (2008). It can be shown that in the long run steady-state, capital/output ratio (β) is equal to the ratio of savings rate and the sum of population growth rate (n) and the growth rate of TFP (v) since the depreciation rate (δ) is assumed to approach to zero in the long run:

$$g = n + v + \delta = n + v \qquad (7.3)$$

Piketty defines this as the long-run path of the capitalist economy implying that the only exit from falling into the infinite accumulation of capital and zero rate of return is to have a positive structural growth rate of population and total factor productivity ($n + v$).

The second theoretical source of advocating for profit-led growth can be found in the innovation theories in capitalist development, which started from Schumpeter (1934) and were extended by Griliches and Schmookler (1963) and Schmookler (1966). Acemoglu (2008: 420–421) reviews the neoclassical models of innovation and finds potential profit and market size are the most important incentives for innovation. Griliches and Schmookler (1963) and Schmookler (1966) argue that firms' investments for creative innovations are a part of their profit maximization activity. The replacement effect by Arrow et al. (1961) and Arrow (1962) suggests that the monopoly's incentive for innovation is lower than the competitive firm because the monopolist expects that a new creative innovation would replace its existing profits and, therefore, it has lower incentive for innovation than the potential entrants.

Acemoglu (2008) explains why *ex post* monopoly power is also an important determinant for innovation. The reason why there is a difference in incentive structure between competitive firms and a monopolist is due to appropriability effect. The appropriability effect is the effect on innovation-leading firms who are usually not able to appropriate enough consumer surplus because the private value of an innovation is lower than social value being created from product or process innovation. Acemoglu argues that, since there could be business-stealing effects, there is a tendency for excessive innovation. Acemoglu (2008: 430) notes that the monopolistic completion model by Dixit and Stiglitz (1977) suggests the mark-up profits by monopolistic competitors are independent of the number of firms and the profits of innovation can be created despite the increase in the number of products and processing equipment and machineries.

The third theoretical source of advocating for profit-led growth can be found in the theory of human capital. As pointed out by Piketty (2014), one of the most important determinants for a sustainable growth path of the capitalist economy is to have a positive growth rate of population which is usually decomposed by quantity of population and quality of human capital. Becker and Barro (1986), Galor and Weil (2000) and Galor (2005) have endogenized the quantitative growth of population and found that there could be a trade-off between quantitative labor supply and qualitative labor supply. In addition the models of Galor and Zeira (1993) and Banerjee and Newman (1993) have endogenized the qualitive population growth and have argued that unequal income distribution and imperfect credit markets in developing economies tend to hinder the formation of human capital. In this context, Aghion and Bolton (1997) and Piketty (1997) have argued that income inequality hinders the formation of human capital through investments in entrepreneurship and, therefore, profit-led growth is crucial to lead innovation and maintain a sustainable level of quantitative and qualitative population growth.

Empirical tests on the Kaldor-Verdoorn Law

Empirical results for OECD countries

Empirical tests on the validity of the Kaldor-Verdoorn Law and the relative merit of wage-led growth vs. profit-led growth have been carried out mostly by post-Kaleckians. There have been two types of empirical tests: one is to have a direct test of the Kaldor-Verdoorn Law by regressing the effect of aggregate demand on labor productivity growth and the other is to run the causality test between aggregate demand (or real wages) and labor productivity growth. All of the existing empirical tests are summarized in Appendix Tables.

As summarized in Table 7.A.1, Kaldor (1967) found a significant positive coefficient of output growth (defined as Verdoorn coefficient) on labor productivity growth from 12 OECD-country dataset during the period of 1934–35 to 1963–64. His estimates of the

Verdoorn coefficient was 0.446 with output growth rate being the only explanatory variable and 0.356 when the gross investment/output ratio was added. Later empirical estimates of the Verdoorn coefficient rages from 0.1 to 0.25 for the United States (1960–2007) and 0.3–0.6 for the UK (1960–2007) by Hein and Tarassow (2009) and 0.3–0.6 by McCombie (2002), Strom and Naastepad (2009) and Hein and Tarassow (2009) for Europe (1960–2007).

Empirical tests on the effect of real wages on labor productivity growth as summarized in Table 7.A.2 includes Marquetti (2004) who finds a causality from real wage increase to labor productivity growth and no reverse causality from the US data during the period of 1869–1999. Naastepad (2006) estimates the elasticity of real wage on labor productivity growth in the Netherlands as 0.52, and Storm and Naastepad (2009) estimate 0.50–0.55 from OECD-20 dataset (1984–2004). Vergeer and Kleinknecht (2010–11) found estimated elasticity in the range of 0.31–0.39 from a panel data of OECD countries (1960–2004), and Hein and Tarassow (2009) estimate 0.30 from the data of OECD-6 country data set (1960–2007).

The empirical study by Onaran and Galanis (2013) decomposes aggregate demand into consumption, investment and net exports. He estimates the impact of the increase in profit rate rather than real wages and, therefore, can be interpreted as the impact of profit-led growth on three aggregate demand components. They also estimated the effect of 1 percent increase in profit share by each country upon total aggregate demands in selected OECD countries and major emerging economies and a simultaneous increase by 1 percent of profit share on all total aggregate demand to simulate the effect of increase in profit share on global aggregate demand as summarized in Table 7.A.3. The increase of profit share by 1 percent by individual country is estimated to result in all negative impacts on aggregate demand, including Euro Area-12 (–0.133), the United States (–0.808), Japan (–0.034) and Korea (–0.115), except China (1.932), South Africa (0.729), Australia (0.268), Canada (0.148), Argentina (0.075) and India (0.075). The estimated coefficients from the simultaneous simulation of increase in profit share by all sample countries were mostly negative, including EU Area-12 (–0.245), the United States (–0.921), Japan (–0.179) and Korea (–0.864), except China (1.115), South Africa (0.390) and Australia (0.172). Onaran and Galanis (2013) conclude that profit-led growth is likely to produce negative impacts on aggregate demand except relatively resource-rich countries with larger domestic market size. It should be noted that both Japan and Korea are expected to produce negative impacts of increase in profit share on aggregate demand even though both countries have relatively larger net exports. In addition, Korea seems more vulnerable than Japan to global simultaneous increase in profit share.

Causality tests between aggregate demand increase and labor productivity growth by EU-9 dataset and East Asia dataset

We have run a regression of value-added growth as dependent variable and labor productivity growth as independent variable and its reversed version to test Granger causality using EU-KLEMS dataset for EU-9 countries. The result is summarized in Table 7.1 and shows that in all EU-KLEMS 9 member countries the causality is accepted and runs from aggregate demand (Value-added: GDP) increase to labor productivity increase. The reverse causality from labor productivity growth to GDP growth is not accepted. Therefore, in general, EU-9 countries' dataset accepts the Kaldor-Verdoorn Law.

The causality test was carried out from the data set of four East Asian countries and is summarized in Table 7.2. The Kaldor-Verdoorn Law is accepted with the causality running from aggregate income (demand) growth to labor productivity growth in Korea (both annual and quarterly data), Japan (quarterly data) and China (annual data). It is not accepted in Japan (annual data) and Taiwan (annual data). The reverse causality is accepted only in Korea (both annual and quarterly data) and Japan (annual data). Therefore, we can conclude that the Kaldor-Verdoorn Law is partly accepted in East Asia and has a mixed evidence.

Lastly we have run a causality test between real wage increase and labor productivity from the data set of KIP database, JIP database and the World Bank's China database for the period of 1970–2014 (annual data). The unit root tests for real wages and labor productivity indicate that there is a co-integration (a long-run relationship in both untransformed and log-transformed variables as summarized in Table 7.3. Based on the result of unit root tests, we have conducted Granger causality test, which is also often called as Granger non-causality test because its null hypothesis is that there is no causality from an independent variable to the dependent variable. The causality test results accept the existence of causality from real wages to labor productivity in Korea and China but not in

Table 7.1 Causality test between value-added and labor productivity in EU

Country	Variables	Chi-square	Prob > chi2
Austria (annual data) 1970–2012	Value-added → Labor productivity (O)	3.63174	0.0372
	Labor productivity → Value-added (X)	0.57791	0.5665
Belgium (annual data) 1970–2012	Value-added → Labor productivity (O)	2.71543	0.0801
	Labor productivity → Value-added (X)	0.25864	0.7736
UK (annual data) 1970–2012	Value-added → Labor productivity (O)	4.57575	0.0174
	Labor productivity → Value-added (X)	0.38651	0.6824
Finland (annual data) 1970–2012	Value-added → Labor productivity (O)	11.2190	0.0002
	Labor productivity → Value-added (X)	1.28178	0.2918
France (annual data) 1970–2012	Value-added → Labor productivity (O)	3.63876	0.0373
	Labor productivity → Value-added (X)	0.95138	0.3965
Germany (annual data) 1970–2012	Value-added → Labor productivity (O)	2.59964	0.0890
	Labor productivity → Value-added (X)	1.18257	0.3188
Italy (annual data) 1970–2012	Value-added → Labor productivity (O)	5.13740	0.0112
	Labor productivity → Value-added (X)	0.02065	0.9796
Netherlands (annual data) 1970–2012	Value-added → Labor productivity (O)	7.16991	0.00025
	Labor productivity → Value-added (X)	2.35950	0.1093
Spain (annual data) 1970–2012	Value-added → Labor productivity (O)	7.17648	0.0026
	Labor productivity → Value-added (X)	1.36270	0.2700

Source: www.euklems.net/index3.shtml accessed on 10 May 2016.

Table 7.2 Causality test between income and labor productivity in East Asia

	Variables		Chi-square	Prob > chi2
Korea (annual data) 1972–2012	Income → Labor productivity (O)		6.7624	0.009
	Labor Productivity → Income (O)		8.9496	0.003
Korea (quarterly data)	Variables		Chi-square	Prob > chi2
	Income → Labor productivity (O)		124.97	0.000
	Labor Productivity → Income (O)		107.84	0.000
Japan (annual data) 1975–2011	Variables		Chi-square	Prob > chi2
	Income → Labor productivity (X)		2.5281	0.112
	Labor Productivity → Income (X)		0.94377	0.331
Japan (quarterly data)	Variables		Chi-square	Prob > chi2
	Income → Labor productivity (O)		165.29	0.000
	Labor Productivity → Income (O)		341.66	0.000
China (annual data) 1982–2010	Variables		Chi-square	Prob > chi2
	Income → Labor productivity (O)		25.938	0.000
	Labor Productivity → Income (X)		2.3367	0.126
Taiwan (annual data) 1998–2013	Variables		Chi-square	Prob > chi2
	Income → Labor productivity (X)		0.89859	0.343
	Labor Productivity → Income (X)		0.46952	0.493

Source: Korea – The Bank of Korea ECOS and KIP Database, Japan – JIP Database, Taiwan – Asia KLEMS Database and China – World Bank website and Hitotsubashi University CIP Database.

Table 7.3 Unit root tests for real wages and labor productivity in East Asia (1970–2014)

Test statistics for	Variable	Constant, no trend ADF lag I			Constant and trend ADF lag I		
		Korea	Japan	China	Korea	Japan	China
No unit root	LW	−1.57	−2.43	−0.34	−0.57	−3.37	−3.52*
	LPL	−1.14	−2.67*	−1.21	−0.5	−1.37	−2.66
One unit root	DLW	−3.72***	−4.91***	−4.71***	−4.45***	−4.86***	−4.42**
	DLPL	−4.03***	−3.66***	−2.97*	−4.31***	−4.55***	−2.97

Notes: LW, log-transformed real wages; LLP, log-transformed labor productivity. The ADF regression with constant α and time trend t is

$$\Delta y_t = \alpha + \beta t + \rho y_{t-1} + \sum_{j=1}^{p} \theta_j \Delta y_{t-1} + e_t,$$

where y is the variable of interest, e is a white noise term and j = 1,....,p are the ADF lags.

 * significant at 10 percent
 ** significant at 5 percent
 *** significant at 1 percent

Source: Author compilation

Table 7.4 Granger causality tests between real wages and labor productivity for Korea, Japan and China (1970–2014)

H0		Lag Length	F value
Korea	LW does not granger cause LPL	1	3.09*
	LPL does not granger cause LW	1	0.68
Japan	LW does not granger cause LPL	1	0.27
	LPL does not granger cause LW	1	2.45
China	LW does not granger cause LPL	1	4.57**
	LPL does not granger cause LW	1	2.02

Notes: LW, log-transformed real wages; LLP, log-transformed labor productivity.
* significant at 10 percent
** significant at 5 percent
Source: Author compilation

Japan. The reverse causality from labor productivity growth to real wage increase seems non-existent in all East Asian countries.

Summary and conclusion

With a brief survey on the global trend toward increasing income inequality and decreasing wage share in national income, we have examined the theoretical background of two contesting economic and political ideologies – wage-led growth and income-led growth. The post-Kaleckian models, which is the main theoretical model of wage-led growth, suggest that the increase in wage share or real wages are likely to induce labor productivity growth validating the Kaldor-Verdoorn Law. On the other hand, the neoclassical models emphasize the importance of profits as incentives for innovation and human capital investment and therefore maintaining positive growth rates of total factor productivity and quantitative and qualitative population to avoid infinite accumulation of capital and convergence toward zero profit.

We have reviewed earlier empirical studies and found that the validity of wage-led growth has been mostly accepted. However, the empirical result of Onaran and Galanis (2013) have shown that profit-led growth could generate positive aggregate demand effects on some of the resource-rich countries such as China, India, South Africa and Australia while it generates negative impacts on the EU Area, the United States, Japan and Korea. We have also run the regression of GDP growth and real wage growth on labor productivity growth from East Asian countries' datasets. The causality test results accept the existence of causality from real wages to labor productivity in Korea and China but not in Japan. The reverse causality from labor productivity growth to real wage increase seems non-existent in all East Asian countries.

At the same time, we have to recognize that the merit of profit-led growth may not be easily demonstrated because it calls for empirical tests based on firms' long run data of profits and innovation and investments in human capital. Therefore, we can conclude that the debate on relative merits of wage-led growth and profit-led growth is far from being over.

Appendix

Table 7.A.1 Empirical test results of the Kaldor-Verdoorn Law

1. Kaldor (1967)	Industrial sectors of OECD 12 countries (manufacturing, electricity, gas, water etc., public service and construction) 1935–54, 1963–64 annual data
	(1) P = 0.888 + 0.446X R^2 = 0.847
	(0.060)
	(2) E = −.0888 + 0.554X R^2 = 0.893
	(0.060)
	(3) P = 0.527 + 0.356X + 0.048I R^2 = 0.880
	(0.079) (0.029)
	(4) P = 0.709 + 0.268X + 0.073I[1] R^2 = 0.960
	(0.047) (0.017)
	(5) X = 2.06 + 1.614E R^2 = 0.893
	(0.176)
	(6) X = 0.835 + 1.367E + 0.097I R^2 = 0.940
	(0.168) (0.037)
	(7) X = 0.937 + 1.320E + 1.105I[1] R^2 = 0.986
	(0.085) (0.018)
	(X = output growth rate, P = labor productivity growth rate, E = employment growth rate, I = aggregate investment/output rate)
	Estimates of Verdoorn coefficient
2. McCombie (2002: 106)	0.3–0.6
3. Storm and Naastepad (2008)	0.3–0.6
4. Hein and Tarassow (2010) (1960–2007)	0.3–0.6 (Europe) Lower than 0.3–0.6 (UK) 0.1–0.25 (the United States)

Notes: 1 OECD 11 countries' data except Canada

Source: Kaldor (1967), McCombie (2002), Storm and Naastepad (2008), Hein and Tarassow (2009), and Marquetti (2004).

Table 7.A.2 Summary of the multiplier effects at the national and global level

	The effect of a 1% increase in the profit share in only on country on private excess demand/Y	The effect of a 1%t increase in the profit share in only on country on % change in aggregate demand (A*multiplier)	The effect of a simultaneous 1% increase on private excess demand/Y (includes effects of changes in P_m)	The effect of a simultaneous 1% increase on the % change in aggregate demand (C*multiplier (including effects of Yrw))
	A	B	C	D
Euro area-12	−0.084	−0.133	−0.119	−0.245
UK	−0.025	−0.030	−0.107	−0.214
US	−0.388	−0.808	−0.426	−0.921
Japan	−0.014	−0.034	−0.043	−0.179
Canada	0.122	0.148	−0.020	−0.269
Australia	0.190	0.268	0.122	0.172
Turkey	−0.208	−0.459	−0.325	−0.717
Mexico	0.096	0.106	0.025	−0.111
Korea	−0.063	−0.115	−0.161	−0.864
Argentina	0.054	0.075	0.022	−0.103
China	1.574	1.932	1.289	1.115
India	0.018	0.040	−0.012	−0.027
South Africa	0.490	0.729	0.356	0.390

Source: Onaran and Galanis (2013), Table 13.

Table 7.A.3 Empirical tests on the effect of real wage on productivity growth

Author	Country (Period)	Empirical test result
1. Marquetti (2004)	United States (1869–1999)	Granger causality test: Increase in real wage → increase in labor productivity (o) Increase in real wage → increase in labor productivity (x)
2. Naastepad (2006)	Netherlands	1% increase in real wage → 0.52% increase in labor productivity
3. Storm and Naastepad (2009)	OECD-20 countries (1984–2004)	Restricted or adjusted labor market system → increase in productivity increase in real wage → increase in productivity (elasticity: 0.50–0.55)
4. Vergeer and Kleinknecht (2010–11)	OECD countries (1960–2004) Panel data	Strong labor market system → higher long-run growth increase in real wage → increase in productivity (elasticity: 0.31–0.39)
5. Hein and Tarassow (2009)	OECD-6 countries (1960–2007)	increase in real wage → increase in productivity (elasticity: 0.30)

Source: Lavoie and Stockhammer (2012: 21) and Marquetti (2004).

Bibliography

Acemoglu, D. 2008. *Introduction to Modern Economic Growth*. Princeton: Princeton University Press.

Aghion, P., and P. Bolton. 1997. "A Theory of Trickle-Down Growth and Development." *The Review of Economic Studies* 64(2): 151–172.

Arrow, K. J. 1962. "Economic Welfare and the Allocation of Resources for Invention." In *The Rate and Direction of Inventive Activity: Economic and Social Factors*. Princeton: Princeton University Press, pp. 609–626.

Arrow, K. J., H. B. Chenery, B. S. Minhas, and R. M. Solow. 1961. "Capital-Labor Substitution and Economic Efficiency." *The Review of Economics and Statistics*: 225–250.

Atkinson, A. B., T. Piketty, and E. Saez. 2009. "Top Incomes in the Long Run of History." *National Bureau of Economic Research*, No. w15408.

Banerjee, Abhijit V., and Andrew F. Newman. 1993. "Occupational Coice and the Pocess of Dvelopment." *Journal of political economy*, 101(2).

Baran, P., and P. Sweezy. 1966. *Monopoly Capital: An Essay on the American Social and Economic Order*, Modern Reader Paperbacks, New York and London.

Barro, Robert J., and Xavier Sala-i-Martin. 2004. *Economic Growth*. 2nd edition. Cambridge, MA: The MIT Press.

Becker, G. S., and R. J. Barro. 1986. "A Reformulation of the Economic Theory of Fertility." *National Bureau of Economic Research*, No. w1793.

Bhaduri, A. 1986. *Macroeconomics: The Dynamics of Commodity Production*. London: Macmillan.

Bhaduri, A., and S. Marglin. 1990. "Unemployment and the Real Wage: The Economic Basis for Contesting Political Ideologies." *Cambridge Journal of Economics* 14(4): 375–393.

Bleaney, M. F. 1976. *Underconsumption Theories: A History and Critical Analysis*. London: Lawrence and Wishart.

Blecker, R. A. 1989. "International Competition, Income Distribution and Economic Growth." *Cambridge Journal of Economics* 13(3): 395–412.

Blecker, Robert A. 2010. "Open Economy Models of Distribution and Growth." in E. Hein and E. Stockhammer (eds), *A Modern Guide to Keynesian Macroeconomics and Economic Policies*, Edward Elgar.

Boyer, R. 1988. *The Search for Labour Market Flexibility: The European Economies in Transition*. New York: Oxford University Press.

Cho, T., J. Kim, and P. Schreyer. 2015. "Measuring the Evolution of Korea's Material Living Standards 1980–2012." *Journal of Productivity Analysis* 44(2): 157–173.

Dixit, A. K., and J. E. Stiglitz. 1977. "Monopolistic Competition and Optimum Product Diversity." *The American Economic Review*: 297–308.

Dray, Mark, and Anthony P. Thirlwall. 2011. "The Endogeneity of the Natural Rate of Growth for a Selection of Asian Countries." *Journal of Post Keynesian Economics* 33(3): 451–468.

Dumenil, G., and D. Levy. 1993. *The Economics of the Profit Rate.* Aldershot: Edward Elgar.

Dutt, A. K. 1987. "Alternative Closures Again: A Comment on Growth, Distribution and Inflation." *Cambridge Journal of Economics* 11(1): 75–82.

Galor, O. 2005. "From Stagnation to Growth: Unified Growth Theory." *Handbook of Economic Growth* 1: 171–293.

Galor, O., and D. N. Weil. 2000. "Population, Technology, and Growth: From Malthusian Stagnation to the Demographic Transition and Beyond." *American Economic Review*: 806–828.

Galor, O., and J. Zeira. 1993. "Income Distribution and Macroeconomics." *The Review of Economic Studies* 60(1): 35–52.

Granger, C. 1969. "Investigating Causal Relations by Econometric Models and Cross-Spectral Methods." *Econometrica* 37: 99–126.

Griliches, Z., and J. Schmookler. 1963. "Inventing and Maximizing." *The American Economic Review*: 725–729.

Hein, E., and A. Tarassow. 2009. "Distribution, Aggregate Demand and Productivity Growth: Theory and Empirical Results for Six OECD Countries Based on a Post-Kaleckian Model." *Cambridge Journal of Economics*, bep066.

Hicks, J. 1932. *The Theory of Wages.* London: Macmillan.

Kaldor, N. 1957. "A Model of Economic Growth." *The Economic Journal*: 591–624.

Kaldor, N. 1961. *Capital Accumulation and Economic Growth.* London: Macmillan, 177–222.

Kaldor, N. 1967. *Strategic Factors in Economic Development, New York State School of Industrial and Labour Relations.* Ithaca: Cornell University.

Kalecki, M. 1971. "Selected Essays on the Dynamics of the Capitalist Economy 1933–1970." *CUP Archive.*

Keynes, J. M. 1936. *The General Theory of Employment, Interest and Money.* London: Macmillan.

Kurz, Heinz D. 1990. *Capital, Distribution and Effective Demand: Studies in the Classical Approach to Economic Theory*, Cambridge: Polity Press.

Lavoie, Marc. 1995. "The Kaleckian Model of Growth and Distribution and its Neo-Ricardian and Neo-Marxian Critiques." *Cambridge Journal of Economics*, 19, 789–818.

Lavoie, M., and E. Stockhammer. 2012. *Wage-Led Growth: Concept, Theories and Policies.* Basingstoke: Palgrave Macmillan.

León-Ledesma, M. A., and A. P. Thirlwall. 2002. "The Endogeneity of the Natural Rate of Growth." *Cambridge Journal of Economics* 26(4): 441–459.

Marquetti, A. 2004. "Do Rising Real Wages Increase the Rate of Labor-Saving Technical Change? Some Econometric Evidence." *Metroeconomica* 55(4): 432–441.

Marx, K. 1979. *Value, Price and Profit.* Chicago: Charles H. Kerr.

McCombie, John and A. P. Thirlwall. 1994. *Economic Growth and the Balance-of-Payments Constraint*, Palgrare Macmillan UK.

McCombie, J. 2002. "Increasing Returns and the Verdoorn Law From a Kaldorian Perspective." *JSL McCombie, M. Pugno, and B. Soro*: 64–114.

Naastepad, C. W. M. 2006. "Technology, Demand and Distribution: A Cumulative Growth Model With an Application to the Dutch Productivity Growth Slowdown." *Cambridge Journal of Economics*: 403–434.

Naastepad, C. W. M., and S. Storm. 2010. *Feasible Egalitarianism: Demand-Led Growth, Labour and Technology*. Cheltenham, UK and Northampton: Edward Elgar Publishing.

Nyeon, Kim Nak and Jong Il Kim. 2013. "A Reconsideration of Income Distribution Indicators in Korea", *Journal of Korean Economic Analysis*, Vol. 19 No.2, 1-50, Panel for Korean Economic Analysis and Korea Institute of Finance (in Korea).

Onaran, Ö., and G. Galanis. 2013. "Is Aggregate Demand Wage-Led or Profit-Led? A Global Model." In *Wage-Led Growth: An Equitable Strategy for Economic Recovery*. Basingstoke: Palgrave Macmillan, 71–99.

Piketty, T. 1997. "The Dynamics of the Wealth Distribution and the Interest Rate With Credit Rationing." *The Review of Economic Studies* 64(2): 173–189.

Piketty, T. 2014. *Capital in the Twenty-First Century*. The Belknap Press of Harvard University Press, Cambridge, MA.

Pyo, Hak K. 2015. "The Empirical Test of the Piketty Propositions Using Long-Run Statistical Data of Korea." *Korea Economic Forum* 8(1) (in Korean).

Pyo, Hak K. 2018 (forthcoming). "Chapter23 Productivity and Economic Development" in E. Grifell-Tatje, C. A. K. Lovell and R. C. Sickles (eds), *The Oxford Handbook of Productivity Analysis*, The Oxford Unversity Press.

Rowthorn, B. 1981. *Demand, Real Wages and Economic Growth*. London: North East London Polytechnic.

Samuelson, P. 1965. "A Theory of Induced Innovation Along Kennedy-Weisacker Lines." *Review of Economics and Statistics* 47: 343–356.

Schmookler, J. 1966. *Invention and Economic Growth*. Cambridge, MA, Havard University Press.

Schumpeter, J. A. 1934. *The Theory of Economic Development: An Inquiry Into Profits, Capital, Credit, Interest, and the Business Cycle*, vol. 55. New Brunswick, London: Transaction Publishers.

Setterfield, M., and J. Cornwall. 2002. "A Neo-Kaldorian Perspective on the Rise and Decline of the Golden Age." In M. Setterfield (ed.), *The Economics of the Demand-Led Growth: Challenging the Supply-Side Vision of the Long Run*. Cheltenham: Edward Elgar.

Solow, R. M. 1956. "A Contribution to the Theory of Economic Growth." *The Quarterly Journal of Economics* 70(1): 65–94.

Steindl, J. 1952. *Maturity and Stagnation in American Capitalism*, No. 4. New York: NYU Press.

Storm, S., and C. W. M. Naastepad. 2009. "Labor Market Regulation and Productivity Growth: Evidence for Twenty OECD Countries (1984–2004)." *Industrial Relations: A Journal of Economy and Society* 48(4): 629–654.

Taylor, Lance. 1991. *Income Distribution, Inflation, and Growth: Lectures on Structuralist Macroeconomic Theory*. The MIT Press, Cambridge, Massachusetts.

Taylor, L. 1988. *Varieties of Stabilization Experience: Towards Sensible Macroeconomics in the Third World*. Oxford: Clarendon Press.

Thirlwall, A. P., and J. McCombie. 1994. *Economic Growth and the Balance of Payments Constraint*. Grã-Bretanha (primeira publicação): Macmillan Press LTD.

Vergeer, R., and A. Kleinknecht. 2010. "The Impact of Labor Market Deregulation on Productivity: A Panel Data Analysis of 19 OECD Countries (1960–2004)." *Journal of Post Keynesian Economics* 33(2): 371–408.

Chapter 8

Declining rate of return on capital and the role of intangibles in Japan

An empirical study using Japanese KLEMS (JIP) database

Tsutomu Miyagawa, Miho Takizawa, Konomi Tonogi and Kyoji Fukao

Introduction

Since the Global Financial Crisis, many advanced countries have suffered from slow growth rates. In his lecture at the IMF in 2013, Summers warned that the United States and advanced countries in Europe might follow the Japanese economy and suffer from a similar long-term stagnation that Japan has seen since the collapse of the bubble economy in the United States.[1] He and his followers emphasized that the decline in capital formation and the real interest rate have led to the slow growth rate in advanced countries.[2]

As Summers pointed out, the slowdown in capital accumulation in Japan has been dramatic. Figure 8.1 shows the growth rates in private capital formation in the first three years of the recovery period in the 2000s. We find that the growth rate has gradually slowed down and the growth rate during the 'Abenomics' period is the lowest of the three recovery periods.

This slow capital accumulation led to stagnated growth in Japan. In particular, the gap in economic growth between Japan, the United States and East Asian countries in the 2000s is not a result of the gap in the contributions in labor input but of the gap in contributions in capital input as shown in growth accounting in Figures 8.2a, 8.2b, 8.2c 8.2d.

Before Summers pointed out the issues of the falling real interest rate and corporate profit rate, Japanese economists argued that it was the inefficiency of capital which led to the low real interest rate and profit rate. Ando et al. (2003) and Hayashi (2006) were critical of the fact that corporate savings in Japan were used for inefficient

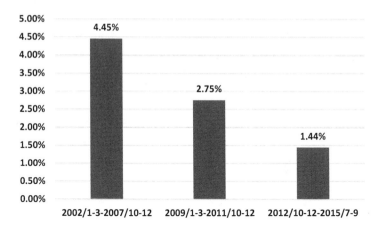

Figure 8.1 Annual growth rate in capital formation in the recovery periods in Japan

Source: System of National Accounts.

capital formation that induced low corporate profit. Based on the arguments by Ando et al. (2003) and Hayashi (2006), Saito (2008) argued that over-investment crowds out consumption and generates welfare loss. Fukao et al. (2016) also confirmed that the over-investment in the 1980s and the 1990s led to a high capital/output ratio and a low rate of return on capital. Miyagawa (2004, 2005) suggested that the low corporate profit rate in the 1990s was caused by a high labor share and low total factor productivity (TFP) growth.[3]

However, the discussions on the falling rate of return on capital have changed since the Global Financial Crisis. According to the Japanese KLEMS (Japan Industrial Productivity, JIP) Database, the real capital stock in Japan has fallen since the Global Financial Crisis despite the historically low interest rate and expanding monetary policy. Thwaites (2015) argued that the decrease in nominal investment under the falling real interest rate for the past two decades in the industrialized economies is caused by the following three factors. First, the price of capital has fallen rapidly. Second, households have increased their debt for holding residential assets and for consumption. Third, firms invest in intangibles more than in tangibles. Murase and Ando (2014) showed the possibility of

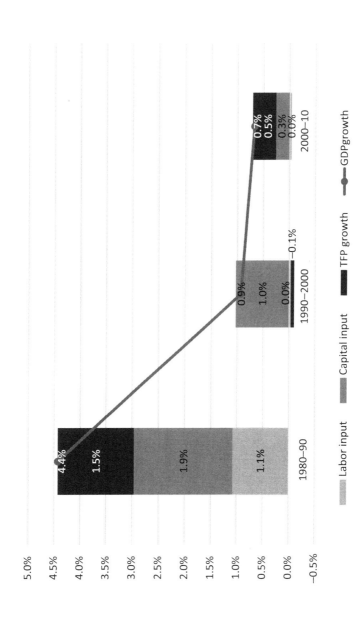

Figure 8.2a Growth accounting in Japan

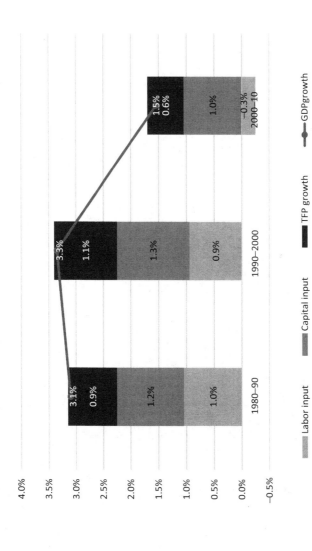

Figure 8.2b Growth accounting in the United States

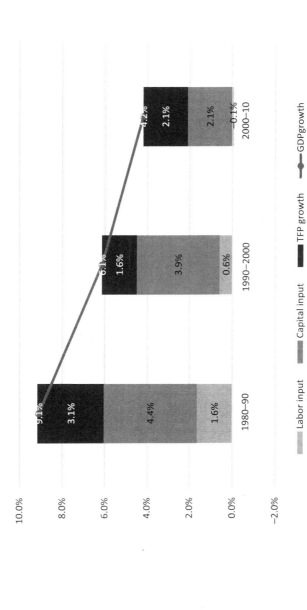

Figure 8.2c Growth accounting in Korea

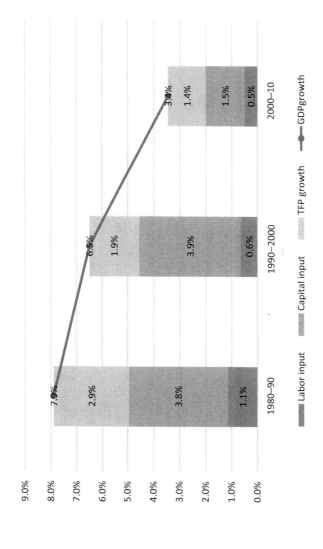

Figure 8.2d Growth accounting in the Republic of China

steady state where economic agents hold money instead of capital under weak governance. This allows for a high labor share and a zero interest rate. Benigno and Fornaro (2015) also show an equilibrium that represents a secular stagnation by combining a standard short-run Keynesian model and an endogenous growth model. In this equilibrium, underemployment and low potential growth coexist under zero interest rates and pessimistic expectation on future growth.

These studies in the 2010s imply that factor shares and innovations induced by R&D and other intangibles play crucial roles in falling real rates of interest or corporate profit rate. Then, we focus on long-term movements in rate of return on capital by using the JIP Database and examine whether wage rate and innovation factors affect rate of return on capital by estimating a modified factor price frontier model.[4]

Movements in rate of return on capital are broken down into capital/output ratio and capital share. We find that the capital/output ratio is on an upward trend as Fukao (2012) found. In particular, the capital/output ratio in the service sector is very high. Although capital share in the 2000s recovered from that in the 1990s, it was still lower than that in the 1980s. In addition, the relative variance of the average rate of return on capital in the service sector has become larger and the number of industries where we find negative rate of return has increased.

To be more precise, we estimate the modified factor price frontier model, which incorporates intangibles to the standard model, by using industry-level data and examine what kind of factors affect rate of return on capital. Estimation results show, first, that the increase in wage rate has negative impact on the rate of return on capital as we expect in the standard factor price frontier. Second, larger investment in IT and human resources leads to higher rate of return on capital. Third, in the service sector, the effects of investment in IT and human resources are more important than those of other factors. These results suggest, and the policy implication is, that the government should undertake a comprehensive innovation policy which not only stimulates investment in R&D but also promotes firms to utilize IT and human resources more effectively.

In the next section, we examine the movements in rate of return on capital, capital/output ratio and capital share by using the JIP Database. In the third section, we estimate modified factor frontier model to examine the determinants of the profit rate. In the last section, we summarize our results and show some policy implications.

Why has the rate of return on capital declined?

We show two types of real gross rate of return on capital in the market sector in Figure 8.3 by using the JIP database.[5] The first measure is the average real rate of return on capital. We obtain this measure by dividing the sum of the operating surplus and consumption of fixed capital by real capital stock.[6] The second measure is the marginal rate of return on capital (marginal product of capital = MPK), which is obtained by the following equation.

$$MPK = \frac{\partial Y}{\partial K} = \alpha * \frac{Y}{K} \tag{8.1}$$

Y represents value-added or output, K represents capital stock and α represents capital share. Then, we measure the marginal rate of return on capital by dividing capital share by capital/output (value-added) ratio.[7][8]

Figure 8.3 shows that both rates of return on capital in the 2000s were lower than those in the 1980s. However, the average rate of return was restored in the 2000s after its fall in the 1990s, although the marginal rates of return have been on a downward trend since the collapse of the bubble economy. Hence, the gap between the average and the marginal rate of return has widened in the 2000s. This gap implies that Japanese firms have concentrated on the businesses that earn high profits by restructuring after the financial crisis in Japan, while the rate of return on new investment has declined.

Following Equation 8.1, we break down the marginal rate of return into capital/output ratio and capital share. Figure 8.4 shows movements in capital/output ratio. Not only the capital/output ratio in the market sector but also the capital/output ratio in the manufacturing and the service sectors have been on an upward trend as Fukao et al. (2016) pointed out.[9] We find that the increase in the capital/output ratio in the service sector after the collapse of the bubble economy has led to the increase in the capital/output ratio in the market economy.

Figure 8.5 shows movements in capital share. Capital share in the market sector was greater than 30 percent in the 1980s. However, it has been on a downward trend and it was around 30 percent in the

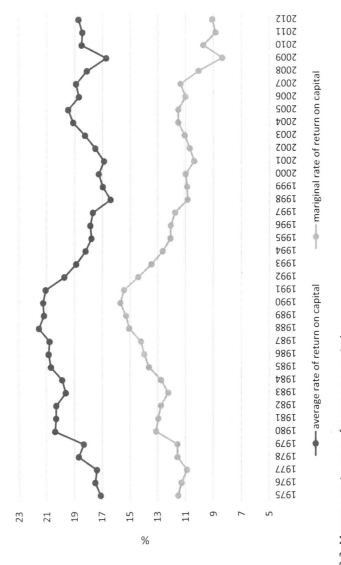

Figure 8.3 Movements in rate of return on capital

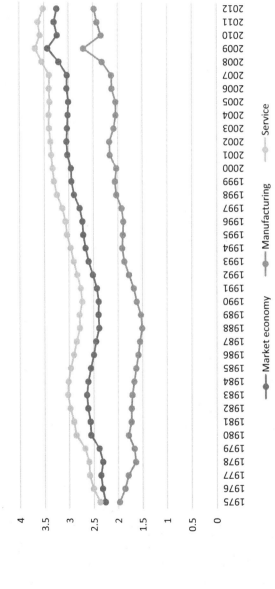

Figure 8.4 Capital/output ratio in Japan

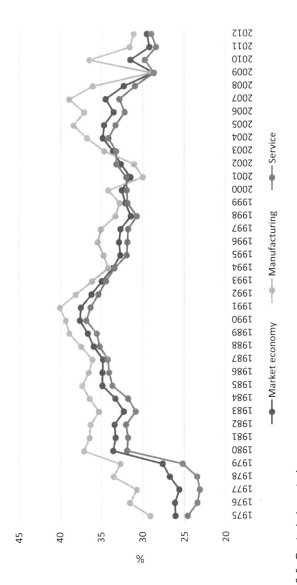

Figure 8.5 Capital share in Japan

2010s as Ando et al. (2003), Miyagawa (2004, 2005) pointed out. Capital shares in each sector show a different movement from that in the market sector. The capital share in the manufacturing sector seems to be cyclical. It was restored in the 2000s after its fall in the 1990s. On the other hand, the capital share in the service sector shows an upward trend. This upward trend may be generated by the rising share of irregular workers whose wages are cheaper than regular workers.

Figures 8.6a and 8.6b show the marginal rate of return on capital by industry in 1980 and 2012. We find not only that the number of industries with negative rates of return has increased but also there are vast differences in rate of return on capital by industry.[10] We show variances and relative standard deviations (=standard deviation/mean) in the average rate of return on capital in Table 8.1. In Table 8.1, variances in the rates of return in the service sector have become larger in the 21st century, while those in the market and the manufacturing sectors have decreased as the rates of return falls. The relative standard deviations in the service sector also have increased, which affects the increase of the relative standard deviations in the market economy.

Finally, we compare rate of return on capital in Japan with those in EU countries.[11] As EUKLEMS database does not show the rate of return at the aggregate level, we choose the rates of return on capital at the chemical, transportation, retail and information service industries (Figures 8.7a, 8.7b, 8.7c, 8.7d). In the four industries, the rates of return on capital in the Japanese industries are relatively low. However, the rates of return on capital in the EU countries declined drastically when the Global Financial Crisis occurred – especially, the rates of return on capital in the information service industry in Japan, Germany and the Netherlands in the late 2000s. The exceptions are rates of return on capital in the chemical and information service industries in the UK.

However, as the movements of rates of return on capital at the industry level are volatile, we are not able to make consistent explanations only by examining them. So, we will examine some factors that affect rates of return on capital through estimation using industry level data in Japan.

Estimating the factor price frontier

In this section, in order to establish the factors affecting the rates of return on capital, we empirically examine the factor price frontier

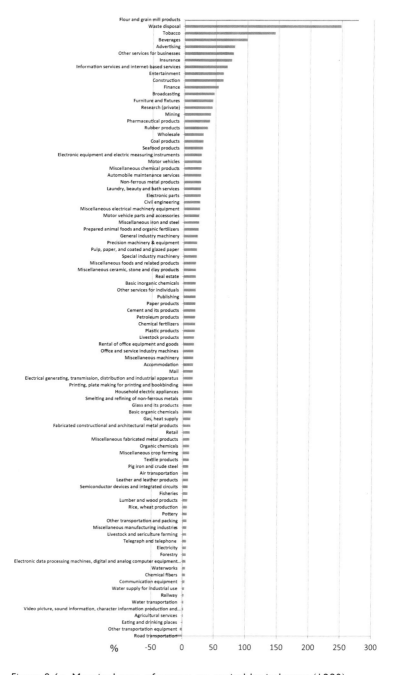

Figure 8.6a Marginal rate of return on capital by industry (1980)
Source: Authors' calculations using JIP Database 2015.

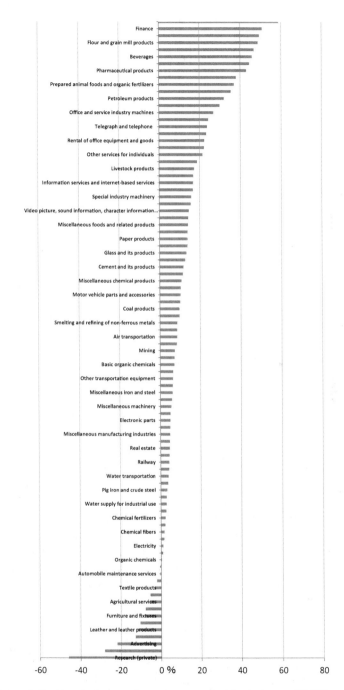

Figure 8.6b Marginal rate of return on capital by industry (2012)
Source: Authors' calculations using JIP Database 2015.

214 Tsutomu Miyagawa et al.

Table 8.1 Variances and relative standard deviations in the average rate of return on capital

		1990	2000	2012
Market economy	Variances	1179.8	652.3	453.2
	Relative S.D.	1.3	1.4	1.7
Manufacturing	Variances	1535.0	786.1	191.2
	Relative S.D.	1.3	1.4	1.1
Service	Variances	837.0	566.3	953.2
	Relative S.D.	1.1	1.3	2.0

Source: Authors' calculations using JIP Database 2015.

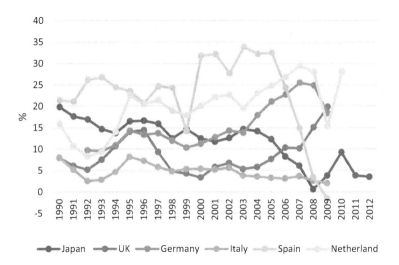

Figure 8.7a Rates of return on capital in the chemical industry

(FPF). Although Bruno and Sachs (1985) estimated the FPF considering material inputs to examine the effects of changes in oil price on the macroeconomy, we assume the following simple production function.[12]

$$Y = F(L, K; T) \tag{8.2}$$

Y is value-added, L is labor input, K is capital input and T is a technological factor.

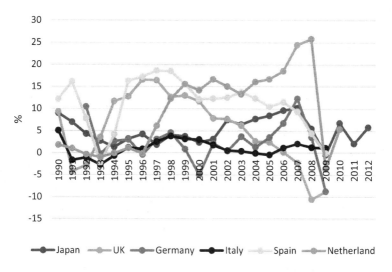

Figure 8.7b Rates of return on capital in the transportation equipment industry

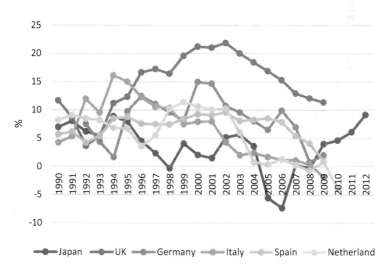

Figure 8.7c Rates of return on capital in the retail industry

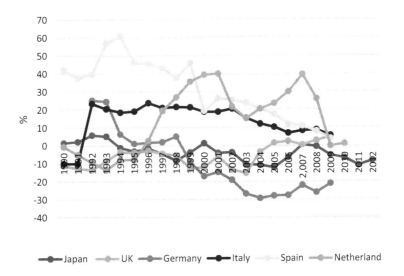

Figure 8.7d Rates of return on capital in the information service industry

When we assume that the production function is linearly homogeneous in factor inputs and firms minimize their costs, the following equation is obtained:

$$\ln r = a' - (\frac{\alpha}{\beta})\ln w + \lambda t + \delta j \tag{8.3}$$

In this expression, α and β are labor income share and capital income share, respectively.

Ln r and ln w denote the log of the real rate of return on capital, and the log of the real wage respectively. In order to account for the time-series components affecting Ln r, the model also contains t as the technology factor and j as the cyclical factor.

When we assume that the technological factor is positively correlated with intangibles such as IT, R&D and other intangibles, Equation 8.2 is rewritten as follows.

$$\ln r_{jt} = const. + a_1 \ln w_{jt} + a_2 \ln(\frac{IT_{jt}}{K^{IT}_{jt}})$$
$$+ a_3 \ln(\frac{RD_{jt}}{K^{RD}_{jt}}) + a_4 \ln(\frac{HR_{jt}}{K^{HR}_{jt}}) + a_5 \ln Y_{jt} + \mu_j + \eta_t + \varepsilon_{jt} \tag{8.4}$$

In this expression, IT and K^{IT} account for the capital formation (i.e., investments) in information technology and its capital stock, respectively while RD and K^{RD} denote the capital formation in R&D and its capital, respectively.[13] Furthermore, HR and K^{HR} are used to include the capital formation in human resources and its capital stock as the additional factors affecting FPF. Y is the log of value-added by industry as a control variable. Subscription j and t correspond to the industry and the time, while μ_j and η_t denote industry and year fixed effects.[14,15]

We include the additional variables in the right-hand side of the equation due to our presumption that productivity growth pushes up the FPF. As a proxy for productivity variable, IT, R&D and human capital investments are used. Such presumptions based on the discussion in Corrado et al. (2009) indicate that the contribution of intangible capital deepening, especially that of IT capital, to labor productivity growth is high in the US. In order to verify this presumption, we study the effects of intangibles on the rate of return on tangible capital through the estimation of the equation above.

Given the presumption that an increase in labor share (decline in capital share) would decrease the rate of return on capital, we predict the sign of a coefficient as $a_1 < 0$. Then, $a_2 < 0$, $a_3 < 0$, $a_4 < 0$ can also be predicted because an increase in intangible investments is expected to shift up the FPF. Thus, intangibles have positive effects on the rate of return on tangible capital.

The data we use in the present study is obtained from the JIP 2015 database. Note that our analysis focuses on the market economy over the periods from 1985 to 2012, which consists of 92 industries. Table 8.A.1 in the Appendix provides a more detailed description of our data set. Table 8.2 shows the summary statistics for the variables used in our analysis.

For the rate of return on capital, which we use for our dependent variables, both the marginal and average rates of return are employed. Table 8.3 shows the results of the industry-level fixed-effect estimation for the market economy. A dependent variable in column (1) is marginal rate of return on capital and a dependent variable in column (2) is average rate of return on capital. First, we can see that the coefficient on wage is negative and significant in both estimations, which is consistent with our expectation. Second, the coefficient on the IT investment ratio is positive and significant in both estimations. Third, the coefficient on the R&D investment ratio is negative and significant, suggesting that R&D investments

Table 8.2 Summary statistics: market economy 1985–2012

Variables	Definitions	Mean	Std. Dev	Min	Max	Obs
r_marginal	Marginal rate of return on capital	22.674	26.287	0.022	237.888	1,762
r_average	Average rate pf return on capital	22.431	30.083	0.027	385.338	1,762
w	Wage	3.438	3.194	0.456	34.304	1,762
IT/K_{IT}	Capital formation in IT over IT capital stock	0.360	0.061	0.144	0.609	1,762
RD/K_{RD}	Capital formation in R&D over R&D capital stock	0.185	0.069	0.034	0.577	1,762
HR/K_{HR}	Capital formation in Human Resources over Human Resources capital stock	0.378	0.061	0.195	0.560	1,762
Y	Value-added	3781351	5651996	47902.62	3.87E+07	1,762
ln r_marginal	Log of marginal rate of return on capital	−1.899	0.954	−8.422	0.867	1,762
ln r_average	Log of average rate pf return on capital	−1.921	0.947	−8.208	1.349	1,762
ln w	Log of wage	1.044	0.547	−0.785	3.535	1,762
ln IT/K_{IT}	Log of capital formation in IT over IT capital stock	−1.037	0.170	−1.939	−0.495	1,762
ln RD/K_{RD}	Log of capital formation in R&D over R&D capital stock	−1.752	0.374	−3.386	−0.550	1,762
ln HR/K_{HR}	Log of capital formation in R&D over R&D capital stock	−0.987	0.164	−1.635	−0.580	1,762
ln Y	Log of value-added	14.455	1.164	10.777	17.472	1,762

Notes: All the variables are converted into values in constant prices for the year 2000.

Source: We obtained the data from JIP2015 database.

Table 8.3 Basic estimation results in the market economy

Dependent variable	Marginal rate of return on capital			Average rate of return on capital		
	(1)			(2)		
	Coef.	Std. Err		Coef.	Std. Err	
ln w	−0.661	0.058	***	−1.208	0.060	***
ln IT/K_{IT}	0.124	0.067	*	0.169	0.069	**
ln RD/K_{RD}	−0.176	0.041	***	−0.134	0.043	***
ln HR/K_{HR}	0.216	0.094	**	0.311	0.097	***
ln Y	1.407	0.048	***	1.314	0.050	***
Constant	−17.181	0.662	***	−14.893	0.687	***
	Fixed-effects model			Fixed-effects model		
Number of obs	1,762			1,762		
Number of groups	70			70		
Prob > F	0			0		
R-sq:						
within	0.5515			0.515		
between	0.008			0.0001		
overall	0.0523			0.0231		

Source: Authors' calculations using JIP Database 2015.

do have negative impacts on the rate of return on capital, which is highly counter-intuitive. Fourth, nonetheless, the coefficient on the human resource (HR) investment ratio is positive and significant, suggesting that larger investment in HR in fact leads to higher rates of return on capital.

The negative coefficient on the R&D investment is a puzzling result. However, as knowledge capital which is accumulated by R&D investment contributes to the increase in future capital, it may not contribute to the short-run profitability.

Given these baseline results, we implement an additional subsample analysis. Namely, we have divided our sample into the manufacturing and service sectors. In Table 8.4, the estimation results in the manufacturing sector contrast to those in the service sector. While the coefficient of real wage in the manufacturing sector is negative and significant, that in the service sector is positive and insignificant. While coefficients of intangibles do not show expected signs in the manufacturing sector, those of IT and human resources in the

Table 8.4 Estimation results by industry

Dependent variable: Marginal rate of return on capital

	Manufacturing sector			Service sector		
	(1)			(2)		
	Coef.	Std. Err		Coef.	Std. Err	
ln w	−0.880	0.062	***	0.136	0.249	
ln IT/K_{IT}	−0.006	0.071		0.434	0.233	*
ln RD/K_{RD}	−0.070	0.046		−0.401	0.121	***
ln HR/K_{HR}	−0.006	0.097		1.399	0.346	***
ln Y	1.618	0.054	***	1.057	0.206	***
Constant	−19.692	0.730	***	−12.725	3.119	***
	Fixed-effects model			Fixed-effects model		
Number of obs	1,335			274		
Number of groups	52			12		
Prob > F	0			0		
R-sq:						
within	0.6429			0.3725		
between	0.0052			0.0418		
overall	0.0327			0.0589		

Source: Authors' calculations using JIP Database 2015.

service sector are positive and significant as in the market economy. The estimation results suggest that intangibles, especially IT and human resources, are crucial factors for profitability improvement in the service sector, because the shares of investment in IT and human resources in the service sector are very large as shown in Figure 8.8.

From the estimate results based on the sample covering the whole market economy and the service sector, we found that the coefficients on human resources investment ratio (a_4) are positive and significant. This suggests that growth in human resources is crucial for the rise of the rate of return on capital. Given Figure 8.9, which shows that the investments in human resources from 1980 to 2012 experienced the rapid decrease in investments in human resources since 2000, we can conjecture that the rapid decrease in investments in human resources might have led to the low rate of return on capital.

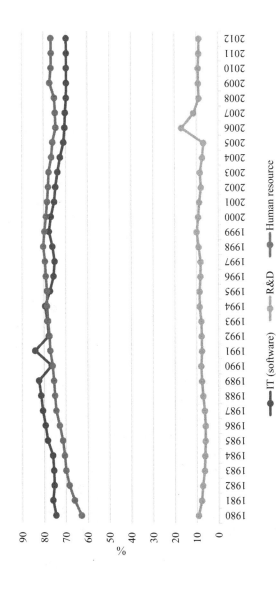

Figure 8.8 Share of the service sector in intangible investment

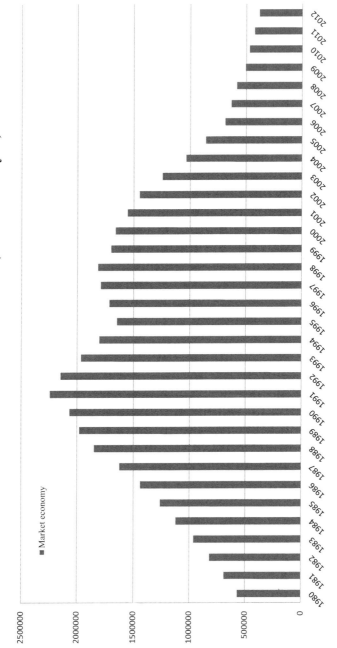

Figure 8.9 Investments in human resources, 1980–2012

Conclusion and policy implications

Since the collapse of the bubble economy, the Japanese economy has suffered from long-term stagnation. Advanced countries in the United States and Europe are following the Japanese experiences after the Global Financial Crisis. One of the main issues on long-term stagnation is the low growth rate induced by the stagnated capital formation under low interest rate. In this paper, we focus on the movements in the real rate of return on capital to understand secular stagnation by using the Japanese KLEMS (JIP) database.

First, we break down the rate of return on capital into the capital/output ratio and the capital share. We find that the capital/output ratio has an upward trend. In particular, the capital output ratios in the service sector are very high, which indicates that service industries have accumulated inefficient capital stock. These findings are consistent with the argument in Fukao et al. (2016). On the other hand, the capital share seems to be cyclical, but the capital share in the 2000s is lower than that in the 1980s as Ando et al. (2003) and Miyagawa (2004, 2005) pointed out. The downward trend in the rate of return on capital leads to the number of industries with negative profit rate. In addition, the greater relative standard deviation in the service sector indicates that industry-level factors affect the dispersion of rate of return on capital in this sector. When we compare the rate of return in Japan with those in the EU countries in the four industries, we find that the rate of return on capital in Japan is relatively low in many industries. However, rates of return in many industries in the EU countries declined dramatically when the Global Financial Crisis occurred.

Based on these findings, we estimate a profit function based on the factor price frontier developed by Bruno and Sachs (1985). In factor price frontier theory, the profit rate is affected by factor prices and productivity. As determinants of productivity, we choose some intangibles such as IT investment and R&D investment. As an important feature associated with the Japanese economy, while the level of IT investment and R&D investment are relatively high in Japan, the rate of return on capital, which could potentially benefit from such high investments, is low. In order to clarify the mechanism governing this feature, we empirically examine the factor price frontier through the estimation of the extended version of the model in Bruno and Sachs (1985).

From the obtained estimate results, first, we can see that higher real wage is associated with lower rate of return as expected from the shape of standard factor price frontier. This might imply that a policy measure intending to directly increase wages does not necessarily stimulate capital formation. Second, a puzzling result, R&D investments have negative or not significant effect on the rate of return on tangible capital. This implies that R&D investment may contribute to short-run profitability negatively, although it contributes to future profitability. Third, an important result, strong positive effects associated with investment in IT and human resources on the rate of return on capital can be seen in the results for the market economy. It is important to note that such a result is confirmed despite the rapid decline in the investments on human resources since 2000 in Japan shown in Figure 8.9.[16] Such a result provides some support for government to encourage expenditure in human resources.

The arguments by Benigno and Fornaro (2015) that we are not able to escape from aggregate demand policy and need aggressive innovation policy to escape from a stagnation trap are associated with policy implications from our estimation results. The aggregate demand policy implemented through an increase in wages is insufficient to induce aggressive capital formation. We need a bold innovation policy that includes not only accumulation in human resources but also organizational reforms that vitalize the complementary effect between tangibles and intangibles.

Appendix

Table 8.A.1 Data definition

Variables	Definitions	Constructions
r_marginal	Marginal rate of return on capital	Capital share × (Value-added/ Net capital stock)
r_average	Average rate of return on capital	(Operating surplus + Consumption of fixed capital)/ Net capital stock
w	Wage rate	Labor share × value-added/ Man-hours
IT	Capital formation in information technology (IT)	See Chun et al. (2017)
K_{IT}	IT capital stock	See Chun et al. (2017)
RD	Capital formation in R&D over R&D capital stock	See Chun et al. (2017)
K_{RD}	R&D capital stock	See Chun et al. (2017)
HR	Capital formation in human resources	See Chun et al. (2017)
K_{HR}	Human resources capital stock	See Chun et al. (2017)

Notes: All the variables are converted into values in constant prices for the year 2000.

Source: We obtained the data from JIP 2015 database.

Notes

1 See also Summers (2015).
2 Solow (2014) also discussed the secular stagnation induced by the low capital accumulation on the IMF website (www.imf.org/external/pubs/ft/fandd/2014/09/nobels.htm, accessed 17 July 2017).

3 Measuring the equilibrium interest rate in Japan, Kamata (2009) did not find clear evidence that the rate fell. As for the measurement in the long-term equilibrium interest rate in the United States, see Hamilton et al. (2015).
4 Many studies on investment behavior in Japan suggest that profit rate (or Tobin's Q indicating future profitability) is the most important determinant of capital formation. See Hayashi (2000).
5 The JIP database is published on the website of Research Institute of Economy, Trade and Industry (www.rieti.go.jp/en/database/JIP2015/index.html, accessed 17 July 2017)
6 Operating surplus and consumption of fixed capital are deflated by the investment deflator by industry.
7 The KLEMS type database like the JIP database assumes that the marginal rate of return on capital in each asset is captured as the capital service of this asset. This assumption implies that each capital is utilized efficiently. However, as Basu and Fernald (2001), Miyagawa et al. (2006) showed the capital utilization rate fluctuates in the short run. In addition, Jorgenson et al. (2007) and Fukao et al. (2012) showed that there is a gap between rate of return on capital at the aggregate level and that at the industry level due to the misallocation of capital input.
8 In Figure 8.3, Y is measured by value-added.
9 The service sector in our paper consists of the non-manufacturing industries except agriculture, forestry, fishing and mining industries in the market sector.
10 Nomura (2004) also found large variances in rates of return on capital by industry. As we use the JIP database, the rate of return on capital is measured by activity base. Firms combine some of the activities listed in JIP database.
11 We obtain the EUKLEMS data updated in March 2011 on the following website: www.euklems.net/, accessed 17 July 2017. In the EUKLEMS database, as the marginal rate of return on capital is endogenously determined, we compare only average rate of return at the industry level. In addition, as the rate of return in the EU KLEMS database does not include capital consumption, we measure rate of return on capital without capital consumption in Japan.
12 The simple FPF theory is explained in Chapter 2 in Bruno and Sachs (1985).
13 Note that the 'IT investments' used in the estimations do not account for the investment on hardware associated with IT but only for the investments in software.
14 In order to explicitly focus on the rate of return on tangible capital, we subtract the contribution of custom software from the rate of return on capital, which originally includes the contribution of intangibles.
15 According to the Monthly Labor Survey compiled by Ministry of Health, Labor and Welfare, real wage has been declining since 2000. Contrary to this widely used statistic, the data series accounting for real wage used in the present paper, which is obtained from JIP database, shows the increasing trend over the period. The discrepancy between these data series is partly due to the inclusion of the income associated with self-employed in the JIP database.

16 Fukao and Otaki (1993) and Otaki (1995) provided a model where conventional capital formation is associated with human capital accumulation. Otaki and Yaginuma (2014) emphasized that skill in human capital is crucial for firm growth.

Bibliography

Ando, Albert, Dimitris Christelis, and Tsutomu Miyagawa. 2003. "Inefficiency of Corporate Investment and Distortion of Saving Behavior in Japan." In Magnus Blomstrom, Jennifer Corbett, Fumio Hayashi, and Anil Kashyap (eds.), *Structural Impediments to Growth in Japan*. Chicago: The University of Chicago Press.

Basu, Susanto, and John Fernald. 2001. "Why Is Productivity Procyclical? Why Do We Care?" In Charles Hulten, Edwin R. Dean, and Michael J. Harper (eds.), *New Developments in Productivity Analysis*. Chicago: The University of Chicago Press.

Benigno, Geanluca, and Luca Fornaro. 2015. "Stagnation Traps." Paper presented at the *IMF Conference on Secular Stagnation, Growth, and Real Interest Rate*, Florence, Italy, June 18–19.

Bruno, Michael, and Jeffery Sachs. 1985. *Economics of Worldwide Stagflation*. Cambridge, MA: Harvard University Press.

Chun, Hyunbae, Tsutomu Miyagawa, Hak Kil Pyo, and Konomi Tonogi. 2017. "Do Intangibles Contribute to Productivity Growth in East Asian Countries? Evidence from Japan and Korea." in Dale W. Jorgenson, Kyoji Fukao, and Marcel P. Timmer (eds.), *The World Economy Growth or Stagnation?*. Cambridge: Cambridge University Press.

Corrado, Carol, Charles Hulten, and Daniel Sichel. 2009. "Intangible Capital and U.S. Economic Growth." *Review of Income and Wealth* 55: 658–660.

Fornaro, L. 2015. "Financial Crises and Exchange Rate Policy." *Journal of International Economics* 95(2): 202–215.

Fukao, Kyoji, Kenta Ikeuchi, Hyeog Ug Kwon, YoungGak Kim, Tatsuji Makio, and Miho Takizawa. 2016. "The Structural Causes of Japan's Lost Decades." in Dale W. Jorgenson, Kyoji Fukao, and Marcel P. Timmer (eds.), *The World Economy Growth or Stagnation?*. Cambridge: Cambridge University Press.

Fukao, Kyoji. 2012. *Lost Two Decades and the Japanese Economy*. Tokyo: Nihon Keizaisinbun Publishing Company (in Japanese).

Fukao, Kyoji, Tsutomu Miyagawa, Hak Kil Pyo, and Keun Hee Rhee. 2012. "Estimates of Total Factor Productivity, the Contribution of ICT, and Resource Reallocation Effects in Japan and Korea." In Matilde Mas and Robert Stehrer (eds.), *Industrial Productivity in Europe Growth and Crisis*. Cheltenham: Edward Elgar.

Fukao, Kyoji, and Masayuki Otaki. 1993. "Accumulation of Human Capital and the Business Cycle." *Journal of Political Economy* 101: 73–99.

Hamilton, James D., Ethan S. Harris, Jan Hatzius, and Kenneth D. West. 2015. "The Equilibrium Real Funds Rate: Past, Present, and Future." Paper presented at the *IMF Conference on Secular Stagnation, Growth, and Real Interest Rate*, Florence, Italy, 18–19 June.

Hayashi, Fumio. 2000. "The Cost of Capital, Q, and the Theory of Investment Demand." In Lawrence Lau (ed.), *Econometrics Vol. 2, Econometrics and the Cost of Capital*. Cambridge, MA: MIT Press.

Hayashi, Fumio. 2006. "The Over-Investment Hypothesis." In Lawrence R. Klein (ed.), *Long-Run Growth and Short-Run Stabilization: Essays in Memory of Albert Ando*. Cheltenham: Edward Elgar.

Jorgenson, Dale, Mun S. Ho, John Samuels, and Kevin Stiroh. 2007. "The Industry Origins of the American Productivity Resurgence." *Economic Systems Research* 19: 229–252.

Kamata, Koichiro. 2009. "On the Equilibrium Real Interest Rate in Japan." In Kyoji Fukao (ed.), *Macro Economy and Industrial Structure*. Tokyo: Keio University Press (in Japanese).

Miyagawa, Tsutomu. 2004. "Long-Term Stagnation in the Japanese Economy From the Viewpoint of the Supply Side." In Koichi Hamada and Akiyoshi Horiuchi (eds.), *Economic Crisis in Japan*. Tokyo: Nihon Keizai Shimbunsha (in Japanese).

Miyagawa, Tsutomu. 2005. *Economic Analysis of Long-Tern Slumps: Structural Change and Globalization*. Tokyo: The University of Tokyo Press (in Japanese).

Miyagawa, Tsutomu, Yukie Sakuragawa, and Miho Takziawa. 2006. "Productivity and Business Cycles in Japan: Evidence From Japanese Industry Data." *The Japanese Economic Review* 57: 161–186.

Murase, Hideaki, and Koichi Ando. 2014. "Long-Term Stagnation in Japan and Structural Change in Capital Accumulation." In Akiyoshi Horiuchi, Masaharu Hanazaki, and Junichi Nakamura (eds.), *The Japanese Economy: Financial Development and Corporate Behavior in a Changing Environment*. Tokyo: The University of Tokyo Press (in Japanese).

Otaki, Masayuki. 1995. *Theory of Business Cycles A Structural Analysis of the Contemporary Japanese Economy*. Tokyo: The University of Tokyo Press (in Japanese).

Otaki, Masayuki, and Hisashi Yaginuma. 2014. "Conflict Between Management Rights and Firm Growth." In Akiyoshi Horiuchi, Masaharu Hanazaki, and Junichi Nakamura (eds.), *The Japanese Economy: Financial Development and Corporate Behavior in a Changing Environment*. Tokyo: The University of Tokyo Press (in Japanese).

Saito, Makoto. 2008. "On Substitutability between Household Consumption and Capital Formation." In Kazumi Asako, Shinsuke Ikeda, Hidehiko Ichimura, and Hideshi Ito (eds.), Current Issues in Modern Economics 2008. Tokyo: Toyo Keizai Shimposha (in Japanese).

Solow, Robert. 2014. "Secular Stagnation." Presented at the IMF website. www.imf.org/external/pubs/ft/fandd/2014/09/nobels.htm, accessed 17 July 2017.

Summers, Lawrence. 2015. "Demand Side Secular Stagnation." *American Economic Review Papers and Proceedings* 105(5): 60–65.

Thwaites, Gregory. 2015. "Why Are Real Interest Rates So Low? Secular Stagnation and the Relative Price of Capital Goods." Paper presented at the *IMF Conference on Secular Stagnation, Growth, and Real Interest Rate*, Florence, Italy, 18–19 June.

Chapter 9

The industry-level productivity of Taiwan in 1981–2010

Evidence from Taiwan KLEMS database

Yih-ming Lin, Tsu-tan Fu, Hsing-chun Lin, and Wei-Hsin Kong

Introduction

Taiwan has experienced extraordinary economic growth since the 1960s. Its gross domestic product (GDP) average annual growth rate was higher than 8 percent during the period 1961–90, which corresponds to the Taiwan Economic Miracle (Krugman 1994; Young 1992, 1994, 1995). Taiwan's economic growth slowed down in the late 1990s and become sluggish in the 2000s as a result of a sequence of severe negative impacts from the Asian financial crisis, the worldwide economic recession after the dot-com bubble, the recent Global Financial Crisis, and Europe's latest financial debt crisis. In addition, strong competition from newly industrialized and emerging economies also cut into the profit margins of Taiwan's information and communications technology (hereinafter ICT) industries. The GDP growth rate of Taiwan dropped to 3.8 percent during 2000–10. From the historical evidence, Taiwan has a successful story on economic growth in the past decades, which may be attributed to appropriate industrial policies taken by the government at different developmental stages. It has successfully developed and modernized its economy to near-Western levels in a short period. On the other hand, the economic development of Taiwan has been stagnated by severe challenges, such as the Global Financial Crisis, the rise of mainland China, and the cross-strait relation. It is thus important and necessary to investigate the key drivers behind Taiwan's diversified economic performance at the industrial level during each time period.

As productivity is often regarded as the main engine for long-term economic growth, it is equally crucial to examine the major factors affecting changes in a country's economic growth in the past decades. A qualitative description of the major productivity policies and movements taken in Taiwan under different time periods is needed before discussing the issues and challenges in improving future productivity. The growth accounting approach is able to identify the source of growth for an economy. In the productivity literature on Taiwan's industries, most studies focus on firm level productivity in a specific industry, such as the banking industry (Chen and Yeh 2000; Huang and Fu 2009; Huang et al. 2014) and hotel industry (Chen and Soo 2007; Yu and Chen 2016). There have been few studies regarding the aggregate economic productivity of Taiwan's economy, except Chang and Luh (2000) and Fu and Lin (2015). Chang and Luh (2000) employed the Malmquist index to identify the sources of productivity growth in ten Asian economies using national level data, including Taiwan. Fu and Lin (2015) identified drivers of economic growth in Taiwan over the last 50 years and found that both TFP and the labor productivity index increased steadily over time, but the magnitude of labor productivity growth has been higher than TFP growth in the last decades. Furthermore, it is hard to find the seminal works discussing the productivities of the industry level for Taiwan's economy.

This paper aims to improve our understanding of this country's economic growth performance at the industry level during the past three decades (1981–2010) based on data availability. To reach this purpose, we construct the Taiwan KLEMS Database, in which the economy is divided into 31 industries based on the Asia KLEMS manual (Pyo et al. 2012). Following the methodology developed by Jorgenson and Griliches (1967), Jorgenson et al. (1987) and Jorgenson et al. (2005) and the Asia KLEMS manual (Pyo et al. 2012), we decompose output growth into contributions from capital (K), labor (L), and intermediate inputs (energy (E), materials (M), and services (S)) as well as total factor productivity (TFP). The KLEMS approach has been adopted to analyze the comparisons of multi-year, multi-country origin of economic growth in developed countries, such as the United States (Jorgenson, Gollop, and Fraumeni 1987; Jorgenson et al. 2005, 2007), Europe (Timmer et al. 2010; O'Mahony and Timmer 2009), and Japan (Jorgenson et al. 1987; Jorgenson and Nomura 2007; Fukao et al. 2011). We further conduct cross-period and cross-industry comparisons on the structures of industry output growth and the origin of productivity growth in Taiwan.

The structure of this paper is outlined as follows. Section 2 briefly sketches Taiwan's industrial development and related policies. Section 3 introduces the methodology used with some descriptions on data resources and variables employed. Section 4 analyzes the structure of Taiwanese industry based on value-added industry weight and growth rate. Section 5 conducts empirical cross-industry and cross-period comparisons on the sources of output growth analyses. The paper ends with some concluding remarks.

Taiwan's main industrial development strategies

Taiwan's economic development took off in the 1960s. In the beginning, the focus was on light industries, whereby the government policy targeted the development of these industries for import substitution, achieving an average high annual GDP growth rate of over 10.2 percent, which is called the 'import substitution' stage. In the 1970s, heavy and chemical industries grew rapidly due to the government's export promotion policy, which is called the 'export expansion' stage. With cheap production costs and the availability of a high-quality labor force prior to the 1980s, Taiwan's export expansion policy was successfully pursued. Annual GDP growth rates reached 9.27 percent on average during the period 1971–80, as shown in Figure 9.1.

Since 1980, Taiwan has encountered and overcome a considerable amount of challenges. In political terms, Taiwan became a truly democratic society with the appearance of a powerful opposition party, thus making Taiwanese society more diversified. In the economic arena, the exchange rate of New Taiwan dollars (NT$) strongly appreciated from NT$40 per US$1 in 1985 to NT$25 per US$1 in 1992. That upward trend in the value of Taiwan's currency caused inflation and asset bubbles. The stock market soared to new highs and the real estate market rose dramatically. As Taiwan's low-cost wages began to gradually increase, a large number of labor-intensive industries lost their comparative advantage in the middle of the 1980s. In order to survive, manufacturers were forced to move their production bases to Southeast Asia or to mainland China.

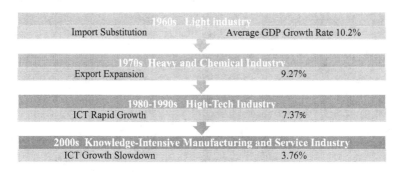

Figure 9.1 Overview of Taiwan's industrial development
Source: Summarised in this study.

Economic liberalization and internationalization

In order to solve the increasing trade disputes with the United States due to the economic imbalance, in the early 1980s the Taiwan government implemented a policy of economic liberalization, which included trade liberalization, the lifting of foreign exchange rate controls, and deregulation of its financial sector. In 1991, the government approved the establishment of 15 new private commercial banks, while several new private banks were set up through the reorganization of trust companies and credit cooperatives. This brought about a rapid increase in the number of commercial banks in Taiwan. Furthermore, some new areas of business for banks, such as commercial papers and short-term certificates, were allowed in the financial market.

With the aforementioned gradual increase in labor cost and land cost, many large firms that lost their competitiveness in traditional manufacturing industries moved overseas starting from the late 1980s. These manufacturers invested in mainland China and Southeast Asian countries, such as Vietnam, Indonesia, Thailand, Philippines, Malaysia, etc. The industries that moved their production overseas included paper and plastics, basic metals, textile products, garments, fur and leather goods, wood and bamboo products, rubber products, and other labor-intensive industries. This increase in Taiwan's foreign direct investment (FDI) resulted in major structural changes to the country's economic development.

The manufacturing sectors kept decreasing, while service sectors started to rise.

ITRI and technical support of NSTP

In order to maintain continued growth, the government's industrial policy turned toward a greater emphasis on upgrading industrial technology, with capital- and technology-intensive industries replacing the more labor-intensive industries. Founded and sponsored by the Taiwan government, the Industrial Technology Research Institute (ITRI) is a non-profit R&D organization engaging in applied research and technical services. ITRI's main tasks are the undertaking of industry-research technology and product R&D, along with the diffusion of the results of their work among private manufacturers. ITRI provides technical support and services for small and medium enterprises (SMEs). With the support of the National Science and Technology Project (NSTP), ITRI has gradually grown bigger and stronger.

The main objective of NSTP is to encourage industry to undertake R&D. NSTP promotes the development of ICT industries, fosters the upgrading of traditional industries (modernization and automation), establishes the basic infrastructure for industrial development, improves the efficient use of resources, and solves common problems shared by industries. ITRI and NSTP both carry out R&D work and transfer the results to private manufacturers, thus making a significant, impressive contribution to industrial upgrading. By disseminating both technology and talent, ITRI has played a vital role in transforming Taiwan's economy from a labor-intensive industry to a high-tech industry. Numerous well-known, high-tech companies in Taiwan, such as the global leaders in the semiconductor industry, TSMC and UMC, can trace their origins to ITRI.

The establishment of HSIP

Once the first oil crisis happened in the 1970s, the government realized that Taiwan's industrial development was based too much on a labor-intensive structure. The government fully understood the necessity for pursuing a policy to develop high-tech, high value-added industries. In order to attract investment from foreign hi-tech manufacturers, the government realized the need to construct a suitable investment environment. The Hsinchu Science-based Industrial Park (HSIP) was therefore founded for high-tech industries targeting ICT products and was established similarly to Silicon Valley in California. No one can doubt HSIP's contribution to Taiwan's economic development and its major impact on stimulating the development of ICT industries.

Firms located within HSIP enjoy tax incentives and tariff exemptions and deductions, which are the main factors attracting companies to invest and set up inside the Park. In addition, HSIP helps in the diffusion of technology by encouraging manufacturers to recognize and reap the benefits of congregating together. In 1997, there were 245 companies located in the Park, employing a total of 68,410 workers. Up to date, more than 400 high-tech companies with more than 120,000 workers, mainly involved in the semiconductor, computer, telecommunication, and optoelectronics industries, have been established in the park. Its 400 technology companies accounted for 10 percent of Taiwan's GDP in 2007. The government policy of subsidizing research and development (R&D) and sponsoring cooperative research has certainly helped to heighten the rapid technological progress in the high-tech industries, which grew quickly during the 1980s and then became the dominant business sector in the 1990s.

Tax incentives under the statute of upgrading industries

In the mid-1980s, with the appreciation of Taiwan's currency, labor and land costs began to rise, making labor-intensive industries lose their competitiveness. With the need to accelerate the process of industrial upgrading, improve products' value-added, and help domestic firms' competitiveness, the 'Statute of Upgrading Industries' was passed and implemented on January 1, 1991. The main contents of the statute are provisions for tax incentives (tax credits, tax exemptions, and tax deferrals) to encourage manufacturers to undertake R&D, to implement automation, and to promote the development of ICT industries.

Promotion of the semiconductor industry

In 1976, 37 young engineers were dispatched to the US to undergo training. These young engineers not only brought back technology, but also established a Complementary Metal Oxide on Silicon (CMOS) plant at one of the ITRI laboratories. The government invested in excess of NT$400 million in the development of the domestic semiconductor industry and signed various agreements with foreign semiconductor manufacturers, such as RCA, for technology transfer and personnel training during the late 1970s. In addition, the government also directed plans to bring together private sector capital and to transfer technology to private companies. During the 1980s, the government directed the establishment of United Microelectronic Corporation (UMC) and Taiwan Semiconductor Manufacturing Company (TSMC). A number of small design companies were then set up in HSIP. With the government's investment in the semiconductor industry and the establishment of UMC and TSMC, not only was production process technology being continuously improved, but various other semiconductor-related technologies were also innovated, including circuit design, mask production, packaging and testing, and so on.

Taiwan's economic growth slowed down in the late 1990s and become sluggish in the 2000s as a result of a sequence of negative impacts such as the Asian financial crisis in 1997, the worldwide economic recession in 2000 due to the dot-com bubble, the Global Financial Crisis in 2008, and Europe's sovereign debt crisis in 2011. Up to now, Taiwan's focus industries include Information and Communications, Electronics and Optoelectronics, Material, Chemical and Nanotechnology, Medical Device and Biomedical, Mechanical and Systems, Green Energy, and Environment.

Methodology

Growth and productivity accounts

In order to investigate the contribution of each input on economic growth, we follow the growth accounting methodology provided by the Asia KLEMS manual (2012), which was developed by Jorgenson and Griliches (1967) and associates as outlined in Jorgenson, Gollop, and Fraumeni (1987) and more recently in Jorgenson et al. (2005). It is assumed that industry gross output is a function of capital, labor, intermediate inputs, and technology. Following the notation of the Asia KLEMS manual (2012), the aggregate industrial production functions are assumed to be separable in these inputs:

$$Y_i = f^i(X_i, K_i, L_i, T), \quad i = 1, 2, \ldots, n, \tag{9.1}$$

where Y_i is the output quantity of industry i, K_i is an index of capital service flow, L_i is an index of labor service flow, T represents the technology status, and X_i is an index of intermediate inputs, which consists of the intermediate inputs purchased from other domestic industries and imported products. Intermediate inputs (X_i) include energy (E_i), materials (M_i), and service (S_i) inputs in this model.

Under the assumptions of constant returns to scale and competitive markets, the value of output is equal to the value of all inputs:

$$p_Y^i Y_i = p_X^i X_i + p_K^i K_i + p_L^i L_i, \quad i = 1, 2, \ldots, n, \tag{9.2}$$

where p_Y^i denotes the price of output of industry i, p_X^i denotes the price of intermediate inputs, p_K^i denotes the price of capital services, and p_L^i denotes the price of labor services. The value share of each input is defined as follows:

$$v_{it}^X = \frac{P_{it}^X X_{it}}{P_{it}^X Y_{it}}; \; v_{it}^L = \frac{P_{it}^L X_{it}}{P_{it}^L Y_{it}}; \; v_{it}^K = \frac{P_{it}^K X_{it}}{P_{it}^K Y_{it}} \tag{9.3}$$

The assumption of constant returns to scale implies $v_{it}^X + v_{it}^L + v_{it}^K = 1$.

The standard growth accounting decomposition of output growth in the contribution of each input and TFP can be expressed as:

$$\Delta TFP^i = \Delta \ln Y_i - \bar{v}_X^i \Delta \ln X_i - \bar{v}_k^i \Delta \ln K_i - \bar{v}_L^i \Delta \ln L_i, \tag{9.4}$$

where the contribution of each input is defined as the product of the input's growth rate and its two-period average revenue share. Furthermore, we define the quantity of output in industry j as an aggregate of M distinct outputs using the Tornqvist index:

$$\Delta \ln Y_{it} = \sum_{j=1}^{m} \bar{v}_{ijt}^Y \Delta \ln Y_{it} \tag{9.5}$$

Here, $\bar{v}_{ijt}$ denotes the two-period average share of product j in the nominal value of output. The value share of each product is defined as follows:

$$v_{ijt}^Y = (\sum_i p_{ijt}^Y Y_{ijt})^{-1} p_{ijt}^Y Y_{ijt} \tag{9.6}$$

Here, $p_{i,j}^Y$ is the basic price received by industry i for selling commodity j. Similarly, the intermediate input quantity index for industry i is defined analogously by:

$$\Delta \ln X_{it} = \sum_i \bar{v}_{ijt}^X \Delta \ln X_{it} \qquad (9.7)$$

Here, $v_{ijt}^X = (\sum_i p_{ijt}^X X_{ijt})^{-1} p_{ijt}^X X_{ijt}$, and P_{ij}^x is the price paid by industry i for using product j.

Intermediate inputs are typically divided into three groups: energy (E), materials (M), and services (S). We next follow Jorgenson et al. (1987) and assume that aggregate services are a translog function of the services of individual types. Hence, the corresponding index of capital and labor services input is a translog quantity index of individual types, indexed by l, and given by:

$$\begin{aligned}\Delta \ln L_i &= \sum \bar{v}_{Ll}^i \Delta \ln L_{Li} \\ \Delta \ln K_i &= \sum \bar{v}_{kl}^i \Delta \ln K_{ki}\end{aligned} \qquad (9.8)$$

where weights are given by the average shares of each type in the value. Therefore, we can obtain:

$$\begin{aligned}\Delta TFP^i &= \Delta \ln Y_i - \bar{v}_X^i \left\{ \bar{v}_{XE}^i \Delta \ln E_i + \bar{v}_{XM}^i \Delta \ln M_i + \bar{v}_{XS}^i \Delta \ln S_i \right\} \\ &\quad - \bar{v}_K^i \cdot \sum \bar{v}_{Kk}^i \Delta \ln K_{Ki} - \bar{v}_L^i \cdot \sum \bar{v}_{Ll}^i \Delta \ln L_{Li}\end{aligned} \qquad (9.9)$$

Taiwan KLEMS database

We construct the Taiwan KLEMS database following the Asia KLEMS manual, in which the economy is divided into 31 industries (the 32nd sector, 'extra-territorial organizations and bodies', in the Asia KLEMS manual is not available). The data resources are based on the data published by the Directorate General of Budget, Accounting and Statistics, Taiwan (DGBAS) for the period 1981–2010. For the output data (Gross output and Value-added), we utilize the National Income Survey data (93 SNA) and convert 65 sectors into 31 sectors. Intermediate inputs (II) include energy (E), materials (M), and services (S). The data come from the Intermediate Inputs of the national income series. The inputs of energy, materials, and services are calculated by applying the shares of E, M, and S from the Taiwan Input-output tables for each industry.

Following the methodology developed by Jorgenson et al. (1987) and Jorgenson et al. (2005) and the Asia KLEMS manual (2012), we decompose the output growth into contributions of capital, labor, and intermediate inputs (energy, materials, and services) as well as total factor productivity. The details of the construction of the Taiwan KLEMS database are reported in Fu et al. (2016).

To calculate capital service, we need the capital stock measurement for the detailed assets. Thus, the perpetual inventory method (PIM) approach is employed. First, we need to find a benchmark year of capital stock of each asset (including ICT assets and Non-ICT assets) and the series of Fixed Capital Formation for each industry. Incorporating the appropriate depreciation rate, we can get the series of capital stock of each asset for each industry. We employ the following formula to calculate the capital price for each type of asset:

$$p_{k,t}^K = p_{k,t-1}^I i_t + \delta_k p_{k,t}^I [p_{k,t}^I - p_{k,t-1}^I] \tag{9.10}$$

where δ_k is the depreciation rate of asset type k, i_t is the interest rate in period t, and $p_{k,t}^I$ is the asset type k price index of the Fixed Capital Formation. Labor data include labor compensation and working hour data. We employ the raw survey data from Manpower, which has been conducted every May since 1977. There are about 60,000 observations in this survey every year. There are 18 types of labor included, which are distinguished on the basis of age, gender, and educational attainment for each industry. Compiling the manpower data with Employees' Earnings Survey, we can obtain labor compensation and working hour data for each industrial level.

Economic performance of Taiwan: 1981–2010

Industry structural change in Taiwan

We first examine the trend and the structural change of Taiwan's economic development for the past decades. Table 9.2 shows that the industry weights of primary, secondary, and tertiary industries are 6.13 percent, 44.75 percent, and 49.11 percent in 1981–90, respectively. For the period 2001–10, their industry weights are 1.73 percent, 30.99 percent, and 67.27 percent, respectively. We can conclude that the industry weights for the primary and secondary sectors decrease over time and that the importance of tertiary industries has risen in the past three decades, as shown in Table 9.1 and Figure 9.2.

From Figure 9.2, it is easy to find that 1987 could be the turning point for Taiwan's economic development. Before 1987, the weights of tertiary and non-tertiary industries are almost equal. After 1987, the weights for secondary industries decrease gradually over time and never revert. In 2010, the tertiary industries accounted for more than two-thirds of the Taiwan GDP output. Around 1987, some important events affected Taiwan's economic development, including the strong appreciation of the local currency and the economic liberalization policy. Those events made labor-intensive industries lose their competitiveness. In order to survive, labor-intensive manufacturers were compelled to relocate their production bases to Southeast Asia or to mainland China, which explained the main reason why the manufacturing industries shrank since the late 1980s.

As for value-added weights for the 31 sectors, Table 9.2 shows the level and some changes in industry weight in the last three decades. In 1981, we find that '3 Food products, beverages and tobacco', '4 Textiles, textile products, leather, etc.', '13 Electrical and optical equipment', and '17 Construction' are important sectors among secondary industries, whereas '27 Public administration and defense, etc.', '19 Wholesale trade and commission trade', '20 Retail trade, etc.', and '25 Real estate activities' are those with the highest weight in the tertiary industries. However, Table 9.2 shows that except for '13 Electrical and optical equipment' and '11 Basic and fabricated metal', the industry weights of most others in the secondary industries decreased over time. On the contrary,

Table 9.1 Industry value-added weights of primary, secondary, tertiary, and manufacturing industries by sub-period

unit:%

	1981–90	1991–2000	2001–10	1981–2010
Primary	6.13	3.10	1.73	3.66
Secondary	44.75	34.70	30.99	36.82
Manufacturing	35.55	27.03	26.29	29.62
Tertiary	49.11	62.19	67.27	59.53

Source: Calculations based on Taiwan KLEMS database, August 2015.

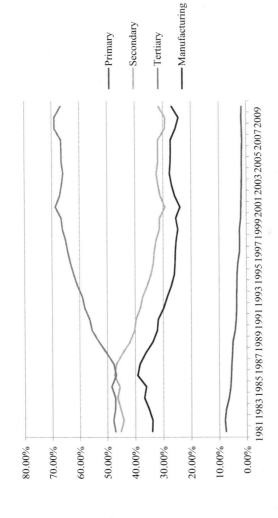

Figure 9.2 Taiwan industrial structure, 1981–2010

Source: Calculations based on Taiwan KLEMS database, August 2015.

Table 9.2 Industry value-added weights by selected year

unit:%

Sector	Industry number and name	1981	1990	2000	2010
Primary	1. Agriculture, hunting and forestry	7.65	4.24	2.08	1.69
Secondary	2. Mining and quarrying	2.16	0.68	0.52	0.48
	3. Food products, beverages and tobacco	4.48	3.33	1.47	1.24
	4. Textiles, textile products, leather and footwear	6.96	4.47	1.88	0.82
	5. Wood and products of wood and cork	0.65	0.41	0.08	0.07
	6. Pulp, paper, paper products, printing and publishing	1.57	1.29	0.73	0.63
	7. Coke, refined petroleum products and nuclear fuel	1.30	1.14	1.38	1.09
	8. Chemicals and chemical products	2.50	2.82	2.25	3.23
	9. Rubber and plastic products	1.42	2.10	1.26	0.70
	10. Other non-metallic mineral products	1.69	1.43	0.70	0.47
	11. Basic metals and fabricated metal products	2.94	3.99	3.55	3.30
	12. Machinery, nec	0.98	1.28	1.18	1.27
	13. Electrical and optical equipment	4.31	5.46	8.37	12.08
	14. Transport equipment	2.39	2.42	1.56	1.26
	15. Manufacturing nec; Recycling	2.80	2.01	1.04	0.65
	16. Electricity, gas and water supply	3.40	2.81	2.06	1.35
	17. Construction	5.69	4.61	3.22	2.90
Tertiary	18. Sale, maintenance and repair of motor vehicles	1.16	1.44	1.33	1.23
	19. Wholesale trade and commission trade	6.17	6.23	9.41	10.94
	20. Retail trade, except motor vehicles and motorcycles	5.78	5.76	6.97	6.67
	21. Hotel and restaurants	0.90	1.67	2.09	2.05
	22. Transport and storage	4.27	4.40	3.93	3.02

23. Post and telecommunications	1.62	1.72	2.50	1.95
24. Financial intermediation	4.22	7.77	8.58	6.51
25. Real estate activities	5.09	6.42	8.88	8.86
26. Renting of m&eq and other business activities	1.70	2.02	3.39	4.88
27. Public admin. and defense; Compulsory social security	9.01	9.29	8.16	7.48
28. Education	2.74	3.06	4.22	4.74
29. Health and social work	0.75	1.60	2.63	3.09
30. Other community, social and personal services	3.22	3.51	3.87	4.55
31. Private households with employed persons	0.47	0.61	0.71	0.80

Source: Calculations based on Taiwan KLEMS database, August 2015.

Table 9.2 also presents that most of the industry weights in the tertiary industries increased over time. As a result, we find in 2010 that there are only three industries with a relatively high weight among secondary industries, which are '13 Electrical and Optical equipment', '11 Basic and fabricated metal products', and '8 Chemicals and chemical products'. In the tertiary sector, we can find the value-added weights are generally relatively large compared to those of secondary industries. '19 Wholesale trade and commission trade', '25 Real estate activities', '27 Public administration and defense, etc.', '20 Retail trade, etc.', and '24 Financial intermediation' are the industries with a relatively high weight in tertiary industries.

Cross-period comparisons of value-added growth at the industry level

Table 9.3 presents the average annual growth of industry value-added for the last three decades. The average growth rate in 1981–90 was 7.35 percent, but it decreased substantially in the later two decades. Among the 31 industries, we note from Table 9.3 that only four sectors among the secondary industries had an average annual growth rate higher than 7 percent during the period 1981–2010: '13 Electrical and optical equipment', '8 Chemicals and chemical products', '11 Basic metals and fabricated metal products', and '12 Machinery, nec'. Furthermore, '13 Electrical and optical equipment' is the only sector industry with average annual growth higher than 10 percent among secondary industries. On the contrary, only two sub-industries, '22 Transport and storage' and '27 Public administration and defense; Compulsory social security', among tertiary industries have an annual growth rate lower than 7 percent during the same period. Generally speaking, all sub-industries in tertiary industries have higher average growth rates than the sub-industries in secondary industries.

Cross-period comparisons on the annual growth rate at the industry level can also be seen in Table 9.3. The growth rate for the 31 industries ranged from 18.35 percent (industry #29 during 1981–90) to –7.36 percent (industry #5 during 1991–2000) and varied by sub-period, implying the importance of analysis at the industry level. Furthermore, we also see that the growth rates in the

Table 9.3 Growth of industry value-added by period

unit:%

Sector	Industry number and name	1981–90	1991–2000	2001–10	1981–2010
Primary	1. Agriculture, hunting and forestry	3.36	1.35	0.85	1.80
Secondary	2. Mining and quarrying	-2.97	5.83	2.20	1.85
	3. Food products, beverages and tobacco	6.62	0.26	1.24	2.57
	4. Textiles, textile products, leather and footwear	5.02	-0.23	-5.37	-0.37
	5. Wood and products of wood and cork	4.76	-7.36	1.29	-0.62
	6. Pulp, paper, paper products, printing and publishing	7.77	2.72	1.54	3.88
	7. Coke, refined petroleum products and nuclear fuel	8.52	10.34	0.56	6.40
	8. Chemicals and chemical products	11.26	6.18	6.57	7.89
	9. Rubber and plastic products	14.26	3.33	-2.89	4.58
	10. Other non-metallic mineral products	8.10	1.23	-1.01	2.59
	11. Basic metals and fabricated metal products	13.31	7.27	2.22	7.40
	12. Machinery, nec	12.89	7.60	3.69	7.89
	13. Electrical and optical equipment	12.54	12.73	6.62	10.56
	14. Transport equipment	10.04	4.05	0.84	4.80
	15. Manufacturing nec; Recycling	6.24	1.80	-1.65	1.99
	16. Electricity, gas and water supply	7.82	5.34	-1.26	3.83
	17. Construction	7.58	4.87	1.89	4.68
Tertiary	18. Sale, maintenance and repair of motor vehicles	12.40	7.64	2.13	7.21
	19. Wholesale trade and commission trade	10.03	12.57	4.46	8.98
	20. Retail trade, except motor vehicles and motorcycles	9.89	10.34	2.52	7.50
	21. Hotel and restaurants	16.77	10.64	2.76	9.83
	22. Transport and storage	10.24	7.31	0.33	5.81

(Continued)

Table 9.3 (Continued)

unit:%

Sector	Industry number and name	1981–90	1991–2000	2001–10	1981–2010
	23. Post and telecommunications	10.62	12.16	0.46	7.65
	24. Financial intermediation	16.70	9.44	0.19	8.50
	25. Real estate activities	12.50	11.69	2.93	8.92
	26. Renting of m&eq and other business activities	11.85	13.61	6.60	10.65
	27. Public admin. and defense; Compulsory social security	10.26	7.15	2.07	6.36
	28. Education	11.15	11.66	4.11	8.90
	29. Health and social work	18.35	13.41	4.55	11.89
	30. Other community, social and personal services	10.87	9.43	4.57	8.20
	31. Private households with employed persons	12.81	9.97	4.16	8.85

Source: Calculations based on Taiwan KLEMS database, August 2015.

earlier period are generally higher than those of the latter periods, no matter what industry.

Output growth at the industry level

Output growth is defined to be the addition of value-added and intermediate inputs. Table 9.4 presents the growth of industry output for the past three decades (1981–2010). Despite the rates of growth output being different from those of value-added, by comparing Tables 9.3 and 9.4, one can see that the growth rate ranks of the 31 industries in gross output and in value-added are quite similar. Except for '13 Electrical and optical equipment', the growth rates of gross output in secondary industries are generally lower than those of tertiary industries. In general, the growth rates of the latter are relatively high. Cross-period comparison of the growth rate in industry output also indicates vast differences between sub-industries and sub-periods.

TFP growth at the industry level

As in the standard growth accounting practice, TFP is defined as the residual contribution that is unexplained by factor inputs. The resulting TFP growth for each industry can be found in Table 9.5, which shows that the figures of TFP growth in secondary industries are relatively lower than the figures in tertiary industries. The TFP growth rate of the '13. Electrical and optical equipment' industry is the highest among secondary industries, while the TFP growth rate of 'Post and telecommunications' is the largest among the tertiary industries, meaning the impact of the industrial policy not only affects structural change, but also influences the TFP growth rate.

Table 9.5 also lists the cross-period comparisons on the annual growth rate of TFP at the industry level. Generally speaking, the growth rates in the earlier period are higher than those of the latter periods, especially in secondary industries. More than 60 percent of secondary industries TFP growth rates are negative in the period 2000–10, while most of the TFP growth rates are positive for the period 1981–90. Similarly, it is easy to find that the performance of tertiary industries is better that those of secondary industries for each sub-period.

Table 9.4 Growth of industry gross output by period

unit:%

Sector	Industry number and name	1981–90	1991–2000	2001–10	1981–2010
Primary	1. Agriculture, hunting and forestry	3.96	−0.25	−0.99	0.80
Secondary	2. Mining and quarrying	0.45	0.01	−0.26	0.05
	3. Food products, beverages and tobacco	5.36	0.27	0.04	1.77
	4. Textiles, textile products, leather and footwear	3.09	−1.04	−3.53	−0.62
	5. Wood and products of wood and cork	1.09	−8.31	−1.29	−2.97
	6. Pulp, paper, paper products, printing and publishing	6.06	1.97	1.17	2.96
	7. Coke, refined petroleum products and nuclear fuel	4.12	4.99	2.64	3.91
	8. Chemicals and chemical products	9.15	7.57	5.35	7.30
	9. Rubber and plastic products	12.81	3.32	−2.16	4.38
	10. Other non-metallic mineral products	6.46	3.13	−0.33	2.97
	11. Basic metals and fabricated metal products	9.90	7.74	0.49	5.91
	12. Machinery, nec	11.85	7.21	4.35	7.67
	13. Electrical and optical equipment	12.96	13.91	8.98	11.92
	14. Transport equipment	8.56	3.89	2.30	4.79
	15. Manufacturing nec; Recycling	6.40	0.19	−1.09	1.67
	16. Electricity, gas and water supply	7.17	7.04	2.19	5.41
	17. Construction	6.59	4.18	−0.68	3.25
Tertiary	18. Sale, maintenance and repair of motor vehicles	12.30	3.60	2.08	5.78
	19. Wholesale trade and commission trade	9.00	7.95	4.24	7.00
	20. Retail trade, except motor vehicles and motorcycles	7.88	6.80	2.44	5.63
	21. Hotel and restaurants	14.86	7.85	1.75	7.92
	22. Transport and storage	7.43	6.80	1.93	5.32

23. Post and telecommunications	11.26	16.10	4.15	10.47
24. Financial intermediation	15.93	6.94	1.55	7.87
25. Real estate activities	9.66	6.91	2.64	6.29
26. Renting of m&eq and other business activities	9.16	11.35	4.69	8.38
27. Public admin. and defense; Compulsory social security	7.58	2.55	0.23	3.31
28. Education	7.86	8.23	3.37	6.44
29. Health and social work	14.86	9.45	2.25	8.65
30. Other community, social and personal services	8.91	7.19	3.81	6.56
31. Private households with employed persons	9.79	5.74	3.30	6.16

Source: Calculations based on Taiwan KLEMS database, August 2015.

Table 9.5 Growth of industry TFP by sub-period

unit:%

Sector	Industry number and name	1981–2010	1981–90	1991–2000	2001–10
Primary	1. Agriculture, hunting and forestry	0.03	(0.34)	0.11	0.29
Secondary	2. Mining and quarrying	(13.92)	(3.76)	(5.36)	(31.61)
	3. Food products, beverages and tobacco	(0.90)	0.05	(1.38)	(1.29)
	4. Textiles, textile products, leather and footwear	(0.51)	(0.15)	(0.92)	(0.43)
	5. Wood and products of wood and cork	0.35	0.44	0.22	0.39
	6. Pulp, paper, paper products, printing and publishing	(0.05)	(0.52)	(0.37)	0.69
	7. Coke, refined petroleum products and nuclear fuel	(0.96)	(0.68)	(1.66)	(0.51)
	8. Chemicals and chemical products	(0.19)	1.26	(1.13)	(0.56)
	9. Rubber and plastic products	0.62	2.04	0.06	(0.08)
	10. Other non-metallic mineral products	(0.01)	0.46	(0.35)	(0.09)
	11. Basic metals and fabricated metal products	0.09	0.99	0.33	(0.95)
	12. Machinery, nec	0.37	1.05	0.64	(0.53)
	13. Electrical and optical equipment	1.31	1.42	1.43	1.11
	14. Transport equipment	(0.46)	0.48	(1.41)	(0.35)
	15. Manufacturing nec; Recycling	(0.24)	0.75	(0.26)	(1.09)
	16. Electricity, gas and water supply	0.68	2.72	(1.36)	0.88
	17. Construction	(1.35)	0.58	(0.23)	(4.21)
Tertiary	18. Sale, maintenance and repair of motor vehicles	2.12	2.63	2.47	1.30
	19. Wholesale trade and commission trade	3.28	3.21	3.78	2.85
	20. Retail trade, except motor vehicles and motorcycles	2.76	4.01	4.14	0.25
	21. Hotel and restaurants	1.18	4.40	2.30	(2.85)
	22. Transport and storage	0.27	0.18	0.10	0.53

23. Post and telecommunications	4.14	1.30	7.67	3.16
24. Financial intermediation	1.97	4.19	1.48	0.46
25. Real estate activities	0.80	1.01	1.13	0.28
26. Renting of m&eq and other business activities	(0.56)	(0.82)	(0.38)	(0.50)
27. Public admin, and defense; Compulsory social security	0.45	1.22	0.64	(0.43)
28. Education	1.85	2.43	2.54	0.64
29. Health and social work	1.31	2.69	0.99	0.38
30. Other community, social and personal services	(0.99)	0.91	(4.41)	0.73

Source: Calculations based on Taiwan KLEMS database, August 2015.

Sources of gross output growth at the industry level

Sources of industry output for the whole sample period (1981–2010)

Standard growth accounting decomposes gross output (GO) growth into the contribution of each input and TFP. In other words, the growth rate of GO can be decomposed into contributions of K, L, II, and TFP on GO growth. Table 9.6 presents the results of such decomposition for the 30 industries[1] in 1981–2010, while Table 9.7 presents such decomposition in the percentage share for each input. Despite the results of such decomposition varying by industry, we still can easily see that the contribution from intermediate inputs (II) (sum of energy (E), materials (M), and services (S)) dominates the growth, which is followed by contribution from capital (K), then labor (L), and finally TFP in secondary industries. However, we also find that intermediate inputs contribute about 70 percent of output growth in secondary industries with low TFP contribution. In fact, TFP is negative in many industries in secondary sector. Among the intermediate inputs, the shares of material (M) contribute the largest proportion in secondary industries. We also discover that the contribution of labor is quite small.

Comparing to the secondary sector, the contribution of intermediate inputs is generally not so significant, however, in tertiary industries. From Table 9.6, we easily see that the contribution from intermediate inputs (II) (sum of energy (E), materials (M), and services (S)) still dominates the growth, but is not so significant, followed by the contribution from TFP, then capital (L), and finally labor (L) in tertiary industries. The contribution of intermediate inputs accounts for 30–50 percent of output growth in these industries. The TFP contribution as well as that of capital (K) is more important for these industries. Among the intermediate inputs, the share of services (S), not material (M), contributes the largest proportion. We also can find that the contribution of labor is still quite low in tertiary industries.

Tables 9.6 and 9.7 show that such inputs' dominant contribution effect may differ by industries in both the secondary and tertiary sectors. For example, among all factor contributions in '21 Hotel and restaurant', II has the largest contribution share (49 percent), K has the second largest share (26 percent), and L has the lowest

Table 9.6 Sources of industry output growth (in growth rate): 1981–2010

unit:%

Sector	Industry number and name	GO	ConK	ConICT	Con Non-ICT	ConL	ConE	ConM	ConS	ConII	TFP
Primary	1. Agriculture, hunting and forestry	0.80	1.11	0.20	0.91	−0.89	0.01	0.21	0.33	0.55	0.03
Secondary	2. Mining and quarrying	0.05	13.36	4.06	7.32	−0.62	0.07	0.87	0.28	1.22	(11.92)
	3. Food products, beverages and tobacco	1.77	1.34	0.49	0.85	−0.06	0.04	0.81	0.55	1.39	(0.90)
	4. Textiles, textile products, leather and footwear	−0.62	0.48	0.07	0.42	−0.66	−0.01	−0.12	0.20	0.07	(0.51)
	5. Wood and products of wood and cork	−2.97	0.32	0.10	0.22	−1.26	−0.16	−1.66	−0.57	−2.38	0.35
	6. Pulp, paper, paper products, printing and publishing	2.96	0.70	0.09	0.60	0.14	0.13	1.13	0.92	2.18	(0.05)
	7. Coke, refined petroleum products and nuclear fuel	3.91	2.56	0.31	2.25	−0.01	1.07	0.69	0.56	2.32	(0.96)
	8. Chemicals and chemical products	7.30	1.86	0.62	1.24	0.07	0.28	4.39	0.88	5.55	(0.19)
	9. Rubber and plastic products	4.38	0.44	0.14	0.31	0.04	0.11	2.44	0.71	3.27	0.62
	10. Other non-metallic mineral products	2.97	1.35	0.21	1.14	−0.12	0.01	1.02	0.72	1.75	(0.01)
	11. Basic metals and fabricated metal products	5.91	1.09	0.33	0.76	0.29	0.12	3.38	0.94	4.44	0.09
	12. Machinery, nec	7.67	0.76	0.35	0.40	0.42	0.07	4.28	1.77	6.12	0.37
	13. Electrical and optical equipment	11.92	1.48	0.62	0.86	0.43	0.22	5.83	2.64	8.70	1.31
	14. Transport equipment	4.79	1.33	0.30	1.02	0.09	0.05	2.77	1.01	3.83	(0.46)
	15. Manufacturing nec; Recycling	1.67	1.23	0.38	0.86	−0.40	0.00	0.53	0.54	1.08	(0.24)
	16. Electricity, gas and water supply	5.41	2.45	0.77	1.67	0.00	1.06	0.72	0.51	2.28	0.68
	17. Construction	3.25	1.99	−0.01	2.00	0.06	0.00	1.79	0.75	2.54	(1.35)

(Continued)

Table 9.6 (Continued)

unit:%

Sector	Industry number and name	GO	ConK	ConICT	Con Non-ICT	ConL	ConE	ConM	ConS	ConII	TFP
Tertiary	18. Sale, maintenance and repair of motor vehicles	5.78	0.38	0.19	0.20	0.80	0.10	1.15	1.24	2.48	2.12
	19. Wholesale trade and commission trade	7.00	0.28	0.04	0.23	1.22	0.06	0.30	1.85	2.21	3.28
	20. Retail trade, except motor vehicles and motorcycles	5.63	0.81	0.44	0.37	0.15	0.15	0.31	1.46	1.92	2.76
	21. Hotel and restaurants	7.92	2.07	0.97	1.10	0.78	0.56	1.58	1.76	3.90	1.18
	22. Transport and storage	5.32	2.14	0.23	1.90	0.06	0.03	1.15	1.67	2.85	0.27
	23. Post and telecommunications	10.47	3.36	0.73	2.64	0.42	0.13	0.69	1.73	2.55	4.14
	24. Financial intermediation	7.87	2.65	0.75	1.90	1.17	0.02	0.18	1.88	2.08	1.97
	25. Real estate activities	6.29	3.94	0.32	3.62	0.18	0.01	0.60	0.76	1.37	0.80
	26. Renting of m&eq and other business activities	8.38	3.08	1.15	1.93	2.10	0.07	1.33	2.35	3.75	(0.56)
	27. Public admin. and defense; Compulsory social security	3.31	0.96	0.11	0.84	0.83	0.01	0.25	0.81	1.07	0.45
	28. Education	6.44	0.20	0.05	0.16	3.10	0.16	0.54	0.60	1.29	1.85
	29. Health and social work	8.65	1.67	0.52	1.14	2.03	0.21	1.79	1.65	3.64	1.31
	30. Other community, social and personal services	6.56	4.20	0.68	3.52	0.30	0.14	0.85	2.05	3.05	(0.99)

Source: Calculations based on Taiwan KLEMS database, August 2015.

Table 9.7 Sources of industry output growth (in % share): 1981–2010

unit:%

Sector	Industry number and name	GO	ConK	ConICT	Con Non-ICT	ConL	ConE	ConM	ConS	ConII	TFP
Primary	1. Agriculture, hunting and forestry	100.00	138.61	25.01	113.60	−111.46	1.44	26.53	41.08	69.05	3.80
Secondary	2. Mining and quarrying	100.00	24758.51	7517.52	13553.93	−1141.50	128.42	1612.22	522.44	2263.08	−22093.03
	3. Food products, beverages and tobacco	100.00	75.91	27.90	48.02	−3.66	2.10	45.73	31.05	78.88	−51.13
	4. Textiles, textile products, leather and footwear	100.00	−78.65	−10.57	−68.08	106.86	1.57	19.03	−31.88	−11.28	83.07
	5. Wood and products of wood and cork	100.00	−10.81	−3.44	−7.37	42.51	5.34	55.74	19.02	80.11	−11.81
	6. Pulp, paper, paper products, printing and publishing	100.00	23.49	3.14	20.35	4.56	4.39	38.18	31.08	73.64	−1.69
	7. Coke, refined petroleum products and nuclear fuel	100.00	65.51	7.89	57.62	−0.36	27.33	17.65	14.34	59.31	−24.47
	8. Chemicals and chemical products	100.00	25.48	8.53	16.95	1.02	3.87	60.20	12.05	76.12	−2.63
	9. Rubber and plastic products	100.00	10.08	3.09	6.98	0.93	2.54	55.85	16.33	74.72	14.27
	10. Other non-metallic mineral products	100.00	45.50	7.23	38.27	−4.03	0.27	34.27	24.23	58.77	−0.24
	11. Basic metals and fabricated metal products	100.00	18.37	5.57	12.80	4.86	2.04	57.28	15.91	75.23	1.54
	12. Machinery, nec	100.00	9.89	4.62	5.27	5.46	0.96	55.85	23.08	79.89	4.76
	13. Electrical and optical equipment	100.00	12.41	5.19	7.22	3.59	1.86	48.94	22.18	72.98	11.02
	14. Transport equipment	100.00	27.69	6.36	21.33	1.86	1.08	57.86	21.06	80.00	−9.56
	15. Manufacturing nec; Recycling	100.00	73.62	22.41	51.21	−23.84	0.08	31.91	32.31	64.30	−14.08
	16. Electricity, gas and water supply	100.00	45.22	14.25	30.97	−0.01	19.59	13.27	9.36	42.23	12.57
	17. Construction	100.00	61.41	−0.24	61.64	2.00	0.12	55.05	23.08	78.25	−41.65

(Continued)

Table 9.7 (Continued)

unit:%

Sector	Industry number and name	GO	ConK	ConICT	Con Non-ICT	ConL	ConE	ConM	ConS	ConII	TFP
Tertiary	18. Sale, maintenance and repair of motor vehicles	100.00	6.59	3.21	3.38	13.79	1.73	19.83	21.41	42.98	36.65
	19. Wholesale trade and commission trade	100.00	3.93	0.63	3.30	17.48	0.85	4.35	26.45	31.64	46.95
	20. Retail trade, except motor vehicles and motorcycles	100.00	14.37	7.81	6.56	2.67	2.67	5.45	25.90	34.02	48.94
	21. Hotel and restaurants	100.00	26.17	12.29	13.88	9.79	7.01	19.91	22.27	49.19	14.84
	22. Transport and storage	100.00	40.17	4.41	35.76	1.14	0.50	21.63	31.46	53.58	5.10
	23. Post and telecommunications	100.00	32.12	6.96	25.16	4.02	1.24	6.60	16.51	24.34	39.51
	24. Financial intermediation	100.00	33.71	9.52	24.20	14.85	0.20	2.25	23.94	26.39	25.04
	25. Real estate activities	100.00	62.65	5.09	57.56	2.84	0.18	9.55	12.02	21.76	12.76
	26. Renting of m&eq and other business activities	100.00	36.80	13.72	23.08	25.11	0.80	15.87	28.08	44.75	−6.67
	27. Public admin. and defense; Compulsory social security	100.00	28.88	3.39	25.49	25.12	0.42	7.54	24.41	32.37	13.63
	28. Education	100.00	3.15	0.70	2.45	48.08	2.46	8.32	9.26	20.04	28.73
	29. Health and social work	100.00	19.26	6.06	13.20	23.47	2.43	20.66	19.04	42.13	15.14
	30. Other community, social and personal services	100.00	64.04	10.39	53.65	4.56	2.20	12.93	31.32	46.45	−15.05

Source: Calculations based on Taiwan KLEMS database, August 2015.

share (9.79 percent). In '23 Post and telecommunications', the TFP share is 39.51 percent, the K share is 32.12 percent, the II share in only 24 percent, and the L share is only 4.02 percent. For '28 Education', L has the dominant share of contribution (48.08 percent) with capital at a low contribution (3.15 percent).

Sources of industry output growth: cross-period comparisons

Tables 9.8, 9.9, and 9.10 present sources of industry output growth analyses (in growth rate (Tables a) and in percentage share (Tables b)) for the periods 1981–90, 1991–2000, and 2001–10, respectively. These tables show that the contributions of each input exhibit the same pattern similar to those in the whole sample period (1981–2010). The contribution of intermediate inputs (II) (sum of energy (E), materials (M), and services (S)) still dominates the growth in both secondary and tertiary sectors. TFP seems to have a larger contribution in the early decade (1981–90) than in the later decades (1991–2000, 2001–10). In contrast, the contribution share from K (ConK) increases over time. Such results seem consistent with the change of Taiwan's industrial structure, in which the size of secondary (manufacturing) sectors with a relatively high contribution share in intermediate input (II) decreased over time.

Since there are 30 industries with different decomposition results, in this subsection we choose three important and representative industries to show the vast differences at the industry level in Taiwan. The study selects '13 Electrical and optical equipment', '19 Wholesale and commission trade', and '23 Post and telecommunications'.

The sector with the largest industry weight and growth rate among secondary industries is '13 Electrical and optical equipment'. It is also regarded as one of most important ICT-producing industries in Taiwan. Taking it as an example, we find the contribution shares of II to be high during every period, but the size of each share falls over time. The contribution from M also dominates other intermediate inputs. The reduced contributions from K and L are much smaller than that from II. TFP shows an insignificant impact on growth. The results can be seen in Table 9.11.

The sector with the biggest industry weight among tertiary industries is '19 Wholesale and commission trade'. We find the contribution shares of factor inputs to be dominated by TFP and II over the three decades. As shown in Table 9.12, the contribution of material

Table 9.8a Sources of industry output growth (in growth rate): 1981–90

unit:%

Sector	Industry number and name	GO	ConK	ConICT	Con Non-ICT	ConL	ConE	ConM	ConS	ConII	TFP
Primary	1. Agriculture, hunting and forestry	3.96	1.81	0.37	1.43	−0.54	0.04	2.21	0.77	3.03	(0.38)
Secondary	2. Mining and quarrying	0.45	3.71	0.00	3.71	−1.17	−0.11	1.36	0.43	1.68	(3.66)
	3. Food products, beverages and tobacco	5.36	1.20	0.11	1.09	−0.06	0.07	3.32	0.77	4.16	(0.02)
	4. Textiles, textile products, leather and footwear	3.09	0.74	0.01	0.73	−0.42	0.09	2.39	0.44	2.92	(0.24)
	5. Wood and products of wood and cork	1.09	0.52	0.01	0.51	−0.55	0.14	−0.51	1.05	0.68	0.30
	6. Pulp, paper, paper products, printing and publishing	6.06	1.02	0.02	1.00	0.48	0.24	3.41	1.44	5.08	(0.76)
	7. Coke, refined petroleum products and nuclear fuel	4.12	1.93	0.02	1.91	0.10	2.27	−0.98	1.48	2.77	(2.95)
	8. Chemicals and chemical products	9.15	0.85	0.08	0.76	0.12	0.23	5.76	0.93	6.92	1.03
	9. Rubber and plastic products	12.81	0.68	0.00	0.68	0.37	0.26	7.99	1.48	9.73	1.77
	10. Other non-metallic mineral products	6.46	1.43	0.01	1.42	0.06	0.41	2.48	1.62	4.51	0.05
	11. Basic metals and fabricated metal products	9.90	1.01	0.02	0.99	0.51	0.24	5.78	1.38	7.39	0.75
	12. Machinery, nec	11.85	0.27	0.01	0.26	0.75	0.12	7.68	1.98	9.78	0.93
	13. Electrical and optical equipment	12.96	0.71	0.04	0.67	0.45	0.20	8.20	1.99	10.38	1.21
	14. Transport equipment	8.56	1.01	0.14	0.86	0.23	0.11	5.92	0.82	6.85	0.37
	15. Manufacturing nec; Recycling	6.40	0.99	0.00	0.99	0.21	0.08	3.28	1.10	4.46	0.66
	16. Electricity, gas and water supply	7.17	2.01	0.34	1.67	0.07	1.83	−0.45	0.99	2.37	0.89
	17. Construction	6.59	1.07	0.02	1.05	−0.07	0.01	3.91	1.09	5.01	0.57

Tertiary	18. Sale, maintenance and repair of motor vehicles	12.30	0.83	0.16	0.67	2.46	0.24	3.55	2.60	6.38	2.38
	19. Wholesale trade and commission trade	9.00	1.32	0.19	1.12	1.40	0.04	0.61	2.42	3.07	3.18
	20. Retail trade, except motor vehicles and motorcycles	7.88	1.16	0.16	1.00	−0.58	0.17	1.09	2.03	3.29	3.84
	21. Hotel and restaurants	14.86	1.72	0.37	1.36	1.16	1.83	2.77	2.98	7.58	2.57
	22. Transport and storage	7.43	3.15	0.60	2.55	0.23	0.01	1.43	2.44	3.88	0.17
	23. Post and telecommunications	11.26	6.48	1.43	5.05	1.10	0.15	1.21	1.02	2.37	1.15
	24. Financial intermediation	15.93	5.15	1.56	3.59	2.51	0.04	0.60	3.44	4.08	4.15
	25. Real estate activities	9.66	5.48	1.76	3.72	0.22	0.01	2.45	0.49	2.95	1.00
	26. Renting of m&eq and other business activities	9.16	3.78	0.91	2.87	1.81	0.04	2.14	2.21	4.39	(0.87)
	27. Public admin. and defense; Compulsory social security	7.58	1.20	0.18	1.02	1.16	0.18	1.38	2.44	4.00	1.04
	28. Education	7.86	0.23	0.06	0.17	3.58	0.28	0.85	0.49	1.62	2.16
	29. Health and social work	14.86	2.53	0.67	1.86	3.12	0.27	4.23	2.02	6.51	2.43
	30. Other community, social and personal services	8.91	3.38	0.53	2.85	0.45	0.27	1.42	2.48	4.17	0.64

Source: Calculations based on Taiwan KLEMS database, August 2015.

Table 9.8b Sources of industry output growth (in % share): 1981–90

unit:%

Sector	Industry number and name	GO	ConK	ConICT	Con Non-ICT	ConL	ConE	ConM	ConS	ConII	TFP
Primary	1. Agriculture, hunting and forestry	100.00	45.66	9.45	36.21	(13.66)	1.07	55.98	19.49	76.54	(9.61)
Secondary	2. Mining and quarrying	100.00	817.61	0.23	817.38	(258.86)	(23.87)	300.54	94.09	370.76	(805.64)
	3. Food products, beverages and tobacco	100.00	22.48	2.08	20.40	(1.06)	1.28	62.01	14.35	77.65	(0.34)
	4. Textiles, textile products, leather and footwear	100.00	24.07	0.29	23.78	(13.77)	2.81	77.44	14.40	94.64	(7.75)
	5. Wood and products of wood and cork	100.00	47.23	0.50	46.73	(50.42)	12.75	(46.40)	96.24	62.58	27.86
	6. Pulp, paper, paper products, printing and publishing	100.00	16.79	0.32	16.47	7.91	3.91	56.23	23.71	83.84	(12.45)
	7. Coke, refined petroleum products and nuclear fuel	100.00	46.92	0.46	46.46	2.37	55.05	(23.71)	35.81	67.15	(71.49)
	8. Chemicals and chemical products	100.00	9.27	0.92	8.35	1.33	2.49	62.99	10.16	75.64	11.26
	9. Rubber and plastic products	100.00	5.27	(0.04)	5.31	2.86	2.04	62.39	11.54	75.97	13.86
	10. Other non-metallic mineral products	100.00	22.16	0.23	21.93	1.00	6.28	38.40	25.07	69.75	0.80
	11. Basic metals and fabricated metal products	100.00	10.23	0.24	9.99	5.13	2.39	58.37	13.90	74.65	7.59
	12. Machinery, nec	100.00	2.30	0.10	2.19	6.34	1.01	64.78	16.71	82.51	7.85
	13. Electrical and optical equipment	100.00	5.48	0.34	5.14	3.49	1.56	63.23	15.31	80.10	9.37
	14. Transport equipment	100.00	11.74	1.68	10.06	2.67	1.28	69.12	9.59	79.99	4.32
	15. Manufacturing nec; Recycling	100.00	15.41	(0.04)	15.44	3.32	1.30	51.19	17.12	69.61	10.36
	16. Electricity, gas and water supply	100.00	28.05	4.68	23.36	0.97	25.49	(6.23)	13.83	33.09	12.41
	17. Construction	100.00	16.22	0.29	15.94	(0.99)	0.16	59.30	16.55	76.01	8.61

Tertiary	18. Sale, maintenance and repair of motor vehicles	100.00	6.75	1.30	5.45	19.98	1.97	28.84	21.11	51.91	19.39
	19. Wholesale trade and commission trade	100.00	14.62	2.16	12.46	15.60	0.39	6.79	26.89	34.07	35.32
	20. Retail trade, except motor vehicles and motorcycles	100.00	14.70	2.05	12.65	(7.32)	2.14	13.88	25.72	41.74	48.75
	21. Hotel and restaurants	100.00	11.60	2.48	9.12	7.83	12.29	18.63	20.07	50.99	17.30
	22. Transport and storage	100.00	42.38	8.10	34.28	3.04	0.07	19.26	32.89	52.22	2.29
	23. Post and telecommunications	100.00	57.59	12.71	44.88	9.81	1.29	10.72	9.05	21.07	10.23
	24. Financial intermediation	100.00	32.34	9.77	22.57	15.74	0.28	3.74	21.58	25.59	26.04
	25. Real estate activities	100.00	56.76	18.26	38.50	2.27	0.15	25.31	5.04	30.51	10.31
	26. Renting of m&eq and other business activities	100.00	41.28	9.92	31.36	19.74	0.47	23.32	24.17	47.96	(9.46)
	27. Public admin. and defense; Compulsory social security	100.00	15.83	2.35	13.48	15.28	2.36	18.23	32.20	52.79	13.74
	28. Education	100.00	2.92	0.72	2.20	45.56	3.54	10.76	6.27	20.56	27.42
	29. Health and social work	100.00	17.02	4.53	12.49	21.01	1.79	28.48	13.57	43.84	16.35
	30. Other community, social and personal services	100.00	37.93	5.98	31.96	5.04	3.04	15.93	27.83	46.80	7.18

Source: Calculations based on Taiwan KLEMS database, August 2015.

Table 9.9a Sources of industry output growth (in growth rate): 1991–2000

unit:%

Sector	Industry number and name	GO	ConK	ConICT	Con Non-ICT	ConL	ConE	ConM	ConS	ConlI	TFP
Primary	1. Agriculture, hunting and forestry	(0.25)	1.02	(0.08)	1.09	(1.24)	0.00	(0.55)	0.41	(0.13)	0.10
Secondary	2. Mining and quarrying	0.01	5.56	0.43	5.13	(0.41)	0.09	0.09	0.03	0.21	(5.45)
	3. Food products, beverages and tobacco	0.27	1.81	0.62	1.19	(0.14)	0.01	(0.61)	0.58	(0.02)	(1.39)
	4. Textiles, textile products, leather and footwear	(1.04)	0.59	0.06	0.53	(0.82)	0.00	(0.46)	0.56	0.10	(0.92)
	5. Wood and products of wood and cork	(8.31)	0.20	(0.02)	0.22	(2.13)	(0.47)	(4.29)	(1.85)	(6.61)	0.69
	6. Pulp, paper, paper products, printing and publishing	1.97	0.84	0.10	0.74	0.07	0.37	(0.26)	1.32	1.43	(0.74)
	7. Coke, refined petroleum products and nuclear fuel	4.99	3.92	0.08	3.84	(0.12)	1.35	1.18	0.32	2.85	(3.00)
	8. Chemicals and chemical products	7.57	2.96	0.72	2.24	0.16	0.58	3.06	1.94	5.58	(1.71)
	9. Rubber and plastic products	3.32	0.56	0.29	0.27	0.10	0.28	1.05	1.27	2.60	(0.22)
	10. Other non-metallic mineral products	3.13	1.98	0.08	1.90	(0.24)	(0.19)	0.88	1.04	1.74	(0.16)
	11. Basic metals and fabricated metal products	7.74	1.14	0.17	0.97	0.28	0.22	3.90	1.86	5.98	0.11
	12. Machinery, nec	7.21	0.47	(0.01)	0.48	0.39	0.09	3.45	2.16	5.71	0.55
	13. Electrical and optical equipment	13.91	1.39	0.31	1.08	0.52	0.23	6.03	4.31	10.57	1.20
	14. Transport equipment	3.89	1.90	0.10	1.80	0.01	0.02	1.84	1.54	3.40	(1.43)
	15. Manufacturing nec; Recycling	0.19	1.36	0.17	1.19	(0.85)	(0.02)	(0.61)	0.58	(0.05)	(0.24)
	16. Electricity, gas and water supply	7.04	5.01	1.95	3.05	(0.03)	1.02	1.52	0.88	3.43	(2.38)
	17. Construction	4.18	0.63	(0.04)	0.67	0.37	(0.00)	1.98	1.42	3.41	(0.23)

Tertiary	18. Sale, maintenance and repair of motor vehicles	3.60	(0.11)	0.09	(0.20)	0.60	0.02	(0.32)	0.94	0.64	2.45
	19. Wholesale trade and commission trade	7.95	(0.66)	(0.19)	(0.47)	2.22	0.05	(0.03)	2.59	2.61	3.74
	20. Retail trade, except motor vehicles and motorcycles	6.80	(0.01)	0.34	(0.35)	1.00	0.11	(0.23)	1.80	1.68	4.03
	21. Hotel and restaurants	7.85	1.13	0.11	1.02	0.56	0.30	0.83	2.75	3.87	2.00
	22. Transport and storage	6.80	2.86	0.03	2.83	0.18	0.08	1.02	2.56	3.66	0.02
	23. Post and telecommunications	16.10	3.97	0.91	3.05	0.34	0.28	1.16	2.67	4.12	7.39
	24. Financial intermediation	6.94	2.53	0.57	1.97	1.18	(0.01)	(0.02)	1.77	1.74	1.49
	25. Real estate activities	6.91	4.44	(0.63)	5.07	0.29	(0.01)	0.11	0.94	1.04	1.14
	26. Renting of m&eq and other business activities	11.35	4.00	1.70	2.30	2.03	0.19	1.17	4.33	5.69	(0.57)
	27. Public admin. and defense; Compulsory social security	2.55	1.65	0.21	1.43	0.32	(0.09)	(0.04)	0.07	(0.05)	0.73
	28. Education	8.23	0.31	0.09	0.22	3.86	0.17	0.57	0.80	1.53	2.37
	29. Health and social work	9.45	2.92	1.14	1.78	1.69	0.32	1.06	2.47	3.85	0.68
	30. Other community, social and personal services	7.19	7.49	1.12	6.36	0.37	0.14	1.04	2.56	3.74	(4.55)

Source: Calculations based on Taiwan KLEMS database, August 2015.

Table 9.9b Sources of industry output growth (in % share): 1991–2000

unit:%

Sector	Industry number and name	GO	ConK	ConICT	Con Non-ICT	ConL	ConE	ConM	ConS	ConII	TFP
Primary	1. Agriculture, hunting and forestry	100.00	(408.80)	31.03	(439.83)	498.81	(1.43)	219.14	(165.22)	52.49	(41.07)
Secondary	2. Mining and quarrying	100.00	60630.24	4742.46	55887.78	(4470.53)	995.23	1000.59	342.90	2338.72	(59393.66)
	3. Food products, beverages and tobacco	100.00	677.44	233.20	444.24	(53.44)	2.46	(227.01)	216.79	(7.76)	(518.70)
	4. Textiles, textile products, leather and footwear	100.00	(57.07)	(6.00)	(51.07)	78.63	(0.02)	44.41	(54.30)	(9.91)	88.36
	5. Wood and products of wood and cork	100.00	(2.46)	0.24	(2.70)	25.61	5.65	51.62	22.27	79.54	(8.34)
	6. Pulp, paper, paper products, printing and publishing	100.00	42.48	5.11	37.37	3.80	18.61	(13.38)	67.34	72.57	(37.46)
	7. Coke, refined petroleum products and nuclear fuel	100.00	78.49	1.65	76.84	(2.33)	26.96	23.59	6.51	57.06	(60.19)
	8. Chemicals and chemical products	100.00	39.08	9.56	29.52	2.11	7.70	40.37	25.64	73.70	(22.60)
	9. Rubber and plastic products	100.00	16.87	8.64	8.23	3.16	8.46	31.46	38.26	78.18	(6.66)
	10. Other non-metallic mineral products	100.00	63.23	2.46	60.77	(7.65)	(6.06)	28.25	33.31	55.49	(5.01)
	11. Basic metals and fabricated metal products	100.00	14.74	2.21	12.54	3.68	2.82	50.42	24.08	77.32	1.44
	12. Machinery, nec	100.00	6.56	(0.12)	6.68	5.41	1.29	47.86	29.99	79.15	7.59
	13. Electrical and optical equipment	100.00	10.01	2.23	7.78	3.77	1.64	43.33	31.00	75.97	8.60
	14. Transport equipment	100.00	48.82	2.59	46.24	0.15	0.42	47.29	39.51	87.23	(36.61)

	15. Manufacturing nec; Recycling	100.00	717.99	88.17	629.82	(451.64)	(12.21)	(321.65)	306.67	(27.19)	(126.95)
	16. Electricity, gas and water supply	100.00	71.08	27.71	43.37	(0.49)	14.52	21.65	12.51	48.68	(33.79)
Tertiary	17. Construction	100.00	15.20	(0.91)	16.12	8.85	(0.02)	47.53	34.03	81.55	(5.58)
	18. Sale, maintenance and repair of motor vehicles	100.00	(3.11)	2.36	(5.48)	16.61	0.60	(8.96)	26.20	17.84	68.06
	19. Wholesale trade and commission trade	100.00	(8.34)	(2.40)	(5.94)	27.92	0.57	(0.32)	32.57	32.81	47.04
	20. Retail trade, except motor vehicles and motorcycles	100.00	(0.20)	4.94	(5.14)	14.66	1.59	(3.38)	26.50	24.71	59.25
	21. Hotel and restaurants	100.00	14.34	1.35	12.99	7.08	3.81	10.51	34.96	49.28	25.49
	22. Transport and storage	100.00	42.09	0.48	41.61	2.65	1.18	14.94	37.68	53.80	0.28
	23. Post and telecommunications	100.00	24.64	5.68	18.95	2.12	1.75	7.21	16.62	25.58	45.91
	24. Financial intermediation	100.00	36.54	8.16	28.38	17.03	(0.11)	(0.36)	25.51	25.04	21.50
	25. Real estate activities	100.00	64.34	(9.11)	73.45	4.17	(0.10)	1.55	13.64	15.09	16.49
	26. Renting of m&eq and other business activities	100.00	35.28	15.01	20.27	17.92	1.70	10.31	38.15	50.16	(5.06)
	27. Public admin. and defense; Compulsory social security	100.00	64.59	8.42	56.17	12.49	(3.47)	(1.39)	2.75	(2.12)	28.51
	28. Education	100.00	3.73	1.06	2.67	46.84	2.02	6.87	9.69	18.58	28.83
	29. Health and social work	100.00	30.88	12.06	18.82	17.92	3.36	11.18	26.16	40.70	7.15
	30. Other community, social and personal services	100.00	104.16	15.61	88.55	5.15	1.92	14.47	35.66	52.05	(63.29)

Source: Calculations based on Taiwan KLEMS database, August 2015.

Table 9.10a Sources of industry output growth (in growth rate): 2001–10

unit:%

Sector	Industry number and name	GO	ConK	ConICT	Con Non-ICT	ConL	ConE	ConM	ConS	ConII	TFP
Primary	1. Agriculture, hunting and forestry	(0.99)	0.57	0.32	0.25	(0.86)	(0.00)	(0.83)	(0.15)	(0.99)	0.28
Secondary	2. Mining and quarrying	(0.26)	29.85	11.33	12.75	(0.32)	(0.01)	1.20	0.40	1.60	(25.62)
	3. Food products, beverages and tobacco	0.04	1.00	0.71	0.29	0.01	0.04	(0.04)	0.32	0.32	(1.29)
	4. Textiles, textile products, leather and footwear	(3.53)	0.14	0.12	0.03	(0.71)	(0.11)	(2.03)	(0.39)	(2.53)	(0.43)
	5. Wood and products of wood and cork	(1.29)	0.26	0.31	(0.05)	(1.04)	(0.12)	(0.06)	(0.73)	(0.91)	0.39
	6. Pulp, paper, paper products, printing and publishing	1.17	0.27	0.15	0.12	(0.11)	(0.20)	0.48	0.05	0.33	0.69
	7. Coke, refined petroleum products and nuclear fuel	2.64	1.77	0.80	0.98	(0.01)	(0.29)	1.70	(0.03)	1.39	(0.51)
	8. Chemicals and chemical products	5.35	1.67	1.01	0.66	(0.05)	0.03	4.49	(0.23)	4.30	(0.56)
	9. Rubber and plastic products	(2.16)	0.11	0.11	0.00	(0.32)	(0.19)	(1.15)	(0.53)	(1.87)	(0.08)
	10. Other non-metallic mineral products	(0.33)	0.65	0.53	0.12	(0.17)	(0.15)	(0.17)	(0.41)	(0.73)	(0.09)
	11. Basic metals and fabricated metal products	0.49	1.09	0.76	0.33	0.09	(0.08)	0.71	(0.37)	0.26	(0.95)
	12. Machinery, nec	4.35	1.48	1.02	0.46	0.15	0.01	2.06	1.18	3.25	(0.53)
	13. Electrical and optical equipment	8.98	2.25	1.44	0.81	0.31	0.23	3.51	1.57	5.31	1.11
	14. Transport equipment	2.30	1.04	0.65	0.39	0.05	0.04	0.87	0.65	1.56	(0.35)
	15. Manufacturing nec; Recycling	(1.09)	1.33	0.92	0.41	(0.49)	(0.05)	(0.79)	0.00	(0.84)	(1.09)
	16. Electricity, gas and water supply	2.19	0.28	(0.02)	0.30	(0.03)	0.41	0.96	(0.30)	1.06	0.88
	17. Construction	(0.68)	4.19	(0.00)	4.19	(0.12)	0.00	(0.31)	(0.23)	0.54	(4.21)

Tertiary										
18.	Sale, maintenance and repair of motor vehicles	2.08	0.47	0.31	0.16	(0.50)	0.05	0.45	0.31	0.81	1.30
19.	Wholesale trade and commission trade	4.24	0.28	0.14	0.13	0.06	0.10	0.36	0.60	1.05	2.85
20.	Retail trade, except motor vehicles and motorcycles	2.44	1.32	0.79	0.52	(0.04)	0.18	0.14	0.60	0.92	0.25
21.	Hotel and restaurants	1.75	3.34	2.39	0.95	0.65	(0.33)	1.26	(0.31)	0.61	(2.85)
22.	Transport and storage	1.93	0.50	0.11	0.39	(0.21)	(0.01)	1.03	0.09	1.11	0.53
23.	Post and telecommunications	4.15	(0.04)	(0.09)	0.05	(0.11)	(0.04)	(0.24)	1.42	1.14	3.16
24.	Financial intermediation	1.55	0.52	0.20	0.32	(0.05)	0.01	0.00	0.60	0.62	0.46
25.	Real estate activities	2.64	2.05	(0.03)	2.08	0.03	0.03	(0.57)	0.81	0.27	0.28
26.	Renting of m&eq and other business activities	4.69	1.53	0.81	0.72	2.44	(0.04)	0.76	0.50	1.22	(0.50)
27.	Public admin. and defense; Compulsory social security	0.23	0.05	(0.05)	0.10	1.05	(0.03)	(0.48)	0.08	(0.44)	(0.43)
28.	Education	3.37	0.07	(0.01)	0.08	1.90	0.04	0.23	0.49	0.76	0.64
29.	Health and social work	2.25	(0.36)	(0.23)	(0.14)	1.38	0.05	0.32	0.49	0.86	0.38
30.	Other community, social and personal services	3.81	1.65	0.38	1.27	0.09	0.04	0.14	1.16	1.34	0.73

Source: Calculations based on Taiwan KLEMS database, August 2015.

Table 9.10b Sources of industry output growth (in % share): 2001–10

unit:%

Sector	Industry number and name	GO	ConK	ConICT	ConNon-ICT	ConL	ConE	ConM	ConS	ConLL	TFP
Primary	1. Agriculture, hunting and forestry	100.00	(57.60)	(32.32)	(25.28)	86.38	0.18	83.89	15.35	99.42	(28.20)
Secondary	2. Mining and quarrying	100.00	(11434.80)	(4340.07)	(4884.21)	122.37	3.16	(461.27)	(153.98)	(612.09)	9814.00
	3. Food products, beverages and tobacco	100.00	2789.73	1978.35	811.38	18.10	110.46	(111.66)	895.93	894.73	(3602.56)
	4. Textiles, textile products, leather and footwear	100.00	(4.07)	(3.36)	(0.72)	20.13	3.01	57.58	11.17	71.76	12.18
	5. Wood and products of wood and cork	100.00	(20.36)	(24.21)	3.86	80.61	9.02	4.29	57.09	70.40	(30.65)
	6. Pulp, paper, paper products, printing and publishing	100.00	22.80	12.99	9.82	(9.75)	(17.23)	40.64	4.56	27.96	58.98
	7. Coke, refined petroleum products and nuclear fuel	100.00	67.09	30.11	36.98	(0.45)	(10.92)	64.50	(1.04)	52.54	(19.19)
	8. Chemicals and chemical products	100.00	31.19	18.79	12.40	(0.99)	0.56	83.99	(4.26)	80.29	(10.48)
	9. Rubber and plastic products	100.00	(5.11)	(5.09)	(0.02)	14.66	8.97	53.22	24.53	86.72	3.73
	10. Other non-metallic mineral products	100.00	(195.75)	(160.08)	(35.66)	49.92	45.70	49.78	124.52	220.00	25.83
	11. Basic metals and fabricated metal products	100.00	225.24	156.83	68.41	18.63	(16.79)	146.52	(77.14)	52.59	(196.46)
	12. Machinery, nec	100.00	34.01	23.53	10.48	3.40	0.28	47.22	27.20	74.70	(12.10)
	13. Electrical and optical equipment	100.00	25.12	16.07	9.05	3.43	2.59	39.07	17.45	59.11	12.35
	14. Transport equipment	100.00	45.36	28.43	16.92	2.06	1.53	38.02	28.26	67.81	(15.23)

15. Manufacturing nec; Recycling	100.00	(121.58)	(84.45)	(37.12)	45.25	4.37	72.33	(0.23)	76.47	99.86
16. Electricity, gas and water supply	100.00	12.64	(0.85)	13.49	(1.37)	18.53	43.73	(13.88)	48.38	40.35
Tertiary										
17. Construction	100.00	(612.17)	0.19	(612.37)	17.94	(0.38)	46.04	33.29	78.95	615.28
18. Sale, maintenance and repair of motor vehicles	100.00	22.46	14.77	7.69	(23.96)	2.46	21.76	14.77	38.99	62.52
19. Wholesale trade and commission trade	100.00	6.51	3.37	3.14	1.48	2.26	8.43	14.13	24.82	67.18
20. Retail trade, except motor vehicles and motorcycles	100.00	54.07	32.55	21.52	(1.71)	7.23	5.54	24.76	37.53	10.11
21. Hotel and restaurants	100.00	190.91	136.63	54.29	37.06	(19.01)	71.98	(17.93)	35.04	(163.02)
22. Transport and storage	100.00	25.75	5.51	20.24	(10.75)	(0.45)	53.45	4.53	57.53	27.47
23. Post and telecommunications	100.00	(1.07)	(2.17)	1.10	(2.77)	(0.90)	(5.88)	34.30	27.53	76.31
24. Financial intermediation	100.00	33.73	13.18	20.55	(3.06)	0.90	0.18	38.73	39.81	29.51
25. Real estate activities	100.00	77.63	(1.16)	78.79	1.22	1.02	(21.46)	30.80	10.36	10.80
26. Renting of m&eq and other business activities	100.00	32.62	17.29	15.33	51.95	(0.78)	16.25	10.57	26.04	(10.61)
27. Public admin. and defense; Compulsory social security	100.00	20.02	(21.54)	41.56	457.71	(13.93)	(210.53)	33.35	(191.11)	(186.62)
28. Education	100.00	2.20	(0.23)	2.43	56.41	1.25	6.78	14.47	22.50	18.90
29. Health and social work	100.00	(16.18)	(9.98)	(6.20)	61.36	2.35	14.01	21.66	38.01	16.80
30. Other community, social and personal services	100.00	43.32	9.85	33.46	2.42	0.95	3.74	30.47	35.16	19.10

Source: Calculations based on Taiwan KLEMS database, August 2015.

Table 9.11 Sources of GO growth for the electrical and optical equipment industry

Period	ConK	ConICT	Con Non-ICT	ConL	ConE	ConM	ConS	ConII	TFP
1981–2010	12.41	5.19	7.22	3.59	1.86	48.94	22.18	72.98	11.02
1981–90	5.48	0.34	5.14	3.49	1.56	63.23	15.31	80.10	9.37
1991–2000	10.01	2.23	7.78	3.77	1.64	43.33	31.00	75.97	8.60
2001–10	25.12	16.07	9.05	3.43	2.59	39.07	17.45	59.11	12.35

Source: Calculations based on Taiwan KLEMS database, August 2015.

Table 9.12 Sources of GO growth for the wholesale and commission trade industry

Period	ConK	ConICT	Con Non-ICT	ConL	ConE	ConM	ConS	ConII	TFP
1981–2010	3.93	0.63	3.30	17.48	0.85	4.35	26.45	31.64	46.95
1981–90	14.62	2.16	12.46	15.60	0.39	6.79	26.89	34.07	35.32
1991–2000	(8.34)	(2.40)	(5.94)	27.92	0.57	(0.32)	32.57	32.81	47.04
2001–10	6.51	3.37	3.14	1.48	2.26	8.43	14.13	24.82	67.18

Source: Calculations based on Taiwan KLEMS database, August 2015.

is quite small. Instead, we can find that the contribution from service dominates other intermediate inputs. Furthermore, it should be noted that TFP has increased over time and became the dominant driver in 2001–10. The contribution of L is significant in the early decades, but gradually fell over time. The contribution of K is relatively low in these industries. The results discussed can be demonstrated in Table 9.12.

The sector with the biggest annual growth rate among tertiary industries is '23 Post and telecommunications'. This industry is also regarded as a major ICT-using industry in Taiwan. We find that it had quite a high contribution share from K in 1981–90, high shares from II and TFP in 1991–2000, and a very high share from TFP in 2001–10. We list the contribution shares of its factor inputs in Table 9.13. The structure of sources of output growth for this industry changes dramatically fast, which seems to fit in with the characteristic of the Post and Telecommunications Industry.

Table 9.13 Sources of GO growth for the post and telecommunications industry

Period	ConK	ConICT	Con Non-ICT	ConL	ConE	ConM	ConS	ConII	TFP
1981–2010	32.12	6.96	25.16	4.02	1.24	6.60	16.51	24.34	39.51
1981–90	57.59	12.71	44.88	9.81	1.29	10.72	9.05	21.07	10.23
1991–2000	24.64	5.68	18.95	2.12	1.75	7.21	16.62	25.58	45.91
2001–10	(1.07)	(2.17)	1.10	(2.77)	(0.90)	(5.88)	34.30	27.53	76.31

Source: Calculations based on Taiwan KLEMS database, August 2015.

Based upon the above discussions, we may conclude that the contribution share of II to industry output in most tertiary industries tends to be smaller than those for the secondary industries.

Concluding remarks

In the last several decades, Taiwan's industrial policy focused on how to help high-tech industries, such as ICT, '13 Electrical and Optical Equipment,' and '23 Post and telecommunications.' The strategies included the establishment of science-based industrial parks; technological support from national research institutes; national planning, tax incentives, and special support for the development of the local semiconductor industry; and so on. It is clear that significant structural changes happened in the past decades. The industry weights for primary and secondary industries have decreased over time, while the importance of tertiary industries has risen during the period 1981–2010. The industry weights of most of the secondary industries fell, except for 'Electrical and optical equipment' and 'Basic and fabricated metal'. On the contrary, most tertiary industries increased their weights over 1981–2010. It is thus shown that the industrial policy is a significant factor influencing industrial structural change.

The empirical results show that the output growth rate for the 31 industries ranged from 11.92 percent to –2.97 percent in 1981–2010 and varied by sub-period. The results also present that the structure of the factor contribution share differed by industry. However, in general, the contribution share from intermediate inputs dominates that from other inputs (capital and labor) for most sectors in secondary industries. In several industries, such as food products and textile, rubber and plastics, their growth rates of labor input are negative. However, such inputs' dominant contribution effect differs by sector in the tertiary industries. This indicates the importance of growth decomposition analysis at the industry level.

We also find that the TFP growth rate of '13 Electrical and optical equipment' is the highest among secondary industries, while the TFP growth rate of '23 Post and telecommunications' is the largest among tertiary industries. This means that the industrial policy not only impacts structural change, but also influences the TFP growth rate. We find that capital is the main driver to value-added (VA) output growth and intermediate inputs are the main driver to gross output (GO) growth. Among those intermediate inputs, we find that the contribution share from materials input (ConM) outweighs those from other inputs (capital and labor) for most secondary industries. We also find that the contribution share of the services input (ConS) plays a dominant role on GO growth for most tertiary industries. Furthermore, our cross-period comparison results indicate that the roles of the contribution shares of K and II have decreased over time, whereas the contribution from TFP has increased over time. Lastly, tertiary industries have had higher growth rates as well as higher TFP than the secondary industries over the last three decades in Taiwan.

Note

1 The last industry, "31. Private households with employed persons", is dropped in TFP analysis in this study since there is no intermediate input data of this industry.

Bibliography

Chang, C. C., and Y. H. Luh. 2000. "Efficiency Change and Growth in Productivity: The Asian Growth Experience." *Journal of Asian Economics* 10: 551–570.

Chen, C. F., and K. T. Soo. 2007. "Cost Structure and Productivity Growth of the Taiwanese International Tourist Hotels." *Tourism Management* 28: 1400–1407.

Chen, T. Y., and T. L. Yeh. 2000. "A Measurement of Bank Efficiency, Ownership and Productivity Changes in Taiwan." *Service Industries Journal* 20: 95–109.

Chun, H., Hak K. Pyo, and K. H. Rhee. 2008. "Multifactor Productivity in Korea and an International Comparison: Data and Productivity Estimates of the Korea Industrial Productivity Database." *Seoul Journal of Economics* 21(4): 7.

Fu, T. T., and Y. M. Lin. 2015. "Productivity in Retrospect – Republic of China." In Tsu-Tan Fu (ed.), *Productivity in the Asia-Pacific: Past, Present & Future*, commemorating the 50th Anniversary of the APO Special Publication. Japan: Asia Productivity Organization. ISBN: 978-92-833-2437-9.

Fu, T. T., Y. M. Lin, H. C. Lin, and W.H. Kong. 2016. "The Construction of Taiwan KLEMS Growth and Productivity Accounts and Database." Manuscript, in Chinese.

Fukao, K., T. Miyagawa, H. K. Pyo, and R. H. Rhee. 2011. "Estimates of Total Factor Productivity, the Contribution of ICT, and Resource Reallocation Effects in Japan and Korea." *Global COE Hi-Stat Discussion Paper Series* 177.

Huang, Cliff J., and T. T. Fu. 2009. "Uncertainty and Total Factor Productivity in the Taiwanese Banking Industry." *Applied Financial Economics* 19: 753–766.

Huang, M. Y., J. C. Juo, and T. T. Fu. 2014. "Metafrontier Cost Malmquist Productivity Index: An Application to Taiwanese and Chinese Commercial Banks." *Journal of Productivity Analysis* 44: 321–325.

Jorgenson, Dale, Mun S. Ho, Kevin Stiroh. 2005. *Productivity, volume 3: Information Technology and the American Growth Ressurgence*. Cambridge, MA: MIT Press.

Jorgenson, D. W., F. M. Gollop, and B. M. Fraumeni. 1987. *Productivity and U.S. Economic Growth*. Cambridge, MA: Harvard University Press.

Jorgenson, D. W., and Z. Griliches. 1967. "The Explanation of Productivity Change." *Review of Economic Studies* 34: 249–283.

Jorgenson, D. W., M. Koroda, and M. Nishimizu. 1987. "Japan-US. Industry-Level Productivity Comparisons: 1960–1979." *Journal of the Japanese and International Economies* 1: 1–30.

Jorgenson, D. W., Mun S. Ho, J. Samuels, and K. J. Stiroh. 2007. Industry Origins of the American Productivity Resurgence. *Economic Systems Research* 19(3): 229–252.

Jorgenson, D. W., and K. Nomura. 2007. "The Industry Origins of the US–Japan Productivity Gap." *Economic Systems Research* 19(3): 315–341.

Krugman, P. 1994. "The Myth of Asia's Miracle." *Foreign Affairs* 73(6): 62–78.

O'Mahony, M., and M. P. Timmer. 2009. "Output, Input and Productivity Measures at the Industry Level: The EU KLEMS Database." *Economic Journal* 119: F374–F403.

Pyo, Hak, K. H. Rhee, and H. Chun. 2012. *Asia KLEMS Growth and Productivity Accounts, Version 1.0. Draft and Proposal, Part 1 Methodology*. Asia KLEMS Consortium.

Timmer, Marcel P., Robert Inklaar, Mary O'Mahony and Bart van Ark. 2010, Economic Growth in Europe. *A Comparative Industry Perspective*, Cambridge University Press.

Young, A. 1992. "A Tale of Two Cities: Factor Accumulation and Technical Change in Hong Kong and Singapore." *NBER Macroeconomics Annual*: 13–64.

Young, A. 1994. "Lessons From the East Asian NICs: A Contrarian View." *European Economic Review* 38: 964–973.

Young, A. 1995. "The Tyranny of Numbers: Confronting the Statistical Realities of the East Asian Growth Experience." *Quarterly Journal of Economics* 110: 641–680.

Yu, M. M., and L. H. Chen. 2016. "Productivity Growth of Taiwanese International Tourist Hotels in a Metafrontier Framework." *Cornell Hospitality Quarterly* 57: 38–50.

Chapter 10

Total factor productivity and the sources of Singapore's economic growth

Measurement, insights, and projection[1]

Dale W. Jorgenson and Khuong M. Vu

Introduction

Total factor productivity (TFP) has long been considered the main source of economic growth and a major driver of a nation's advancement toward prosperity. However, this conventional wisdom has been challenged by the growth experiences of the East Asian newly industrialized countries (NICs), which include South Korea, Taiwan, Hong Kong, and Singapore. These economies have experienced remarkably high GDP growth for long periods in spite of their surprisingly low TFP growth (TFPG). Tsao (1985), Young (1992, 1995), and Kim and Lau (1994) are among the first studies to point out this paradox (Table 10.1).

Most studies have drawn dismal conclusions regarding the growth performance of the NICs. Young (1995) concluded that whereas 'the growth of output [. . .] in the newly industrialized countries is virtually unprecedented, the growth of TFP in these economies is not'; Kim and Lau (1994) argued that 'the hypothesis that there has been no technical progress during the postwar period cannot be rejected for the four East Asian newly industrialized countries.'

Among the four NICs, the problem of low TFPG appeared most acute for Singapore. Young (1995) and Kim and Lau (1994) are consistent in estimating that TFPG accounted for a very small share (less than 5 percent) of Singapore's output growth. This problem, indeed, had been brought up much earlier for Singapore. Tsao (1982, 1985) showed that productivity growth in Singapore's manufacturing sector during 1970–79 was nearly nil (0.08 percent),

Table 10.1 Output and TFP growth in NICs from selected previous studies[i]

Unit:%

Period	S. Korea		Taiwan		Hong Kong		Singapore	
	Output	TFP	Output	TFP	Output	TFP	Output	TFP
Tsao (1985)*	–	–	–	–	–	–	8.3	0.08
Young (1995)**	10.3	1.7	8.9	2.1	7.3	2.3	8.7	0.2
Kim and Lau (1994)***	8.6	−0.05	9.4	2.6	7.8	2.0	8.9	0.4

Notes: *For Singapore's manufacturing sector in 1970–9. **The period is 1966–90; TFPG estimates in Young (1995) for S. Korea and Taiwan exclude agriculture. ***TFPG is from the study's conventional estimates; the period is 1960–90 for S. Korea, 1953–90 for Taiwan, 1966–90 for Hong Kong, and 1964–90 for Singapore.

Source: compiled by authors.

i Among the studies on TFP growth in the NICs, Young (1992, 1995) and Kim and Lau (1994) are the earliest works with comprehensive comparative analyses of all four economies.

while its output grew rapidly at 8.3 percent during the same period. Young (1992), who compared the growth performance between Singapore and Hong Kong, showed that Singapore's TFPG was extremely low relative to Hong Kong's. This sharp contrast sparked a fervent debate about Singapore's growth model and implications for its interventionist economic policy. With Singapore as the focal point, Krugman (1994) adopted a blunt pessimistic view about the East Asian growth model. He compared the growth in these economies with the Soviet Union, which also achieved outstanding growth through rapid input accumulation for a long period before its economic stagnation and eventual collapse in 1991. Krugman (in 1994) predicted: 'from the perspective of the year 2010, current projections of Asian supremacy extrapolated from recent trends may well look almost as silly as 1960-vintage forecasts of Soviet industrial supremacy did from the perspective of the Brezhnev years' (p. 78).

Hsieh (2002) challenged the pessimistic views of Singapore's growth model by applying dual approach growth accounting to estimate TFPG. He found that the primal and dual estimates of TFPG for Singapore are vastly different: while the primal estimate based on the standard approach ranges between –0.69 to –0.22 percentage points, the dual estimate varies from 1.52 percent to 2.16 percent. That is, using the primal estimate of TFPG, one may conclude that there has been no technological progress in Singapore's economic growth, whereas the dual estimate of TFPG suggests the opposite conclusion: technological progress has played an important role in Singapore's growth. Hsieh (2002) concluded that, given the difficulties associated with constructing the data for standard primal accounting exercises, the dual approach provides a more reliable estimate of TFPG; hence, technological progress indeed has played an important role in Singapore's growth.

At least until 2010, reality has tended to support Hsieh's conclusion. Singapore's rapid growth since its independence in 1965, which, on average, was 7.4 percent for 1965–2009,[2] has placed Singapore among the world's top ten nations in per capita GDP (measured in purchasing power parity). Singapore's economy is forecasted to grow between 7 percent and 9 percent in 2010 after a contraction of 2 percent in 2009, when the world suffered a severe global economic crisis.

Our paper is motivated by the strikingly opposing conclusions about Singapore's growth drawn by Krugman and Hsieh. Why do these two prominent scholars have such contradictory views about a real story that has played out for decades? What are the main factors behind their clashing opinions: measurement or personal views? What can policy makers and economists alike learn from Singapore's economic growth model? Can we predict the growth of Singapore over the next decade?

Our paper aims to answer these questions. In section 2, we analyze Singapore's growth pattern and the sources of its output and labor productivity growth. Our growth accounting decomposition method takes into account the contributions of information technology capital and labor quality and thus allows us to more accurately estimate TFPG. In section 3, we discuss the pattern of TFPG in Singapore, shedding light on the debate regarding the high output growth–low TFPG paradox observed for the NICs, especially Singapore. In section 4, we show that our growth accounting decomposition framework can be turned into a helpful model for predicting labor productivity growth. This model takes into account the contribution of the quality of capital and labor inputs in addition to other sources of growth, enabling policy makers to act more effectively in promoting economic growth. We apply this model to predict Singapore's growth over the next decade, from 2009–19. Finally, in section 5, we make concluding remarks. The appendices at the end of our paper elaborate on the data estimation, growth decomposition, and growth prediction procedures presented in sections 2 and 4.

Understanding the sources of Singapore's growth

Data and growth accounting framework

The main dataset used for this exercise is from Statistics Singapore. Additional sources of data include Infocomm Development Authority of Singapore (IDA) for data on the ICT sector and Conference Board for data on total hours worked.[3]

Our growth decomposition exercise also requires a series of data estimation tasks, which include:

- Income share of labor input
- Labor quality index
- Investment flows in ICT
- Capital stocks

- Harmonized ICT deflators
- Rental prices of Capital and Capital services

The details of these estimation procedures are provided in Appendices A and B at the end of this paper.

Our decomposition framework is based on the extended production possibility frontier (PPF) model introduced by Jorgenson et al. (2005):

$$Y = A \cdot X(K_{nict}, K_{ict}, H, L_Q) \tag{10.1}$$

where gross domestic product Y is produced from an aggregate input function X of capital and labor services. The capital services are rendered by non-ICT capital K_{nict} and ICT capital K_{ict}. The non-ICT capital K_{nict} consists of three non-ICT capital vintages – non-residential buildings and structures, transport equipment, and machinery and equipment; however, the ICT capital K_{ict} comprises computer hardware, computer software, and telecommunication equipment. The labor services are from labor input L, which is a product of total hours worked H and labor quality index L_Q ($L = H \cdot L_Q$). The total factor productivity (TFP) A represents a Hicks-neutral augmentation of the aggregate input function.

Under the neoclassical assumptions of competitive markets and constant returns to scale, Equation 10.1 can be transformed into a growth accounting decomposition:

$$\Delta \ln Y = \bar{v}_{K_{ict}} \Delta \ln K_{ict} + \bar{v}_{K_{nict}} \Delta \ln K_{nict} \\ + \bar{v}_L \Delta \ln H + \bar{v}_L \Delta \ln L_Q + \Delta \ln A \tag{10.2}$$

where $\bar{v}$ is the average share in total factor income of the subscripted input over the two periods of the change. All variables are expressed in logarithmic first differences ($\Delta \ln$) to represent their growth rates. The assumption of constant returns to scale of the aggregate input function implies that

$$\bar{v}_K = \bar{v}_{K_{ict}} + \bar{v}_{K_{nict}} = 1 - \bar{v}_L$$

Equation 10.2 implies that GDP output growth can be decomposed into:

- The contribution of capital input ($\bar{v}_{K_{ict}} \Delta \ln K_{ict} + \bar{v}_{K_{nict}} \Delta \ln K_{nict}$), which consists of the contribution of ICT capital services

($\bar{v}_{K_{ict}} \Delta \ln K_{ict}$) and the contribution of non-ICT capital services ($\bar{v}_{K_{nict}} \Delta \ln K_{nict}$);
- The contribution of labor input ($\bar{v}_L \Delta \ln H + \bar{v}_L \Delta \ln L_Q$), which consists of the contribution of total hours worked ($\bar{v}_L \Delta \ln H$) and the contribution of labor quality improvement ($\bar{v}_L \Delta \ln L_Q$); and
- TFPG ($\Delta \ln A$).

For the period for which the data on labor quality and ICT capital are not available (1965–90), we treat the aggregate capital as non-ICT capital and labor input as labor hours worked. Therefore, the output growth accounting decomposition in Equation 10.2 can be simplified as

$$\Delta \ln Y = \bar{v}_K \Delta \ln K^o + \bar{v}_L \Delta \ln H + \Delta \ln A^o \qquad (10.2')$$

where the superscript 'o' indicates the estimate does not account for the contributions of labor and capital quality. It is easy to see that $\Delta \ln A^o$ in Equation 10.2', in general, is likely greater than $\Delta \ln A$ in Equation 10.2. In other words, TFPG estimated in the framework of Equation 10.2' tends to be larger than TFPG in Equation 10.2. The reason is straightforward: TFPG estimated in Equation 10.2' captures the contributions of labor and capital quality, which are positive for a longer period in most cases.

Equation 10.2 can be rewritten to decompose the growth of the average labor productivity (ALP) as

$$\Delta \ln y = \bar{v}_{K_{ict}} \Delta \ln k_{ict} + \bar{v}_{K_{nict}} \Delta \ln k_{nict} + \bar{v}_L \Delta \ln L_Q + \Delta \ln A \qquad (10.3)$$

where $y = Y/H$ is ALP and $k = K/H$ is capital deepening.

Equation 10.3 shows that three factors contribute to ALP growth:

- ICT and non-ICT capital deepening ($\bar{v}_{K_{ict}} \Delta \ln k_{ict} + \bar{v}_{K_{nict}} \Delta \ln k_{nict}$), which captures the effects of these capital vintages in capital-labor substitution;
- Labor quality improvement ($\bar{v}_L \Delta \ln L_Q$); and
- TFP growth ($\Delta \ln A$).

For the growth accounting decomposition framework, in which the contributions of labor quality and ICT capital are not extracted from TFPG, Equation 10.3 is simplified as

$$\Delta \ln y = \bar{v}_K \Delta \ln K^o + \Delta \ln A^o \qquad (10.3')$$

That is, labor productivity growth is simply contributed to by capital deepening and TFPG.

Singapore's growth patterns

The pattern of Singapore's economic growth since its independence in 1965 can be characterized by three main features: *intervention*, *vulnerability*, and *resilience*.

Intervention: The government's interventionist policy has a powerful effect on the dynamics of growth. Since its independence, the Singaporean government has adopted interventionist policies to promote economic growth and development. The policies range from attracting and cultivating foreign direct investment (FDI) to promoting domestic businesses and from targeting strategic industries to upgrading the factor conditions. These policies have evolved over time and have had strong effects on the pattern of Singapore's growth.

Vulnerability: The Singapore economy is highly vulnerable to external shocks. Singapore, by its legacy and development strategy, has a large and export-reliant manufacturing sector, of which the major industries, such as electronics, petroleum, chemicals, and shipbuilding, are large-scale and highly cyclical. As a result, any turmoil in the global environment can cause a severely adverse effect on the economy.

Resilience: The economy is able to bounce back robustly from a shock. As shown in Figure 10.1, since 1965 Singapore has experienced five major external shocks: the 1973–75 oil crisis, the 1985 global trade slowdown, the 1997–98 Asian financial crisis, the 2008–09 global economic turmoil, and the Post 9/11 Economic Recession. Although Singapore's growth dropped sharply in the periods associated with these shocks, the robustness of its recovery from each shock was remarkable.

Based on the features of Singapore's economic growth, we divided the 1965–2008 timeframe into two main periods: 1965–90 and 1990–2008. The first period, 1965–90, was characterized by the government's export-led industrialization efforts to promote quantitative growth through rapid capital accumulation. The second period, 1990–2008, was marked by the government's strategic plan to transform Singapore into a developed nation with an emphasis on qualitative development.[4] The second period was also characterized by the accelerating pace of globalization, which was fostered by the end of the Cold War in 1991, the rise of Asia, and the rapid penetration of information technology in many countries, including Singapore.

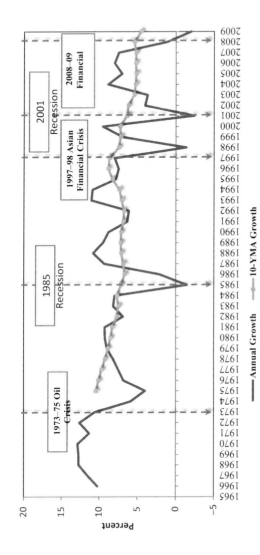

Figure 10.1 GDP growth, 1965–2009
Source: Statistics Singapore.

The first period, 1965–90, was further split into two subperiods: 1965–80 and 1980–90. In the subperiod of 1965–80, the main objectives of government policy were to promote growth through attracting FDI to create jobs and expand productive capacity (Peebles and Wilson 1996). During this subperiod, Singapore achieved fast growth but was also hit hard by the worldwide recession in 1974–75 caused by the 1973 oil crisis. Singapore's growth in the subperiod of 1980–90 was shaped by the government's policies launched in the late 1970s and early 1980s to restructure industry with a focus on high-tech manufacturing and high value-added services.[5] The economy in this subperiod, however, also experienced a recession in 1985, which was partly caused by the slump in global demand, especially from the United States (Rigg 1988).

For the period 1990–2008, we examine three six-year subperiods, 1990–96, 1996–2002, and 2002–08. The first subperiod (1990–96) witnessed the booming of Singaporean and other East Asian economies. The second subperiod (1996–2002) was marked by three major external shocks – the Asian financial crisis of 1997–98, the dotcom crash in 2000, and the 9/11 terrorist attack in 2001, all of which dealt harsh blows to Singapore's economy. In the last subperiod (2002–08), Singapore bounced back vigorously with high growth before it was hit again by the global economic crisis in 2008–09.

We decompose the sources of Singapore's output and productivity growth for the two periods, 1965–90 and 1990–2008, and their subperiods as presented above. The results are discussed in subsection 2.3 below.

Sources of output and labor productivity growth

The growth decomposition results are reported in Table 10.2 (for output) and Table 10.3 (for labor productivity). For the period of 1965–90 and its two subperiods, 1965–80 and 1980–90, due to data limitations, the contributions to growth of labor quality and ICT capital are not estimated. The sources of output growth for this period and its subperiods, therefore, are from capital (which is all treated as non-ICT capital), labor hours worked, and TFPG. As pointed out in subsection 2.1, TFPG estimated for this period should be considered as 'raw TFPG', which also includes the contributions of labor and capital quality and, hence, is slightly larger than its actual contribution.[6]

Table 10.2 Sources of GDP growth, 1965–2008

Period	1965–90			1990–2008			
Subperiod	65–80	80–90	65–90	90–96	96–02	02–08	90–08
Growth Contribution in Percentage Points							
Real GDP Growth	9.7	7.2	**8.7**	8.3	4.1	6.0	**6.2**
Capital Inputs	7.9	3.8	**6.2**	4.5	3.5	2.7	**3.6**
· ICT Capital	—	—	—	1.0	1.1	0.9	**1.0**
· Non-ICT Capital	7.9	3.8	**6.2**	3.6	2.4	1.8	**2.6**
Labor Input	1.9	1.7	**1.8**	2.1	1.3	3.0	**2.1**
· Labor Quality	—	—	—	-0.1	0.2	0.9	**0.3**
· Hours Worked	1.9	1.7	**1.8**	2.2	1.1	2.1	**1.8**
TFP	-0.1	1.7	**0.6**	1.7	-0.7	0.4	**0.5**
Growth Contribution in Share (%)							
Real GDP Growth	100.0	100.0	**100.0**	100.0	100.0	100.0	**100.0**
Capital Inputs	81.1	52.8	**71.8**	54.4	84.5	44.2	**57.8**
· ICT Capital	—	—	—	11.6	25.7	14.5	**15.7**
· Non-ICT Capital	81.1	52.8	**71.8**	42.8	58.7	29.7	**42.1**
Labor Input	20.1	23.8	**21.3**	25.3	31.3	50.0	**34.7**
· Labor Quality	—	—	—	-1.3	5.4	15.2	**5.6**
· Hours Worked	20.1	23.8	**21.3**	26.6	25.9	34.8	**29.1**
TFP	-1.2	23.3	**6.9**	20.3	-15.7	5.8	**7.5**

Source: Authors.

Table 10.3 Sources of labor productivity growth, 1965–2008

Period	1965–90		1965–90	1990–2008			1990–2008
Subperiod	65–80	80–90	65–90	90–96	96–02	02–08	90–08
Contribution in Percentage Points							
Labor Productivity Growth	5.9	3.8	**5.1**	4.2	2.2	1.9	**2.7**
Capital Deepening	6.0	2.2	**4.5**	2.6	2.6	0.6	**1.9**
· ICT Capital	—	—	—	0.8	1.0	0.6	**0.8**
· Non-ICT Capital	6.0	2.2	—	1.8	1.6	0.0	**1.1**
Labor Quality	—	—	—	−0.1	0.2	0.9	**0.3**
TFP	−0.1	1.7	**0.6**	1.7	−0.7	0.4	**0.5**
Growth Contribution in Share (%)							
Labor Productivity Growth	100.0	100.0	**100.0**	100.0	100.0	100.0	**100.0**
Capital Deepening	102.0	56.4	**88.2**	62.4	119.7	31.8	**70.6**
· ICT Capital	—	—	—	18.9	45.3	32.2	**28.9**
· Non-ICT Capital	102.0	56.4	—	43.5	74.5	−0.4	**41.7**
Labor Quality	—	—	—	−2.5	10.2	49.3	**12.6**
TFP	−2.0	43.6	**11.8**	40.1	−30.0	18.9	**16.8**

Source: Authors.

For the period of 1990–2008 and its three subperiods, 1990–96, 1996–2002, and 2002–08, the growth decomposition is complete. The contribution of capital input comprises ICT and non-ICT capital, whereas the contribution of labor inputs includes those of labor hours worked and labor quality. The contribution of TFPG in this period, therefore, is more accurately estimated.

The results of the sources of output and labor productivity growth provide more insights into the pattern of Singapore's growth over each period and subperiod. We will discuss these results in subsection 2.2.

The overall results for the 25-year period of 1965–90 show that capital input was the main driver of Singapore's growth. Capital input contributed 71.8 percent to GDP growth and 88.2 percent to labor productivity growth for the entire period (Tables 10.2 and 10.3). Meanwhile, TFPG was 0.6 percentage points and accounted for only 6.9 percent of GDP growth and 11.8 percent of labor productivity growth. The pattern of the sources of growth over this 25-year period, however, changed markedly over its two subperiods, which implies that changes in the government's policy had a profound impact on the country's growth pattern.

Over the first subperiod of 1965–80, capital input contributed 7.9 percentage points, or over 80 percent, of Singapore's superior GDP growth of 9.7 percent (Table 10.2). The pattern reflects the success of Singapore's government policy of promoting growth through massive capital accumulation. The contribution of hours worked, however, was 1.9 percentage points, which was comparable to other subperiods. Meanwhile, TFPG was negative; hence, the increase in labor productivity of 5.9 percent over this subperiod was totally driven by capital deepening (102 percent) (Table 10.3). The very low TFPG found for this subperiod is consistent with the results from previous studies, especially Tsao (1985), who found that TFPG was only 0.8 percent points in the manufacturing sector in 1970–79. There are several possible explanations for the low TFPG in Singapore over the subperiod of 1965–80. First, the government's policy might have overemphasized the effort to foster capital accumulation at the expense of resource allocation efficiency. Second, a large portion of capital investment in long-term foundations of growth, such as infrastructure and urban development, may not affect short-term GDP growth. Third, the oil crisis and world economic recession in 1973–75 raised the cost of production and reduced the profitability of Singapore's business sector, which certainly caused an adverse effect on Singapore's TFPG.

In the second subperiod, 1980–90, the government embarked on its 'second industrial revolution' strategy, which focused on shifting the economy towards higher value-added activities. The results were impressive. The average growth rates of GDP and labor productivity were lower, at 7.2 percent and 3.8 percent (Tables 10.2 and 10.3), respectively, but the growth efficiency notably improved. The contribution of capital input to output growth declined to 3.8 percentage points, or a 52.8 percent share, while raw TFPG rose to 1.7 percentage points, or a 23.3 percent share. At the same time, capital deepening accounted for 56.4 percent of labor productivity, while TFPG claimed the remaining share of 43.6 percent. These results are consistent with Toh and Ng (2002) and Akkemik (2007), who found that TFPG was negligible in the early stages of Singapore's development but have substantially increased since the late 1980s. The heavy capital deepening invested in the previous subperiod, which built the foundation for long-term growth, might also contribute to this improved performance.

Singapore's growth in the second period, from 1990 to 2008, slowed down relative to the period of 1965–90, from 8.7 percent to 6.2 percent in GDP and from 5.1 percent to 2.7 percent in labor productivity growth (Tables 10.2 and 10.3). However, the contributions of ICT capital and labor quality became notable in this period. The share of capital input in growth decreased but remained high, at 57.8 percent for output and 70.6 percent for labor productivity. ICT capital made up nearly one fourth of the contribution of capital input to output and productivity growth. The contribution of labor input accounted for about one-third of GDP growth, of which one sixth came from labor quality improvement. The contribution of labor quality added 0.3 percent to output and labor productivity growth. TFPG remained small at 0.5 percent, but its share rose slightly to 7.5 percent of output growth and 16.8 percent of labor productivity growth. The contribution of TFPG could have been larger if we had employed the approach used for the period of 1965–90, in which we did not squeeze out the contributions of labor and capital quality.

Over the three six-year subperiods of the 1990–2008 period, a few trends were observed. First, the contribution of ICT capital to growth was substantial and stable at about 1.0 percent for output growth and 0.6–1.0 percent for labor productivity (Tables 10.2 and 10.3). Moreover, the share of ICT capital in the contribution of capital input to output growth rose from about one fifth in 1990–96 to about one-third in 1996–2002 and 2002–08. The share of ICT in the contribution of capital deepening to labor productivity growth rose even faster, from less than one-third in 1990–96 to nearly 100 percent in 2002–08. At the same time, the contribution of non-ICT capital steadily declined, from 3.6 percent in 1990–96 to 2.4 percent in 1996–2002 to 1.8 percent in 2002–08.

Second, labor input played an increasing role in output growth, from 25.3 percent in 1990–96 to 31.3 percent in 1996–2002 to 50 percent in 2002–08 (Table 10.2). The labor quality also increased significantly over the three subperiods, from –0.1 percent in 1990–96 to 0.2 percent in 1996–2002 to 0.9 percent in 2002–08. One concern, however, was the steady decline in labor productivity growth over the three subperiods, from 4.2 percent in 1990–96 to 2.2 percent in 1996–2002 to 1.9 percent in 2002–08 (Table 10.2). Relative to the 1965–90 period, the contribution of labor input (even if labor quality was excluded) to output growth in the 1990–2008 period rose significantly, while labor productivity growth dropped from 5.1 percent in 1965–90 to 2.7 percent in 1990–2008. This trend, in part, reflects the maturation of Singapore's economy. However, it was also likely associated with the government policy that emphasized GDP growth instead of labor productivity, which unintentionally encouraged firms to seek cheap labor from neighboring countries to expand their businesses.

Third, TFPG remained low for the entire period of 1990–2008, but its magnitude fluctuated markedly over the three subperiods; the external environment seemed to be a critical determining factor. TFPG was negative during the turmoil of the subperiod of 1996–2002.

TFPG in Singapore: a brief discussion

Our finding of low TFPG in Singapore, as presented in section 2, is consistent with the findings from most previous studies, including Tsao (1985), Young (1992, 1995), and Kim and Lau (1994). That is, our study supports the existence of low TFPG in Singapore. The main challenge, however, is how to use this fact to enhance our understanding of the roles of TFPG and technological progress in economic growth. In this spirit, we use the insights gained in this study to answer three questions related to Singapore's low TFPG:

- What could explain the low TFPG in Singapore?
- What could explain why Singapore's TFPG is lower than Hong Kong's?
- Why was the dual estimate of Singapore's TFPG computed by Hsieh (2002) rather high?

What could explain the low TFPG in Singapore?

The low TFPG in Singapore can be explained partly by three interrelated factors: *dependency on external trade*, *vibrancy of the business sector*, and *government policy*.

- *Dependency on external markets:* Throughout its development, Singapore's economy has been very dependent on external trade. In fact, the economy's openness, measured by its total trade to GDP ratio, has historically been very high: 267 percent in 1965, 287 percent in 1970, 428 percent in 1980, 361 percent in 1990, 378 percent in 2000, and 446 percent in 2005.[7] Although openness allows a small economy such as Singapore's to efficiently allocate resources and to acquire global knowledge, the disadvantage caused by its high dependency on external markets and its exposure to intense international competition is significant. In fact, the prices of Singapore's manufactured products tend to fall faster (or rise less quickly) than the costs of its supply inputs. Figures 10.2 and 10.3, respectively, show the price trends of Singapore's two major categories of manufactured products, 'machinery and transport equipment' and 'chemicals and chemical products.'[8]
- On the other hand, as shown in Figure 10.4, the low TFPG in Singapore is based on longer-term measures such as the ten-year moving average. However, this low TFPG was not caused by a steadily low TFPG pattern but by the sharp plummeting of TFPG during the years associated with external economic downturns, which are 1973–75 (the first oil crisis), 1985 (the global trade slump), 1997–98 (the Asian financial crisis), 2000–02 (the dotcom crash and the 9/11 terrorist attack), and 2008–09 (the global economic crisis). The acute vulnerability of Singapore's TFPG to external shocks can be explained in

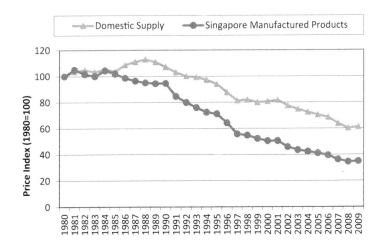

Figure 10.2 Price index: machinery and transport equipment
Source: Statistics Singapore.

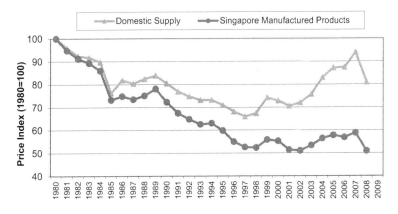

Figure 10.3 Price index: chemicals and chemical products
Source: Statistics Singapore.

two ways. First, these shocks reduce the utilization of equipment and employed labor during the period,[9] which lowers the output rate per unit of input used. Second, global economic turmoil also lowered the prices of Singapore's major manufactured

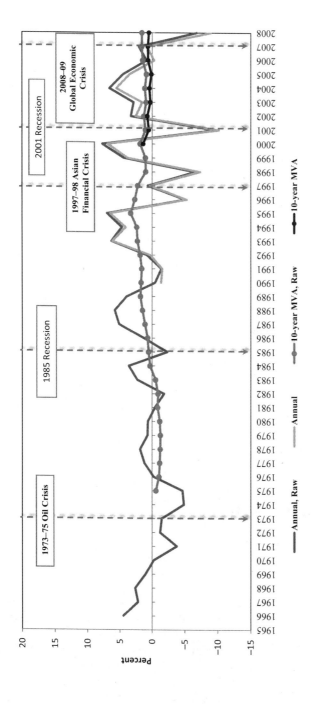

Figure 10.4 TFP growth

Notes: Raw TFPG is TFPG from which the contributions of ICT capital and labor quality are not excluded; MVA stands for moving average.

Source: Authors.

products, such as electronics and chemicals, reducing the value of each output unit produced by Singapore's firms. As a result, the effect of these shocks on TFPG tended to be more severe than their effect on GDP growth for Singapore during the periods of turmoil.

- *Vibrancy of the business sector:* Aw et al. (2001), examining the case of the Taiwanese manufacturing sector, found that the productivity differential between entering and exiting firms is an important source of industry-level productivity growth. This vibrancy in Singapore is low due to its small population (about one fifth of Taiwan's) and its more rigid structure in the manufacturing sector, which has been dominated by MNCs. Consequently, Singapore's productivity growth from this kind of dynamism of the businesses was expected to be low.
- *Government policy:* Singapore's government pursued an export-led growth strategy, of which the export-oriented manufacturing sector has been a key driver. This policy has tended to establish a rigid economic structure based on a large export-dependent manufacturing sector. Although this policy is effective in pushing for rapid growth to catch up with the industrialized nations, its consequence may be a low TFPG. On the other hand, Singapore's government policy has devoted much attention to building the foundation of long-term development, which ranges from urban planning to environmental protection to housing development. These investments, while beneficial to the economy in the long run, may not affect TFPG in the short and medium terms.

Why is Singapore's TFPG lower than Hong Kong's?

In 1965, Singapore's per capita income level was about 70 percent of Hong Kong's, but Singapore has caught up and stayed on par with Hong Kong on this measure since 1999. Singapore's rapid growth has been driven by export-led industrialization and intensive capital accumulation.

Possible reasons for Singapore's lower TFPG relative to Hong Kong's seem to be associated with three interrelated characteristics of the economies of Singapore and Hong Kong, which we touched on in subsection 3.1: the manufacturing sector's share of GDP, legacy, and development approach. With its economic strategy of relying on the manufacturing sector to drive rapid growth, Singapore has maintained a large manufacturing sector at around 25 percent of GDP, of which the major products, such as electronics and chemicals, are highly pro-cyclical. At the same time, this share for Hong Kong has rapidly declined from over 20 percent in the early 1980s to less than 5 percent in the 2000s (Figure 10.5). However, Singapore's openness, or trade to GDP ratio, has also been notably higher than Hong Kong's (Figure 10.6). A combination of a large manufacturing sector dominated by large firms and a higher degree of exposure to external trade, therefore, could be a major factor causing Singapore to be more vulnerable to external shocks than Hong Kong, especially on TFPG.

Legacy may be another factor behind Singapore's lower TFPG relative to Hong Kong. Huff (1987) observed that Singapore seemed less advantageous than Hong Kong at the inception of industrialization. The Chinese revolution provided Hong Kong with a large influx of Shanghai capitalists complete with finance and machinery. This legacy may be a significant factor contributing to the vibrancy of Hong Kong's indigenous business sector, which allowed Hong Kong to achieve higher TFPG than Singapore.

Singapore's development approach, in which the government has made substantial and steady investments in building a long-term foundation for growth, may also be a factor behind Singapore's lower TFPG. The investments, which range from greenery to pollution control and from urban planning to housing, are not captured fully by TFPG in the short and medium terms; however, they have helped Singapore to enhance and sustain its long-term growth prospects. In fact, Singapore has consistently been ranked notably higher than Hong Kong on most factors underlying quality of life, especially air quality.[10]

Why was the dual estimate of Singapore's TFPG computed by Hsieh (2002) rather high?

Hsieh (2002) employed the dual approach to growth accounting to estimate TFPG for the NICs. The results of the study (Table 10.4) show that the estimates of TFPG resulting from the dual and primal approaches are similar for Korea, Hong Kong, and Taiwan but much different for Singapore. The estimate of Singapore's TFPG from the dual approach was 2.16 percent, whereas it was –0.22 percent using the primal approach. Hsieh argued that the large discrepancy between the two estimates of TFPG for Singapore

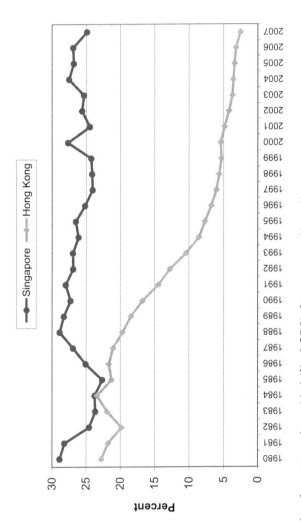

Figure 10.5 Manufacturing, value-added (% of GDP): Singapore vs. Hong Kong
Source: Data from Penn World Table, version 6.3.

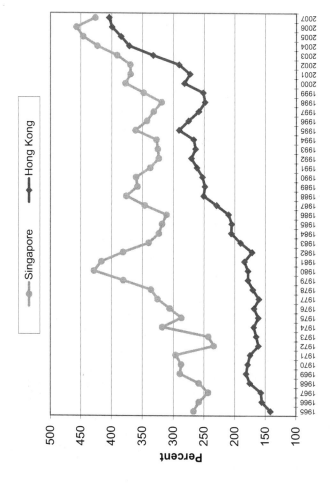

Figure 10.6 Openness: Singapore vs. Hong Kong
Source: Data from Penn World Table, version 6.3.

Table 10.4 TFPG estimated by Hsieh (2002) for the NICs

Unit:%

Economy (Real interest rate used, period)	Labor share	Annual growth rate of		Dual TFPG	Primal TFPG
		Rental price of capital	Wages		
Korea (Curb market loan, 1966–90)	0.703	–3.95	4.38	1.91	1.70
Singapore (Average lending rate, 1968–10)	0.511	1.64	2.67	2.16	–0.22
Hong Kong (Prime lending rate, 1966–91)	0.628	–1.13	4.05	2.12	2.30
Taiwan (Curb loan rate, 1966–90)	0.739	–0.36	5.26	3.79	2.60

Source: Compiled by authors.

is due to the errors in its national accounts, which tend to overstate investment expenditures.

Notes: These estimates are from Hsieh (2002, Table 10.1). The dual TFPG is estimated as $TFPG_{dual} = s_K \hat{r} + s_L \hat{W}$, where s_K and s_L are the capital and labor income shares, while $\hat{r}$ and $\hat{w}$ are the growth rates of the rental capital (r) and wage (w). The primal TFPG is estimated based on the traditional method: $TFPG_{primal} = \hat{Y} - s_K \hat{K} + s_L \hat{L}$, where $\hat{Y}$, $\hat{K}$, and $\hat{L}$ are the growth rates of GDP (Y), capital input (K), and labor input (L). The two sets of TFPG estimates should be the same if the identity $Y = rK + wL$ holds and the two estimates use the same set of data.

Hsieh's argument about errors in Singapore's national accounts may explain the reduced estimates of TFPG in Singapore. However, they should not be the main source of the large discrepancy between the dual and primal estimates of Singapore's TFPG. We find that the large difference between the two estimates in Hsieh (2002) emanates from the use of the lending rate as a proxy for the rental price of capital. In fact, the rental price of capital should not be estimated independent of the income share of capital. Furthermore, our estimate of the growth of the rental price of capital for the period 1968–90 is –1.77 percent, which is far different from Hsieh's estimate of 1.64 percent (Table 10.4).[11] That is, if Hsieh (2002) had used our estimated growth of the rental price of capital (–1.77 percent), his dual estimate of TFPG for Singapore would have been 0.65 percent. That is, using the dual approach to growth accounting should not change the finding of Singapore's low TFPG.

Projecting Singapore's growth over the 2009–19 period

We have shown evidence supporting Singapore's low TFPG. However, we find it to be a special feature of the economic growth model of a small open country without natural resources that fosters rapid growth by deeply integrating itself into the world economy with large manufacturing and services sectors. Taking this reality into account, we are not as pessimistic about Singapore's future prospects as Krugman (1994) was. Instead, we attempt to predict what growth rate Singapore could achieve over the next decade.

In 2008, after over four decades of impressive growth, Singapore's per capita GDP has been comparable to the US level, at 106 percent of the US level on PPP terms and 81 percent on the exchange rate (Table 10.5). However, the gap between Singapore and the United States is large on many key indicators that determine the long-term income level: labor productivity (63 percent), years of schooling (66 percent), and capital deepening (capital stock/worker, 53 percent). One of the main reasons for this contrast is that the employment-to-population ratio for Singapore (62 percent) is 1.28 times higher than it is for the United States (48.3 percent).

Table 10.5 Selected indicators of economic development: Singapore vs. the United States

Indicator	Singapore	United States	Singapore relative to the United States
Per capita GDP (US$)	37,597	46,350	81%
Per capita GDP (PPP$)	49,321	46,350	106%
Productivity (US$)	60,641	95,964	63%
Employment/Population	62.0%	48.3%	1.28 times
Education (years of schooling)	8.12	12.25	66%
Capital Stock/Worker (US$)	159,485	302,285	53%
Capital Stock/GDP	2.63	3.15	83%

Source: WDI (for per capita GDP); Conference Board (for employment); Barro and Lee (2000) for education attainment; BEA (for capital stock for the United States).

These comparative data provide some recommendations for how Singapore can promote its growth in the next decade. First, it is more urgent for Singapore to promote labor productivity growth than GDP growth because its labor productivity gap with the United States is much larger than the income gap. Second, promoting labor productivity growth appears to be an essential way for Singapore to sustain high GDP growth because it will not be able to fuel growth with more labor participation due to its already high employment-to-population ratio. Third, the main channels for Singapore to promote growth in the years to come will be raising labor quality (education), enhancing capital deepening, and TFPG.

We use these insights to predict Singapore's labor productivity and output growth over the next decade (2009–19). Equation 10.3 for growth accounting decomposition, introduced in section 2, can be transformed into a model for predicting productivity growth as follows (see Appendix 3 for more details):

$$\Delta \ln y = \left(\frac{1-\bar{v}_L}{\bar{v}_L}\right)\Delta \ln K_Q + \left(\frac{1-\bar{v}_L}{\bar{v}_L}\right)\tau + \Delta \ln L_Q$$
$$+ \left(\frac{1}{\bar{v}_L}\right)\Delta \ln A \qquad (10.4)$$

where K_Q denotes the quality of capital input, which is defined as the ratio of the capital service flow K to the productive capital stock S. Growth in K_Q captures the dynamics of capital stock structure shifting towards ICT; $\bar{v}_L$ is the average income share of labor; and τ represents the gap between the growth rates of the productive capital stock S and GDP Y.

The projection model shown in Equation 10.4 suggests that the labor productivity growth is driven by growth in capital quality, labor quality, capital intensity, and TFP. The income share of labor input is rather stable within the range of (0.49, 0.55).

We project the growth of labor productivity and output over the 2009–19 period using three scenarios: pessimistic, base case, and optimistic. For labor income share ($\bar{v}_L$) and labor quality growth ($\Delta \ln L_Q$), which we surmise will be rather stable over the 2009–19 period, our assumptions are common to all three scenarios. We assume that these two parameters are similar to the means of their ten-year moving averages observed for 2000–08.

For the remaining parameters, which are τ ($\Delta \ln K - \Delta \ln S$), capital quality growth ($\Delta \ln K_Q$), and TFPG ($\Delta \ln A$), we use alternative assumptions that vary by scenario as follows. For each of these parameters, we compute the 25th percentile, the median, and the 75th percentile of the set of its ten-year moving averages observed for the past five years.[12] We assume that over the period of 2009–19, this parameter will take the 25th percentile value for the pessimistic scenario, the median for the base case, and the 75th percentile for the optimistic scenario.

With regard to employment growth, the US Census has forecasted that the annual growth of Singapore's natural population aged 15–64 will be as low as 0.13 percent for the period of 2009–19. Taking into account that the inflow of foreign labor added about one percentage point to Singapore's employment growth in the past decade and the government's new policy emphasizes more strict controls on foreign labor, we assume that employment growth will be 0.50 percent for the pessimistic scenario, 0.75 percent for the base case, and 1.0 percent for the optimistic scenario.

The assumptions and projection results, together with the actual information for the period of 1998–2008, are reported in Table 10.6. One may notice that the period of 1998–2008 seems to be an outlier with regard to our assumptions. In fact, this period included a series of external shocks caused by the Asian financial crisis that erupted in 1997, the dotcom crash in 2000, the 9/11 terrorist attack in 2001, and the global financial crisis in 2008–09. As a result, the growth of capital intensity (τ) and the growth of capital quality ($\Delta \ln K_Q$) were outliers in the sets of their ten-year moving averages. At the same time, the growth rates of labor quality and labor employment were unusually high due to the government's efforts to

Table 10.6 Projected productivity and output growth, 2009–19

	Actual 1998–2008	Pessimistic	Base Case	Optimistic
Labor share, $\bar{v}_L$	0.532	0.539	0.539	0.539
Labor quality growth, $\Delta \ln L_Q$	1.24	0.53	0.53	0.53
$\tau = \Delta \ln K - \Delta \ln S$	0.08	0.25	0.50	1.20
Capital quality growth, $\Delta \ln K_Q$	0.29	0.44	0.53	0.67
TFPG, $\Delta \ln A$	0.51	0.43	0.51	0.63
Employment growth	2.92	0.50	0.75	1.00
Productivity growth	2.52	1.91	2.35	3.29
GDP Growth	5.45	2.41	3.10	4.29

Source: Authors.

promote growth by fostering the contribution of labor inputs. We believe that the period of 1998–2008 does not characterize what we will see in the next decade. This anticipation explains why our assumptions for the period of 2009–19 differ significantly in some aspects from what we observed for the period of 1998–2008.

Our growth model offers three advantages. First, it explicitly indicates the channels for promoting labor productivity growth, which are capital quality and labor quality (raising $\Delta \ln K_Q$ and $\Delta \ln L_Q$), capital deepening and capital intensity (raising τ), and TFPG. Second, it allows policy makers to examine these sources of growth for the past period to see what changes in policy should be made to enhance growth and make it more sustainable. Finally, our model makes good use of the information from past observations to set our assumptions for each of the three scenarios.

Our projections show that the growth of labor productivity and GDP for the period of 2009–19 will be 2.35 percent in the base case, 1.91 percent for the pessimistic scenario, and 3.29 percent for the optimistic scenario, while the actual rate for the period 1998–2008 was 2.52 percent. Our base case falls in the targeted range of 2–3 percent productivity growth that the Singapore government has set for the next decade.[13] However, our projections for the pessimistic (1.91 percent) and optimistic scenarios (3.29 percent) are slightly outside of this range. These projections imply that Singapore's government should foresee possible larger fluctuations of labor productivity growth outside of its targeted range, which will likely be related to the effort to increase capital deepening and capital intensity.

Singapore's GDP growth over the next decade will depend on its labor productivity growth and its policy on attracting foreign labor. Our projections of Singapore's GDP growth for the 2009–19 period are 3.10 percent for the base case, 2.41 percent for the pessimistic scenario, and 4.29 percent for the optimistic scenario vis-à-vis the actual rate of 5.45 percent during the period of 1998–2008. Our projected rates of GDP growth for the base case and optimistic scenario are within the 3–5 percent range targeted by Singapore's government, while the projection for the pessimistic case is below this range.

Conclusion

Singapore has been a focal point of the debate on the East Asian growth model, in which total factor productivity growth (TFPG) is unusually low relative to remarkable output growth. Although computing TFPG is rather simple, understanding it has proven to be a challenge. Abramovitz (1993) commented that TFPG, or the residual, 'was clearly not a measure of the advance of applied knowledge alone' and called the residual 'some sort of measure of ignorance' (p. 218). On the other hand, Lewis (1984) pointed out that one of the main weaknesses was the widening gap between economics and economic history in development economics. The points made by Abramovitz and Lewis tend to suggest that the economist should not simply use our current understanding of a theory to criticize a surprising reality; rather, he or she should carefully examine the reality to advance the field's understanding of the theory. We believe that Singapore's growth model is an excellent case for us to improve our understanding of the main drivers of a miraculous growth process in a small open economy and of the extent to which TFPG can be thought of as representative of technological progress.

Our paper contributes to the debate on the paradox of high output growth with low TFP growth observed for the NICs, especially Singapore, in three ways: measurement, insights, and conjectures for the future. On the measurement facet, we provide a rigorous test of the sources of Singapore's labor productivity and output growth over the course of its development since 1965. Our results show that TFPG in Singapore was only approximately 0.5–0.6 percent for a long period, which verifies Singapore's low TFPG. Our growth accounting decomposition framework, which takes into account the contributions of information technology and labor quality, not only improves our estimates of the sources of Singapore's growth but also provides a plausible model to predict the country's growth over the next decade.

Regarding insights, we found that Singapore's low TFPG was caused not by a steady low TFPG but by acute vulnerability to external shocks in the years of global turmoil. In fact, TFPG in Singapore plunged sharply in the years of external shocks but remained fairly high in normal times. We argue that Singapore's large export-reliant manufacturing sector, with a rather rigid structure, a small domestic market, and a government development policy focusing on long-term foundations for growth, is the main factor explaining why Singapore's TFPG has been so low relative to its remarkable GDP growth over the past four decades. Our study also provides insights into the debate on the important points raised by previous notable studies, such as what factors cause TFPG in Singapore to be lower than it is in Hong Kong (Young 1992) and why the dual estimate is much higher than the primal estimate of TFPG for Singapore (Hsieh 2002).

Our projection results show that for the base case, Singapore will achieve labor productivity growth of 2.35 percent and GDP growth of 3.10 percent over the next decade. These figures are, respectively, 1.91 percent and 2.41 percent for the pessimistic scenario and 3.29 percent and 4.28 percent for the optimistic scenario.

Appendix A

Labor income share and labor quality index

Labor income share

We have (from Singapore's Annual Yearbook of Statistics):

$$Y = CE + GOS + GOSO + TPI + SD, \qquad (10.A1)$$

where Y is GDP, CE is 'Compensation of Employees', 'GOS is Gross Operating Surplus', $GOSO$ is 'Gross Operating Surplus of Others',[14] TPI is 'Taxes on Production & Imports', and SD is 'Statistical Discrepancy'. We assume that the share of labor income in the three ambiguous items – $GOSO$, TPI, and SD – is the same as the labor income share in the total economy v_L, which implies

$$v_L Y = CE + v_L(GOSO + TPI + SD) \qquad (10.A2)$$

Equation 10.A2 can be rewritten to estimate the labor income share

$$v_L = \frac{CE}{Y - GOSO - TPI - SD} \qquad (10.A3)$$

Under the neoclassical assumption of constant returns to scale, the income share of capital input can simply be computed as $v_K = 1 - v_L$.

Labor quality

We follow Jorgenson et al. (2005) in constructing the labor quality index for Singapore. Given the data available, we divide Singapore's employment into 12 worker groups according to two dimensions – educational attainment and gender. Educational attainment consists of six levels of education – Primary and Below, Lower Secondary, Secondary, Post Secondary, Diploma, and Degree; while gender includes male and female categories.[15]

The aggregate volume of labor input L_t for year t is defined as a Tornqvist index of the individual components:

$$L_t = \prod_l (H_{l,t})^{\bar{v}_{l,t}} \tag{10.A4}$$

where $H_{l,t}$ is the total hours worked by worker group l ($l = 1,2,3,\ldots,12$) in year t. $\bar{v}_{l,t}$ is the two-period average weight of worker group l in time t. The weight of worker group l is defined as its share of the value of labor compensation, which is computed as

$$v_{l,t} = \frac{W_{l,t} H_{l,t}}{\sum_l W_{l,t} H_{l,t}} \tag{10.A5}$$

and hence, $\bar{v}_{l,t} = \frac{1}{2}[v_{l,t} + v_{l,t-1}],$ (10.A6)

where $W_{l,x}$ is the average wage of worker group l.

The labor quality index is obtained from the ratio of the volume of labor input to total hours worked:

$$L_{Q_t} = \left(\frac{L_t}{H_t}\right) \tag{10.A7}$$

Appendix B

Capital stocks and capital services

Estimating ICT investment series

ICT investment is the major measure of ICT diffusion in a country. ICT investment is divided into three ICT capital goods: computer hardware, telecommunication equipment, and software.[16]

To estimate current-price ICT investment flows in an ICT asset type, we follow a method based on the approach used by Timmer and Ark (2005), which includes two main steps. In the first step, we use the Singapore Input–Output Tables 2000 to derive current-price investment (defined as gross fixed capital formation) in each of the three ICT asset types for the year 2000.[17]

In the second step, we project annual ICT investment series for each ICT capital asset based on the investment figures for the year 2000 and the assumption that the nominal growth of investment in each ICT asset type is proportional to the growth in the domestic market for that product category.

We use the following formula to estimate investment $I_{i,t}$ in ICT asset i for year t:

$$I_{i,t} = \left(\frac{R_{i,t}}{R_{i,2000}}\right)^{\alpha} \cdot I_{i,2000} \qquad (10.\text{B}1)$$

where $R_{i,t}$ is the domestic spending of Singapore on ICT asset i in year t. The parameter α ($0 < \alpha$) is used to adjust the growth rate of the spending by the specific business sector relative to that of the overall domestic market. To be conservative, we choose $\alpha = 0.5$.

Harmonized ICT deflation

Schreyer (2002) introduces methods to deflate nominal ICT investment flows (in current local currency) to constant price series. These methods use the US hedonic price[18] index as a base to construct the deflator for that asset for a non-US country.

Because Singapore is an open economy, we chose the exchange rate-based approach from the methods suggested by Schreyer, which implies:

$$\Delta \ln P_{ict}^{singapore} = \Delta \ln P_{ict}^{US} + \Delta \ln e_{US}^{singapore} \quad (10.B2)$$

That is, for a given ICT asset type, its Singapore price change over a period of interest is equal to its US price change plus the change in the Singapore–US exchange rate.

Capital stocks

The quantity of capital stock for asset[19] i is constructed based on the 'perpetual inventory method' (PIM) as:

$$S_{i,T} = S_{i,T-1}(1-\delta_i) + I_{i,T} = \sum_{t=0}^{\infty}(1-\delta_i)^t I_{i,T-t} \quad (10.B3)$$

where $S_{i,T}$ is the capital stock in year T for asset type i, δ_i is the constant rate of depreciation,[20] and $I_{i,T-t}$ is the constant price investment flow in year $T-t$.

Capital services

The steps to estimate capital services for each of the six capital assets follow Jorgenson et al. (2005).

Capital services quantity

The quantity of capital services rendered by capital asset i in year T is defined as:

$$K_{i,T} = \frac{(S_{i,T} + S_{i,T-1})}{2} \quad (10.B4)$$

Rental price of capital services

The rental price $c_{i,T}$ of capital services from capital good i in period T is obtained based on the assumption that the typical investor in period $T-1$ who invests in this capital asset at price $p_{i,T-1}$ would get a return rate that must justify the nominal rate of return r_T observed for the economy and the remaining market price of the asset. Under the market equilibrium condition, we have:

$$p_{i,T-1}(1+r_T) = c_{i,T} + (1-\delta_i)p_{i,T} \tag{10.B5}$$

Equation 10.B5 suggests the formula for computing the rental price, $c_{i,T}$:

$$c_{i,T} = r_T p_{iT-1} + \delta_i p_{i,T} - \pi_{i,T} p_{i,T-1} \tag{10.B6}$$

where $\pi_{i,T} = (p_{i,T} - p_{i,T-1})/p_{i,T-1}$ is the asset's price change over the period.

Income share of a capital good

The income share $v_{i,T}$ of capital services from capital good i in year T is computed as

$$v_{i,T} = \frac{K_{i,T}}{Y_T} c_{i,T} \tag{10.B7}$$

where Y_T is GDP in current prices in year T.

Nominal rate of return

The income capital share v_K computed from Appendix A can be expressed as

$$v_K = \sum_i v_{i,T} \tag{10.B8}$$

Combining Equations 10.B6, 10.B7, and 10.B8 yields

$$v_K = \sum_i \frac{K_{i,T}}{Y_T}(r_T p_{i,T-1} + \delta_i p_{i,T} - \pi_{i,T} p_{i,T-1}) \tag{10.B9}$$

The nominal rate of return r_T (based on the ex-post approach), therefore, can be estimated from Equation 10.B8 as

$$r_T = \frac{\left\{v_K Y_T + \sum_i K_{i,T}\pi_{i,T} p_{i,T-1} - \sum_i K_{i,T}\delta_i p_{i,T-1}\right\}}{\sum_i K_{i,T} p_{i,T-1}} \tag{10.B10}$$

Appendix C

Growth predicting model

From Equation 10.3 in the main text, ICT and non-ICT capital services inputs are combined to obtain the composite overall capital services K, with a corresponding income share given by $\bar{v}_K$ as follows:

$$\Delta \ln y = v_K \Delta \ln K + \bar{v}_L \Delta \ln L_Q + \Delta \ln A \qquad (10.C1)$$

where y is the labor productivity (ratio of total output Y to total labor hours worked H), k refers to capital deepening (ratio of capital services K to total labor hours worked H), L_Q is the labor quality, and A is TFP.

We define capital quality K_Q as the ratio of total capital services K to the aggregate capital stock S:

$$K_Q = \frac{K}{S} \qquad (10.C2)$$

Growth in the capital quality K_Q indicates that each unit of capital stock can render a higher value of capital services. This growth has been associated with the shift of the capital structure toward ICT capital.

Furthermore, we introduce another measure, τ, to capture the increase in capital intensity, which is computed as the gap between the growth rate of capital stock S and GDP:

$$\tau = \Delta \ln S - \Delta \ln Y \qquad (10.C3)$$

Combining (C2) and (C3) yields

$$\Delta \ln K_Q = \Delta \ln K - \Delta \ln S = \Delta \ln K - (\tau + \Delta \ln Y)$$
$$= \Delta \ln k - \tau - \Delta \ln y \qquad (10.C4)$$
$$\rightarrow \Delta \ln k = \Delta \ln K_Q + \tau + \Delta \ln y \qquad (10.C5)$$

Substituting Equation 10.C5 into Equation 10.C1 results in

$$\Delta \ln y = \bar{v}_K (\Delta \ln K_Q + \tau + \Delta \ln y) + \bar{v}_L \Delta \ln L_Q + \Delta \ln A \quad (10.6)$$

Equation 10.C6 can be rearranged into a model for predicting labor productivity growth as

$$\Delta \ln y = \left(\frac{1-\bar{v}_L}{\bar{v}_L}\right) \Delta \ln K_Q + \left(\frac{1-\bar{v}_L}{\bar{v}_L}\right) \tau$$

$$+ \Delta \ln L_Q + \left(\frac{1}{\bar{v}_L}\right) \Delta \ln A \quad (10.C7)$$

And GDP growth is derived from 10.C7 as

$$\Delta \ln y = \Delta \ln y + \Delta \ln H \quad (10.C8)$$

where $\Delta \ln H$ is the projected growth of the total labor hours worked.

Notes

1 The authors acknowledge the financial support of the NUS LKYSPP and the research assistance of Kris Harley and Nguyen Chi Hieu.
2 It is also worth noting that Singapore's success has allowed the government to substantially build up its financial strength, from an empty coffer in 1965 to hundreds of billions of US dollars in sovereign funds (the total assets owned by Singapore's two sovereign funds, GIC and Temasek, in 2017 are estimated at $556 billion. Source: SWF Institute, www.swfinstitute.org/sovereign-wealth-fund-rankings/, accessed June 17, 2017).
3 The employment data from Statistics Singapore are only available in terms of number of workers. The employment data provided by the Conference Board, which includes both the number of workers and hours worked, are available at www.conference-board.org/economics/database.cfm, accessed June 1, 2016.
4 Ministry of Trade and Industry, *The Strategic Economic Plan Towards a Developed Nation*. Report of the Economic Planning Committee, 1991.
5 These restructuring policies, referred to as the 'second industrial revolution', were initiated in 1979 (Peebles and Wilson 1996).
6 In our rough estimate, TFPG for this period is inflated by about 0.1–0.2 percentage points.
7 Source: data from Penn World Table, version 6.3.
8 Notes: The Singapore Manufactured Products Price Index monitors price changes of locally manufactured commodities, while the Domestic Supply Price Index measures the changes in the price level of goods

manufactured locally or imported that are retained for use in the domestic economy by the government, business, or household sectors. Data for the years prior to 1980 are not available. The two categories 'machinery and transport equipment' and 'chemical and chemical product' together have a 65.5 percent weight in Singapore's manufactured product price index (Source: Sing Stat). The price indices have tended to decline over time because Singapore's dollar has been on an appreciation trend, from S$2.49 per US$1 in 1975 to 2.09 in 1980 to 1.75 in 1990 to 1.73 in 2000 to 1.43 in 2008.

9 Wu and Ping (2002) pointed out the problem of excess capacity during a recession.
10 According to the 'Quality of Living global city rankings – Mercer survey, 2008' by Mercer LLC, Singapore ranked 34th out of 218 global cities, while Hong Kong was 72nd. In addition, Singapore ranked highest among Asian cities.
11 It is worth noting that our estimates of other parameters, such as labor share and wage growth, are fairly similar to Hsieh's (2002).
12 The ten-year moving average of parameter X observed for year T (T = 2004, . . ., 2008) is defined as the average of X over the period [T-10, T].
13 Singapore aims to achieve 2–3 percent productivity growth and 3–5 percent GDP growth over the next decade (source: Report of the Singapore's Economic Strategies Committee (ESC), February 2010, available at www.esc.gov.sg/attactments/ESC%20Report.pdf, accessed August 31, 2016).
14 The 'Others' here include unincorporated enterprises and non-profit institutions.
15 Employment data are estimated by EPG, MAS. Shares of employed persons in the 12 worker groups are calculated using survey-based data from the Labor Force Survey (LFS) and applied to administrative employment records from CPF. Median wage data were obtained directly from the LFS. For population census years (1990, 1995, 2000 and 2005) when the LFS was not conducted, a simple interpolation method is applied.
16 Computer hardware consists of the products included in industry 30, and telecommunication equipment comprises the products in industry 32 in the International Standard Industrial Classification System (ISIC) rev. 3 (Timmer and Ark 2005).
17 I-O codes for the three ICT asset types are as follows: Computer hardware: 64, 65, 67–70; Telecommunication equipment: 66, 71, 72, 120; Software (and related IT services): 128.
18 The hedonic price index for the ICT assets (computer hardware, telecommunication equipment, and software) is provided by the Bureau of Economic Analysis (BEA).
19 The six asset types examined in this exercise are: computer hardware, computer software, telecommunication equipment, non-residential buildings and other structures, transport equipment, and non-ICT machinery.
20 We use the geometric depreciation rates provided by Jorgenson et al. (2005) and Timmer et al. (2003): 0.315 for computer hardware and

computer software, 0.11 for telecommunication equipment, 0.132 for non-IT machinery, 0.191 for transportation equipment, and 0.028 for non-residential buildings and other structures.

Bibliography

Abramovitz, Moses. 1993. "The Search for the Sources of Growth: Areas of Ignorance, Old and New." *The Journal of Economic History* 53(2): 217–243.

Akkemik, K. Ali. 2007. "TFP Growth and Resource Allocation in Singapore, 1965–2002." *Journal of International Development* 19(8): 1059–1073.

Aw, Bee Yan, Xiaomin Chen, and Mark J. Roberts. 2001. "Firm-Level Evidence on Productivity Differentials and Turnover in Taiwanese." *Journal of Development Economics* 66(1): 51–86.

Barro, Robert J. and Jong-Wha Lee. 2000. International Data on Educational Attainment Updates and Implications: National Bureau of Economic Research.

Hsieh, C. T. 2002. "What Explains the Industrial Revolution in East Asia? Evidence From the Factor Markets." *American Economic Review* 92(3): 502–526.

Huff, W. G. 1987. "Patterns in the Economic Development of Singapore." *The Journal of Developing Areas* 21(3): 305–326.

Jorgenson, Dale W., Mun S. Ho, and Kevin J. Stiroh. 2005. *Productivity, Volume 3: Information Technology and the American Growth Resurgence.* Cambridge, MA: MIT Press.

Kim, J. I., and L. J. Lau. 1994. "The Source of Economic Growth in the East Asian Newly Industrializing Countries." *Journal of the Japanese and International Economies* 8(3): 235–271.

Krugman, Paul. 1994. "The Myth of Asia's Miracle." *Foreign Affairs* 73(6): 62–78.

Lewis, W. Arthur. 1984. "The State of Development Theory." *American Economic Review* 74(1): 1–10.

Peebles, Gavin, and Peter Wilson. 1996. *The Singapore Economy.* Cheltenham, Brookfield: Edward Elgar Publishing.

Rigg, Jonathan. 1988. "Singapore and the Recession of 1985." *Asian Survey* 28(3): 340–352.

Schreyer, P. 2002. "Computer Price Indices and International Growth and Productivity Comparisons." *Review of Income and Wealth*, 48: 15–31.

Timmer, Marcel P., and Bart Van Ark 2005. "Does Information and Communication Technology Drive EU-US Productivity Growth Differentials?." *Oxford Economic Papers*, 57(4): 693–716.

Timmer, Marcel P. & Ypma, Gerard & Ark, Bart van der, 2003. "IT in the European Union: driving productivity divergence?," GGDC Research Memorandum 2003 63, *Groningen Growth and Development Centre*, University of Groningen.

Toh, Mun Heng, and Ng Wai Choong. 2002. "Efficiency of Investments in Asian Economies: Has Singapore Over-Invested?" *Journal of Asian Economics* 13(1): 52–71.

Tsao, Y. 1982. "Growth and Productivity in Singapore: A Supply Side Analysis." PhD Thesis, Harvard University.

Tsao, Y. 1985. "Growth Without Productivity." *Journal of Development Economics* 18: 25–38.

Wu, Friedrich, and Thia Jang Ping. 2002. "Total Factor Productivity With Singaporean Characteristics: Adjusting for Impact of Housing Investment and Foreign Workers." *Economic Survey of Singapore*, Third Quarter: 45–55.

Young, A. 1992. "A Tale of Two Cities: Factor Accumulation and Technical Change in Hong Kong and Singapore." In *NBER Macroeconomics Annual 1992*. Cambridge, MA: MIT Press.

Young, A. 1995. "The Tyranny of Numbers: Confronting the Statistical Realities of the East Asian Growth Experience." *Quarterly Journal of Economics* 110(3): 641–680.

Chapter 11

Russia since 1995
Natural gas, catching up and informality[1]

Ilya B. Voskoboynikov

Introduction

Recent decades after transition from plan to market were turbulent for the Russian economy. They include a transformational output fall until 1998 up to the level of around 60 percent relative to 1990, quick recovery in 1999–2008 with outstanding 6.7 percent yearly average GDP growth rates, and stagnation after the global crisis of 2008 with growth rates 1.7 percent in 2009–15.[2] In addition, the Russian economy was affected by intensive structural transformations, drastic shocks in terms of trade, and expanding of the informal economy. What were main proximate sources of the Russian economy growth all these years? What is the relative importance of each of them?

Since the pioneering study of Solow (1957) the standard kit to answer these questions is growth accounting, which represents output growth rates as the sum of contributions of inputs and multifactor productivity (MFP). While the link between the contribution of inputs, such as labor or capital, and output growth have no need of additional explanations, the meaning of MFP can be explained, following Harberger (1998),[3] by the ability of an industry or the economy to diminish real costs of production. Much of the current literature on growth accounting of the Russian economy at macro level pays particular attention to MFP as the main source of growth. Using various sources of data on labor and capital,[4] paying special attention to such measurement aspects as capacity utilization (Jorgenson and Vu 2013; Entov and Lugovoy 2013), terms of trade (Kaitila 2016) or taking into account its natural capital (Brandt, Schreyer, and Zipper 2017), it points at MFP as the main driver of Russian growth.

At the same time, another strand of the literature on Russian growth[5] provides arguments why it can be fuelled by oil price and the rainfall money from export of Russian oil and gas. These explanations deal with fluctuations of real exchange rate, the level of rents, and the poor quality of domestic financial intermediation as potential drivers or constraints for growth. However, it is not clear how all these factors diminish real costs of production. In other words, if oil prices do influence Russian growth, why does the growth accounting decomposition unveil MFP as the main driver of growth, rather than, say, capital and investments, fuelled by rainfall money from oil and gas export?

A shift from total economy to the level of industries seems to be the key to deal with these questions. Recent studies on this (Timmer et al. 2010; Jorgenson, Fukao, and Timmer 2016) show that industry-level growth accounting is more promising and precise, taking into account industry-specific sources of growth and processes of inputs' reallocation. The purpose of this chapter is to review and update recent research into the supply-side industry-level sources of growth of the Russian economy.[6] It reports that oil and gas money fuelled Russian growth in the form of capital services in extended mining and low-skill intensive services. The contribution of capital input was higher in the years of soaring oil prices. One more factor of growth was catching up, which is rooted in the fact that Russia, as well as other Central and East European socialist economies (CEEs) on the eve of transition from plan to market, were backwards in technologies in comparison with advanced economies. Similar to CEEs, in the years after transition Russian manufacturing outperformed the West in productivity growth. This provided a remarkable contribution to aggregate productivity. Before 2008 Russia also gained from MFP growth in financial and business services, because the initial level of these sectors was low even in comparison with CEEs. Finally, the remarkable peculiarity of the Russian economy is the expanding share of informal labor, especially in years of outstanding growth before 2008. This makes Russia, to a certain extent, similar to India (Vries et al. 2012). Splitting industries into formal and informal segments and estimating the contribution of labor reallocation, I report that expanding informality slows down labor productivity growth.

The chapter has been organized in the following way. The second section provides an aggregate view of sources of Russian growth in 1995–2012, considering separately three periods of growth – the post-transition recession until 1998, the recovery period in 1999–2008, and the post-crisis stagnation. It also reveals relative importance of intra-industry sources of growth and labor reallocation. The third section focuses on structural change of the Russian economy. In particular, it deals with the influence of labor reallocation and its impact on labor productivity growth, considering labor flows between industries, as well as between formal and informal segments within industries. The fourth section delves into intra-industry sources of growth, showing what industries contributed more to aggregate capital intensity and TFP. The fifth section concludes, summarizing lessons that can be learned from the case of Russia in the global perspective.

Sources of aggregate labor productivity growth

Long run GDP growth of the Russian economy at the level of almost 3 percent per year in 1961–2012, represented in Figure 11.1, seems moderate. At the same time, it is highly inhomogeneous.

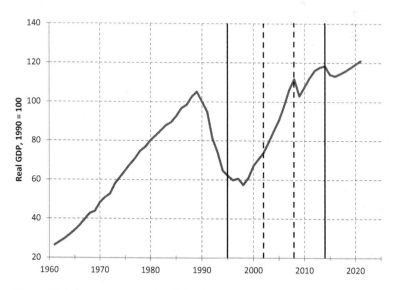

Figure 11.1 Long run growth of the Russian economy (1990 = 100)

Source: Kuboniwa and Ponomarenko (2000), Ponomarenko (2002), Rosstat, IMF WEO database, January 2016.

Long growth slowdown before transition in 1990 was followed by the transformational fall with negative rates –6.8 percent in 1991–98, common for all former socialist economies in Europe (Campos and Coricelli 2002). The post-transition jump off in 1999–2008 with growth rates of 6.7 percent brought Russia in line with the largest booming emerging economies – India, China, and Brazil – which formed the BRIC club. However, after the global financial crisis of 2008 the Russian economy entered the period of stagnation, which continues until present. Focusing on the post-transition period after 1995 and using the neoclassical growth accounting framework, I answer the question, what proximate factors contributed to growth in these years.

As shown by Stiroh (2002), growth of labor productivity, defined as the ratio of real value-added and hours worked ($z = Z/H$), can be represented as a function of capital intensity ($k = K/H$), multifactor productivity (A) and the reallocation of hours worked (R):

$$\Delta \ln z = \sum_j \bar{v}_{Z,j}^{GDP} \cdot \Delta \ln z_j + \left(\sum_j \bar{v}_{Z,j}^{GDP} \cdot \Delta \ln H_j - \Delta \ln H \right)$$
$$= \sum_j \bar{v}_{Z,j}^{GDP} \cdot \Delta \ln z_j + R$$
$$= \sum_j \bar{v}_{Z,j}^{GDP} \cdot \bar{v}_{K,j}^{Z} \Delta \ln k_j + \sum_j \bar{v}_{Z,j}^{GDP} \cdot \Delta \ln A_j + R, \quad (11.1)$$

where $\bar{v}_{Z,j}^{GDP}$ – the yearly average share of sector j in total value-added and $\bar{v}_{K,j}^{Z}$ is the yearly average capital share in value-added of sector j. The reallocation term R captures changes in labor productivity growth, caused by the difference of the share of an industry in value-added and hours worked. It is positive if industries with the above average share of value-added show positive growth of employment shares.

Table 11.1 represents real value-added growth rates decomposition in 1995–2012 and three sub periods, 1995–2002, 2003–07 and 2008–12. The first period covers the last years of the transformational recession and first years of recovery;[7] the second one includes years of fast growth and the last one deals with stagnation. Real value-added growth rate is represented as the sum of hours worked (the second row) and labor productivity (the third row). As can be seen, the role of variation in employment is marginal. Indeed, of the total 3.7 percent growth in 1995–2012 it explains only 0.2. Low and negative population growth, as well as relatively low change in unemployment rates, makes labor input stable.

Table 11.1 Sources of economic growth of the Russian economy in 1995–2012 (contributions in p.p.)

	1995–2002	2003–07	2008–12	1995–2012
Aggregate real GDP growth	2.78	7.14	1.03	3.74
Hours worked	−0.09	0.83	−0.13	0.22
Aggregate labor productivity	2.86	6.31	1.16	3.52
Labor reallocation	1.31	0.72	0.09	0.76
Intra-industry labor productivity growth	1.55	5.59	1.08	2.76
MFP	1.63	3.17	−1.61	1.16
Capital intensity	−0.33	2.26	2.47	1.38
Labor composition	0.25	0.15	0.22	0.22

Source: Timmer and Voskoboynikov (2016).

Notes: Extended mining includes mining, fuel and wholesale trade; other goods includes utilities and construction; market services incorporates retail, hotels and restaurants, transport, post and telecom, financial and business services. Numbers may not sum exactly because of rounding.

In turn, aggregated labor productivity growth is contributed by labor reallocation and intra-industry growth. Its contribution is growth enhancing and slows down from almost half of the total labor productivity growth in 1995–2002 to nil after the global crisis. On the one hand, this pattern can illustrate the final stages of transition from plan to market. The differences between productivity levels become smaller; the structure of the economy becomes more balanced, once multiple distortions of the planned economy period disappeared. On the other hand, the post-crisis stagnation could terminate labor reallocation, because in stagnation workers prefer to postpone changes of workplaces, avoiding the risks of losing jobs.

The last three rows of the table represent intensive (MFP) and extensive (capital intensity, which is defined as growth rates of capital services per hour worked) components of intra-industry productivity growth, as well as the contribution of labor composition. As it follows from the last column, the role of capital intensity seems the largest one, which makes Russian growth extensive and contradicts the bulk of the literature. Why is that? As it follows from the data of the last two periods – years of relatively high oil prices and huge inflow of export revenues – capital intensity provided the lion's share of labor productivity growth. In contrast, in years of relatively low oil prices, MFP dominated, while the capital intensity contribution was small and negative. This can be explained not only by the fact that in years of low investments discards exceeded installations of new equipment, but also because the rental price of old, but serviceable, "communist" capital[8] tended to zero. Finally, the contribution of labor composition is positive and stable, but relatively small. It varies around 0.2 p.p.

These findings suggest a contrasting picture of Russian aggregate productivity growth. In the initial period it was driven by the process of diminishing costs and the lack of investments. Starting from early 2000s, growing oil prices and export revenues provided resources for investments, which can be seen in the increasing role of capital intensity. This resolves the puzzle of intensive growth in years of soaring oil prices, discussed in the introduction, if the oil and gas sectors provide the substantial contribution to aggregate capital intensity growth. However, for this the aggregate level perspective is not very informative. Further steps are needed for clarification as to which sectors contribute more to aggregate capital intensity. Another important limitation of the aggregate view is the lack of information about the labor reallocation process. That is why the following sections shift focus to the level of industries and the processes that accompany the structural change.

Structural change, informality and labor productivity growth

The economic structure of command economies was unbalanced in favor of manufacturing and agriculture. That is why it is little wonder that intensive structural change and labor reallocation with the extension of market services and shrinking manufacturing was one of a few basic stylized facts, common for all economies in transition (Campos and Coricelli 2002).

The case of Russia is not an exception. Table 11.2 reports changes in shares of value-added in six major sectors of the Russian economy. As can be seen from the table, the share of agriculture and manufacturing shrank from 25.6 percent in 1995 to 14.5 percent in 2012, while services expanded from 42.2 percent to 47.7 percent. At the same time, in contrast with many other post-transition economies, Russia is a resources-exporting country. Growth of global oil prices after 1999 lead to the remarkable extension of its mining and mining-related industries, combined with the "Oil, Gas and Wholesale trade" sector,[9] from 18.2 percent in 1995 to almost

Table 11.2 Aggregate GDP growth and structural change in 1995–2012

	Share of value-added (%)		Growth rates (%)	Contributions (pp)
	1995	2012	1995–2012	1995–2012
Total	100.00	100.00	3.74	3.74
Market economy	86.10	81.04	3.87	3.24
Agriculture	7.61	3.87	1.23	0.07
Extended mining	20.13	26.92	4.30	1.01
Manufacturing	17.99	11.62	2.50	0.37
Other goods	12.05	9.93	2.70	0.30
Market services	28.33	28.70	5.22	1.49
Non-market services	13.90	18.96	3.07	0.50

Source: Own calculations based on Russia KLEMS. See main text.

Notes: Extended mining includes mining, fuel and wholesale trade; other goods includes utilities and construction; market services incorporates retail, hotels and restaurants, transport, post and telecom, financial and business services.

a quarter in 2012. The increasing role of extended mining and market services predetermines the leading contribution of these sectors in aggregate growth. Market services show the highest growth rates 5.2 percent, which contribute 1.5 p.p. (= 5.2 × ½ × (28.3% + 28.7%)) of 3.7 percentage growth, or 40 percent. Extended mining and market services in total provide two thirds of total aggregate growth rates, while the impact of agriculture and manufacturing is much lower and almost the same as for non-market services.

As follows from the development patterns of many developing economies, intensive structural change can be accompanied by a structural bonus hypothesis, which states that during industrial development, factor inputs shift to more productive branches. One might expect that post-transition economies would enjoy growth-enhancing structural change, because elimination of multiple command-economy distortions would provide a more efficient inputs allocation. However, Table 11.1 reports that this was not the case in Russia. Indeed, such drastic changes in the structure of the Russian economy starting from 1995 are not accompanied with the substantial contribution of labor reallocation to aggregate labor productivity growth.

Dealing with this, I suggest three different explanations.[10] The initial point for the first one is the fact that productivity gains from the shift to a more balanced industrial structure are more the higher the initial inter-sectoral productivity gaps. From this perspective, being industrialized and much more developed, the CEE economies and Russia do not have much room for this. Indeed, McMillan and Rodrik (2011: 56) note, that high gaps are a feature of underdevelopment. Figure 11.2 demonstrates how a measure of economy-wide productivity gaps, the coefficient of variation of the log of sectoral labor productivities, decays over the course of development in 1995. Being the least developed in the sample, India is placed on the top-left corner of the graph, while developed economies, e.g., Germany, are grouped in the right-bottom one. The figure also shows that the CEE economies, including Russia, are more developed, than most developing economies, and closer to developed economies in terms of variation in productivity gaps.

The second explanation comes from the observation that the structural change in post-transition countries shifts these economies to services. In turn, long run productivity growth in services can be lower than in, say, manufacturing.[11] That is why the expansion of services can lead to the slowdown of the aggregate labor productivity *growth* (the Baumol effect). At the same time, aggregate

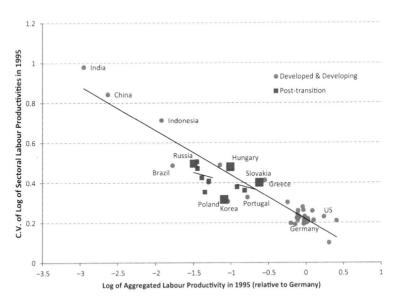

Figure 11.2 Inter-sectoral productivity variation and aggregate labor productivity levels in 1995

Source: Voskoboynikov (2014).

productivity growth varies also because of labor inflow to industries with higher productivity *levels* (the Denison effect). Controlling this, I report the decomposition of aggregate labor productivity growth in Russia and ten CEE economies in 1995–2007 into these two effects. Results are presented in Figure 11.3.

The figure represents aggregate labor productivity growth in 2007 relative to 1995 as the sum of the three components: intra-industry growth, the Baumol effect and the Denison effect. Interestingly, in all economies in the sample labor reallocation between different productivity *levels* was growth enhancing, while the reallocation effect between industries with different *growth rates* is growth reducing. For example, in the case of Estonia total reallocation was growth reducing, because the Baumol component exceeded

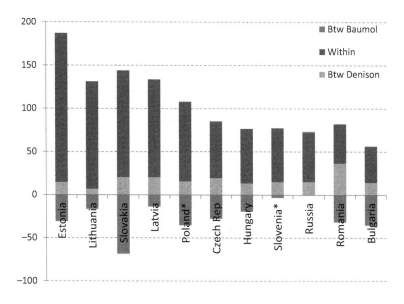

Figure 11.3 Labor reallocation in CEE and Russia (1995–2007)

Source: own calculations, using socio-economic accounts of World Input Output Database (Timmer et al. 2016, 5), available at www.wiod.org/release13. Accessed on 24 September 2016. See also main text.

Results are presented for market sectors of the economies.

Labor productivity is split into the contribution within industries (within) and the effect of labor reallocation between industries due to differences between labor productivity levels (Btw Denison) and growth rates (Btw Baumol). TRAD decomposition is used (see more on the approach in Voskoboynikov (2017)).

* – for Poland and Slovenia results are reported for 1995–2006.

the Denison one. Generalizing these observations it is interesting to note that, as far as post-transition economies grow, they enjoy some gains from improvements of their industrial structure because of the shift of labor to industries with higher productivity levels in line with the projection of McMillan and Rodrik (2011: 56). At the same time, the total contribution of labor reallocation can be small or even negative because of the expansion of low-growing, stagnant industries.

Finally, the influence of labor reallocation on productivity growth in Russia can be sensitive to the expansion of the informal segment of the economy. As follows from Figure 11.4, of the three and half million jobs increase in 2013 relative to 2000, about nine million were added in the informal segment, while six an half were lost by the formal one. Workers lost formal jobs mostly in agriculture and manufacturing, and only trade created some formal jobs. At the same time, informality grew in trade, construction, small

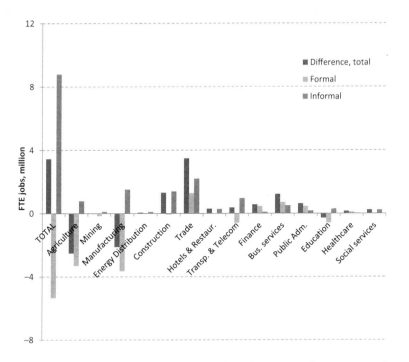

Figure 11.4 The change of the number of workers in total economy and major sectors in 2000–13

Source: Rosstat.

manufacturing firms and transport. Informality expanded even in years of outstanding growth before 2008. What was the impact of this formal–informal reallocation to aggregate labor productivity, taking into account that in the case of India the expansion of the informal economy is growth reducing (Vries et al. 2012)?

This impact can be estimated within the same framework of the shift–share analysis. For this each industry should be split into formal and informal segments. Using Russian National Accounts and the satellite account of labor inputs, this can be done starting from 2005 onwards. Following the Russian National Accounting system, I qualify a worker as informal if her job is not in the corporate sector. De Vries et al. (2012) show that the impact of this split would be in relative contributions of within and between components of the shift–share decomposition. Specifically, a certain part of the reallocation effect in the 'no-split' case can be interpreted as the impact of the intra-industry sources, or the other way around. For example, assume that a worker leaves a capital-intensive job in a big car service station for a small informal car-repairing workshop. In the 'no-split' case this is considered as the fall of labor productivity within the car-repairing industry. However, in the 'informal split' case productivity in both 'car-repairing' sub-industries, the 'formal' and the 'informal' ones, remains the same, but the worker contributes to aggregate labor reallocation negatively.

The contribution of labor reallocation to aggregate productivity growth in 2005–12 is represented in Figure 11.5. In the no-split case, labor reallocation contributed around 2.6 p.p., of which 4.4 p.p. belonged to the Denison effect, and –1.8 p.p. to the Baumol effect.[12] Once informality is taken into consideration, the total reallocation effect becomes smaller. In other words, if we take into account labor reallocation to informality explicitly, the role of intra-industry sources becomes stronger, but a transfer of a worker to the informal sector contributes to the reallocation effect negatively. This result is consistent with the finding of de Vries et al. (2012) for India. Another important insight of Figure 11.5 is that the contraction of the reallocation effect takes place mostly because the Denison effect becomes weaker, which means that labor reallocation to informality influences aggregate productivity growth mostly because of the difference between formal and informal segments in productivity *levels*, rather than *growth rates*.[13]

Taken together, the results of this section suggest that the influence of structural change on aggregate labor productivity growth is more sophisticated than it might be expected from the simple

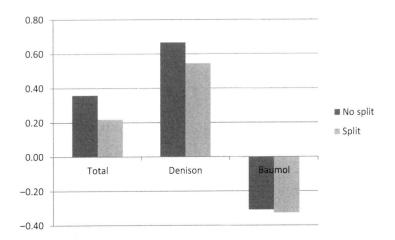

Figure 11.5 Informal split, labor reallocation and aggregate labor productivity growth contributions to yearly average growth rates (p.p.)

Source: (Voskoboynikov 2017; Voskoboynikov 2014).

Note: GEAD approach for the shift–share analysis (Tang and Wang 2004)

shift–share decomposition (1). Indeed, a relatively small contribution of the reallocation effect can be the net effect of two different phenomena, the Denison effect and the Baumol effect, which affect in different directions and cancel each other. Next, this combination of the two effects is common for all post-transition economies. Finally, the expansion of informality in the Russian economy makes the impact of growth-enhancing structural change weaker.

However, the main conclusion of the aggregate shift–share analysis remains unchanged. Namely, intra-industry sources of productivity growth are stronger than the reallocation effects. In the following section I consider these sources in detail.

Capital intensity, multifactor productivity, and convergence in industries

The sources of intra-industry labor productivity growth include accumulation of human and physical capital, intangible assets, and multifactor productivity. The latter is usually interpreted as the outcome of technological change, but could also be explained by temporary disequilibrium, caused by a delayed reaction to technological changes in previous periods, terms of trade, low mobility of labor and capital, as well as various competitive barriers (Reinsdorf 2015).

Transmission of oil and gas export revenues to the supply side sources of growth should be identified not only because of a substantial capital contribution at the aggregate level, but also in the sectoral composition of the aggregate capital input. It is confirmed by data reported in Table 11.3. As can be seen from the table, the extended oil and gas sector demonstrates the second largest yearly average capital growth rates among sectors of the market economy at the level of 3.8 percent in 1995–2012.[14] It contributes almost one quarter of market economy capital intensity growth rates. At the same time, market services enjoyed the highest capital inflow of 5.2 percent per year. This is also not surprising. Large investments came to retail, which was underdeveloped in early transition. McKinsey ("Unlocking Economic Growth in Russia" 1999, 5; Bakatina et al. 2009, 65) reports that by 1999 only 1 percent of retail fell on modern supermarkets, while in ten years this share increased to the level of 35 percent. Huge investments were made in telecommunications both because of its technological backwardness in the planned economy period and the IT revolution. Last, but not least, financial and business services expanded in these years.

Table 11.3 Labor, capital services, and MFP in 1995–2012, sectoral contribution

	Growth rates (%)			Contributions (p.p.)		
	Labor	Capital Intensity	MFP	Labor	Capital Intensity	MFP
Total	0.98	2.77	1.16	0.98	2.77	1.16
Market economy	0.91	2.64	1.30	0.76	2.21	1.09
Agriculture	−1.48	0.65	1.31	−0.08	0.04	0.08
Extended mining	1.56	2.24	0.43	0.37	0.53	0.10
Manufacturing	−0.83	2.35	2.13	−0.12	0.35	0.32
Other goods	0.59	3.12	0.60	0.07	0.34	0.07
Market services	1.87	3.34	1.87	0.53	0.95	0.53
Non-market services	1.37	3.45	0.40	0.22	0.57	0.07

Source: Own calculations based on Russia KLEMS. See main text.

Notes: Extended mining includes mining, fuel and wholesale trade; other goods includes utilities and construction; market services incorporates retail, hotels and restaurants, transport, post and telecom, financial and business services.

At the same time, agriculture and manufacturing, the planned economy 'priority sectors', suffered from low or even negative capital inflow, which could be caused by overinvestment of the planned-economy decades. As can be seen from the table, capital inflow in manufacturing made up only 1.5 percent per year, while in agriculture capital shrank with rates of −0.8 percent. Interestingly, positive growth rates of capital intensity indicate that in total capital/labor ratio in both sectors grew, because the outflow of labor exceeded the outflow of capital. Both market services and extended mining provide two thirds of aggregate capital-intensity contribution.

The sector of market services is also one of the most productive. It provides the largest contribution to aggregate MFP growth, being the second best in MFP growth. Timmer and Voskoboynikov (2014) explain this with the initial underdevelopment of financial and business services not only in comparison with the West, but also relative to many former socialist economies of Central and Eastern Europe. Such banking services as credit cards, consumer credits, or brokerage services, available in many countries for many decades, were novel in Russia in early transition. This provided many opportunities for catching up, which is reflected in outstanding MFP growth of these industries.

Interestingly, two other leading productive sectors are manufacturing, which demonstrates the best MFP growth 2.13 percent, and agriculture with 1.3 percent. At the same time, since their share shrank from a quarter in 1995 to a modest 15 percent in 2012, their contribution to aggregate MFP growth is relatively modest. Against this background, the role of extended mining seems stagnant and inefficient, so that its role in aggregate productivity growth is close to nil. Such inefficiency is also confirmed by sector studies.[15]

Conclusion

Comparison of an economy with similar countries is a powerful tool for understanding its specific features. What group of countries does the Russian economy belong to? A quarter of a century ago it was the backbone of the Soviet Union and of the socialist camp. So, naturally, it was among the Central and East Europe (CEE) economies with relatively high GDP per capita. Some of them successfully converge with the developed economies of Western Europe. Indeed, similar to CEEs, Russian manufacturing demonstrates high MFP growth. At the same time, high growth in the unfavorable institutional environment makes Russia comparable with India and China. All this makes the picture of Russian growth sophisticated.

Indeed, market services contribute more than two-thirds of the aggregate growth because of capital intensity in retail and telecom, and technology catching up in financial and business services. The role of extending mining is evident in high growth rates of capital services. Traditional sectors, manufacturing and agriculture, seem progressive in terms of productivity growth, but their contribution to aggregate productivity is less sound.

Structural change generated growth-enhancing labor reallocation, which was strong in early transition and faded out in the post-crisis stagnation. At the same time, strong labor reallocation to informality, which makes Russia, to a certain extent, similar to India, influences aggregate labor productivity growth negatively. Finally, labor composition provides positive small contribution to growth in all stages of Russian post-transition development.

All in all, this growth structure makes the future of the Russian economy uncertain. Russian dependence on oil and gas export makes growth unstable. Structural change does not provide a strong impact on growth. At the same time, we observe such sources of sustainable growth as MFP contribution of manufacturing and agriculture, as well as improvements in labor quality. Unfortunately, these sources are not strong enough for making sustainable growth high in the upcoming decade.

Notes

1 A preliminary version of this chapter has been presented at the 4th World KLEMS conference in Madrid on 23 May 2016.
2 The Russian Statistics Office (Rosstat). Retrieved on 24 September 2016 from www.gks.ru/free_doc/new_site/vvp/vvp-god/tab3.htm.
3 See more about this in e.g. Hulten (2001).
4 See literature review in Timmer and Voskoboynikov (2016).
5 Rautava (2004); Gaddy and Ickes (2005); Connolly (2011).
6 Voskoboynikov (2017); Timmer and Voskoboynikov (2016).
7 The through point in 1998 was avoided to diminish biases on TFP because of the short-term capacity utilization effects.
8 The concept of communist capital was suggested by Campos and Coricelli (2002). It is defined as capital installed in years of planned economy in a different institutional environment. It could become serviceable, but obsolete in years after transition.
9 The true size of mining in the Russian economy and its contribution to economic growth were widely discussed in the literature (Gurvich 2004; Kuboniwa et al. 2005; World Bank 2005). An extended oil and gas sector includes organizations that are involved in the process of extraction, transportation, and wholesale trade of oil and gas. Some of them have establishments in different industries, such as mining, wholesale trade, fuel, and pipeline transport. Because of strong vertical

integration and transfer pricing its share in total value-added exceeds mining. Following Timmer and Voskoboynikov (2016) the present study assumes that all this extended mining sector includes mining, wholesale trade, and fuel. At the same time, I recognize the limitations of this split. On the one hand many firms in wholesale trade are not related with energy exports. On the other hand, some pipeline transportation organizations fall within transport in sector 'market services'.
10 We know from micro-level studies of manufacturing firms (e.g. of Brown and Earle (2003)) that labor reallocation intensified in early transition and subsided within a few years. So, one of the explanations of the observed reallocation pattern is that the present study does not cover first years of transition with the most intensive labour flows. However, this strand of the literature overlooks labour flows between manufacturing and the rest of the economy.
11 Baumol (1967); Baumol et al. (1985).
12 Ilya B. Voskoboynikov and Gimpelson (2015, tab. 8).
13 Voskoboynikov (2014) discusses this effect in detail.
14 Capital growth rates can be calculated from Table 11.3 as the sum of labour and capital intensity growth rates. In the case of extended mining this is 1.56% + 2.24% = 3.8%.
15 See, e.g., Ahrend and Tompson (2004); McKinsey (2009).

Bibliography

Ahrend, Rudiger, and William Tompson. 2004. "Russia's Gas Sector: The Endless Wait for Reform?" *OECD Economic Department Working Papers* ECO/WKP(2004)25 (402).
Bakatina, Daria, Jean-Pascal Duvieusart, Vitaly Klintsov, Kevin Krogmann, Jaana Remes, Irene Shvakman, and Yermolai Solzhenitsyn. 2009. "Lean Russia: Sustaining Economic Growth through Improved Productivity." McKinsey Global Institute. https://www.mckinsey.com/global-themes/employment-and-growth/lean-russia-sustaining-economic-growth.
Baumol, William J. 1967. "Macroeconomics of Unbalanced Growth: The Anatomy of Urban Crisis." *American Economic Review* 57(3): 415–426.
Baumol, William J., Sue Anne Batey Blackman, and Edward N. Wolff. 1985. "Unbalanced Growth Revisited: Asymptotic Stagnancy and New Evidence." *American Economic Review* 75(4): 806–817.
Brandt, Nikola, Paul Schreyer, and Vera Zipper. 2017. "Productivity Measurement with Natural Capital." *Review of Income and Wealth* 63(S1): S7–21. https://doi.org/10.1111/roiw.12247.
Brown, J. David, and John S. Earle. 2003. "Job Reallocation and Productivity Growth Under Alternative Economic Systems and Policies: Evidence From the Soviet Transition." *HSE Working Paper*, no. WP/2003/05.
Campos, Nauro F., and Fabrizio Coricelli. 2002. "Growth in Transition: What We Know, What We Don't, and What We Should." *Journal of Economic Literature* 40(3): 793–836.
Connolly, Richard. 2011. "Financial Constraints on the Modernization of the Russian Economy." *Eurasian Geography and Economics* 52(3): 428–459.

Entov, Revold M., and Oleg V. Lugovoy. 2013. "Growth Trends in Russia After 1998." In Michael Alexeev and Shlomo Weber (eds.), *The Oxford Handbook of the Russian Economy*. Oxford: Oxford University Press.

Gaddy, Clifford G., and Barry W. Ickes. 2005. "Resource Rents and the Russian Economy." *Eurasian Geography and Economics* 46(8): 559–583.

Gurvich, Evsey. 2004. "Makroėkonomicheskaia Otsenka Roli Rossiĭskogo Neftegazovogo Kompleksa [Macroeconomic Role of Russia's Oil and Gas Sector]." *Voprosy Ėkonomiki* (10): 4–31.

Harberger, Arnold C. 1998. "A Vision of the Growth Process." *American Economic Review* 88(1): 1–32.

Hulten, Charles R. 2001. "Total Factor Productivity: A Short Bibliography." In Charles R. Hulten, Edwin R. Dean, and Michael J. Harper (eds.), *New Developments in Productivity Analysis*. Chicago, London: The University of Chicago Press, 1–53.

Jorgenson, Dale W., Kyoji Fukao, and Marcel P. Timmer, eds. 2016. *Growth and Stagnation in the World Economy*. Cambridge: Cambridge University Press.

Jorgenson, Dale W., and Khuong Minh Vu. 2013. "The Emergence of the New Economic Order: Growth in the G7 and the G20." *Journal of Policy Modeling* 35(3): 389–99. https://doi.org/10.1016/j.jpolmod.2013.03.001.

Kaitila, Ville. 2016. "GDP Growth in Russia: Different Capital Stock Series and the Terms of Trade." *Post-Communist Economies* 28(2): 129–145.

Kuboniwa, Masaaki, and Aleksey N. Ponomarenko. 2000. "Revised and Enlarged GDP Estimates for Russia, 1961–1990." In Kōnosuke Odaka, Yukihiko Kiyokawa, and Masaaki Kuboniwa (eds.), *Constructing a Historical Macroeconomic Database for Trans-Asian Regions*. Tokyo Garden Palace, Tokyo: Institute of Economic Research, Hitotsubashi University, 109–127.

Kuboniwa, Masaaki, Shinichiro Tabata, and Nataliya Ustinova. 2005. "How Large Is the Oil and Gas Sector of Russia? A Research Report." *Eurasian Geography and Economics* 46(1): 68–76.

McMillan, Margaret, and Dani Rodrik. 2011. "Globalization, Structural Change, and Productivity Growth." In Mark Bacchetta and Marion Jansen (eds.), *Making Globalization Socially Sustainable*. Geneva: International Labour Office; World Trade Organization, 49–84. www.wto.org/english/res_e/booksp_e/glob_soc_sus_e.pdf, accessed 24 September 2016.

Ponomarenko, Aleksey N. 2002. *Retrospektivnye Natsional'nye Scheta Rossii: 1961–1990 [Retrospective Russian National Accounts in 1961–1990]*. Moscow: Finansy i statistika.

Rautava, Jouko. 2004. "The Role of Oil Prices and the Real Exchange Rate in Russia's Economy – a Cointegration Approach." *Journal of Comparative Economics* 32(2): 315–327.

Reinsdorf, M. 2015. "Measuring Industry Contributions to Labour Productivity Change: A New Formula in a Chained Fisher Index Framework." *International Productivity Monitor* 28: 3–26.

Solow, Robert M. 1957. "Technical Change and the Aggregate Production Function." *Review of Economics and Statistics* 39(3): 312–320.

Stiroh, Kevin J. 2002. "Information Technology and the U.S. Productivity Revival: What Do the Industry Data Say?" *American Economic Review* 92(5): 1559–1576.

Tang, Jianmin, and Weimin Wang. 2004. "Sources of Aggregate Labour Productivity Growth in Canada and the United States." *Canadian Journal of Economics* 37(2): 421–44.

Timmer, Marcel P., and Ilya B. Voskoboynikov. 2014. "Is Mining Fuelling Long-Run Growth in Russia? Industry Productivity Growth Trends since 1995." *Review of Income and Wealth* 60 (Supplement Issue S2): S398–422.

Timmer, Marcel P., Robert Inklaar, Mary O'Mahony, and Bart van Ark. 2010. *Economic Growth in Europe*. Cambridge: Cambridge University Press.

Timmer, Marcel P., Erik Dietzenbacher, Bart Los, Robert Stehrer, and Gaaitzen J. de Vries. 2015. "An Illustrated User Guide to the World Input–Output Database: The Case of Global Automotive Production." *Review of International Economics* 23(3): 575–605. https://doi.org/10.1111/roie.12178.

Timmer, Marcel P., and Ilya B. Voskoboynikov. 2016. "Is Mining Fuelling Long-Run Growth in Russia? Industry Productivity Growth Trends in 1995–2012." In *Growth and Stagnation in the World Economy*, edited by Dale W. Jorgenson, Kyoji Fukao, and Marcel P. Timmer, 281–318. Cambridge University Press.

"Unlocking Economic Growth in Russia." 1999. Moscow: McKinsey Global Institute.

Voskoboynikov, Ilya Borisovich. 2014. *Economic Growth in Russia: A Comparative Perspective*. Groningen: University of Groningen, SOM Research School.

Voskoboynikov, Ilya B. 2017. "Structural Change, Expanding Informality and Labour Productivity Growth in Russia." 18/2017. BOFIT Discussion Papers. Helsinki: Bank of Finland. http://urn.fi/URN:NBN:fi:bof-201711291674.

Vries, Gaaitzen J. de, Abdul A. Erumban, Marcel P. Timmer, Ilya B. Voskoboynikov, and Harry X. Wu. 2012. "Deconstructing the BRICs: Structural Transformation and Aggregate Productivity Growth." *Journal of Comparative Economics* 40(2): 211–227.

World Bank. 2005. *Russian Federation: From Transition to Development*, vol. March. Washington, DC: World Bank.

Chapter 12

Accounting for the role of information and communication technology in China's productivity growth[1]

Harry X. Wu and David T. Liang

Introduction

Since the 1990s, the world economy has been driven by two most important and mutually enhancing engines, that is, globalization through trade and direct investment, thanks to the market-oriented reforms in emerging economies, especially China, and information and communication technologies (ICT) that have been quickly maturing for the majority of manufacturing industries as a result of the rapid decline in the prices of ICT equipment. Figure 12.1 shows a time profile of China's dynamic production growth of personal computers, integrated circuits and semi-conductors vis-à-vis the gross output of manufacturing industries as a whole over the period 1990–2015. The annual compound growth rate of these ICT products is indeed very impressive as 40.7, 31.8 and 22.7 percent, respectively, compared to 14.7 percent of the manufacturing sector as a whole. China's rapid emergence as the world largest manufacturing powerhouse cannot be appropriately assessed without understanding the role of ICT in China's output and productivity growth.

In one of the pioneer studies that account for the role of ICT in advanced economies, Jorgenson (2001) shows that the growth of ICT capital services in the United States jumped from 11.5 percent per annum over the period 1990–15 to 19.4 percent over the period 1995–99, which was in sharp contrast to the growth of non-ICT capital services increasing merely from 1.7 to 2.9 percent. Particularly over the period 1995–99, ICT products (both equipment and software) contributed 0.5 percentage points (ppts) out of 0.75 percent annual TFP growth, accounting for nearly 67 percent

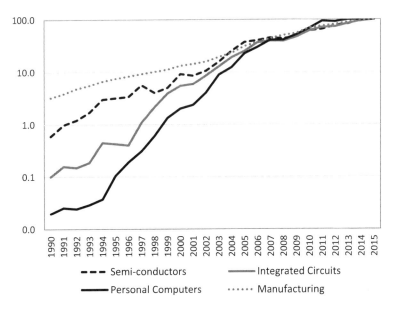

Figure 12.1 China's production of ICT products vis-à-vis gross output of manufacturing (2015 = 100)

Source: Authors' calculation based on official data in physical units (NBS 2013: 515, updated). Manufacturing gross output data are measured at 1990 prices, based on CIP 3.

of the aggregate TFP, even though it only accounted for 29 percent of the US 4.08 percent annual GDP growth.

In the case of Europe, O'Mahony and van Ark (2003) show that for 15 EU member states during the period 1995–2001, ICT-producing industries enjoyed a labor productivity growth of 7.5 percent per annum, much faster than that of the total economy of 1.7 percent per annum. Focusing on ICT investment and economic growth in nine OECD countries, Colecchia and Schreyer (2002) also find that, along with a significant decline in the prices of ICT capital goods over the period 1980–2000, all these countries experienced a remarkable increase in the rate of investment in ICT equipment. On average, ICT capital contributed between 0.2 and 0.5 ppts to annual economic growth, ranging from 2.0 to 3.8 percent per annum. Particularly for the second half of the 1990s, this rose to 0.3 to 0.9 ppts per year out of 1.0 to 5.6 percent annual output growth. In a comparative study of Japan and South Korea, Fukao et al. (2009) also find that the growth of ICT investment in the two economies was phenomenal during the period 1995–2005, by 13.1 and 15.5 percent per annum, respectively. However, it concludes that aggregate TFP appears to be more attributable to ICT-producing industries than to ICT-using industries for both Japan and Korea.

However, lack of statistics on ICT investment at industry level has prevented us from directly identifying and measuring individual Chinese industries with a specific role and a level of importance in ICT. We therefore adopt an indirect approach to bypass this problem by reclassifying all the 37 industries in the CIP data set into ICT-specific groups, using the ICT-making and asset-based ICT-using criteria in the US case (Jorgenson et al. 2005a). Obviously, in doing so, we arbitrarily assume that the extent to which individual industries are exposed to the impact of ICT, either producing or using, is the same in China as in the United States. This is by no means an ideal solution to the ICT data problem, but it provides an important perspective for examining the role of ICT in the Chinese economy.

We examine the so-grouped CIP data in a growth accounting model *a la* Jorgenson (Jorgenson 2001; Jorgenson et al. 2005a) that specifies the role of individual industries in an aggregate production possibility frontier (APPF) framework and also incorporates Domar aggregation to account for the interactions of individual industries within the system. This model allows us to decompose China's productivity growth into the contribution of ICT-specific groups and the factor reallocation effect across the groups. Our preliminary results have shown that ICT-producing and ICT-using manufacturing industries appear to be the most important driver of China's productivity growth over the entire period 1981–2012. While sharing 29 percent of China's 9.38 percent annual value-added growth, these industries contributed 149 percent to China's 0.83 percent annual aggregate TFP growth.

The rest of the paper is organized as follows. Section 2 introduces the aggregate production possibility frontier framework incorporating Domar weights for industry aggregation, especially designed for ICT-specific grouping. Section 3 explains the updated and revised CIP data and the ICT-specific industry grouping in this study. Section 4 reports and interprets the growth accounting results. Section 5 concludes this study with prioritized tasks for future research.

Accounting for the industry origin of TFP

The role of ICT in an economy can be more possibly examined by Jorgenson's aggregate production possibility frontier (APPF) framework that incorporates Domar weights for industry aggregation to account for the industry origin of growth and productivity. The widely used aggregate production function (APF) approach to TFP analysis is implicitly subject to very stringent assumptions that for all (underlying) industries 'value-added functions exist and are identical across industries up to a scalar multiple' and 'the aggregation of heterogeneous types of capital and labor must receive the same price in each industry' (Jorgenson et al. 2005a). Given heavy government interventions and institutional set-ups that cause market imperfections in China, the APF approach is undoubtedly inappropriate for the growth accounting exercise of the economy, especially when the performances of specified industries are to be compared economy wide.

The APPF approach in growth accounting relaxes the strong assumption that all industries are subject to the same value-added production function to account for the industry origin of aggregate growth (Jorgenson 1966). The Domar weights-based aggregation was introduced into the APPF framework in Jorgenson et al. (1987) to exercise direct aggregation across industries to account for the role of American industries in the changes of aggregate inputs. This approach has been used in Jorgenson and Stiroh (2000), Jorgenson (2001) and Jorgenson et al. (2005a, 2005b) to quantify the role of information technology (IT)-producing and IT-using industries in the US economy.

To illustrate this aggregation methodology, let us begin with a production function where industry gross output is a function of capital, labor, intermediate inputs and technology indexed by time. We use individual industries as building blocks, which allow us to explicitly trace the sources of the aggregate productivity growth and input accumulation to the underlying industries. Focusing on an industry-level gross output production function given by Equation 12.1, each industry, denoted by a subscript j, purchases distinct intermediate inputs, capital and labor services to produce a set of products:

$$Y_j = f_j(K_j, L_j, X_j, T) \tag{12.1}$$

where Y is output, K is an index of capital service flows, L is an index of labor service flows and X is an index of intermediate inputs including energy, materials and services, purchased from domestic and/or international markets. Note that all input variables are indexed by time but this is suppressed for notational convenience.

Under the assumptions of competitive factor markets, full input utilization and constant returns to scale, the growth of output can be expressed in the cost-weighted growth of inputs and technological change:

$$\Delta \ln Y_j = \bar{v}_j^K \Delta \ln K_j + \bar{v}_{jt}^L \Delta \ln L_j + \bar{v}_j^X \Delta \ln X_j + v_j^T \qquad (12.2)$$

where $\bar{v}_j^K$, $\bar{v}_j^L$ and $\bar{v}_j^X$ are two-period averages of nominal weights of input $v_j^K = \dfrac{P_j^K K_j}{P_j^Y K_j}$, $v_j^L = \dfrac{P_j^L L_j}{P_j^Y K_j}$ and $v_j^X = \dfrac{P_j^X X_j}{P_j^Y K_j}$, respectively. Note that under constant returns to scale $v_j^K + v_j^L + v_j^X = 1$, which is controlled by the industry production accounts in nominal terms. Each element on the right-hand side of Equation 12.2 indicates the proportion of output growth accounted for respectively by the growth of capital services ($\bar{v}_j^K \Delta \ln K_j$), labor services ($\bar{v}_j^L \Delta \ln L_j$), intermediate materials ($\bar{v}_j^X \Delta \ln X_j$) and total factor productivity (v_j^T).

Clearly, Equation 12.2 requires a proper measure of input services by different types of each input. For example, it requires a measure for labor services provided by different types of labor with specific demographic, educational and industrial attributes, as discussed in pioneering studies by Griliches (1960), Denison (1962) and Jorgenson and Griliches (1967). In doing so, it relaxes the usual strong assumption that treats numbers employed or hours worked as if they are homogeneous. The growth of total labor input is hence defined as a Törnqvist quantity index of individual labor types as follows:

$$\Delta \ln L_j = \sum_h \bar{v}_{h,j} \Delta \ln H_{h,j} \qquad (12.3a)$$

where $\Delta \ln H_{h,j}$ indicates the growth of hours worked by each labor type h (with specific gender, age and educational attainment) and its cost weights $\bar{v}_{h,j}$ given by two-period average shares of each type in the nominal value of labor compensation controlled by the labor income of industry production accounts.

The same user-cost approach is also applied to K and X to account for the contribution of different types of capital asset (Z_k) and intermediate input (X_x) in production with type-specific, two-period average cost weight defined as $\bar{v}_{k,j}$ and $\bar{v}_{x,j}$, respectively:

$$\Delta \ln K_j = \sum_k \bar{v}_{k,j} \Delta \ln Z_{k,j} \quad (12.3\text{b}) \text{ and}$$

$$\Delta \ln X_j = \sum_x \bar{v}_{x,j} \Delta \ln X_{x,j} \quad (12.3\text{c})$$

It should be noted that the Equations from 12.2 through the whole set of 12.3 also explicitly express the methodological framework for the CIP industry-level data construction that is linked to and controlled by the national production and income accounts.

Using the value-added concept, Equation 12.2 can be rewritten as:

$$\Delta \ln Y_j = \bar{v}_j^V \Delta \ln V_j + \bar{v}_j^X \Delta \ln X_j \quad (12.4)$$

where V_j is the real value-added in j and v_j^V is the nominal share of value-added in industry gross output.

Through rearranging Equations 12.2 and 12.4, we can obtain an expression for the sources of industry value-added growth (i.e. measured in terms of input contributions):

$$\Delta \ln V_j = \frac{\bar{v}_j^K}{\bar{v}_j^V} \Delta \ln K_j + \frac{\bar{v}_j^L}{\bar{v}_j^V} \Delta \ln L_j + \frac{1}{\bar{v}_j^V} v_j^T \quad (12.5)$$

Growth of aggregate value-added by the APPF approach is expressed as weighted industry value-added in a Törnqvist index:

$$\Delta \ln V = \sum_j \bar{w}_j \Delta \ln V_j \quad (12.6)$$

where w_j is the share of industry value-added in aggregate value-added. With ICT-specific grouping, we can rewrite Equation 12.6 as:

$$\begin{aligned}\Delta \ln V = &\sum_{j \in ICT-P} \bar{w}_j \Delta \ln V_j + \sum_{j \in ICT-U1} \bar{w}_j \Delta \ln V_j \\ &+ \sum_{j \in ICT-U2} \bar{w}_j \Delta \ln V_j + \sum_{j \in NonICT-1} \bar{w}_j \Delta \ln V_j \\ &+ \sum_{j \in NonICT-2} \bar{w}_j \Delta \ln V_j + \sum_{j \in NonICT-3} \bar{w}_j \Delta \ln V_j \end{aligned} \quad (12.6\text{a})$$

where the grouping notation ICT-P stands for ICT-producing industries, ICT-U1 for ICT-using in manufacturing and ICT-U2 for ICT-using in services, and where NonICT-1 stands for non-ICT group in manufacturing, NonICT-2 for non-ICT in services and NonICT-3 in others (see next section for the grouping and Appendix Table for the details of industries in each group).

By combining Equations 12.5 and 12.6, we can have a new expression of aggregate value-added growth by weighted contribution of industry capital growth, industry labor growth and TFP growth:

$$\Delta \ln V \equiv \sum_j \bar{w}_j \Delta \ln V_j$$
$$= \sum_j \left(\bar{w}_j \frac{\bar{v}_j^K}{\bar{v}_j^V} \Delta \ln K_j + \bar{w}_j \frac{\bar{v}_j^L}{\bar{v}_j^V} \Delta \ln L_j + \bar{w}_j \frac{1}{\bar{v}_j^V} v_j^T \right) \quad (12.7)$$

Through this new expression, we have introduced the well-known Domar weights in our industry aggregation (Domar 1961), i.e. a ratio of each industry's share in total value-added (w_j) to the proportion of the industry's value-added in its gross output (v_j^v).

If we maintain the stringent assumption that capital and labor inputs have the same marginal productivity in all industries, we can define aggregate TFP growth as:

$$V^T \equiv \sum_j \bar{w}_j \Delta \ln V_j - \bar{v}^K \Delta \ln K - \bar{v}^L \Delta \ln L \quad (12.8)$$

However, this assumption is not likely to hold, particularly in the case of China as argued above. It is therefore interesting to look at the difference of the two measurement approaches. By subtracting Equation 12.7 from Equation 12.8 and rearranging, we can show how the aggregate TFP growth is attributed to Domar-weighted industry TFP growth and to the effect of factor reallocation across industries (Jorgenson et al. 2005a):

$$V^T = \left(\sum_j \frac{\bar{w}_j}{\bar{v}_j^V} v_j^T \right) + \left(\sum_j \frac{\bar{w}_j}{\bar{v}_j^V} v_j^T \Delta \ln K_j - \bar{v}_K \Delta \ln K \right)$$
$$+ \left(\sum_j \frac{\bar{w}_j}{\bar{v}_j^V} v_j^L \Delta \ln L_j - \bar{v}_L \Delta \ln L \right) \quad (12.9)$$

The *reallocation* terms in the second and third brackets can be simplified as:

$$v_T = \sum_j \frac{\bar{w}_j}{\bar{v}_j^V} v_j^T + p^K + p^L \tag{12.9'}$$

It should be noted that the Domar-weighted industry TFP growth term $\sum_j \frac{\bar{w}_j}{\bar{v}_j^V} v_j^T$ can also be expressed as the Domar-weighted sum of ICT-specific group TFP growth (see Equation 12.6a for group denotation):

$$\sum_j \frac{\bar{w}_j}{\bar{v}_j^V} v_j^T = \sum_{j \in ICT-P} \frac{\bar{w}_j}{\bar{v}_j^V} v_j^T + \sum_{j \in ICT-U1} \frac{\bar{w}_j}{\bar{v}_j^V} v_j^T$$
$$+ \sum_{j \in ICT-U2} \frac{\bar{w}_j}{\bar{v}_j^V} v_j^T + \sum_{j \in NonICT-1} \frac{\bar{w}_j}{\bar{v}_j^V} v_j^T \tag{12.9'}$$
$$+ \sum_{j \in NonICT-2} \frac{\bar{w}_j}{\bar{v}_j^V} v_j^T + \sum_{j \in NonICT-3} \frac{\bar{w}_j}{\bar{v}_j^V} v_j^T$$

Equation 12.9 expresses the aggregate TFP growth in terms of three sources: Domar-weighted industry TFP growth, reallocation of capital and reallocation of labor across industries. This Domar weighting scheme ($\bar{w}_j / \bar{v}_j^V$), originated by Domar (1961), plays a key role in the direct aggregation across industries of the Jorgensonian growth accounting framework. A direct consequence of the Domar-aggregation is that the weights do not sum to unity, implying that aggregate productivity growth amounts to more than the weighted average of industry-level productivity growth (or less, if negative). This reflects the fact that productivity change in the production of *intermediate inputs* do not only have an 'own' effect but in addition they lead to reduced or increased prices in downstream industries, and that effect accumulates through vertical links. As elaborated by Hulten (1978), the Domar aggregation method establishes a consistent link between the industry-level productivity growth and the aggregate productivity growth. Productivity gains of the aggregate economy may exceed the average productivity gains across industries because flows of intermediate inputs between industries contribute to aggregate productivity by allowing productivity gains in successive industries to augment one another. The same logic can explain productivity losses.

The next two terms reflect the impact on aggregate TFP growth of the reallocation effect of capital (ρ^K) and labor (ρ^L) across industries, respectively. Each of the reallocation term is obtained by subtracting cost-weighted aggregate factor (capital or labor) input growth from the Domar-weighted input growth across industries. It should be noted that both theoretically and methodologically, when these terms are not negligible, it indicates that industries do not face the same factor costs, which suggests a violation of the assumption of the widely used aggregate approach. However, one should not expect a significant reallocation effect in an economy where there is a well-developed market system. This is a very useful analytical tool for the Chinese case where strong government interventions in resource allocation may have caused severe market distortions (Hsieh and Klenow 2009; Wu 2016).

DATA and ICT-specific industry grouping

The CIP data – a brief introduction

This study uses updated and revised CIP (China Industrial Productivity) data based on the publicly available CIP 3.0 (see Wu 2015; Wu and Ito 2015; Wu et al. 2015 for the construction of the CIP data and details of data sources and problems). The principle of the CIP data construction adheres to the underlying theory as expressed in Equation 12.2 as well as in the set of Equation 12.3. This means that in the case of input and output data the CIP industry accounts are made coherently consistent with the Chinese national accounts as control totals as given in the official input–output system, reconstructed and interpolated for the time series of the accounts (Wu and Ito 2015). It should be noted that in constructing industry accounts we do not, or are unable to, challenge the official national accounts data except for necessary consistency adjustments. Therefore, the widely reported and discussed data falsification problems should be born in mind when interpreting our results.[2]

In the case of employment data, the CIP industry accounts are built on all available employment statistics and surveys, reconstructed to ensure consistency with population censuses as control totals. Workers include both employees and self-employed (farming households and self-employed retailers and transporters), cross-classified by gender, age and educational level. Besides, the labor compensation at industry level is controlled by the national income accounts (Wu et al. 2015). In the absence of national investment matrix, however, despite tremendous efforts have been made to reconstruct industry investment flows, the lack of coherence between individual industries and the national accounts has remained as a major obstacle to establishing economy-wide consistency in the productivity analysis for the Chinese economy (Wu 2015).

The revision of the nominal input and output data is based on the lately available Chinese 2012 input–output tables. Accordingly, updated national accounts data for the period 2007–12 are used to interpolate the input–output series between the 2007 and 2012 tables replacing the extrapolated series from 2007 onwards in CIP 3.0. The nominal accounts are double-deflated by a producer price index (PPI) matrix, constructed based on official PPIs for the agricultural and industrial sectors and relevant components of the consumer price index (CPI) for service industries (Wu and Ito 2015). However, our PPI revision is still domestic transactions-based by nature, that is, it has not yet been able to take into account the effect of the price changes of imported intermediate inputs. This may however induce some biases to industries that have been heavily depending on imported materials, including many Chinese ICT producers.

ICT-specific industry grouping

Since we are interested in how ICT has affected the productivity performance in the Chinese economy, the whole economy could be divided into two large sectors, ICT sector and non-ICT sector. This kind of technology is diffused among industries by means of ICT capital assets and skilled labor. Therefore, to explore the role of ICT we may consider distinguishing industries that are highly related to information technology from those are not through their intensity of using ICT equipment. The ICT intensity is defined as the share of ICT capital stock on total equipment capital stock.

In the absence of ICT equipment data, we opt for using the US criteria for ICT intensity in capital stock in the present study. This is justifiable because empirical studies have shown that the diffusion of ICT has similarities across countries (van Ark et al. 2002; O'Mahony and De Boer 2002). We may also argue that the rapid globalization through direct investment and trade in manufacturing has enhanced such diffusion. Following Jorgenson et al. (2005a), we first take the median of ICT intensity of all industries in 1995 as the benchmark and then define the industries whose ICT intensity exceeds the median as intensive users of ICT and those below the median as non-ICT industries. Besides, ICT producers should be distinguished from ICT users. As explained by Jorgenson (2001), on the one hand, as ICT-producing industries become more efficient, more ICT equipment and software can be produced using the same cost. This raises the productivity of ICT producers and contributes to aggregate TFP growth through ICT users. On the other hand, investment in ICT equipment leads to the growth of productive capability in ICT-using industries as labor is working with more efficient equipment. Such an increase in the deployment of ICT affects TFP growth only if there are spillovers from ICT producers to ICT users.

To better investigate the industry origin of the ICT impact on the aggregate TFP performance, we also feel necessary to distinguish manufacturing and services industries in ICT users and non-ICT users. Therefore, we categorize the 37 CIP industries into six groups as defined in Equation 12.6a, namely ICT-producing, ICT-using in manufacturing, ICT-using in services, non-ICT manufacturing, services and others (see Table 12.A.1 for details). This grouping is guided by our desire to study differences across industries that vary in ICT-using intensity. Although such breakdown is somewhat subjective, causal inspection suggests that it is reasonable.

For example, three industries, 'electronic and telecommunication equipment' (CIP21), 'instruments and office equipment' (CIP22) and 'post and telecommunication services' (CIP30) are primary producers of ICT capital goods and should be distinguished from ICT users and non-ICT users. Industries such as 'electric equipment' (CIP20) and 'transport and storage' (CIP29) are considered most ICT-intensive users, hence should be labeled as ICT-using in manufacturing and ICT-using in services, respectively. Industries like 'coal mining' (CIP02) and 'real estate activities' (CIP32) are not ICT-intensive and hence are grouped into non-ICT in manufacturing and non-ICT in services accordingly. Finally, to differentiate non-ICT-intensive agriculture and construction from the above groups, we put them into the non-ICT group in 'other industries'.

Based on the above discussion, we conjecture that the productivity growth of ICT-producing and ICT-using manufacturing groups may generally outperform the remaining groups. We may also expect the latter group, as the one using ICT equipment most intensively and benefited by the spillover effect of the former, growing more rapidly than the former group, hence being the most important contributor to the aggregate TFP growth.

Empirical results

Sources of gross output growth by ICT-specific group

Let us begin with an examination of ICT-specific group level sources of growth as reported in Table 12.1 for each sub-period based on a gross output production function as expressed in Equation 12.2. In Figure 12.2 we depict the gross output-based TFP in index for each group. Note that the so-estimated group TFP is not intended to be analytical with any theoretical underpinning; rather it serves as a residual indicator ignoring any connection with other industry or the rest of the economy. This is however a necessary starting point because in the ultimate analysis these groups are used as building blocks of the national economy and originators of aggregate productivity growth.

As shown in Figure 12.2, among the six groups only the ICT-producing and the ICT-using manufacturing demonstrate a positive linear trend in the growth of total factor productivity, but the former was twice as fast as the latter over the entire period in question (as suggested by the estimated coefficients from the simple regression models in Figure 12.2). Such a gap in TFP performance between the two groups may reflect that the price decline of ICT components, which were mainly used by Chinese ICT makers, was faster than that of ICT equipment facing Chinese ICT users.

It is also interesting to see that in the case of the ICT-producing group there was a short-term jump in TFP growth following China's WTO entry, implying that this group was likely benefitted by the WTO-induced greater exposure to the world ICT market albeit shocked by the global financial crisis (GFC). There were nonetheless no WTO and GFC effects observed in the ICT-using manufacturing group that appears to have undergone a much steadier TFP trend. In sharp contrast, all other groups including the ICT-using services group generally experienced little TFP improvement following China's WTO entry.

The estimated sources of gross output growth in Table 12.1 and their relative contributions expressed in percentage shares in Figure 12.3 can help better understand the TFP indices presented in

Table 12.1 Sources of gross output growth in China by ICT-specific industry group

(Gross output-weighted annual growth rate in percent)

Group	Y	L¹	K¹	X²	TFP	Y	L¹	K¹	X²	TFP
	1981–1991					1991–2001				
ICT-producing	21.21	0.53	3.55	10.45	6.69	26.12	0.61	3.44	16.52	5.55
ICT-using manufacturing	13.32	0.30	2.13	6.94	3.95	12.85	0.06	2.24	8.56	1.99
ICT-using services	9.84	1.66	3.15	4.60	0.43	7.08	0.92	5.03	4.38	-3.26
Non-ICT manufacturing	7.97	0.42	2.82	6.08	-1.36	10.92	0.13	1.64	7.06	2.09
Non-ICT services	6.98	1.09	3.05	3.63	-0.79	9.30	2.44	4.39	7.10	-4.63
Non-ICT other sectors	6.94	0.55	1.27	3.18	1.94	9.02	0.37	2.04	5.76	0.85
	2001–2007					2007–2012				
ICT-producing	25.76	0.87	3.05	17.37	4.46	13.01	0.59	1.72	9.88	0.83
ICT-using manufacturing	18.49	0.43	2.39	13.45	2.22	11.92	0.07	1.95	8.92	0.98
ICT-using services	12.09	0.72	4.54	5.79	-0.48	12.99	0.66	5.77	7.29	-0.73
Non-ICT manufacturing	15.04	0.51	2.26	11.68	0.58	11.39	0.03	2.52	8.14	0.69
Non-ICT services	10.53	1.61	5.66	4.80	-1.54	6.62	1.53	5.38	2.49	-2.77
Non-ICT other sectors	8.31	-0.44	2.36	6.86	-0.48	7.61	-0.63	3.37	6.21	-1.34

Source: Authors' calculation based Equation 12.2 using updated and revised CIP 3.0 data.

Notes: 1) All primary factor inputs are measured in flows of factor services rather than stocks. 2) Intermediate inputs include all materials, energy and services that are purchased by producers.

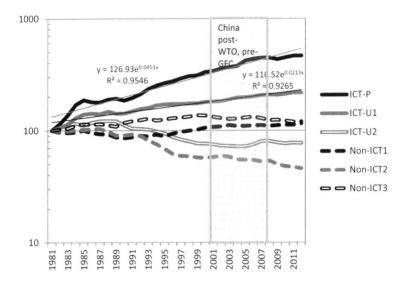

Figure 12.2 Total factor productivity index by ICT-specified group (1981 = 100)

Source: As Table 12.1.

Notes: ICT-P: producing; ICT-U1: using in manufacturing; ICT-U2: using in services; non-ICT1: manufacturing; non-ICT2: services; non-ICT3: others.

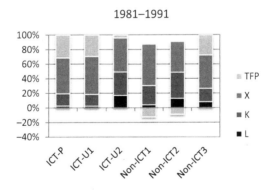

Figure 12.3 Sources of gross output growth in China by ICT-specific industry group (Gross output growth = 100 percent)

Source: Authors' calculation based Table 12.1.

Notes: ICT-P: producing; ICT-U1: using in manufacturing; ICT-U2: using in services; non-ICT1: manufacturing; non-ICT2: services; non-ICT3: others.

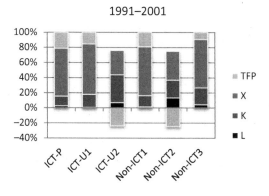

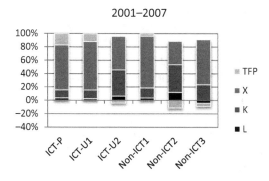

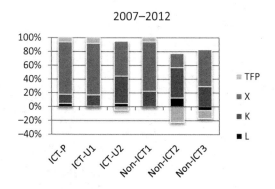

Figure 12.3 (Continued)

Figure 12.2. Based on these estimates, we can summarize three points worth noting. Firstly, ICT-related sectors were indeed outstanding performers in terms of gross output growth. The ICT-producing group was the champion over each sub-period despite radical policy regime shifts or macroeconomic shocks. This group was followed by the ICT-using manufacturing group before the GFC shock. During China's post-WTO period 2001–07, these two groups achieved a very high growth rate of 25.8 and 18.5 percent per annum, respectively. However, in the wake of GFC while they lost steam like many others and considerably slowed down to 13.0 and 11.9 percent, the ICT-using services group accelerated (Table 12.1).

Secondly, even in the case of outstanding output growth, the ICT-related industries were still increasingly driven by the rise of intermediate inputs, reflected by a rising ratio of input materials growth to gross output growth, i.e. $\Delta \ln X_j / \Delta \ln Y_j$ using our denotations. In the case of ICT-producing, based on Table 12.1, the $\Delta \ln X_j / \Delta \ln Y_j$ ratio rose from 0.42 in 1981–91 to 0.63 in 1991–2001, 0.68 in 2001–07 and further 0.76 in 2007–12. In the case of ICT-using manufacturing, this ratio also rose from 0.52 to 0.67, 0.73 and 0.75 accordingly. In these two cases, since the contribution to gross output growth by labor and capital inputs was more or less stable over time, this implies an inevitable decline in the TFP growth, that is, as reported in Table 12.1, 6.69, 5.55, 4.46 and 0.83 percent per annum for the former over each sub-period and 3.95, 1.99, 2.22 and 0.98 percent per annum for the latter (see Figure 12.3 for relative factor contributions).

This was also generally phenomenal in other groups, mainly services, though there was no clear trend in some cases. For example, a similar rise in $\Delta \ln X_j / \Delta \ln Y_j$ is also observed in non-ICT other sectors covering mainly agriculture and construction, from 0.46 in 1981–91 to 0.64 in 1991–2001, and then further to an average of 0.83 over the rest through 2012. Consequently, this group's TFP growth declined from 1.94 percent in 1981–91 to 0.85 in 1991–2001, –0.48 in 2001–07, and further to –1.34 percent in 2007–12 (Table 12.1 and also see Figure 12.3).

Thirdly, while both ICT and non-ICT manufacturing industries experienced a decline or sometime stability in the ratio of capital input growth to gross output growth, i.e. $\Delta \ln K_j / \Delta \ln Y_j$, both ICT and non-ICT services experienced a rise of the ratio rather substantially in some cases. We could observe that, over the entire period, the $\Delta \ln K_j / \Delta \ln Y_j$ ratio of the ICT-producing group declined from 0.17 to 0.13 and in the case of ICT-using manufacturing it stayed at around 0.16. In sharp contrast, it rose from 0.32 to 0.44 in the case of ICT-using services and from 0.44 to 0.81 in the case of non-ICT services. This largely explains their poor TFP performances over time (Table 12.1 and Figure 12.3).

ICT-specific group contribution to aggregate growth and source of growth

The above observations provide what the CIP data may imply in a less analytical manner or largely in a descriptive way in that there is no connection whatsoever between industries economy-wide through market and government industry-specific policies as well as affected by institutional deficiencies. However, from the observations, we have seen that these ICT-specific groups have performed very differently in their output growth and sources of the growth over time, which well justifies the importance of taking into account industry heterogeneity as discussed in our methodological section *a la* Jorgenson (2001). We devote this sub-section to examine group contributions to China's aggregate value-added growth that is made through the gross output growth of individual groups and industries, in parallel to the scrutiny of the sources of the aggregate value-added growth. The results are summarized in Table 12.2.

As shown in the first panel of Table 12.2, adopting double-deflation procedures and using the industry weights from our ICT-specific industry grouping, the Chinese economy achieved a real value-added growth of 9.38 percent per annum over the period 1981–2012. On average, the three ICT-related groups made up 47 percent of China's GDP growth (4.46 ppts out of the 9.38 percent of annual growth), or 29 percent if focusing only on ICT-related manufacturing. This 29 percent contribution is represented by 2.71 ppts out of the 9.38 percent annual growth, of which 0.74 ppts could be attributed to ICT-producing and 1.97 to ICT-using manufacturing. As expected, the latter group, as the one using ICT equipment most intensively and benefited by the spillover effect of the former, indeed expanded more rapidly, hence being the most important contributor to the aggregate GDP and TFP growth (see Table 12.4 on TFP growth).

The largest GDP contributor was nevertheless the non-ICT manufacturing group that accounted for 27 percent (2.54 ppts) of the

Table 12.2 Sources of aggregate value-added growth in China, 1981–2012

(Contributions are share-weighted growth rate in percent)

	1981– 91	1991– 2001	2001– 07	2007– 12	1981– 2012
Industry contribution to value-added growth					
Value-added growth due to (%)	8.81	8.85	11.37	9.22	9.38
– ICT-producing	0.52	0.67	1.25	0.68	0.74
– ICT-using manufacturing	2.15	1.86	2.34	1.37	1.97
– ICT-using services	1.37	0.99	2.82	2.74	1.75
– Non-ICT manufacturing	1.73	3.10	2.55	3.04	2.54
– Non-ICT services	0.79	0.41	1.48	0.72	0.79
– Non-ICT other sectors	2.25	1.81	0.93	0.68	1.60
Factor contribution to value-added growth					
Value-added growth due to (%)	8.81	8.85	11.37	9.22	9.38
– Capital input:	5.82	7.00	9.45	10.39	7.64
– Stock	5.83	7.08	9.54	10.38	7.68
– Capital quality (composition)	−0.01	−0.08	−0.09	0.02	−0.04
– Labor input:	1.12	1.12	0.59	0.25	0.88
– Homogeneous hours	1.07	0.69	0.54	−1.00	0.51
– Labor quality (composition)	0.06	0.43	0.05	1.26	0.37
– Aggregate TFP	1.86	0.72	1.32	−1.42	0.86

Source: Authors' estimates.

GDP growth. This should not be a big surprise given the nature of China's catch up through export-oriented manufacturing. It is clear now that the estimates of gross output growth in Table 12.1 cannot be easily translated into the estimates of value-added growth in Table 12.2 without properly considering the different roles of industries interacted and connected through their intermediate inputs.

The estimated TFP performance was highly unstable over time with the highest TFP growth achieved in the initial reform stage in the 1980s and the worst in the wake of GFC.[3] Of the economy-wide 9.38 percent annual value-added growth for the entire period, the contribution of capital input was 7.64 ppts, labor input 0.88 ppts, and TFP growth 0.86 ppts on average. This means that the Chinese economy relied 81.4 percent of its real value-added growth on the growth of capital input, 9.4 percent on the growth of labor input and the rest 9.2 percent on total factor productivity growth. Over time, the contribution of capital input increased from 66.1 percent in the 1980s to 83.1 percent post WTO and then even jumped to 112.7 percent post GFC (10.39 capital input growth versus 9.22 value-added growth in 2007–12, Table 12.2).

On the other hand, the contribution of labor input declined from 12.8 percent in the 1980s to 5.2 percent post WTO and then dropped to only 2.7 percent post GFC. In fact, the decline in hours worked was substantial by 1.0 ppt per annum in 2007–12. This was nonetheless cancelled out by labor quality improvement by 1.26 ppts. The contribution of the quality of capital was insignificant on average.[4]

If the estimated annual aggregate TFP growth rates are translated into an index benchmarked on the initial year 1981 as shown in Figure 12.4, we observe a very volatile TFP performance around its underlying trend (level not rate) with substantial shocks. Using the trend line as a yardstick to identify major shocks, one may find that the shocks are largely institutional. The first TFP drive was

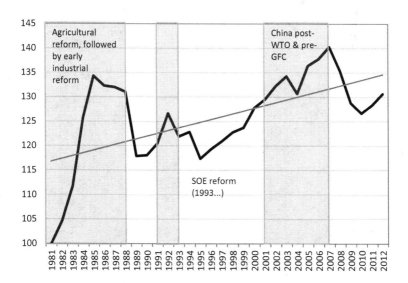

Figure 12.4 An index of China's aggregate total factor productivity (1981 = 100)

Source: Based on results reported in Table 12.2.

observed in the early 1980s associated with China's agricultural reform and more or less maintained by early industrial reform from the mid-1980s. The TFP collapsed following the 1989 political crisis but somewhat recovered in the early 1990s in response to Deng's call for bolder reforms in 1992. But this did not last long before it lost steam along with the SOE reform in 1994. It began to accelerate following China's WTO entry and peaked by the eve of the GFC. Note that the current CIP data is not yet long enough for us to sufficiently examine the post-GFC decline in TFP growth and if it had indeed turned positive after 2010.

Table 12.3 presents the results of a decomposition of China's aggregate value-added per hour worked into changes in capital deepening, labor quality and TFP. This enables us to separate the contribution of hours worked from the contribution of genuine labor productivity improvement and its sources. The Chinese economy once benefited significantly from the increase in hours worked or the so-called 'demographic dividend'. This has, however, declined over time, as shown in Table 12.3, from 2.55 percent per annum in 1981–91 to 1.28 following China's WTO entry. However, in the last period 2007–12, the growth of hours worked turned negative and dropped substantially by 2.33 percent per annum. This clearly indicates the complete loss of the 'demographic dividend'. Although the growth of value-added per hour worked increased from 6.25 to

Table 12.3 Decomposition of aggregate labor productivity growth in China

(Contributions are weighted growth in percent)					
	1981–91	1991–2001	2001–07	2007–12	1981–2012
Growth of labor productivity					
Value-Added Growth (APPF)	8.81	8.85	11.37	9.22	9.38
– Value-added per hour worked	6.26	7.26	10.08	11.55	8.18
– Natural hours[1]	2.55	1.59	1.28	−2.33	1.21
Factor contribution					
Value-Added per hour worked	6.26	7.26	10.08	11.55	8.18
– Capital deepening	4.34	6.10	8.71	11.72	6.94
– Labor quality	0.06	0.43	0.05	1.26	0.37
– TFP growth	1.86	0.72	1.32	−1.42	0.86

Source: Authors' estimates.

Note: 1) Different from user cost-weighted homogeneous hours in Table 12.2.

11.55 percent per annum, it appeared to be increasingly relying on the growth of capital deepening ranging from 4.34 to 11.72 percent per annum. In fact, Table 12.3 shows that the TFP growth was not necessarily in line with, or completely contradictory to, the pace of capital deepening, which suggests serious misallocation of resources.

The ICT-specific industry origin of aggregate TFP growth

In order to explicitly account for differences across ICT-specific groups and their impact on China's aggregate TFP performance, we now introduce the Domar aggregation approach to the APPF framework as given in Equation 12.9 following the ICT studies on the US economy by Jorgenson et al. (2005a and 2005b). This is to account for genuine TFP improvement within industries and factor reallocation effects across industries. The results presented in the first line of Table 12.4 are estimated with the stringent assumption that marginal productivities of capital and labor are the same across all industries, which are the same as those presented in Tables 12.2 and 12.3. As expressed in Equation 12.9, if using Domar weights such an aggregate TFP growth rate can be decomposed into three

Table 12.4 Decomposition of China's aggregate total factor productivity growth: Domar-aggregation vis-à-vis factor reallocation effects

(In percentage points except aggregate TFP growth in percent per annum and)

	1981–91	1991–01	2001–07	2007–12	1981–12
Aggregate TFP growth	1.86	0.72	1.32	−1.42	0.86
1. Domar-weighted TFP growth	1.47	0.63	1.47	−2.08	0.63
– ICT-producing	0.35	0.32	0.56	0.28	0.37
– ICT-using manufacturing	1.33	0.99	0.92	−0.06	0.92
– ICT-using services	0.14	−1.08	1.00	−0.18	−0.14
– Non-ICT manufacturing	−1.05	1.42	−0.05	0.18	0.14
– Non-ICT services	−0.28	−1.41	−0.94	−1.66	−0.99
– Non-ICT other sectors	0.96	0.41	−0.01	−0.65	0.33
2. Reallocation of K (ρ^K)	−0.26	−0.35	−1.33	−0.08	−0.47
3. Reallocation of L (ρ^L)	0.65	0.44	1.19	0.74	0.70

Source: Authors' estimates following Equation 12.9.

additive components, i.e. 1) the change of aggregate TFP originated in industries summed up by Domar weights; 2) the change of capital reallocation across industries; and 3) the change of labor reallocation across industries.

On average of the entire period 1981–2012, China's Domar-weighted TFP growth is estimated at 0.63 percent per annum, compared to the aggregate TFP growth of 0.86 percent per annum. This implies a net factor reallocation effect of 0.23 ppts. Table 12.4 also shows the contribution of each industrial group to the Domar-weighted annual TFP growth (see Table 12.A.2 for the results of individual industries). The biggest contributor to the Domar-weighted aggregate TFP growth was the ICT-using manufacturing group, contributing 0.92 ppts. The ICT-producing group contributed 0.37 ppts. The non-ICT using services was the worst performer, dragging down the Domar weighted TFP growth by 0.99 ppts (Table 12.4). Such a sharp contrast across industry groups in TFP performance can also be observed over different sub-periods, which clearly suggests that treating individual industries homogenous in the growth accounting can substantially distort our view of the productivity performance of the Chinese economy and give no vision of the industry origin of the aggregate TFP performance.

In terms of Domar-weighted TFP growth, both the period of the 1980s and the period post WTO were equally appraisable with a very impressive 1.47 percent annual growth. The ICT-producing and manufacturing groups were the key TFP contributors during the former period and all the three ICT-related groups were positive and significant TFP drivers during the latter period. The post-GFC period 2007–12, however, saw a considerable TFP decline by 2.08 percent per annum, the worst throughout the whole period in question. Yet, the ICT-producing group, together with the non-ICT manufacturing group (0.18), still registered a positive TFP growth of 0.28 percent per annum (Table 12.4).

The effect of factor reallocation

The slower Domar-weighted TFP growth (0.63) compared to the aggregate TFP growth (0.86) implies that the net reallocation of capital and labor is positive. Following Equation 12.9, in Table 12.4 we show that this effect consists of a positive labor reallocation effect (ρ^L) of 0.70 ppts, yet a negative capital reallocation effect (ρ^K) of −0.47 ppts. Figure 12.5 depicts the two reallocation effects as indices benchmarked on the initial time point 1981.

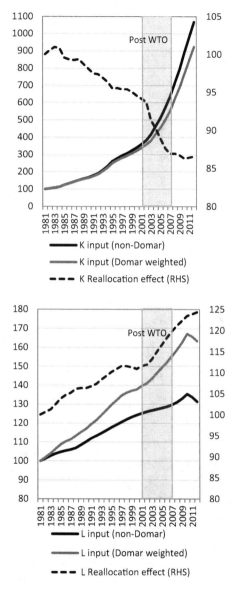

Figure 12.5 Domar and non-Domar weighted factor input indices and reallocation effects (1981 = 100)

Source: Based on results reported in Table 12.4.

It should be noted that such a magnitude of reallocation effect is typically not observed in market economies. Based on their empirical work on the US economy in 1977–2000, Jorgenson et al. (2005a) showed that, first, the reallocation effect was generally negligible and, second, if it was non-negligible for some subperiods, the capital and labor reallocation effects generally moved in opposite directions. Jorgenson et al. (1987) also reported the reallocation of capital that was typically positive and the reallocation of labor that was typically negative for the US economy for the period 1948–79. This is because capital grew more rapidly in industries with high capital service prices, hence high returns on capital, whereas labor grew relatively slowly in industries with high marginal compensation.

In the case of China, such a large magnitude and unexpected sign of capital and labor reallocation effects have two important implications. First, individual industries indeed face significantly different marginal factor productivities suggesting that there are barriers to factor mobility which cause misallocation of resources in the economy. The flip-side of this finding is that corrections to the distortions can potentially be productivity-enhancing, which is good news in terms of much talked about and long-awaited structural reforms.

We find that the effect of labor reallocation remained generally positive over time. This suggests that labor market was much less distorted than the capital market, benefitting from increasing labor mobility along with reforms. Notably, the post-WTO period experienced the most significant productivity gain attributable to labor reallocation (1.19 in 2001–07) which could be driven by the rapid expansion of export-oriented, labor-intensive industries that was in line with China's comparative advantage. Besides, the effect of labor reallocation was also strong in the wake of the GFC (0.74 in 2007–12), reflecting that labor responded more quickly to the changes of market conditions.

The case of capital reallocation is different. It maintained a negative reallocation effect throughout the entire period with the period of post-WTO the worst (−1.33). This may reflect local governments' increasing engagement in the GDP race by promoting local urbanization and a new round of extensive heavy industrialization that has been criticized as repetitious and redundant (Wu 2008).

Concluding remarks

In this study, we apply Jorgensonian APPF industry origin of productivity framework, incorporating Domar weights for industry aggregation, to Chinese ICT-specific industry groups in China's post-reform growth from 1981 to 2012. In the absence of a direct measure of ICT asset, our ICT-specific industry grouping adopts the ICT-intensity criteria used in the US case (Jorgenson et al. 2005a), assuming that the similarities found in the ICT intensity across industries across countries can be reasonably held for China. This allows us to decompose China's productivity growth into the contribution of the so-grouped ICT industries and the factor reallocation effects across the groups.

We show that Chinese ICT-producing and ICT-using manufacturing groups appear to be the most important driver of China's productivity growth over the entire period in question, although we cannot rule out that the so-grouping may to some extent be mixed up with China's most dynamic and productive downstream industries that are close to the most competitive end market and thus less exposed to government direct interventions (Wu 2016). However, ICT-related industries are by nature more market based and more open to international competition than other industries.

We find that while sharing 29 percent of China's 9.38 percent annual value-added growth, these industries contributed 149 percent to China's 0.83 percent annual aggregate TFP growth. This, together with a strong gain from the labor reallocation effect across industries, has enabled the economy to compensate for its heavy productivity losses by services and the economy-wide misallocation of capital resources. This could be good news to Chinese policy makers who have been searching for new engines of China's growth and hoping that technological innovation is the way out for the currently overcapacity and inefficiency-burdened real sector.

This ever first endeavor could be further improved by several challenging data works. The top priority is a proper construction of productive ICT assets for individual industries, controlled by the industry-specific total equipment as currently available in the CIP database. While working on this paper we did explore a commodity flow approach but failed to find a way to allocate ICT commodities among industries. We then attempted to empirically model the relationship between changes in skilled labor and changes in ICT assets using the US data, but have not yet been successful. We do hope that the Chinese statistical authority could listen to researchers' long appeal for establishing national investment matrix that is coherently linked to the national accounts.

Besides, we could consider further improving the CIP industry-specific producer price index to incorporate price changes of imported materials. This is not only to make the price matrix more realistic and reflect the true intermediate costs facing Chinese producers, but more importantly to improve our measure of the real value-added growth for industries that heavily rely on imported parts and materials, among which ICT-related industries should be unquestionably on the top of the list.

Appendix

Table 12.A.1 CIP/China KLEMS industrial classification and ICT-specific grouping

CIP	EU-KLEMS	Grouping	Industry	
01	AtB	Non-ICT3	Agriculture, Forestry, Animal Husbandry and Fishery	AGR
02	10	Non-ICT1	Coal mining	CLM
03	11	Non-ICT1	Oil and gas extraction	PTM
04	13	Non-ICT1	Metal mining	MEM
05	14	Non-ICT1	Non-metallic minerals mining	NMM
06	15	Non-ICT1	Food and kindred products	F&B
07	16	Non-ICT1	Tobacco products	TBC
08	17	Non-ICT1	Textile mill products	TEX
09	18	Non-ICT1	Apparel and other textile products	WEA
10	19	Non-ICT1	Leather and leather products	LEA
11	20	Non-ICT1	Saw mill products, furniture, fixtures	W&F
12	21t22	ICT-U1	Paper products, printing & publishing	P&P
13	23	Non-ICT1	Petroleum and coal products	PET
14	24	Non-ICT1	Chemicals and allied products	CHE
15	25	Non-ICT1	Rubber and plastics products	R&P
16	26	Non-ICT1	Stone, clay, and glass products	BUI
17	27t28	Non-ICT1	Primary & fabricated metal industries	MET
18	27t28	Non-ICT1	Metal products (excl. rolling products)	MEP
19	29	ICT-U1	Industrial machinery and equipment	MCH
20	31	ICT-U1	Electric equipment	ELE
21	32	ICT-P	Electronic and telecommunication equipment	ICT
22	30t33	ICT-P	Instruments and office equipment	INS
23	34t35	ICT-U1	Motor vehicles & other transportation equipment	TRS

(Continued)

Table 12.A.1 (Continued)

CIP	EU-KLEMS	Grouping	Industry	
24	36t37	ICT-U1	Miscellaneous manufacturing industries	OTH
25	E	ICT-U1	Power, steam, gas and tap water supply	UTL
26	F	Non-ICT3	Construction	CON
27	G	ICT-U2	Wholesale and Retail Trades	SAL
28	H	Non-ICT2	Hotels and Restaurants	HOT
29	I	ICT-U2	Transport and Storage	T&S
30	64	ICT-P	Post and Telecommunications	P&T
31	J	ICT-U2	Financial Intermediation	FIN
32	K	Non-ICT2	Real Estate Activities	REA
33	71t74	ICT-U2	Leasing, Technical, Science & Business Services	BUS
34	L	Non-ICT2	Public Administration and Defense	ADM
35	M	Non-ICT2	Education	EDU
36	N	Non-ICT2	Health and Social Security	HEA
37	O&P	Non-ICT2	Other Services	SER

Source: See Wu and Ito (2015) for CIP classification.

Notes: ICT-P: producing; ICT-U1: using in manufacturing; ICT-U2: using in services; non-ICT1: manufacturing; non-ICT2: services; non-ICT3: others.

Table 12.A.2 Industry contributions to value-added and total factor productivity growth: 1981–2012

	Value-Added			Total Factor Productivity		
	VA weight	VA growth	Contribution to aggregate VA growth	Domar weight	TFP growth	Contribution to aggregate TFP growth
AGR	0.195	5.02	1.09	0.313	0.45	0.32
CLM	0.016	4.98	0.07	0.032	−0.03	−0.02
PTM	0.017	−7.34	−0.12	0.026	−12.88	−0.32
MEM	0.005	9.84	0.05	0.014	0.64	0.01
NMM	0.006	10.00	0.06	0.013	2.16	0.03
F&B	0.027	11.35	0.30	0.128	0.29	0.03
TBC	0.012	9.37	0.10	0.018	−3.59	−0.08
TEX	0.026	11.33	0.29	0.112	1.10	0.10
WEA	0.009	15.15	0.13	0.037	1.22	0.04
LEA	0.004	13.95	0.06	0.020	0.84	0.02
W&F	0.007	14.84	0.11	0.027	1.36	0.04

	Value-Added			Total Factor Productivity		
	VA weight	VA growth	Contribution to aggregate VA growth	Domar weight	TFP growth	Contribution to aggregate TFP growth
P&P	0.011	13.60	0.15	0.040	1.32	0.05
PET	0.011	−0.37	−0.04	0.047	−3.98	−0.17
CHE	0.036	15.51	0.55	0.139	1.75	0.23
R&P	0.012	19.10	0.22	0.050	2.43	0.11
BUI	0.025	11.39	0.28	0.079	0.82	0.09
MET	0.031	8.62	0.24	0.140	−0.49	−0.07
MEP	0.012	18.77	0.23	0.052	2.64	0.11
MCH	0.034	14.81	0.53	0.123	3.12	0.34
ELE	0.015	21.24	0.30	0.068	3.08	0.14
ICT	0.015	37.76	0.51	0.079	6.78	0.31
INS	0.003	13.48	0.05	0.011	1.82	0.02
TRS	0.018	21.63	0.40	0.079	3.46	0.22
OTH	0.016	19.78	0.31	0.046	3.81	0.18
UTL	0.027	9.55	0.28	0.109	−0.52	−0.02
CON	0.055	9.48	0.51	0.213	0.13	0.02
SAL	0.077	8.70	0.64	0.144	−0.21	−0.07
HOT	0.019	9.32	0.17	0.053	−1.38	−0.06
T&S	0.051	8.24	0.42	0.105	−1.18	−0.11
P&T	0.013	13.56	0.18	0.024	0.78	0.04
FIN	0.048	10.88	0.44	0.074	2.95	0.05
REA	0.039	9.53	0.36	0.056	−7.71	−0.43
BUS	0.023	8.25	0.25	0.059	−0.90	−0.01
ADM	0.032	11.61	0.38	0.062	1.03	0.07
EDU	0.025	−6.17	−0.16	0.043	−7.33	−0.31
HEA	0.012	−6.20	−0.07	0.032	−5.31	−0.17
SER	0.017	4.27	0.11	0.038	−4.02	−0.10
Sum	**1.000**		**9.38**	**2.707**		**0.63**

Source: See Tables 12.2 and 12.4.

Notes: See Table 12.A.1 for industry abbreviation. Value-added and TFP growth rates are annualized raw growth rates in percent. Industry contribution to VA and TFP growth is weighted growth rate in percentage points. See Equation 12.9 for Domar aggregation.

Notes

1 The earlier versions of this paper were presented at RIETI and OECD seminars. Helpful comments and suggestions from Kyoji Fukao and Colin Webb as well as participants in seminars are gratefully acknowledged. We also thank George Zhang and Zhan Li for timely data support, and Hiroshi Ikari for editorial suggestions for the RIETI DP version of the paper (17-e-111). What is reported in this study are interim results of China Industrial Productivity (CIP) Database Project supported by RIETI's Asian Industrial Productivity Program and the IER of Hitotsubashi University.
2 China's official estimates of GDP growth have long been challenged for upward bias (see Wu 2013, 2014). Alternative estimates have indeed shown slower growth rates than the official accounts. The most affected sectors are manufacturing and so-called 'non-material services' (including non-market services). Wu (2013) shows that the official industrial output index has substantially moderated the impact of external shocks. Besides, Wu (2014) also shows that the 5–6 percent annual growth of labor productivity in 'non-material services' based on official data appears to be too good to be true if considering the international norm of between −1 and +1 percent per annum in the literature (Griliches 1992; van Ark 1996).
3 Table 12.A.2 reports the details for individual industries.
4 This might be due to the limited set of asset types ('structures' and 'equipment') that is available in the current CIP database. If a distinction between ICT and non-ICT assets could be made, a higher measured contribution is to be expected, see Jorgenson and Vu (2013).

Bibliography

Colecchia, Alessandra, and Paul Schreyer. 2002. "ICT Investment and Economic Growth in the 1990s: Is the United States a Unique Case? A Comparative Study of Nine OECD Countries." *Review of Economic Dynamics* 5: 408–442.

Denison, Edward F. 1962. *The Sources of Economic Growth in the United States and the Alternative before Us*. New York: Committee on Economic Development.

Domar, Evsey. 1961. "On the Measurement of Technological Change." *Economic Journal* 71: 709–729.

Fukao, Kyoji, Tsutomu Miyagawa, Hak K. Pyo, and Keun H. Rhee. 2009. "Estimates of Multifactor Productivity, ICT Contributions and Resource Reallocation Effects in Japan and Korea." *RIETI Discussion Papers*, 09-E-021.

Griliches, Zvi. 1960. "Measuring Inputs in Agriculture: A Critical Survey." *Journal of Farm Economics* 40(5): 1398–1427.

Griliches, Zvi. 1992. "Introduction." In Griliches Zvi (ed.), *Output Measurement in the Service Sectors*. Chicago: University of Chicago Press.

Hsieh, C., and P. J. Klenow. 2009. "Misallocations and Manufacturing TFP in China and India." *Quarterly Journal of Economics* CXXIV(4): 1403–1448.

Hulten, Charles. 1978. "Growth Accounting with Intermediate Inputs." *Review of Economic Studies* 45: 511–518.

Jorgenson, Dale W. 1966. "The Embodiment Hypothesis." *Journal of Political Economy* 74(1): 1–17.

Jorgenson, Dale W. 2001. "Information Technology and the U.S. Economy." *The American Economic Review* 91(1): 1–32.

Jorgenson, Dale W., Frank Gollop, and Barbara Fraumeni. 1987. *Productivity and U.S. Economic Growth*. Cambridge, MA: Harvard University Press.

Jorgenson, Dale W., and Z. Griliches. 1967. "The Explanation of Productivity Change." *Review of Economic Studies* 34(3): 249–283.

Jorgenson, Dale W., Mun S. Ho, and Kevin J. Stiroh. 2005a. *Information Technology and the American Growth Resurgence, Productivity Volume 3*. Cambridge, MA: MIT Press.

Jorgenson, Dale W., Mun S. Ho, and Kevin J. Stiroh. 2005b. "Growth of the US Industries and Investments in Information Technology and Higher Education." In Carol Corrado, John Haltiwanger, and Daniel Sichel (eds.), *Measuring Capital in a New Economy*. Chicago: University of Chicago Press.

Jorgenson, Dale W., and Kevin J. Stiroh. 2000. "Raising the Speed Limit: U.S. Economic Growth in the Information Age." Chapter 3 in Dale W. Jorgenson (2001a), 71–150.

Jorgenson, Dale W., and Khuong Vu. 2013. "The Emergence of the New Economic Order: Growth in the G7 and the G20." *Journal of Policy Modeling* 35(3): 389–399.

O'Mahony, M., and Bart van Ark, eds. 2003. *EU Productivity and Competitiveness: An Industry Perspective. Can Europe Resume the Catching-Up Process?* Luxembourg: DG Enterprise, European Union. www.ggdc.net/pub/EU_productivity_and_competitiveness.pdf.

O'Mahony, M., and De Boer. 2002. "Britain's Relative Productivity Performance: Has Anything Changed?" *National Institute Economic Review* 179: 38–43.

van Ark, Bart. 1996. "Sectoral Growth Accounting and Structural Change in Postwar Europe." In B. van Ark and N. Crafts (eds.), *Quantitative Aspects of Post-War European Economic Growth*. Cambridge: Cambridge University Press, 84–164.

van Ark, Bart, Johanna Melka, Nanno Mulder, Marcel Timmer, and Gerard Ypma. 2002. "ICT Investment and Growth Accounts for the European Union, 1980–2000." *Final Report on ICT and Growth Accounting for the DG Economics and Finance of the European Commission*, Brussels.

Wu, Harry X. 2013. "How Fast Has Chinese Industry Grown? – the Upward Bias Hypothesis Revisited." *China Economic Journal* 6(2–3): 80–102.

Wu, Harry X. 2014. "The Growth of 'Non-Material Services' in China – Maddison's 'Zero-Labor-Productivity-Growth' Hypothesis Revisited." *The Economic Review*, Institute of Economic Research, Hitotsubashi University 65(3): 265–283.

Wu, Harry X. 2015. "Constructing China's Net Capital Stock and Measuring Capital Service in China." *RIETI Discussion Papers*, 15-E-006.

Wu, Harry X. 2016. "On China's Strategic Move for a New Stage of Development – a Productivity Perspective." In D. W. Jorgenson, K. Fukao, and M. P. Timmer (eds.), *The World Economy: Growth or Stagnation?* Cambridge: Cambridge University Press, 153–198.

Wu, Harry X., and Keiko Ito. 2015. "Reconstruction of China's National Output and Income Accounts and Supply-Use and Input-Output Accounts in Time Series." *RIETI Discussion Papers*, 15-E-004.

Wu, Harry X., Ximing Yue, and George G. Zhang. 2015. "Constructing Employment and Compensation Matrices and Measuring Labor Input in China." *RIETI Discussion Papers*, 15-E-005.

Wu, Jinglian. 2008. *The Choice of China's Growth Model* [Zhongguo zengzhang moshi jueze]. Shanghai: Yuandong Book Press.

Chapter 13

Source of growth and structural changes in the Indian economy since 1980

Bishwanath Goldar

Introduction

Several studies have noted that a significant acceleration in the pace of economic growth in India took place from around 1980 or from the late 1970s.[1] Before the 1980s, the long-term economic growth rate of India's economy was about 3.5 percent per annum, which has been referred to as the *Hindu rate of growth*.[2] Indeed, this was the average annual growth rate in real gross domestic product (GDP) in India during the period 1950–51 to 1979–80 (or during 1955–56 to 1979–80 or during 1960–61 to 1979–80). In the 1980s, there was a marked step up in the rate of growth in real GDP; the average annual growth rate rose to about 5.5 percent per annum.[3] In the next decade, i.e. the 1990s, the average annual growth rate in real GDP of the Indian economy was slightly higher than 5.5 percent per annum, which accelerated further in the 2000s to reach more than 7 percent per annum. In terms of per capita economic growth, there was a significant increase from 1.7 percent per annum during 1950–80 to 3.8 percent per annum during 1980–2000 (Rodrik and Subramanian 2004: 193–194), which accelerated further to about 5.5 percent per annum during 2000–14.[4]

Rodrik and Subramanian (2004) have asserted that the transition in economic growth in India from around 1980 was grounded in an impressive increase in productivity. According to a set of estimates of total factor productivity (TFP) growth presented by them (Table 13.1 of their paper, estimates made by the IMF), the annual rate of TFP growth in India at the aggregate economy level was 1.17 percent during 1960–70 and 0.47 during 1970–80, which were relatively much higher at 2.89 percent and 2.44 percent during 1980–90 and 1990–2000, respectively. This assertion of Rodrik and Subramanian (2004) that the transition in economic growth in India from around 1980 was grounded in an impressive increase in productivity has been corroborated by the analysis of sources of growth of the Indian economy undertaken by Bosworth, Collins and Virmani (2007).[5] Their study reveals that the increase in India's economic growth rate in the post-1980 period was accompanied by a marked increase in the growth rate of TFP. The rate of growth in TFP in Indian economy went up from 0.2 percent per annum during 1960–80 to 2.0 percent per annum during 1980–2004, thus confirming the assessment of Rodrick and Subramanian (2004).[6] That there was significant acceleration in TFP growth in the Indian economy in the post-1980 period is borne out also by the TFP estimates of Sivasubramonian (2004). According to his estimates, the annual rate of TFP growth in the Indian economy was 1.20 percent during 1960–70 and 0.16 percent during 1970–80, which increased to 2.2 percent during 1980–90 and 2.1 percent during 1990–99. An interesting question that presents itself here is whether the marked acceleration in economic growth that took place in India in the 2000s as compared to the 1980s and 1990s was also accompanied by an accelerated growth in TFP.

The object of this paper is to study the sources of growth and changes in the structure of the Indian economy since 1980. For the core part of the analysis presented in the paper, the period covered is 1980–81 (1980) to 2011–12 (2011). However, for two components of the analysis presented in the paper, the period covered is extended to 2014–15 (2014). The sub-periods considered for the analysis are:

- Sub-period-1: 1980–81 to 1993–94
- Sub-period-2: 1994–95 to 2002–03
- Sub-period-3: 2003–04 to 2011–12 (or 2003–04 to 2014–15)

The division of the time period under study, 1980–81 to 2011–12, into three sub-periods mentioned above for the purpose of the present analysis follows the periodization adopted by Panagariya et al. (2014, Chapter 2) as reflecting three distinct periods of growth of the Indian economy since 1980. In the first sub-period, 1980–93, India's per capita GDP grew at an average annual rate of 2.9 percent. In the second sub-period, 1994–2002, India's per capita GDP grew at an average annual rate of 3.9 percent, and in the final sub-period, 2003–11, the growth rate in per capita GDP was about 6.9 percent per year.[7]

For the components of the analysis where the period covered is extended to 2014–15, the third sub-period has been divided into two parts: 2003–04 (2003) to 2007–08 (2007) and 2008–09 (2008) to 2014–15 (2014) representing the periods before and after the commencement of the recent global economic crisis. These are referred to as sub-periods 3A and 3B.

The first sub-period, 1980–81 to 1993–94, may be taken as a period of initiation of economic reforms in India. Some initial economic reforms were made in the 1980s, especially in the latter half of the 1980s. Then, the process of major trade and industrial reforms in India began from 1991. The year 1991 is a watershed in India's economic history because of major economic policy changes: dismantling of industrial licensing and removal of quantitative restrictions (QRs) on imports of intermediate and capital goods. The years 1991, 1992 and 1993 also saw some reductions in customs duty rates on imports from the high levels prevailing in 1990. The peak rate of customs duty was 150 percent in 1991–92 and it was lower at 85 percent in 1993–94 (subsequently, it was lowered to 65 percent in 1994–95, 50 percent in 1995–96 and 40 percent in 1997–98). The collection rate of customs duty was 47 percent in 1990–91, which fell to 44 percent in 1991–92, 37 percent in 1992–93 and 30 percent in 1993–94 (Goldar 2002).

The second sub-period is marked by consolidation of reforms. Certain important changes in industrial and trade policy made at the end of the first sub-period probably began to be felt by Indian firms in this period, both by manufacturing firms and firms belonging to services and other sectors. Also, significant cuts in tariff rates were made and QRs on imports of consumer goods were lifted so that domestic industries began to feel the effect of import competition in a major way and at the same time had the opportunity to exploit gainfully easier access to imported inputs. Since QRs on imports of intermediate and capital goods were removed in 1991, most goods became freely importable after the removal of QRs on imports of consumer goods in 2000 and 2001. The peak rate of customs duty fell from 65 percent in 1994–95 to 30 percent in 2002–03 (with some exceptions). Import weighted average of tariff rates was about 47 percent in 1993–94, which fell to about 29 percent by 2002–03 (Ahluwalia 2002).

The third sub-period, 2003 to 2011 (or up to 2014), contains a phase of rapid economic growth in India during 2003 to 2007 (partly traceable to the fact that the Indian economy was reaping gains from the economic reforms undertaken earlier and partly to an upturn in the global economy) which was followed by a phase of economic slowdown due to the recent global economic crisis. During this sub-period, substantial cuts were made in tariff rates on imports, bringing them to sufficiently low levels and exposing Indian industries thereby to intense import competition. This process was aided by India entering into a number of free trade or preferential trade agreements. In 2007–08, the peak duty rate for non-agricultural goods was brought down to 10 percent with a few exceptions (20 percentage points lower than the peak duty rate in 2002–03). The average duty rate for manufactured products fell from 31.8 percent in 2001 to 8.6 percent in 2008 and 2009 (World Bank tariff data on manufactured products for different countries).[8] After 2009, there has been not much decline in the MFN (most favored nation) tariff rates. According to data presented in *World Tariff Profiles* (publication of WTO OMC, ITC and UNCTAD), the average tariff rate on non-agricultural goods in India was 10.1 percent in 2009 and 9.8 percent in 2010. It was marginally higher at 10.4 percent in 2012 and 10.2 percent in 2013.

The rest of the paper is organized as follows. The next section outlines the data source used for the study. The third section presents an analysis of the growth rate of the Indian economy in the period 1980–81 to 2014–15 and sub-periods within this period. The analysis is undertaken for the aggregate economy and for broad sectors of the economy. This section also contains a brief analysis of structural changes in the Indian economy. The fourth section is devoted to an analysis of TFP growth in the Indian economy during the period 1980–81 to 2011–12. The methodology of estimation is explained first and then the TFP growth estimates for the Indian economy at the aggregate level and for the manufacturing sector and the market-services sector are presented and discussed. The fifth section contains a cross-country comparative analysis of GDP growth and TFP growth for the period 2003–14 using data for a select set of 17 emerging economies. For this purpose, TFP growth in the Indian economy at the aggregate level is estimated for the period 2003–04 to 2014–15 using a simpler methodology than that in the fourth section. The focus is on a comparison of TFP growth rates in the Indian economy before and after the recent global economic crisis, and how some of the other emerging economies have fared. Finally, in the sixth section of the paper, the main findings of the study are summarized and some concluding remarks are made.

Data sources

The basis source of data for the analysis is the India KLEMS database, 2015. The period covered in this database is 1980–81 to 2011–12.

The main source of data used for the preparation of the India KLEMS database is the *National Accounts Statistics* (NAS), published annually by the Central Statistics Office (CSO), Government of India. The national accounts series with base 2004–05 and the corresponding back series have been used. These data are supplemented by input–output tables (published by the CSO) and *Annual Survey of Industries* (ASI) brought out by the CSO and various rounds of NSSO (National Sample Survey Office) surveys on employment and unemployment, and on unorganized manufacturing.

The details of the procedures that have been adopted to construct time series on gross output, gross value-added, capital stock and capital service, labor input (number of persons employed and labor composition index reflecting changes in labor quality), energy input, materials inputs, and services input, and factor income shares for the various industries (27 industries: see Appendix) for India KLEMS database are provided elsewhere.[9] Therefore, this is not discussed here.

It should be noted that TFP estimates presented in the fourth section paper are primarily based on the India KLEMS database, 2015. Therefore, the period covered is up to 2011–12. The analysis of growth and structural change presented in the next section is based on data drawn from NAS, the 2004–05 series and the more recent 2011–12 series. Because of this, it becomes possible to cover an extended period up to 2014–15. The analysis of TFP growth at the economy level in the fifth section of the paper, which covers the period 2003–04 to 2014–15, is based on India KLEMS, 2015 database combined with data taken from NAS and some other sources.[10] For the cross-country comparative analysis of GDP growth and TFP growth, data have been drawn from the Conferences Board Total Economy Database.[11] In this case too, the period covered is up to 2014.

Indian economy: growth and structural change

Trends in GDP growth at the aggregate level

In the period 1980–81 to 2014–15, the trend growth rate in India's real GDP was about 6.1 percent per year. This growth rate has been estimated by fitting an exponential trend equation to the time series on real GDP for the years 1980–81 to 2014–15.[12] To study the differences in trend growth rate in India's real aggregate GDP among sub-periods, growth rates for sub-periods have been estimated by fitting the kinked-exponential model (Boyce 1986). The estimated trend growth rates in real GDP for the periods 1980–81 to 1993–94, 1993–94 to 2002–03 and 2002–03 to 2014–15 are found to be 5.1, 6.0 and 7.4 percent per annum, respectively.[13] If the third sub-period is split into two parts, as explained earlier, the trend growth rates for the four sub-periods are: 5.1 percent per annum for the period 1980–81 to 1993–94, 5.8 percent per annum for the period 1993–94 to 2002–03, 8.0 percent per annum for the period 2002–03 to 2007–08 and 6.9 percent per annum for the period 2007–08 to 2014–15.

The hike in the trend growth rate in real GDP in the second sub-period compared to that in the first sub-period is statistically significant at 1 percent level of significance and the same holds true for the hike in the trend growth rate in real GDP in the third sub-period in relation to that in the second sub-period. When the trend growth rates are compared between the two parts of the third sub-period (sub-periods 3A and 3B), the growth rate in sub-period 3B is found to be lower than that in sub-period 3A, i.e. the growth rate in GDP came down after the commencement of the global economic crisis. Since India's economic growth is expected to be affected adversely by the global economic crisis, the finding of a fall in GDP growth rate in the post-crisis period is consistent with that expectation. However, the reduction in growth rate is found to be relatively small (by about 1 percentage point only). Also, the decrease in growth rate is statistically significant at 5 percent level, not at 1 percent level. Thus, it appears that the adverse impact of the global economic crisis on the rate of India's economic growth was only modest.

Annual rates of growth in real GDP for the years 1981–82 through 2014–15 are shown in Figure 13.1. These show wide year-to-year variations. The trend growth rates for different sub-periods are superimposed on the annual growth rates in the graph. It is

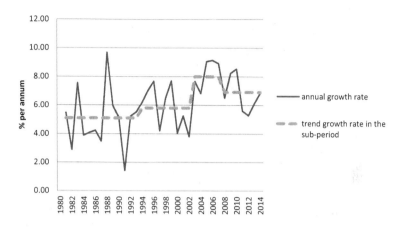

Figure 13.1 Growth rate in real GDP, India, 1981–82 to 2014–15
Source: Author's computations based on NAS.

evident from the graph that in the period 2003–07 there was a significant hike in the trend economic growth rate, and there was relatively a small fall in the trend economic growth rate in the period 2008–14, i.e. the period following the commencement of the recent global economic crisis.

It may be mentioned in passing that GDP growth data in the Conference Board Total Economy Database reveal that a significant reduction in GDP growth rate has taken place in the post-crisis era in a number of emerging economies. These include China (average annual growth rates of 11.7 and 8.8 percent during 2003–07 and 2008–14, respectively), Thailand (5.6 and 2.9 percent), Turkey (6.9 and 3.3 percent), South Africa (4.7 and 2.0 percent) and Russia (7.5 and 1.7 percent). The corresponding figures for India are 8.6 and 7.1 percent per annum during 2003–07 and 2008–14, respectively. It is clear that the deceleration in GDP growth rate has been relatively smaller for India. But, this has been the experience of a number of other emerging economies as well. Examples are: Brazil (4.0 and 3.0 percent during 2003–07 and 2008–14, respectively), Vietnam (7.4 and 5.8 percent), Indonesia (5.5 and 5.7 percent) and Philippines (5.7 and 5.2 percent). Closer to home, Bangladesh achieved an average annual growth rate in GDP of 6.3 percent per annum during 2003–07 and the growth rate was only marginally lower at 6.0 percent per annum during 2008–14. Sri Lanka achieved an average annual growth rate in GDP of 6.4 percent per annum during 2003–07 and an increased growth rate of 6.7 percent per annum during 2008–14. Evidently, India is not an exception in regard to the impact of the global economic crisis on GDP growth of emerging economies. As in the case of India, several other emerging economies have experienced only a small reduction in their GDP growth rate in the post-crisis period. Some emerging economies have even experienced an increase in the growth rate of GDP in the post-crisis period, for example, Indonesia and Sri Lanka. This point is pursued further later in the paper.

Sectoral growth performance

Let us now consider the growth performance of different broad sectors of the Indian economy. The estimated trend growth rates in real GVA (gross value-added) in broad sectors of the Indian economy during the period 1980–81 to 2014–15 and in various sub-periods are shown in Table 13.1. The estimation has been done by the kinked exponential model.

It is seen from Table 13.1 that trend growth rates in real GVA in the mining and electricity sectors were significantly lower in the period 1993–94 to 2002–03 as compared to the period 1980–81 to 1993–94. This was more than compensated by a significant increase in the trend growth rates in real GVA in construction, market services and non-market services. As a result, there was an increase in the growth rate in real GVA (or GDP) at the aggregate economy level in second sub-period compared to the first sub-period. Comparing the trend growth rates in real GVA between the period 1993–94 to 2002–03 and 2002–03 to 2007–08, it is found that there was a significant increase in the trend growth rate in the latter period in the manufacturing, electricity, construction and market services sectors. This led to a significant hike in the growth rate in real GDP at the aggregate economy level.

Even though the period 2008–09 to 2014–15 is marked by the global economic crisis, the trend growth rate in real GVA in this period is significantly lower than that in the period 2002–03 to 2007–08 in only three cases out of the seven broad sectors considered. These are construction, manufacturing and market services. In the case of market services, the fall in the growth rate in the latter period was statistically significant but small in magnitude, from 10 percent per annum to 9.2 percent per annum. In the case

Table 13.1 Trend growth rates in real GVA in various sub-periods, aggregate Indian economy and broad sectors

Sector	Sub-periods				
	1980–81 to 1993–94	1993–94 to 2002–03	2002–03 to 2007–08	2007–08 to 2014–15	1980–81 to 2014–15
Agriculture, forestry and fishing	3.2	2.7	3.0	3.5	3.0
Mining and quarrying	6.8	3.9**	4.9	3.3	5.0
Manufacturing	5.7	5.9	8.8**	6.4*	6.4
Electricity, gas and water supply	8.5	5.3**	6.4*	5.7	6.6
Construction	4.4	6.1**	12.3**	5.2**	6.5
Market services	6.8	8.0**	10.0**	9.2*	8.1
Non-market services (covering community, social & personal services)	5.5	6.5*	5.9	6.8	6.1
Total Economy GDP	5.1	5.8**	8.0**	6.9*	6.1

Source: Author's computations based on NAS.

*, ** Significantly different from the estimated trend growth rate in the previous sub-period at 5 and 1 percent level of significance respectively.

of manufacturing, the fall in growth rate was relatively bigger, from 8.8 percent per annum to 6.4 percent per annum. In the case of construction, the fall was much bigger, from 12.3 percent per annum to 5.2 percent per annum.[14] The reductions in the growth rates in real GVA of manufacturing, construction and market services get reflected in a statistically significant fall in the growth rate of the aggregate economy. Another interesting observation from Table 13.1 is that the trend growth rate in agriculture and allied activities was higher in the period 2002–03 to 2007–08 as compared to the period 1993–94 to 2002–03, and the growth rate went up further in the period 2007–08 to 2014–15.

Structural change

Turning now to the structural changes in the Indian economy, it may be seen from Figure 13.2 that in the period 1980–81 to 2014–15 there was a clear downward trend in the share of agriculture and allied activities in aggregate GDP, a virtual stagnation in the share

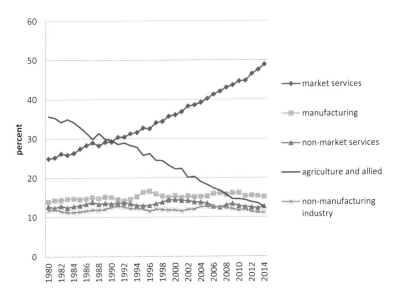

Figure 13.2 Share of broad sectors in aggregate GDP (at 2004–05 prices), India, 1980–2014

Source: Author's computations based on NAS.

of manufacturing and a clear upward trend in the share of market services. These trends are well recognized and much discussed in the literature on India's economic development. What is important to note from Figure 13.2 is that the share of non-market services in aggregate GDP did not increase over time, and therefore the growing share of services in India's aggregate GDP is essentially caused by the rising share of market services. As regards the stagnation in the share of manufacturing in aggregate GDP (about 14 percent both in 1980–81 and 1992–93, and marginally higher at about 15 percent in 2014–15 in NAS data),[15] some observations are made later in the paper contesting the validity of this commonly held perception.

Since there has been a large and almost steady increase in the share of market services in GDP during 1980–81 to 2014–15, it would be interesting to find out which industries within the market services sector are mainly responsible for the observed trend. The relative shares of seven industries in total GVA of the market services sector are shown in Figure 13.3. These seven industries

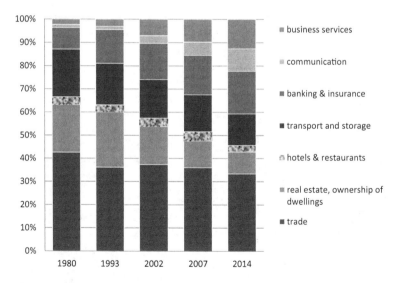

Figure 13.3 Relative share of different industries in total GVA of the market services sector (at 2004–05 prices)

Source: Author's computations based on NAS.

Note: Shares of different industries in aggregate GVA (at 2004–05 prices) of market services sector in India is shown in the figure.

together constitute the market services sector. The relative shares are shown for five years: 1980–81, 1993–94, 2002–03, 2007–08 and 2014–15.

It is evident from Figure 13.3 that the relative share of banking and insurance (covers banking, insurance and various other financial services, and thus corresponds to KLEMS industry 'Financial Services' in the Appendix), communication (includes postal services, courier services and telecommunications, and thus corresponds to KLEMS industry 'Post and Telecommunication' in the Appendix) and business services in aggregate GVA of the market services sector has increased substantially between 1980–81 and 2014–15. In 1980–81, the relative share of these industries was about 13 percent, which increased to about 40 percent by 2014–15. In 1980–81, these three industries accounted for about 3 percent of the aggregate economy GDP, which increased over time to reach about 20 percent by 2014–15.

A similar analysis undertaken for manufacturing reveals that the share of wearing apparel, chemicals and chemical products, rubber, plastic and petroleum products, electrical machinery and transport equipment in aggregate GVA of manufacturing increased from about 21 percent in 1980–81 to about 41 percent in 2014–15 (see Figure 13.4). The relative share of textiles (other than wearing apparel) fell by about four percentage points. The relative share of the basic metals industry did not change much between 1980–81 and 2014–15, though during 1980–81 to 2012–13 there was a 4 percentage points fall with smart recovery thereafter. For the rest of the industries, it is found that their relative share in total manufacturing GVA fell by about 17 percentage points during the period 1980–81 to 2014–15.

Trends in TFP growth: economy, manufacturing and market services

Methodology

As mentioned earlier, the India KLEMS database, 2015, contains time series data on output, labor input, capital input, materials input, energy input, services input and factor income shares for the period 1980–81 to 2011–12 for 27 industries which together constitute the entire economy (the list of industries given the Appendix). The time

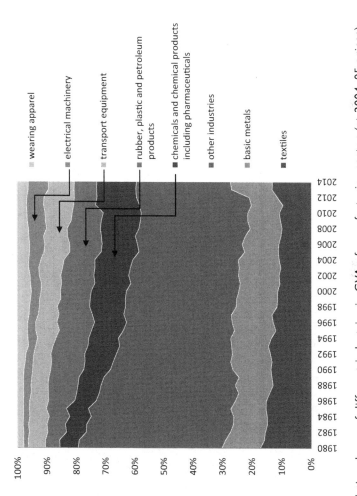

Figure 13.4 Relative shares of different industries in GVA of manufacturing sector (at 2004–05 prices)

Source: Author's computations based on NAS.

Note: Shares of different industries in aggregate GVA (at 2004–05 prices) of the manufacturing sector in India is shown in the figure.

series on output and intermediate inputs are available at both current prices and at 2004–05 prices. Labor input has two components: number of persons employed and an index of labor quality for each industry. The labor quality index captures the changes in the composition of workers in terms of their educational attainment. Time series on both capital stock and capital services input are available. The difference between the growth rates in capital stock and capital services represents improvement in quality of capital input (which may alternatively be termed as asset composition effect).

Given these data, TFP growth rates have been computed for each of the 27 industries for each year in the period 1980–81 to 2011–12. Let Y denote output, Z denote inputs {capital (K), labor (L), energy input (E), materials input (M) and services input (S)} and v factor income shares. For each industry j, the growth rate in TFP in year t is computed as:

$$TFPG_t^j = \Delta \ln A_t^j = \Delta \ln Y_t^j - \sum_i \bar{v}_i^j \Delta \ln Z_{i,t}^j \quad (13.1)$$

$$\bar{v}_i = \frac{\left[v_i(t) + v_i(t-1)\right]}{2}, i = K, L, M, E, S \quad (13.2)$$

Aggregate level estimates of TFP growth for the entire economy, manufacturing sector and market services sector have been made by using essentially the production possibility frontier approach (details available in Jorgenson et al. 2005, Chapter 8). For some analyses, aggregation of industry-level TFP growth rates to the economy level has been done by using the Domar weights (see Domar 1961).

The application of the production possibility frontier approach for deriving TFP growth rates at the economy level may be briefly explained. The steps are given below:

(1) For each industry each year, the growth rate in real value-added [$\Delta ln V_j$] has been computed by using the following equation:

$$\Delta \ln Y_j = \bar{v}_{V,j} \Delta \ln V_j + \bar{v}_{X,j} \Delta \ln X_j \quad (13.3)$$

In this equation, Y is deflated gross output, and X is deflated intermediate input. Given the time series on Y and X (or its three components, M, E and S), and the share of value-added and intermediate inputs in output (at current prices) denoted by

$\bar{v}_{V,j}$ and $\bar{v}_{X,j}$, the growth in real value-added is computed for each industry each year. Note that the bars represent averages of current and previous year.

(2) Having computed real value-added growth for each industry for each year, this is aggregated at the economy level by using the Tornqvist index. Thus, for each year, the computation is done by using the following equation:

$$\Delta \ln V = \sum_j \bar{w}_j \Delta \ln V_j \qquad (13.4)$$

In this equation, w_j is the share of industry j in aggregate economy value-added at current prices. The bar represents the average of current and previous year.

(3) The labor and capital inputs are aggregated in a similar manner. To aggregate the growth rate in the number of persons employed in individual industries (denoted by $\Delta ln N_j$), the following equation is applied:

$$\Delta \ln N = \sum_j \bar{w}_j^L \Delta \ln N_j \qquad (13.5)$$

In this equation, $\bar{w}_j^L$ is the share of industry j in aggregate income of labor across industries. The bar represents average of current and previous year. To aggregate growth in labor quality index in individual industries (denoted by $\Delta ln D_j$), the following equation is used:

$$\Delta \ln D = \sum_j \bar{w}_j^L \Delta \ln D_j \qquad (13.6)$$

Aggregation of industry-level growth in capital services, denoted by $\Delta ln K_j$, and growth in capital stock, denoted by $\Delta ln C_j$, is done in a similar manner. The equations are:

$$\Delta \ln K = \sum_j \bar{w}_j^K \Delta \ln K_j \qquad (13.7)$$

$$\Delta \ln C = \sum_j \bar{w}_j^K \Delta \ln C_j \qquad (13.8)$$

In these two equations, $\bar{w}_j^K$ is the share of industry j in aggregate income of capital across industries. The bar represents the average of current and previous year.

(4) Having obtained the growth rate in real value-added $\Delta ln V$ (which is implicitly double deflated, see Equations 13.3 and 13.4), labor input $\Delta ln N$ and $\Delta ln D$ (Equations 13.5 and 13.6) and capital input $\Delta ln K$ (Equation 13.7) and making use of the time series on the income share of labor and capital in gross value-added at the aggregate economy level, the growth rate in TFP is computed for each year by applying the Tornqvist index.

(5) It should be noted that if the number of persons is simply aggregated by taking $N^*(t) = \sum_j \{N_j(t)\}$ and similarly the capital stock is simply aggregated by taking $C^*(t) = \sum_j \{C_j(t)\}$, then the difference between $\Delta ln N(t)$ and $\Delta ln N^*(t)$ is the effect of the reallocation of persons employed across industries. Similarly, the difference between $\Delta ln C(t)$ and $\Delta ln C^*(t)$ gives the effect of reallocation of capital stock across industries.

TFP growth estimates

The average annual growth rate in TFP in the Indian economy during the period 1980–81 to 2011–12 (obtained by the method explained above) is found to be 0.9 percent per annum. The corresponding figures for the manufacturing sector and the market services sectors are 2.6 and 1.1 percent per annum, respectively.

For the aggregate economy, the average annual growth rates in TFP in the three sub-periods, 1980–81 to 1993–94, 1994–95 to 2002–03 and 2003–04 to 2011–12, were 0.77, 0.60 and 1.53 percent per annum, respectively. Clearly, there has been a significant acceleration in TFP growth in the third sub-period. This has accompanied an acceleration in growth in real (double-deflated) GVA: 5.2 percent per annum during 1980–81 to 1993–94, 5.5 percent per annum during 1994–95 to 2002–03 and 8.1 percent per annum during 2003–04 to 2011–12. Combining the first two sub-periods, the growth rate in TFP was 0.7 percent per annum during 1980–81 to 2002–03 and 1.5 percent per annum during 2003–04 to 2011–12.

Table 13.2 presents a decomposition of output (real GVA) growth in the Indian economy into its sources. This is shown for the periods 1980–81 to 1993–94, 1994–95 to 2002–03, 2003–04 to 2011–12, 1980–81 to 2002–03 and the entire period 1980–81 to 2011–12.

It is seen from Table 13.2 that growth in capital stock (new investments in fixed assets) is the prime source of growth of the

Table 13.2 Sources of growth, Indian economy, 1980–81 to 2011–12, by sub-period (percent per annum)

	1980–81 to 1993–94	1994–95 to 2002–03	2003–04 to 2011–12	1980–81 to 2002–03	1980–81 to 2011–12
Real GVA growth	5.22	5.49	8.14	5.33	6.15
Contributions of:					
– Persons	1.10	0.78	0.51	0.97	0.84
– Reallocation of persons	0.49	0.33	0.70	0.43	0.51
– Labor quality	0.37	0.24	0.34	0.32	0.32
– Capital stock	2.28	2.83	4.35	2.50	3.04
– Reallocation of capital stock	0.10	0.40	0.42	0.23	0.28
– Capital quality (asset composition effect)	0.10	0.30	0.28	0.18	0.21
Total primary inputs growth	4.45	4.88	6.61	4.63	5.20
TFP growth	0.77	0.60	1.53	0.70	0.94

Source: Author's computations based on India KLEMS database, 2015.

Indian economy followed by the growth in the number of persons employed. Considering the entire period under study, 1980–81 to 2011–12, the growth rate in real GVA was about 6.1 percent per annum of which the combined contribution of growth in capital stock and persons employed was about 3.9 percent per annum i.e. nearly two-thirds. The contribution of improvements in labor and capital quality (effects of changes in composition) was about 0.5 percentage points, and the contribution of reallocation of persons and capital stock was about 0.8 percent per annum. This leaves a residual of 0.9 percentage points per annum as the growth rate in TFP.

Making a comparison between the periods 1980–81 to 2002–03 and 2003–04 to 2011–12, it is found that the growth rate in real GVA went up from 5.33 percent per annum to 8.14 percent per annum, an increase of about 2.8 percentage points. A dominant part of this increase in real GVA growth is explained by a faster growth rate in capital stock; the contribution of this factor going up from 2.50 percentage points per annum during 1980–81 to 2002–03 to 4.35 percentage points per annum during 2003–04 to 2011–12. Thus, the acceleration in GDP growth in the period since 2003 was largely due to a hike in the rate of investment in fixed assets. The contribution of increases in the number of persons employed came down in the latter period, which was made up to a large extent by the enhanced contribution of industrial reallocation of persons working. The growth rate in TFP was 0.7 percent per annum during 1980–81 to 2002–03 and this rose to 1.5 percent per annum during 2003–04 to 2011–12. Thus, a higher rate of accumulation of fixed capital, a reallocation of labor to more productive industries and a faster growth rate in TFP by and large explain the marked acceleration in GDP growth that took place in the Indian economy in the period since 2003–04.

It has been noted above that the growth rate in TFP in the Indian economy went up from 0.7 percent per annum during 1980–81 to 2002–03 to 1.5 percent per annum during 2003–04 to 2011–12. The corresponding figures for manufacturing are 1.3 and 5.6 percent per annum respectively and those for market services are 0.8 and 1.7 percent per annum respectively (Figure 13.5). These estimates show that TFP growth in manufacturing had been faster than that in market services, especially in the period since 2003–04.

The finding of a fast growth in TFP in manufacturing in the period 2003–04 to 2011–12 calls for an investigation, particularly

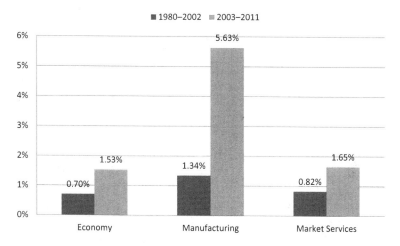

Figure 13.5 TFP growth rate (percent per annum), Indian economy, by sub-period
Source: Author's computations based on India KLEMS database, 2015.

of the underlying estimates of growth rates in real GVA in manufacturing. Figure 13.6 makes a comparison of growth rates in single deflated GVA (obtained from the NAS) and those obtained by computing double deflated GVA with the help of the Tornqvist index (as in Equations 13.3 and 13.4). It is found that for the economy as a whole the growth rates in single deflated and double deflated GVA are not much different. This also holds true for the market services sector. However, for manufacturing, there are significant differences between the growth rates in real GVA obtained by the single deflated method and those obtained by the double deflated method. The application of the double deflated method (which is considered more appropriate) leads to much higher estimated growth rates in manufacturing real GVA. The growth rate in real GVA in manufacturing during 2003–04 to 2011–12 is found to be about 7.9 percent per annum by the single deflated value-added method whereas this is found to be about 12.8 percent per annum by the double deflated value-added method. This observed high rate of growth in double deflated GVA in manufacturing provides an explanation for the observed high rate of growth in TFP in this sector of about

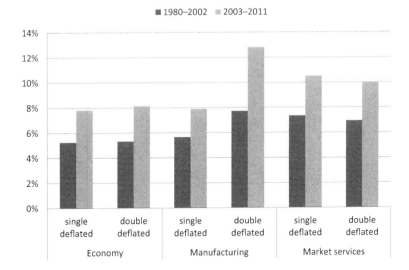

Figure 13.6 Growth rate in real GVA (percent per annum), by sub-period
Source: Author's computations based on India KLEMS database, 2015.

5.6 percent per annum during the period 2003–04 to 2011–12, as shown in Figure 13.5.

It is important to draw attention to the fact that when double deflated GVA is used, the share of manufacturing in aggregate GVA is not stagnant (see Figure 13.7). Rather, there is a clear upward trend (from about 10 percent in 1980–81 to about 22 percent in 2011–12). This calls into question a widely held impression or view among economists and researchers in India that the share of manufacturing in aggregate GDP has been virtually stagnant in the last three decades or more (to observe the contrast, see Figure 13.1).

Figure 13.6 uses annual growth rates in real GVA series that has been formed on the basis of Equations 13.3 and 13.4. The computation of these growth rates implicitly involves double deflation, since these are derived from real gross output and real intermediate input series both deflated by their respective price indices. Figure 13.7 uses double deflated GVA series that has been constructed by subtracting the constant-price values of energy, materials and services from the constant-price values of gross output, different deflators

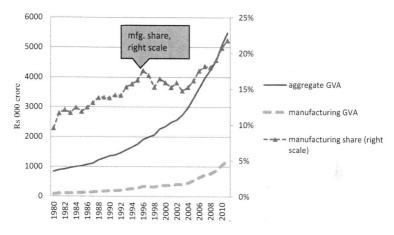

Figure 13.7 Double deflated GVA, aggregate economy and manufacturing, and share of manufacturing

Source: Author's computations based on India KLEMS database, 2015.

Note: One crore = 10 million

being used for output and intermediate inputs. Both figures clearly point toward an upward trend in the share of manufacturing in aggregate level double deflated GVA (in Figure 13.6, on the basis of difference in growth rates, and in Figure 13.7, on the basis of the line plot of the share of manufacturing).

Industry contributions to aggregate level real GVA and TFP growth

Contributions of different constituent industries toward output growth acceleration and TFP growth acceleration in the Indian economy in the period since 2003–04 are depicted in Figures 13.8 and 13.9, respectively. Between 1980–2002 and 2003–11, the growth rate in real (double deflated) GVA in the Indian economy at aggregate level increased by about 2.8 percentage points (from about 5.3 percent per annum to about 8.1 percent per annum). The largest contributors to this increase in the pace of economic growth were construction, business services, trade, transport and storage, petroleum refining, financial services, post and telecommunication, chemicals and chemical products and transport equipment (in that

Figure 13.8 Contribution of different industries to GVA growth acceleration in the period since 2003–04 (2003–11 minus 1980–2002) (percent per annum)

Source: Author's computations based on India KLEMS database, 2015.

Note: Methodology for this analysis is the same as in Jorgenson et al. (2005, Table 8 and Figure 8.2).

order). The contribution of these industries adds up to almost the entire hike in the growth rate of real GVA in the Indian economy in the period 2003–11 as contrasted to the period 1980–2002.

As regards the hike in the growth rate of TFP (from 0.7 percent per annum during 1980–81 to 2002–03 to 1.5 percent per annum during 2003–04 to 2011–12), the main contributors to the acceleration in TFP growth are petroleum refining, agriculture and allied activities, financial services, post and telecommunication, transport and storage, chemicals and chemical products, public administration and defense, textiles, textile products, leather and leather products, and construction (in that order) (Figure 13.9). All these industries achieved an improvement in the rate of TFP growth in the latter period and, taken together, these industries were the dominant source of the hike in TFP growth achieved by the Indian economy.

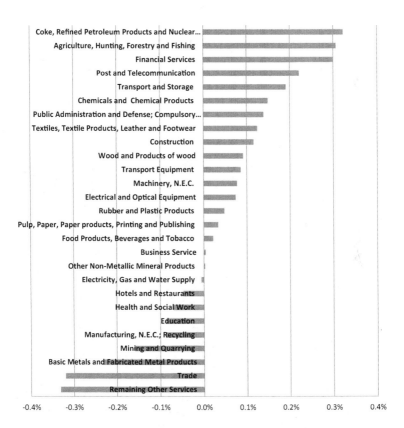

Figure 13.9 Contribution of different industries to aggregate level TFP growth acceleration in the period since 2003–04 (2003–11 minus 1980–2002) (percent per annum)

Source: Author's computations based on India KLEMS database, 2015.

Note: For this figure, aggregate level TFP growth rate estimate has been formed on the basis of Domar aggregation of industry-level TFP growth estimates. This has been done for the periods 1980–2002 and 2003–11, and then the difference has been taken. Methodology for this analysis is the same as in Jorgenson et al. (2005, Table 8 and Figure 8.4).

Figure 13.10 shows the annual average rates of TFP growth in select industries for the periods 1980–81 to 2002–03 and 2003–04 to 2011–12.[16] It reveals that post (including courier service) and telecommunications, financial services and petroleum refining achieved a marked increase in TFP growth rate in the latter period. Although the hike in the rate of TFP growth was relatively smaller in the case of agriculture and allied activities, the contribution made by this industry to the increase in TFP growth rate at the aggregate level is comparable to that of post and telecommunications, financial services and petroleum refining. The explanation lies in the relatively larger weight given to agriculture and allied activities industry on account of its relatively bigger share in aggregate GVA. This point applies more or less also to chemicals and chemical products, public administration and defense, transport and storage, textiles and leather products and construction. It is interesting to note that TFP growth in construction was negative for the periods, 1980–81 to 2002–03 and 2003–04 to 2011–12. However, the performance was relatively better (lower fall in TFP) in the period 2003–11 than that in 1980–2002.

Cross-country perspective: GDP growth and TFP growth

How does India compare with other emerging economies in terms of GDP growth and TFP growth in recent years? This is the question that is addressed next using data for a select set of emerging economies. The period considered for the analysis is 2003–14. The Conference Board Total Economy Database (as was available in October 2016) is the basic data source used for this analysis.

The Conference Board database provides estimates of TFP growth in the Indian economy from 1990 to 2014. The estimates for the years 2003–14 yield an annual average growth rate of 1.90 percent per annum. The average annual growth rates for 2003–07 and 2008–14 are found to be 2.61 and 1.39 percent per annum, respectively, indicating the growth rate in TFP fell by about 1.2 percentage points in the post-crisis period.

Using the India KLEMS database, 2015, along with data from other sources, an estimate of TFP growth in the Indian economy has been made for the period 1980–81 to 2014–15 with a view to making a comparison with the Conference Board estimates. The GDP series obtained from NAS has been used as the measure

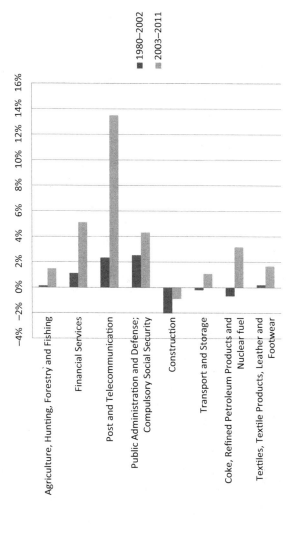

Figure 13.10 TFP growth rate, 1980–2002 and 2003–11, select KLEMS industries (percent per annum)
Source: Based on India KLEMS database, 2015.

of output. The series on 'number of persons employed' has been extended to 2014–15 using population projections and the work participation rates for 2011, 2012 and 2013 given in *Report on Employment-Unemployment Survey* of the Ministry of Labour and Employment (Reports for 2011–12, 2012–13 and 2013–14 have been used). The labor quality index was aggregated to the economy level for the period 1980–81 to 2011–12 by using the Tornqvist index (Equation 13.6) for the TFP growth estimates presented in the previous section. This time series on growth rate in labor quality index at the economy level has been extended to 2014–15 by linear extrapolation. The fixed capital stock series available in the India KLEMS database, 2015, for the period up to 2011–12 has been extended to 2014–15 by using data on gross fixed capital formation for the next three years taken from the new National Account series (with adjustments made for depreciation). The growth rate in capital quality index at the aggregate economy level computed for the period up to 2011–12 for the purpose of the analysis in the previous section has been extended to the next three years by using linear extrapolation. Similarly, the share of labor income in GVA available from 1980–81 to 2011–12 has been extended until 2014–15 by linear extrapolation. From the estimates of TFP growth for Indian economy obtained in this manner, the average annual growth rate in TFP is found to be 1.91 percent per annum for the period 2003–04 to 2014–15 which is almost the same as the TFP growth rate in the estimate made by the Conference Board. For the sub-periods 2003–04 to 2007–08 and 2008–09 to 2014–15, the average annual growth rates in TFP are found to be 2.85 and 1.23 percent, respectively, which is broadly consistent with the estimates of the Conference Board.

According to Conference Board data on TFP growth, TFP growth rate in Indian economy fell by about 1.2 percentage points between pre and post-crisis periods. The fall in the growth rate of GDP was about 1.5 percentage points. There are other emerging economies which experienced a larger fall in the rate of TFP growth. These include the Russian Federation (4.7 percentage points fall), China (3.5 percentage points fall), South Africa (2.7 percentage points fall) and Turkey (2.7 percentage points fall). Analyzing data for a select set of 17 emerging economies, it is found that the economies which experienced a bigger fall in the growth rate of TFP as compared to India also commonly suffered a bigger fall in the growth rate of GDP. On the other hand, the countries which experienced a smaller fall in the rate of TFP growth as compared to India had a smaller decrease in the rate of GDP growth. This is depicted in Figure 13.11. There is a significant positive correlation between the change in the rate of growth in TFP and the change in the rate of growth in GDP. The correlation coefficient is 0.68. It is interesting to observe that the observation for India in the plot is almost on the regression line (true for other BRICS countries as well). Thus, India's growth experience in the post-crisis is not exceptional. Rather, in some ways, it is in line with the experiences of other emerging economies. In other words, India's GDP growth did not decrease much in the post-crisis period because the crisis did not result in any marked slowdown in the rate of TFP growth in the Indian economy. How could the Indian economy avoid a major decline in TFP growth, even as the global economic crisis hit the export markets, is a moot question. This is a matter for further investigation and outside the scope of this paper.

Conclusion

This paper examined the sources of growth and changes in structure of the Indian economy in the period 1980–81 to 2014–15. It was observed that there was a marked acceleration in GDP growth in the period since 2003–04 which was accompanied by an accelerated growth in TFP. The trend growth rates in real GDP in the periods 1980–81 to 1993–94 and 1993–94 to 2002–03 were 5.1 and 5.8 percent per annum, respectively, while that in the period 2002–03 to 2014–15 was higher at 8.0 percent per annum. Similarly, the average annual growth rate in TFP in the Indian economy increased from 0.7 percent per annum during 1980–81 to 2002–03 to 1.5 percent per annum during 2003–04 to 2011–12. Looking into the industry origins of TFP growth acceleration in the period 2003–04 to 2011–12, it was found that the main contributors to the acceleration in TFP growth at the aggregate economy level are petroleum refining, agriculture and allied activities, financial services, post and telecommunication, transport and storage, chemicals and chemical products, public administration and defense, textiles, textile products, leather and leather products, and construction.

The analysis of sources of growth revealed that GDP growth in India is mainly attributable to increases in fixed capital stock and the number persons working, and the contribution of improvements in quality of labor and capital inputs and reallocation of labor and

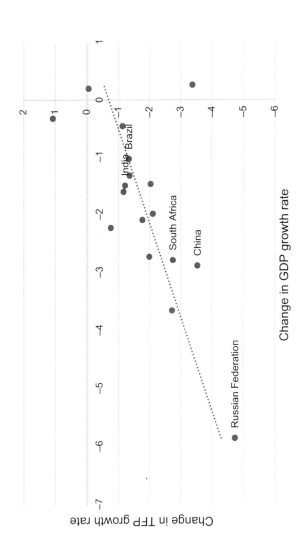

Figure 13.11 Changes in GDP growth rate and TFP growth rate (2008–14 vs. 2003–07), emerging economies, cross-country plot (percent per annum)

Source: Author's computations from Conference Board Total Economy Database.

Note: The countries included in the analysis are Bangladesh, Brazil, Chile, China, India, Indonesia, Mexico, Philippines, Poland, Russian Federation, South Arica, South Korea, Sri Lanka, Taiwan, Thailand, Turkey and Vietnam.

capital across industries is relatively minor. Also, the marked acceleration in economic growth that took place in India in the period since 2003 is found to be mostly traceable to an increased rate of accumulation of fixed capital, a reallocation of labor to more productive industries and a faster growth rate in TFP.

One important finding of the study is that the share of non-market services in aggregate GDP did not increase over time, and therefore the growing share of services in India's aggregate GDP is essentially caused by the rising share of market services. A deeper analysis revealed that the increasing share of market services in aggregate GDP is basically traceable to the growth dynamism of financial services, post and telecommunication services and business services. The relative share of banking and insurance, post and communication and business services in aggregate GDP of the market services sector increased substantially between 1980–81 and 2014–15, from about 13 percent to about 40 percent.

Another finding is that the growth rate of manufacturing based on double deflated GVA is much higher than that obtained by single deflated GVA. The implication is that *National Accounts Statistics*, which presents estimates of real GVA in manufacturing based on single deflation, may not be correctly showing the growth performance of the manufacturing sector. For the period 2003–04 to 2011–12, for example, the growth rate in single deflated GVA in manufacturing given by NAS is about 7.9 percent per annum, whereas the growth rate based on double deflated GVA obtained in this study using the India KLEMS database is about 12.8 percent per annum. Accordingly, TFP growth rate in manufacturing in the period 2003–04 to 2011–12 based on double deflated GVA is found to be as high as 5.63 percent per annum, well above the TFP growth rate in market services at 1.65 percent per annum. Based on double deflated GVA for manufacturing and that for the entire economy, it is found that there was a clear upward trend in the share of manufacturing in aggregate GVA. It increased from about 10 percent in 1980–81 to about 22 percent in 2011–12. This calls into question a widely held perception or view that there has been a virtual stagnation in the share of manufacturing in GDP in the last three decades or more. This matter needs further investigation.

Analysis of GDP growth and TFP growth for the period 2003–04 to 2014–15, split into the sub-periods 2003–04 to 2007–08 and 2008–09 to 2014–15 (before and after the commencement of the recent global economic crisis), revealed that there was a fall in the growth rates of GDP and TFP in the latter period, i.e. the period since 2008–09. TFP growth rate in the Indian economy fell by about 1.2 percentage points between pre- and post-crisis periods. The fall in the growth rate of GDP was about 1.5 percentage points. Since the Indian economy is expected to be affected adversely by the global economic crisis, the dip in the growth rates of GDP and TFP is expected. The analysis indicated that the adverse effect of the recent global economic crisis on the pace of economic growth in India was only modest. However, a closer examination of the data for India when considered along with such data for a set of other emerging economies brought to the fore the fact that India's performance has been not exceptional, but broadly in line with the experience of other emerging economies. Indeed, several emerging economies have performed better than India. Also, if one considers a regression line between the change in GDP growth rate and change in TFP growth rate, the observation for India (and those for other BRICS countries) is almost on the regression line. Thus, it appears that the global crisis did not cause a major fall in India's GDP growth rate because there was no large fall in the growth rate of TFP. An important question is: when a number of emerging economies have experienced a fall in the growth rate of TFP by about 3 percentage points or more in the post-crisis period, why this did not happen in India (and in several other emerging economies). Perhaps, this is related to the degree of trade dependence or to the structure of the economy (say, in terms of the share of services in GDP). This remains an issue to be investigated in future.

Appendix

Table 13.A.1 List of KLEMS industries in India KLEMS database, 2015

1	Agriculture, Hunting, Forestry and Fishing
2	Mining and Quarrying
3	Food Products, Beverages and Tobacco Products
4	Textiles, Textile Products, Leather and Footwear
5	Wood and Products of Wood
6	Pulp, Paper, Paper products, Printing and Publishing
7	Coke, Refined Petroleum Products and Nuclear Fuel
8	Chemicals and Chemical Products
9	Rubber and Plastic Products
10	Other Non-Metallic Mineral Products
11	Basic Metals and Fabricated Metal Products
12	Machinery, not elsewhere classified
13	Electrical and Optical Equipment
14	Transport Equipment
15	Manufacturing, not elsewhere classified; recycling
16	Electricity, Gas and Water Supply
17	Construction
18	Trade
19	Hotels and Restaurants
20	Transport and Storage
21	Post and Telecommunication
22	Financial Services
23	Public Administration and Defense; Compulsory Social Security
24	Education
25	Health and Social Work
26	Business Services
27	Other Services

Source: Author's Compilation based on India KLEMS database, 2015.

Acknowledgments

I am grateful to Prof. K.L. Krishna for his comments and suggestions on the previous version of the paper. The study is primarily based on the India KLEMS dataset, 2015, which was prepared with financial support of the Reserve Bank of India. I thank the members of the India KLEMS team for the contributions they have made for the construction of the dataset. These include Deb Kusum Das, Suresh Chand Aggarwal, Abdul A. Erumban, Pilu Chandra Das and Shomak Chakraborty.

Notes

1 See Rodrik and Subramanian (2004), Virmani (2006) and Balakrishnan and Parameswaran (2007). Rodrik and Subramanian (2004) state that there was a break in India's economic growth around 1980. According to Virmani (2006) and Balakrishnan and Parameswaran (2007), a break in India's economic growth occurred in 1978–79. Also see in this context the studies undertaken by Williamson and Zagha (2002), De Long (2003), Wallack (2003) and Hausmann et al. (2004). For a review of literature on this issue, see Lal (2008).
2 On 'Hindu rate of growth', see Raj (1984) and Virmani (2004, 2006), among others.
3 Even though the average growth rate of the Indian economy in the 1980s was higher than that during the previous three decades, doubts have been raised on whether the hike in growth rate was statistically significant or whether it is right to date the growth turn-around to the late 1970s. Ghate and Wright (2012), for instance, take the position that the turn-around in India's economic growth took place in 1987.
4 Growth rate computed by using data on per capita net national income at constant prices taken from *Economic Survey*, 2015–16, Ministry of Finance, Government of India (Table 1.1, Page A2).
5 See, in this context, Krishna (2007) in Vaidyanathan and Krishna (eds.) where several TFP growth studies for India for the period 1950–2000 are reviewed.
6 Goldar and Mitra (2010) report that most of the increase in the TFP growth rate at the aggregate level in the post-1980 period is traceable to improved TFP growth performance of the services sector.
7 The average annual growth rate in per capita net national income at constant prices was 6.4 percent during 2003–11 and 6.0 percent during 2003–14, as against a growth rate of 2.8 percent during 1980–93 and 3.9 percent during 1994–2002.
8 http://data.worldbank.org/indicator/TM.TAX.MANF.SM.AR.ZS?locations=IN, accessed September 17, 2016.
9 See, for instance, Estimates of Productivity Growth for the Indian Economy, Report, Reserve Bank of India, available at https://rbi.org.in/

Scripts/PublicationReportDetails.aspx?ID=785, accessed October 10, 2016. Information on the data base is available also at the Asia KLEMS website: file:///C:/Documents%20and%20Settings/uits/My%20Documents/Downloads/Source%20and%20notes%20(India).pdf, accessed October 10, 2016.

10 It may be mentioned here that ASI data for 2011–12 in respect of two industries have been corrected in January 2016. In the available NAS publications for the 2004–05 series, the required correction to registered manufacturing gross output and value-added has not been made by the CSO since it has meanwhile shifted to a new NAS series with base 2011–12. In preparing the data series for this study, this correction in ASI data has been incorporated in the NAS data. The correction affects the estimates of gross output, value-added and intermediate input for two industries, namely (1) chemicals and chemical products and (2) basic metals. This has an impact on the estimate for the manufacturing sector GVA and aggregate level GDP.

11 www.conference-board.org/data/economydatabase/, accessed October 7, 2016.

12 To construct the time series on real GDP, data on real GDP have been taken from NAS publications. GDP data for the years 1980–81 to 2011–12 have been taken from National Accounts series with base 2004–05 (*National Accounts Statistics*, 2014, CSO and Back series published in 2011). For subsequent years, such data have been taken from the new National Accounts series with base 2011–12 (see *National Accounts Statistics*, 2016, CSO). The two series, one with base 2004–05 and the other with base 2011–12, have been joined by splicing (after making a correction to the reported GDP for 2011–12 in the previous series, as explained in endnote 10). The growth rates (over previous year) in real gross value-added (GVA) for the years 2012–13 to 2014–15 computed from data taken from the new National Accounts series (NAS, 2016) have been applied to the old series (with base 2004–05) to extend it to 2014–15. The same method has been applied to construct GVA series at disaggregate level.

13 Since the kinked exponential model is used, the terminal year between two sub-periods is included in both sub-periods when presenting the trend growth rate estimates.

14 Why the growth rate in construction fell sharply in the period 2008–09 to 2014–15 is puzzling. To ascribe this entirely or principally to the global economic crisis would obviously not be right.

15 In the new national accounts series with base 2011–12, the share of manufacturing in aggregate GVA is higher at 17 percent. This is attributable to differences in methodology and data sources used.

16 These TFP growth rates are based on the gross output function and are therefore not comparable to estimates TFP growth for manufacturing sector, market services sector or the economy presented in Figure 13.5 and Table 13.2 (since the latter category of estimates are based on a value-added function).

Bibliography

Ahluwalia, Montek S. 2002. "Economic Reforms in India Since 1991: Has Gradualism Worked?" *Journal of Economic Perspectives* 16(3): 67–88.

Balakrishnan, P., and M. Parameswaran. 2007. "Understanding Economic Growth in India: A Prerequisite." *Economic and Political Weekly* 42(27&28): 2915–2922.

Boyce, James K. 1986. "Kinked Exponential Models for Growth Rate Estimation." *Oxford Bulletin of Economics and Statistics* 48(4): 385–91.

De Long, B. 2003. "India Since Independence: An Analytic Growth Narrative." In Dani Rodrik (ed.), *In Search of Prosperity: Analytic Narratives on Economic Growth*. Princeton: Princeton University Press, 184–204.

Domar, E. D. 1961. "On the Measurement of Technological Change." *Economic Journal* 71(284): 709–729.

Ghate, Chetan, and Stephen Wright. 2012. "The 'V-Factor': Distribution, Timing and Correlates of the Great Indian Growth Turnaround." *Journal of Development Economics* 99(1): 58–67.

Goldar, Bishwanath. 2002. "Trade Liberalization and Manufacturing Employment: The Case of India." *Employment Paper* no. 2002/34, International Labour Organization, Geneva.

Goldar, Bishwnath, and Arup Mitra. 2010. "Productivity Increase and Changing Sectoral Composition: Contribution to Economic Growth in India." In Pulin Nayak, Bishwanath Goldar, and Pradeep Agrawal (eds.), *India's Economy and Growth*. New Delhi: SAGE Publications, 35–68.

Hausmann, Ricardo, Lant Pritchett, and Dani Rodrik. 2004. "Growth Accelerations." *NBER Working Paper* No. 10566, National Bureau of Economic Research, Cambridge, MA.

Jorgenson, D., M. S. Ho, and K. J. Stiroh. 2005. *Information Technology and the American Growth Resurgence*. Cambridge, MA: The MIT Press.

Krishna, K. L. 2007. "What Do We Know About the Sources of Economic Growth in India?" In A. Vaidyanathan and K. L. Krishna (eds.), *Institutions and Markets in India's Development: Essays for K.N. Raj*. New Delhi: Oxford University Press, 45–69.

Lal, Deepak. 2008. "An Indian Economic Miracle?" *Cato Journal* 28(1): 11–33.

Panagariya, Arvind, Pinaki Chakraborty, and M. Govinda Rao. 2014. *State level Reforms, Growth and Development in Indian States*. Oxford: Oxford University Press.

Raj, K. N. 1984. "Some Observations on Economic Growth in India Over the Period 1952–53 to 1982–83." *Economic and Political Weekly* 19(41): 1801–1804.

Rodrik, Dani, and Arvind Subramanian. 2004. "From 'Hindu Growth' to Productivity Surge: The Mystery of the Indian Growth Transition." *IMF Staff Papers* 52(2): 193–228.

Sivasubramonian, S. 2004. *The Sources of Economic Growth in India: 1950–51 to 1999–2000*. New Delhi: Oxford University Press.

Virmani, Arvind. 2004. "India's Economic Growth: From Socialist Rate of Growth to Bharatiya Rate of Growth." *Working Paper* No. 122, Indian Council for Research on International Economic Relations, New Delhi, February. www.icrier.org/pdf/wp122.pdf, accessed September 28, 2016.

Virmani, Arvind. 2006. "India's Economic Growth History: Fluctuations, Trends, Breakpoints, and Phases." *Indian Economic Review* 41(1): 81–103.

Wallack, Jessica Seddon. 2003. "Structural Breaks in Indian Macroeconomic Data." *Economic and Political Weekly* 38(41): 4312–4315.

Williamson, John, and Roberto Zagha. 2002. *From Slow Growth to Slow Reform*. Washington, DC: Institute for International Economics.

Chapter 14

Productivity slowdown in Brazil 2000–13

General performance and sectoral contributions[1]

David Kupfer and Thiago Miguez

Introduction

Productivity is a strategic element for growth and development in any emergent country. Nevertheless, in the 21st century a new key challenge has been raised in the form of a puzzle: how to increase productivity without reducing the totality of jobs. Although it is a well-known issue in the economic debate, the paradoxical relationships between productivity, jobs and growth nowadays refers to a problem that has been profoundly aggravated. The novelty is the sharp jobless feature of several cutting-edge innovations in the new productive paradigm led by Information and Communication Technologies (ICT).

The challenges of the new era must be addressed from two different perspectives. The first perspective may require adjustments in both macro- and microeconomic frameworks, which in turn will necessarily involve new management models, new inter-firm relationships concerning competition and cooperation, new labor regulations and so on. The other perspective adds new socio-political elements to this debate, as it refers to the different historical backgrounds and national characteristics that make each productivity dynamic so unique. In consequence, the job–productivity paradox always implies reengineering of work processes, according to the first perspective, and the redesign of international division of labor models, according to the second one.

However, in Brazil, things run different. Both the perspective of macro–micro changes and the one related to the international integration of the economy have remained more or less frozen in the last decades. For that reason, an increase in productivity is currently a major concern in Brazilian economy. Even though during the 2000s

Brazil experienced small, but positive GDP growth rates, the low levels of productivity growth displayed during these years are a sign that something is not working well. With a view to address this issue, the newly adopted Brazilian industrial policy, *Brasil Mais Produtivo* (More Productive Brazil), focuses on helping MSMEs increase their productivity levels. In addition, the publication of a two-volume book discussing the performance and causes behind Brazilian productivity by the Instituto de Pesquisas Econômicas Aplicadas (IPEA) shows that this issue is becoming a priority in academic debate too.

The aim of this chapter is to show how Brazilian labor productivity has performed in the 2000–13 period. In order to do that, we have a brief section to discuss some analytical references relating productivity growth to economic and Gross Fixed Capital Formation (GFCF) growth. The third section presents a general overview of the Brazilian economy and the labor productivity for the entire economy. The fourth section shows the numbers for Brazilian labor productivity, in a sectoral perspective, although by sectoral we mean 'Agriculture', 'Mining and Quarrying' and 'Manufacturing'. The fifth section brings a shift-share analysis aiming to understand which factors may explain the low evolution of Brazilian labor productivity. In the last section are the conclusions.

Some analytical references

According to the Convergence Theory, popular among scholars of the 'growth accounting' methodology, emergent countries tend to show higher growth rates than developed countries. These catching-up processes occur due to three main reasons. The first one is a consequence of the small amount of capital accumulated in emergent countries, which implies a large room for it to increase. The second reason has demographic causes, generally associated with higher possibilities of expansion of the economically active population, which is consistent with a higher rate of GDP growth. The third reason is related to the effects of the international diffusion of technologies, which allow emergent countries to benefit from fast ways of incorporating innovation, reducing their productivity gap between developed economies.

Of course, Brazil is not apart from this framework. But, differently from other emergent countries, the Brazilian economy has presented a relatively low rate of productivity growth in the 2000s. The causes behind this slowdown in Brazilian productivity are diverse and deep-rooted and a detailed analysis of this issue is not within the scope of this chapter. It is remarkable that this low performance took place despite the directions and intensity of economic changes which Brazil experienced along these years. Indeed, since 1999, when a typical balance of payment crisis irrupted, leading to the adoption of the so-called 'macroeconomic tripod' (inflation targeting, fiscal contraction and floating exchange rate), the country experienced three different growth patterns: (1) an export-led pattern during 2000–04; (2) a more generalized growth pattern during 2004–10, especially consumption and GFCF; and (3) a (low) consumption-led pattern since then.

Why any of these accumulation patterns were not effective to boost aggregate productivity is a puzzle that still awaits solution. However, the sources of such long-term poor performance might be found in some structural causes. The main hypothesis behind the argument presented in this chapter is that the main cause of the low rate of productivity increase is associated with the slow pace of capital formation in the Brazilian economy, mainly in manufacturing and infrastructure services activities. This assumption is in line with the well-known stylized fact that embodied technical change is one of the key sources of productivity growth in a developing economy. In this hypothesis, the poor result in productivity gains performance can be explained by a specific structural rigidity prevailing in the Brazilian economy: companies prefer to preserve allocative flexibility instead of making irreversible decisions to invest in fixed capital formation. This kind of structural rigidity is observed in both intrasectoral and intersectoral dimension. In the first one, there is the case of lack of capacity expansion of existing companies and difficulty of entry of new companies in many activities. In the second case, we can mention the weakness of structural change process in Brazil in the past decades; this means that Brazilian production has not moved toward more sophisticated goods or services.

Thus, in this kind of micro–macro framework, the companies with more survival capacity expand by acquiring the less successful ones. By doing so, the major companies capture market share without expanding their greenfield (or even brownfield) capacity and without renovating their facilities. Enterprises which operate in stagnant markets tend to only introduce minor innovations such as the replacement of machinery only in critical stages of the productive process and only partial adoption of new organizational methods of the work process. Often, technology updating demands massive investment especially in capital-intensive industries, which are very important in the Brazilian pattern of industrial specialization. However, such capital formation is less attractive when there are no favorable perspectives of revenue growth. Therefore, productivity either stops growing or grows very slowly, leading to a vicious circle on the perspectives of economic growth.

The next sections present some results about the behavior of labor productivity in Brazil. Although in an early stage, we expected that the application of KLEMS methodology to Brazilian national account statistics will generate a rich data set that will contribute to refine the quality of data. When available, these new data surely will be useful to clarify some dimensions of the productivity puzzle in Brazil.[2]

General overview

As we can see in Figure 14.1, during the 2000–13 period, the Brazilian economy experienced three different stages: (1) 2000–04; (2) 2004–10; and (3) 2010–13. The 2000–04 period was marked by low GDP growth (2.3 percent p.a.) due mainly to low dynamism in household consumption,[3] in spite of the positive contribution of increasing surplus showed by the trade balance at this time.

In the second period, 2004–10, the Brazilian economy achieved one of its best moments in many past decades (4.1 percent p.a.). It is important to notice that this high economic growth happened with all demand elements contributing positively to it, especially household consumption and GFCF. Both foreign and domestic factors can help to explain this good performance. On the foreign side, the rise in the commodities prices was also followed by a rise in the exports quantum.[4] On the domestic side, we can mention: (1) the income rise of social classes with higher propensity to consume;[5] (2) the expansion of credit lines for durable goods and real estate properties; (3) the recovery of government spending, especially investments; and (4) the very response of the investments, helping to virtuous circle.

Though, in the third period, 2010–13, the Brazilian economy entered again into a period of medium to low economic performance (2.9 percent p.a.). This time, even though household consumption was still growing, other demand elements started to show a lower dynamism, especially government spending and exports.

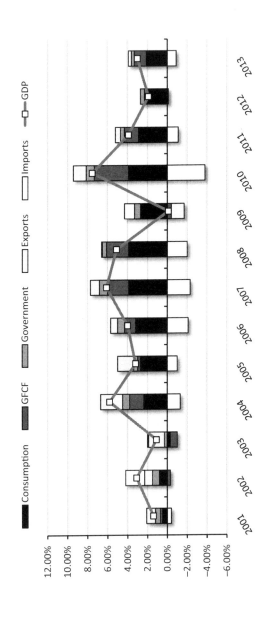

Figure 14.1 GDP annual growth rate – demand elements contributions (2001–13)
Source: GIC-IE/UFRJ Database.

In fact, the GDP growth rate of −0.1 percent during the last quarter of 2013 was the beginning of the current Brazilian economic recession, which 'officially'[6] started in the middle of 2015. This recession is still going on after seven consecutive quarters (the cumulative GDP loss is now in −7.4 percent) and shows no signs of reverse at least in the next few quarters.

These movements in GDP had strong influence in Brazilian labor productivity, as we can see in Figure 14.2. As expected, the figure confirms the pro-cyclical behavior of productivity which prevails in Brazil,[7] but, unfortunately, labor productivity did not achieve numbers that can be considered at least satisfactory. During the years 2000–04, of less economic performance, productivity growth had it worst results, limited to an annual average rate of 0.2 percent p.a. During 2004–10, the most dynamic period, we can see a better average rate of 2.1 percent p.a. While in 2010–13 there was a decrease to 1.2 percent p.a., expecting an even lower trend for the next few years. Summing up, during 2000–13 the cumulative productivity growth was 18.3 percent, which means an annual average of only 1.3 percent p.a. This means that the good period the Brazilian economy enjoyed in the past years was not enough to make the country's labor productivity grow for a long period at strong rates.

Nevertheless, an important relation the numbers reveal is that there was a strong connection between GFCF growth and labor productivity growth. Figure 14.3 makes it very easy to see. Indeed, we can also see that there was an even stronger connection between labor productivity growth and the GFCF growth when we only consider its 'Machine and equipment' share. This result reinforces the role that machine and equipment acquisitions have to spread technological innovations throughout the economy, helping this way to increase labor productivity.

However, what probably makes labor productivity an urgent topic in Brazil is not its own growth. The concern about productivity is usually related to competitiveness, which is a relative variable. In this sense, the adjective 'low' that is commonly given to Brazilian productivity growth comes from the perspective that Brazil has been left behind by other countries in recent years. The worst consequence of this relative low performance is that Brazil is showing signs of losing its competitiveness, especially in manufacturing activities.[8] The increasing of the manufacturing trade deficit is usually pointed to as evidence (SQUEFF 2012).

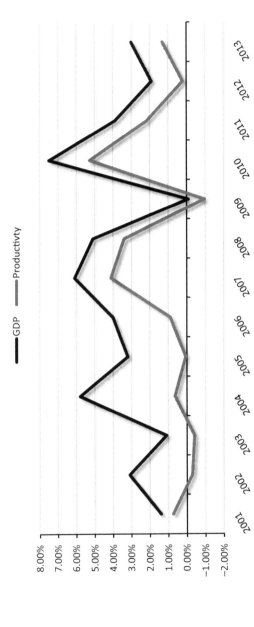

Figure 14.2 Productivity and GDP growth rates (2001–13)
Source: GIC-IE/UFRJ Database.

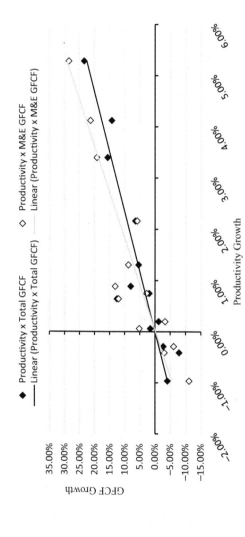

Figure 14.3 Correlation between productivity and GFCF growth (2001–13)
Source: GIC-IE/UFRJ Database.

As an example of relative productivity performance, Miguez and Moraes (2014) compare Brazilian productivity with those in Germany, the United States, Mexico and China. The study has found that Brazilian productivity has moved further from the benchmarks and closer to the lowest productivities countries. The relation 'Best Country/Brazil' that was 6.6 times in 1995 had increased to 7.1 times in 2009, which means a small difference against Brazil. At the same time, the comparison 'Brazil/lowest country' was '8.6' in 1995 and '3.0' 2009, almost three times closer in such a short period. Both movements confirm how Brazilian productivity has been growing slowly when compared to other countries. It is also important to highlight that the same pattern is trailed by most activities, more prominently in the case of lowest productivity countries reaching Brazil.

In summary, despite the good periods of GDP and GFCF growth during recent years, they were not enough to make Brazil achieve a better performance on labor productivity. This is especially disturbing when international experiences are considered. However, to achieve a full diagnosis it is necessary to consider sectoral performances, which is the next section topic.

Sectoral performance

The main objective of this section is to show that the pattern followed by labor productivity in most activities was not necessarily the same, either in size or in direction. In fact, this reinforces all the structural differences present in Brazil – typical of a developing and unequal economy. However, before we continue, it is important to mention that the focus here will remain on those industries with 'physical' outputs, such as 'Agriculture', 'Mining and Quarrying' and 'Manufacturing'. The reason for this restriction is that it is more difficult to settle a connection (especially in short run analysis) between what we can call 'physical productivity' and 'economic productivity'.[9]

In a general perspective, 'Agriculture' had the best labor productivity growth during the 2000–13 period. Figure 14.5 allows us to see it had a much better performance than the average of the Brazilian economy. In fact, it had not only an excellent average evolution rate of 6.2 percent p.a. (accumulating 106.0 percent), but, maybe even more important, it also had a sustainable growth, showing positive rates in most of the 13 years. We can say this

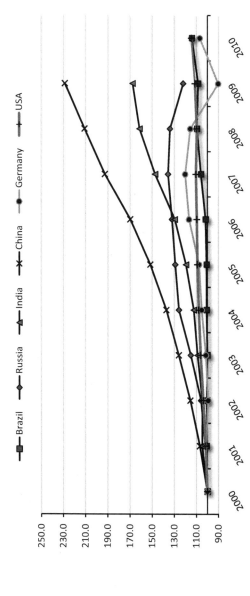

Figure 14.4 Productivity evolution in selected countries (2000 = 100)

Source: GIC-IE/UFRJ Database.

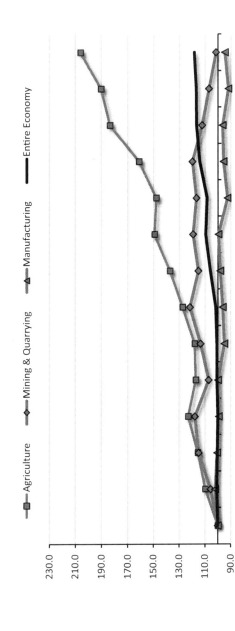

Figure 14.5 Sectoral labor productivity 2000–13 (2000 = 100)
Source: GIC-IE/UFRJ Database.

result comes from a combination of both continuous investments growth (6.7 percent p.a)[10] and a big fall in the 'Agriculture' share in the number of persons engaged (−1.7 percent p.a.).

However, we cannot see the same positive results for 'Mining and Quarrying'. During the short period 2000–03, we can see a consistent evolution rate of 8.5 percent p.a. On the other hand, in the period 2003–10, it has presented unstable growth, alternating positive and negative rates, that have made its general performance to stay around the same level achieved in 2003. Then, what we can see is a downward trend until 2013 that brought labor productivity back to the initial levels. The main activities in this sector for the Brazilian economy are 'Extraction of Oil and Gas' and 'Mining of Iron Ore'. Despite both of them having shown a high growth rate in its investments (more than 10 percent p.a.), the rise in demand made the number of persons engaged in these activities also grow, more than the value-added had.[11]

The situation for 'Manufacturing' was even worse, as shown in Figure 14.5. It is possible to notice a slightly downward trend, making 'Manufacturing' labor productivity finishing in 2013 in a worst position than in 2000. In addition, unlike 'Mining and Quarrying', it is not possible to see even a short period of good performance. In the same way, most activities that compose 'Manufacturing' have had negative results. As an example of these results, we can mention that 19 of the 29 activities presented a negative (cumulative) growth rate from 2000 to 2013, which means that they have ended 2013 at a lower level that they were in 2000. In addition, only four activities achieved better growth than the general economy average (bigger than 18.3 percent for the entire period).

Shift-share analysis

A brief review

Usually, productivity growth responds to both better activities performance or movements in the labor share to those activities with above the average performance. The next topic in our analysis tries to find out how these movements in labor productivity happened. Did the economy not achieve a better result because of its activities own performance? Did the movements in the labor force, i.e. structural change, have a major role? To help answer these questions a decomposition of the labor productivity, also known as shift-share, is done. The main idea in this kind of decomposition is to capture the contribution of each factor exposed. Usually the main factors that are measured in shift-share analyses are the contributions from activities productivity growth ('within effect') and those from changes in labor shares across the activities ('between effect' or 'structural change').

A few methods of shift-share decompositions are available. Exploring some of this variety, Fevereiro and Freitas (2015) make a comparison between three different shift-shares methods. The first one is the traditional shift-share method, which they have called TRAD, which is a simpler decomposition, similar to those applied in Timmer and Szirmai (2000) and Macmillan and Rodrik (2011), for example. The second one is that developed in Tang and Wang (2004), which they have called GEAD.[12] And the third one is based on Diewert (2008) and Diewert (2013), which they have called Modified-GEAD. The main difference between these methods is the concern with the influence that relative prices can exert in productivity measurement. Using this kind of decomposition, it is possible to identify three different contributions to labor productivity growth: (1) the within effect; (2) the between effect (structural change); and (3) the change in relative prices effect. According to the authors, the Modified-GEAD method is the one that best deals with the changes in relative price.[13]

For the Brazilian economy, we can mention applications of shift-share analysis in Rocha (2007), Squeff and De Negri (2014) and Fevereiro and Freitas (2015). The first one applies the TRAD method in order to analyze the influence of structural change[14] in the productivity growth in the 'Mining & Quarrying' and 'Manufacturing' industries. The period studied is 1970–2001 and the data used are the respective industries surveys. Among the results found are that structural change had presented a negative contribution in most of the years, which means that employment flows went to those activities with lower productivity levels. Therefore, the productivity growth of the own activities (the within effect) was responsible for the biggest share in the aggregate productivity growth.

On the other hand, Squeff and De Negri (2014) apply the Modified-GEAD method for the 2000–12 period combining two sets of data. The first one, covering the 2000–09 period, is from the System of National Accounts (SNA)[15] and contain data for 56 activities. The second one, covering the 2009–12 period, is from the Quarterly National Accounts[16] and, although covering a longer period, it only contains data for 12 activities.[17] This time, what the results tell us is a more balanced distribution between the within and the between effects and a small contribution from the changes in relative prices. Also, both the within and between effects have positively contributed to the productivity growth rate of the period. According to the authors, this means that the explanation for the low productivity growth in the period is less for reasons related to structural changes and more because the within effect was not high enough.

The last study, Fevereiro and Freitas (2015), explores three different shift-share methods. Though, not only its methodological aspects are considered; they also do so having in perspective the numbers for the Brazilian economy. The data set used is the same in each method: the SNA Ref.-2010 for the 2000–11 period with information for 12 activities. The conclusion in methodological aspects is that the decomposition with best results is the Modified-GEAD as it deals better with the change in relative price effects. Regarding the numbers, all three methods lead in the same direction: even though the between effect provided a positive contribution, the low productivity growth rate is better explained because the within effect was not high enough.

Methodology

In accordance with the methodological conclusions of Fevereiro and Freitas (2015), the method applied in the present chapter is the Modified-GEAD. However, the data set used here is the Brazilian SNA Ref. 2010 for the 2000–13 period for 51 activities, which means a larger covering with a better set of activities. Notwithstanding, the same criteria used in the previous section is valid here: there will be detailed data only in activities related to 'Agriculture', 'Mining and Quarrying' and 'Manufacturing'. The sum of the other activities is shown as 'Other Activities'.[18]

As basic concepts, let the economy Nominal Value-Added (Y_t) be the sum of all activities Nominal Value-Added (Y_t^i) and that they are their price (P_t^i) multiplied by their Real Value-Added (X_t^i).

$$P_t \cdot X_t = Y_t = \sum Y_t^i = \sum P_t^i \cdot X_t^i \qquad (14.1)$$

Labor productivity at any time t (Z_t) is the relation between Real Value-Added (X_t) and Persons Engaged (L_t). At the same time, the aggregate productivity (Z_t) (i.e., for the entire economy) is the sum of all 51 activities productivity weighted by its share in Persons Engaged (l_t^i).

$$Z_t = \frac{X_t}{L_t} \tag{14.2}$$

$$Z_t = \sum Z_t^i . l_t^i \text{ where } l_t^i = \frac{L_t^i}{L_t} \tag{14.3}$$

Rearranging Equation 14.2 with the information in Equations 14.1 and 14.3, we have

$$\begin{aligned}
Z_t &= \frac{\frac{Y_t}{P_t}}{L_t} = \frac{Y_t}{P_t . L_t} = \frac{\sum Y_t^i}{P_t . L_t} = \frac{\sum P_t^i . X_t^i}{P_t . L_t} \\
&= \sum \frac{P_t^i . X_t^i . L_t^i}{P_t . L_t . L_t^i} = \sum \frac{X_t^i . L_t^i . P_t^i}{L_t^i . L_t . P_t} \\
&= \sum Z_t^i . l_t^i . p_t^i, \text{ where } p_t^i = \frac{P_t^i}{P_t}
\end{aligned} \tag{14.4}$$

In Equation 14.4, the p_t^i means the relative price index.

Now, if we consider the share of each activity on the value-added ($s_{Y_t}^i$), the growth rate of each activity for labor productivity (γ_i), share of persons engaged (σ_i) and relative prices index (ρ_i),

$$s_{Y_t}^i = \frac{Y_t^i}{Y_t} \tag{14.5a}$$

$$\gamma_i = \frac{Z_t^i}{Z_{t-1}^i} - 1 \tag{14.5b}$$

$$\sigma_i = \frac{l_t^i}{l_{t-1}^i} - 1 \tag{14.5c}$$

$$\rho_i = \frac{p_t^i}{p_{t-1}^i} - 1 \tag{14.5d}$$

At the expense of not going to much deeper into equations, the final equation of the Modified-GEAD method is

$$\dot{Z}_t = \sum \Delta Z_i + \sum \Delta l_i + \sum \Delta p_i, \text{ where} \tag{14.6}$$

$$\Delta Z_t = s^i_{Y_{t-1}} \cdot \gamma^i \left\{ 1 + \frac{1}{2}\rho^i + \frac{1}{2}\sigma^i + \frac{1}{3}\rho^i\sigma^i \right\} \quad (14.6a)$$

$$\Delta l_t = s^i_{Y_{t-1}} \cdot \sigma^i \left\{ 1 + \frac{1}{2}\gamma^i + \frac{1}{2}\rho^i + \frac{1}{3}\gamma^i\rho^i \right\} \quad (14.6b)$$

$$\Delta p_t = s^i_{Y_{t-1}} \cdot \rho^i \left\{ 1 + \frac{1}{2}\gamma^i + \frac{1}{2}\sigma^i + \frac{1}{3}\gamma^i\sigma^i \right\} \quad (14.6c)$$

On Equation 14.6, $\dot{Z}_t$ means the productivity growth rate for the entire economy. Equation 14.6a is the within effect, Equation 14.6b is the between effect and Equation 14.6c is the relative prices effect. Although this equation is totally additive, including the activities contributions in each share, an important interpretation aspect is relevant. The only contribution that can be intrinsically attributed to the activities is the within effect. Because the between effect and the relative prices effect correspond to relative movements, they cannot be analyzed individually for each activity, only when aggregate to the entire economy.

Shift-share results for the Brazilian labor productivity growth

As previously discussed, we can consider three distinct moments for the Brazilian economy during the 2000–13 period: (1) 2000–04; (2) 2004–10; and (3) 2010–13. Accordingly, these were also the periods used for the shift-share analysis, besides, of course, the entire period 2000–13. In Table 14.1, we can find the shift-share results for these periods for the entire economy.

Just like the other shift-share studies for the Brazilian economy, once again we have found evidence that, after the year 2000, the

Table 14.1 Effects contributions to the Brazilian labor productivity growth rate (accumulated growth)

Effect	2000–04	2004–10	2010–13	2000–13
Within	0.4%	6.0%	0.1%	6.6%
Between	0.3%	7.2%	3.4%	11.8%
Relative Prices	0.0%	0.1%	−2.1%	0.0%
Total	0.7%	13.3%	1.4%	18.3%

Source: GIC-IE/UFRJ Database.

between effect had a positive effect on productivity growth. At the same time the performance of the within effect is the major factor responsible for the low evolution of Brazilian labor productivity. During 2000–04, when the economy was at a slow pace of growth, not only the total labor productivity had a bad performance, but also the separate effects. Even though they were positive, they were equally very low. This probably reflects a situation of less investments and job opportunities, which diminishes the potentiality of productivity gains.

However, the worst situation occurs in the 2004–10 period. Though the Brazilian economy had presented better results for GDP and GFCF growth, the within effect did not achieve a better contribution than the between effect, although it had shown a better result than in previous years. This period was certainly the best in decades that Brazil could have increased its labor productivity. Later, when looking for the activities data, we can make better evaluations on why this might have happened.

Finally, the period 2010–13 was once again one of low growth in Brazil, putting an end to the short best period in decades for its economy. As we have seen, this has also led to low performance in labor productivity. However, this time, not only the within effect had a bad contribution, but the relative prices effect had shown an expressive negative contribution of –2.1 percent.[19] Probably the effects of the crisis on commodities prices played an important part in this situation.

Now, looking from a sectoral perspective, Figures 14.6, 14.7, 14.8 and 14.9 bring us the shift-share results for activities and for the four periods we analyze (2000–13, 2000–04, 2004–10 and 2010–13). In relation to these figures, it is important to highlight two points. Firstly, as discussed in the methodological section, the only effect we can attribute to each activity separately is the within effect. Therefore, the figures reflect this interpretation. The second point is that we are showing only four sectors: 'Agriculture', 'Mining and quarrying', 'Manufacturing' and 'Other activities'. Nonetheless, as all the estimations were made with all the 51 activities, they reflect the sum of each activity that compound them.[20]

As we can see in all four figures above, 'Agriculture' is the sector with the best results – not only during the entire period 2000–13,

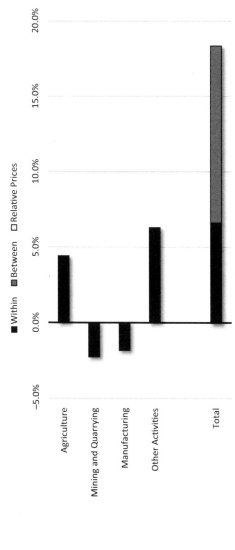

Figure 14.6 Brazilian activities labor productivity shift-share 2000–13
Source: GIC-IE/UFRJ Database.

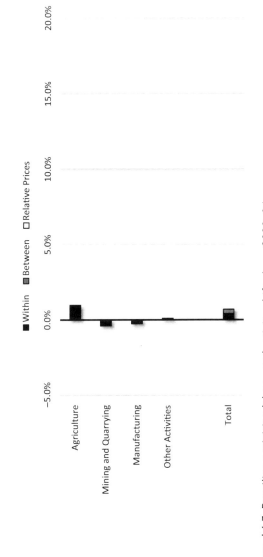

Figure 14.7 Brazilian activities labor productivity shift-share 2000–04
Source: GIC-IE/UFRJ Database.

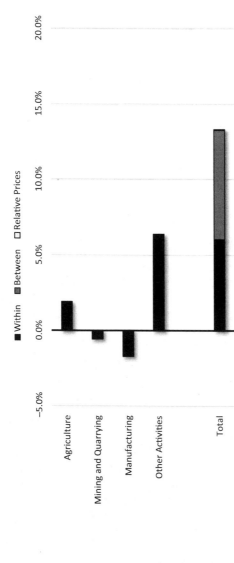

Figure 14.8 Brazilian activities labor productivity shift-share 2004–10
Source: GIC-IE/UFRJ Database.

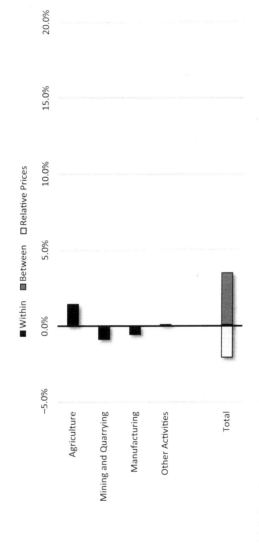

Figure 14.9 Brazilian activities labor productivity shift-share 2010–13
Source: GIC-IE/UFRJ Database.

but also in all the analytical intervals we use. In fact, this consistent result is also present in the two activities that compound it, 'Crop and forestry' and 'Animal production and fishing', especially the first one. When we consider the 4.4 percent contribution from the within effect in the 2000–13 years, 3.3 percent came from 'Crop and forestry'. This activity also invested more than 'Animal production and fishing' in the period (Miguez 2016). For these numbers, we can say that, despite a low participation in total GDP (around 5 percent), 'Agriculture' was one of the main contributors to labor productivity growth in Brazil.

However, we cannot say the same about 'Mining and quarrying'. In an opposite situation to 'Agriculture', it had presented a negative within effect in all periods considered. Because it is a compound of activities that are strongly connected with commodities (oil, iron ore, etc.), this sector is very affected by the Modified-GEAD methodology and its purge of the change in relative prices from the within effect. For the Brazilian economy, the most important activity in this sector is 'Extraction of oil and gas', which had a within effect of −1.6 percent during 2000–13, the biggest part of the −2.3 percent within effect of all 'Mining and quarrying'. Another important activity, especially for its exports, 'Mining of iron ore' also had a negative performance of −0.7 percent in the same period. This pattern is basically the same for all the intervals: negative within effects for 'Extraction of oil and gas' and 'Mining of iron ore', with 'higher' contributions from the first one, and null contributions from the other activity 'Other mining and quarrying'.

The situation for 'Manufacturing' is not different. Just like 'Mining and quarrying' we have negative results for the within effect in all periods. Even worst, this situation comes from contributions in most of its activities. When considering the total 'Manufacturing' within effect of −1.8 percent for the entire 2000–13 period, from the 29 activities in it, 18 had negative contributions. Between them, we can find traditional activities of the Brazilian economy, such as 'Food and beverage' (−0.7 percent) and 'Machinery and equipment' (−0.7 percent). Besides that, on the opposite side, from the 11 activities with positive within effects, only two of them have a relevant positive contribution, 'Computer, electronic and optical products' (0.1 percent) and 'Motor vehicles, trailers and semi-trailers' (0.3 percent); the other nine activities had all individual contributions of less than 0.1 percent and a collective production of only 0.6 percent. Indeed, the situation is the same when we look to the other periods. There are a similar number of activities with positive contributions and only a few of them have a significant and punctual positive contribution. However, we consider that the worst results were in the 2004–10 years, when the economy was at a good point but, in contrast, the accumulated within effect in the 'Manufacturing' sector was negative at −1.7 percent.

When looking to the entire economy we can see a large contribution from the between effect for labor productivity growth. Therefore, if Brazil may not, in the near future, count on a 'demographical bonus', it looks like the structural change, in this case meaning jobs flowing from lower productivity activities to higher productivity activities, can still be an important source of aggregate labor productivity growth.

However, it seems that in Brazil these flows are coming from 'Agriculture' and going mostly to the 'Services' sector.[21] Even though 'Services' might have a higher productivity level than 'Agriculture', in Brazil they are not what we can call 'high productive services'; in fact they are also low productivity activities (Arbarche 2015). As a result, this could limit the size of the between effect in the next few years if this characteristic in the 'Service' sector persists and if 'Agriculture' productivity continues to grow.

Since the between effect had a good contribution and the relative price effect had a null effect (as expected, except for the 2010–13 period), there are few doubts that, indeed, the within effect is primarily responsible for the low evolution of the Brazilian economy. Apart from 2004–10, and even so thanks to 'Agriculture' and 'Other activities', the within effect had a poor performance. The question that persists is why the within effect had such a lower performance, especially in a period where the investments were rising.

Conclusions

During the 2000–13 period, Brazil had reached a good moment in its economy, especially during the years 2004–10 when GDP and the GFCF achieved expressive growth rates and a general positive effect spread throughout the economy. Low unemployment rates, better income distribution and strong poverty reduction are among the main characteristics of these years. In contrast, labor productivity did not achieve such good results. The cumulative progress in labor productivity during the entire period was only 18.3 percent, a worst result than in developed and other BRIC economies.

These results contributed to put productivity as a major concern in Brazil. In addition, there has been recent discussions that Brazil might be losing its 'demographical bonus', which means that rises in the working population will not be a possible source of economic growth in the near future and productivity will need to rise (Bonelli 2014). However, this idea is linked to the mainstream vision that productivity leads economic growth, and not that productivity may be one of the ways that an economy might be reacting to growth. Nevertheless, the evidence of low productivity performance can imply competitiveness questions, especially when the international comparison evidences a disadvantage (Miguez and Moraes 2014).

Meanwhile, the shift-share analysis has shown that structural change, the between effect, still has an important role in labor productivity growth. It certainly could soften any (improbable) effect from an end in the 'demographical bonus'. In fact, with the current depression in Brazil, as long as the unemployment rate continues to rise, or keep its high levels,[22] any problems from labor restriction is unlikely to happen. Another result from the shift-share analysis was that the main explanation for the low evolution of labor productivity was the low performance of the within effect. From a sectorial perspective, apart from the good contribution from the 'Agriculture' activities, we could see that the 'Mining and quarrying' and 'Manufacturing' activities were mainly responsible for this.

However, this prevalence of the within effect as the main cause of Brazilian low productivity does not necessarily mean that efforts in rising productivity in the 'firm level' should be a top priority. Questions about what we produce are still very important. We need to consider if the portfolio in our activities are concentrated in high or low value-added products and services. For example, is Brazil producing the top technological products or are our factories producing low value-added products? The services we are specialized in, are they strongly connected with R&D activities? How good is the connection between our services and our manufacturing activities? Are they improving each other? When taking this into consideration, the role of industrial policy is of obvious importance. Nonetheless, initiatives like 'Advanced Manufacturing' and the 'Industry 4.0' are now gaining space in developed economies.

Appendix

Table 14.A.1 Activities labor share (% total)

Activity	2000	2004	2010	2013
Agriculture, forestry and fishing	**21.2%**	**20.4%**	**15.8%**	**13.1%**
Crop and forestry	10.0%	9.6%	7.6%	6.3%
Animal production and fishing	11.2%	10.8%	8.2%	6.8%
Mining and quarrying	**0.2%**	**0.3%**	**0.3%**	**0.3%**
Extraction of oil and gas	0.0%	0.0%	0.1%	0.1%
Mining of iron ore	0.0%	0.0%	0.0%	0.1%
Other mining and quarrying	0.2%	0.2%	0.2%	0.2%
Manufacturing	**10.5%**	**10.8%**	**11.8%**	**11.8%**
Food and beverage	1.8%	2.0%	2.2%	2.3%
Tobacco products	0.0%	0.0%	0.0%	0.0%
Textiles	0.7%	0.7%	0.6%	0.6%
Wearing apparel	1.8%	1.8%	1.8%	1.8%
Shoes and other leather products	0.6%	0.6%	0.6%	0.5%
Products of wood and cork, except furniture	0.6%	0.6%	0.5%	0.4%
Pulp, paper and converted paper products	0.2%	0.2%	0.2%	0.2%
Printing and reproduction of recorded media	0.2%	0.2%	0.2%	0.2%
Refined petroleum products and coke	0.0%	0.0%	0.0%	0.0%
Alcohol (ethanol)	0.1%	0.1%	0.1%	0.1%
Basic chemicals	0.1%	0.1%	0.1%	0.1%
Manufacture of man-made fibers	0.0%	0.0%	0.0%	0.0%
Pharmaceutical products and preparations	0.1%	0.1%	0.1%	0.1%
Pesticides and other agrochemical products	0.0%	0.0%	0.0%	0.0%

(Continued)

Table 14.A.1 (Continued)

Activity	2000	2004	2010	2013
Cleaning and polishing preparations, perfumes and toilet preparations	0.2%	0.2%	0.2%	0.1%
Paints, varnishes and similar coatings, printing ink and mastics	0.0%	0.0%	0.0%	0.0%
Other chemical products n.e.c.	0.0%	0.0%	0.0%	0.0%
Rubber and plastics products	0.4%	0.4%	0.5%	0.5%
Cement and other non-metallic mineral products	0.6%	0.6%	0.6%	0.7%
Manufacture of basic iron and steel	0.1%	0.1%	0.1%	0.1%
Manufacture non-ferrous metals	0.1%	0.1%	0.1%	0.1%
Other fabricated metal products, except machinery and equipment	0.7%	0.7%	0.8%	0.8%
Machinery and equipment n.e.c.	0.5%	0.7%	1.0%	1.0%
Domestic appliances and other electrical equipment	0.2%	0.2%	0.2%	0.3%
Computer, electronic and optical products	0.2%	0.2%	0.2%	0.2%
Motor vehicles, trailers and semi-trailers	0.2%	0.2%	0.2%	0.2%
Parts and accessories for motor vehicles	0.2%	0.3%	0.4%	0.3%
Other transport equipment	0.1%	0.1%	0.1%	0.1%
Furniture and other manufacturing	0.8%	0.8%	0.8%	0.7%
Other activities	**68.0%**	**68.5%**	**72.1%**	**74.8%**
Total	**100.0%**	**100.0%**	**100.0%**	**100.0%**

Source: GIC-IE/UFRJ Database using IBGE.

Table 14.A.2 Shift-share results for accumulated labor productivity growth rate 2000–13

Activity	Within Effect	Between Effect	Relative Prices Effect	Productivity Growth
Agriculture, forestry and fishing	**4.4%**	**−3.0%**	**−0.7%**	**0.7%**
Crop and forestry	3.3%	−2.0%	−0.6%	0.7%
Animal production and fishing	1.1%	−0.9%	−0.1%	0.0%

Activity	Within Effect	Between Effect	Relative Prices Effect	Productivity Growth
Mining and quarrying	**−2.3%**	**2.7%**	**3.2%**	**3.5%**
Extraction of oil and gas	−1.6%	1.9%	1.9%	2.2%
Mining of iron ore	−0.7%	0.7%	1.2%	1.2%
Other mining and quarrying	0.1%	0.0%	0.1%	0.1%
Manufacturing	**−1.8%**	**2.7%**	**−1.6%**	**−0.7%**
Food and beverage	−0.7%	0.6%	1.2%	1.0%
Tobacco products	0.0%	0.0%	0.1%	0.0%
Textiles	−0.1%	0.0%	−0.1%	−0.2%
Wearing apparel	−0.3%	0.0%	0.1%	−0.2%
Shoes and other leather products	−0.1%	0.0%	0.1%	0.0%
Products of wood and cork, except furniture	0.0%	−0.1%	0.0%	−0.1%
Pulp, paper and converted paper products	0.1%	0.0%	−0.3%	−0.2%
Printing and reproduction of recorded media	0.0%	0.0%	−0.1%	−0.2%
Refined petroleum products and coke	0.1%	0.0%	−1.7%	−1.6%
Alcohol (ethanol)	0.0%	0.1%	−0.1%	0.0%
Basic chemicals	0.0%	0.0%	−0.3%	−0.3%
Manufacture of man-made fibers	−0.1%	0.0%	0.0%	−0.1%
Pharmaceutical products and preparations	0.1%	0.0%	−0.3%	−0.1%
Pesticides and other agrochemical products	0.0%	0.0%	0.1%	0.1%
Cleaning and polishing preparations, perfumes and toilet preparations	0.1%	−0.1%	−0.1%	−0.1%
Paints, varnishes and similar coatings, printing ink and mastics	0.0%	0.0%	0.0%	0.0%
Other chemical products n.e.c.	−0.1%	0.0%	0.1%	0.0%
Rubber and plastics products	−0.2%	0.1%	0.2%	0.1%
Cement and other non-metallic mineral products	−0.1%	0.1%	0.2%	0.2%
Manufacture of basic iron and steel	−0.1%	0.1%	0.4%	0.4%
Manufacture non-ferrous metals	0.0%	0.0%	0.0%	0.0%
Other fabricated metal products, except machinery and equipment	0.1%	0.1%	−0.2%	0.0%

(Continued)

Table 14.A.2 (Continued)

Activity	Within Effect	Between Effect	Relative Prices Effect	Productivity Growth
Machinery and equipment n.e.c.	−0.7%	0.9%	0.3%	0.5%
Domestic appliances and other electrical equipment	−0.1%	0.1%	0.0%	0.1%
Computer, electronic and optical products	0.1%	0.1%	−0.1%	0.1%
Motor vehicles, trailers and semi-trailers	0.3%	0.2%	−0.5%	0.0%
Parts and accessories for motor vehicles	−0.1%	0.2%	0.3%	0.3%
Other transport equipment	0.0%	0.3%	−0.3%	0.0%
Furniture and other manufacturing	0.1%	−0.1%	−0.2%	−0.2%
Other activities	6.3%	9.4%	−0.9%	14.7%
Total	**6.6%**	**11.8%**	**0.0%**	**18.3%**

Source: GIC-IE/UFRJ Database.
Obs: the light gray values cannot be interpreted individually

Table 14.A.3 Shift-share results for accumulated labor productivity growth rate 2000–04

Activity	Within Effect	Between Effect	Relative Prices Effect	Productivity Growth
Agriculture, forestry and fishing	**1.0%**	**−0.3%**	**0.5%**	**1.2%**
Crop and forestry	0.8%	−0.2%	0.5%	1.2%
Animal production and fishing	0.1%	−0.1%	0.0%	0.0%
Mining and quarrying	**−0.4%**	**0.6%**	**0.9%**	**1.1%**
Extraction of oil and gas	−0.4%	0.6%	0.6%	0.7%
Mining of iron ore	0.0%	0.0%	0.2%	0.2%
Other mining and quarrying	0.0%	0.0%	0.1%	0.1%
Manufacturing	**−0.3%**	**0.7%**	**2.2%**	**2.6%**
Food and beverage	−0.1%	0.2%	0.2%	0.3%
Tobacco products	0.0%	0.0%	0.0%	0.0%
Textiles	0.0%	0.0%	0.0%	−0.1%
Wearing apparel	−0.2%	0.0%	−0.1%	−0.3%
Shoes and other leather products	0.0%	0.0%	0.1%	0.1%
Products of wood and cork, except furniture	0.0%	0.0%	0.1%	0.1%

Activity	Within Effect	Between Effect	Relative Prices Effect	Productivity Growth
Pulp, paper and converted paper products	0.1%	0.0%	−0.1%	0.0%
Printing and reproduction of recorded media	0.0%	0.0%	0.0%	−0.1%
Refined petroleum products and coke	0.1%	0.0%	0.3%	0.4%
Alcohol (ethanol)	0.0%	0.0%	−0.1%	−0.1%
Basic chemicals	0.0%	0.1%	0.4%	0.5%
Manufacture of man-made fibers	0.0%	0.0%	0.1%	0.1%
Pharmaceutical products and preparations	0.0%	0.0%	0.0%	0.0%
Pesticides and other agrochemical products	0.0%	0.0%	0.2%	0.2%
Cleaning and polishing preparations, perfumes and toilet preparations	0.0%	0.0%	−0.1%	−0.1%
Paints, varnishes and similar coatings, printing ink and mastics	0.0%	0.0%	0.0%	0.0%
Other chemical products n.e.c.	0.0%	0.0%	0.1%	0.1%
Rubber and plastics products	0.0%	0.0%	0.1%	0.1%
Cement and other non-metallic mineral products	0.0%	0.0%	0.1%	0.0%
Manufacture of basic iron and steel	0.0%	0.1%	0.8%	0.8%
Manufacture non-ferrous metals	0.0%	0.0%	−0.1%	−0.1%
Other fabricated metal products, except machinery and equipment	0.1%	0.0%	−0.1%	0.0%
Machinery and equipment n.e.c.	−0.2%	0.3%	0.2%	0.3%
Domestic appliances and other electrical equipment	0.0%	0.0%	−0.1%	−0.1%
Computer, electronic and optical products	0.1%	0.0%	0.0%	0.1%
Motor vehicles, trailers and semi-trailers	0.2%	0.0%	0.0%	0.2%
Parts and accessories for motor vehicles	−0.1%	0.1%	0.2%	0.3%
Other transport equipment	−0.1%	0.2%	0.1%	0.2%
Furniture and other manufacturing	0.0%	−0.1%	0.0%	−0.1%
Other activities	0.1%	−0.8%	−3.5%	−4.2%
Total	0.4%	0.3%	0.0%	0.7%

Source: GIC-IE/UFRJ Database.

Obs: the light gray values cannot be interpreted individually

Table 14.A.4 Shift-share results for accumulated labor productivity growth rate 2004–10

Activity	Within Effect	Between Effect	Relative Prices Effect	Productivity Growth
Agriculture, forestry and fishing	1.9%	−1.5%	−1.6%	−1.2%
Crop and forestry	1.4%	−1.0%	−1.5%	−1.1%
Animal production and fishing	0.5%	−0.5%	−0.1%	−0.1%
Mining and quarrying	**−0.6%**	**1.1%**	**0.7%**	**1.3%**
Extraction of oil and gas	−0.4%	0.8%	0.0%	0.4%
Mining of iron ore	−0.2%	0.4%	0.7%	0.8%
Other mining and quarrying	0.0%	0.0%	0.1%	0.1%
Manufacturing	**−1.7%**	**2.1%**	**−1.2%**	**−0.8%**
Food and beverage	−0.2%	0.2%	0.7%	0.6%
Tobacco products	0.0%	0.0%	0.1%	0.1%
Textiles	0.0%	0.0%	−0.1%	−0.1%
Wearing apparel	−0.1%	0.0%	0.2%	0.2%
Shoes and other leather products	0.0%	0.0%	0.0%	0.0%
Products of wood and cork, except furniture	−0.1%	−0.1%	0.0%	−0.2%
Pulp, paper and converted paper products	0.0%	0.0%	−0.2%	−0.1%
Printing and reproduction of recorded media	0.0%	0.0%	−0.1%	−0.1%
Refined petroleum products and coke	−0.6%	0.2%	−0.3%	−0.7%
Alcohol (ethanol)	0.0%	0.1%	0.0%	0.0%
Basic chemicals	0.1%	−0.1%	−0.7%	−0.7%
Manufacture of man-made fibers	−0.1%	0.0%	−0.1%	−0.1%
Pharmaceutical products and preparations	0.1%	0.0%	−0.2%	0.0%
Pesticides and other agrochemical products	0.0%	0.0%	−0.2%	−0.1%
Cleaning and polishing preparations, perfumes and toilet preparations	0.0%	0.0%	0.1%	0.1%
Paints, varnishes and similar coatings, printing ink and mastics	0.0%	0.0%	0.0%	0.0%
Other chemical products n.e.c.	0.0%	0.0%	0.0%	0.0%
Rubber and plastics products	−0.1%	0.1%	0.1%	0.1%
Cement and other non-metallic mineral products	0.0%	0.1%	0.1%	0.2%

Activity	Within Effect	Between Effect	Relative Prices Effect	Productivity Growth
Manufacture of basic iron and steel	−0.2%	0.1%	−0.4%	−0.5%
Manufacture non-ferrous metals	−0.1%	0.1%	0.1%	0.1%
Other fabricated metal products, except machinery and equipment	−0.1%	0.1%	0.1%	0.1%
Machinery and equipment n.e.c.	−0.5%	0.6%	0.1%	0.2%
Domestic appliances and other electrical equipment	−0.1%	0.1%	0.1%	0.2%
Computer, electronic and optical products	−0.1%	0.1%	0.0%	0.1%
Motor vehicles, trailers and semi-trailers	0.2%	0.2%	−0.2%	0.2%
Parts and accessories for motor vehicles	−0.1%	0.2%	0.1%	0.2%
Other transport equipment	0.1%	0.1%	−0.4%	−0.2%
Furniture and other manufacturing	0.0%	0.0%	−0.2%	−0.1%
Other activities	**6.4%**	**5.5%**	**2.1%**	**14.0%**
Total	**6.0%**	**7.2%**	**0.1%**	**13.3%**

Source: GIC-IE/UFRJ Database.

Obs: the light gray values cannot be interpreted individually

Table 14.A.5 Shift-share results for accumulated labor productivity growth rate 2010–13

Activity	Within Effect	Between Effect	Relative Prices Effect	Productivity Growth
Agriculture, forestry and fishing	**1.4%**	**−1.1%**	**0.4%**	**0.7%**
Crop and forestry	1.0%	−0.8%	0.3%	0.6%
Animal production and fishing	0.4%	−0.3%	0.1%	0.1%
Mining and quarrying	**−0.9%**	**0.6%**	**1.4%**	**1.2%**
Extraction of oil and gas	−0.6%	0.3%	1.4%	1.1%
Mining of iron ore	−0.3%	0.3%	0.1%	0.1%
Other mining and quarrying	0.0%	0.0%	0.0%	0.0%

(Continued)

Table 14.A.5 (Continued)

Activity	Within Effect	Between Effect	Relative Prices Effect	Productivity Growth
Manufacturing	**−0.6%**	**0.3%**	**−3.8%**	**−4.1%**
Food and beverage	−0.3%	0.1%	0.3%	0.1%
Tobacco products	0.0%	0.0%	0.0%	0.0%
Textiles	−0.1%	0.0%	0.0%	0.0%
Wearing apparel	0.0%	0.0%	−0.1%	−0.1%
Shoes and other leather products	0.0%	0.0%	0.0%	0.0%
Products of wood and cork, except furniture	0.1%	0.0%	0.0%	0.0%
Pulp, paper and converted paper products	0.0%	0.0%	−0.1%	−0.1%
Printing and reproduction of recorded media	0.0%	0.0%	0.0%	0.0%
Refined petroleum products and coke	0.0%	0.0%	−3.1%	−3.1%
Alcohol (ethanol)	0.0%	0.0%	0.0%	0.0%
Basic chemicals	−0.1%	0.1%	−0.1%	−0.1%
Manufacture of man-made fibers	0.0%	0.0%	−0.1%	−0.1%
Pharmaceutical products and preparations	0.0%	0.0%	−0.1%	−0.1%
Pesticides and other agrochemical products	0.0%	0.0%	0.1%	0.1%
Cleaning and polishing preparations, perfumes and toilet preparations	0.0%	0.0%	0.0%	0.0%
Paints, varnishes and similar coatings, printing ink and mastics	0.0%	0.0%	0.0%	0.0%
Other chemical products n.e.c.	0.0%	0.0%	0.0%	0.0%
Rubber and plastics products	−0.1%	0.0%	0.0%	−0.1%
Cement and other non-metallic mineral products	0.0%	0.0%	0.0%	0.0%
Manufacture of basic iron and steel	−0.1%	0.1%	0.2%	0.1%
Manufacture non-ferrous metals	0.0%	0.0%	0.0%	0.0%
Other fabricated metal products, except machinery and equipment	0.1%	0.0%	−0.2%	−0.1%
Machinery and equipment n.e.c.	0.0%	0.1%	−0.1%	−0.1%

Activity	Within Effect	Between Effect	Relative Prices Effect	Productivity Growth
Domestic appliances and other electrical equipment	0.0%	0.0%	0.0%	0.0%
Computer, electronic and optical products	0.1%	0.0%	−0.2%	0.0%
Motor vehicles, trailers and semi-trailers	−0.1%	0.0%	−0.2%	−0.2%
Parts and accessories for motor vehicles	0.0%	−0.1%	−0.1%	−0.1%
Other transport equipment	0.0%	0.1%	−0.1%	0.0%
Furniture and other manufacturing	0.0%	−0.1%	0.0%	0.0%
Other activities	**0.1%**	**3.6%**	**−0.1%**	**3.6%**
Total	**0.1%**	**3.4%**	**−2.1%**	**1.4%**

Source: GIC-IE/UFRJ Database.

Obs: the light gray values cannot be interpreted individually

Notes

1 The opinions, findings, conclusions or recommendations expressed in this paper are those of the authors and do not necessarily reflect the view of any institutions to which they are affiliated.
2 In Brazil, KLEMS Database is being elaborated under the responsibility of GIC-IE/UFRJ (Industry and Competitiveness Research Group, Institute of Economics, Federal University of Rio de Janeiro) in collaboration with ECLAC.
3 To illustrate part of this low performance we can mention the high unemployment rate around 11.5 percent in 2002.
4 There is a discussion in Brazil if the medium- and long-term effects of the rise in the commodities share in the total exports are causing a 'premature' deindustrialization of the Brazilian economy. For a few examples that go deep into Brazilian deindustrialization topic, see Bresser-Pereira, L. 2012. *Doença Holandesa e Indústria*. São Paulo: FGV Editora and Squeff, G. 2012. "Desindustrialização: Luzes e Sombras no Debate Brasileiro." *Working Paper 1747*.
5 Thanks to an expansion of social programs, the fall in the unemployment rate and the rises in minimum and average wages.
6 Two consecutive negative GDP results in 2015-I (−1.0 percent) and 2015-II (−.3 percent).
7 The procyclicality of the productivity growth is a much-discussed topic in economics, especially for labor productivity. One can check Bhaumik, S. 2011. "Productivity and the Economic Cycle." *BIS Economic*

Paper 12 for a good review of the discussion and an explanation of the main hypothesis.
8 Productivity would not be, for sure, the only cause, but it certainly has it share.
9 As the name suggests 'physical productivity' is calculated in physical measures, such as units, meters, hours, and it is also related to the entire final product (e.g., we can say that Car Plant A that produces 100 cars/hour is more productive than Car Plant B that produces 90 cars/hours). However, it is very difficult – not to say impossible – to have a physical productivity measure for the entire economy. To deal with this problem, economic productivity is measured in monetary values. In addition, what is usually used as a reference is not the production value, but the value-added. Therefore, it is possible that these differences cause some distortions in the connections between both patterns, and it can get even worse when not dealing with tangible or commodities products, such as services.
10 From now on, the reference for mentions related to sectoral investments (GFCF) is Miguez, T. 2016. "Evolução da Formação Bruta de Capital Fixo na Economia Brasileira 2000–2013: Uma Análise Multissetorial a partir das Matrizes de Absorção de Investimento (MAIs)." PhD diss., Federal University of Rio de Janeiro. There, the author develops a methodology to estimate GFCF for 53 activities.
11 An important note must be added here. Actual data shows that most of the nominal rise in the value-added was, in fact, due to the rise in commodities prices. While the cumulative price index was 605.7 percent for 'Extraction of Oil and Gas' and 1486.4 percent for 'Mining of Iron Ore', the volume index was only 68.4 percent and 61.0 percent, respectively. However, there was a previous version of this data – that is extracted from the Brazilian SNA – that covered the 2000–11 period, showing lower values for the price index and bigger values for volume index for these activities. As expected, the results for productivity in this case were better. Fevereiro, J., and F. Freitas. 2015. "Produtividade do Trabalho e Mudança Estrutural: Uma Comparação entre Diferentes Métodos de Decomposição a partir da Experiência Brasileira entre 2000–2011." Paper presented at the *VIII Encontro Internacional da Associação Keynesiana Brasileira*, Uberlândia, Minas Gerais, August 19–21 is a reference using these numbers. It is not known by the authors the nature of such change.
12 GEAD = Generalized Exactly Additive Decomposition.
13 See Fevereiro, J., and F. Freitas. 2015. "Produtividade do Trabalho e Mudança Estrutural: Uma Comparação entre Diferentes Métodos de Decomposição a partir da Experiência Brasileira entre 2000–2011." Paper presented at the *VIII Encontro Internacional da Associação Keynesiana Brasileira*, Uberlândia, Minas Gerais, August 19–21.
14 Remembering that, in this case, 'structural change' means changes in the composition of employment between activities.
15 The SNA is based on 'Reference Years'. The data used by Squeff, G., and F. De Negri. 2014. "Produtividade do Trabalho e Mudança Estrutural no Brasil nos Anos 2000" in F. De Negri and L. Cavalcante (eds.),

Produtividade no Brasil: Desempenho e Determinantes, Vol. 1: Desempenho. Brasília: IPEA/ABDI is in what we call SNA-Ref. 2000. This data covers the period 2000–09. The newest version of Brazilian SNA data is the SNA-Ref. 2010.
16 The Quarterly National Accounts is the more up-to-date economic data in Brazil. However, it has a 'temporary' and incomplete character. The final and complete version of the data is the SNA, when Supply and Use Tables (and others) are released and the information contains details for more activities.
17 It is important to notice that when using the shift-share analysis, having less activities means that the between effect is worst estimated, because it 'reduces possibilities' of employment changes. Imagine that there are data only for 'Manufacturing' but not for the activities that are inside it. In that case, it is not possible to see when someone changes job between, for example, 'Manufacture of textiles' to 'Manufacture of rubber and plastics products'.
18 Despite this aggregation, all the calculus was made using the 51 activities. As mentioned, using a bigger number of activities is especially important for better estimations of the between effect, but it is also important to a better estimation of relative prices changes. However, the low connection between 'physical productivity' and 'economic productivity' is still valid, that is the reason for the aggregation.
19 This result draws attention because usually what we can expect from this effect are lower contributions. Otherwise it means that the relative prices in the economy are changing fast, which is usually not a good situation, typical of hyperinflations or heavy macroeconomic adjustments.
20 This was merely a 'didactical' choice, as detailed explanation for each activity is provided. However, there are tables with the complete results, with all effects for all activities in the attachments.
21 In the attachments, we can see the changes in labor share across activities. While there is a loss in the 'Agriculture' share, we can see a rise in the 'Service' share.
22 It is probably going to end 2016 around 11.0 percent (11.5 million people).

Bibliography

Arbarche, J. 2015. "Produtividade no Setor de Serviços." In F. De Negri and L. Cavalcante (eds.), *Produtividade no Brasil: Desempenho e Determinantes, Vol. 2: Determinantes.* Brasília: IPEA/ABDI.

Bhaumik, S. 2011. "Productivity and the Economic Cycle." *BIS Economic Papers n° 12.*

Bonelli, R. 2014. "Produtividade e Armadilha do Lento Crescimento." In F. De Negri and L. Cavalcante (eds.), *Produtividade no Brasil: Desempenho e Determinantes, Vol. 1: Desempenho.* Brasília: IPEA/ABDI.

Bresser-Pereira, L. 2010. *Doença Holandesa e Indústria.* São Paulo: FGV Editora.

Diewert, W. 2008. "On the Tang and Wang Decomposition of Labour Productivity Growth Into Sectoral Effects." *Discussion Paper 08-06*, Department of Economics, University of British Columbia, Vancouver.

Diewert, W. 2013. "Decomposition of Productivity Growth Into Sectoral Effects." Paper presented at the *IARIW-UNSW Special Conference on Productivity Measurement, Drivers and Trends*, Sydney, Australia, November 26–27.

Fevereiro, J., and F. Freitas. 2015. "Produtividade do Trabalho e Mudança Estrutural: Uma Comparação entre Diferentes Métodos de Decomposição a partir da Experiência Brasileira entre 2000–2011." Paper presented at the *VIII Encontro Internacional da Associação Keynesiana Brasileira*, Uberlândia, Minas Gerais, August 19–21.

McMillan, M., & Rodrik, D. 2011. Globalization, structural change and productivity growth. In M. Bacchetta, & M. Jense (Eds.), Making globalization socially sustainable (pp. 49–84). Geneva: International Labour Organization and World Trade Organization.

Miguez, T. 2016. "Evolução da Formação Bruta de Capital Fixo na Economia Brasileira 2000–2013: Uma Análise Multissetorial a partir das Matrizes de Absorção de Investimento (MAIs)." PhD diss., Federal University of Rio de Janeiro.

Miguez, T., and Moraes, T. 2014. " Produtividade do Trabalho e Mudança Estrutural: Uma Comparação Internacional com Base no World Input-Output Database (WIOD) 1995–2009" In F. De Negri and L. Cavalcante (eds.), *Produtividade no Brasil: Desempenho e Determinantes, Vol. 1: Desempenho*. Brasília: IPEA/ABDI.

Rocha, C. 2007. "Produtividade do trabalho e mudança estrutural nas indústrias brasileiras extrativa e de transformação, 1970–2001." *Brazilian Journal of Political Economy* 27(2): 221–241.

Squeff, G. 2012. "Desindustrialização: Luzes e Sombras no Debate Brasileiro." *Working Paper n° 1747*, IPEA, Brasília.

Squeff, G., and F. De Negri. 2014. "Produtividade do Trabalho e Mudança Estrutural no Brasil nos Anos 2000." In F. De Negri and L. Cavalcante (eds.), *Produtividade no Brasil: Desempenho e Determinantes, Vol. 1: Desempenho*. Brasília: IPEA/ABDI.

Tang, J. and W. Wang. 2004. "Sources of Aggregate Labour Productivity Growth in Canada and the United States", *The Canadian Journal of Economics* 37, 421–444.

Timmer, M., and A. Szirmai. 2000. "Productivity Growth in Asian Manufacturing: The Structural Bonus Hypothesis Examined." *Structural Change and Economic Dynamics* 11: 371–392.

Chapter 15

Argentina growth failure

An overview from ARKLEMS+LAND growth and productivity accounts

Ariel Coremberg

Introduction

Argentina was one of the richest countries of the world at the beginning of the twentieth century. Its per capita income was 80 percent of the United States, very similar to Australia and Canada, which shares natural resource base characteristics. But at the beginning of the twenty-first century, Argentina's GDP per capita was only one-third of per capita income of Australia and Canada.

The commodity prices boom during the first decade of the twenty-first century impacted on Argentina as well as other natural resource dependent economies by a significant consumption and GDP growth. But, Argentina presents a growth mismatch during the last seven years, after showing 'Chinese rates' at the beginning of the twenty-first century.

This failure of economic development is well-known by academics and policy makers qualifying this as a resource curse and Dutch disease case. But growth accounting does not usually include natural capital based on compatible metrics and does not take into account the recovery short run effects taking account of the volatile and high amplitude of Argentina GDP behavior.

This chapter analyzes Argentina's growth profile and productivity by an overview of ARKLEMS+LAND database, which allows to take into account the effect of natural resource and short run recovery effects.

Methodology of ARKLEMS database 3.0

ARKLEMS+LAND is a research project on the measurement, analyses and international comparisons of the sources of economic growth, productivity and competitiveness of the Argentinean economy at macro and industry level. As the Argentinean counterpart of

WorldKLEMS, the project adapts the KLEMS framework (Capital, Labor, Energy, Material and Service Inputs) developed by Pr. Dale Jorgenson (Harvard University), who leads the WORLDKLEMS project together with Marcel Timmer (Groningen University) and Bart Van Ark (Conference Board).

The research takes into account international experience on the measurement of economic growth profile and productivity: WORLDKLEMS, EUKLEMS, OECD, Instituto Valenciano de Investigaciones Económicas (IVIE), ASIA-KLEMS, LA-KLEMS, BEA, BLS, ERS-USDA, CSLS and recent economic literature on measurement of productivity and sources of growth.

The ARKLEMS+LAND project is organized by a team of Argentinean academics and researchers from the University of Buenos Aires, with more than 20 years of experience in KLEMS measurements of sources of growth, national accounts and other issues in measurement and economic analyses. This project is audited by a prestigious academic committee.

The main outcome of ARKLEMS+LAND research is a database on produced capital, human capital, natural resources, the effect of ICTs, technological progress and productivity by industry, which allows the analysis and international comparison of Argentina's growth profile.

Special features of Latin America and Argentina have been considered: natural resources (agricultural land and subsoil assets), public infrastructure, non-observed economy (NOE), informality and segmentation in labor markets, economic cycle and crisis effects on productivity performance, among others.

The paper is structured as follows. Section 2 described the methodology of every components of source of growth which are divided by workpackages.[1] Section 3 presents main findings of accounting GDP growth of Argentina during the last two decades by ARKLEMS+LAND series. Section 4 presents a brief discussion, taking into account growth diagnoses based on the database about what kind of growth strategies could Argentina follow to increase resilience to trade of terms reversion in order to achieve sustainable growth.

Workpackages

WP1: output and intermediate input accounts

Output (Q) as well as the rest of the components of source of growth is measured by Tornqvist volume index, defined as follows:

$$\frac{Q_t^T}{Q_{t-1}^T} = \prod_{i=1}^{n} \left(\frac{Q_{it}}{Q_{it-1}}\right)^{\frac{1}{2}(v_{it}+v_{it-1})} \tag{15.1}$$

where Q_t^T is the Tornqvist aggregate of period t, Q_{it} is the output of industry i of the aggregate and v_{it} is the nominal share of the component i in the aggregate (at 1 digit of ISIC classification). It is worth to point out that in the case of GDP and output, Tornqvist aggregation allows including output and GDP composition change.

Argentina GDP growth is positive bias from 2007, as it is recognized by academics, domestic and international public opinion, since political intervention in the whole Argentinean statistical system (INDEC-National Statistics Institute). This important issue cannot be ignored in order to measure the sources of growth and productivity avoiding obvious distortions. The ARKLEMS project, thanks to previous experience in national accounts of his team, reproduce GDP series by industry with a high level of disaggregation from 1993 to present, calculated with the same sources and methods similar to those traditionally used by national accounts for the purposes of checking the reliability and consistency of the official series. Following traditional Argentinean national accounts methodology and sources, ARKLEMS could reproduce official GDP from 1993 to 2007. After that year, however, an important gap appears showing a positive bias of official GDP. Methodology and detailed results are reported in Coremberg (2014). Some of this finding is presented in section 3.

We construct supply and use tables, following traditional national accounts, which allow constructing intermediate inputs by product by every industry taking into account input–output data from the economic census and reliable prices and volume index at high detail.

WP2: produced capital

The approach of EUKLEMS (2007, 2009) based on the aggregation of capital assets by user costs at industry level is followed. The measurement includes more than 80 different types of assets at a very detailed level: from dwelling units, transport equipment, machinery, public and private non-residential construction, other agricultural assets as livestock and agricultural construction.[2] The update 3.0 version of net capital stock and capital services takes into account a revision of the previous version of the database according to the most recent economic and population census and updates of other registers. Tornqvist aggregation by capital type is made by user costs:

$$\frac{K_t^T}{K_{t-1}^T} = \prod_{i=1}^{n} \left(\frac{K_{it}}{K_{it-1}}\right)^{\frac{1}{2}(v_{it}+v_{it-1})} \qquad (15.2)$$

v_{it} is the share of each asset in the value of total capital compensation. The weights are user cost (rental price) of each asset. This procedure allows to take into account that the contribution of computers to growth, for example, are higher than buildings, because their marginal productivity (proxied by marginal costs) is higher (duration is high and negative relative prices trend).

In the case of imported capital inputs, we apply the so-called international prices methodology which consists in the use of export price index of capital goods from the countries import origin (due to the lack of domestic index) for all types. This implies an hedonic adjustment of imported capital goods if the suppliers use this kind of methodology; according to the Argentinean case, the imports origin comes from developed countries (the United States mostly). It is worth to point out that in the ICT case[3] this methodology is in fact the price harmonization method as applied by EUKLEMS (2008) which allows the intertemporal and international comparability of ICT investment and capitalization intensity and the quality adjustment of ICT contribution to Argentinean economic growth.[4]

WP3: natural capital

ARKLEMS+LAND includes a measurement of agricultural land and subsoil assets, taking into account the role of agricultural and mineral exports in Argentina as well as natural resource dependent economies.

The contribution of agricultural land (pastures and cultivated land) to economic growth is given by the growth of land areas, weighted by the share of agriculture land rent in total Argentinean GDP. This rent was estimated taking into account rent/value ratios from detailed statistics of agricultural land rents classified by zone type.[5] Agricultural land has been valued taking into account market prices of approximately 150 counties classified according to location and size.[6] Agricultural areas growth has been classified for more than 136 different crops and other activities (cereals, oil crops, industrial crops, fruits, vegetables and pastures).

The contribution of subsoil areas to economic growth is calculated as the mineral extracted (including oil and gas) from subsoil deposits weighted by the share of mining rent in aggregated GDP. Mineral rents were calculated as the difference between gross operating surplus of the mining sector and imputed return rate of fixed assets of the sector.[7]

The exclusion of natural capital from growth accounting could impact in an important bias of measured MFP, where natural resource intensive sectors have an important share of the GDP. As pointed out by Schreyer (2010), Brandt et al. (2013) and Coremberg (2015), the exclusion of non-produced assets could bias measured MFP. Productivity growth could be biased if natural capital service input is not taken into account in growth accounting.

However, natural capital services in Argentina grew at a negligible rate. Agricultural land grew at a moderate rate that compensate subsoil assets services negative rate. More details presented not only for Argentina but also for oil and gas rich countries are reported in Coremberg (2015).

WP4: labor and human capital

The Tornqvist index of labor services input L is given by:

$$\frac{L_t^T}{L_{t-1}^T} = \prod_{i=1}^{n}\left(\frac{H_{it}}{H_{it-1}}\right)^{\frac{1}{2}(v_{it}+v_{it-1})} \quad (15.3)$$

where H is hours worked by labor type i and v are the weights given by the average shares of each type in the value of labor compensation:

$$v_{j,t} = \frac{W_{j,t}H_{j,t}}{\sum_j W_{j,t}H_{j,t}} \quad (15.4)$$

vj,t: labor compensation shares by labor characteristics.
wj: hours wage

Characteristics of labor input are typical personal attribute as genre, age and education. But Argentina, as well as the Latin American region generally, is characterized by informal labor markets and the important non-observed economy (NOE). ARKLEMS+LAND database measured jobs and labor income also by occupational categories by industry: registered and non-registered employee and total persons engaged. Labor compensation of non-salaried workers was extracted from mixed income the imputation of average wage of workers with the same characteristics.[8] The estimation consistently compiled data from household surveys, social security registers and population census in order to obtain income generation accounts by industry with the same level of aggregation of output and the other inputs.

Labor composition change is defined as:

$$\frac{d \ln L^q}{dt} = \frac{d \ln L}{dt} - \frac{d \ln H}{dt} \qquad (15.5)$$

This effect reflects human capital as input contribution to GDP growth, according to Lucas (1998), Azariadis (1990) and Coremberg (2010). So if labor input grew through 'high-quality' groups, registered or formal employees, experience, high education, etc., their role in explanation of GDP and labor productivity growth is relevant.

WP5: productivity accounts

Source of economic growth of natural capital dependent and unstable economies

The exhaustive growth accounting which enables to identify sources of growth as a Tornqvist index of output of an industry i, as:

$$\frac{d \ln Q}{dt} = \bar{v}_{K^S_{i,t}} \frac{d \ln K^S_{i,t}}{dt} + \bar{v}_{L^S_{i,t}} \frac{d \ln L^S_{i,t}}{dt} + \frac{d \ln A_{i,t}}{dt} \qquad (15.6)$$

where Q is the output of industry i, K^s are capital services by capital type,[9] L^s is the labor input by type, X is the intermediate input and A is multifactor productivity (MFP). $\bar{v}$ is the two-period average of compensation share of each input in the nominal output.

Labor productivity dynamism is the weighted result of changes in capital intensity (capital services per hour worked), labor composition change and MFP:

$$\frac{d \ln Q}{dt} - \frac{d \ln H}{dt} = \sum v_{K^S_i} \left(\frac{d \ln K^S_i}{dt} - \frac{d \ln H}{dt} \right) \\ + v_L \frac{d \ln L^q}{dt} + \frac{d \ln A}{dt} \qquad (15.7)$$

Adjustment by utilization effects

This paper follows the methodology presented in Coremberg (2008) in order to identify long run MFP, positive movements of the production function sustainable in the long run, from short run productivity fluctuations due to utilization effects. Utilization effects are defined as changes of labor intensity, hours worked by job and capital utilization. Adjustment by utilization effects enables to identify the productivity cyclical gains that are transitory and not sustainable in the long run as it is shown by Bernanke and Parkinson (1990) and Basu, Fernald and Shapiro (2001). Labor intensity and capital utilization procyclical change at high rates according to Argentina GDP amplitude and volatility, as it is reported in Coremberg (2008) and section 3.

Taking into account that Argentina GDP accumulates a GDP drop of more than 10 percent during hyperinflation (1987–90) and flight to quality crises (1998–2002), and very important recoveries at high rates, utilization effects could not easily be set aside without distorting interpretation of MFP and GDP growth profile. For example, the capacity utilization indicator of the manufacturing sector fluctuates from a minimum of 55 percent in 2002 up to 85 percent at the 2008 cyclical peak, very similar to the previous cycle (1989–90 and 1998).

Capital utilization is more hard to measure because there is no agreement of how to measure by every industry. According to research of the Argentinean case as reported by Coremberg (2008, 2009), this variable is proxied by labor intensity by industry.[10]

If we do not adjust growth accounting from this issue, we could erroneously ascribe a sustainable GDP growth profile based on 'technology effects', instead of short run but not long run sustainable cost reductions from utilization effects. We named MFP adjusted by utilization effects as long run MFP vs short run MFP without any adjustment.

Industry origins of productivity gains

The disaggregation of MFP at industry level is very important for the diagnosis of a country's economic growth profile. The productivity gains or losses at an aggregate level could be the result of a significant heterogeneity due to idiosyncratic differences in the characteristics of firms within sectors and to differences in sectors that could be explained by productivity differentials.

Growth sustainability requires that a great share of the gains in productivity have their origin in what we have called strict MFP: continuous and permanent improvements in the production process organization, that is to say that the economy takes advantage of the quality of inputs improvements, externalities, increasing returns, as well as input and output reallocation across industries, instead of productivity gains originated in cyclical or temporary phenomena. But it is also relevant that dynamic sectors should generate not only within productivity gains but also macroeconomic relevant externalities, increasing returns, complementarities, etc. to the rest of the economic sectors, with the capacity to maintain the living standards, profits and productivity continuously in the long run (dynamic efficiency).[11]

The key analysis is in which industry origins macroeconomic productivity gains. A consistent aggregation of MFP of different economic sectors is the methodology presented in Jorgenson et al. (1987) and extended in Jorgenson et al. (2007). This methodology demonstrates that departing from the growth accounting equation (Equation 15.3) set out for each industry j, where in addition to the primary inputs, intermediate inputs are included:

$$\Delta \ln Q_j = \bar{v}_{K,i} \Delta \ln K_j + \bar{v}_{L,i} \Delta \ln L_j + \bar{v}_{X,i} \Delta \ln X_i + \Delta \ln A_i \quad (15.8)$$

Aggregating by industry, it can be demonstrated that aggregate MFP results in:

$$\Delta A_T = \sum \frac{\bar{w}_j}{\bar{v}_{V,j}} \Delta A_{T,j} \quad (15.9)$$

Improvements in sector gross output MFP can be due to the sum of two factors: a direct effect on industry output and an indirect effect generated by the productive linkage when the output from one sector is sold to other industries. When the indirect effect is not taken into account, there could be a bias in the sector MFP contribution to aggregate MFP growth.

This equation links the changes in industry MFP with aggregate MFP. The weight reflects the ratio between the shares of sector value-added in GDP w_j and each industry's value-added coefficient v_{vj}, that in practice results in the so-called Domar weights: the ratio between industry output and GDP, which are typically greater than 1.[12]

Argentina growth profile

Introduction

The source of the growth of Argentina is decomposed by period according to GDP cycle. The analyses concentrate on source of growth during recoveries and long run by peak-to-peak comparisons.[13]

- 1st recovery 1990–98: corresponds to the positive initial phase of the convertibility plan, after the 1980s lost decade until the end of the Tequila effect.
- 2nd recovery 2002–10 (last available year for the present economic cycle): presents macroeconomic inward development regime.
- Long run peak to peak 1998–2010: enables the comparison between the maximum level of GDP local (2010 is the last available data).

The figures showing the contributions also include an analysis of the 1990–2001 and 1990–2010 periods, which correspond to periods of market and convertibility economic reforms of the past decade and of the entire period being analyzed.

Argentina has experienced several structural changes during the last two decades in a context of strong economic instability and important modifications in the macroeconomic regime which had an impact on the sustainability of long run growth. The structural reforms which were implemented at the beginning of the last decade[14] initially generated an apparent important rise in the productivity of the Argentinean economy, even when the adoption of the convertibility exchange regime and the increase in foreign capital inflows caused a significant real appreciation of the domestic currency, generating a high deficit in the current account. It was expected that the ICT investment boom, access to imported capital goods, human capital improvement and the increase of productivity of the service sector originated in the implemented economic regime, which continues at present, would generate sufficient productivity gains to compensate lower real exchange rate and sustain long run growth. However, the macroeconomic regime of the 1990s did not achieve the expected results in terms of sustainability of growth. The economic crisis which took place at the beginning of the twenty-first century showed the internal weakness of the

Argentinean economy, caused by the inconsistency of the economic policy (twin non-sustainable deficits).

The new economic policy regime inherited from the 1998–2002 depression based on high real exchange rate (also known as 'competitive exchange rate'), the consumption boom and the recovery of commodities prices, especially of agricultural and farming goods, in whose production Argentina has a competitive advantage, enable the resurgence of economic growth. One of the expected phenomena was that this new demand-driven macroeconomic regime would be sustainable in the sense that it would not only generate important trade surplus but also it would sustain them as permanent productivity gains in the tradable sectors with a significant influence in the productivity of the whole economy. But the current world economy growth slowdown and terms of trade reversion cast doubt on whether the Argentinean structural productive profile is sustainable in the long run.

This section aims at identifying the changes in Argentina's growth profile through an exhaustive growth accounting analysis at industry and aggregated level. It takes into account the main recommendations from recent economic literature in terms of the analysis and the measurement of the main sources of growth.

This paper tries to identify whether the potential existence of externalities from special inputs such as human capital and ICT as well as the productivity and efficiency dynamic effects from non-tradable sectors in the past decade and tradable sectors and natural resources intensive industries in the present decade has been able to sustain the economic growth in long run productivity gains.

Aggregate source of growth

The main findings of ARKLEMS GDP estimation in order to adjust distortions, reported in detail by Coremberg (2014) from official data from the National Statistics Institute, are:

1. GDP ARKLEMS reproduced official series from 1993 to 2007. After that year, however, an important gap appears. INDEC GDP grew 15.9 percent between 2007 and 2012 and ARKLEMS GDP 29 percent.
2. The gap does not depend on official CPI index manipulation but mainly is due to discretionary political intervention on individual industries that implied changing the original national

accounts methodology that it is not correlated with original data source.
3. There was no structural change in GDP trend between the 1990s (5.5 percent annual rate) and the recent growth episode. Argentina grew at similar rates in 1990–98 and 2002–08 (5.9 percent annual rate), which are periods that reflect the important recovery of production after high depression episodes (hyperinflations at the end of the lost 1980s decade and the big depression 1998–2002).
4. Argentina had the worst GDP growth of Latin America in the long run.

According to Figure 15.1, Argentina was the country that grew less between cyclical peaks (1998–2012), inclusive less than Brazil and Mexico. Moreover, Argentina grew at 2 percent (0.5 percent per capita) average annual rate between recent cyclical peaks, a little bit less than the long run trend (1900–2012).

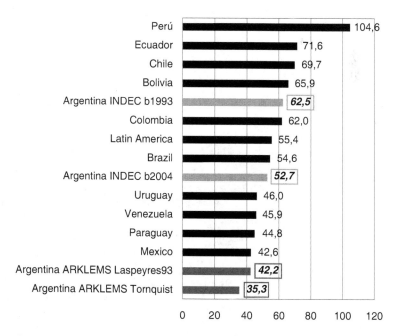

Figure 15.1 GDP growth of Latin America, 1998–2012
Source: ECLAC, INDEC and ARKLEMS+LAND.

Official national accounts over biased GDP growth: 30 percent vs 15 percent nearly from 2007 to 2014. Indeed, political manipulation impacted on all industries by doubling the growth of industry, trade and quadrupling in the case of the financial sector.

The following findings take into account the reproducible ARKLEMS series in order to not impute a positive bias to MFP.[15,16] Taking into account the aggregate methodology, economic growth profile in Argentina was an extensive type mostly driven by the accumulation of factors. As it is shown in Figure 15.2, Argentina's economic growth was driven by factor contribution for 1990–2010 periods and between cyclical peaks.[17]

Non ICT capital was the main asset which contributed to the dynamic of capital services. The utilization effect has an important role during the recovery and recession phases of the economic cycle, being more important during the more recent one (2002–10), but not necessarily between cyclical peaks as it is shown in Figure 15.3. ICT capital input contributed with 20 percent of GDP growth. In addition, the greater user life (non-existent depreciation in the case of non-produced assets) and the real capital gains due to changes in asset prices (to a lesser extent) are the reasons explaining the substantial reduction in the importance of construction and natural resources in productive capital and inversely in the case of ICT productive services.

Labor input explained nearly half of the factor's contribution to GDP growth independent of the period, but its composition was very different by subperiods as it is revealed in Figure 15.4.

Between GDP cyclical peaks, during the convertibility period (1990–2001) and total period (1990–2010), labor input contribution was explained equally by labor quality and by net jobs creation.[18] But the performance of labor input and its composition were very different during the positive phases of the GDP cycle under consideration. Labor input utilization proxied by labor intensity has an important role only during the turning points of the economic cycle, being its contribution nearly is equal between both positive phases. Labor input contribution was higher during the post-2002 crisis than at the beginning of the 1990s, mainly because net job creation was nearly the double of the previous decade. But, labor composition change during the post-2002 period was less than the previous positive phase. This difference is mainly due to the effect of labor hoarding and returns to skills behavior.

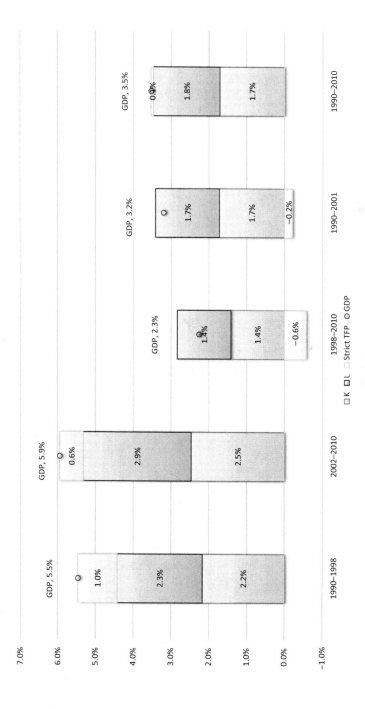

Figure 15.2 Source of Argentina economic growth
Source: ARKLEMS+LAND.

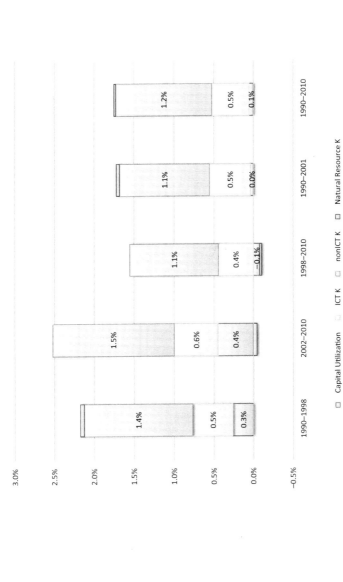

Figure 15.3 Source of Argentina capital service input contribution
Source: ARKLEMS+LAND.

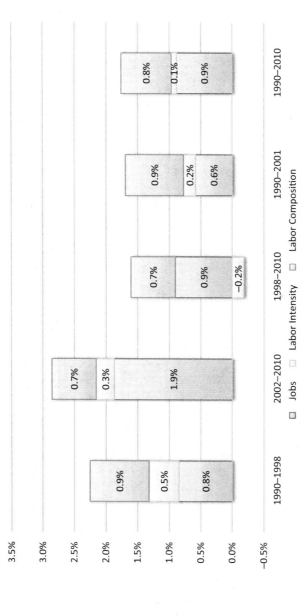

Figure 15.4 Argentina labor input contribution by component
Source: ARKLEMS+LAND.

During the initial phase of the economic reforms implementation in the previous decade, net job creation substantially diminished causing an important increase in unemployment. Likewise, this phenomenon of the lower labor demand growth caused a significant change in the labor structure, which was orientated to retaining skilled workers (labor hoarding).[19] At the same time, the returns to skills, education and experience improved during the 1990s because of a skill-biased technology change effect. The latter was due to increases in technological change embodied in the imported capital goods, which had an impact on human capital demand as a complementary input.[20] The subsequent recovery 2002–10 was generated with a substantially higher real exchange rate and therefore with lower labor costs than in the previous decade, encouraging the increase in labor demand for less skilled workers, who had lost their jobs in the previous decade. This phenomenon provoked a less dynamic labor composition change, even though the weight of registered employment began to increase after 2004. Moreover, the positive labor composition effect during the 1990s could be ascribed, as it is cited before, to a skill-biased technology change effect of the trade openness in favor of more educated workers but the reason for the positive effect during the current macroeconomic regime could be the moderate increase of the wage gap in favor of formal labor force formalization of the labor force, more than the wage gap in favor of educated workers.

Figure 15.5 shows the source of growth during the two recoveries. The following figure puts all inputs by type together allowing the analysis of GDP growth patterns: factor accumulation, input quality improvement, apparent productivity gains disaggregated by cyclical productivity gains and long run productivity gains (strict MFP):

Growth performance of the last recent recoveries during shows a moderate similar performance. But, as it was shown before, between cyclical maxima, 1998–2010, the activity level grew at a moderate rate of 2.3 percent per year, mainly explained by the contribution of primary inputs. Economic growth has an extensive growth profile. It is almost explained by factors accumulation. Nearly half of the productivity performance is explained by short run phenomena as changes in utilization of inputs. The net or strict MFP, once inputs are adjusted by factor utilization and labor composition, shows a positive but moderate growth during the recovery of the 1990s and at half rate during the present economic resurgence. The significant cyclical contribution of factor utilization to GDP economic cycle can be verified

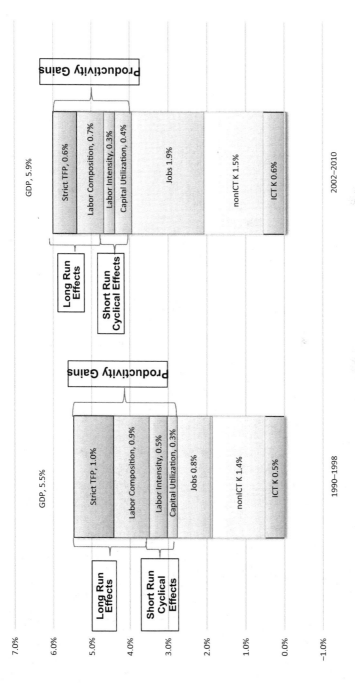

Figure 15.5 Source of Argentina economic growth
Source: ARKLEMS+LAND.

in the MFP dynamic, which is less pronounced if no adjustment by input utilization or labor composition is made, as Figure 15.6 shows:

Short run MFP gains were explained mostly by short run fluctuations during the recovery periods. Long run productivity dynamic explains only the rest, having a negative trend between cyclical peaks. It is worth mentioning that, after the crisis, the strict MFP is showing a lower trend than the 1990s decade showing some kind of asymmetric and hysteresis effect of the 2002 crisis and post-political economy effect on the efficiency of the economy.[21]

Aggregate source of labor productivity growth

According to Figure 15.7, labor productivity presents a positive trend in the whole period (1 percent average annual growth) for both types of labor input, being the performance during the positive years of convertibility the most dynamic subperiod.

Both indicators of labor productivity exhibit procyclical behavior, but as one can expect the performance of hourly productivity has been more procyclical than the job indicator. This effect is a consequence of usual procyclical labor intensity (hours/jobs) due to more flexibility of hours worked than in the jobs indicator. But what are the main drivers of labor productivity during the convertibility plan and the 'competitive exchange rate regime'? According to their main source, is labor productivity dynamics sustainable in the long run? The main conclusions about the source of GDP growth repeat themselves for the labor productivity case.

Labor productivity grew at a very moderate rate between cyclical peaks; the negative trend of strict MFP was exactly compensated by the contribution of capital intensity. So the slow labor productivity growth is almost explained by labor composition change. Argentina generates improvement in the quality of labor and jobs, but there is an MFP slowdown at the same time. As it is analyzed by Azariadis and Drazen (1990), human capital could be wasted.

Industry origin of Argentina's MFP slowdown

ARKLEMS database allows to research what kind of industries were behind the macroeconomic MFP slowdown.[22]

The most dynamics sectors that contribute most to macro MFP during the total period analyzed was manufacturing and transport and communications but with less dynamism during recoveries as it is shown in Figure 15.9.

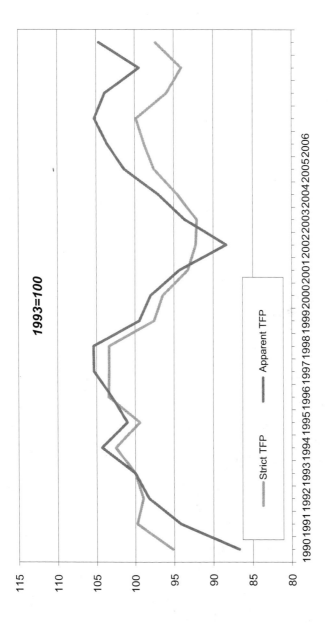

Figure 15.6 TFP of Argentina
Source: ARKLEMS+LAND.

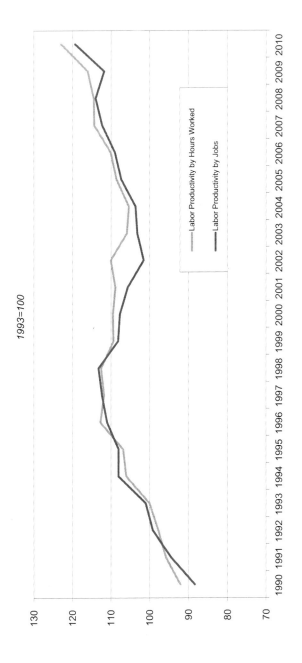

Figure 15.7 Labor productivity in Argentina
Source: ARKLEMS+LAND.

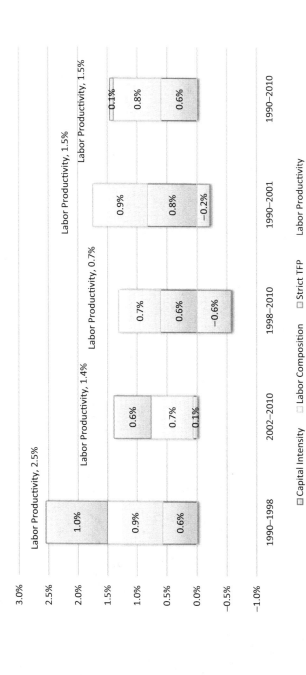

Figure 15.8 Sources of Argentina's labor productivity growth
Source: ARKLEMS+LAND.

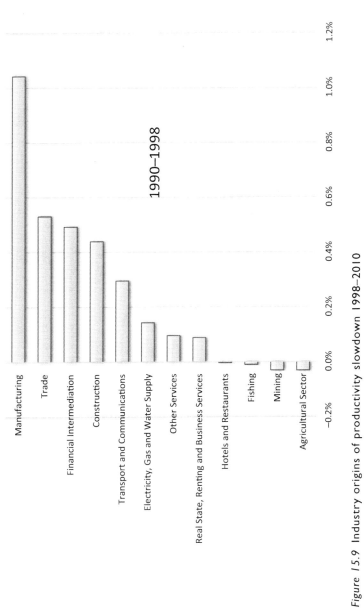

Figure 15.9 Industry origins of productivity slowdown 1998–2010
Source: ARKLEMS+LAND.

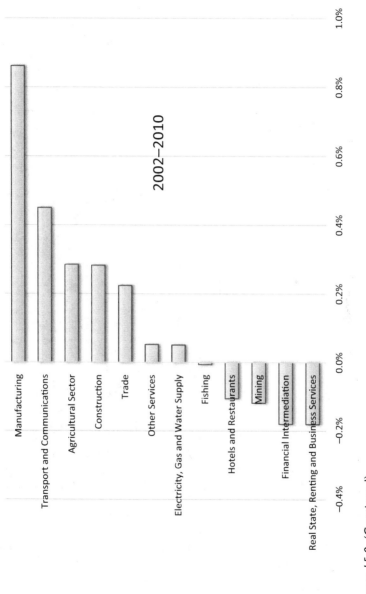

Figure 15.9 (Continued)

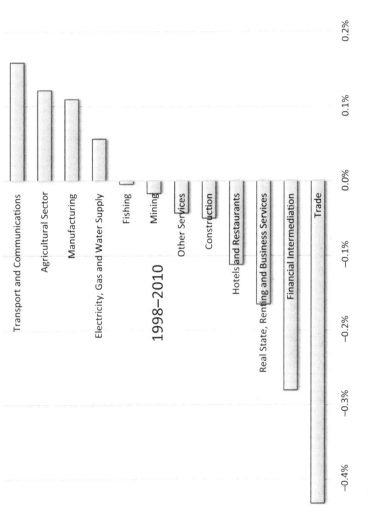

Figure 15.9 (Continued)

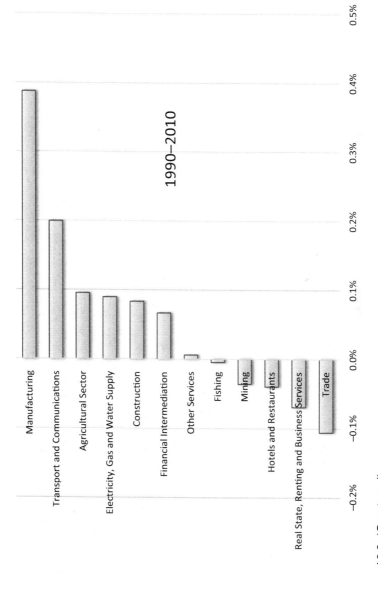

Figure 15.9 (Continued)

During positive phases of the cycle, the most productive dynamic sectors are those that have correlation with the incentives given by the changes in the real exchange rate at the beginning of each macroeconomic regime. During the 1990s recovery, non-tradable sectors, mainly financial intermediation, trade, construction, transport and communications and public administration, partly encouraged by the significant appreciation of the domestic currency during the convertibility plan. The last cyclical phase 2002–10, marked by an initial high real exchange rate, with an MFP close to half of the previous decade, took place from mainly tradable sectors as manufacturing and agricultural sector but also transport and communications, construction and trade.

MFP slowdown between cyclical peaks is mainly due to the negative contribution of the non-tradable sectors: private services (trade, financial intermediation, business services, hotels and restaurants), construction and also mining that could not be offset by the contribution of the transport and communications sectors, manufacturing and agricultural industries. It should be noted that this behavior of productivity stagnation of the services would be analogous to the so-called 'Baumol disease'.

It is worth to point out that literature on developed countries finds the opposite case, during a similar period. Triplett and Bosworth (2003) and Van Ark et al. (2008) have pointed out that contrary to Baumol (1967), 'Baumol's Disease Has Been Cured', as a result of the high productivity performance of the service sector. However, there are important measurement issues of output and productivity of service sectors not only in developing countries but also developed. These measurement issues could translate into a significant bias of growth accounting. Moreover, already that the central variable: the output of the services (or its outcome and quality) is not clearly defined in national accounts exist alternative measurements and a broad debate on the matter.

The MFP of the agricultural sector, manufacturing, transport and communications (direct and indirect measures through the value chain) was not sufficient to encourage a greater dynamism in the other sectors, generating a decline in productivity at the macro level. The Argentine economy does not gain advantage from the alleged efficiency of so-called strategic sectors in each regime macroeconomic since they do not generate sufficient externalities, complementarities, increasing returns to the rest of the economy (despite the incentives of the real exchange rate) as to provoke positive and sustainable productivity gains relevant at the macro level.

Conclusions

ARKLEMS+LAND Growth and Productivity Accounts offers a new set of data that provide researchers, policy makers, media and others with a rich source of information on the sources of growth by input type and industry.

By traditional Argentinean national accounts methodology and supplementary statistics in combination with state-of-the-art growth accounting techniques, this database allows one to detect the key areas of growth and offers a more precise measurement of the sources of growth at the industry level and is important for the analysis of the causes of the growth slowdown. In particular, the breakdown of capital and labor inputs into asset types and labor categories is an important step toward a more adequate assessment of the growth sources and less biased measures of multifactor productivity growth. ARKLEMS+LAND takes into account some key characteristics of unstable and land-rich economies. The database offers an adjustment by short run utilization effects, labor input takes into account also labor composition by registered and non-registered employee as well as self-employed and natural capital contribution to growth (agricultural land and subsoil assets).

The ARKLEMS+LAND Growth and Productivity database revealed that Argentina has shown an extensive growth profile due to productivity slowdown. Since 1990, Argentina has shown an important GDP growth, but with high amplitude and volatile performance, following the typical unstable behavior and continuous change in economic policy regimes.

The 1990s macroeconomic regime was characterized by structural reforms based on the 'Washington Consensus': deregulation. Privatization, openness of financial and trade flows and high appreciation of domestic currency that it is supposed to generate enough incentives to sustain growth on productivity. Labor productivity grew substantially, especially during the 1990s, based on factor accumulation and utilization but also on input quality improvement, especially human capital formation and ICT intensity. But MFP grew only on short-run utilization effects.

Tradable and non-tradable sectors were the main industries that contributed to MFP performance in every recovery phase, following the signals of real exchange rate fluctuations. However, the incentives caused by the relative prices were not sufficient to compensate the latent uncertainty about the possible inconsistency of economic policy.

The new economic policy regime inherited from the 2002 crisis based on initial high real exchange rate (also known as 'competitive exchange rate') and 'demand driven impulse' and the recovery of commodities prices, especially of agricultural and farming goods, in whose production Argentina has a competitive advantage, have enabled the resurgence of the Argentinean economy. But, despite positive MFP dynamism of tradable sectors before the recent global collapse, once direct and indirect effects are taken into account, their contribution to aggregate MFP were not enough to compensate the negative performance of service sectors in order to generate significant aggregate MFP gains.

The current world economic growth slowdown, terms of trade reversion, dollar appreciation and the prospect of a future increase in US interest rates leads to a high level of uncertainty about the resilience of developing countries, above all the Argentinean economy. The recent emergence of BRICH and the role of agricultural and farm global suppliers like Argentina in the global valued-added chain and their role in terms of generating jobs and better living standards of their society are being questioned.

Argentina could not evade its label as a growth failure case since the last century: weak productivity performance and inconsistent macroeconomic through inflation and unstable economy challenge present policy makers to change economic policy to future sustainable growth and competitiveness.

One alternative (not the best welfare one, but feasible) is to adopt an international negotiations strategy and domestic policy to increase the supply of exports in spite of the negative trend in external prices. But, in order to sustain future strong productivity gains, long run growth and living standards, the Argentinean economy needs to adopt first macroeconomic consistent economic policy to lower inflation and increase stability followed by public policy to allow productivity gains in every sector. Therefore, at the same time the Argentine economy makes structural changes toward more dynamic efficient sectors, Argentina should have accomplished a technological and human capital upgrading of natural resources intensive industries through significant within industry productivity gains with positive dynamic spillovers to the rest of the economy. Once the sectoral upgrading has been achieved, more industries (intensive but also non-intensive in natural resources) could become net exporters with higher value-added and long run within efficiency gains.

The key variable to sustain this kind of policy is: productivity. So, 'putting relative prices right' or 'peaking the leader' policies are not enough to support a growth strategy. Needless to say that this kind of pro-productivity strategy, which must be conducted through country-specific institutions and social safety nets, must be accompanied by macroeconomic stability and consistency in line with the incentives to promote investment and production in every kind of activity.

Notes

1. An exhaustive previous version is Coremberg (2009b).
2. See Coremberg (2009b) for more detail.
3. This work considers as ICT asset the computers, telecommunication equipment and software (own estimation).
4. As a result of these adjustments, Argentina presented an important dynamism in its TICS investment intensity, going from 12 percent in 1990 to 5 percent in 2006, though this level is lower than the levels presented by OECD countries such as the United States (18.5 percent), UK (20.1 percent), Australia (13 percent), Portugal (11.5 percent) or even Spain (7 percent).
5. In fact, the user cost of agriculture and farming land is being estimated by 'rental equivalent' approach as pointed out by Coremberg (2004) and OECD (2008).
6. This methodology permits to obtain the wealth value of land without recurring to apply net present value (NPV) assumptions. For a measurement of land following NPV at international level, see World Bank (2005, 2011).
7. The results were made consistent comparing the resulting rent to the estimated resource value, resulting rent ratios (or user cost) of the resources for Argentina. (Equivalent to the sector's WAC rates according to experts in the mining and oil sector.)
8. Jorgenson et al. (2005), BLS (1993), Schwerdt and Turunen (2006), EUKLEMS (2007), Coremberg (2010) followed a similar approach.
9. Including main produced capital aggregates services: ICT and nonICT, domestic and imported (more than 100 different types) and natural capital (agricultural land and subsoil services).
10. There are no reliable surveys on capital utilization by industry in Argentina. Following Coremberg (2008, 2009b) and Basu and Fernald (2001), we adjust capital utilization to take into account labor intensity, which allows to take into account cyclical effects as labor hoarding, double shifts and part-time jobs, extra hours worked.
11. See Timmer and Szirmai (2000), Ocampo (2008) and Pérez (2007).
12. Jorgenson et al. (1987) and Jorgenson et al. (2007) present an extended version of the equation, where the terms 'reallocation' are added. However, as in Jorgenson and Stiroh (2000) present for the US case, as well as in their estimation for Argentina, these terms were not significant.
13. So we exclude accounting GDP growth during the big crisis. After the negative shock until 1998 when the slump period 1998–2002 is the partially stagnated period which could not retakes a strong positive trend at high rates after dot.com crisis of the beginning of 21st century, which is one of the main fundamentals under the so-called 'drinks effects' (Tequila-Mexico, Vodka -Russia, Caipirina-Brazil and Tango-Argentina effects).

14 Exchange rate convertibility regime and real appreciation of the domestic currency, external trade and financial openness, privatization, deregulation and concession of public services, etc.
15 See Coremberg (2014) and Coremberg and Wierny (2014). This allows taking into account several economic phenomena that impact on the GDP cycle since 2008 and it is not recognized in the official series as: the severe agricultural drought, the H1N1 flu epidemic and the international crisis during 2008 and 2009, post recovery in 2010 and the important GDP slowdown since 2011 up to present.
16 Some literature uses MFP as gross output by weighted inputs but we must take into account that MFP at aggregate level is a synonym of MFP.
17 Capital input contribution to growth is given by the growth weighted sum of services provided by non ICT capital, TIC capital and natural resources and its utilization effect. Labor factor contribution to GDP growth results as a consequence of the growth in the amount of jobs, labor intensity (utilization effect) and labor composition effect.
18 This paper follows Davis, Haltiwanger and Schuh (1996) concepts, met job creation equal is the difference between jobs creation and job destruction.
19 See Bernanke and Parkinson (1990).
20 The analyses of these important phenomena would exceed the space of this paper but it could be inferred that the important capital imports growth during the last decade could generate a skill-biased technological change in the sense of Acemoglu (2002).
21 See Gopinath and Neiman (2012).
22 Source of growth by industry is currently under revision and update. MFP of this section corresponds to Domar aggregation of MFP by industry. As it is pointed out before, Domar reallocation effects are negligible. For the purpose of international comparison, non-market sectors have been excluded from the analysis, as traditionally performs the EUKLEMS.

Bibliography

Acemoglu, Daron. 2002. "Technical Change, Inequality and the Labor Market." *Journal of Economic Literature* 40(1): 7–72.
Azariadis, C., and A. Drazen. 1990. "Threshold Externalities in Economic Development." *The Quarterly Journal of Economics* 105(2): 501–526.
Basu, S., J. G. Fernald, and M. D. Shapiro. 2001. "Productivity Growth in the 1990's: Technology, Utilization, or Adjustment?" National Bureau of Economic Research, WP 8359, July.
Baumol, W. J. 1967. "Macroeconomics of Unbalanced Growth: The Anatomy of Urban Crisis." *The American Economic Review* 57(3): 415–426.
Bernanke, Ben, and M. Parkinson. 1990. "Procyclical Labor Productivity and Competing Theories of the Business Cycle: Some Evidence from Interwar US Manufacturing Industries." *NBER WPN.* 3503.
BLS. 1993. "Labor Composition and US Productivity Growth, 1948–1990." *Bureau of Labor Statistics Bulletin 2426*, Bureau of Labor Statistics, Washington, DC.

Brandt, N., P. Schreyer and V. Zipperer. 2013. "Productivity Measurement with Natural Capital ", *OECD Economics Department Working Papers*, No. 1092, OECD Publishing, Paris, http://dx.doi.org/10.1787/5k3xnhsz0vtg-en

Coremberg, Ariel. 2004. *Estimación del Stock De Capital En Argentina. Fuentes, Métodos y Resultados*. Dirección Nacional de Cuentas Nacionales.

Coremberg, Ariel. 2008. "The Measurement of MFP in Argentina in 1990–2004: A Case of the Tyranny of Numbers, Economic Cycles and Methodology." *International Productivity Monitor N° 17*, Fall. www.csls.ca/ipm/17/IPM-17-coremberg.pdf

Coremberg, Ariel. 2009a. "Origen Factorial y Sectorial de la Declinación de la Productividad Argentina." In Fransisco García Perez and A. Coremberg (eds.), *Fuentes del Crecimiento y Productividad en Europa y América Latina*. FBBVA.

Coremberg, Ariel. 2009b. "Measuring Source of Growth of an Unstable Economy: Argentina: Productivity and Productive Factors by Asset Type and Industry." Methods and Series, ECLAC Buenos Aires Office, Estudios y Perspectivas 41 (in Spanish).

Coremberg, Ariel. 2010. "The Economic Value of Human Capital and Education in an Unstable Economy: the Case of Argentina." *International Association for Research in Income and Wealth (IARIW), 31st General Conference*, St-Gallen, Switzerland, August 22–28. www.iariw.org/papers/2010/8cCoremberg.pdf.

Coremberg, Ariel. 2014. "Measuring Argentina's GDP Growth." *World Economics* 15(1): 1–32.

Coremberg, A. and M. Wierny. 2014. "PBI INDEC Base 2004: Nuevos Mitos sin Respaldo," *Foco Económico* http://focoeconomico.org/2014/05/26/nuevos-mitos-sin-respaldo-las-nuevas-cuen-tas-oficiales-del-pbi-ano-base-2004/

Coremberg, Ariel. 2015. "Natural Resource and Human Capital as Capital Services and Its Contribution to Sustainable Development and Productivity KLEMS+ N (Natural Capital) Approach. IARIW-OECD Conference: W(h)ither the SNA? Human Capital." *Growth and Productivity in the SNA*.

Davis, S., John C. Haltiwanger, and S. Scott. 1996. *Job Creation and Destruction*. Cambridge, MA: The MIT Press.

EUKLEMS. 2007. "EU KLEMS Growth and Productivity Accounts." Prepared by Timmer, Marcel, Ton van Moergastel, Edwin Stuivenwold, Gerard Ypma, Mary O'Mahony and Mari Kangasniemi. www.euklems.net.

EUKLEMS. 2008. "EU KLEMS Growth and Productivity Accounts." Prepared by Timmer, Marcel, Mary O'Mahony and Bart Van Ark" www.euklems.net.

EUKLEMS. 2009. "EU KLEMS Growth and Productivity Accounts." Prepared by O' Mahony ,Mary and Marcel P. Timmer. www.euklems.net.

Gopinath, Gita, and B. Neiman. 2012. "Trade Adjustment and Productivity in Large Crises." *American Economic Review* 104(3), May: 793–831.

Jorgenson, Dale W., F. M. Gollop, and B. M. Fraumeni. 1987. *Productivity and US Economic Growth*. Cambridge, MA: Harvard University Press.

Jorgenson, Dale W., Mun S. Ho, J. D. Samuels, and K. J. Stiroh. 2007. "Industry Origins of the American Productivity Resurgence." *Economic Systems Research* 19(3), September: 229–252.

Jorgenson, Dale W., Mun S. Ho, and K. J. Stiroh. 2005. *Information Technology and the American Growth Resurgence.* Cambridge, MA: MIT Press (Productivity, Vol. 3).

Jorgenson, Dale W., and K. Stiroh. 2000. "Raising the Speed Limit: U.S. Economic Growth in the Information Age." *Brookings Papers on Economic Activity* 1: 125–211.

Lucas, Robert E. Jr. 1998. "On the Mechanics of Economic Development." *Journal of Monetary Economics* 22: 3–42.

Ocampo. 2008. "La búsqueda de la eficiencia dinámica: dinámica estructural y crecimiento económico en los países en desarrollo." *Revista de Trabajo* • Año 4 • Número 5 • Enero – Julio 2008, MTSS, Bs.As., Argentina.

OECD. 2008. *Measuring Capital.* Paris: OECD.

Pérez, Fransisco. 2007. *Claves del Desarrollo a Largo Plazo de la Economía Española.* Fundación BBVA. (*Keys to Long Term Development of the Spanish Economy.* BBVA Foundation.)

Schreyer, Paul. 2010. "Measuring Multi-Factor Productivity When Rates of Return Are Exogenous." Chapter 2 in W. E. Diewert, B. M. Balk, D. Fixler, K. J. Fox, and A. O. Nakamura (eds.), *Price and Productivity Measurement: Volume 6 – Index Number Theory.* Trafford Press, 13–40. www.vancouvervolumes.com and www.indexmeasures.com.

Schwerdt, G., and J. Turunen. 2006. "Growth in Euro Area Labour Quality." WP, European Central Bank.

Susanto, Basu and John G. Fernald. 2001. "Why Is Productivity Procyclical? Why Do We Care?," *NBER Chapters, in: New Developments in Productivity Analysis,* pages 225–302 National Bureau of Economic Research, Inc.

Timmer, Marcel P., and A. Szirmai. 2000. "Productivity Growth in Asian Manufacturing: The Structural Bonus Hypothesis Examined." *Structural Change and Economic Dynamics* 11(4): 371–392.

Triplett, Jack E., and Barry P. Bosworth. 2003. "Productivity Measurement Issues in Services Industries: 'Baumol's Disease' Has Been Cured." *FRBNY Economic Policy Review,* September.

Van Ark, B., M. O'Mahony, and M. P. Timmer. 2008. "The Productivity Gap Between Europe and the United States: Trends and Causes." *The Journal of Economic Perspectives* 22(1): 25–44.

World Bank. 2005. *Where Is the Wealth of Nations.* Washington, DC: Word Bank

World Bank. 2011. *The Changing Wealth of Nations: Measuring Sustainable Development in the New Millennium.* Washington, DC: Word Bank.

Chapter 16

Determinants of total factor productivity in Mexico
1991–2014

*Francisco Guillén Martín and
Alfredo Henestrosa Orozco*

Introduction

The main objective of this paper is to identify some determinants of Total Factor Productivity (TFP), which allow us to observe the elements that determine the positive or negative productivity growth.

With the data generated in publishing the Total Factor Productivity Model KLEMS by the National Institute of Statistics and Geography (INEGI), six analytical indicators identified as determinants of productivity growth were calculated.

This document consists of four sections. In the first section, the main factors that determine TFP growth are identified.

The second section shows the same results as they relate to the TFP and Total Contribution Factor (TCF) as a complement to the analysis of these determinants; similarly, also it shows the contribution of each of the KLEMS factors in the TCF and the growth of production, through graphics, allows a better appreciation of trends in the determinants.

In the third section, the determinants of productivity considered herein are described: Service cost of capital, Capital Productivity, Income (cost) per unit of capital, Labor service price, Labor productivity and Unit labor cost. Furthermore, the results achieved in each for total TFP of the Mexican economy. Primary, Secondary and Tertiary: an opening by economic sectors is also presented. It should be noted that the methodology used is attached to the calculations made by the Bureau of Labor Statistics[2] of the United States on determinants of productivity.

In the fourth and final section, the general conclusions are presented, emphasizing the importance of understanding and interpreting the usefulness of each determinant.

Finally, it is clear that the analysis of the determinants of productivity growth outlined in this document is under investigation, so we can present changes in the future. In this respect the results and opinions are not the responsibility of INEGI, but of the authors.

Neoclassical models attribute an important part of TFP growth to technological progress. However, not only technological progress is the main determinant of growth because there are different combinations of factors (technological innovation, human capital and capital accumulation), that determine it.

Among the determinants of TFP growth, we find:

- The creation, transmission and absorption of knowledge.
- Technology adoption and absorptive capacity.
- Supply factors and efficient allocation.
- Health.
- Infrastructure.
- The structural change and reallocation of resources.
- Financial system.
- Trade.
- Institutions and invariants.
- Competition.
- Social dimension.
- Environment.

Results of total factor productivity and total factor contribution

The results published[3] by the National Institute of Statistics and Geography until now is for 1990–2014, base 2008 series; it is clear that these results start updating and dissemination three months after closing the calculation of Goods and Services Accounts System of National Accounts of Mexico, which is the input and the main base for carrying out this task.

Figure 16.1 shows the results observed TFP. Higher levels of this indicator were recorded in 1996 and 2010, the first with a residual of 2.76, and the second with 1.71. The lowest levels were set in 1995 and 2009; the first with a residual of –3.89 and the second with –3.56.

It is clear that the decrease of TFP in these two years is associated with the fall in the value of output of the economy. The situation in 1995 was caused by the lack of international reserves in the country, which caused the devaluation of the Mexican peso. In the international context, this crisis was called 'Tequila Effect.'

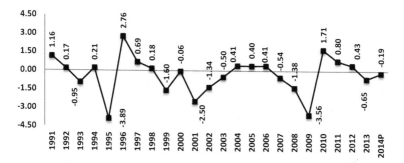

Figure 16.1 Total factor productivity, 1991–2014 series (percentage annual growth rates)
Source: SNAM. Total Factor Productivity.
Note: P preliminary figures.

In 2009, the drop in production was associated with the economic crisis in Mexico in 2008–09, also with the US slowdown, coupled with other internal events, especially the H1N1 influenza epidemic that hit the country since April 2009.

Similarly, in 2001, the fall of the TFP 2.50 as residual has its origin in a drop in production of 1.12 percent, because Mexico suffered the effects of the global economic slowdown, particularly in the United States. Exports, production and employment fell. The weakening of economic activity was reflected in a significant loss of formal employment, especially in those sectors most closely linked to export activity.

Figure 16.2 shows the behavior Value of Production and keeps the TFP association with Total Contribution Factor (TCF), the latter two shows a parallel trend.

In Figure 16.3 the contribution of the five factors KLEMS (Capital Services, Labor Services, Energy, Materials and Services) is observed.

In the following Table 16.1, in the series of 1991 to 2014, the Capital Service is the factor that has a major contribution to the TFC; in contrast energy input has a lower contribution. Moreover, the highest level is presented by TFC in 1997 with a rate of 6.14, highlighting the input materials in that year was the one who contributed more energy and as mentioned by the lower contribution. The lowest level was recorded in 1995 with a rate of –2.29, equally

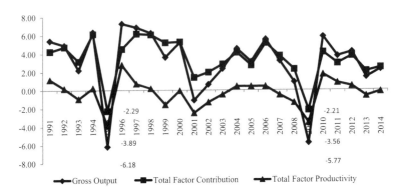

Figure 16.2 Total factor productivity, the total factor contribution and gross output (percentage annual growth rates)
Source: SNAM. Total Factor Productivity.

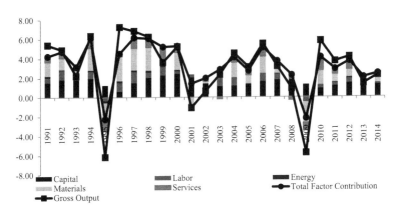

Figure 16.3 Contribution total factor (percentage annual growth rates)
Source: SNAM. Total Factor Productivity.

influenced by the low contribution of material inputs. It is noteworthy that in 2014, Service and Materials Capital have a major contribution in this year's TFC has a rate of 2.42.

Determinants of productivity

We use the theoretical framework of the calculations performed by the Bureau of Labor Statistics of the United States on the main

Table 16.1 Total factor productivity (percentage annual growth rates)

Variables	A				L	E	M	S	B	A − B = C
	Production	K			Labor	Energy	Producer goods	Services	Contribution of factors	TFP
		Capital	TIC	NO TIC						
1991	5.40	1.53	0.04	1.49	0.50	0.21	1.42	0.59	4.24	1.16
1992	4.90	1.85	0.10	1.75	0.97	0.06	1.19	0.66	4.73	0.17
1993	2.20	1.80	0.13	1.67	0.76	0.05	0.32	0.23	3.15	−0.95
1994	6.33	1.96	0.13	1.84	0.72	0.13	2.28	1.03	6.12	0.21
1995	−6.18	1.23	0.00	1.23	−0.39	−0.22	−1.52	−1.39	−2.29	−3.89
1996	7.25	0.60	−0.05	0.65	0.90	0.18	2.52	0.29	4.49	2.76
1997	6.84	1.48	0.05	1.43	1.15	0.16	2.24	1.11	6.14	0.69
1998	6.23	2.00	0.12	1.88	0.55	0.22	2.36	0.92	6.05	0.18
1999	3.58	2.24	0.19	2.05	0.88	0.10	0.78	1.17	5.18	−1.60
2000	5.20	2.42	0.29	2.14	0.24	0.15	1.78	0.66	5.26	−0.06
2001	−1.12	2.04	0.27	1.77	0.30	−0.04	−0.70	−0.22	1.38	−2.50
2002	0.62	1.40	0.12	1.28	−0.04	0.01	0.21	0.38	1.96	−1.34
2003	2.33	1.11	0.07	1.04	1.37	0.15	0.42	−0.22	2.83	−0.50
2004	4.50	1.15	0.08	1.06	0.87	−0.02	1.53	0.57	4.09	0.41
2005	3.08	1.36	0.08	1.28	−0.01	−0.04	0.87	0.50	2.69	0.40
2006	5.51	1.59	0.12	1.47	0.84	−0.03	1.72	0.98	5.11	0.41
2007	3.16	1.77	0.20	1.57	0.60	0.05	0.51	0.77	3.71	−0.54
2008	0.87	1.77	0.12	1.64	0.41	0.06	0.35	−0.34	2.26	−1.38
2009	−5.77	1.29	0.11	1.17	−0.48	−0.03	−2.17	−0.82	−2.21	−3.56
2010	5.81	0.90	0.10	0.80	0.34	−0.03	1.47	1.43	4.11	1.71
2011	3.70	1.14	0.05	1.10	0.32	0.07	0.78	0.58	2.90	0.80
2012	4.15	1.45	0.10	1.35	0.45	0.12	0.77	0.92	3.71	0.43
2013	1.39	1.40	0.09	1.31	0.06	0.07	0.36	0.15	2.04	−0.65
2014	2.23	1.28	0.10	1.18	0.15	−0.03	0.71	0.30	2.42	−0.19

Source: SNAM. Total Factor Productivity.

determinants of productivity and analysis of the various determinants of productivity. For this work they evaluated and considered those variables related to capital and labor or employment, and found the following:[4]

- Capital service price.
- Capital productivity.
- Income per unit of capital.
- Price of labor service.
- Labor productivity.
- Unit labor cost.

So, the theory and practice of each frame is described below.

Capital service prices

The capital service price is defined as the ratio of compensation to capital and service of capital. Considering capital services as aggregations of Laspeyres, Paasche and Fisher flows of productive capital stocks using the user cost of capital to determine the weights type.

$$P_{SK} = \frac{GOS}{Serv_K} \qquad (16.1)$$

where:
P_{SK} Capital service prices
Gos Gross Operating Surplus
$Serv_k$ Capital services

The P_{SK} indicator shows the price per effective unit of capital used in a production unit. Also, we could understand as a kind of 'compensation' that the machines would receive for their work in the production process, as in the case of workers; which mean that a higher ratio of zero represents that assets contribute more in gross operating surplus; this is due to the increase in service prices capital. That is, the price or payment for capital service material impacts on production costs. Down year to year this ratio means that assets are being used efficiently than in the previous year, therefore this causes a drop in production costs reflected in lower capital contribution factor in the production and therefore increased productivity.

In the case of Mexico, we see in Figure 16.4, the behavior of the price of capital services is growing; 2008 standing out with the highest price of the service and this capital of $11.6; however, the lowest price of the series presented in 1995, and its value of $6.1. Therefore, we can see that the price of service capital has an upward trend, except for the years 1995, 2003 and 2009, a slightly lower level are presented.

Capital productivity

Capital productivity is defined as the ratio between the index of the actual product and the index of capital services.

$$\rho_K = \frac{Y}{Serv_K} \tag{16.2}$$

where:
ρ_K Capital productivity
Y Gross Value-Added
$Serv_k$ Capital service

The indicator ρ_K represents the amount of product obtained by a unit of capital used in production. Therefore the positive productivity of capital either means higher production with lower consumption of the capital service or that the growth of production remained and a decline in the consumption of capital services was observed.

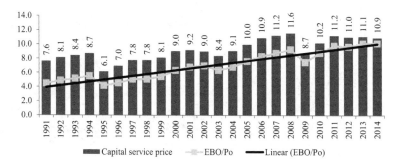

Figure 16.4 Service cost of capital, 1991–2014 series (dollars)
Source: SNAM. Total Factor Productivity.

In the case of Mexico, shown in Figure 16.5: capital productivity with a downward trend in the series studied. Productivity registered capital is highest in 1991 with a value of $71.3, followed by 1992 with a value of $69.1; in contrast, the lowest productivity was recorded in 2014 with a value of $12.7.

Income (cost) per unit of capital

The income per unit of capital we understand it as: the cost of producing a volume of production of goods and services is attributed to the use of capital.

$$C_K = \frac{GOS / Serv_K}{\rho_K} \qquad (16.3)$$

where:
C_K Income per unit of capital
Gos Gross Operating Surplus
ρ_K Capital productivity
$Serv_k$ Capital service

The C_K indicator refers to the cost per unit of capital; ie it is the representation of each unit of capital services with respect to GOS, which is that for every unit of capital services a certain amount of product is obtained.

Or, this indicator relates the price of capital service with the productivity of capital, ie, the production cost, considering the observed price levels of service capital and capital productivity. Therefore, a

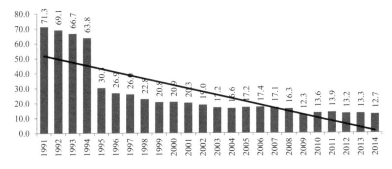

Figure 16.5 Capital productivity, 1991–2014 series (dollars)
Source: SNAM. Total Factor Productivity.

higher ratio means a higher price for the service of capital or low productivity of capital, meaning thereby increasing the costs per unit of capital, or an increase in revenue per unit of capital; in the end it represents a major expense in production.

In the case of Mexico, we observed in Figure 16.6, the trend of income per unit of capital presents an upward trend, the highest level recorded in 2011 and 2013 at a cost of $30.5; in contrast, the lowest level lies at a cost of $15.1 in 1995. It is noteworthy that in the early years of the 1990s income per unit of capital has been low compared to recent years recent where income is higher; this is due to structural change in the economy, from a closed, centrally planned economy in the early years of the 1990s to a more open economy with large investments in different economic sectors, such as tourism, the automotive industry, among others. Therefore, the country has a potential for growth, and only detracts reduce this cost through more efficient use of its assets to thereby reduce the prices of capital services.

In Figure 16.7, the behavior of the price of the service of capital, income (cost) per unit of capital and capital productivity is shown. The first two with an increasing trend, affecting the productivity of capital with a downward trend in the series studied. In the early years of the series when the price was low then capital productivity was high and therefore income per unit low capital. All told, in the final years of the series the gap between the price of capital services and productivity are reversed.

Significantly, the situation observed in the fall of 1995 productivity compared to 1994, which was caused by the 1995 crisis where the exchange rate shot up to almost 100 percent; ie in 1994 the exchange rate was approximately 3 pesos per dollar and by 1995 the exchange rate reached levels of approximately 6 pesos per

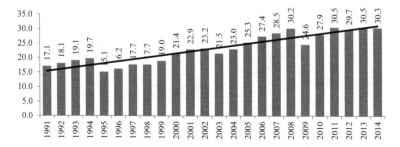

Figure 16.6 Capital income unit, 1991–2014 series (dollars)
Source: SNAM. Total Factor Productivity.

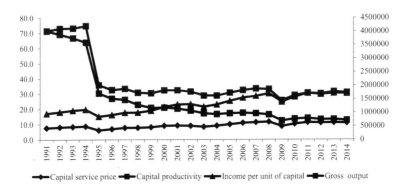

Figure 16.7 Analytical indicators related to capital factor, series 1991–2014 (dollars)

Source: SNAM. Total Factor Productivity.

dollar. From 1995 to date, the price of assets has grown influenced by the level of the exchange rate, which had an impact on interest rates making credit more expensive.

This behavior of low productivity should, according to analysis by the National Development Plan 2013–18, in its program to democratize Productivity 2013–18, due to a low availability of financing, making it more expensive which directly affects the country's chances to develop productive enterprises. Also the processes of entrepreneurship, innovation and research and technological development require a gestation period so that funding is crucial. This is not just a problem of insufficient bank credit, but also not having access to private capital markets.

Price of labor service

The price of labor service is defined as the quotient obtained by dividing the remuneration for labor service.

$$P_{SL} = \frac{Rem}{Serv_L} \qquad (16.4)$$

where:
P_{SL} Price of labor service
Rem Remunerations
$Serv_L$ Labor service

The P_{SL} indicator shows the price per effective hour worked. That is how much was paid for each unit of labor service involved in the production process. Therefore, increasing year to year this indicator means a higher average wage of actual hours worked.

For Mexico, these results are shown in the Figure 16.8. The price of labor service in the series studied has increasing values, its lowest level in 1995 is located with a price of $1.8, in contrast to 2014 whose price is $4.2.

Labor productivity

Labor productivity is defined as the ratio between actual production index and the index of hours worked jobs.

$$\rho_L = \frac{Y}{Serv_L} \qquad (16.5)$$

where:
ρ_L Labor productivity
Y Gross value-added
$Serv_L$ Labor service

The ρ_L indicator shows how much output is produced by a unit factor of labor employed in production. That is, positive labor productivity means higher production with less growth in consumption of the workforce, or growth of production against a decline in the consumption of the labor force that remained were reported.

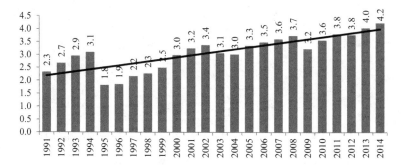

Figure 16.8 Price of labor service, 1991–2014 series (dollars)
Source: SNAM. Total Factor Productivity.

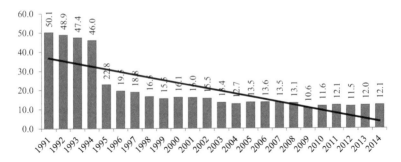

Figure 16.9 Labor productivity, 1991–2014 series (dollars)
Source: SNAM. Total Factor Productivity.

In the case of Mexico, the following was observed in Figure 16.9: the level of the highest labor productivity in the series studied presented in 1991 with a value of $50.1; in contrast, the lowest level was presented in 2009 worth $10.6.

Cost per labor unit

Unit labor cost is defined as the ratio between compensation per hour worked labor service between labor productivity.

$$C_L = \frac{\frac{Rem}{Serv_L}}{P_L} \qquad (16.6)$$

where:
C_L Unit labor cost
Rem Remuneration
ρ_L Labor productivity
$Serv_L$ Labor service

The C_L indicator shows the cost per effective hour worked by a unit of labor productivity. That is, when the ratio is greater than one means that the wage compensation relative to labor service is higher than labor productivity, so the unit labor costs rise, which means less use of the workforce, which affects higher costs for labor services. The positive change rates between one year against another means a higher cost for labor services, resulting from reduced efficiency of hours worked, compared with the previous year.

In the case of Mexico, we see in Figure 16.10 that 2013 had the highest unit labor cost with a value of $26.3, against that observed in 1995, with $12.4.

In Figure 16.11, we find the behavior of growing labor cost per unit and the price of stable employment service, which caused labor productivity, show a slightly decreasing trend in the series studied. It is interesting to analyze the results of this graph into two parts, the first is the 1991–98 series and the second is the 1999–2014 series; in the first, a positive productivity is observed and, second, the series becomes negative despite prices labor service and labor service costs present a negative trend. In this situation we observe that low labor productivity in the second series is caused by low production or an increase in hours worked have no impact on production growth. The reasons for the low growth may be many, but one of the reasons is the informal sector which contributes negatively on labor productivity in the country.

Significantly, the situation observed in the fall of labor productivity in 1995 compared to 1994 was caused by the 1995 crisis where the level of production reported a sharp drop; ie, companies had to lay off staff at a lower level than the drop in production, impacting the growth of unit labor costs in the range of 1995–2014.

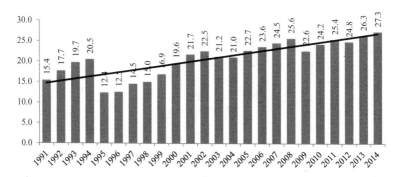

Figure 16.10 Unit labor cost, 1991–2014 series (dollars)
Source: SNAM. Total Factor Productivity.

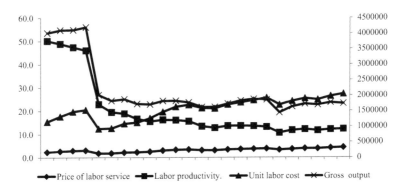

Figure 16.11 Analytical indicators related to the labor factor, 1991–2014 series (dollars)
Source: SNAM. Total Factor Productivity.

Determinants of TFP by sector: primary, secondary and tertiary

In the primary sectors are considered agricultural economic activities, forestry and fishing; in the secondary sector economic activities of mining, manufacturing, construction and electricity generation; and finally, in the tertiary sector, all economic activities of services are included.

Primary sector

Figure 16.12 presents the trend in the price of capital services is positive in the study period, the highest level was in 2013 and 2014 whose prices are $14.1 and $13.5, respectively; in contrast, the lowest level was in 1995 and 1999 with prices of $6.8 and $7.6, respectively.

In the case of capital productivity trend in the study years it has been negative, where in 2009 the lowest level with a productivity of $11.0 and in 1991 with a productivity of $57.6 presents the highest level of the series.

The trend of income per unit of capital services has been positive, where the lowest level is presented in 1995 with an income of $21.6 and the highest level in 2011 with an income of $39.8.

Figure 16.13, concerning analytical indicators of the labor factor in the primary sector found that the price trend is stable for labor

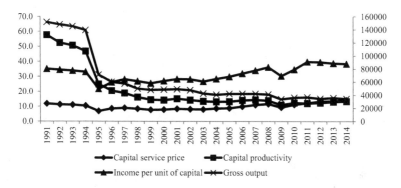

Figure 16.12 Primary sector: analytical indicators of the capital factor (dollars)

Source: SNAM. Total Factor Productivity.

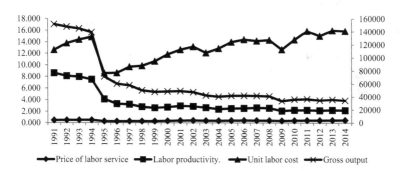

Figure 16.13 Primary sector: analytical indicators of the labor factor (dollars)

Source: SNAM. Total Factor Productivity

service. The highest level is presented with a price of $0.5 in 1993; in contrast the lowest price with a value of $0.3 is in 1996.

In the case of labor productivity the trend it is negative. The lowest level of the series studied was in 2009 with a value of $2.1; in contrast, the highest level is presented in 1991 with a value of $8.6.

The trend of unit labor costs has been positive during the study period. The lowest level is presented in 1995 with a value of $8.6; in contrast, the highest level is in 2013 at a cost of $15.9.

Secondary sector

In Figure 16.14, the service price of capital has a stable trend with a slight upward trend, unlike income per unit of capital, the lowest level of the series in 1995 with a price of $10.3 and the highest level in the period 2011 with a price of $21.2.

On the other hand, capital productivity of the secondary sector has a negative trend. The highest level of the series in 1991 is a value of $135.3; in contrast, the year with the lowest level is 2009 with a productivity of $20.6.

The income per unit of capital has a growing trend. The year 2011 has the highest level studied with an income of $33.9 and 1995 the lowest level with an income of $13.8.

In Figure 16.15, associated with analytical indicators of the labor factor of the secondary sector, the indicator on the price of labor service has an upward trend in the period, the lowest level presented in 1995 with a price of $1.9; in contrast, the highest level is presented in 2014 with $3.7.

On the other hand, labor productivity has a negative trend in the study period. The highest level is in 1991 with a value of $57.9; in contrast, the lowest level ranks in 2009 with $13.0.

The trend of unit labor cost in the study period is up, where the highest level is presented in 2008 with $20.7 and the lowest level in 1995 with $9.0.

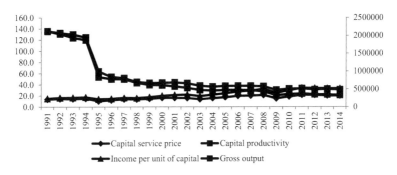

Figure 16.14 Secondary sector: analytical indicators of the capital factor (dollars)

Source: SNAM. Total Factor Productivity.

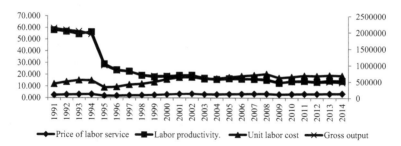

Figure 16.15 Secondary sector: analytical indicators of the labor factor (dollars)
Source: SNAM. Total Factor Productivity.

Third sector

In Figure 16.16, the price of capital services trend presented in the analysis period is growing, with the highest level in 2008 with a price of $8.8 and the lowest level in 1995 with a price of $4.8.

In the case of capital productivity, a decreasing trend in the study period is presented. The highest level is presented in the study in 1991 with a value of $53.1. The lowest level was recorded in 2009 with $10.0.

The income per unit of capital is a growing trend in the study period, with the highest level in 2013 with an income of $28.4; in contrast, the lowest level is in 1995 with $15.3.

In Figure 16.17, concerning analytical indicators of the labor factor in the tertiary sector, the price of labor service has a growing trend, the highest level in 2014 with a price of $5.4, unlike the year 1995 with a price of $2.3 which has the lowest level of the series.

On the other hand, labor productivity has a decreasing trend, the lowest level presented in 2009 with a value of $11.9; in contrast, the highest level in 1993 with a productivity of $45.8.

The cost per labor unit has a growing trend. The highest level of the series is in 2014 at a cost of $30.6; in contrast, the lowest level was in 1995 at $14.8.

Conclusions

These six determinants of productivity of this exercise let analyze the factors that influence the behavior of TFP. In this paper the

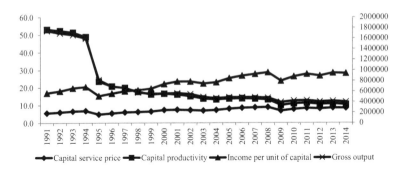

Figure 16.16 Tertiary sector: analytical indicators of the capital factor (dollars)
Source: SNAM. Total Factor Productivity.

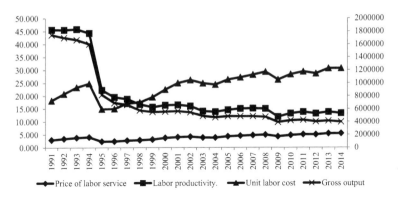

Figure 16.17 Tertiary sector: analytical indicators of the labor factor (dollars)
Source: SNCM. Total Factor Productivity.

basic capital and labor were considered, based on their prices, productivity and income and costs. Therefore, in this exercise it was noted that the service of capital is one of the factors that have a material impact on the total contribution of the factors, and to a lesser extent labor services, so this exercise was focused rather on the two factors mentioned above.

The results of labor productivity and capital show that prices of capital and labor have a material impact on unit costs of capital and labor service. In the part of the productivity of capital, we see that the price of capital service is the one that causes an increase in production costs; this is probably due to increased borrowing costs to finance productive activities, applied mainly in the acquisition of non-financial assets.

Additionally, it should be noted the situation observed in the fall of 1995 productivity compared to 1994, which was caused by the 1995 crisis where the exchange rate shot up to almost 100 percent; ie in 1994 the exchange rate was approximately 3 pesos per dollar and by 1995 the exchange rate reached levels approximately 6 pesos per dollar. From 1995 to date, the price of assets has grown influenced by the level of the exchange rate, which had an impact on interest rates making credit more expensive.

With respect to labor productivity, it is worth to note the rising of the unit per labor cost, even though the price of labor is stable, so the causes can be as diverse as the effect of the informal sector in the economy; but what is technically verifiable is that due to a decline in labor productivity, influenced by an increase in hours worked ineffective.

Likewise, the situation observed in the fall of labor productivity in 1995 compared to 1994 was caused by the 1995 crisis where the level of production reported a sharp drop; ie, companies had to lay off staff at a lower level than the drop in production, impacting the growth of unit labor costs in the range of 1995–2014.

Finally, it should be mentioned that the development of these indicators represent valuable information for decision makers, along with the new challenges and recent economic phenomena occurring in the global economy, particularly with regard to global value chains, which are increasingly becoming important in production and in the so called growth accounting, along with the impact observed in the total contribution of factors of production.

Notes

1 www.bls.gov/bls/productivity.htm, accessed July 8, 2016.
2 www.bls.gov/mfp/mprtech.pdf, accessed July 8, 2016.
3 You can check the following link: www.inegi.org.mx/est/contenidos/proyectos/cn/ptf/default.aspx, accessed July 8, 2016.

4 It should be noted that to meet the objectives of this work only six determinants were studied; the Bureau of Labor Statistics of the United States, however, has a growing list of determinants.

Bibliography

Benhabid, J., and M. Spielgel. 1994. "The Role of Human Capital in Economic Development: Evidence From Aggregate Cross Country Data." *Journal of Monetary Economics* 34(2): 143–173.

Bureau of Economic Analysis. 2007. *Technical Information About the BLS Multifactor Productivity Measures*. www.bls.gov/mfp/mprtech.pdf, accessed July 8, 2016.

Greenwood, J., and B. Jovanovic. 2006. "Contabilidad del crecimiento." *Cuadernos económicos de ICE No72*.

Harris, R. 2002. "Social Policy, Inequality and Productivity: What Are the Linkages?" *The Review of Economic Performance and Social Progress* 2.

Instituto Nacional de Estadística and Geografía. 2013. *Sistema de cuentas nacionales de México: productividad total de los factores 1990–2011*. Instituto Nacional de Estadística y Geografía. www.inegi.org.mx/est/contenidos/proyectos/cn/ptf/default.aspx, accessed July 8, 2016.

Isaksson, A. 2005. "Determinants of Total Factor Productivity: An Assessment of Recent Evidence." *mimeo*, UNIDO, Vienna.

Isaksson, A. 2007. *Determinants of Total Factor Productivity: A Literature Review*. Vienna: Research and Statics Branch, United Industrial Development Organization.

Jorgenson, Dale W., and Kevin J. Stiroh. 2000. "Raising the Speed Limit: U.S. Economic Growth in the Information Age." *OECD Economics Department Working Papers* no. 261. www.oecd.org.

OECD. 2001. *Measuring Productivity Manual*. www.oecd.org, accessed July 8, 2016.

OECD. 2009. *Measuring Capital OCDE Manual*. 2nd edition. www.oecd.org, accessed July 8, 2016.

Romer, P. 1990. "Endogenous Technological Change." *Journal of Political Economy* 98(5): S71–S102.

Schmitz, James, A. Jr. 2005. "What Determines Productivity? Lessons From the Dramatic Recovery of the U.S and Canadian Iron Ore Industries Following Their Early 1980s Crisis." *Journal of Political Economy* 113(13): 582–625.

Syverson, C. 2010. "What Determines Productivity?" *Working Paper 15712*, National Bureau of Economic Research. www.nber.org/papers/w15712, accessed July 8, 2016.

UK Office of Fair Trading. 2007. *Productivity and Competition: An OFT Perspective on the Productivity Debate*. https://pdfs.semanticscholar.org/53db/2a9698301bb1270e79635ca4da80bea2810d.pdf, accessed July 8, 2016.

Chapter 17

What do we know about productivity in Arab economies

The challenges of generating multifactor productivity (MFP) estimates at industry level

Homagni Choudhury and Deb Kusum Das

Introduction

The Arab world has witnessed major economic, political and social changes since the onset of the Arab spring in 2011. Despite the rapidly spreading and worsening political turmoil, as well as, in many cases, an unstable internal socio-political environment, many of the Arab countries in transition, which include Egypt, Jordan, Libya, Morocco, Tunisia and Yemen, have more or less maintained macroeconomic stability (IMF 2014). However, these countries have not been able to generate the kind growth rates required for a meaningful reduction in poverty and creation of jobs. Notwithstanding diversity of conditions, there is need to advance structural reforms to foster higher and more inclusive growth. It is well known that Arab countries do not rank very high in terms of global competitiveness.[1] Further, in some of the Arab countries, there has been uneven implementation of structural reforms carried out in the mid-1980s. The important question to pose is – *has growth delivered following such reforms in the Arab world?*

In order to understand growth and its dynamics, it is becoming increasingly important to obtain multifactor productivity (MFP) estimates. The role of MFP improvements is catalysis for enhancing growth in the economy. Further, in recent times, in the examination of sources of growth the role of factor accumulation and MFP have assumed tremendous academic importance across the world, in developing and emerging countries as well as the developed world.

Several authors have examined the growth and MFP aspects for Arab countries (see, Pipitone 2009, for example), and particularly the role of technological progress in select countries in the Mediterranean region. These studies conclude that physical capital is the key factor of economic growth. The contribution of human capital seems rather low, although it has a positive value. The role of MFP is particularly variable, but it is significant in many transition countries and in all the countries which have recorded the highest economic growth rates.

Given this backdrop, this chapter aims to explore aspects of productivity dynamics in the Arab world and assess the challenges for estimating MFP using the North African countries of Egypt, Morocco and Tunisia as a particular case. Estimation of MFP productivity is at the heart of understanding the growth paradigm and the effects of economic reforms on growth and development. As such we attempt to explore the possibility of empirically estimating MFP using a KLEMS framework for the North African countries of Egypt, Morocco and Tunisia. This in turn allows us to set the context for estimation of MFP productivity for the Arab world, identifying the challenges and laying a roadmap for an Arab KLEMS database.

Our choice of working with the three North African countries to explore challenges for estimation of MFP for the Arab world is conditioned by several factors. First, the choice of Egypt, Morocco and Tunisia lies in the fact that they have a similar economic, sociopolitical and cultural structure and therefore have, to some degree, relatively similar political economy factors affecting economic performance and manufacturing productivity. Specifically, these three countries have adopted market-oriented reforms in the recent past beginning in the mid-1980s. Economic growth, in all three countries, is highly driven by services, and manufacturing sectors. The role of agriculture has declined over the years in growth, but it still employs a large proportion of the workforce. Also, the three countries have similar trading partners and FDI sources, and they share common demographic characteristics such as language, religion, culture and have, to some degree, a similar history of macroeconomic events, policy regimes and level of development of the financial sector. Second, when it comes to economic policy, Egypt, Morocco and Tunisia have witnessed a gradual liberalization of both the external sector and internal reforms resulting in a growing financial and economic system (Mühlberger and Semmelmann

2010; Creane et al. 2006; Achy 2005). Finally, an important common point to note for these three countries is that they are all non-oil dependent unlike other North African countries like Libya and Algeria, which are major exporters of oil. In addition, the geographical and strategic location of the North African region is of great significance. Lying in the northernmost part of the African continent, Egypt, Morocco and Tunisia occupy a unique position in the international community. They enjoy a favorable strategic position; they are advantageously located on the crossroads among different continents and this important geographical location could benefit these countries to have a great potential to attract significant foreign investments and to access various markets, which clearly has implications for firm performance, manufacturing productivity and overall growth.

The rest of the chapter is structured as follows. In section 2, we present a background to understanding growth dynamics in the Arab world in general and for the three North African countries under study, in particular. Section 3 outlines various aspects of productivity estimation in general and the KLEMS framework for estimation of MFP productivity in particular. We assess the practical challenges and requirements for estimating MFP for the Arab world by empirically examining the available data and literature for the three North African countries in section 4, which in turn is used to create a roadmap for phase wise creation of an Arab KLEMS dataset. Section 5 presents some concluding remarks and lays the way forward for estimating MFP productivity for the Arab world.

Understanding the growth dynamics in the Arab world: the case of Egypt, Morocco and Tunisia

This section presents a background to the growth performance of the economies in this study in the context of growth dynamics in the Arab world. The countries of Egypt, Morocco and Tunisia are situated in the northernmost part of the African continent. The geopolitical classification of these countries by the United Nations puts them under North Africa, along with Algeria, Libya, Sudan and Western Sahara.[2] These three countries are also members of the Arab League (the League of Arab states), which is a regional organization of 22 Arab countries in and around North Africa, the horn of Africa and Arabia. But when it comes to an academic discourse of these countries, they are generally studied under the umbrella of the Middle East and North African Economies (MENA) – the MENA region is comprised of a range of Arab[3] countries with diverse social and economic histories and resource base (Messkoub 2008). In Table 17.2, we present selected macroeconomic indicators for the three countries that we consider along with the averages for all MENA and developing MENA countries for comparison. While both real GDP and per capita real GDP show positive trends since the 1980s, it is evident that growth has slowed down in the wake of ongoing political and social turmoil in the region in general and in these three countries in particular following the Arab spring of 2011. Since 2011, most Arab countries have been affected by social unrest, increase in energy (for oil importers) and commodity prices, recessionary impacts affecting both private and public sectors, increased uncertainty for investors and greater demands for expansionary expenditure for economic recovery and social justice. The unrest has already had a huge direct cost, and has also led to a fall in economic activity and increase in unemployment (ILO 2012). Given this background, it is important to understand the growth paradigm in the Arab region in general and the three countries under study in particular. To this end, we first outline the macroeconomic aspects of growth in the Arab world in section 2.1. We then set out the macroeconomic profile of the three countries that we consider in this study to assess the challenges of estimating MFP.

Macro aspects of growth in the Arab world

The historic growth performance of the Arab world has been more or less disappointing. In comparison to other developing countries, the MENA region showed better performance in the 1970s, but since the 1980s the region as a whole witnessed complete stall in growth and very slow growth since the mid-1990s (see Figure 17.1). Following the 'lost decade' of the 1980s, the rate of economic growth in the region showed some signs of improvement. While growth rates averaged 3.5 percent per annum in the 1990s and further increased to over 4.5 percent in the decade leading up to the Arab spring, which are significantly high by historical standards, the fact remains that the economic performance of the Arab countries remained poor in comparison to all world regions[4] (see Figure 17.2). When population growth is factored in, the increase in per capita incomes is far less impressive (ILO 2012).

Table 17.1 Selected macroeconomic indicators for Egypt, Morocco, Tunisia and MENA

	Real GDP[1]				Real GDP Growth				Per capita real GDP[2]			
	1980	1990	2000	2010	2014	1980–89	1990–99	2000–10	2011–14	2013–14	1980	1990	2000	2010	2014
Egypt	29.10	49.50	75.40	121.02	131.40	0.0572	0.0423	0.0478	0.0206	0.0218	670.57	878.22	1,103.44	1,475.13	1,466.98
Morocco	22.50	35.30	46.70	75.50	87.10	0.0459	0.0292	0.0452	0.0358	0.0252	1,110.73	1,401.45	1,595.77	2,315.26	2,527.18
Tunisia[3]	11.70	16.60	26.40	40.60	43.30	0.0345	0.0494	0.0434	0.0218	0.0249	1,830.03	2,033.42	2,758.46	3,847.59	3,979.43
MENA (All)	674.20	796.90	1,184.50	1,888.70	2,145.90	0.0123	0.0442	0.0472	0.0319	0.0216	3,642.74	3,133.23	3,758.55	4,906.30	5,140.46
MENA (Developing countries)[4]	271.50	368.60	526.70	826.80	853.00	0.0194	0.0427	0.0442	0.0078	−0.0003	1,627.03	1,628.76	1,890.42	2,494.49	2,387.21

Source: Authors' calculations based on World Development Indicators, World Bank.

Notes:
1 Real GDP is in billions of 2005 USD.
2 Per capita Real GDP is in 2005 USD.
3 2014 figures not available for Tunisia; instead 2013 is reported under 2014 and 2011–13 and 2012–13 under 2011–14 and 2013–14 respectively.
4 MENA (Developing countries) includes Algeria, Djibouti, Egypt, Iran, Iraq, Jordan, Lebanon, Libya, Morocco, Syria, Tunisia, West Bank and Gaza, and Yemen.

Table 17.2 GDP per capita growth and inflation for Arab, MENA and other developing regions, 2010–14

Regions	GDP per capita growth (annual%, constant LCU)						Inflation (GDP Deflator, annual%)					
	2010	2011	2012	2013	2014	2010–14	2010	2011	2012	2103	2014	2010–14
MENA (All)	2.76	1.68	2.31	0.52	0.19	1.49	10.56	13.45	4.43	2.26	0.96	6.33
MENA (Developing only)	3.29	−3.30	1.75	−0.85	−1.90	−0.20	11.78	9.01	4.99	3.93	2.03	6.35
Arab World	2.12	1.27	3.91	0.92	0.08	1.66	11.08	15.29	4.43	1.64	0.79	6.65
East Asia and Pacific (Developing only)	9.10	7.69	6.67	6.41	6.05	7.19	4.12	4.38	2.50	1.85	2.61	3.09
Latin America and Caribbean (Developing only)	4.80	3.12	1.94	1.59	0.61	2.41	5.55	5.68	3.93	2.72	3.68	4.31

Source: Authors' calculations based on World Development Indicators, World Bank.

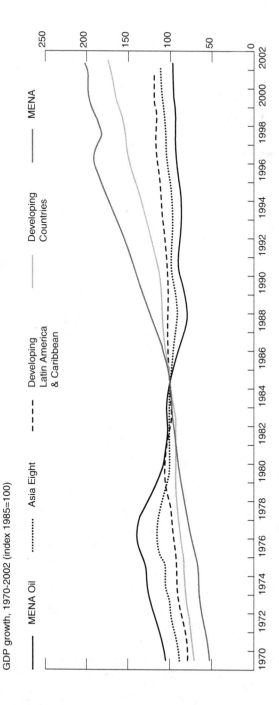

Figure 17.1 Arab countries had a low GDP per capita growth in the 1980s and 1990s
Source: ILO (2012).

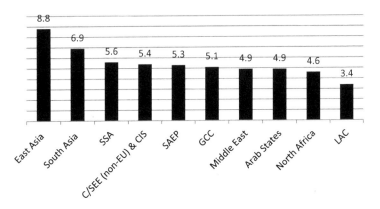

Figure 17.2 GDP growth in the Arab states (and three sub-regions) in the 2000s Relative to the Rest of the World
Source: ILO (2012).

However, the employment scenario in the Arab world in comparison to the rest of the world, despite low levels of growth, has been substantially positive. The elasticity of employment with respect to output averaged 0.69 between 2009 and 2010 (ILO 2012), which is not only high by historical standards,[5] but also significant in the backdrop of the fact that this period saw a conscious shift of the policy stance of the government on its role as employers of last resort, at least until the Arab spring of 2011. Figure 17.3 shows that the employment–output elasticity in each of the three Arab sub-regions (Middle-east, North Africa and Gulf Cooperation Council) was more than double that achieved by their Asian counterparts.

The implication of relatively low economic growth rates but high employment elasticities in the Arab region is that productivity in the Arab world growth has lagged behind other regions (see Figure 17.4). As a matter of fact, the Arab region had the lowest productivity growth compared to any other region (except Latin America) in the decade of the 2000s. ILO (2012) notes that North Africa achieved slightly higher productivity growth than the Middle East, with the respective annual rates being 1.5 percent and 1.2 percent, as against a world average of 1.8 percent.

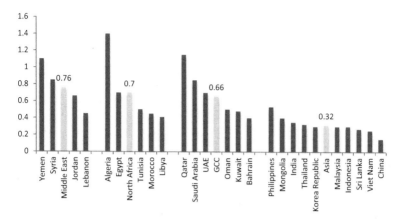

Figure 17.3 Employment elasticity with respect to output in the Arab world and Asia, 2000–10

Source: ILO (2012).

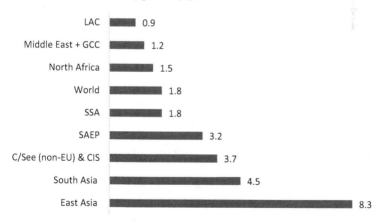

Figure 17.4 Productivity gains in the Arab region in the 2000s in comparison to the rest of the world

Source: ILO (2012).

Note: LAC: Latin America and Caribbean, GCC: Gulf Cooperation Council, SSA: Sub-Saharan Africa, SEAP: South East Asia and Pacific, C/See: Central and South Eastern Europe, CIS: Commonwealth of Independent States.

Given the preceding discussion on the historical economic performance of the Arab world, it is worthwhile to note that this period coincides with a period that saw the initiation of the economic reforms in most Arab countries starting in the late 1980s and gaining momentum in the 1990s. While this section does not attempt to outline country-specific episodes of policy changes in the Arab world, it is important to emphasize that Arab countries resemble other developing countries in the sense that they had adopted widespread market-based reforms including macroeconomic stabilization, trade liberalization and openness to FDI in line with the Washington consensus. There is a huge volume of literature that has reviewed the nature and effects of such reforms in the Arab world and the consensus is that the Arab countries have failed to fully exploit benefits from partial and half-hearted reforms (see, for example, Hoekman and Zarrouk 2000; Hoekman and Messerlin 2002; Abed 2003; Zarrouk 2003; Nunnenkamp 2004, among others).

Turning on to more recent economic performance, and against the backdrop of deepening and spreading social unrest and civil conflicts within the Arab region, the Arab countries in transition (Egypt, Jordan, Libya, Morocco, Tunisia and Yemen) seem to have maintained macroeconomic stability – growth has remained positive, inflation is in single digits (except for Egypt), and budget deficits in most countries have begun to decline in 2014 (IMF 2014). In Figure 17.5, we present the growth performance of the Arab world as well as MENA countries in comparison to other developing countries between 2010 and 2014, which clearly shows that the MENA-developing countries have witnessed a rebound of growth since it fell in 2010–11 following the Arab spring. However, GDP growth in the Arab world remains remarkably low in comparison to developing countries in East Asia and Latin America. Similarly, we present the growth in GDP per capita and inflation rates in the Arab and MENA regions between 2010 and 2014 in Table 17.2, and it is quite clear that the region as a whole has underperformed in comparison to other developing regions in the world.

Finally, to conclude this sub-section, most Arab countries in transition have by now either initiated or announced ambitious reforms targeting generalized energy subsidies and other current expenditures. These reforms are aimed to create space for better targeted social protection for the poor, and higher spending on

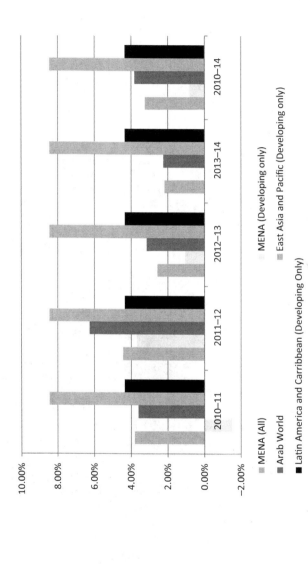

Figure 17.5 Growth in GDP for Arab, MENA and other developing regions, 2010–14

Source: Authors' calculations based on based on World Development Indicators, World Bank.

Note 1: 2010–11, 2011–12, 2012–13 and 2013–14 growth rates represent GDP growth between two respective years.

Note 2: 2010–14 growth rate is the average growth of GDP in the period 2010–14.

infrastructure, healthcare and education. While these are significant first steps in pursuing the medium-term growth agenda, the fact is that progress has been uneven across the Arab world, and reforms of tax policy, civil service and public financial management remain quite slow. Other areas of reform including banking and financial sectors, governance, business climate and labor markets also need immediate attention (IMF 2014).

Macroeconomic profile of Egypt, Morocco and Tunisia

The three countries of Egypt, Morocco and Tunisia constitute some of the key members of the North African sub-region of the Arab world. Bordered on the north by the Mediterranean basin, these three countries have a favorable strategic location at the crossroads of three continents, namely, Africa, Asia and Europe. Arabic is the main official language in each of the three countries, although French is widely used in business and commerce in Tunisia and Morocco, while English is more common in Egypt. Despite having a common language and a similar cultural and religious background, the countries have considerable differences in terms of geographic size as well as sizes and composition of population and standards of living.

When it comes to economic structure, the three countries are again quite similar in the sense that services has the dominant share in GDP for each (48.5 percent for Egypt, 55 percent for Morocco and 59 percent for Tunisia in 2010) (Aboukhdir 2015). With regards to the services sector, financial services, tourism, transport, telecom and information services dominate the scene in each of the three countries. The share of manufacturing in GDP is also very similar for Egypt, Morocco and Tunisia – roughly 16–17 percent in each of the countries. All the three countries are exporters of manufacturing goods and are non-oil dependent countries. Despite these commonalities in their economic structures, there is some evidence that Morocco and Tunisia are relatively more diversified economies than Egypt (see, Aboukhdir 2015 and references therein).

Like many other developing countries, Egypt, Morocco and Tunisia in the 1970s adopted inward-looking import substitution industrialization (ISI) and development strategies actively planned and implemented by the state (Yol 2009; Harrigan and El-Said 2010). However, since the mid-1980s, these countries have continuously attempted to shift their restrictive ISI policy regime toward a more market-oriented regime by adopting trade and investment reforms. Foreign investment in the form of FDI and export-led growth replaced import-substitution industrialization as a result of these unprecedented market-based reforms (Aboukhdir 2015). Since then, the governments in these countries have been undertaking economic reforms with the underlying aim to transform the economies from closed economies into open economies and to expand the role of the private sector. Dillman (2001) notes: 'they started with stabilization programs, followed by structural adjustment, limited privatization, and encouragement of foreign investment'. Further, over the last three decades, these countries, along with pursuing a program of economic reforms based on the Washington consensus, have also seen an active role of the government in emphasizing and encouraging a strong and growing financial system aimed to enhance overall economic growth and to complement the economic reforms by encouraging the strengthening of institutions that would facilitate financing of businesses and commerce (Achy 2005; Mühlberger and Semmelmann 2010).

Industrial productivity in KLEMS format

This section explains the economics of MFP measurement, both from the perspective of an overall economy and industrial sectors.[6] Our focus here is on MFP rather than the widely used labor productivity. The motivation behind this lies in the growing importance and increasing use of the concept in understanding growth dynamics. Improving efficiency of resource usage including labor resource constitutes an important means of enhancing growth which in turn is expected to raise living standards and reduce inequality of earnings and hunger and deprivation of its people. Hulten (2009) argues how income per capita and the closely related output per worker are key determinants of national living standards. He reviews the field of growth accounting and brings out the evolution in the literature in an attempt to explain the historical patterns of these indicators. The concept of MFP is the most important yardstick of overall performance of an economy as it is often an important source of growth in labor productivity.[7] In this context, the seminal work by Jorgenson et al. (1987), which has been recognized as the new framework for productivity measurement, uses growth accounting methods to explain sources of growth, which often are an important aspect of any study of living standards and development. Given this motivation, in this section, we underline the significance of the measure of MFP both from the perspective of understanding output per worker and sources of output growth. We first outline what is meant by MFP and the different methods of measurement of MFP based on both econometric and non-econometric techniques in sections 3.1 and 3.2, respectively. In section 3.3, we discuss the KLEMS framework for measuring productivity, which is followed by a discussion of measurement of MFP growth under this framework in section 3.4 and its data requirements in terms of variables which capture MFP in section 3.5. The final section, section 3.6, highlights the analytical usefulness of using the KLEMS framework in the empirical research of growth dynamics in both advanced and emerging economies.

Measuring MFP

Productivity is a mechanism to convert inputs into output – it is often addressed as a ratio of output to inputs. Further, productivity is a key indicator in the assessment of economic performance of the economy as well as sectors which comprise the economy. The part of economic growth that cannot be explained by increased utilization of capital and labor inputs is measured by MFP. Therefore, economics of productivity remains central to understanding of the forces driving the overall growth of a country.

There are many different productivity measures. The choice between them depends on the purpose of productivity measurement and, in many instances, on the availability of data. Broadly, productivity measures can be classified as single factor productivity measures (relating a measure of output to a single measure of input) or MFP measures (relating a measure of output to a bundle of inputs). Another distinction, of particular relevance at the industry or firm level, is between productivity measures that relate some measure of gross output to one or several inputs and those which use a value-added concept to capture movements of outputs (OECD manual 2001).

Methods of MFP computation

There are four main methodologies used by the various studies to measure MFP growth: (1) Production function Approach (PFA); (2) Stochastic Frontier Approach (SFA); (3) Growth Accounting

Approach (GAA); and (4) Data Envelopment Analysis (DEA), which are broadly classified into two groups – frontier approach and non-frontier approach. The frontier approach identifies the role of technical efficiency in overall firm performance, whereas the non-frontier approach assumes that firms are technically efficient. This difference results in different interpretations of MFP growth under the two approaches. SFA and DEA are frontier approaches, while GAA and PFA non-frontier approaches. These approaches are further categorized according to the estimation techniques: parametric and non-parametric methods. The parametric approach employs econometric technique and, in this approach, the deviation of actual output from the maximum output is decomposed into two parts, viz., the statistical noise and inefficiency. In the parametric method, an explicit functional form is specified for the frontier and the parameters are estimated econometrically using sample data for inputs and output. This implies that the accuracy of the derived estimates is sensitive to the functional form specified. On the other hand, the non-parametric method is parameter free and does not assume any functional form. The major drawback of this method is that no direct statistical tests can be carried out to validate the estimates. PFA and SFA are parametric methods and they directly estimate the parameters of the inputs, while GAA and DEA are non-parametric approaches. In recent times, some researchers have used a modified semi-parametric approach developed by Olly and Pakes (1996) and Levinsohn and Petrin (2003) for estimating MFP. Kathuria et al. (2013), in the context of productivity measurement in Indian manufacturing, found that the MFP estimates based on three different techniques – growth accounting (non-parametric), production function approach accounting for endogeneity (semi-parametric method based on Levinson and Petrin technique) and stochastic production frontier (parametric) – are vastly different from each other.[8]

KLEMS framework

In this section, we discuss in detail the MFP growth estimation methodology in the KLEMS framework, which is based on growth accounting approach. A major advantage of growth accounts is that it is embedded in a clear analytical framework rooted in production functions and the theory of economic growth. It provides a conceptual framework within which the interaction between variables can be analyzed, which is of fundamental importance for policy evaluation. There are three main indices within the growth accounting approach for estimating MFP growth. These are Kendrick arithmetic index, Solow geometric index and the Tornqvist index. In the KLEMS framework, it is desirable to estimate MFP growth using Tornqvist index method. This method considers a Trans Log (TL) functional form of the basic production function. This methodology is developed under standard assumptions of perfect competition, constant return to scale and income shares of the intermediate inputs summing to unity. This method does not assume that technological progress is Hicks-neutral.

Productivity estimates are also sensitive to measurement of variables, besides being sensitive to the specific methodology used. For every variable there are different possible ways to adapt the available data and each of these is liable for criticism. There has been a long debate over the appropriate measurement procedure of output and inputs. Studies on productivity either used gross value-added or value of gross output as an appropriate measure of level of production. The choice between value-added and gross output is critical, as the measures of output determines the choice of factor inputs. Value-added restricts the set of factors of production to labor and capital, while gross output broadens the set by incorporating intermediate inputs (materials, energy and services). Different estimation techniques and measurement procedure of inputs and output have produced a great deal of variation in MFP growth estimates.[9] On the basis of this, we can conclude that the methodology of variable measurement, the specified structure of the production function and MFP growth estimation techniques play a crucial role in productivity growth estimation process.

The MFP estimates computed under the KLEMS framework uses gross output as a measure of level of production incorporating labor, capital as well as intermediate inputs. One advantage of using value of gross output rather than gross value-added is that it incorporates the fact that intermediate inputs (material, energy, services) are as important as factor inputs (labor, capital) in a production process (Gollop and Jorgenson 1980). KLEMS framework not only gives importance to all the intermediate inputs, but it also allows estimating the individual contribution of all inputs in the growth process. It is relevant to mention that the methodology for the construction of factors of production in this framework is also different. KLEMS framework measures labor input adjusting composition information (age, gender and education) instead of total number of person engaged. Capital services in place of capital stock is used which incorporate inter industry as well as over the period asset wise versatility. The detailed discussion on variables construction is undertaken in section 3.4.

MFPG in KLEMS framework

This section deals with the methodology of measurement of MFP growth for individual industries in the KLEMS framework. The methodology developed by Jorgenson and his associates and presented in Jorgenson et al. (2005) is adopted. This methodology has been followed recently in Timmer et al. (2010) for the European Union and the United States.

Let the production function for industry j be denoted by

$$Y_j = f_j(K_j, L_j, E_j, M_j, S_j, A_j) \tag{17.1}$$

where Y is industry gross output, K is capital input, L is labor input, E is energy input, M is material input, S is services input and A is an indicator of technology, all for industry j. All variables vary over time t, but the t subscript is not shown explicitly, for the sake of simplicity. To estimate MFP growth, we begin with the fundamental accounting identity for each industry where the value of output equals the value of inputs,

$$P_{Y,j}Y_j = P_{K,j}K_j + P_{L,j}L_j + P_{E,j}E_j + P_{M,j}M_j + P_{S,j}S_j \tag{17.2}$$

P_Y denotes the price of output, P_K, P_L, P_E, P_M and P_S are the prices of capital, labor, energy, material and services, respectively. Under specific assumptions of constant returns to scale and competitive markets, we can define MFP growth as

$$\Delta \ln A_j^Y = \Delta \ln Y_j - v_{K,j}^Y \Delta \ln K_j - v_{L,J}^Y \Delta \ln L_j$$
$$- v_{E,j}^Y \Delta \ln E_j \quad v_{M,j}^Y \Delta \ln M_j - v_{S,j}^Y \Delta \ln S_j \tag{17.3}$$

where
$v_{i,j}^Y = 0.5\,(v_{i,j,t}^Y + v_{i,j,t-1}^Y)$ is the two period average share of input i (i = K, L, E, M, S).

Data requirements

As mentioned earlier, two types of output measures can be used to calculate MFP: Gross Value-Added (GVA) and Gross Output. In the KLEMS framework, all the participating countries measure MFP using both types of output. The MFP estimates are computed using a value-added production function incorporating labor and capital inputs, while the gross output production function also incorporates other intermediate inputs. The relevant variables are therefore, GVA, GVO, capital (K), labor (L), energy (E), material (M) and service inputs (S).

GVA: Gross value-added of a sector is defined as the value of output less the value of its intermediary inputs. If GVA is used as a measure of output, nominal value-added needs to be converted into real value-added. This conversion can be done with either single deflation (SD) or double deflation (DD) method. It is desirable to use double deflation method as it separately deflated the output with output price index and intermediate inputs with appropriate deflators, while single deflation method deflates nominal value-added by output price index.

Gross output: The gross output of an industry is defined as the value of industry production using primary factors like labor, capital and intermediate inputs purchased from other industries. Nominal value of gross output is deflated by suitable output price index to acquire real value of gross output.

Labor input: In order to construct the labor input series, the majority of the earlier studies have used the total number of persons engaged in the industry as the measure of labor input, while few studies have used total man hours worked or wages and salary bills for estimating labor input. Some studies also made adjustment in labor input incorporating labor quality in terms of training, experience and education level. It is appropriate to estimate the labor input incorporating the composition information (age, gender and education). The measurement of labor composition is essentially an attempt to distinguish one labor type from others taking into account the embodied human capital in each person. The contribution to output by each person also comes from this embodied capital.

Capital input: In the literature of productivity, measurement of capital is considered as the most difficult and complex among all variables. There has been a long debate over the measurement approaches for nature of capital and its role in production. There is no universally accepted method for its measurement and, as a result, several methods have been employed to estimate capital input. Most of the studies follow perpetual inventory method for measuring capital stock as capital input. In KLEMS framework capital services is considered as a measure of capital input for production. For the measurement of capital services we need capital stock estimates for detailed assets and the shares of capital remuneration in total output value.

Intermediate inputs: The KLEMS framework identifies three main categories of intermediate inputs, namely – energy input (E), material input (M) and services input (S). Intermediate inputs are broken down into energy, material and services, based on input output transaction tables. Energy input includes coal, liquefied petroleum gas, petrol, diesel, electricity and lubricants. Material input includes the raw materials, components, chemicals and packing materials during an accounting year. Services input includes all the expenses related to services purchased, such as water supply, transport charges, storage and communication expenses, insurance and banking charges, medical and hotel bills, R&D and education fees. In the case of intermediate inputs, it is important to construct an appropriate deflator for deflating the nominal values of intermediate inputs.

KLEMS based productivity in developed and emerging economies

The KLEMS method of measuring MFP and the data set that it generates for this purpose are meant to support empirical and theoretical research in the area of economic growth as well as facilitate the conduct and analysis of policies aimed at supporting a revival of productivity and competitiveness in both advanced economies as well as emerging markets around the world. These policies require comprehensive measurement tools to monitor and evaluate progress. The construction of the database should also support the systematic production of high-quality statistics on growth and productivity using the methodologies of national accounts and input–output analysis.

In developed countries, studies using KLEMS technique have assessed the industry origins of US–Japan productivity growth (Jorgenson and Nomura 2007), the productivity gap between Europe and the United States (Van Ark et al. 2008), information technology and Japanese growth (Jorgenson and Motohasi 2005), productivity in Japan, the United States and the European Union (Fukao and Miyagawa 2007) and examination of sectoral gaps between the United States, Japan and Germany (Conrad and Jorgenson 1995). The sources of growth at the industry level in several developed countries have also been analyzed (Pyo et al. 2007 for Korea; Jorgenson and Nomura 2005 for Japan; Jorgenson et al. 2007 for the United States). For emerging markets like India, China and several economies of Latin America and East Asia, the development of the KLEMS dataset is still under construction or refinements – notable papers in public domain include productivity growth under varying policy regimes in India (Das et al. 2015), measurement and interpretation of China's MFP 1980–2012 (Harry Wu 2014), structural changes and productivity growth in Thailand (Srihuang 2015).[10]

We conclude that for the developed world, several research papers have been published on the international comparison of Japan and the United States, the United States and the European Union. These papers examine several aspects of the overall growth comparison–productivity gap between two countries or competitiveness across industrial sectors of two different countries thereby exploring the quality data set that exists for such comparisons. For emerging countries, examining industry origins of overall growth is perhaps the first quality research on an important topic like this that is made possible by the construction of KLEMS dataset.[11]

Growth and productivity in the Arab world – Egypt, Morocco and Tunisia

It is well known that economic growth in Arab countries has been weak when compared to other developing regions of the world. Further, there is tremendous diversity in growth performance within the Arab world, ruling out any single factor to account for the poor performance. It is important to figure out what specific factors can account for the regions poor growth record. We find that exogenous shocks, policy failures and institutional deficiencies (Nunnenkamp 2004) are some of the factors which have been highlighted, though economic policy failure seems to be strongly advocated for the underlying poor growth. However, we also find evidence of the resilience of Arab countries to the global financial crisis during the 2006–07 periods. A study by Aly and Strazicich (2011) finds that out of three selected African countries, while Egypt and Tunisia experienced some transitory effect in economic growth during the financial crisis, Morocco had no significant impact on its economic growth.

In the following sections, we review the literature on growth and productivity in the selected countries – Egypt, Morocco and Tunisia – with a view to review the existing estimates of MFP and examine the deficiencies in the estimates of MFP. In section 4.2 we examine the available data sources for the Arab world – in particular, we utilize information from Total Economy database (TCB) and UNIDO industrial database to compute estimates of productivity and comment on the nature of available data. In the following section, we highlight the challenges in building a KLEMS type data set for Arab world and also prepare a list of minimum variables to have effective comparison of Arab countries in an international perspective.

Growth and productivity in Morocco, Egypt and Tunisia – review of available estimates from select studies

In this section, we review three country studies with respect to Egypt (Morsy et al. 2014), Morocco (Chemingui and Isaksson 2007) and Tunisia (Chaffai et al. 2006) to examine the nature of productivity estimates and their implications for analyzing growth and productivity. The three countries chosen are Arab countries in transition and belong to the MENA sub-category as defined in section 2. As noted earlier, despite a challenging internal socio-political environment, the three countries have broadly maintained macroeconomic stability.

The paper by Chemingui and Isaksson (2007) attempts to estimate and analyze productivity change at the economy level for Morocco. The time period extends till 2000 beginning 1960. Two measurement methods to compute MFP have been used – Solow sources of growth and DEA techniques. The study finds a significant contribution of MFP as a source of economic growth.[12] Further, capital grew much faster than labor input during the entire period. The paper also reports data on labor productivity, capital deepening and overall MFP – computed via growth accounting and DEA techniques. In addition, overall MFP computed by DEA method is decomposed into technical change and technical efficiency. Taking the full period into consideration, we find annual change in technical efficiency to be positive and outweighing the negative contribution of technical progress and accounting for positive MFP in the period. The paper further highlights several factors that could account for poor trends in productivity performance – policy failure, weak infrastructure, high tariffs and inefficient financial set up as possible determinants.

Based on a careful review of the paper, we make the following observations. First, the paper uses an outdated method for accounting and analyzing an important phenomenon like economic growth. The building of a KLEMS-type data set instead will allow for more sophisticated analysis of MFP (as well as sources of growth) both at the aggregate and disaggregate sectoral level, thereby allowing us to understand the industry origins of both MFP and growth. Second, the paper does not undertake a detailed explanation of the sources of data for constructing the MFP estimates using two alternative methods. In addition, the construction of capital input is listed as a reference without any details, though some discussion of income shares of labor is made in the paper. Third, the paper does not undertake any rigorous econometric analysis of explaining the determinants of poor trends in observed productivity, except for a descriptive account of possible factors.

The study on Tunisian manufacturing (Chaffai et al. 2006) attempts to explain if MFP in manufacturing is converging or catching up with OECD countries. The period of study is from 1983–2002 and covers six manufacturing sub-groups – food processing, electrical and *metal* products, chemical activities, textile clothing and leather, building materials and ceramics and miscellaneous products. The industrial sector covers around 18 percent of Tunisian GDP. The MFP calculation is based on a basic neoclassical growth model with constant returns. The dataset is from the Institute National De la Statistique (INS) and derives from National Accounts.[13] The MFP growth rates show varied performances among the subsectors and changes in inputs have been important. The authors also undertake a decomposition of MFP into between sectors and within sectors (Bernard and Jones 1996) and find that within sector performance accounts for a large percentage of total manufacturing gains. The paper also makes an attempt to examine an international MFP convergence between Tunisia and other OECD countries.

The following observations should be noted. First, the paper uses outdated Solow growth accounting for explaining economic growth and the data set is confined to only labor and capital and thereby does not take into account the role of intermediate inputs – notably energy in accounting for observed MFP in manufacturing. The construction of capital input does not take into account the services of capital and uses perpetual inventory method. Second, the paper is weak in the estimation and analysis of observed productivity and does not make any attempt to use the industry origins of aggregate MFP growth thereby disregarding the benefits of a disaggregated approach. Third, the analysis of the observed MFP is undertaken with a narrow focus on studying whether there is a catch up to OECD levels – only four sectors show a decrease in MFP gap when compared to the efficient subsets of OECD countries.

The final paper is on Egypt (Morsy et al. 2014), which attempts to understand why growth in Egypt failed to raise labor productivity (as a proxy for overall productivity). For labor productivity calculations, real GDP data is from the Ministry of Planning and International Cooperation (MPIC). Further, the annual employment data is obtained from Egypt's annual labor force survey carried out by CAPMAS.[14] The study covers nine sectors of Egypt's economy covering agriculture as well as manufacturing along with selected services sub-groups. The study highlights that Egypt's productivity gaps across sectors are high, thereby suggesting that structural transformation in the form of redistribution of labor is desirable. The decomposition of labor productivity growth shows large disparities between within sectors and reallocation effects. The study concludes that no large-scale labor reallocation from low to high productivity sectors has taken place within Egypt's economy, but at the same time some low value-added sectors have expanded at the expense of more productive sectors thereby lowering overall productivity in the economy.

The paper attempts to identify the reasons why Egypt's economic growth has not been able to address issues of unemployment and poverty in Egypt. Our review of the paper raises the following observations. First, the paper is on growth performance but measures labor productivity and then comments on the weak nature of growth. To comment whether growth is weak or strong, one needs estimates of MFP unless it justifies a link between labor productivity and growth, which the paper does not and this forms a major drawback of the paper. Second, an attempt is also made to link structural transformation pattern observed in Egypt's economy to labor reallocation aspects using the decomposition of labor productivity to between and within sector effects. Third, an econometric evaluation of structural change is attempted with a few chosen indicators of the macroeconomic environment.

In concluding the review of the three papers on the three countries, it may be pointed out that these three countries have adopted market-oriented reforms in the recent past beginning in the early 1990s. As noted in section 2, when it comes to economic policy, Egypt, Morocco and Tunisia have witnessed a gradual liberalization of both the external sector and internal reforms resulting in a strong growing financial and economic system. Overall, we conclude the following criticisms with regard to estimating and evaluating productivity in the Arab region in general based on our review of the three countries from the MENA sub-region.

(1) Given the background, understanding the sources of growth in these economies by a carefully executed method of MFP estimation becomes essential for a rigorous analysis of growth. In this respect most of the studies either use a Solow growth accounting or DEA analysis based on labor and capital, thereby ignoring a gross output based KLEMS-type production process which allows analysis on aspects such as labor quality, innovation and role of intermediate inputs in the growth process.

(2) The questions of addressing industry origins of aggregate productivity growth have been largely ignored in the studies mentioned on account of non-availability of detailed disaggregated information on the broad sectors of the economy. In this way, we could capture not only which industries contribute most to the aggregate productivity growth but also which industries contribute most to the increased use of labor and capital as well as intermediate inputs. In accounting for productivity improvements, however, this forms a major limitation of the reviewed studies in analyzing productivity changes.

(3) Estimates of productivity computed using sophisticated methods like the KLEMS approach helps understand the sectoral dynamics within the overall aggregate economy numbers. However, except for Tunisia, none of the other studies focus on explaining manufacturing productivity. The papers on Morocco and Egypt confine the studies to aggregate economy, thereby ignoring many questions which are important to understanding the economics of observed productivity growth in Arab countries especially related to manufacturing activity.

(4) None of the studies elaborate on the database they use to compute the productivity estimates. It is well known that productivity estimates are sensitive to measurement of labor and capital even when using a value-added approach in the conventional growth accounting methods. In the paper on Egypt, mention is made of the CAPMAS and other data sources used to quantify labor productivity estimates, whereas in the other papers on Morocco and Tunisia, some aspects of database especially in the context of input measurement need to be more explicit. The databases which form the core of the research papers need to be elaborated more in order to understand the extent of richness and quality that exists in data sources.

(5) All the three papers outline possible determinants of observed productivity performance (economy level – Egypt and Morocco, and manufacturing level – Tunisia); however, none of them attempt a rigorous examination using a quantitative framework – econometric analysis to ascertain links between possible determinants on the one hand and productivity on the other hand. This forms a possible drawback in evaluating the trends in observed productivity.

In conclusion, it can be seen from the limited review of literature that two core problems exist – one is methodology of estimating productivity – moving away from standard Solow aggregate function approach to a KLEMS-based disaggregate production function approach and, secondly, exploring the data sources available to undertake such sophisticated MFP estimates. Unless these are resolved, there will remain some level of skepticism on the studies examining the empirical dynamics of Arab countries economic growth.

KLEMS-based MFP estimates in Arab countries – exploring data availability

Analysis of growth relies on a good measurement of MFP – be it at the economy level or sectoral level as it is often seen that MFP plays an important role in explaining economic growth. Further, it also allows comparison of growth slowdown or enhancement between regions using estimates of MFP (Van Ark et al. 2008). In case of our three Arab countries, as noted in section 2, we find evidence that growth has been weak and poor integration of the Arab world to the global economy has hindered its growth prospects and will continue to do so unless the quality of domestic policies improves integration of this region to the global world. Fundamental to increasing growth here is the role of MFP and, unless we have good measurement of MFP estimates, the foundations of any analysis of observed growth will have its limitations.

Our focus here is on the application of growth accounting (GA) methodology to estimate MFP growth. The GA methodology has undergone several sophistications since the 1950s since the seminal work of Tinbergen (1942), Solow (1957), Denison (1962) and Jorgenson and Griliches (1967). Jorgenson et al. (1987) allocated the sources of US economic growth to the level of individual industries, by allowing MFP estimation at the level of individual industries, based on a KLEMS production function. This in turn allowed growth contributions of capital (K), labor (L), energy (E), material (M) and services (S) inputs as well as the composition of these inputs to identify quality changes. This has opened avenues for comparative productivity comparison across countries based on disaggregated sectors. Further, it has also allowed examination of productivity gaps between regions (the United States and Europe, the United States and Japan) to determine the drivers of productivity change at the sectoral levels across countries or group of countries.

Given this background, our attempt in this section is therefore to explore the databases available for the Arab region to undertake estimation of MFP estimates for Arab economies at the industry level. In addition, these estimates will allow comparison across Arab countries as well as undertaking rigorous examination of drivers of productivity growth. To this effect, we list two data sources – the Total Economy Database provided for select Arab countries by The Conference Board (hereafter TCB) and the UNIDO databases (UNIDO industrial database and UNIDO productivity database).[15] The first set of estimates cover the aggregate economy and the second set of estimates cover industrial sectors at ISIC2, 3 and 4 digit levels of disaggregation on major indicators of industrial performance.

TCB database: TCB provides data on productivity at three levels: (1) labor productivity as captured by the ratio of output to labor input, (2) MFP based on growth accounting technique along with estimates of labor and capital inputs' contribution to observed GDP growth. The primary inputs are further classified into labor quality and labor quantity and capital services – ICT as well as non-ICT, and (3) regional information on GDP, employment (and labor productivity) and MFP for 21 regions covering the period 1990–2015. Of the three different data sets, the longest time series is available for indicators on labor productivity, whereas the other subsets confine to the period 1990–2015. The database is for aggregate economy level and covers several countries in Africa including Egypt, Morocco and Tunisia. We present below some estimates compiled from TCB database below.

For the aggregate economy as a whole we were able to present labor productivity and MFP growth rates for the period 1990–2014 and sub-periods 1990–99 and 2000–14 for our three MENA countries – Egypt, Morocco and Tunisia (see Figures 17.6 and 17.7). We find evidence of higher labor productivity growth in Tunisia among the three countries under study. However, in case of MFP both the region as a whole and Egypt and Morocco have poor growth performance, the exception being Tunisia. In Tunisia, also we experienced a decline in growth rate in the second half of 2000s. The lack of industry level (as well disaggregated sectoral) information inhibits any serious examination of sources of low productivity growth at the aggregate level.

However, TCB database allows examining the economics of productivity change at the aggregate level by decomposing factor inputs into labor quality and employment and taking into consideration the role of ICT and non-ICT capital inputs in accounting for aggregate value-added growth at the economy level. Using the data available, we were able to construct graphs of yearly growth rate in the following variables – labor quality, employment proxied by labor persons and both ICT and non-ICT capital services and MFP growth for selected economies of Arab world – Egypt, Morocco and Tunisia.

Figure 17.8 highlights several interesting points. First, for all the selected countries we find evidence of sharp year-to-year variations in growth rates across all variables. Second, in case of labor person growth, while Egypt and Tunisia show the same pattern of growth, there are tremendous jumps and declines in the Morocco employment growth rate. Third, all three countries show a decline in labor quality in the 2000s; whereas for Tunisia the sharp decline occurs only around 2011, the trend for the other two begins in the early 2000s and stabilizes by the end of 2010. Fourth, for capital services, it is evident that there has been a spurt in growth for all three countries; however, ICT capital services growth rates are better

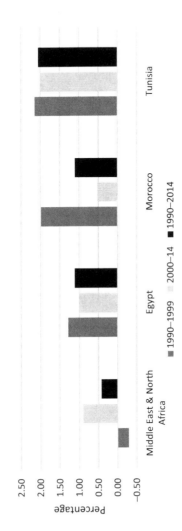

Figure 17.6 Decade-wise labor productivity growth for Egypt, Morocco, Tunisia and Middle East and North Africa, 1990–2014

Source: Author's calculation based on TCB database.

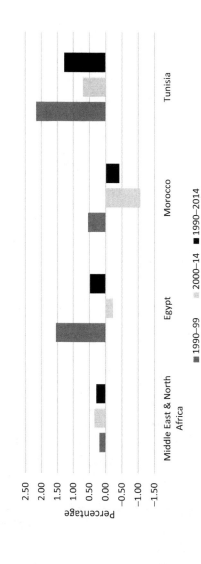

Figure 17.7 Decade-wise MFP growth for Egypt, Morocco, Tunisia and Middle East and North Africa, 1990–2014

Source: Author's calculation based on TCB database.

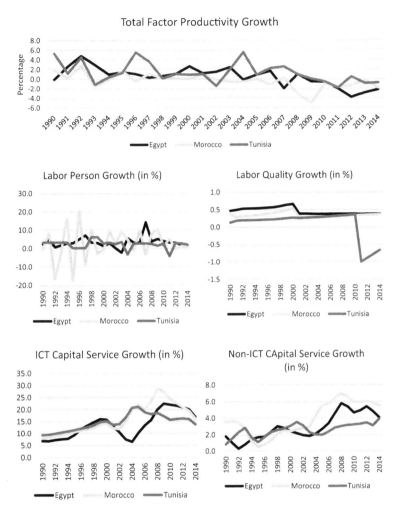

Figure 17.8 MFP growth and input growth for Egypt, Morocco and Tunisia, 1990–2014

Source: Author's calculation based on TCB database.

than non-ICT capital services for the countries. Fifth, as regards MFP, there is no discernible pattern available as there is evidence of sharp yearly fluctuation across the three countries.

The TCB forms a rich and quality database encompassing the framework of productivity measurement; however, growth accounting is based on the value-added approach and not on the KLEMS framework of productivity measurement (Jorgenson et al. 1987). The estimates at productivity change at aggregate level do not allow any serious examination of sources of economic growth and especially assessing the industry origins of aggregate MFP growth.

UNIDO industrial database: This database is the only comparable database across countries of the world – emerging as well as developing. It maintains data at ISIC (international standard industrial classification) sectorial level and provides disaggregated data on industrial sectors for the following indicators – number of establishments, number of employees, wages and salaries, output, value-added, gross fixed capital formation and number of female employees. Further, these variables are available for more than 150 manufacturing sectors and subsectors. It would be important to point out that data available does not allow for any sophisticated measurements of MFP. The only measure which perhaps can be constructed with the available information is the output/value-added-based measures of labor productivity. However, this does not seem feasible unless one has price deflators for the disaggregated sectors/subsectors of the industries. Further, it may not be available at detailed ISIC REV 3 or REV 4 for many countries present in the database thereby raising serious concerns for using UNIDO database for any serious research on aspects of productivity growth in developing and emerging world including African and Arab regions and their sub-regions. We undertook a detailed examination of the data availability for few variables – output, value-added, number of employees and gross fixed capital formation (as a crude proxy for capital stock) and find that, except for Morocco, the data availability for Egypt and Tunisia does not allow any examination of issues connected to growth and productivity.

The UNIDO industrial statistics can be a rich data source for comparative analysis of productivity performance at the industry level for various regions and countries, if some additional variables are constructed to allow meaningful estimates of MFP and partial productivities across countries on selected industrial categories. We need sophisticated measurements of both primary inputs – labor and capital as well as intermediate inputs (energy, materials and services) as such inputs account for a significant role in MFP growth. The rich UNIDO database by industries can be a formidable data source for our examination and understanding of issues connected related to aggregate growth and MFP at the economy level and finding linkages to industry details as possible explanations for sources of aggregate growth.

UNIDO productivity database: We now examine the third data source in our attempt to examine the data sources for undertaking MFP research in Arab countries. This new unique database for 112 countries contains variables which allow us to estimate levels and growth rates of aggregate productivity numbers. The three selected Arab countries are listed as developing countries in the database. Multiple measures of MFP growth are provided in the World Productivity Database based on growth accounting, frontier analysis and regression analysis. We concentrate on the growth accounting method of measuring MFP in order to compare this with the TCB measures of productivity. Four measures are highlighted including Hicks and Harrod neutral technical change and dynamic growth accounting inclusive of Hicks and Harrod technical changes.[16] We present some estimates of aggregate MFP using data for our chosen countries – Egypt, Morocco and Tunisia in Figures 17.9 and 17.10.

In addition, we could also compile some crude measure of partial productivities – capital per workers and income per worker for selected countries. The database for these variables is for large time points beginning in 1960 and thus allows for a significant time series database to observe how these measures have behaved over large periods of time for the countries. The details of the construction of labor input including schooling and health as well as capital input are covered in the overview of the database.

Our assessment of three different data sources in the context of measuring MFP for Arab countries at the disaggregate industry level indicates the dearth of quantitative as well as qualitative database for undertaking any examination of the empirics of growth and productivity for developing countries from the Arab world – the assessment of how input and MFP growth of each industry contributes to aggregate value-added or even output. In particular, the absence of data pertaining to industry level for crucial variables like employment – and its division into age, gender and education; capital – machines and equipment and software/hardware does not allow us to make any conjectures on which industries contribute most to aggregate productivity growth or which industries contribute more to use of software/hardware (read ICT capital) and skills of labor. This information could be rich data sources for examining sources of growth especially in the context of Arab world. The

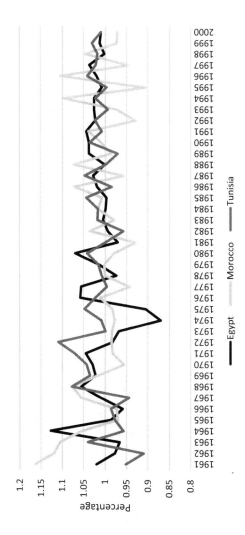

Figure 17.9 MFP growth for Egypt, Morocco and Tunisia, 1960–2000

Source: Author's calculation based on UNIDO productivity database.

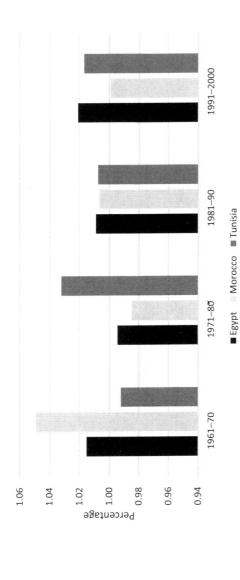

Figure 17.10 Decade-wise MFP growth for Egypt, Morocco and Tunisia, 1960–2000

Source: Author's calculation based on UNIDO productivity database.

seminal work by Angus Maddison[17] on *Growth and Modernity in World Economy* could be taken forward with the help of such database which understands and allows for examination of aggregate productivity through its industry roots.

The challenges of building an Arab KLEMS dataset

As indicated earlier in the chapter, the KLEMS dataset comprises the new framework for understanding growth and productivity.[18] The genesis of KLEMS dataset started with the development of EU KLEMS database for understanding the productivity differential between the United States and Europe. As of now, such databases are available for over 40 countries around the world comprising developing and emerging countries of Asia, Latin America and the developed world – the United States, Japan, Canada, Korea and member countries of Europe. The EU KLEMS database made it possible to analyze many issues which are pertinent to the modern world economy – the role of high skilled labor as well as information technology in driving growth. In addition, issues such as productivity growth versus capital accumulation in accounting for economic growth in the developing world (Krugman hypothesis for East Asian countries) in emerging market economies like India and China.

The EU KLEMS database has largely been constructed on the basis of data from national statistical institutes (NSIs) and processed according to harmonized procedures. These procedures were developed to ensure international comparability of the basic data and to generate growth accounts in a consistent and uniform way. Cross-country harmonization of the basic country data has focused on a number of areas including a common industrial classification and the use of similar price concepts for inputs and outputs but also consistent definitions of various labor and capital types. Importantly, this database is rooted in statistics from the National Accounts and follows the concepts and conventions of the System of National Accounts (SNA) framework, and its European equivalent (ESA), in many respects (O' Mahony and Timmer 2009).

To develop a KLEMS-type database[19] for the Arab world in general, and the three MENA countries under study in particular, we need to construct the following variables in order to examine sources of growth and MFP. We need information on output and inputs for any estimation of productivity. KLEMS dataset provides measures of output both in terms of value-added and gross output.

This needs to be supplemented by constructing for inputs – labor, capital and intermediate inputs (energy, materials and services). The KLEMS database provides data at detailed industry level, but also for other breakups – total economy, market economy, market services, non-market services, total goods production, etc.[20] All aggregations of output and input volumes across industries use Tornqvist quantity index. The variables covered can be split into two main groups: (1) labor productivity variables and (2) MFP productivity variables. The first category includes data needed to construct labor productivity (output per hour worked) – nominal and real series of output and employment. The variables belonging to the second category are also referred to as 'growth accounting variables' and are not always directly available from national accounts data without additional assumptions – time series of capital services, labor services and MFP. These series are based on a theoretical model of production and require some additional assumptions.

There are several challenges to building an Arab KLEMS dataset – output measurement and input measurements. The output series is primarily taken from NA sources. It has been observed that measurement challenges are more severe for output from services than for goods production. Further, converting nominal values of outputs, both goods and services,[21] lies in establishing a price series at disaggregate industry levels.[22] For construction of intermediate inputs, we need the supply-use tables (SUT) and the National Accounts information to arrive at the estimates of material, energy and services inputs at the level of individual industries.[23]

Primary inputs: Labor and capital offers multiple challenges in providing accurate measurement of these inputs. At the international level labor accounts in the EU KLEMS deal with information on (1) the quantity (persons and working hours) and (b) the quality (distribution of quantities by age, gender and education level) of labor input by industry. In the backdrop of this requirement it would be important to assess the nature of data available on the quantity and quality of labor in the context of Arab countries. The capital flow accounts of the Arab KLEMS should be akin to that of EU KLEMS,[24] and therefore these need to be prepared using concepts and methods same as or similar to those adopted for EU KLEMS. Therefore, quantity indices of capital input have to be constructed and time series on the values of capital compensation (at current prices) have to be built for various industries comprising the individual Arab economies. A distinction is to be made between ICT (information and communication technology) capital input and non-ICT capital input and the corresponding capital compensation for these two categories of capital inputs, as done for EU KLEMS. Thus, six variables of interest are: (1) CAP: Capital Compensation (in local currency million); (2) CAPIT: ICT Capital Compensation (in local currency million); (3) CAPNIT: Non-ICT Capital Compensation (in local currency million); (4) CAP_QI: Capital services, volume index (2000 = 100); (5) CAPIT_QI: ICT Capital services, volume index (2000 = 100) (6) CAPNIT_QI: Non-ICT Capital services, volume index (2000 = 100)

Intermediate inputs: A major objective of the KLEMS database is to provide productivity estimates at the industry level using the gross output production function with capital, labor and intermediate inputs as inputs and covering the entire economy of a country. For the construction of intermediate inputs, especially energy, material and services, it builds upon a time series of Supply and Use tables (SUTs). This time series of SUTs traces the supply and use of all commodities in the economy as well as the payments for primary factors, labor and capital. Jorgenson et al. (2005) give a schematic presentation of the two tables (see p. 100). The Supply or Make table indicates for each industry the composition of its output by product (or commodity). This table is used to derive industry gross output indices using the Tornqvist formula. The USE table indicates for each industry the product composition of its intermediate inputs and value-added components. This data is used to calculate the intermediate input index and the input weights for growth accounting (see Timmer et al. 2010).

Arab KLEMS database in an international perspective – minimum list of variables

The requirements of the Arab KLEMS database appear to be quite stringent compared to the available data in the public domain on the one hand and, on the other, KLEMS-based MFP where at the detailed industry, as the role of intermediate inputs in production is fully acknowledged is the most sophisticated estimation procedure. Further, 'Domar' aggregation of KLEMS productivity estimates across industries provides an accurate picture of the contributions of industries to aggregate MFP change. Finally, the benefit of developing a KLEMS framework is to be a part of the world KLEMS database network and in turn be able to undertake international comparison of growth and productivity of the Arab world with other regions of the world as well as within the Arab economies.

Our first priority in building an Arab KLEMS dataset is to explore how many subsectors are feasible within the overall economy in order to capture industry details. KLEMS datasets have allowed disaggregation of the overall economy into sectors producing goods and services, and a further disaggregation of services into market services and non-market services. The goods production industries have been further declassified as (1) consumer manufacturing (food products, textiles including leather and footwear, and manufacturing not elsewhere classified such as recycling; (2) intermediate manufacturing (wood, paper, coke, chemicals, rubber and plastic, non-metallic products, basic metals); (3) investment goods (machinery, transport); (4) electrical machinery including post and communication; and (5) other goods production – mining, electricity, construction and agriculture). We however find that different country KLEMS database have adopted this framework to create own industrial classifications.[25]

Second, we specify below the list of variables that we need to develop, in order to have meaningful estimates of MFP and an examination of the underlying estimates. Two types of estimates – labor productivity and MFP – have been arrived at using the KLEMS dataset in various countries. For the first category, we need the following variables: (1) gross output in current and constant prices, (2) gross value-added at current and constant prices, (3) compensation of employees, operating surplus and taxes minus subsidies in production, (4) number of persons engaged (thousands), (5) number of employees (thousands), (6) total hours worked by persons engaged (millions) and (7) total hours worked by employees (millions). In addition to construct measures of labor quality, we need information by gender (M or F), information by age (age classes can be decided) and educational attainments (number of categories can be decided).

To construct measures of MFP, we need labor accounts as discussed above and also variables representing capital input. The KLEMS capital accounts are in terms of capital services as opposed to capital stock, which is widely used in productivity studies. The assets covered by EU KLEMS capital accounts are fixed assets as defined in ESA 95 with the exception of inventories, land and natural resources. To maintain consistency with EU KLEMS, the estimates of capital stock for industries should provide break-up into ICT and non-ICT capital and further break-up into seven types of assets: three types of assets belonging to ICT capital, (1) office and computing equipment, (2) communication equipment and (3) software; and four types of assets belonging to non-ICT capital, (1) transport equipment, (2) other machinery and equipment, (3) residential buildings and (4) non-residential structures. Considerable difficulties are likely to be faced in constructing capital stock series for various industries with this level of asset type details. Therefore, we need to explore the availability of information across different Arab countries and decide on some common asset type on which information may be easily available.

Further, KLEMS dataset also requires current and constant prices of intermediate inputs energy, material and services as inputs. Whether it will be possible to construct series of intermediate inputs by industry groups will be dictated by the availability of Supply-Use Tables (SUTs). In EU KLEMS, these were generally available on a frequent basis from 1995 onward for many countries but not in the period before. In many countries like India, SUT tables are only available for benchmark years and thus an interpolation is necessary to create a consistent time series of intermediate inputs.

In summary, we have identified in this section the variables that need to be constructed in order to have MFP estimates by industry for Arab economies. Toward this end, we suggest the following phase-wise creation of the Arab KLEMS dataset:

STEP 1: Identify all data sources within the Arab world that are already in the public domain in consultation with statistical agencies which prepare National Accounts.
STEP 2: Create a list of subsectors of overall economy within Arab economies and one that also allows international comparison at broad sectoral levels.
STEP 3: Create estimates of labor productivity by industry.
STEP 4: Create MFP by industry using a value-added specification of production function and incorporate sophisticated measurement of labor and capital inputs.
STEP 5: Create MFP by industry using a gross output specification of production function and incorporating sophisticated measurement of labor and capital inputs as well as intermediate inputs.

Conclusions

The chapter attempted to explore aspects of productivity dynamics in the Arab world and assess the challenges for estimating MFP productivity using the MENA (sub-region of the Arab countries) countries of Egypt, Morocco and Tunisia as a particular case. Estimation of MFP is at the heart of understanding growth paradigm and the effects of economic reforms on growth and development. Therefore, we attempted to explore the possibility of empirically estimating MFP using a KLEMS framework for the MENA countries of Egypt, Morocco and Tunisia. This in turn has set the context for estimation of MFP for the Arab world and allowed us to identify the challenges and lay a roadmap for an Arab KLEMS database. Our review of select empirical papers points to use of old and outdated techniques for measuring MFP. This in turn does not allow a serious as well as a rigorous analytical examination of the empirics of growth – an issue we found to be of utmost significance in the context of Arab economies given their attempts at transition to a new socio-economic and politico-economic order.

There are several challenges in attempting KLEMS-type MFP estimation. The core of this challenge lay in constructing a KLEMS data set available now for more than 40 economies in both developed and emerging markets like India and China. The requirements of constructing both primary and intermediate inputs for Arab KLEMS database appear to be quite stringent compared to the available data in the public domain. The majority of the countries where this dataset has been developed or work is in progress have drawn heavily from the National Accounts of all individual countries. In addition, these variables have been constructed in active association with the national statistical institutes.

We have outlined a phased manner of development of the Arab KLEMS dataset. It may be important to point out that the dataset may need to be structured around a few strong assumptions and also allow for building a time series when no consistent yearly data are available through the technique of interpolation, while there may be costs involved on those account which may question the quality and accuracy of the dataset, but the potential benefits in the long run through the availability of data which allows serious examination of growth dynamics in the Arab world are too enormous to be bogged down by some data shortcomings.

Notes

1 According to the global competitiveness index (2014–15), Morocco (72), Tunisia (87) and Egypt (119) rank lowly among a group of 144 countries (see Global Competitive Report, World Economic Forum).

We also find that the UAE (12), Qatar (16) and Saudi Arabia (24) are the three top Arab countries in this list.
2 http://millenniumindicators.un.org/unsd/methods/m49/m49regin.htm accessed on 1 February 2016.
3 There is no standardized definition of MENA. Different organizations define the region as consisting of different territories. One definition includes a range of non-Arab countries (like Cyprus, Iran and Turkey, among other) along with the standard Arab countries. In this paper, we use MENA as a sub-region of the Arab world, as used in ILO (2012), unless stated otherwise. The ILO (2012) uses the broad term Arab world to include three sub-regions: Middle East (Iraq, Jordan, Lebanon, occupied Palestinian territory (ie West Bank and Gaza), Syria and Yemen), North Africa (Algeria, Egypt, Libya, Morocco, Sudan and Tunisia) and the states of the Gulf Cooperation Council (Bahrain, Kuwait, Qatar, Oman, Saudi Arabia and the United Arab Emirates). In contrast, the World Bank excludes Sudan from MENA and includes Djibouti, Iran and Israel along with the rest of the states included in the ILO definition above. Further, according to World Bank, the Arab world comprises Algeria, Bahrain, Comoros, Djibouti, Egypt, Iraq, Jordan, Kuwait, Lebanon, Libya, Mauritania, Morocco, Oman, Qatar, Saudi Arabia, Somalia, Sudan, Syrian Arab Republic, Tunisia, United Arab Emirates, West Bank and Gaza, and Yemen.
4 With the exception of Latin America.
5 However, the ILO notes: 'The significance of the relatively high value of employment-to-output elasticity should not be overstated in a context where informality plays an important role. In the presence of rapidly increasing labour supply, it is not surprising to find high employment growth, to some extent irrespective of output growth. This is because in the end jobseekers need to be employed somewhere, and, if they end up in the informal economy, their contribution to output growth will be understated. Under such labour surplus conditions, changes in the labour market take place mainly through low quality of jobs and employment at low wages' (ILO 2012).
6 See Tangen (2002), for an understanding of productivity as a concept.
7 See Hulten (2001) for an elaborate history of MFP concept.
8 Kathuria et al. (2013) compare different productivity estimation techniques on the basis of seven different key factors between two study periods 1994–2000 and 2001–05, and found that all methodologies have some limitations.
9 Diewrt (2015) presents some new insights in the gross value-added versus gross output based production function and implications for MFP measurements.
10 For an update on country studies from Asia, see the presentations made at the 3rd ASIA KLEMS conference in Taipei in August 2015.
11 See the presentations made in the 2nd World KLEMS conference at Harvard University, August 2012 on selected countries to have an idea of research issues from emerging economies of Latin America.
12 For capital measurement issues, the paper refers to Isaksson (2006). The labor input is measured as total labor force.

13 A value-added production function with labor and capital stock is used. The capital stock is computed using perpetual inventory method. The sensitivity of MFP to different depreciation rates has also been taken into consideration.
14 Several alternative sources are used for international comparison: GGDC-10 sector database; GGDC-African sector database for Sub-Saharan Africa as well as socio-economic accounts from World Input–Output databases.
15 UNIDO also publishes world productivity indicators for around 40 countries of the Sub-Saharan Region. For details, see Isaksson (2006).
16 For details, see Isaksson (2006).
17 See the seminal work by Maddison (2005).
18 See Jorgenson (2009) for a brief history of productivity measurement.
19 See the chapter titled 'The EU KLEMS database' in Timmer et al. (2010), for an appraisal of data requirement for constructing a KLEMS dataset. One can also refer O' Mahony and Timmer (2009) for detailed aspects of KLEMS data creation.
20 The EU KELMS database was constructed for a 'minimum list' of industries. This was necessitated due to variations in level of details across countries, industries and variables due to data limitations in different countries. This minimum ensures comparison across countries. MFP information is provided for 14 EU countries and Hungary, Slovenia and Czech Republic (NEW EU countries) and Australia, Japan and the United States. The MFP dataset consists for 31 industrial sectors. For all other countries, labor productivity database has been compiled for 62 industries.
21 See the discussion of services sector output measurement in O'Mahony and Timmer (2009).
22 It may be noted that GDP for Arab countries is available by (1) total commodity-producing sectors – agriculture, hunting, forestry and fishing, mining and quarrying, manufacturing, construction, and electricity, gas and water; (2) total productive services sector – trade, restaurants and hotels, transport, storage and communications, financing, banking and insurance; and (3) total social services sectors – accommodation, government services and others. Also, see El-Khoury (2012), National accounts of Arab countries: selected indicators, contemporary Arab Affairs.
23 It may be a good idea to explore and understand the construction of intermediate inputs from different country perspectives. EU KLEMS database, LA KLEMS database, India KLEMS as well as China KLEMS databases as different countries make an attempt to follow the EU KLEMS method while at the same time recognizing the limitations of SUT tables in their own countries.
24 See Van Ark et al. (2007).
25 The India KLEMS database consists for 26 subsectors of the overall economy. However, the number of subsectors for which basic output, input and productivity data has been compiled varies across different countries. See EU KLEMS sub-classifications: EU-25, EU-15, EU-10 and Euro zone. Similarly, the different LA countries have different subsectors for the overall economy.

Bibliography

Abed, G. T. 2003. "Unfulfilled Promise: Why the Middle East and North African Region Has Lagged in Growth and Globalization." *Finance & Development* 40(1): 10–14.

Aboukhdir, A. A. 2015. "Foreign Direct Investment, Economic Growth and the Role of Financial System Development: Findings From the North African Region." Unpublished PhD Thesis, Aberystwyth University, January.

Achy, L. 2005. "Financial Liberalization, Saving, Investment and Growth in MENA Countries." In S. Neaime and N. A. Colton (eds.), *Money and Finance in the Middle East: Missed Opportunities or Future Prospects?* Research in Middle East Economics, vol. 6. Amsterdam: Emerald Group Publishing Limited, 67–94.

Aly, H. Y., and M. C. Strazicich. 2011. "Global Financial Crisis and Africa: Is the Impact Permanent or Transitory? Time Series Evidence From North Africa." *The American Economic Review*: 577–581.

Bernard, A. B., and C. I. Jones. 1996. "Comparing Apples to Oranges: Productivity Convergence and Measurement Across Industries and Countries." *The American Economic Review*: 1216–1238.

Chaffai, M. E. A., P. Plane, and D. Triki. 2006. "Total Factor Productivity in Tunisian Manufacturing Sectors Convergence or Catch-Up With OECD Members?" Middle East and North Africa Working Paper series no 45, Office of the Chief Economist, The World Bank.

Chemingui, M. A., and A. Isaksson. 2007. "Explaining Productivity Change in Morocco." Staff Working Paper 09/2007, Research and Statistics Branch, UNIDO, Vienna.

Conrad, K., and D. Jorgenson. 1995. "Productivity Levels in Germany, Japan and US." In Dale W. Jorgenson (ed.), *International Comparisons of Productivity Growth*, vol. 2. Cambridge, MA: MIT Press.

Creane, G., R. Goyal, M. Mobarak, and R. Sab. 2006. "Financial Sector Development in the Middle East and North Africa." IMF Working Paper WP/04/201.

Das, D. K., A. Azeez, and P. Chandra. 2015. "Productivity Dynamics in Indian Industries – Input Re-Allocation and Structural Change." *IARIW Conference*, August 23.

Denison, E. F. 1962. *Sources of Economic Growth in the United States and the Alternatives Before Us.* Published by "Committee For Economic Development" as a Supplementary Paper No. 13.

Diewrt, W. E. 2015. "Decompositions of Productivity Growth Into Sectoral Effects." *Journal of Productivity Analysis* 43(3): 367–387.

Dillman, B. 2001. "Facing the Market of North Africa." *Middle East Journal* 55(20): 198–215.

El-Khoury, G. 2012. "Population and Vital Statistics in Arab Countries: Selected Indicators." *Contemporary Arab Affairs* 5(1): 177–183.

Fukao, K., and T. Miyagawa. 2007. "Productivity in Japan, the US, and the Major EU Economies: Is Japan Falling Behind?" *RIETI Discussion Papers Series* 2007-046.

Gollop, F., and D. Jorgenson. 1980. "US Productivity Growth by Industry, 1947–73." In *New Developments in Productivity Measurement*. Chicago: University of Chicago Press, 15–136.

Harrigan, J. R., and H. El-Said. 2010. "The Economic Impact of IMF and World Bank Programs in the Middle East and North Africa: A Case Study of Jordan, Egypt, Morocco and Tunisia, 1983–2004." *Review of Middle East Economics and Finance* 6(2): 1–25.

Hoekman, B. M., and P. Messerlin. 2002. *Initial Conditions and Incentives for Arab Economic Integration: Can the European Community's Success Be Emulated?* Washington, DC: The World Bank.

Hoekman, B. M., and J. Zarrouk. 2000. *Catching Up With the Competition: Trade Opportunities and Challenges for Arab Countries*. Ann Arbor: University of Michigan Press.

Hulten, C. 2001. "Total Factor Productivity – A Short Biography. New Developments in Productivity Analysis." *NBER*.

Hulten, C. 2009. "Growth Accounting." *NBER Working Paper* 15341.

ILO. 2012. *Rethinking Economic Growth: Towards Productive and Inclusive Arab Societies. Lebanon: ILO Regional Office for the Arab States & UNDP Regional Bureau for Arab States*. Geneva: International Labour Organisation Publication.

IMF. 2014. *Arab Countries in Transition: Economic Outlook and Key Challenges*. Washington, DC: IMF.

Isaksson, A. 2006. "The UNIDO World Productivity Database: An Overview." *International Productivity Monitor* 18(1): 38–50.

Jorgenson, D. W. 2009. *The Economics of Productivity*. Cheltenham, Northampton: Edward Elgar.

Jorgenson, D. W., D. Gollop, and K. Vu. 1987. *Productivity and US Economic Growth*. Cambridge, MA: Harvard University Press.

Jorgenson, D. W., and Z. Griliches. 1967. "The Explanation of Productivity Change." *Review of Economic Studies* 34: 249–283.

Jorgenson, D. W., M. S. Ho, and K. J. Stiroh. 2005. *Information Technology and the American Growth Resurgence*. Cambridge, MA: MIT Press.

Jorgenson, D. W., M. S. Ho, and K. J. Stiroh. 2007. "A Retrospective Look at the US Productivity Growth Resurgence." *Journal of Economic Perspectives* 22(1): 3–24.

Jorgenson, D. W., and K. Motohashi. 2005. "Information Technology and the Japanese Economy." *Journal of the Japanese and International Economies* 19(4): 460–481.

Jorgenson, D. W., and K. Nomura. 2005. "The Industry Origins of the US–Japan Productivity Gap." *Economic Systems Research* 19(3): 315–341.

Jorgenson, Dale, and Koji Nomura. 2007. "The Industry Origins of the U.S.-Japan Productivity Gap." *Economic Systems Research*, 19(3): 315–412.

Kathuria, V., R. S. Raj, and K. Sen. 2013. "Productivity Measurement in Indian Manufacturing: A Comparison of Alternative Methods." *Journal of Quantitative Economics* 11(1&2): 148–179.

Levinsohn, J., and A. Petrin. 2003. "Estimating Production Functions Using Inputs to Control for Unobservables." *Review of Economic Studies* 70: 317–341.

Maddison, A. 2005. *Growth and Modernity in World Economy – the Roots of Modernity*. Washington, DC: The American Enterprise Institute.

Messkoub, M. 2008. *Economic Growth, Employment and Poverty in the Middle East and North Africa*. Geneva: International Labour Office.

Morsy, H., A. Levy, and C. Sanchez. 2014. "Growth Without Changing-a Tale of Egypt's Weak Productivity Growth." *Working Paper* no 172, European Bank for Reconstruction and Development.

Muhlberger, M., and M. Semmelmann. 2010. *North Africa-Mediterranean Neighbours on the Rise*. Deutsche: Deutsche Bank Research.

Nunnenkamp, P. 2004. *Why Economic Growth Has Been Weak in Arab Countries: The Role of Exogenous Shocks, Economic Policy Failure and Institutional Deficiencies*. Kiel: Kieler Diskussionsbeitrage.

O'Mahony, M., and M. Timmer. 2009. "Output, Input and Productivity Measures at the Industry Level: The EU KLEMS Database." *The Economic Journal* 119(538): F374–F403.

OECD. 2001. *OECD Productivity Manual*. Paris: OCED.

Olly, G. S., and A. Pakes. 1996. "The Dynamics of Productivity in Telecommunications Equipment Industry." *Econometrica* 64(6): 1263–1297.

Pipitone, V. 2009. "The Role of Total Factor Productivity in Mediterranean Countries." *International Journal of Euro–Mediterranean Studies* 2(1).

Pyo, H. K., K. H. Rhee, and B. Ha. 2007. "Growth Accounting and Productivity Analysis by 33 Industrial Sectors in Korea (1984–2002)." *Productivity in Asia: Economic Growth and Competitiveness*: 113–145.

Solow, R. M. 1957. "Technical Change and the Aggregate Production Function." *The Review of Economics and Statistics*: 312–320.

Srihuang, S. 2015. "Structural Changes and Productivity Growth in Thailand." *3rd ASIA KLEMS Conference*, Taiwan, August.

Tangen, S. 2002. "Understanding the Concept of Productivity." *Proceedings of the 7th Asia Pacific Industrial Engineering and Management Systems Conference (APIEMS2002)*, Taipei.

Timmer, M., R. Inklaar, M. O'Mahony, and B. van Ark. 2010. *Economic Growth in Europe: A Comparative Industry Perspective*. Cambridge: Cambridge University Press.

Tinbergen, J. 1942. *The Dynamics of Business Cycles: A Study in Economic Fluctuations*. London: Routledge and Kegan Paul.

Van Ark, B., M. O'Mahony, and M. P. Timmer. 2008. "The Productivity Gap Between Europe and the United States: Trends and Causes." *The Journal of Economic Perspectives*: 25–44.

Van Ark, B., M. O'Mahony, and G. Ypma. 2007. "The EU KLEMS Productivity Report: An Overview of Results From the EU KLEMS Growth and Productivity Accounts for the European Union." EU Member States and Major Other Countries in the World, Issue No. 1, March.

Wu, H. X. 2014. "China's Growth and Productivity Performance Debate Revisited." *The Conference Board Economics Working Papers*, No. 14-01, January.

Yol, M. A. 2009. "Testing the Sustainability of Current Account Deficits in Developing Economies: Evidence From Egypt, Morocco, and Tunisia." *Journal of Developing Area* 43(1): 177–197.

Zarrouk, J. 2003. "A Survey of Barriers to Trade and Investment in Arab Countries." In *Arab Economic Integration: Between Hope and Reality*, ed. A. Galal and B. Hoekman. Cairo: Egyptian Center for Economic Studies; Washington, DC: Brookings Institution Press.

Part III

India in the new global order
A productivity perspective

Chapter 18

Dynamics of labor productivity in Indian industry
1980–2011

Suresh Chand Aggarwal

Introduction

Many studies (Kochhar et al. 2006; Islam 2008; Papola and Sahu 2012; Chandrasekhar 2015; Erumban et al. 2015; Krishna 2015) have confirmed that a structural transformation has taken place in the Indian economy whereby service sector is now (2015–16) the largest contributor to GDP at basic prices (53.4 percent) and agriculture contributes only 15.4 percent. However, the pace of transformation has been slow in employment, as agriculture still employs 48 percent of the workforce. This kind of duality cannot happen unless there is a simultaneous structural change happening in the sphere of labor productivity.

Labor productivity shows the volume of output produced per unit of labor input (OECD 2016). It is one of the key indicator of economic performance and is described by OECD (2016) as 'an essential driver of changes in living standard'. It however, also, depends on the use of other inputs, such as capital – both physical and intangible – and technical and organizational change. OECD defines labor productivity as GDP per hour worked[1] and its growth is measured in GDP at constant prices in the national currency of the country.

Though labor input is measured in terms of hours worked, in the case of India the data on hours worked are either not available or are of low quality and, hence, labor input is measured in terms of the number of persons.[2] The concept of labor productivity, therefore, used in the present paper is defined as real output per unit of persons employed. The paper is organized as follows: in the second section, we provide a brief discussion of the literature on structural change and labor productivity. In the third section, methodology and dataset are discussed. The next section discusses the behavior of labor productivity – trends and some of its underlying reasons. The analysis on sources of labor productivity and sectoral decomposition is carried next, and finally, the conclusion.

Literature on structural change and labor productivity

OECD (2016) highlights that measurement of labor productivity is important, as its growth is an indicator of economic growth and it also has its impact on unit labor costs, which is used many a times to judge the country's international competitiveness. OECD (2016) also indicates the existence of a paradox whereby the labor productivity in many developed countries has been falling since mid-1990s despite big technological progress, thus bringing labor productivity in to focus. A plausible explanation given is the structural change in the economies in terms of shift from more productive manufacturing toward growth of lower productivity personal services (p. 18).

The story of India's pattern of economic growth and subsequent structural change during different policy regimes has been summarized in many studies (e.g. Jha 2015; Krishna 2015). The GDP growth rate has been quite remarkable during the period 2001–2011 at 7.9 percent, as compared to 5.6 percent during the earlier decade of 1991–2001 (Krishna 2015). The acceleration of growth in the past two decades has been attributed to, among others, substantial policy changes initiated in the early 1990s, and continued through the 2000s. The period of 2001–2011 has been defined as a period of service-led growth in India by some economists (Das et al. 2015; Ghose 2015), as industrial sector grew at 7.8 percent whereas services registered an impressive annual average growth of 9.4 percent. Consequently, this resulted in a structural transformation featured by a larger share of services sector in the overall GDP, and the several aspects of this structural transformation have been analyzed in the literature (Kochhar et al. 2006; Islam 2008; Papola and Sahu 2012; Chandrasekhar 2015; Erumban et al. 2015; Krishna 2015). The GDP share[3] of the primary sector has declined to just 13.94 percent in 2013–14 (at 2004–05 prices), from 29.53 percent in 1990–91. The share of the services sector, on the other hand, has increased from 42.55 percent to 59.93 percent, and the share of the secondary sector decreased from 27.63 to 26.13 percent, with the share of manufacturing decreasing from

15.08 percent to 14.94 percent.[4] Clearly, this structural transformation has bypassed the secondary sector and has been from the primary to the tertiary sector.

Methodology and dataset[5]

This section discusses the methodology for computing labor productivity in the 27 individual industries in the Indian economy. We find out the trend in labor productivity over the period 1980–2011 and estimate its sources of growth. We also use the decomposition method (Fabricant 1942) to find the within-industry productivity growth component and between component to understand the reallocation or structural change between the industries.

Here, labor productivity is defined as real gross output per unit of person employed. From the growth accounting framework, we find that there is a strong and direct relationship of labor productivity growth with growth in total factor productivity (TFP). It is because growth in output basically depends on the growth in inputs and the efficiency with which these inputs are used, known as TFP, and the inputs used are not only labor and capital but also intermediate inputs. Labor productivity and its sources are based on gross output for the 27 industries but the decomposition for the economy is based on the value added[6] concept following OECD.

Labor productivity and its sources

In the gross output framework, let labor productivity be defined as gross output per person employed, $\mathfrak{z}_j = \frac{Y_j}{N_j}$. Let $k_j = \frac{K_j}{N_j}$ be capital intensity or capital input per person. Then equation 18.4 can also be rewritten to decompose the growth rate of industrial labor productivity. Subtracting growth rate of employment (N)[7] from both sides, TFPG can be computed as the difference between labor productivity growth, contribution from capital deepening, contribution of labor composition and of intermediate inputs. Then,

$$\Delta \ln \mathfrak{z}_j = v^Y_{K,j} \Delta \ln k_j + v^Y_{L,j} \Delta \ln LC_j + \bar{v}^Y_{I,j} \Delta \ln II_j + \Delta \ln A^Y_j \quad (18.1)$$

The sources of labor productivity growth are, therefore, change in capital intensity, change in labor composition, change in intermediate inputs and TFP growth (as shown in Equation 18.1).

Decomposition of labor productivity- within and between effects

Following Erumbun et al. (2015), we have attempted a decomposition analysis of the annual change in the level of labor productivity based on gross output function of the 27 industries over the entire period. It has been divided into within industry productivity change, between industry workers reallocation, and a 'covariance' term indicating a dynamic reallocation. The aggregate labor productivity for all 27 industries is defined as:

$$v^{PF} = \frac{V^{PF}}{L^*} \qquad (18.2)$$

where the numerator is the sum of gross output at fixed prices of all the 27 industries and the denominator is the sum of total persons employed in 27 industries, and v^{PF} is thus the aggregate labor productivity level for all the industries:

$$\Delta v_t^{PF} = \sum_i \Delta v_{i,t} \cdot u_{i,t-1} + \sum_i \Delta u_{i,t} \cdot v_{i,t-1} + \sum_i \Delta u_{i,t} \cdot \Delta v_{i,t} \qquad (18.3)$$

where $u_{i,t}$ is the employment share of industry i in aggregate employment. The first term in Equation 18.3 is the *within effect*, or the effect of productivity change within each industry. It denotes for each industry the sum of change in productivity levels weighted by its respective employment share in the previous period. The second term is *between effect* – a measure of worker reallocation across industries – and is calculated by a change in employment weighted by levels of productivity in the previous period. If it is positive, it suggests that workers move to sectors with above-average *productivity levels*, and this term is often considered as a *static reallocation (or static between) effect* and is also described as the structural change term measuring the movement of workers from low-productive to high-productive industries. The last term in the equation is an interaction of change in employment share and change in productivity, and thus it measures the combined effect of changes in employment shares and sectoral productivity in a period – a *co-variance* or *dynamic reallocation term* (Ghani et al. 2013; Erumbun et al. 2015). Similarly, a positive dynamic reallocation term describes movement of workers to sectors that see positive *productivity growth*.

Data and variables

The source of data used in the current paper is the India KLEMS data base. The data is completely consistent with national accounts. The India KLEMS provides data on value added, gross output, intermediate inputs (all in both current and constant prices)[8] employment by skill types, labor quality, wage share in GDP including estimates for self-employed workers, capital investment and capital services by asset type, along with indicators of labor productivity and total factor productivity.[9] All these data are available for 27 detailed industries over the period 1980–2011. As such, the data can be directly used in growth accounting analysis.

The main source of data used in the India KLEMS is the National Accounts Statistics (NAS), published annually by the Central Statistical Organization. This data is supplemented by Input-Output tables, Annual Survey of Industries (ASI) and various rounds of National Sample Survey Organization (NSSO) surveys on employment and unemployment and unorganized manufacturing. A brief description of the source and construction of these variables is provided in the next section.[10]

Gross output: In India KLEMS, estimates of gross output at current and constant prices are directly obtained from NAS for a few sectors (i.e. agriculture, hunting, forestry and fishing, mining and quarrying), construction and few of the manufacturing sectors. For splitting some other manufacturing sectors, additional information is used from ASI and NSSO. For other sectors, mainly service sectors, where there was no output information available from NAS, input-output transaction tables, which provides gross output and gross value added, are used.

Intermediate inputs: The methodology used[11] for estimating intermediate inputs under India KLEMS is similar to the one used by Jorgenson et al. (2005, Chapter 4) and Timmer et al. (2010, Chapter 3). For each benchmark year, estimates are obtained for material, energy and service inputs used to produce output in the different industries by using the bench mark Input–Output Tables (IOTT) and then linear interpolation is used for the intervening period, assuming a constantly changing technological change, so as to obtain the series for 1980 to 2011 at current prices. Necessary adjustments have been made to these values to ensure consistency with National Accounts data. Necessary weighted deflators (see Balakrishnan and Pushpangadan 1994) for materials, energy and service inputs for each of the industries have been generated by using wholesale price indices published by the Office of the Economic Advisor, Ministry of Commerce and Industry.

Employment and labor composition: Employment data in India KLEMS are based on the usual principal and subsidiary status (UPSS) concept, and are obtained from the quinquennial rounds of Employment and Unemployment Surveys (EUS) published by the National Sample Survey Office (NSSO). Since the EUS do not provide self-employed wage compensation, India KLEMS uses econometrically estimated compensation rates, using demographic and socio-economic characteristics of workers (see Aggarwal and Erumban 2013). Labor composition is based on education and uses the Jorgenson, Gallop and Fraumeni (JGF) methodology.

Capital services: Capital services for the aggregate economy and for industries in India KLEMS are arrived at using Equation 18.4:

$$\Delta \ln K = \sum_{k} \bar{v}_k \Delta \ln K_k; \qquad (18.4)$$

where v_k is the share of each type of capital k in aggregate capital compensation, and is defined as:

$$v_k = \frac{P_{K,k} K_k}{\sum_{K} P_{K,k} K_k} \qquad (18.5)$$

where $P_{K,k}$ is the rental price of capital type k, and $\bar{v}$ in (18.4) is the two-period averages of these shares.

The required investment data by asset type for each sector in three different asset types – construction, transport equipment, and machinery[12] – are gathered by the India KLEMS dataset (2015) from NAS for broad sectors of the economy, the ASI covering the formal manufacturing sector and the NSSO rounds for unorganized manufacturing. These sectoral data are used to construct capital stock using perpetual inventory method.

Labor productivity – trends and behavior

In this section, we first explain the behavior of labor productivity, followed by its decomposition. Labor productivity has been computed by the difference of *growth rate of value of gross output and growth rate of persons employed* by UPSS. The gross output approach is useful at industry level as it accurately reflects the contribution of intermediate inputs also to the growth of labor productivity. At the economy level, the gross output approach may pose problems due to aggregation, and a value-added approach may be better. Estimates of labor productivity are presented later, followed by the decomposition and analysis of labor productivity growth.

The contribution to labor productivity growth comes from four sources: capital deepening, where more or better capital makes labor more productive; labor quality or labor compositional changes; contribution of intermediate input deepening, which reflects the impact of more intermediate-intensive production on labor productivity; and, finally, from TFP growth which contributes to labor productivity point-for point (Jorgensen 2005: 299).

Growth of labor productivity

Labor productivity is a partial measure of productivity and reflects the joint influence of a host of factors; however, the time profile shows how productively labor is used to generate output and reflects the productivity of labor in terms of personal capacities of persons employed or the intensity of their effort. In this section, we provide estimates of growth of labor productivity, which is calculated as gross value of output per person employed. It may be mentioned that there has been substantial structural shift of the labor force from primary sector (where its employment share was 68 percent in 1983 and only 51.3 percent in 2009–10), to services (where the employment share increased from 17.6 percent to 26.7 percent during the same period). However, this has not been commensurate with changes in sectoral share in GDP. While the share of primary sector in GDP reduced from 37 percent to 15.2 percent, the share of services increased from 38.6 percent to 58.8 percent over the same period. It thus reflects how per-worker productivity has changed over the period.

The labor productivity growth rates are presented for the 27 sectors in Table 18.1 and Figure 18.1. It shows that the growth rates vary widely across the industries for the given periods. Looking at these, we find some of those industries which show higher rates of labor productivity growth are post and telecommunication; manufacturing, N.E.C. (Not Elsewhere Classified), recycling; chemical and chemical products; electrical and optical equipment; textile and leather products, whereas sectors like wood and wood

Table 18.1 Growth rate of labor productivity, 1980 to 2011

(% per annum)

Industry No.	Industry/Period	1980–93	1994–2002	2003–11	1980–11
1	Agriculture, Forestry and Fishing	1.26	1.60	5.10	2.48
2	Mining and Quarrying	3.04	4.75	3.58	3.70
3	Food, Products, Beverages and Tobacco	2.80	6.93	8.06	5.53
4	Textiles, Textile Products, Leather and Footwear	5.72	3.97	8.48	6.01
5	Wood and Products of wood	−4.66	−4.99	8.84	−0.83
6	Pulp, Paper, Paper products, Printing and Publishing	4.51	−0.01	9.94	4.78
7	Coke, Refined Petroleum Products and Nuclear fuel	−3.07	8.09	9.11	3.71
8	Chemicals and Chemical Products	4.48	6.40	10.42	6.76
9	Rubber and Plastic Products	3.96	4.79	9.88	5.92
10	Other Non-Metallic Mineral Products	6.30	6.57	6.21	6.35
11	Basic Metals and Fabricated Metal Products	3.43	3.74	8.36	4.95
12	Machinery, N.E.C.	−1.15	7.03	9.23	4.24
13	Electrical and Optical Equipment	3.70	6.55	10.37	6.46
14	Transport Equipment	6.39	6.27	3.97	5.65
15	Manufacturing, N.E.C.; Recycling	5.78	7.67	8.96	7.25
16	Electricity, Gas and Water Supply	5.40	8.22	1.09	4.97
17	Construction	−2.07	0.82	0.67	−0.43
18	Trade	0.48	3.37	6.72	3.13
19	Hotels and Restaurants	1.66	4.99	4.22	3.37
20	Transport and Storage	1.94	2.97	5.21	3.19
21	Post and Telecommunication	2.05	9.79	20.12	9.54
22	Financial Services	2.94	7.30	5.75	5.02
23	Business Services	3.18	6.69	4.84	4.68
24	Public Administration and Defense; Compulsory Social Security	3.80	6.31	7.91	5.72
25	Education	2.55	3.62	2.99	2.99
26	Health and Social Work	2.13	0.37	1.29	1.37
27	Other Services	2.55	3.42	−0.77	1.84
	Median	2.94	4.99	6.72	4.78

Note: Labor productivity is here defined as real gross output per person employed.

Source: Authors' calculations

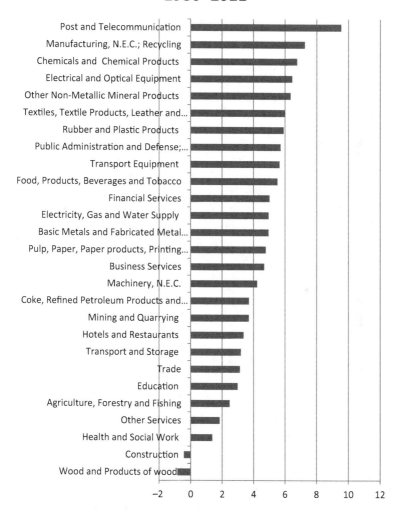

Figure 18.1 Growth Rate of Labor Productivity, 1980–2011 (% per annum)

Source: Authors' calculations

Note: Figure shows the rank-wise position of the industries on growth of labor productivity.

products; construction; health and social work; other services; agriculture, forestry and fishing have lower growth rates in comparison.

The agriculture sector records a two and a half percent growth in labor productivity for the period but it experienced a sharp acceleration in the recent period. In the recent period, substantial improvements in labor productivity growth are also noticed in some of the manufacturing and services sectors which may have fueled improvements for the entire economy. Some of the noticeable sectors showing acceleration are food, products, beverages and tobacco; wood and products of wood; coke, refined petroleum products and nuclear fuel; chemical and chemical products; rubber and plastic products; electrical and optical equipment; basic metals and fabricated metal products; trade; and post and telecommunication. On the other hand, some important sectors have experienced deceleration in labor productivity growth. These are transport equipment; electricity, gas and water supply; health and social work; and other services. It is imperative that for fast economic growth focus be placed on sectors where we witness accelerated labor productivity growth and also efforts be made to pull up labor productivity in the laggard industries.

Labor productivity: sources of growth and sectoral decomposition

Sources of growth in labor productivity

The contribution of the four sources of growth in labor productivity for the 27 sectors for the period 1980 to 2011 is presented in Table 18.2 and Figure 18.2. It is evident that across the 27 sectors, the median contribution of intermediate inputs is 2.5 percentage points out of 4.8 percent followed by 0.98 percentage points by capital deepening; 0.53 percentage points by TFP and 0.11 by labor composition index. In 17 out of 27 industrial sectors, intermediate input deepening contributed the maximum to labor productivity; in three industries TFP contributed the maximum, and only in seven industries capital deepening contributed the maximum to labor productivity. In all the sectors the contribution of labor composition growth has been quite marginal, median being 0.11 except in mining; post and telecommunication; public administration; education; and other services.

Table 18.2 Sources of labor productivity growth, 1980–2011

(% per annum)

Industry No.	Industry/Period	Growth in TFP	Growth in labor composition	growth in capital intensity	growth in intermediate inputs	growth in LP
1	Agriculture, Forestry and Fishing	0.53	0.17	1.24	0.54	2.48
2	Mining and Quarrying	-1.34	0.38	3.18	1.47	3.70
3	Food, Products, Beverages and Tobacco	0.69	0.09	0.41	4.34	5.53
4	Textiles, Textile Products, Leather and Footwear	0.64	0.10	1.16	4.11	6.01
5	Wood and Products of wood	-2.76	0.07	1.53	0.32	-0.83
6	Pulp, Paper, Paper products, Printing and Publishing	0.67	0.15	0.53	3.43	4.78
7	Coke, Refined Petroleum Products and Nuclear fuel	0.45	0.01	1.01	2.24	3.71
8	Chemicals and Chemical Products	1.11	0.09	0.58	4.98	6.76
9	Rubber and Plastic Products	0.91	0.06	1.02	3.93	5.92
10	Other Non-Metallic Mineral Products	0.36	0.11	1.91	3.98	6.35
11	Basic Metals and Fabricated Metal Products	-0.07	0.07	0.85	4.10	4.95
12	Machinery, N.E.C.	0.90	0.22	0.63	2.50	4.24
13	Electrical and Optical Equipment	1.83	0.07	0.46	4.09	6.46
14	Transport Equipment	0.75	0.09	0.73	4.08	5.65
15	Manufacturing, N.E.C.; Recycling	1.49	0.11	0.73	4.92	7.25
16	Electricity, Gas and Water Supply	1.41	0.12	0.98	2.45	4.97
17	Construction	-1.70	0.11	0.29	0.87	-0.43
18	Trade	0.39	0.25	2.21	0.28	3.13
19	Hotels and Restaurants	-0.18	0.09	0.87	2.59	3.37
20	Transport and Storage	0.17	0.15	0.32	2.55	3.19

(Continued)

Table 18.2 (Continued)

(% per annum)

Industry No.	Industry/Period	Growth in TFP	Growth in labor composition	growth in capital intensity	growth in intermediate inputs	growth in LP
21	Post and Telecommunication	5.57	0.29	2.04	1.64	9.54
22	Financial Services	2.28	0.19	1.68	0.87	5.02
23	Business Services	0.22	0.10	1.86	2.50	4.68
24	Public Administration and Defense; Compulsory Social Security	3.05	0.42	0.56	1.69	5.72
25	Education	−0.17	0.30	2.63	0.22	2.99
26	Health and Social Work	−1.12	0.12	1.83	0.54	1.37
27	Other Services	0.45	0.32	0.63	0.44	1.84
	Median	0.53	0.11	0.98	2.50	4.78

Source: Authors' calculations

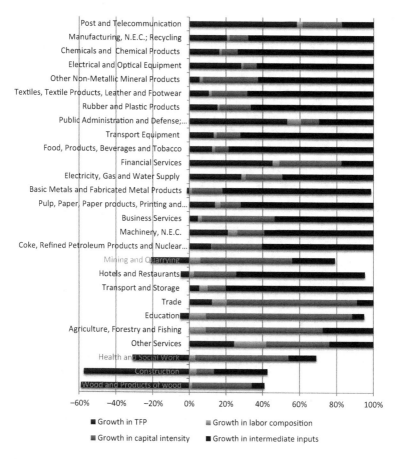

Figure 18.2 Sources of labor productivity growth, 1980–2011 (percent per annum)

Source: Authors' calculations. Industries are in reverse order.

Note: Figure shows the rank-wise position of the industries on growth of labor productivity.

It is either intermediate input deepening or capital deepening which has contributed substantially to labor productivity growth in large number of subsectors of manufacturing industries. On the other hand, the growth of labor productivity in most of the subsectors of services has been fueled by TFP growth, except in hotels and restaurants, transport and storage (intermediate deepening in both), and education and health and social work (capital deepening in both).

We thus find that not only labor productivity growth differs across different industries but the contribution to labor productivity growth also comes from different sources. The most important contribution comes from intermediate inputs in 17 out of 27 industries. It is thus important that we do not ignore the role of intermediate inputs, and instead of focusing on value-added approach, we should focus on gross output measure. But from long-term growth prospects, it is necessary that growth in labor productivity is driven more by TFP growth rather than by factor inputs.

Sectoral decomposition of aggregate labor productivity growth

In this section, we look into the contribution of different sectors and structural change in terms of workers' movement across sectors, to aggregate labor productivity growth. The growth rate of labor productivity, measured as output per worker, over 1986–2011 period, broken down to within industry productivity growth, and static and dynamic reallocation is depicted in Table 18.3 and Figure 18.3. Labor productivity growth has increased from 2.01 percent during 1980–93 to 4.96 percent during 1994–2002 and to 13.78 percent during 2003–2011. This was the period when we find acceleration, more than double, in aggregate labor productivity growth compared to previous period.

Figure 18.3 also provides the magnitude of the reallocation effects – both static and dynamic in relation to the within-industry

Table 18.3 Decomposition of labor productivity growth for the total economy based on gross output, 1980–2011 and subperiods

	1980–93	1994–2002	2003–2011	1980–2011
Within Industry productivity	1.18	4.11	10.26	4.66
Static reallocation	0.89	0.91	3.66	1.70
Dynamic reallocation	−0.05	−0.06	−0.14	−0.08
Aggregate productivity	2.01	4.96	13.78	6.28

Source: Author calculation using India KLEMS data

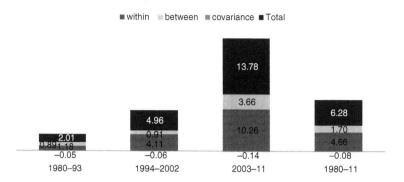

Figure 18.3 Decomposition of labor productivity growth for the total economy based on gross output – 1980–2011 and subperiods

Source: Author calculation using India KLEMS data

productivity growth. If workers are moving into industries with above-average productivity levels, the static reallocation term will be positive, and if workers are moving to industries that witness faster productivity growth, the dynamic reallocation term will be positive. In general, aggregate productivity growth is explained majorly by within-industry productivity growth, and the remaining part can be attributed to between or structural change. The impact of overall reallocation has been throughout positive and is in accordance with the recent findings in McMillan and Rodrik (2011) and de Vries et al. (2012). On average, the negative structural change effect has been larger in the period 2003–11, whereas it has been lower in the period 1980–93. The static effect has been lower during the earlier period, and it has increased substantially since 2003.

In Figure 18.4, annual data is used to further follow the evolution of reallocation effects. When looking at static and dynamic effects separately, we observe that, on average, there have been almost no dynamic reallocation effects throughout the period. The dynamic effects have been contributing less and mostly negative in most of the years, suggesting that employment was hardly generated in sectors which were witnessing faster productivity growth. The static reallocation effect, however, has been positive throughout the period, with steep rise since 2004–05, suggesting a positive structural change effect. In some of the recent years, dynamic effect is also positive, though very small. In general, the effect of structural

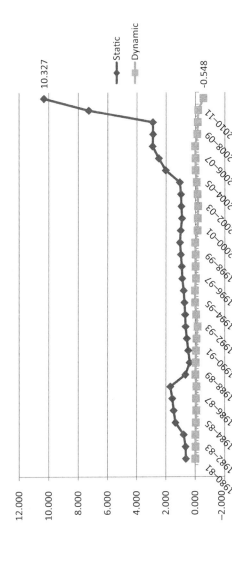

Figure 18.4 Labor reallocation effects in labor productivity decomposition
Source: Author calculation using India KLEMS data

change, in terms of workers moving to sectors of high productivity level, on labor productivity growth has been positive, though the magnitude of the effect varies substantially over years.

Conclusion

This chapter has estimated labor productivity for 27 industries across all sectors of the Indian economy for the period 1980–2011, wherein labor productivity has been computed by the difference of *growth rate of value of gross output and growth rate of persons employed* by UPSS. The chapter has used the gross output approach as it accurately reflects the contribution of intermediate inputs also to the growth of labor productivity. It finds that growth of labor productivity is different among the industries where post and telecommunication grew the fastest with a growth rate of more than 9.5 percent, followed by manufacturing, N.E.C., and chemical and chemical products. On the other extreme are industries like wood and products of wood, and construction, which have negative growth in labor productivity. Even health and social work, agriculture, forestry and fishing, and education have very low (less than 3 percent) growth of labor productivity. An important concern here is that if labor productivity growth is low in these key industries which together employ almost half of workforce, then how are we going to improve the economic condition of these employed? This is pertinent, as the living conditions of workers generally depend on their labor productivity. The status of labor productivity becomes more adverse when we analyze the sources of growth of labor productivity. The contribution to labor productivity growth is calculated from four sources: namely capital deepening, labor quality or labor compositional changes, contribution of intermediate input deepening, and finally from TFP growth. The sources of growth of labor productivity are not only different for different industries, but in most of them it is either the growth in intermediate inputs (17 industries out of 27) or growth in capital intensity (7 industries out of 27), which basically means it is factor accumulation that is leading to a growth in labor productivity. The contribution of both, growth in labor composition and TFP growth in growth of labor productivity, is marginal. So more than the quality of factors, it is the quantity which is the main source of labor productivity growth. From a long-term perspective of growth of the economy, it is growth in TFP and growth in labor composition which is desirable and sustainable and not the growth in factor accumulation.

Industry decomposition of labor productivity growth shows that aggregate productivity growth is explained majorly by within-industry productivity growth, and between or structural change explains the remaining part. The static reallocation has been positive and substantial in the entire period 1980–2011, suggesting a positive structural change effect. The dynamic effects have been mostly negative and small in most of the years, suggesting that employment was hardly generated in sectors which were witnessing faster productivity growth.

What could be the reasons for slow growth in labor productivity and what is way forward are the questions which need further and deeper investigation. One plausible reason which could be explored is the very low proportion of labor in regular job employment and the pre-dominance of self-employed and casual labor. Traditionally labor productivity is low not only in traditional sectors like agriculture where even in 2011–12, 48 percent of the workforce is employed but also in casual and self-employment. So, the only long-term solutions are to increase employment in the regular wage employment and provide the necessary infrastructure, financing and skill training to labor so as to improve the labor composition as well as TFP growth.

Notes

1 OECD (2016) suggests that GDP be measured as gross value added in market prices. But for international comparison of labor productivity levels, the series of GDP in national currency and at current prices must be converted to a common currency, US dollar, using PPPs.
2 The number of persons employed in India refers to persons usually employed either in *principal* or in *subsidiary activities* for *major period of the year*.
3 Source: Planning commission, GOI (2015).
4 With a change in base to 2011–12 and in methodology, the new shares in 2013–14 at 2011–12 prices are 17.22 percent, 31.68 percent (18.08 percent for manufacturing), and 51.09 percent, respectively, for agriculture & allied, industry, and services sectors.
5 This section is drawn heavily from the three presentations made by Aggarwal (2015), Das (2015) and Erumbun et al. (2015) in the RBI workshop held in December 2015 at the Delhi School of Economics under the India KLEMS Productivity Research project being undertaken at Centre for Development Economics (CDE), Delhi School of Economics (DSE), Delhi, and sponsored by Reserve Bank of India. These papers provide more details about the methodology and data.

6 As mentioned earlier, gross output is more appropriate at industry level and value added at the aggregate economy level.
7 Note that we measure labor input by taking account of heterogeneity among different type of employees, in terms of education, and therefore the concept of labor input (L) is different from the concept of employment (N). So whereas the latter is measured as the number of persons employed, labor input includes both the number of persons employed and labor composition (L=N*LC).
8 India KLEMS use a double deflation approach to construct constant-price value-added series (see Balakrishan and Pushpangadan, 1994 for a first use of double deflation in Indian manufacturing).
9 For details about the definition and measurement of these variables, refer to India KLEMS data manual (2015).
10 See Das et al. (2015) for a detailed discussion on the construction of these variables.
11 Ibid. (2015).
12 Land and livestock have also been included in investment data for agricultural sector as separate assets.

Bibliography

Aggarwal, Suresh Chand, and A. A. Erumban. 2013. "Labor Input for Measuring Productivity Growth in India: Methodology and Estimates." *Mimeo*.

Aggarwal, Suresh Chand, et al. 2015. "Structural Changes in Employment in India, 1980–2011." Paper presented at the *India KLEMS Conference*, Delhi School of Economics, New Delhi, India, December 17.

Balakrishnan, P., and K. Pushpangadan. 1994. "Total Factor-Productivity Growth in Manufacturing Industry: A Fresh Look." *Economic and Political Weekly* 29(31), July 30: 2028–2035.

Chandrasekhar, C. P. 2015. "Promise Belied: India's Post Independence Industrialization Experience." In C. P. Chandrasekhar (ed.), *Economics: Indian Industrialization*, Vol. I, ICSSR Research Surveys and Explorations. New Delhi: Oxford University Press.

Das, Deb Kusum, et al. 2015. "Productivity Dynamics in India's Service Sector: An Industry-Level Perspective." Paper presented at the *India KLEMS Conference*, Delhi School of Economics, New Delhi, India, December 17.

Erumban, A. A., et al. 2015. "Relative Importance of Sectors and Structural Change in Overall Economic Growth in India." Paper presented at the *India KLEMS Conference*, Delhi School of Economics, New Delhi, India, December 17.

Fabricant, S. 1942. "Employment in Manufacturing, 1899–1939: An Analysis of its Relation to the Volume of Production." National Bureau of Economic Research, Inc.

Ghani, Ejaz, Kerr, William R. and O'Connell, Stephen D. 2013. "The Exceptional Persistence of India's Unorganized Sector", *Policy Research Working Paper no.6454* (May 2013), Economic Policy and Debt Department, Poverty Reduction and Economic Management Network, World Bank.

Ghose, Ajit K. 2015. "Service-Led Growth and Employment in India." In K. V. Ramaswamy (ed.), *Labor, Employment and Economic Growth in India*. New Delhi, India: Cambridge University Press.

Islam, R. 2008. "Has Development and Employment Through Labor Intensive Industrialization Become History?" In Kaushik Basu and R. Kanbur (Eds), *Arguments for a Better World: Essays in Honour of Amartya Sen, Vol. II: Society, Institutions and Development*. Oxford: OUP.

Jha, Praveen. 2015. "Labor Conditions in Contemporary India." In Prabhat Patnaik (Ed.), *Economics: Macroeconomics*, Vol. III, ICSSR Research Surveys and Explorations. New Delhi: Oxford.

Jorgenson, D., M.S. Ho, and K.J. Stiroh. 2005. *Information Technology and the American Growth Resurgence*, Cambridge, The MIT Press.

Kochhar, K., U. Kumar, R. Rajan, A. Subramanian, and I. Tokattidis. 2006. "India's Pattern of Development: What Happened, What Follows." *Journal of Monetary Economics* 535: 981–1019.

Krishna, K. L. 2015. "Industrial Development and Policies Since Independence: Growth Without Employment." In Uma Kapila (ed.), *Indian Economy Since Independence*. New Delhi, India: Academic Foundation.

McMillan, M. S., and D. Rodrik. 2011. "Globalization, Structural Change and Productivity Growth." National Bureau of Economic Research, No. w17143.

OECD. 2016. *OECD Economic Outlook*. Paris: OECD, November.

Papola, T. S., and Sahu Partha Pratim. 2012. *Growth and Structure of Employment in India: Long-Term and Post-Reform Performance and the Emerging Challenge*. New Delhi, India: Institute for Studies in Industrial Development.

Planning Commission, Government of India. 2015. *Data-book Compiled for use of Planning Commission*. planningcommission.nic.in/data/datatable, page5.

Timmer, Marcel P., Robert Inklaar, Mary O'Mahony, and Bart van. Ark. 2010. *Economic Growth in Europe: A Comparative Industry Perspective*. Cambridge: Cambridge University Press.

Vries, Gaaitzen J. de, Abdul A. Erumban, Marcel P. Timmer, Ilya B. Voskoboynikov, and Harry X. Wu. 2012. "Deconstructing the BRICs: Structural Transformation and Aggregate Productivity Growth." *Journal of Comparative Economics*, 40(2): 211–27.

Chapter 19

Total factor productivity in Indian organized manufacturing

The story of the noughties

Pilu Chandra Das

Introduction

Historically, industrial development has always had a crucial role to play in the transition of developing economies into developed economies. In this process, productivity plays a significant role in achieving a high rate of industrial growth and in sustaining a robust industrial performance. In developing countries, economic liberalization implies a major shift in the economy from a regulatory and protective regime to a free and market-oriented environment by significantly reforming the policies related to industry, trade and macroeconomic environment. A liberalized economic policy is expected to enhance the productivity performance through increasing competition among industries, adoption of advanced technology and encouraging investment in the productivity enhancing facilities. Competition among firms is expected to lead to cost reduction, and consequently to an improvement in efficiency and productivity, while superior technology is expected to utilize inputs efficiently.

During the immediate post-independence period, establishment of an industrial base and broad-based industrial development was formulated as one of the most important objectives for the Indian economy. But, after three decades of industrial growth under planning, in the early 1980s, Indian policy makers took the initiative to change the industrial policy framework. Some of the major changes that occurred during 1980s were reduction in entry barriers and abolishing of the "License-Permit" Raj. But the most significant changes in economic policy in the Indian economy took place after the 1991 financial crisis, as the economy liberalized and moved toward privatization of economic activities which were under state control. The policy makers had not only changed industrial policy but also changed policy on trade, technology and capital flow to create a dynamic industrial environment. These were aimed at introduction of new technology and processes, promotion of foreign direct investment (FDI) and trade liberalization. These reforms not only had a significant impact on the industrial sector, but also affected the entire economy.

Several studies have attempted to analyze the productivity performance of the organized Indian manufacturing sector during the 1990s at both aggregated and disaggregated levels. Most of these studies observed that there has been a fall in total factor productivity (TFP) growth rate in the 1990s compared to 1980s, and this result holds across different firms and industries (Balakrishnan et al. 2000; Goldar 2000; Das 2003; Goldar and Kumari 2003; Virmani and Hashim 2011). Some other studies found marginal but insignificant improvements in TFP performance (Krishna and Mitra 1998; Unel 2003; Bollard et al. 2011). Goldar and Kumari (2003) attribute this unsatisfactory TFP performance to poor capacity utilization during the 1990s. Another argument was that the adverse effects of macroeconomic condition – such as excessively small scale of firms, exit barriers, high concentration and poor market integration – offset the favorable effect of economic reform (Goldar 2014). Virmani and Hashim (2011) attribute the unsatisfactory TFP performances to the lag between reforms and impact of reform on productivity growth, mainly because of structural transformation as well as introduction of completely new (unfamiliar) technology as a result of economic reform. In other words, it may suggest that the economic reforms have short-term adverse effects on productivity growth. However, after some time and after a process of structural adjustment and industrial restructuring, reforms are expected to have positive and favorable effects on productivity performance. In the context of this suggestion, it is important to analyze the productivity performances of Indian manufacturing sector during the 2000s to examine whether productivity growth in the 2000s is better than that was in the 1990s.

This study aims to estimate and analyze the Indian organized manufacturing sector's growth and productivity performance during 2000–01 to 2009–10. The study undertakes a comparison of TFP growth for selected three-digit industries to evaluate the Indian manufacturing sector's productivity performance in detail. It will also estimate the relative contribution of TFP growth to output growth in order to examine whether the growth of output of the Indian manufacturing sector has been driven by productivity growth or by input expansion. A majority of the earlier studies usually applied the value added function or the KLEM (capital-labor-energy-materials) production function as the basic framework.[1] Banga and Goldar (2007) and Virmani and Hashim (2011) are the only two studies that estimate the contribution of each input to output growth to document the sources of output growth. But their estimates on the sources of output growth were also at the aggregate level or at the two-digit disaggregated level. To analyze the productivity performance and sources of output growth in Indian organized manufacturing, this study use the KLEMS production function as an underlying production function framework.[2] We consider a set of 51 three-digit organized manufacturing industries.[3] Combined value added shares of these industries are around 90 percent of the total organized manufacturing sector.

The second section reviews the literature on productivity growth in Indian organized manufacturing industry for the periods of 1980s and 1990s. Detailed discussion on methodologies used in this study, along with the availability of the dataset and the variable constructions, are presented in the third section. The estimates of total factor productivity using growth accounting approach are presented in the fourth section, which also documents the contribution of TFP growth and input expansion to output growth. The final section provides the summary and conclusion of the study.

Productivity performance in India's organized manufacturing sector: a review

In this section, we discuss the productivity performance of Indian organized manufacturing sector in the post-economic reform periods. As mention earlier in the introduction, major changes in Indian industrial policy occurred in the mid-1980s and early-1990s. Several studies investigated the impact of the 1990s' economic reform on the productivity performance in the Indian organized manufacturing sector at the aggregate level as well as the disaggregated level. The following studies specifically document the productivity growth performance during the 1990s: Balakrishnan et al. (2000), Banga and Goldar (2007), Bollard et al. (2011), Das (2003), Ghosh (2010), Goldar (2004), Goldar and Kumari (2003), Krishna and Mitra (1998), Srivastava (2000), Trivedi et al. (2000), Unel (2003) and Virmani and Hashim (2011). Most of the studies except

Krishna and Mitra (1998), Unel (2003) and Bollard et al. (2011) did not find any statistically significant evidence which indicates that economic reform has had a favorable effect on the productivity performance of the organized manufacturing sector.

Krishna and Mitra (1998) and Balakrishnan et al. (2000) use the same production function framework developed by Halls (1988) based on firm level data for selected manufacturing industries to examine the effect of trade reform on competition and TFP growth pattern. Krishna and Mitra (1998) observe that after 1990s' economic reform, there was an increase in productivity growth rate in all industries except transport equipment. Balakrishnan et al. (2000) estimate productivity growth of 2,300 firms spread over five industry groups: machinery, transport equipment and parts, textiles, textile products and chemicals (which experienced the most significant tariff reduction), during 1988–89 to 1991–98. They did not find any evidence of acceleration in productivity growth in the post-reform periods.

Unel (2003) observes that the average annual TFP growth rate for aggregate manufacturing sector was 2.5 percent for the period 1991–92 to 1997–98, as compared to 1.8 percent for the period 1979–80 to 1990–91. Bollard et al. (2011) use plant level ASI data for the period 1980 to 2004 and growth accounting methodology developed by Basu and Fernald (1997) to estimate TFP growth. They observe that TFP growth rate in the 1993–2004 was higher as compare to earlier subperiods.

The claim of an increase in productivity growth in the first-half of the 1990s made by Unel (2003) was examined by Goldar (2004). He finds that the average annual TFP growth rate in the post-reform period had declined to 1 percent from 2.4 percent in the pre-reform period, which contradicted the findings of Unel's study. Using the gross output function framework, Goldar (2004) also concludes that the productivity performance of the post-reform period has been deteriorated. Based on ASI data set, Trivedi et al. (2000) use three different methodologies: single deflation, double deflation of nominal value added, and gross output specification of the production function, to estimate the TFP growth rate for selected manufacturing sectors for the period 1980–81 to 1997–98. Findings of all three methods indicate a much lower growth rate during the period 1991–98. Using data for about 3,000 public limited companies Srivastava (2000) analyze the pattern of productivity growth and technical efficiency in Indian manufacturing industry during

1980s and 1990s. Applying both the growth accounting and production function approaches, he noticed that there was a decrease in TFP growth rate during the 1990s. Goldar and Kumari (2003) estimate TFP growth rate for aggregate manufacturing as well as for 17 two-digit industry groups in the period 1980–82 to 1997–98. Findings of this study indicated a slowdown in TFP growth during 1990s. Comparing between two time periods, they find that 12 industrial groups depicted a positive TFP growth rate in the pre-liberalization phase and 11 groups showed positive growth rate in the post-liberalization period, whereas TFP growth rate of 11 groups worsened in the 1990s.

Das (2003) has tried to analyze the TFP growth pattern and contribution of TFP growth to the output growth of 75 three-digit industries for four different trade reform periods between 1980 and 2000. He observes that the average annual TFP growth rate was positive for 43 and 34 industries in the 1980s and 1990s, respectively, and that the TFP growth in the 1990s was lower than the 1980s. His study also observed that factor inputs had a major contribution to output growth, while TFP had a very low contribution (7 percent per annum over the period 1980–90 and insignificant or negative contribution during 1990s) to the output growth. In another related study, Das and Kalita (2009) find that TFP performance was worse in the 1990s as compared to 1980s.

Banga and Goldar (2007) include services as an input in production function (KLEMS) to estimate the contribution of services sector to output growth. They found that annual TFP growth rate of aggregate organized manufacturing for the post-reform period was reduced by 0.6 percentage points compared to the pre-reform period. They also find that relative contribution of services growth to output growth had risen to 25.5 percent during 1989–90 to 1999–00 from 0.8 percent per annum during 1980–81 to 1988–89. Studies by Ghosh (2010) and Virmani and Hashim (2011) re-examine the productivity performance in the 1980s and 1990s as well as early 2000s to investigate the impact of economic reform on productivity. Ghosh has not found any statistically significant evidence which indicates that productivity growth in the post-reform period was higher as compared to the pre-reform period. Using the translog index method based on the KLEMS production function framework, Virmani and Hashim (2011) observe that eight industry groups out of 12 showed productivity growth in the post-reform period compared to the pre-reform period.

Even though the major objective of the liberalized industrial policy was industrial growth by improving efficiency and productivity through optimum utilization of existing capacity, our assessment of the studies shows that TFP growth rate in the 1990s deteriorated compared to in the 1980s, and this decline seemed to hold across different firms and industries levels. The productivity performance of Indian registered manufacturing industries during the 1980s and 1990s is presented in Table 19.1.

Methodology and data sources

This section discusses in detail the TFP growth estimation methodologies used for estimation, along with the data sources and the construction of variables. As stated in its introduction, this chapter estimates the total factor productivity of the Indian manufacturing sector using the growth accounting approach and the production function approach for the period 2000–01 to 2009–10.

Growth accounting approach

Total factor productivity is the ratio of output to all inputs, which can be defined as the shift in an aggregate production function (Solow 1957).[4] The rate of growth of TFP is defined as the rate of growth of output with respect to time, holding all inputs constant. There are three main indices within the growth accounting approach for estimating TFP growth. These are the Kendrick Arithmetic Index, the Solow Geometric Index and the Törnqvist Index. For calculating TFP growth, this study uses the Tornqvist Index method.[5] This method considers translog (TL) production functional form. Basic assumptions of this methodology are perfect competition, constant return to scale and income shares of the intermediate inputs sum to unity. This method also does not assume that technological progress is Hicks-neutral.

In this study, we assume a simple KLEMS production framework for each industry. On the basis of this production function we calculate the TFP growth rate applying growth accounting estimation approaches:

$$Y_i = f(K_i,\ L_i,\ E_i,\ M_i,\ S_i;\ t) \qquad (19.1)$$

Y represents real gross output, L labor input, K real capital stock, M real material input, E real energy input, S real services input, and

Table 19.1 Selective productivity studies in India – a brief review

Study	Estimation Approach	Output Measure	Inputs Included	Period	TFP Growth Rate (Percent per Annum)
Goldar (2000)	GAA	RVASD	K and L	1981–82 to 1989–90	4.52
				1990–91 to 1997–98	1.86
		RVADD			8.97
					2.92
		RGO	K, L and I		2.13
					0.9
Trivedi et al. (2000)	GAA	RVADD	L and K	1981–82 to 1990–91	3.06
				1990–91 to 1997–98	1.96
		RGO	L, K and N		1.26
					0.63
Unni et al. (2001)	GAA	RVASD	K and L	1978–79 to 1984–85	−0.26
				1984–85 to 1989–90	4
				1989–90 to 1994–95	−1.28
Goldar and Kumari (2003)	GAA	RGO	K, L and I	1981–82 to 1990–91	4.27
				1990–91 to 1997–98	1.6
Unel (2003)	GAA	RVASD	K and L	1979–80 to 1990–91	1.8
				1991–92 to 1997–98	2.5
Das (2003)	GAA	RGO	K, L, E and M	1980–81 to 1989–90	7.3
				1990–91 to 1999–00	−0.18
Goldar (2004)	GAA	RVASD	K, L, E and M	1979–80 to 1990–91	2.14
				1991–92 to 1997–98	—
				1991–92 to 1999–00	1.57
	PFA	RGO			2.23
					1.08
					1.63

(Continued)

Table 19.1 (Continued)

Study	Estimation Approach	Output Measure	Inputs Included	Period	TFP Growth Rate (Percent per Annum)
Mukherjee and Ray (2005)	DEA	RGO	K, L1, L2, E and M	1985–86 to 1990–91	0.96
				1990–91 to 1995–96	0.96
				1995–96 to 1999–00	0.91
Banga and Goldar (2007)	PFA	RGO	K, L, E, M and S	1980–81 to 1989–90	0.88
				1989–90 to 1999–00	0.26
Das and Kalita (2009)	GAA	RGO	K, L, E and M	1980–81 to 1989–90	0.65*
				1990–91 to 1999–00	0.31*
Virmani and Hashim (2011)	GAA	RGO	K, L, E, M and S	1992–93 to 1997–98	0.73
				1998–99 to 2001–02	−0.14
				2002–03 to 2005–06	1.89
Kathuria, Raj and Sen (2011)	GAA	RVASD	K and L	1994–95 to 2000–01	−8.30 (−7.13)
				2000–01 to 2005–06	−3.33 (−9.66)
	LP			1994–95 to 2000–01	8.86 (−4.01)
				2000–01 to 2005–06	−1.59 (−16.00)
Bollard et al. (2011)	GAA (Basu & Fernald)	RVADD	K and L	1980–81 to 1992–93	3.5
				1992–93 to 2004–05	8.4

Notes: GAA represents growth accounting approach, PFA–production function approach, MI–Malmquist Index, LP – Levinsohn and Petrin approach.
RVASD–real value added single deflation, RVADD–real value added double deflation, and RGO–real gross output.
* Domar aggregation of TFP growth estimates of three-digit industries.
TFP growth rates shown in parentheses are for unorganized sector.

Source: Author's compilations

t is time. Subscripts i refer to industry. After total differentiation and dividing by Y, for each industry the equation 1 becomes:

$$\begin{aligned}
dY/dt(1/Y) = &(\partial Y/\partial L)(dL/dt)(1/Y) \\
&+(\partial Y/\partial K)(dK/dt)(1/Y) \\
&+(\partial Y/\partial E)(dE/dt)(1/Y) \\
&+(\partial Y/\partial M)(dM/dt)(1/Y) \\
&+(\partial Y/\partial S)(dS/dt)(1/Y) \\
&+\partial Y/\partial t(1/Y)
\end{aligned} \quad (19.2)$$

$$\begin{aligned}
dY/dt(1/Y) = &(\partial Y/\partial L)(dL/dt)(1/Y)(L/L) \\
&+(\partial Y/\partial K)(dK/dt)(1/Y)(K/K) \\
&+(\partial Y/\partial E)(dE/dt)(1/Y)(E/E) \\
&+(\partial Y/\partial M)(dM/dt)(1/Y)(M/M) \\
&+(\partial Y/\partial S)(dS/dt)(1/Y)(S/S) \\
&+\partial Y/\partial t(1/Y)
\end{aligned} \quad (19.3)$$

$$\begin{aligned}
d\ln Y/dt = &(\partial Y/\partial L)(L/Y)(d\ln L/dt) \\
&+(\partial Y/\partial K)(K/Y)(d\ln K/dt)(1/Y) \\
&+(\partial Y/\partial E)(E/Y)(d\ln E/dt) \\
&+(\partial Y/\partial M)(M/Y)(d\ln M/dt) \\
&+(\partial Y/\partial S)(S/Y)(d\ln S/dt)+\partial\ln Y/\partial t
\end{aligned} \quad (19.4)$$

Under the assumptions of perfect competition, each industry is price takers in product and factor markets. Factor prices are equal to their respective marginal products. So

$$(\partial Y/\partial L)(L/Y) = wL/Y = (Total\,emoluments)/(\text{Gross output})$$
$$= \text{Value share of labor}$$

Similarly we can replace the elasticities in the Equation 19.4 with the value shares.

$$\begin{aligned}
\partial lnY/\partial t = d lnY/dt - [&S_L(dlnL/dt) \\
&+S_K(dlnK/dt)+S_E(dlnE/dt) \\
&+S_M(dlnM/dt)+S_S(dlnS/dt)\}]
\end{aligned} \quad (19.5)$$

where S_L, S_K, S_E, S_M and S_S are the value shares of capital, labor, energy, material and services input, respectively. Under the assumption of constant return to scale, all the value shares sum up to unity.

In other words, TFP growth is equal to the growth of output minus a value-share-weighted average of the growth of inputs. And under the further assumption that the production function is translog, it can be shown that the average growth of TFP over the discrete interval t–1 to t is measured exactly by the following Törnqvist index:

$$\begin{aligned} \text{Ln}\left[\text{TFP}(t)/\text{TFP}(t-1)\right] = &\ \text{Ln}\left[O(t)/O(t-1)\right] - 1/2\left[S_k(t) + S_k(t-1)\right] \\ &\ \text{Ln}\left[K(t)/K(t-1)\right] - 1/2\left[S_l(t) + S_l(t-1)\right] \\ &\ \text{Ln}\left[L(t)/L(t-1)\right] - 1/2\left[S_e(t) + S_e(t-1)\right] \\ &\ \text{Ln}\left[E(t)/E(t-1)\right] - 1/2\left[S_m(t) + S_m(t-1)\right] \\ &\ \text{Ln}\left[M(t)/M(t-1)\right] - 1/2\left[S_s(t) + S_s(t-1)\right] \\ &\ \text{Ln}\left[S(t)/S(t-1)\right] \end{aligned}$$

(19.6)

where, S_l, S_k, S_m, S_e and S_s are the income shares of labor, capital, materials input, energy input and services input for the years (t) and (t–1).

Data and variables

To analyze the Indian organized manufacturing sector's growth and productivity performance during 2000–01 to 2009–10, this study considers a set of 51 three-digit organized manufacturing industries. The selection of industries has been guided by the fact that these industries together account for a large percentage of registered manufacturing value added. Combined value added shares of these industries are more than 90 percent of total organized manufacturing sector.

The basic source of data for this study is the Annual Survey of Industries, published by the Central Statistical Organization (CSO), Government of India. Data series have been collected for the following points – gross output, net value added, gross fixed capital stock, depreciation, total persons engaged, total emoluments, fuels consumed, materials consumed and total inputs. Nominal values of output and input have been deflated by suitable price deflators, which have been constructed using Wholesale Price Indices (Office of the Economic Advisor, Ministry of Industry, Government of India) and various yearly volumes of the National Accounts Statistics (CSO). An implicit deflator for capital stock has been constructed with the help of various yearly volumes of the National Accounts Statistics published by CSO, Government of India. For the purposes of deflating nominal values, we have to construct suitable weighted price index. Input-Output transaction tables (published by CSO) have been used for computing appropriate weight for each materials and services input. Real output and input series of 51 three-digit industries have been aggregated to obtain the data series for the aggregate organized manufacturing sector.

Output: In this study, value of gross output has been used as the measure of output. Nominal value of gross output has been obtained from ASI for each three-digit industry. Nominal figures have been deflated by the wholesale price index (with 2004–05 as the base year), obtained from the Office of the Economic Advisor, Ministry of Industry, Government of India. Since industry-specific price deflators were not directly available from wholesale price indices for each of the 51 industries, a weighted average price index has been constructed with the help of commodity weights and wholesale price index.

Labor: Total number of persons engaged in industries available in ASI has been taken as the measure of labor input.[6] Total persons engaged represents the number of persons employed by the factory, whether for wages or not, and engaged in any manufacturing process. It also includes persons engaged in administrative office, store-keeping section, welfare section and family members who are actively engaged in the work of the factory. However, this measure of labor input assumes that workers and other employees are perfect substitutes. Total emoluments are used to compute the income share of labor.

Capital: In the literature of productivity, measurement of capital stock is always considered the most difficult and complex among all variables. There has been a long debate over the measurement approaches for nature of capital and its role in production. Due to unavailability of data series on directly observable flow of capital services, capital stock is considered as measure of capital input and assumed that the flow of capital services is proportional to the stock of capital. There is no universally accepted method for its measurement and, as a result, several methods have been employed to estimate capital stock. A majority of the studies on productivity estimation follow the perpetual inventory method for measuring the capital stock variable, while some of the studies have simply used the book values of capital stock.[7] Perpetual inventory method construct the time series of capital stock step by step using the time series data on book-value of fixed capital stock and the implicit deflator for capital stock. In this study, net fixed capital stock at constant prices has been used as the measure of capital input. The construction of net fixed capital series by the perpetual inventory method requires (1) benchmark net fixed capital stock, (2) real net investment series and (3) implicit deflator for capital stock.

For calculating benchmark net fixed capital stock for each three-digit industry, first we obtained the book value of fixed capital stock (for the year 1990–91) from ASI. For constructing industry-specific implicit deflators for capital stock, we require data on industry-specific shares of land, plant, machinery and equipment in the total capital stock. But neither the ASI nor the NAS provide any information regarding industry-specific shares of land, plant, machinery and equipment. So, in this study, an implicit deflator (at 2004–05 prices) for capital stock has been constructed with the help of data on gross fixed capital formation in organized manufacturing at current and constant prices, obtained from various yearly volumes of the National Accounts Statistics published by CSO, Government of India.

Gross investment series at current prices has been computed for each year using book-values of fixed capital assets and depreciation reported in ASI. The annual gross investment is derived by subtracting the book-value of fixed assets in the previous year from that in the current year and adding to that depreciation in fixed assets in the current year. Then yearly gross investment series at current price is deflated by the implicit deflator for capital stock constructed earlier:

$$I_t = \left(B_t - B_{t-1} + D_t\right) / \text{implicit deflator} \qquad (19.7)$$

where, I, B and D are real gross investment, book-value of fixed capital and depreciation, respectively. Subscript *t* is time.

Time series in real net investment prior to benchmark year has been obtained by subtracting depreciation of fixed capital stock from real gross investment series. The annual rate of discarding of the capital stock was assumed to be 5 percent (assuming the average life of capital stock of 20 years).[8] The net fixed capital stock series has been computed as the sum of benchmark fixed capital stock and real net investment series.

Energy inputs: Total fuels consumed by industries available in ASI have been taken as the measure of energy input. Energy input includes coal, liquefied petroleum gas, petrol, diesel, electricity, lubricants and water. For purposes of this study, wholesale price indices (base 2004–05 = 100) of coal, mineral oil and electricity for industry is used to deflate nominal value of energy input.

Materials input: ASI publishes data series on materials consumed (excludes all intermediate products) for each three-digit industry. Intermediate products are those products which are produced by the factory and used in further manufacturing processes. Materials consumed included the cost of raw materials, components, chemicals and packing materials during an accounting year. Because ASI does not provide a breakup of the materials consumed at the three-digit industry level, we compute breakup of the materials for each three-digit industry with the help of Input Output Transaction Table (IOTT).

For calculating the suitable weighted price index for each three-digit industry, first price indices were constructed for 98 and 105 IOTT sectors with the help of wholesale price indices (base 2004–05 = 100) series and data on gross domestic product at current and constant prices (National Accounts Statistics published by CSO, Government of India). Then we constructed a concordance table between IOTT manufacturing sectors and three-digit manufacturing industries for calculating industry specific breakup of the materials. Onward 2007–08, weights for each of material inputs computed from IOTT 2007–08 and between 2001–02 and 2006–07 IOTT 2003–04 and up to 2001–02 we used IOTT 1998–99 for each three-digit industries.

Services input: Since ASI does not provide data on services purchased by the industrial units, we applied a similar methodology to that adopted by Banga and Goldar (2007). However, the ASI reported that the total expenditure on inputs includes total value of fuels and materials consumed, as well as expenses related to services purchased. The difference between total inputs and the cost of materials and energy has been taken as a measure of services purchased by the industrial units. Industry-specific information on the purchases of services for each three-digit industry was obtained from IOTT. The price index for the services input was computed by applying the methodology similar to the one applied for material inputs. First, price indices were constructed for IOTT service sector. For service inputs, since wholesale price indices are not available, an implicit deflator was constructed using GDP at current and constant prices, obtained from various yearly volumes of the National Accounts Statistics published by CSO, Government of India. Then, weights for each of the services inputs was computed from IOTT table 1998–99 and 2003–04 for each three-digit industries.

Estimates of productivity in organized manufacturing (2000–09)

This study attempts to analyze the Indian organized manufacturing sector's growth and productivity performance during 2000–01 to 2008–09. We examine the TFP growth performance for selected manufacturing industries and estimate the relative contribution of TFP growth and inputs growth to output growth. We consider a set of 51 three-digit manufacturing industries. Before moving on to a discussion of the TFP growth performance, we first examine the industry shares of value added and employment, along with value added growth and labor productivity. However, for analytical feasibility, we aggregate the 51 industries into different subsectors using appropriate aggregation procedures.

We start with the value-added shares of different broad sectors to understand how different sectors behaved over the last decade in order to document the importance of these sectors in our assessment of overall registered manufacturing growth. We distributed the 51 three-digit industries in 18 broad industry groups. Figures 19.1 and 19.2 depict the time-series of changing structure of registered manufacturing in terms of value added and employment shares since 2000 for broad industry aggregates.

We observed from Figure 19.1 that the three industry groups 'Chemical Product', 'Basic Metals' and 'Coke & Petroleum Products' occupy more than 40 percent share of registered manufacturing value added. However, value added share of the Chemical Products in aggregate value added has been declined steadily over the decade and, on the contrary, the share of Coke & Petroleum Products has been continuously increasing, from around 5 percent in 2000–01 to more than 13 percent in 2008–09. Wood and Wood Products depict the lowest value added share of less than 0.3 percent, followed by Medical Instruments and Watches, Manufacturing

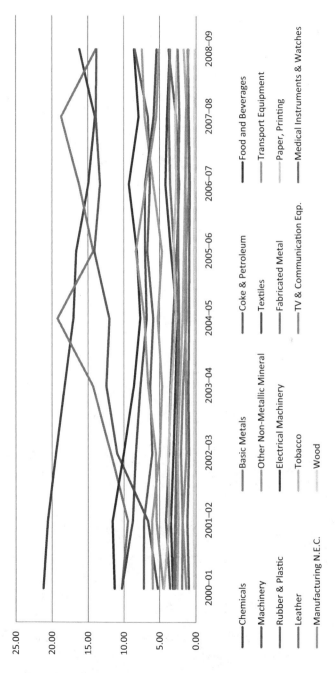

Figure 19.1 Sectoral share in aggregate registered manufacturing value added
Source: Author's calculation based on ASI data

N.E.C., TV and Communication Equipment, and Tobacco occupy less than 1 percent share.

In case of employment share, it is clearly visible from Figure 19.2 that two industry groups: Textiles and Food and Beverages Products – absorbs many more workers than do others, contributing more than 30 percent of registered manufacturing employment. Wood and Wood Products is the worst performer in terms of employment share followed by TV and Communication Equipment, Medical Instruments and Watches. Individually, they comprised around or less than 1 percent of registered manufacturing employment. Chemical Products, Basic Metals, and Coke and Petroleum Products, who have higher value added share, collectively absorb only 17 percent registered manufacturing workforce.

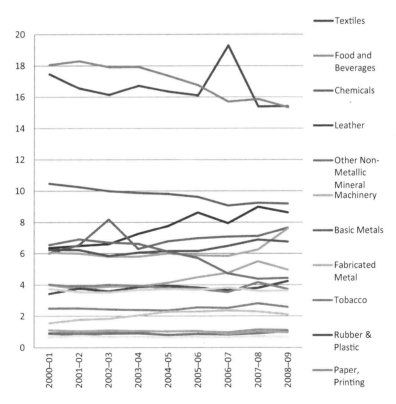

Figure 19.2 Sectoral share in aggregate registered manufacturing employment
Source: Author's calculation based on ASI data

In Table 19.2, we present the gross value added and labor productivity growth estimates along industrial contribution to aggregate value added and labor productivity growth for 18 broad industry groups between 2000 and 2009. GVA growth rate for these classified manufacturing sectors shows wide fluctuation. The wide variations of TFP growth rate ranging from a low of 4.10 percent per annum to a high of 18.40 percent per annum for entire period of analysis. Overall, the aggregate registered manufacturing has been growing at an average of 10.30 percent per annum. Nine industry groups achieve more than 10 percent per annum growth rate, whose combined value added share is around 45 percent. Coke and Petroleum Products have been the fastest-growing sectors in the entire

Table 19.2 Industry contributions to aggregate GVA and LP growth

Industries description	Growth rate (% per Annum) GVA	LP	Industry contribution to aggregate growth GVA	LP
Food products & beverages	7.41	5.41	0.63	0.47
Tobacco products	4.10	4.93	0.07	0.08
Textiles products	4.65	2.18	0.29	0.14
Leather & fur products	10.01	2.17	0.24	0.05
Wood & wood products	8.45	4.45	0.02	0.01
Paper, printing & publishing	5.77	2.66	0.16	0.08
Coke & petroleum products	18.42	12.03	1.89	1.07
Chemical products	8.30	5.90	1.36	1.02
Rubber & plastic products	12.70	6.01	0.40	0.19
Other non-metallic mineral	12.30	5.26	0.70	0.27
Basic metals	9.89	4.88	1.35	0.49
Fabricated metal products	12.26	5.50	0.36	0.15
Machinery	12.88	5.98	0.85	0.38
Electrical machinery	12.51	8.04	0.41	0.25
TV & communication equipm.	9.50	7.32	0.13	0.11
Medical instruments & watches	14.33	8.37	0.14	0.08
Transport equipment & parts	14.12	10.47	0.91	0.64
Manufacturing N.E.C.	8.13	0.24	0.12	0.01
Aggregate registered manufacturing	**10.30**	**6.26**		
Reallocation effect			**0.26**	**0.76**

Source: Author's calculation based on ASI data

period, growing at above 18 percent per annum, followed by Medical Instruments and Watches, and Transport Equipment. Tobacco Products depicts slowest growth among all the industries, growing at around 4 percent per annum during 2000–01 to 2008–09. Textiles Products and Paper, and Printing and Publishing are the other two industries growing around 5 percent per annum. In the case of labor productivity, Coke and Petroleum Products and Transport Equipment are the only two industries which observesmore than 10 percent labor productivity growth, while Manufacturing N.E.C. shows the lowest labor productivity growth around 0.3 percent, followed by Leather and Fur Products, Textiles Products and Paper, and Printing and Publishing.

This study next looks at the contribution of individual sectors' value added growth to the aggregate value added growth in registered manufacturing industries for the period 2000–09. This allows us to extend the scope of growth analysis to the different industries which comprise the economy. The aggregate growth is the weighted sum of industry growth plus a reallocation term R. The reallocation term is positive if the economy shifts from low-growing industries toward high-growing industries. The detailed analysis of the manufacturing sector reveals that much of the growth is accruing to the contribution of Coke and Petroleum Products, Chemical Products, and Basic Metals GVA growth to aggregate value added growth. Labor productivity in the Indian manufacturing sector has been growing substantially over decades, and much of this gain is accruing through acceleration in the contribution of Coke and Petroleum Products, Chemical Products labor productivity to aggregate service labor productivity growth. The labor reallocation effect is positive, suggesting that resources seem to be moving from less-productive services to more-productive services. If workers are moving to industries that witness faster productivity growth, the reallocation term will be positive.

Figure 19.3 has attempted to broadly classify the three-digit industries according to ranges of TFP growth rate. Evidence from figure suggests that around one-quarter of the industries depict negative TFP growth for entire study periods and another quarter of the industries recorded TFP growth between 1 and 2 percent. While only 18 percent and 14 percent of industries respectively attain 2 to 3 percent and 3 to 4 percent TFP growth. Only eight industries or around 15 percent of industries observed high TFP growth (more than 4 percent).

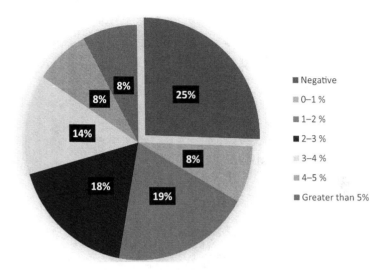

Figure 19.3 Ranges of TFP growth (2000–01 to 2008–09)
Source: Author's calculation based on ASI data

In Figure 19.4, we present the TFP growth estimates for 51 three-digit industries between 2000 and 2009. TFP growth rate for these classified manufacturing sectors shows wide fluctuation, and it also varies across industries. The wide variations of TFP growth rate range from a low of –4.21 percent per annum to a high of 6.87 percent per annum for the entire period of analysis. Thirty-eight three-digit industries recorded positive TFP growth, whose combined value added share is around 80 percent. Only 13 industries with around 20 percent value added share record negative TFP growth. Coke oven products is the worst performer in terms of average annual TFP growth rate, followed by knitted and crocheted fabrics, leather products, and processing and preservation of meat, fish, fruit, vegetables, etc. On the other hand, only four industries recorded TFP growth rate in excess of 5 percent. These industries are air craft and space craft, watches and clocks, TV and radio receivers and office, accounting and computer machinery.

The major observation to be drawn from the previous two figures is that the overall total factor productivity growth rate of registered manufacturing industries shows wide fluctuation. And more than

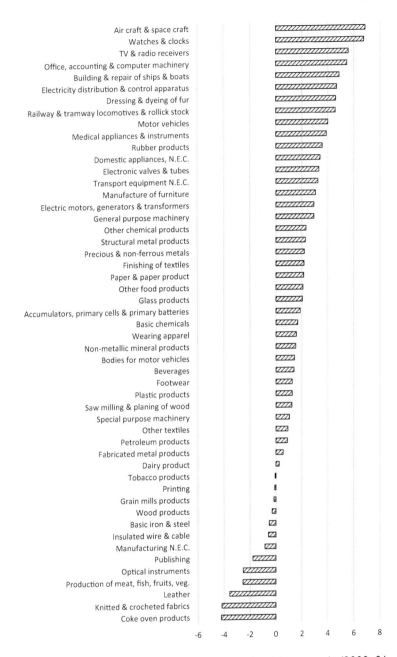

Figure 19.4 Average annual total factor productivity growth (2000–01 to 2008–09)

Source: Author's calculation based on ASI data

50 percent of the industries shows very poor productivity growth around 1 percent per annum. Next, we analyze the TFP growth for the top 10 contributors to value added (Table 19.3).

Evidence from Panel A suggests that the combined value added shares of the top-10 industries are around 64 percent. Basic iron and steel, petroleum products, other chemical products, basic chemicals and spinning, weaving and finishing of textiles industry

Table 19.3 Average annual TFP growth, value added share and industry contribution to aggregate GVA growth

Panel A:

NIC 2004	Industry Description	TFPG	VA Share
271	Basic iron & steel	−0.52	11.41
232	Petroleum products	0.89	10.95
242	Other chemical products	2.31	9.62
241	Basic chemicals	1.67	7.97
171	Finishing of textiles	2.16	6.00
269	Non-metallic mineral products	1.53	5.26
154	Other food products	2.08	3.78
291	General purpose machinery	2.92	3.15
341	Motor vehicles	3.99	3.10
272	Precious & non-ferrous metals	2.19	2.84
	Combined Top 10 Industries	**1.92**[1]	**64.08**

Panel B:

NIC 2004	Industry Description	TFPG	Contribution to Aggregate GVA growth
242	Other chemical products	2.31	1.27
271	Basic iron & steel	−0.52	1.25
232	Petroleum products	0.89	1.18
269	Non-metallic mineral products	1.53	0.62
341	Motor vehicles	3.99	0.52
291	General purpose machinery	2.92	0.45
359	Transport equipment N.E.C.	3.23	0.31
252	Plastic products	1.25	0.28
241	Basic chemicals	1.67	0.27
281	Structural metal products	2.27	0.27
	Combined Top 10 Industries	**1.96**	**6.41**

Source: Author's calculation based on ASI data

Note: 1 simple average

groups specifically are the major contributors to value added. Even though these 10 industries occupy around two-thirds of the organized manufacturing value added share, their average TFP growth rate is 1.92 percent per annum. And all of the industries accept one within the top-10 value added contributors recorded TFP growth below 3 percent per annum. Panel B shows that the combined GVA growth contribution of top-10 industries to aggregate manufacturing is 6.41 percent. Between 2000–01 and 2008–09, registered manufacturing grew at a rate of 10.30 percent per annum. Even though these 10 industries originate around two-third of the organized manufacturing value added growth, their average TFP growth rate is 1.96 percent per annum. Manufacture of motor vehicles and transporting equipment are the only industries which depict more than 3 percent TFP growth.

Table 19.4 documents the decomposition of output growth for 51 three-digit manufacturing industries during 2000–01 to 2008–09. The contribution of an input is defined as the product of value share of the input and the growth rate of the input. Thus, each input contributes to output in proportion to its value share, while TFP contributes to output growth point for point. We observe wide variations in output growth across different manufacturing industries with over 10 percent growth in 30 industries in the period 2000–09. Observing the industry mean and median, we note that the average TFP contribution is around 15 percent for aggregate manufacturing for the entire study period 2000–09. At disaggregate level, the majority of the three-digit industries' TFP growth contribution lies in the range of 0 to 30 percent. Only 14 industries have more than 30 percent TFP contribution, while 10 industries show negative TFP contribution. We also found that about one-half of the output growth contributed by material expansion, followed by service and capital input around 10 to 15 percent. While energy and labor input have a minor contribution to output growth, this implies that most of the industries output growth has still been driven by intensive use of inputs. In the case of material input, only two industries showed negative contribution, followed by services (three industries depicted negative contribution) and capital input (four industries depicted negative contribution).

Summary and conclusion

The present study has sought to analyze the Indian organized manufacturing sector's growth and productivity performance from

Table 19.4 Sources of output growth

| Industry Description | Output Growth | Contribution to Output Growth ||||||
		Employment	Capital	Material	Energy	Services	TFP
Production of meat, fish, fruits, veg.	9.05	0.05	0.36	9.71	0.14	1.34	-2.55
Dairy product	6.37	0.11	0.42	4.66	0.15	0.79	0.25
Grain mills products	8.26	0.05	0.54	6.65	0.15	1.03	-0.16
Other food products	5.83	0.03	0.78	1.75	0.20	0.98	2.08
Beverages	9.75	0.22	1.86	5.51	0.27	0.50	1.39
Tobacco products	0.88	-0.07	1.45	-0.01	-0.01	-0.42	-0.07
Finishing of textiles	5.23	-0.03	0.48	2.02	0.17	0.44	2.16
Other textiles	19.44	0.89	2.15	11.95	0.58	2.95	0.93
Knitted & crocheted fabrics	0.13	0.45	0.68	2.21	0.05	0.91	-4.16
Wearing apparel	9.09	0.79	1.15	3.62	0.17	1.79	1.57
Dressing & dyeing of fur	28.23	1.37	1.19	15.16	1.43	4.48	4.60
Leather	-0.95	0.14	0.37	1.50	0.06	0.55	-3.57
Footwear	9.27	0.59	0.65	4.78	0.17	1.82	1.26
Saw milling & planing of wood	14.43	-0.06	0.47	10.01	0.10	2.69	1.23
Wood products	12.73	0.29	0.78	8.96	0.45	2.56	-0.30
Paper & paper product	8.22	0.17	0.83	4.25	0.11	0.71	2.13
Publishing	-7.11	-1.33	0.78	-3.66	-0.11	-1.00	-1.79
Printing	16.53	0.71	2.33	10.16	0.42	3.01	-0.10
Coke oven products	4.52	0.16	1.55	5.14	-0.03	1.91	-4.21
Petroleum products	14.33	0.04	1.21	11.33	0.17	0.68	0.89
Basic chemicals	5.81	-0.05	0.37	3.26	0.03	0.53	1.67

(Continued)

Table 19.4 (Continued)

Industry Description	Output Growth	Employment	Capital	Material	Energy	Services	TFP
Other chemical products	11.02	0.21	2.09	4.46	0.23	1.72	2.31
Rubber products	12.12	0.23	0.84	6.62	0.22	0.65	3.56
Plastic products	12.64	0.32	1.15	8.25	0.44	1.23	1.25
Glass products	7.83	0.10	0.92	3.14	1.05	0.60	2.03
Non-metallic mineral products	11.24	0.43	2.12	4.19	1.57	1.40	1.53
Basic iron & steel	11.01	0.16	1.43	7.54	1.11	1.29	−0.52
Precious & non-ferrous metals	10.72	0.00	1.18	6.54	0.40	0.41	2.19
Structural metal products	19.32	0.43	2.10	11.90	0.15	2.47	2.27
Fabricated metal products	8.71	0.32	1.29	4.37	0.26	1.91	0.56
General purpose machinery	14.65	0.71	1.41	6.06	0.10	3.44	2.92
Special purpose machinery	12.47	0.23	1.07	7.60	0.09	2.44	1.04
Domestic appliances, N.E.C.	8.62	−0.04	0.61	3.26	−0.04	1.43	3.40
Office, accounting & computer machinery	13.05	0.04	2.05	4.51	0.25	0.73	5.46
Electric motors, generators & transformers	15.58	−0.05	0.78	9.79	0.14	1.99	2.92
Electricity distribution & control apparatus	17.74	0.42	1.31	8.86	0.14	2.34	4.67
Insulated wire & cable	9.81	0.22	0.66	8.74	0.10	0.67	−0.58
Accumulators, primary cells & primary batteries	14.49	0.20	1.79	8.94	0.39	1.31	1.87
Electronic valves & tubes	11.10	0.40	0.26	5.41	−0.08	1.79	3.31
TV & radio receivers	11.62	−0.07	0.52	2.28	−0.02	3.35	5.57
Medical appliances & instruments	11.90	0.50	1.35	4.83	0.12	1.23	3.88
Optical instruments	−5.10	−0.50	0.29	−0.30	−0.27	−1.79	−2.53

Watches & clocks	18.53	0.69	1.66	8.14	0.16	1.11	6.77
Motor vehicles	14.87	0.09	0.94	6.94	0.05	2.87	3.99
Bodies for motor vehicles	21.63	1.28	2.23	13.49	0.30	2.91	1.43
Building & repair of ships & boats	11.89	0.17	2.42	0.37	0.01	4.06	4.86
Railway & tramway locomotives & rollick stock	13.55	-0.36	-0.13	7.02	0.12	2.34	4.56
Air craft & space craft	22.29	1.87	1.17	8.49	0.34	3.56	6.87
Transport equipment N.E.C.	10.66	0.10	1.11	5.32	0.10	0.79	3.23
Manufacture of furniture	8.84	0.44	0.80	4.67	0.29	-0.41	3.05
Manufacturing N.E.C.	19.31	0.32	1.15	13.48	0.06	5.15	-0.85
Industry Mean	**11.02**	**0.26**	**1.12**	**6.15**	**0.24**	**1.59**	**1.65**
Industry Median	**11.10**	**0.20**	**1.11**	**5.51**	**0.15**	**1.34**	**1.67**

Source: Author's calculation based on ASI data

2000–01 to 2008–09 by comparing the TFP growth for selected three-digit industries and examining the sources of output growth. We have considered a set of 51 three-digit organized manufacturing industries, combined value added shares of these industries are around 90 percent of the total organized manufacturing sector. During the entire study period, around 60 percent of the classified manufacturing industries have recorded output growth rate in excess of 10 percent per annum. Output growth for organized manufacturing is 11.02 percent per annum, while TFP growth rate of aggregate organized manufacturing is 1.65 percent per annum. At a disaggregated level, TFP growth of three-digit industries has shown a wide fluctuation, with wide inter-industry variation. TFP growth rate for all classified three-digit organized manufacturing industries has been found between –4.21 percent and 6.87 percent. The results of the study also indicate that TFP growth contribution to output growth is insignificant. We note that the average TFP contribution is around 15 percent for aggregate manufacturing for the entire study period. The TFP contribution also varies across different ranges of output growth. Only 14 industries have more than 30 percent TFP contribution. For aggregate manufacturing, we have found that materials alone contributed most of the output growth at about 55 percent, followed by services and capital input around 15 and 10 percent, respectively. Contribution of labor and energy inputs are insignificant for the entire study period, respectively contributing 2.36 percent and 2.18 percent to output growth.

Comparing findings of this research with the earlier findings for the 1990s, we have found that total factor productivity growth rate to some extent being improved in the 2000s, but TFP contribution to output growth has been insignificant. Our results have also indicated that there exist sharp inter industry differences in productivity performance. Even now, Indian manufacturing sector's output growth has driven by input accumulation. The TFP contribution has also varied across different ranges of output growth. Findings of our study have also indicated that the intermediate inputs contributed most of the output growth, more than the traditional inputs (labor and capital). Material input alone has been contributed more than half of the output growth, followed by services input. Use of services in manufacturing has grown at an accelerated pace in the 2000s compared to any earlier period. The contribution of services to output growth has also increased. Our study may have important implications for further work. First, we need to identify and analyze the causal relation between policy changes, especially trade and industrial and TFP growth, and then explore and examine the causes behind the unsatisfactory performance in terms of TFP by Indian organized manufacturing sector during the post-reform period. Second, we may need a more complete study based on organized and unorganized manufacturing sectors, as well as the services sectors to arrive at a more complete picture of productivity growth.

Notes

1 Banga and Goldar (2007) and Virmani and Hashim (2011) are the only studies which include services as an intermediate input.
2 A more detailed discussion on the factor of production used in this study has been provided in the third section.
3 List of the three-digit organized manufacturing industries are presented in Appendix I, Table 1.
4 See Das (2003).
5 See Das (2003), Goldar (2003).
6 In earlier ASI reports it was denoted as number of employees.
7 Das (2003), Goldar (2004), Banga and Goldar (2007) and Virmani et al. (2011) have employed perpetual inventory method. On the other hand, studies like Kathuria et al. (2010) used the book values of capital stock as capital input.
8 Similar as Unel (2003) and Banga and Goldar (2007).

Bibliography

Balakrishnan, P., K. Pushpangadan, and M. Suresh Babu. 2000. "Trade Liberalisation and Productivity Growth in Manufacturing: Evidence From Firm-Level Panel Data." *Economic and Political Weekly* 35(41): 3679–3682.

Banga, R., and B. Goldar. 2007. "Contribution of Services to Output Growth and Productivity in Indian Manufacturing: Pre- and Post-Reforms." *Economic and Political Weekly* 42(26): 2769–2777.

Basu, Susanto, and John G. Fernald. 1997. "Returns to Scale in U.S. Production: Estimates and Implications." *Journal of Political Economy* 105(2): 249–283.

Bollard, A., P. Klenow, and G. Sharma. 2011. "India's Mysterious Manufacturing Miracle." mimeo, Stanford University.

Das, Deb Kusum. 2003. "Manufacturing Productivity Under Varying Trade Regimes: India in the 1980s and 1990s." *Working Paper*, No. 107, Indian Council for Research on International Economic Relations, New Delhi.

Das, Deb Kusum, and Gunajit Kalita. 2009. "Aggregate Productivity Growth in Indian Manufacturing: An Application of Domar Aggregation." *Working Paper*, No. 239, Indian Council for Research on International Economic Relations, New Delhi.

Ghosh, Saibal. 2010. "Economic Reforms and Manufacturing Productivity: Evidence From India." *EERI Research Paper Series* No 32/2010.

Goldar, B. 2014. "Productivity in Indian Manufacturing in the Post-Reform Period." In *Productivity in Indian Manufacturing: Measurements, Methods and Analysis*, p.75. Routledge.

Goldar, Bishwanath. 2000. "Productivity Growth in Indian Manufacturing in the 1980s and 1990s." Paper presented at conference on Centre for Development Economics, Delhi School of Economics, *Industrialisation in a Reforming Economy: A Quantitative Assessment*, New Delhi, December 20–22.

Goldar, Bishwanath. 2004. "Indian Manufacturing: Productivity Trends in Pre- and Post-Reform Periods." *Economic and Political Weekly* 39(46/47): 5033–5043.

Goldar, Bishwanath, and Anita Kumari. 2003. "Import Liberalization and Productivity Growth in Indian Manufacturing Industries in the 1990s." *The Developing Economies* 41(4): 436.

Hall, R. 1988. "The Relation Between Price and Marginal Cost in US Industry." *Journal of Political Economy* 96: 921–947.

Kathuria V., Rajesh Raj S.N., and Sen K. 2010. "Organised versus unorganised manufacturing performance in the post-reform period". *Economic and Political Weekly*. 45(24): 55–64.

Kathuria V., Rajesh Raj S.N., and Sen K. 2011. "Productivity Measurement in Indian Manufacturing: A Comparison of Alternative Methods". Development Economics and Public Policy Cluster, Institute of Development Policy and Management, School of Environment and Development, University of Manchester, WP No 31/2011.

Krishna, Pravin, and Devashish Mitra. 1998. "Trade Liberalization, Market Discipline and Productivity Growth: New Evidence From India." *Journal of Development Economics* 56(2): 447.

Mukherjee, Kankana, and Subhash C Ray. 2005. "Technical Efficiency and Its Dynamics in Indian Manufacturing: An Inter-State Analysis". *Indian Economic Review*. 40(2): 101.

Solow, Robert M. 1957. "Technical Change and the Aggregate Production Function." *The Review of Economics and Statistics* 39(3): 312–320.

Srivastava, Vivek. 2000. "The Impact of India's Economic Reforms on Industrial Productivity, Efficiency and Competitiveness." Draft of the report Submitted to the National Council of Applied Economic Research, New Delhi.

Trivedi, Pushpa, Anand Prakash, and David Sinate. 2000. *Productivity in Major Manufacturing Industries in India, 1973–74 to 1997–98*. Mumbai: Department of Economic Analysis and Policy, Reserve Bank of India.

Unel, Bulent. 2003. *Productivity Trends in India's Manufacturing Sectors in the Last Two Decades*. Washington, DC: International Monetary Fund (IMF).

Unni, Jeemol, N. Lalitha, and Uma Rani. 2001. "Economic Reforms and Productivity Trends in Indian Manufacturing," *Economic and Political Weekly*, 36(41): 3914–22.

Virmani, M. A., and M. D. A. Hashim. 2011. "J-Curve of Productivity and Growth: Indian Manufacturing Post-Liberalization." International Monetary Fund, no. 11-163.

Chapter 20

A state-level perspective of productivity growth of the Indian organized manufacturing sector

Pushpa Trivedi

Introduction

The National Manufacturing Policy (NMP, henceforth) (Government of India in 2011) aims at increasing the share of manufacturing sector in GDP to about 25 percent by 2021 (i.e., within a decade of its announcement) and creating about 100 million additional jobs during 2011 to 2021. These ambitious targets in a way aim at combining growth of output with growth of employment. The strategy embedded in the NMP is said to be neutral with respect to sectors, location and technology.[1] It may not be out of place to mention here that India's economic growth has been accompanied by sharp inequalities. Chowdhury (2014) concludes that during 2003–04 to 2009–10, regional inequalities have risen, despite the fact that some of the poorer states have registered higher growth rates. In particular, this is true for the post-reform period and for the recent period when India has witnessed high growth rates. The study also demonstrates that the prime source of inequalities has been the differences in the growth of the primary sector, followed by the secondary and tertiary sectors. The concern for regional inequalities is reflected in Ghate and Wright (2013), who find no evidence of either convergence or divergence in real per capita income across the Indian states. In fact, their study indicates that those state that had a higher proportion of their income originating from agricultural and registered manufacturing sector did not contribute to the turnaround in the growth trajectory of the Indian economy. Das et al. (2015) find that the state-level effects have significantly contributed to India's unbalanced growth. In brief, the regional disparities have been a matter of concern and, hence, investigation. For their own survival, the policy makers cannot afford to ignore these regional inequalities and will have to do a tightrope walk in order to promote regionally balanced growth with employment creation.

There has been an outpouring of literature on regional (state-level) growth and regional inequalities in India (Ahluwalia 2002; Ghosh and Deb 2005; Singh et al. 2010). There have been quite a few studies on regional growth of the manufacturing sector and their determinants in the Indian context (see Aghion et al. 2008). In the latter group of studies, the major determinants of output growth performance of the Indian manufacturing sector have been identified to be some proxies of economic reforms, such as trade liberalization (Das 2016), liberalization of norms for foreign direct investment, infrastructure constraints. However, the studies investigating the linkages between productivity in manufacturing sector and its determinants at the state level (Veeramani and Goldar 2005) have been rather few (see Babu and Natarajan 2013, for elaborate review of literature). The same is true about the literature on productivity in the disaggregated manufacturing sector at state levels and their determinants at state levels (Trivedi 2004; Trivedi et al. 2011). A good number of studies have investigated the impact of economic reforms on either output or on productivity growth in the manufacturing sector (Mukherjee and Ray 2005; Deb and Ray 2014).

It may not be out of place to mention here that the two major states of India – Maharashtra and Gujarat – account for almost one-third of India's GDP originating from the manufacturing sector, whereas the corresponding figure for Bihar, which the third most-populous state of India, is merely 1 percent. Given this context, this paper aims to study the growth path of the registered manufacturing[2] sector of the selected states of the Indian economy. In particular, it seeks to answer the two questions. First, is the growth of the organized manufacturing sector has been propelled due to increased application of inputs, or is it due to Total Factor Productivity Growth (TFPG), and if the latter is true then what is the contribution of TFPG to growth? Second, is the growth of organized manufacturing sector accompanied by employment creation in this sector? We seek to answer these questions in the context of 17 selected states[3] of India for 9 major categories of industries.[4] The selection of states was based on the criteria that the state should account for at least 1 percent of the total population of India and then at least 1 percent of share of a state's manufacturing sector in gross output of manufacturing sector of India.

An aggregative analysis of state-level perspective on growth, productivity and employment would mask many differences across states, as different states may have different industries that are prominent in those regions. Hence, this study also attempts a disaggregated analysis at the industry level for each of the selected states. The rest of this paper is organized as follows. In the second section, we provide a synoptic view of the importance of the manufacturing sector of selected states to the manufacturing sector of India. We also provide information on the importance of the manufacturing sector of each selected state in its own gross state domestic product (GSDP) across the various selected states of India, and the importance of each of the selected industries in the registered manufacturing sector of the selected states. In the third section, we detail the coverage of the study (spatial and temporal) and the methodology used for measurement of total productivity. The fourth section presents the estimates of growth, productivity and employment for the selected states and selected industries, and the final section summarizes conclusions emanating from the study.

Manufacturing sector in selected states of India: an overview

Figure 20.1 shows the importance of manufacturing (MFG, henceforth) sector of various states in India's manufacturing sector. This is proxied by the percentage of real state domestic product originating from the manufacturing sector (along with the disaggregation at registered and unregistered segments) to the real GDP of India originating from the manufacturing sector. It can be seen that Gujarat, Maharashtra and Tamil Nadu contribute to more than 10 percent of India's manufacturing sector. These three states alone account for about 42 percent of the GDP originating from the manufacturing sector. In the next category are the states, A&T, Karnataka, UP and West Bengal, which individually account for about 5 to 10 percent of real GDP of India's MFG sector. Together, these four states account for another 25 percent of real GDP of India's MFG sector. In brief, these 7 states account for more than two-thirds of India's real GDP of India's MFG sector. Hence, the growth of productivity in these states will have a greater influence on the overall productivity of manufacturing sector.

Figure 20.2 provides the information on contribution of the manufacturing sector in real SDP of the respective state and also provides the corresponding data for India. It can be seen from Figure 2.2 that the contribution of manufacturing in real SDP of Gujarat, Jharkhand, Maharashtra, Tamil Nadu, Haryana, Chhattisgarh,

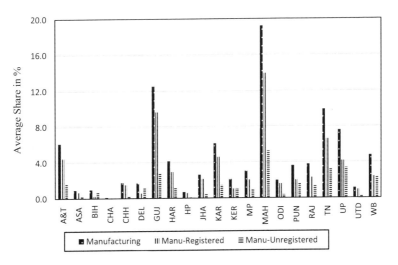

Figure 20.1 Contribution of states' MFG sector to India's MFG sector (2000–13)

Source: Compiled from data sourced from www.mospi.nic.in last accessed on 5-7-2016

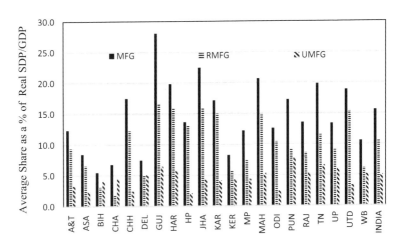

Figure 20.2 Contribution of manufacturing sector in real SDP/GDP (2000–13)

Source: Compiled from data sourced from www.mospi.nic.in last accessed on 5-7-2016

Punjab and Karnataka are above that for the rest of India. The states of Rajasthan, UP, Odisha, Andhra Pradesh and Telangana, Madhya Pradesh and West Bengal form the next layer, wherein, their contribution of their manufacturing sector ranges from 10 to 14 percent.

Table 20.1 provides a synoptic view of the registered manufacturing[5] sector in various states of India.

A few facts from Table 20.1 may be noted. The FBT (Food, Beverages and Tobacco), PT, CHEM, METAL and MTE industries are important from the point of view of output their contribution to India's manufacturing sector (last row of Table 20.1). The FBT is an important industry more or less consistently in all the selected states. The TEX industry is an important industry in Delhi, Punjab, Rajasthan and Tamil Nadu. The PT industry is important industry in Bihar, Kerala, Gujarat, Karnataka, Maharashtra and A&T. The CHEM industry is important in Gujarat, Rajasthan, Maharashtra, West Bengal and MP, where it accounts for more than 10 percent of the value of gross output of the total manufacturing sector in the respective state. The corresponding figure for UP, MP, Kerala and A&T are about 10 percent or so. Thus, the CHEM industry is also well dispersed across the states, as is the case with the FBT industry. In Chhattisgarh, Odisha and West Bengal, metal industry dominates. Except Kerala and Bihar, this industry accounts for about 10 to 15 percent of the value of gross output of the organized manufacturing. MTE accounts for about 55 percent of the value of gross output of the organized manufacturing sector. In Haryana, Kerala, MP and Chhattisgarh, the corresponding figures range between 24 and 30 percent. In Tamil Nadu, West Bengal, Punjab, Karnataka and Gujarat, these figures range between 10 and 20 percent. Thus, this industry also has a significant presence in many states of India, like the FBT, CHEM and METAL industries. In other words, due to differences in capital intensities of various industries, employment and output contributions differ widely across the industries.

Table 20.2 presents the contribution of various industries in employment across the selected states of India.

It can be seen from Table 20.2 that in Kerala and A&T, FBT accounts for nearly half or more than that of the employment (as measured by the total persons engaged) of the organized manufacturing sector. In other states too, this industry has been a significant contributor to employment. The TEX industry too has been a major employment provider within the organized sector. The

Table 20.1 Average share of nominal gross output of selected industries in total gross output of manufacturing output of the state/India (2000–01 to 2012–13)

Srl No	State/Country	FBT	TEX	LEATH	PAPER	RP	PT	CHEM	MET	MTE	SMFG
1	A&T	29.0	4.1	0.0	2.2	3.0	13.7	10.0	15.2	10.2	87.3
2	BIHAR	17.8	0.5	0.5	0.8	0.4	70.1	0.7	4.4	1.4	96.6
3	CHAT	9.6	0.4	0.4	0.0	0.6	1.2	1.2	76.6	2.1	92.3
4	DELHI	27.4	23.0	3.7	1.0	2.8	0.0	8.8	8.4	17.9	93.2
5	GUJ	9.1	7.3	1.2	0.0	1.9	33.8	24.1	10.4	7.6	95.6
6	HAR	11.1	8.8	1.0	1.2	2.0	0.2	4.2	14.0	55.3	97.7
7	JHA	1.7	0.1	N.A.	0.0	0.3	9.2	2.4	62.0	19.6	95.3
8	KAR	16.5	6.7	1.2	0.3	2.6	16.8	7.0	14.1	26.2	91.8
9	KER	19.9	3.9	1.2	1.0	9.6	39.1	9.6	5.1	5.5	94.8
10	MAH	12.5	5.5	1.2	0.1	3.4	15.3	14.0	15.5	26.3	93.8
11	MP	32.0	9.4	1.0	0.9	5.9	2.8	11.6	9.4	16.7	89.7
12	ODI	9.5	0.5	2.8	N.A.	3.3	1.8	10.6	61.8	2.6	92.9
13	PUN	22.4	20.4	3.0	0.8	3.0	0.0	9.0	18.9	18.9	96.4
14	RAJ	16.2	17.6	0.5	0.5	4.3	1.4	14.4	14.2	13.9	83.0
15	TN	10.8	19.3	1.7	3.1	2.5	9.6	7.1	11.8	28.9	94.7
16	UP	25.8	5.4	1.8	2.8	3.3	8.2	10.4	13.2	24.1	95.2
17	WB	13.7	8.3	0.8	2.1	1.6	15.5	13.2	30.1	9.3	94.7
	INDIA	14.7	8.6	1.5	0.9	3.3	15.0	13.3	16.8	20.2	94.1

Source: Calculated from the ASI data sourced from www.epwrfits.in/index.aspx last accessed on 6–7–2016.

Note: SFMG indicates total of all selected manufacturing industries.

Table 20.2 Average share of employees in selected industries in total employees of the state (2000–01 to 2012–13)

Srl No	State/Country	FBT	TEX	LEATH	PAPER	RP	PT	CHEM	MET	MTE	SMFG
1	A&T	48.9	8.1	0.4	2.4	2.9	1.2	8.4	7.2	9.6	89.2
2	BIHAR	22.6	5.7	2.1	1.2	0.5	4.2	2.9	5.0	3.9	48.1
3	CHAT	16.8	1.4	0.9	0.1	3.4	1.7	1.6	62.5	4.2	92.6
4	DELHI	9.1	34.4	4.9	1.5	3.5	0.0	5.0	9.0	22.0	89.4
5	GUJ	9.5	21.9	2.4	0.1	3.8	1.9	21.9	10.6	15.4	89.8
6	HAR	10.3	22.7	1.4	3.0	2.5	0.0	3.6	8.6	41.4	93.6
7	JHA	4.2	0.5	N.A.	0.1	0.7	9.4	3.8	50.3	17.0	86.0
8	KAR	15.1	33.4	1.7	0.6	3.2	0.4	5.7	8.5	23.1	93.0
9	KER	57.1	9.0	1.3	0.8	5.6	1.3	5.3	3.1	5.9	89.4
10	MAH	18.9	12.5	2.0	0.3	4.7	0.9	12.4	13.9	26.1	91.6
11	MP	18.9	16.5	3.0	1.2	7.0	0.6	10.7	9.0	21.2	88.2
12	ODI	18.5	2.6	4.0	—	2.8	1.2	5.4	51.0	2.2	91.9
13	PUN	21.8	23.3	2.4	1.1	3.9	0.1	3.7	12.0	20.4	88.7
14	RAJ	12.6	39.3	1.1	1.6	4.5	0.3	8.4	11.7	14.1	93.5
15	TN	10.9	36.9	1.8	5.8	3.0	0.3	9.5	8.1	16.8	93.1
16	UP	26.6	13.1	2.1	7.2	3.3	0.6	6.7	12.2	17.9	89.6
17	WB	15.5	34.0	1.3	3.3	1.9	1.4	4.9	20.1	11.8	94.2
	INDIA	20.4	20.5	2.2	2.1	3.8	1.0	9.5	12.2	17.9	87.7

Source: Calculated from the ASI data sourced from www.epwrfits.in/index.aspx, last accessed on 6–7-2016.

Note: SFMG indicates total of all selected manufacturing industries.

CHEM industry has been a major employment provider in Gujarat and Maharashtra. The MTE industry also has been a major employment provider, especially in Haryana, Maharashtra, Karnataka, Delhi, MP and Punjab.

Coverage and the methodology used for measurement of TFPG

This study may be considered as a continuation and revision of the previous studies, Trivedi et al. (2000), Trivedi (2003), Trivedi (2004) and Trivedi et al. (2011). This study encompasses 17 major states of India. The states included in this study (arranged in alphabetical order with their abbreviations) have been listed in Table 20.A.1.

The industry groups chosen for investigation in this study are: Food, Beverages and Tobacco (FBT); Textiles and Textile Products (TEX); Leather and Leather Products (LEATH); Paper and Paper Products (PAPER); Manufacture of coke and refined petroleum products (PT); Chemicals and Chemical Products (CHEM); Rubber and Plastic Products (RP); Metal and Metal Products (METAL); and Machinery and Transport Equipment (MTE). Apart from these categories, we also estimate TFPG of the manufacturing sector as a whole, though we exclude recycling and other miscellaneous industries beyond NIC code 36 in NIC 1998 and 2004 and beyond NIC code 31 in NIC 2008.

The growth accounting (GA) framework has been used in this study for estimated TFPG. This approach measures TFPG as the difference between the rate of growth of output and the weighted rates of growth of factor inputs and material inputs. We have used translog index (TLI), using a three input (labor, capital and material) framework (see Equation 20.1). The justification for using the TLI has been provided by Diewert (1976).[6] We have assumed constant returns to scale, which implies that the weights of all inputs sum up to unity.

$$\ln(TFP_t / TFP_{t-1}) = \ln(O_t / O_{t-1}) - \left[(w_t + w_{t-1})/2\right] \\ \ln(L_t / L_{t-1}) - \left[(n_t + n_{t-1})/2\right]\ln(N_t / N_{t-1}) \\ - \left[\{(1-(n_t + w_t)) + (1-(n_{t-1} + w_{t-1}))\}/2\right] \\ \ln(K_t / K_{t-1})$$

(20.1)

The notations used in Equation 20.1 are as follows: O and N denote the value of output and raw materials at constant (1999–2000) prices. L and K denote total persons engaged and real capital stock, respectively. Additionally, w and n are shares of total emoluments and value of total inputs in nominal output, respectively, and ln indicates natural logarithm, whereas subscript t denotes time. The weight of capital input in Equation 20.1 has been obtained as a residual, by subtracting the sum of weights of labor and total inputs from unity.

After calculating the TFPG for each year in the sample period, we have used the arithmetic average and reported the annual average TFPG for the entire period 2000–01 to 2012–13. We have also calculated the annual variations in total persons engaged and value of gross output, wherein the latter has been deflated by the respective Wholesale Price Index (WPI).[7] WPI time-series with different base years have been converted to a common base year, i.e., 1999–2000 base. In order to compile the input price data series, the data on four Input-Output matrices (I-O) have been used. The weights for various inputs used by these industries have been derived by using the I-O 1998–99, 2003–04, 2006–07 and 2007–08 matrices. It may be also noted that due to non-availability of the I-O matrix beyond then is a cause for concern to the researchers, as it is almost a decade since I-O matrix has been provided by the Central Statistical Organization, Ministry of Statistics and Programme Implementation, Government of India. The measurement of TFPG would have been much more accurate if updated details of input use across various industries were available. The details of industry codes of various industries in the above listed I-O matrices have been provided in Table 20.A.1.

TFPG of MFG sector and selected industries: performance of selected states/India

Table 20.3 presents the average annual growth rates of TFP (TFPG) for the selected states and industries and for the organized MFG sector. In Table 20.2, we report the annual average growth rates of real gross output, again for the selected industries and MFG sector (Og). These results are also reported for MFG of the selected states and for India Table 20.3, we report the ratio (in percentages) of the TFPG to Og for selected states, selected industries and also for MFG and for country as a whole. It may be noted that for country as a whole, the annual average TFPG for the period 2000–01 to

Table 20.3 Average annual growth rates of TFP (2000–01 to 2012–13)

Srl No	State/Country	FBT	TEX	LEATH	PAPER	RP	PT	CHEM	METAL	MTE	MFG
1	A&T	0.31	1.94	31.89	−2.23	0.79	1.19	12.75	−0.67	1.51	−0.02
2	BIHAR	0.64	4.08	1.11	−2.83	1.60	−0.14	11.87	−0.49	0.37	0.98
3	CHAT	0.86	3.08	22.46	0.28	15.22	17.99	4.94	−1.49	0.73	1.55
4	DELHI	1.17	0.23	1.01	0.55	3.36	−2.28	4.29	−1.34	2.02	1.10
5	GUJ	0.58	1.79	6.25	0.35	1.75	1.43	4.37	−0.56	1.92	1.98
6	HAR	0.35	1.22	1.96	1.62	2.16	0.11	3.66	−0.87	2.35	1.73
7	JHA	−0.06	3.11	0.00	2.09	2.97	5.63	2.56	−3.11	4.28	0.80
8	KAR	0.08	1.14	4.52	1.02	2.37	1.84	4.44	1.07	2.85	2.49
9	KER	0.86	1.27	5.82	1.82	3.13	1.42	3.87	−1.16	1.54	1.73
10	MAH	0.06	2.52	1.55	1.83	1.82	1.89	4.18	−0.66	1.91	1.63
11	MP	1.00	1.71	−0.46	1.01	3.02	−0.03	4.85	−1.17	2.59	2.04
12	ODI	1.44	3.79	N.A.	1.95	3.17	0.92	6.87	−2.41	2.92	0.61
13	PUN	0.50	1.74	0.32	1.36	1.50	3.07	2.46	−1.03	2.26	1.27
14	RAJ	1.68	1.78	3.22	3.70	−0.50	11.07	4.72	−0.11	3.22	1.26
15	TN	0.89	1.38	1.46	1.81	2.23	1.75	3.96	0.67	2.45	1.89
16	UP	0.34	1.75	1.97	1.00	1.60	4.89	4.37	−0.14	2.68	2.09
17	WB	0.44	1.84	2.09	1.82	3.08	0.97	5.58	−1.24	2.46	1.64
	INDIA	0.16	1.68	1.64	1.01	1.84	2.16	4.52	−0.82	2.37	1.79

Source: Calculated from the ASI data sourced from www.epwrfits.in/index.aspx last accessed on 6–7-2016.

2012–3 is about 1.8 percent (Table 20.3). Given the fact that gross output has increased by 13 percent per annum (pcpa) for the same period (Table 20.4), the contribution of productivity to growth works out to be just about 14 percent (Table 20.5).

As regards performance on the TFPG front (Table 20.3), Karnataka, UP, MP Gujarat and Tamil Nadu performed better as compared to the all-India average. The performance of A&T, Odisha, Jharkhand and Bihar was the worst, and these states witnessed TFPG of even less than 1.0 pcpa, over the period of the study. The TFPG for Haryana, Kerala, West Bengal, Maharashtra, Chhattisgarh, Punjab, Rajasthan was less than that witnessed at the all-India level, but was higher (1.0 pcpa) for the period under investigation.

As regards industries, the CHEM and MTE industries performed better and, hence, pulled up the overall TFPG. The RP and PT industries also performed rather well. However, given their negligible weight in the MFG sector, it was mainly the former two industries that witnessed somewhat better performance on the TFPG front pulled the overall TFPG of MFG sector. Growth of real output for MFG has been in double digits, except for Delhi, West Bengal and A&T. This period also covers the period when the industries could have been impacted by the global financial crisis. Thus, considering this, the output growth record of India's MFG sector is rather impressive. However, the performance of TFPG is far from impressive.

Across the states, for the FBT (which is a major industry, both in terms output and employment contribution), the highest productivity contribution was witnessed by Rajasthan to the extent of just about 11 percent.

The variation in growth of the TEX industry across the states has been higher than that witnessed by the FBT industry. Delhi, Punjab, Rajasthan and Tamil Nadu are the major textiles producers. Among these states, the highest TFPG for TEX is witnessed by Rajasthan (1.78 pcpa) and the lowest by Delhi (0.23 pcpa). Maximum contribution of TFPG to output growth among these states has been by Rajasthan, which is just about 15.6 percent.

The Leather, Paper, and Rubber & Plastic industries barely constitute about 6 percent of gross output of the MFG sector. In view of this, even high contribution of TFPG for these industries will not significantly improve the TFPG of the MFG sector as a whole. Even for the PT industry, the TFPG is rather low in those states in which this industry dominates.

Table 20.4 Average annual growth rates of real gross output (2000–01 to 2012–13)

Srl No	State/Country	FBT	TEX	LEATH	PAPER	RP	PT	CHEM	METAL	MTE	MFG
1	A&T	5.6	14.0	51.2	7.4	20.3	21.0	12.0	12.9	7.3	8.8
2	BIHAR	15.9	4.3	-0.4	52.9	38.1	15.8	23.4	45.0	12.9	11.7
3	CHAT	16.4	2.4	36.9	-0.7	21.8	13.7	20.6	15.9	43.8	14.5
4	DELHI	15.3	9.8	11.8	8.2	6.7	88.0	10.8	7.6	7.9	7.9
5	GUJ	10.9	12.2	13.8	35.1	18.2	21.9	9.9	19.2	15.0	12.8
6	HAR	12.8	21.1	14.2	17.6	14.4	37.3	14.7	17.7	15.4	14.9
7	JHA	13.2	19.1	N.A.	30.4	20.1	11.0	4.7	11.7	9.1	20.1
8	KAR	14.1	15.1	10.3	14.6	18.2	22.0	17.1	17.2	16.7	15.4
9	KER	11.9	7.1	20.8	81.1	12.0	15.1	6.8	9.1	10.5	10.0
10	MAH	11.3	7.5	10.3	17.3	13.5	15.8	12.7	15.9	12.9	12.1
11	MP	11.4	7.7	8.3	9.9	17.1	29.0	9.8	11.5	13.1	11.0
12	ODI	17.7	5.6	N.A.	16.5	11.0	80.9	10.7	18.8	6.8	15.9
13	PUN	10.6	14.3	20.4	17.1	11.5	77.0	12.9	12.0	12.4	12.6
14	RAJ	15.1	11.4	29.2	21.1	17.3	43.7	17.1	16.1	16.1	16.0
15	TN	12.4	13.5	14.0	16.0	66.4	14.8	7.6	18.5	19.2	14.9
16	UP	9.7	12.8	10.9	20.9	13.0	69.3	11.0	14.2	12.8	11.7
17	WB	12.9	6.6	9.5	19.9	14.2	12.5	7.6	9.7	5.8	8.1
	INDIA	11.2	11.1	11.3	15.8	15.3	14.6	12.2	14.3	14.1	12.9

Source: Calculated from the ASI data sourced from www.epwrfits.in/index.aspx last accessed on 6–7-2016.

Table 20.5 Ratio of annual average TFPG to annual average growth rate of real gross output (2000–01 to 2012–13)

Srl No	State/Country	FBT	TEX	LEATH	PAPER	RP	PT	CHEM	METAL	MTE	MFG
1	A&T	5.54	13.86	62.29	−30.14	3.89	5.67	106.25	−5.19	20.68	−0.23
2	BIHAR	4.03	94.88	−277.50	−5.35	4.20	−0.89	50.73	−1.09	2.87	8.38
3	CHAT	5.24	128.33	60.87	−40.00	69.82	131.31	23.98	−9.37	1.67	10.69
4	DELHI	7.65	2.35	8.56	6.71	50.15	−2.59	39.72	−17.63	25.57	13.92
5	GUJ	5.32	14.67	45.29	1.00	9.62	6.53	44.14	−2.92	12.80	15.47
6	HAR	2.73	5.78	13.80	9.20	15.00	0.29	24.90	−4.92	15.26	11.61
7	JHA	−0.46	16.29	N.A.	6.87	14.79	51.00	54.94	−26.54	47.14	3.98
8	KAR	0.57	7.55	43.88	6.99	13.02	8.36	25.96	6.22	17.07	16.17
9	KER	7.23	17.89	27.98	2.24	26.08	9.40	56.91	−12.75	14.67	17.30
10	MAH	0.53	33.60	15.05	10.58	13.48	11.96	32.91	−4.15	14.81	13.47
11	MP	8.77	22.21	−5.54	10.20	17.66	−0.10	49.49	−10.17	19.77	18.55
12	ODI	8.14	67.68	N.A.	11.82	28.82	1.14	64.21	−12.82	42.94	3.84
13	PUN	4.72	12.17	1.57	7.95	13.04	3.99	19.07	−8.58	18.23	10.08
14	RAJ	11.13	15.61	11.03	17.54	−2.89	25.33	27.60	−0.68	20.00	7.88
15	TN	7.18	10.22	10.43	11.31	3.36	11.82	52.11	3.62	12.76	12.68
16	UP	3.51	13.67	18.07	4.78	12.31	7.06	39.73	−0.99	20.94	17.86
17	WB	3.42	27.75	21.91	9.13	21.71	7.76	73.23	−12.84	42.20	20.37
	INDIA	1.43	15.14	14.51	6.39	12.03	14.79	37.05	−5.73	16.81	13.88

Source: Derived from data presented in Table 20.4 and 20.5.

The performance of the CHEM industry has been the best as compared to the other industries. The TFPG for this industry has been 4.52 pcpa, as compared to the corresponding figure of 1.79 for the MFG sector. More than one-third of growth in output can be ascribed to the TFPG in the CHEM industry. The growth of this industry is also widely dispersed across the various states of the country.

The METAL industry has been the worst performer as regards TFPG, though the growth performance of this industry was rather good. Due to the negative TFPG of this industry in most of the states, growth of this industry has been marked by a greater growth in inputs as compared to the growth of output. It may also be pertinent to note that it is a major industry in the MFG sector.

Another important industry in MFG is MTE. Its performance in terms of growth and TFPG has been good. In fact, it is the second-best industry in terms of performance of TFPG. However, at the national level the contribution of TFPG to growth of this industry is merely 16.8 percent. Some states have performed very well in the MTE industry, but their share in the MTE industry is rather low and, hence, the somewhat lower contribution of this TFPG of this industry to the growth of real output.

Summary and conclusions

We now relate employment growth, TFPG, growth of output and to contribution of TFPG to output growth (Table 20.6). The major industries like FBT, TEX, CHEM, METAL and MTE witnessed growth in employment to the extent of 1.2 pcpa, 3.4 pcpa, 2.9 pcpa, 5.0 pcpa and 4.8 pcpa, respectively. Thus, industry-wise, it was the METAL and MTE industries that pulled up the growth of employment in the MFG sector during the period of the study. As regards the regional growth in employment, except for Delhi and Jharkhand, all other states witnessed positive rates of growth of employment. Rajasthan, Odisha, Haryana, Tamil Nadu, Karnataka, Bihar, Punjab and Chhattisgarh witnessed employment growth rates higher than the national average. Maharashtra, Gujarat and UP, which are large states, also witnessed employment growth rates of around 3.0 pcpa. A&T and West Bengal were the poor performers, which witnessed employment growth of less than 1 pcpa. As mentioned earlier, Delhi and Jharkhand were the worst performers, where the growth in organized manufacturing sector can be characterized as the 'jobloss growth'.

Table 20.6 Average annual growth rates of employment (2000–01 to 2012–13)

Srl No	State/Country	FBT	TEX	LEATH	PAPER	RP	PT	CHEM	METAL	MTE	MFG
1	A&T	-2.5	7.4	32.7	3.4	6.0	22.3	4.9	3.5	1.7	0.8
2	BIHAR	5.4	-1.4	-7.5	15.3	8.2	-0.7	9.5	4.8	14.8	4.9
3	CHAT	6.4	-3.3	34.9	-0.6	3.3	6.2	6.8	5.7	22.6	4.3
4	DELHI	5.5	-0.3	1.2	0.8	-5.2	259.2	-9.1	-2.0	-3.9	-2.3
5	GUJ	2.2	3.3	4.6	19.2	7.3	18.1	1.9	8.4	4.4	2.9
6	HAR	-0.2	12.7	3.8	8.7	7.7	12.7	4.8	6.5	7.3	5.6
7	JHA	-1.1	-1.4	N.A.	9.2	-0.7	-1.7	4.6	-0.4	1.6	-0.2
8	KAR	2.4	6.9	2.4	6.3	9.1	10.6	6.0	7.6	6.7	5.0
9	KER	2.9	0.0	0.7	32.5	2.0	2.0	-0.6	2.1	3.5	1.5
10	MAH	2.2	0.1	1.0	3.8	5.6	5.0	4.9	6.5	4.6	3.2
11	MP	3.0	-1.1	2.3	4.7	7.8	13.4	3.6	3.6	2.3	1.9
12	ODI	5.2	-5.5	N.A.	0.8	3.9	40.2	-0.7	9.8	-0.4	5.9
13	PUN	1.7	5.9	11.4	1.0	0.3	26.2	3.7	3.6	3.5	4.6
14	RAJ	5.6	3.2	11.8	12.8	14.2	14.2	7.7	7.9	9.0	6.9
15	TN	2.6	7.3	5.1	7.6	22.2	9.6	-0.7	7.4	8.7	5.2
16	UP	0.0	5.3	1.8	12.4	2.4	28.0	-1.0	7.1	2.8	2.7
17	WB	2.6	0.0	2.5	14.3	4.7	3.7	-1.1	2.1	-1.8	0.7
	INDIA	1.2	3.4	2.7	7.1	5.6	2.8	2.9	5.0	4.8	3.4

Source: Calculated from the ASI data sourced from www.epwrfits.in/index.aspx last accessed on 6–7-2016.

Taking the national perspective as a whole for the period 2000–1 to 2012–13, the overall observations are as follows. The output growth performance of this sector for the said period was rather impressive, given that the global financial crisis and greater trade openness of the Indian economy. Real output of the organized MFG sector in many states witnessed double-digit output growth. The floor for this variable across the states was about 8.0 pcpa. Despite the somewhat impressive performance of the organized MFG sector, the share of the MFG sector in India's GDP has been rather stagnant. During the period of the study, the share of total manufacturing sector in India's GDP has increased merely by 1.0 percent. The respective figures for registered and unregistered manufacturing sectors were 1.5 and –0.6 percent. Expecting it to increase almost by 10 percent by 2021 requires a radical departure from the past in terms of productivity performance. It is not clear as to how the targets of NMP 2011 can be achieved.

The TFPG performance was not impressive, if we judge its role in explaining the growth of real output. The TFPG explained just about 14 percent of growth of the MFG sector. The highest contribution of the TFPG to growth was witnessed by West Bengal, which recorded very low growth rate of employment (0.7 pcpa) as compared to the national average (3.4 pcpa). However, if compare the performance of TFPG in absolute terms then as indicated by the previous studies, such as Das (2016), Trivedi (2004), and Trivedi et al. (2011), the TFPG for MFG was merely 1.0 pcpa for the period 1980–81 to 2009–10, 1980–81 to 2000–01, and 1980–81 to 2003–04. The growth performance has improved during the subsequent periods and also the TFPG has improved. However, the contribution of the TFPG to growth seems to be more or less stagnant, and the growth process seems to be induced mainly by more resource use. Following Krugman (1994), this seems to be the result of perspiration rather than inspiration and, hence, policy makers must view the sustainability of the resource-intensive growth process with caution.

As regards employment generation, the targets set by NMP 2011 seem to be too ambitious. During the period of the study, total employment in organized industry in India increased from about 7.75 million people (2000–01) to about 12.08 people (2012–13). Assuming that these are only 20 percent of persons engaged in the MFG, the total labor force in India's manufacturing sector in 2012–13 would be around 60 million people. In other words, during the period of the study (13 years), about 21 million people have been absorbed in India's manufacturing sector. The target set in NMP 2011 is to create about 100 million jobs by 2021. Again, it is not very clear as to which regions and which industries can be relied upon to fulfill these targets. The study undertaken in this paper does not allow us to be optimistic as regards fulfilling the agenda of NMP 2011.

Appendix

Table 20.A.1 Selected states and their abbreviations used

1	A&T	Andhra Pradesh & Telangana
2	BIH	Bihar
3	CHH	Chhattisgarh
4	DEL	Delhi
5	GUJ	Gujarat
6	HAR	Haryana
7	JHA	Jharkhand
8	KAR	Karnataka
9	KER	Kerala
10	MP	Madhya Pradesh
11	MAH	Maharashtra
12	ODI	Odisha
13	PUN	Punjab
14	RAJ	Rajasthan
15	TN	Tamil Nadu
16	UP	Uttar Pradesh
17	WB	West Bengal

Source: Author's Compilation

Table 20.A.2 Industry codes and description of selected industries

NIC 1998 & NIC 2004	NIC 2008	Industry
15 – Manufacture of Food Products & Beverages	10 – Food Products 11 – Beverages	FBT
16 – Manufacture of Tobacco Products	12 – Tobacco Products	
17 – Manufacture of Textiles	13 – Textiles	TEX
18 – Manufacture of Wearing Apparel Dressing & Dyeing of Fur	14 – Wearing Apparel	
19 – Tanning & Dressing of Leather Manufacture of Luggage, Hand bags, Saddlery, Harness & Footwear	15 – Leather & Related Products	LEATH
21 – Manufacture of Paper & Paper Products	17 – Paper & Paper Products	PAPER
23 – Manufacture of Coke, Refined Petroleum Products and Nuclear Fuel	19 – Manufacture of coke and refined petroleum products	PT
24 – Manufacture of Chemicals & Products	20 – Chemicals & Chemical Products 21 – Pharmaceuticals, Medicinal Chemical & ...	CHEM
25 – Manufacture of Rubber & Plastic Products	22 – Rubber & Plastics Products	RP
27 – Manufacture of Basic Metals	24 – Basic Metals	METAL
28 – Manufacture of Fabricated Metal Products, Except Machinery & Equipment	25 – Fabricated Metal Products, Except Machinery & Equipment	
29 – Manufacture of Machinery & Equipments N.E.C	26 – Computer, Electronic & Optical Products	
30 – Manufacture of office, Accounting & Computing Machinery	27 – Electrical Equipment	
31 – Manufacture of Electrical Machinery & Apparatus N.E.C.	28 – Machinery & Equipment N.E.C	
32 – Manufacture of Radio, Television & Communication Equipment & Apparatus	29 – Motor Vehicles, Trailers & Semi-Trailers	
33 – Manufacture of Medical, Precision & Optical Instruments, Watches & Clocks		
34 – Manufacture of Motor Vehicles, Trailers & Semi-Trailers	30 – Other Transport Equipment	MTE
35 – Manufacture of Other Transport Equipment		

Source: Compiled by the Author from NIC 1998, NIC 2004 & NIC 2004, Central Statistical Organization, Ministry of Statistics and Programme Implementation, Government of India.

Table 20.A.3 Codes of industries in various I-O matrices used for compiling input price index

Industries	I-O 1998–99	I-O 2003–04, 2006–07 and 2007–08
FBT	18+33–40	21+38–45
TEX	41–49	46–54
LEATH	54–55	59–60
PAPER	52–53	57–58
RP	56–57	61–62
PT	58–59	63–64
CHEM	60–68	65–73
METAL	73–77	77–80
MTE	78–98	81–105
MFG	18+33–98	81–015

Source: Compiled by the Author from I-O 1998–99, 2003–04, 2006–07 and 2007–08 matrices. These matrices have been sourced from National Accounts Statistics, Central Statistical Organization, Ministry of Statistics and Programme Implementation, Government of India.

Notes

1 NMP, however, recommends the incentive for promoting green technologies.
2 The registered manufacturing sector includes factories registered under the Factory Act, 1948, which employ 10 or more workers, either working currently or working on any day of the preceding 12 months and using power. If the manufacturing process is carried on without the aid of power, the minimum employment for a manufacturing factory which is reregistered is 20 workers.
3 See the list of selected states and abbreviations used for the same in Annexure 1.
4 See the list of selected industries (also their NIC codes) and abbreviations used for the industries in Annexure 2.
5 Terms 'Organized' and 'Registered' have been used interchangeably in this study and from here onward, we refer to the registered manufacturing sector as the manufacturing sector so as to economize on word count.
6 TLI imposes fewer *a priori* restrictions on the underlying form of the production function or the technology. It has the advantage that it can be used for the discrete time analysis.
7 WPI 1993–94 series and 2003–04 series were converted to obtain a common base year 1999–2000.

Bibliography

Aghion, Philippe, Robin Burgess, Stephen J. Redding, and Fabrizio Zilibotti. 2008. "The Unequal Effects of Liberalization: Evidence From Dismantling the License Raj in India." *American Economic Review* 98: 1397–1412.

Ahluwalia, Montek S. 2002. "State Level Performance Under Economic Reforms in India." In Anne Krueger (ed.), Economic Policy Reforms and the Indian Economy. Chicago: University of Chicago Press: 91–128.

Babu, Suresh M., and Rajesh Raj S. Natarajan. 2013. "Growth and Spread of Manufacturing Productivity Across Regions in India." *SpringerPlus* 2: 53. www.springerplus.com/content/2/1/53, accessed on January 20, 2017.

Chowdhury, Samik. 2014. "Regional Disparity in India – a Study of Three Decades Using a Comparable Database." Paper presented for the *IARIW 33rd General Conference Rotterdam*, The Netherlands, August 24–30. www.iariw.org/papers/2014/Chowdhury2 Paper.pdf, accessed August 3, 2016.

Das, Deb Kusum. 2016. "Trade Policy and Manufacturing Performance: Exploring the Level of Trade Openness in India's Organized Manufacturing in the Period 1990-2010." *DRG Study* No. 41, Reserve Bank of India, Mumbai. https://rbidocs.rbi.org.in/rdocs/ Publications/PDFs/41DRG33B9 D69D7B6941B1A81ADEC2E172C71D.PDF, accessed June 5, 2016.

Das, Samarjit, Chetan Ghate, and Peter E. Robertson. 2015. "Remoteness, Urbanization, and India's Unbalanced Growth." *World Development* 66: 572–587. http://dx.doi.org/10.1016/j.worlddev.2014.09.013c, accessed July 5, 2016.

Deb, Arnab K., and Subhash C. Ray. 2014. "Total Factor Productivity Growth in Indian Manufacturing: A Biennial Malmquist Analysis of Inter-State Data Source." *Indian Economic Review* 49(1): 1–25.

Diewert, W. E. 1976. "Exact and Superlative Index Numbers." *Journal of Econometrics* 4: 115–145.

Ghate and Wright. 2013. "Why Were Some Indian States So Slow to Participate in the Turnaround?" *Economic & Political Weekly* XLVIII(13), March 30: 118–127.

Ghosh, Buddhadeb, and Prabir Deb. 2005. "Investigating the Linkage Between Infrastructure and Regional Development in India: Era of Planning to Globalisation." *Journal of Asian Economics* 15: 1023–1050.

Government of India. 2011. *National Manufacturing Policy 2011*. Manufacturing Policy Division, Department of Industrial Policy & Promotion, Ministry of Commerce & Industry. http://dipp.nic.in/English/Policies/National_Manufacturing_Policy_25October 2011.pdf, accessed July 6, 2016.

Krugman, Paul.1994. "The Myth of Asia's Miracle", *Foreign Affairs*, 73: 62–78.

Mukherjee, Kankana, and Subhash C. Ray. 2005. "Technical Efficiency and Its Dynamics in Indian Manufacturing: An Inter-State Analysis." *Indian Economic Review*, New Series 40(2), July–December: 101–125.

Singh, Nirvikar, Jake Kendall, R. K. Jain, and Jai Chander. 2010. "Regional Inequalities in India in the 1990s: Trends and Policy Implications." *DRG Study* No. 36, Reserve Bank of India, Mumbai. https://rbidocs.rbi.org.in/rdocs/Publications/PDFs/NSSD170510F.pdf, accessed January 18, 2017.

Trivedi, Pushpa. 2003. "Growth and Productivity in Selected Manufacturing Industries in India: A Regional Perspective." # 375, *Visiting Research Fellow Series*, Institute of Developing Economies, Chiba, Japan.

Trivedi, Pushpa. 2004. "An Inter-State Perspective on Manufacturing Productivity in India: 1980–81 to 2000–01." *Indian Economic Review*, New Series 39(1): 203–237.

Trivedi, Pushpa, A. Prakash, and D. Sinate. 2000. "Productivity in Major Manufacturing Industries in India: 1973–74 to 1978–79." *Development Research Group*, Study No. 20, Department of Economic Analysis and Policy, Reserve Bank of India, Mumbai.

Trivedi, Pushpa, L. Lakshmanan, Rajeev Jain and Yogesh Kumar Gupta. 2011. "Productivity, Efficiency and Competitiveness of the Indian Manufacturing Sector", Study No. 37, *Development Research Group*, Reserve Bank of India.

Veeramani, C., and Bishwanath Goldar. 2005. "Manufacturing Productivity in Indian States: Does Investment Climate Matter?" *Economic and Political Weekly* 40(24), June 11–17: 2413–2420.

Major Data Sources

Annual Survey of Industries. New Delhi: Ministry of Planning, Government of India. www.epwrfits.in/index.aspx, accessed July 6, 2016.

Input Output Transactions Tables. New Delhi: Central Statistical Organisation, Ministry of Planning, Government of India.

National Accounts Statistics. New Delhi: Central Statistical Organization, Ministry of Planning, Government of India.

Wholesale Price Index. New Delhi: Office of Economic Advisor, Ministry of Industry, Government of India. www.eaindustry.nic.in, accessed July 5, 2016.

Chapter 21

Size and productivity in Indian manufacturing sector[1]

Arup Mitra and Chandan Sharma

Introduction

In the literature, the importance of total factor productivity (TFP) is highlighted in order to explain growth differences across countries (Howitt 2000). Improving TFP in manufacturing, in particular, is recognized as an effective way of enhancing the overall performance and catching up with other better performers, i.e., the convergence hypothesis. Manufacturing is capable of experiencing rapid productivity gains largely through technical progress, innovation, externalities, economies of scale, and knowledge spill-over (Kaldor 1966; Murphy et al. 1989). These productivity gains can be further realized at the macroeconomic level through structural transformation and changes in resource allocation from less- to more-productive firms and sectors (Bernard and Jensen 1999).

This chapter has three objectives. First, we present a review of literature on TFPG in India. Second, using a recent firm-level survey data we estimate TFP of the Indian manufacturing firms and attempt to analysis the productivity differential among different sizes of firms. Finally, we provide policy suggestions and discussion on enhancing output and productivity growth of the Indian manufacturing.

Broad trends in TFP growth across sectors: a review

In order to present a broad profile of productivity growth across certain major sectors of the Indian economy, this study refers largely to the report titled "Estimates of Productivity Growth for Indian Economy" (India KLEMS project at ICRIER in collaboration with the Reserve Bank of India, Goldar 2014). Unlike many other studies which are largely confined to some of the specific segments of the economy, this study covers the entire economy for a considerably long period of time (1980–81 through 2008–09). The following sectors are considered in the analysis:[2] Agricultural, Mining and Quarrying, Manufacturing industries, Electricity, Gas and Water supply, Construction, and Services comprising both market and nonmarket services.

The study by Bosworth et al. (2007) and Bosworth and Maertens (2010) show that the growth rate in TFP in the services sector by and large exceeded that in industry and agriculture, particularly between 1980 and 2004 (Table 21.1). At the aggregate level, TFPG shot up to 2 percent per annum from 1980 onward, with almost no productivity growth (0.2 percent per annum) prior to that. Since the aggregate economic growth rate has been mostly services driven, the rapid productivity growth in the services sector also contributed to the overall productivity growth.

From Table 21.2, it is evident that as per all the three estimates shown by Goldar et al. (2014), productivity growth decelerated marginally in the agriculture sector in the 2000s compared to the period 1980–1999. The manufacturing sector productivity growth, on the other hand, registered acceleration in 2000s compared to

Table 21.1 Growth of output and TFP in broad sectors in 1960–2004

(% per annum)		
Total Economy	Output Growth Bosworth et al. (2007)	TFP Growth Bosworth et al. (2007)
1960–1980	3.4	0.2
1980–2004	5.8	2.0
Agriculture		
1960–1980	1.9	–0.1
1980–2004	2.8	1.1
Industry		
1960–1980	4.7	–0.4
1980–2004	6.4	1.0
Services		
1960–1980	4.9	0.4
1980–2004	7.6	2.9

Source: Bosworth et al. (2007), see Goldar and Mitra (2010)

Table 21.2 Productivity growth at the aggregate level and across sectors (% per annum)

Sector	Estimate 1			Estimate 2			Estimate 3		
	1: 1980/81–1999/00	2: 2000/01–2008/09	1+2: 1980/81–2008/09	1: 1980/81–1999/00	2: 2000/01–2008/09	1+2: 1980/81–2008/09	1: 1980/81–1999/00	2: 2000/01–2008/09	1+2: 1980/81–2008/09
Agriculture, etc.	1.99	1.26	1.81	1.89	1.3	1.68	1.78	0.71	1.52
Mining and quarrying	0.65	−1.03	0.23	0.42	−1.91	−0.17	0.22	−1.59	−0.24
Manufacturing	1.27	3.13	1.74	0.81	2.75	1.30	0.04	2.76	0.73
Utilities	1.51	7.2	2.94	1.22	6.8	2.62	1.14	6.93	2.96
Construction	−3.82	−0.34	−2.95	−4.18	−0.7	−3.31	−4.19	−0.69	−3.31
Services	2.5	2.83	2.59	1.98	2.31	2.07	1.74	2.14	1.84
Total economy	2.23	2.99	2.42	1.52	2.38	1.74	1.11	2.26	1.4

Source: Goldar (2014), KLEMS Project.

Note: Estimate 1 uses labor person and capital stock; Estimate 2 uses labor input and capital stock, and Estimate 3 uses labor input and capital service.

the earlier phase. The services sector maintained a moderate productivity growth of 2.5 and 2.83 percent over period 1 and 2, respectively (Estimate 1). At the aggregate level, the TFPG (2.2 and 3 percent per annum in period 1 and 2, respectively, as per Estimate 1) resembles more or less the productivity growth patterns in the services sector. But the most striking point is that the average productivity growth over 1980/81 through 2008/09 in the manufacturing sector turns out to be lower than that in agriculture or services, though for period 2 (2000/01–2008/09) the manufacturing productivity growth is higher than that in agriculture or services as per all the three alternative estimates.

From the long-run point of view, the sector which is supposed to take the lead role in terms of productivity growth (manufacturing), as suggested in the literature, in fact, does not turn out to be so. Hence, the beneficial effects of productivity growth which are expected to spill over from this sector to the rest of the economy seem to have remained beyond realization. Rapid productivity growth in the manufacturing sector is usually taken in the literature to raise profitability and wages in this sector, which in turn could generate demand for goods produced in other sectors, enabling them to experience rapid expansion in output, productivity and wages. The technology spillover effects are also likely to originate from the manufacturing sector and get transmitted to other sectors. However, the sluggish growth in manufacturing productivity seems to have blocked this link. The rapid productivity growth in other sectors, if any, may have derived the impetus from within the sector itself or somewhere else. For example, the changing technology configurations in the services sector may have enabled the services sector to experience a steady, though not perceptibly high, growth in productivity.

Size of firm and productivity: background

In this section, we present estimates of TFPG based on firm-level data. There are several factors which cause productive differential among firms in the same industry or sector. Theoretical and empirical models have considered several endogenous and exogenous factors which cause productivity growth (e.g., see Craft 1995). These factors largely vary with the size of firms. For example, R&D, technology transfer, and availability of easy and cheap credit are easily accessible to large firms (Biesebroeck 2005). However, some other argue that small firms have the advantage of more flexible management and lower response time to market changes, while larger firms have the advantages of economies of scale, political clout and better access to government credits, contracts and licenses, particularly in developing countries (Jovanovic 1982). To understand the productivity performance of firms, it is important to analyze the productivity and size of firms. Therefore, in the next section, we make an attempt to analyze TFP differential among different size of firms.

Data and measurement of total factor productivity

Data

For empirical analysis in this study, we have taken the recently published data from Enterprise Surveys in India. The survey includes important information related to the business environment. The Enterprise Surveys are conducted by the World Bank and its partners across all geographic regions and cover small, medium, and large companies. The surveys are administered to a representative sample of firms in the non-agricultural formal private economy. The sample is consistently defined in all countries and includes the entire manufacturing sector, the services sector, and the transportation and construction sectors. The Indian survey of business owners and top managers in 9,281 firms were interviewed from June 2013 through December 2014. We focus only on manufacturing firms, which covers 7,169 firms. We have utilized important indicators, such as sales, trade, age, foreign ownership, and size of the firm. Details of these variables are presented in Table 21.3.

Measuring total factor productivity

To test the role of firm size in the context of productivity of firms, we assess the impact of size on TFP. First, we discuss the model used for measuring TFP and subsequently focus on the results. We specify the production function as a value-added function where the dependent variable Q represents gross value added, K represents capital inputs, and N represents number of labor inputs. Since, our data is from a cross-sectional survey, we form the following model:

$$Q_i = f(K_i, N_i)\varphi_i \qquad (21.1)$$

Table 21.3 Data description

Variable	Definition
Log (TFP)	Log of TFP
Log (Workers)	Log of total workers
Log (Capital)	Log to current value of Machinery, vehicles, and equipment
Foreign Tech	=1 if firm has transferred foreign technology, otherwise 0
Large	=1 if firm is a large firm (100+ workers), otherwise 0
Medium	=1 if firm is a medium firm (20–99 workers), otherwise 0
Small	=1 if firm is a small firm (5–19 workers), otherwise 0
Foreign	=1 if firm is a foreign firm (more than 10% owned by private foreign individuals, companies or organizations), otherwise 0
Log(Labor)$_{t-3}$	Log of total workers in t-3 year
Log (GVAD)	Log of sales excluding raw material expenses
Trade	% of export + import to total sales
Age	Age

Source: Authors' estimation.

If we assume the Cobb-Douglass production function and that the TFP index can be written as $\varphi_I = e^{vi}$, the above equation can be specified as

$$Q_i = AK_i N_i e^{vi} \qquad (21.2)$$

which can be transformed into a linear equation using logarithm transform of both sides:

$$\ln Q_i = \ln A + \beta_1 \ln K_i + \beta_2 \ln N_i + v_i \qquad (21.3)$$

where βs are parameters to be estimated. Here, the natural logarithm of the TFP index is equal to the residual term in the econometric production function. The production function estimates are presented in columns 1 and 2 of Table 21.4, which indicate that overall estimation works well and as expected the contribution from labor input is much larger than capital input. Importantly, labor and capital both significantly contribute to production, yet contributions from labor are noticeably higher. The capital elasticity is estimated to be around 0.30, while labor elasticity is around three times that of capital. In the next stage, the TFP index of firms is computed for further analysis.

Table 21.4 Production function estimation

Dependent Variable: Log (GVAD)		
	1	2
Log (Labor)	0.88281**	0.86439**
	(0.01415)	(0.0238)
Log (Capital)	0.29668**	0.30366**
	(0.8828)	(0.0148)
Const	8.7629**	8.73962**
	(0.1871)	(0.2021)
Adj R-squared	0.5897	0.5938
Industry Dummies	No	Yes
Number of obs	2943	2943

Source: Authors' estimation.

TFP of large firms vis-à-vis small firms: comparing distributions

Comparing the distributions: Kernel density estimators

One of the objectives of this paper is to examine whether an association exists between size of firm and productivity levels. For illustration purpose, we use Epanechnikov kernels with optimal bandwidths to smooth the distribution of productivity levels for different sizes of firms and productivity performance. Kernel density estimators divide the sample into non-overlapping intervals, and counts are made of the number of data points within each interval. The estimator utilizes histograms to depict the frequency counts. The bar of the histogram is centered at the midpoint of each interval and its height reflects the average number of data points in the interval. Major advantages of the kernel density estimation is that its estimates are related to its smoothness and independence of the choice of origin corresponding to the location of the bins in a histogram (see Cox 2008). Kernel density estimators approximate the density $f(x)$ from observations on x. We use a kernel density that estimates the kernel function K, as in

$$\widehat{f}_k = \frac{1}{qh} \sum_{i=1}^{n} W_i K\left(\frac{x - X_i}{h}\right) \tag{21.4}$$

where $q = \sum_i w_i$ and weights $w_i = 1$, if firm $i = 1, 2 \ldots, n$. We specifically use the Epanechnikov function as it is the most efficient in minimizing the mean integrated squared error (see Cox 2008).

In Figure 21.1, we plot the smoothed distributions of average log TFP levels for large firms vis-à-vis others. The distribution of the large firms is skewed to relatively right of other firms, which clearly demonstrates productivity superiority of large firms over other. Figure 21.2 compares distribution of small vis-à-vis other firms. The distribution of small firms is skewed toward left, suggesting smaller firms have lower productivity than other firms.

Comparing the distributions: preliminary regression results

In order to compare the productivity distribution of large and small firms, here we further attempt to assess the performance differen-

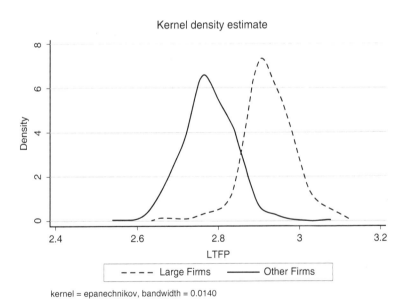

Figure 21.1 Distributions of average log TFP levels for large firms vis-à-vis others

Source: Authors' estimation

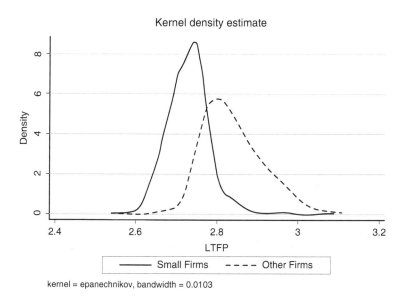

Figure 21.2 Distributions of average log TFP levels for small firms vis-à-vis others

Source: Authors' estimation

tial between the groups. For this purpose, we run the following regression:

$$Z_i = \beta_0 + \beta_1 \text{Large}_i + \beta_2 \text{Small}_i + \varepsilon \quad (21.5)$$

where Z is TFP of firm i, while Large and Small represents large and small firm-specific dummies. The medium-size firms are used as reference in the model. Subscript i indexes firms and ε is disturbance. Estimation result, of Equation 21.5 is reported in Table 21.5. These results, although showing simple relations, nevertheless have the advantage that the estimated coefficients can be interpreted in percentage terms. The results are expected to provide specific percentage differential between large vis-à-vis medium firms and small vis-à-vis medium firms. The results presented in Table 21.5 clearly indicate that large firms are superior to medium-size firms in terms of productivity. Specifically, in terms of TFP,

Table 21.5 Descriptive regressions results

Dependent Variable: LTFP

	1	2
Large	0.11688**	0.11391**
	(0.00261)	(0.0025)
Small	−0.07802**	−0.07461**
	(0.0021)	(0.0021)
Constant	2.8075**	2.7992**
	(0.0013)	(0.0031)
$\bar{R}^2$	0.6246	0.6573
Test of Equality (H_0: Large = Small)	4962.49	4875.24
	(0.00)#	(0.00) #
Industry Dummies	No	Yes
Number of obs	2995	2995
Estimator	OLS	OLS

Note: 1. Standard error in brackets. 2.** Significant at 5 percent critical level. 3. Industry dummies are included in all regressions. # P-value

Source: Authors' estimation.

large firms are estimated to be 11.7 percent more productive in the model without industry dummies, while 11.4 percent more productive in the model with industry dummies. As expected, small firms are estimated to be around 8 percent less productive when industry dummies are not included. On the whole, these findings confirm the results of kernel distribution and endorse that large firms are more productive, whereas the small firms comprise the least-productive group. These findings motivate us to analyze the issue in a comprehensive model.

Main results

To analyze the effects of size of firms, we next estimate the following model:

$$Z_i = \beta_0 + \beta_1 \text{Large}_i + \beta_2 \text{Small}_i + \beta_3 X_i + \varepsilon \quad (21.6)$$

where X is a vector of some important variables which affect productivity of firms. The results are presented in columns 1 to 3 of Table 21.6. Column 1 reports the results without industry dummy. As expected, both size dummies – large and small – are estimated

Table 21.6 Descriptive regressions results

Dependent Variable: LTFP

	1	2
Large	0.11688**	0.11391**
	(0.00261)	(0.0025)
Small	−0.07802**	−0.07461**
	(0.0021)	(0.0021)
Constant	2.8075**	2.7992**
	(0.0013)	(0.0031)
$\bar{R}^2$	0.6246	0.6573
Test of Equality (H_0: Large = Small)	4962.49	4875.24
	(0.00)#	(0.00)#
Industry Dummies	No	Yes
Number of obs	2995	2995
Estimator	OLS	OLS

Note: 1. Standard error in brackets. 2.** Significant at 5 percent critical level. 3. Industry dummies are included in all regressions. # P-value

Source: Authors' estimation.

to be positive and negative, respectively, and statistically significant. Specifically, results suggest that large firms are 9.5 percent to 11 percent more productive than others, while small firms are 7.6 percent to 9 percent less productive. To test the large firms vis-à-vis small firms' productivity differential, we also employ test of equality, which is found to be significant, apparently indicating that their estimated coefficients are significantly different. This result further confirms that size-wise, Indian firms diverge in productivity. These findings support the findings of Bartelsman and Doms (2000), which indicate that large firms corresponded to higher levels of productivity and also enjoyed higher growth, although their productivity levels are dispersed and highly persistent in developed countries. Biesebroeck (2005) also finds for developing countries that firms employing 100 or more workers are more productive and more likely to survive. However, large firms also grow more rapidly and enhance TFP faster. These findings are contrary to the findings of De and Nagaraj (2014), which estimated that small firms in India are more productive.[3]

Our analysis also indicates that trade intensity has a significant impact on productivity but its size is comparatively small. This is quite similar to earlier findings of Sharma and Mishra (2011, 2012,

2015) and Mitra et al. (2016) for India. Foreign firms are found to be 0.7 percent to 2.4 percent more productive than domestic firms. We include number of labor in (Column 3) to control the model and take care of the potential endogeneity problem. This is also found to be statistically significant.

Firm size: a production function approach

To understand the productive dynamics in different categories of firms, we employ an alternative technique to estimate production function for each type of firms: large, medium, and small. Results are presented in Table 21.7, which suggests that labor elasticity is highest among medium firms, followed by small firms. In the large firms, labor elasticity is found to be lowest (0.72) among the different size groups. Elasticity of capital is found to have a similar pattern. These results indicate that the growth in small firms is mainly driven by growth in inputs, but that output growth of large firms is comparatively driven by technology and productivity enhancement. This is indeed an important result which confirms our earlier findings, as well.

Policy initiatives and suggestions for the Indian manufacturing

In this section, we offer a detailed review of the policy initiatives before focusing on the policy implications of our study. The policy suggestions of various studies include trade reforms,

Table 21.7 Production function estimation

	Large	Medium	Small
Labor	0.7254	0.8083	0.76741
	(0.0645)	(0.0617)	(0.0679)
Capital	0.2506	0.33103	0.30223
	(0.0285)	(0.0226)	(0.0272)
Const	10.2141	8.4573	9.1398
	(0.4914)	(0.3591)	(0.3862)
Adj R-squared	0.4418	0.3043	0.2939
Industry Dummies	Yes	Yes	Yes
Number of obs	543	1420	980

Source: Authors' estimation

Note: 1. Standard error in brackets. ** Significant at 5% critical level.

pro-concentration initiatives, labor market reforms, skill upgradation programs, infrastructure-related programs which not only refer to physical but also financial and social infrastructure, efforts to improve accessibility of the enterprises to ICT, and proactive measures to encourage FDI (*foreign direct investment*) and innovation. FDI is expected to bring in foreign technology, which will not only contribute to productivity growth directly but also through spillover effects. Similarly, innovations are expected to develop technology which will contribute to productivity and employment both. There are sufficient indications for improvements to be followed in terms of allocative efficiency, that is, resources to be diverted toward sectors of higher productivity away from sectors of lower productivity. In trying to understand why India's manufacturing sector has not been more dynamic, Dougherty et al. (2009) argue that anti-competitive regulations have deterred firms' expansion and the entry of new firms.

In the reform era (since 1991) in India, the manufacturing sector has witnessed major policy changes. Industrial de-licensing and removal of restrictions on foreign investment have modified the profile of this sector considerably (Aghion et al. 2008). Trade policies have stimulated exports and imports, especially of intermediate and capital goods, since tariff rates have been reduced drastically and the quantitative restrictions on imports were by and large abolished (see Topalova and Khandelwal 2011).

Studies have highlighted the complementarities between trade liberalization and other market reforms, in particular deregulation and further lowering of FDI regulations (Hasan et al. 2006). The issue of the impact of imports on productivity is highly critical, as the trade regime in the pre-reform era was highly restrictive. In 1991, in the aftermath of a balance-of-payments crisis, India embarked on a dramatic import liberalization of the economy as part of an IMF adjustment program. An important part of this reform was to abandon the extremely restrictive import policies. The average tariffs were reduced from about 86 percent in 1989–90 to about 30 percent in 1999–2000. For manufacturing, there was a decline from about 120 percent in 1989–90 to about 33 percent in 1997–98. The non-tariff barriers (NTBs) in manufacturing also fell from 87 percent in 1988–89 to 28 percent in 1999–2000. Within manufacturing, the NTB for machinery and intermediate goods dropped considerably, to only 10 and 12 percent, respectively, in 1995. Currently, almost all commodities are free from quantitative restrictions on imports (see International Trade 2010).

Consequently, imports (both capital and intermediate) surged dramatically in recent years.

The trade policies in the 1990s and the 2000s have dramatically changed the dynamics of India's exports. Policies such as the removal of export restrictions, the simplification of the trade regime, the elimination of the trade monopolies of the state trading agencies, the full convertibility of the domestic currency for foreign exchange transactions, and the policy of export promotion have boosted industrial export growth (Hasan et al. 2003).

In order to encourage firms to innovate and conduct R&D activities, the government has developed a system of fiscal incentives and financial benefits (Sharma 2012; UNIDO 2005). These reforms aimed at making Indian industry (manufacturing) more efficient, technologically up-to-date, and competitive. However, despite these policy changes, the total factor productivity (TFP) growth in manufacturing declined from above 5 percent in the 1980s to less than 2 percent in the 1990s (see Goldar and Kumari 2003; Trivedi et al. 2000). Some other estimates also indicate only marginal improvement in TFP in the 2000s (Kathuria et al. 2010; Sharma and Sehgal 2010). Goldar et al.'s (2014) estimate for the manufacturing sector which shows a marked improvement in the 2000s compared to the average figure combined for the 1980s and the 1990s also lie in the neighborhood of a modest 3 percent per annum. However, some authors have argued that non-traditional ICT-intensive services, which are characterized by a growing tradability, increasing technological sophistication, and low transport costs, are on the forefront of a third industrial revolution, which has started showing up in terms of a revival in productivity growth in the 2000s (see Ghani 2010).

On the labor market front, Goldar (2004) argues that the unions in India have become weaker in the reform period, which caused a slowdown in the growth rate of real product wage rate in the organized manufacturing in the 1990s. Though the labor market regulations have not undergone significant changes, in practical terms the state governments have adopted a pro-employer approach. Given the fact that stricter rules may discourage the industrialization pace, which in turn may affect the revenue earnings of the state, most of the state governments have allowed the employers to adopt several means of flexibility, leading to rapid increases in contractual employment (Tendulkar 2000, 2004; D'Souza 2008). Hence, for all practical purposes, the labor marker regulations cannot be held against sluggish productivity growth in the manufacturing sector. However, strict labor market rules may be discouraging many foreign firms from investing in India. Hypothetically speaking, their inclusion may have contributed to productivity growth. Therefore, a strong case can be made for labor market reforms.

The National Manufacturing Policy (NMP) 2011 promises to create 100 million more jobs and contribute 25 percent to the country's GDP in a decade. In the face of dampening demand and rising cost of capital, the experts in the policy circle believed that it can change the fate of manufacturing in India and turn around the overall economy. The policy addresses in great detail the environment and regulatory issues, and labor laws and taxation, but it is the proposed creation of national manufacturing investment zones (NIMZs) or clustering of manufacturing units that are treated as a unique way of integrating the industrial infrastructure and achieve economies of scale. NIMZs will be developed as integrated industrial townships with world-class infrastructure and land use on the basis of zoning, and clean and energy-efficient technology, with a size of at least 5,000 hectares. The NIMZs will be on the nonagricultural land with adequate water supply, and the ownership will be with the state government. It aims at introducing flexibility in the labor market by offering greater freedom to the employers while hiring and firing. It also enables the sunset industrial units to follow a simplified exit mechanism. At the same time, it insists on workers' rights, which runs the risk of being compromised in the name of flexibility. "Make in India" under the present government is now a flagship initiative. An important feature of the manufacturing policy is its financial and development incentives to the small and medium enterprises. On the whole, the policy promises to increase the share of manufacturing sector to the country's gross domestic product to 25 percent from existing 16 percent by 2020. Formation of smart cities is an attempt to reduce the cost of investment and reap the benefits of concentration. The NMP and the creation of NIMZs seem to be subscribing to the view that concentration can lead to enhanced productivity.

In order to raise the share of the manufacturing sector, the government has identified 25 focus sectors for development. One hundred percent FDI is allowed in all sectors except Space (74 percent), Defense (49 percent), and News Media (26 percent). A key emphasis of the Make in India campaign is to improve "the ease of doing business in these sectors – faster clearances, transparency for permits and financing, as well as efficient e-governance mechanisms." Since the launch of Make in India in September 2014, FDI into the country has witnessed a 48 percent jump in the seven-month period between October 2014 and April 2015, and a 31 percent increase, valued at US$9.50 billion, between April and June 2015. It is still early days, and critical infrastructural developments are needed to convert investment into manufacturing gains. Nevertheless, Make in India affirms that India is "open for business".[4]

For increased industrialization of the work force, the employability of the available labor force must be improved. The skill match index representing the difference between the skill level of the population and the workers is estimated at 73.11, which is quite high (Mitra 2013). In other words, the difference between the skill levels of the potential labor supply and those already working is sizeable. Of course, we need to understand that those who are employed are not necessarily absorbed in demand-induced activities. There are several activities which are repository of surplus labor, not requiring much skill to be pursued. Hence, those who are working are not necessarily better off compared to the non-workers in terms of skill levels. Even then, the mismatch is significant.

The skill mismatch index calculated for different time points from the distribution of workers in each of the activities across various skill levels is again highly significant. The skill gap in the manufacturing sector is seen to be increasing, indicating that, over time, jobs in this activity are becoming more skill based compared to those in other activities, such as construction and transport (Mitra 2013). Therefore, improvement in employability is an important consideration from a policy point of view. For this, skill formation is an essential prerequisite which can be attained by accessing quality education and participating in institutions which impart training in skill formation. Such technical institutions, particularly which provide diplomas, are however few in number and, thus, government initiative is indeed crucial. From the point of view of the quality of vocational education, again greater efforts are called for. Besides, on-the-job training is another important way of eliminating skill mismatches.

The present government's 'Skill India' program is supposed to be a multi-skill program. The objective is to create opportunities for the youth and to develop more of those sectors which have already been put under skill development in the past, and also to identify new sectors for skill development. The Skill India campaign was launched in July 2015 to prepare graduates and workers alike for the skills needed by industry. It aims at imparting training to 400 million by 2022 through the National Skill Development Corporation. "The Ministry of Skill Development and Entrepreneurship was set up in November 2014 to drive the 'Skill India' agenda in a 'Mission Mode' in order to converge existing skill training initiatives and combine scale and quality of skilling efforts, with speed. The Ministry, therefore, proposes to launch the National Mission for Skill Development which will provide the overall institutional framework to rapidly implement and scale up skill development efforts across India. The vision, objectives and design of the Mission, draw on the lessons learnt from the implementation of skill development efforts over the past decade."[5]

Bandyopadhyay[6] (undated) reviewed in detail the industrial policies in India. The Industrial Policy 1991 of the government of India introduced a number of policies for reducing cost, technological and managerial modernization of industries for improving productivity and quality of the products and the international competitiveness. Micro, small, and medium enterprises (MSMEs) received focus, village industries were targeted, infrastructure was to be developed for rural industrialization to take place, and the flagship scheme of the ministry of MSME introduced the cluster development program for the MSMEs. Till 2007, 400 MSME clusters were developed and other ministries also promoted 800 more clusters. A credit-linked capital subsidy scheme for technology upgradation was also introduced. The National Manufacturing Competitive Council, under which the national manufacturing competitive program was introduced, was set up mainly to support the MSMEs. Application of lean manufacturing, design clinic, promotion of ICT in manufacturing sector, setting up of mini tool rooms, technology and quality management support to MSMEs are the main components of the program. Food Processing, Textiles and Garments, Engineering, Consumer Goods, Pharmaceuticals, Capital Goods, Leather, and IT Hardware are among the priority items specifically mentioned in the Common Minimum Program.

The Planning Commission study (2012) discusses the challenges faced by small and medium manufacturing firms, and builds the case for how adopting a cluster approach would enhance productivity of these enterprises. According to the study, the basic requirement for the government to make incisive, relevant, and impactful interventions at the cluster level is to have information on the units within clusters. The requirement of the units in terms of energy, infrastructure, finance, and marketing facility can be assessed and, accordingly, provisions can be made to improve the economic viability of the clusters. For different products, such clusters can be identified in order to extend support, since the cluster-based approach is expected to be highly efficient and cost effective. A study by UNIDO mapped more than 6,000 clusters in traditional handloom, handicrafts, and modern MSME industry segments (as cited by this study, Planning Commission 2012). The Development Commissioner (Handicrafts), Government of India, launched the Baba Saheb Ambedkar Hastshilp Vikas Yojana Scheme (AHVY), which aims at promoting Indian handicrafts by developing artisans' clusters into professionally managed and self-reliant community enterprises.

The McKinsey Report[7] (2001) revealed that there are three main barriers to faster growth and productivity across sectors: the multiplicity of regulations governing product markets and restricting competition and best practices; distortions in the land market; and widespread government ownership of businesses, which promotes inefficiency and wastage. In terms of output to input ratio productivity is measured which brings out the gross inefficiency of the government run units, particularly in the manufacturing sector. In order to overcome these barriers, the government must adopt a deeper, faster process of reform which can remove the bureaucratic delays, fasten the decision-making processes, and strengthen the support system, improving the efficiency of the units.

In the backdrop of these efforts, we may like to recapitulate the findings from our analysis and their policy implications. Our results confirm that, size-wise, Indian firms diverge in terms of productivity. As we plot the smoothed distributions of average log TFP levels for large firms vis-à-vis others, the distribution of the large firms is skewed relatively right to that of other firms, which clearly demonstrates productivity superiority of large firms over others. Similarly, as we compare the distribution of small vis-à-vis other firms, the distribution of small firms is skewed toward the left, suggesting small firms have lower productivity than other firms. Labor elasticity is highest among medium-scale firms, followed by small firms. In the large firms, labor elasticity is lowest among different size groups. The growth in small firms is mainly driven by growth in inputs but output growth of large firms is comparatively driven by technology and productivity enhancement. This is indeed an important result, which confirms our earlier findings as well. Our analysis also indicates that trade intensity has a significant impact on productivity but its size is comparatively small. Too much of support to the small and medium-sized firms in the Indian context tends to make them less competitive. On the other hand, the large firms need to be encouraged for further innovation and technology development. The incentive structure has to be woven appropriately so that large firms divert a great deal of effort and resources to pursue innovation for both technological progress and product improvisation which in turn can expand demand, including exports. The limitations of the small and medium-sized firms in accessing better technology must be realized. Their competitiveness has to improve, for which they need to pursue innovation. Joint effort by groups of small firms keeping in view their common requirements is an option. Besides, the share of small firms in total exports must rise. And for this to happen, the support structure must be linked to their performance.

Conclusion

How does productivity vary across firms? Are large firms more productive than small firms? What other attributes affect firm growth? These are important questions for a country like India, trying hard to boost manufacturing growth. Understanding the relationship between productivity and size is of special interest for India, given the fact that most firms are small and enjoy several exemptions and subsidies. A point of departure in the related literature is the Gibrat's law, which suggests that the performance of firms is independent of its size. However, our findings in this study indicate that firm size is an important factor determining its productivity performance. Large firms are robustly found to have 9–11 percent more productivity than smaller firms. Also, smaller firms are significantly lower in terms of productivity performance in comparison to other firms. The rate of return of inputs is also found to be higher among large firms. More importantly, these results are robust across the alternative analyses. Our findings raise questions on existing industrial policies in the country that aim at encouraging small firms. For example, small and medium-scale firms enjoy several benefits, such as easy and subsidized credit, support for R&D and technology transfer, infrastructure building, and support in selling output in domestic and international markets. However, we do not argue for abolition of these incentives but recommend a better designed and efficient policy that helps the small and medium-scale firms in enhancing their use of technology and augmenting the productivity level. Furthermore, large firms have productivity advantages which also help other firms through several spillover channels. The policy makers need to keep in mind these issues.

Notes

1 Parts of the paper are taken from Mitra, A. 2016. "Productivity Growth in India: Determinants and Policy Initiatives Based on the Existing Literature." *UN-ESCAP Working Paper Series: Macroeconomic Policy and Financing for Development Division*, WP/16/08, June.
2 For manufacturing and services, a number of subsectors have also been considered.
3 De and Nagaraj (2014) have used the Prowess database. Their analysis is heavily based on enter and exit issues. It is noteworthy that the Prowess database does not report entry or exit. A firm can be out of the database but may not be closed down.
4 *India's Economic Initiatives: A Magnet for Investments.* www.indiabriefing.com/news/indias-economic-initiatives-magnet-investments-11247.html/#sthash.XWIa3aDn.dpuf, accessed 21 December 2016.
5 *The National Mission for Skill Development a Framework for Implementation.* http://pibphoto.nic.in/documents/rlink/2015/jul/p201571 502.pdf, accessed 21 December 2016.
6 Bandoypadhyay, M. Undated. "Policies and Programmes for Industrial Development and Technological Innovation in India." *ADB – RETA Final Report*, www.namstct.org/ADB_RETA_Report/Mr_M_Bandyo padhyay.pdf, accessed 21 December 2016.
7 Reference to MckKinsey report "MGI_The_growth_imperative_for_ India.pdf", accessed 21 December 2016.

Bibliography

Aghion, P., R. Burgess, S. Redding, and F. Zilibotti. 2008. "The Unequal Effect of Liberalization: Evidence From Dismantling the License Raj in India." *American Economic Review* 98: 1397–1412.

Bartelsman, E. J., and M. Doms. 2000. "Understanding Productivity: Lessons From Longitudinal Microdata." *Journal of Economic Literature* 38(3): 569–594.

Bernard, Andrew B. and J. Bradford Jensen. 1999. "Exceptional exporter performance: cause, effect, or both?", *Journal of International Economics*, 47: 1–25.

Bosworth, Barry, S. M. Collins, and A. Virmani. 2007. "Sources of Growth in the Indian Economy." *NBER Working Paper* No. 12901, National Bureau of Economic Research, Cambridge, MA.

Bosworth, Barry, and Annemie Maertens. 2010. "Economic Growth and Employmentgeneration: The Role of the Service Sector." In Ejaz Ghani (ed.), *The Service Revolutionin South Asia.* New Delhi: Oxford University Press.

Cox, N. J. 2008. "Speaking Stata: Correlation With Confidence, or Fisher'sz Revisited." *Stata Journal* 8: 413–439.

Crafts, N. F. R. 1995. "Exogenous or Endogenous Growth? The Industrial Revolution Reconsidered." *The Journal of Economic History* 55(4): 745–772.

De, P. K., and P. Nagaraj. 2014. "Productivity and Firm Size in India." *Small Business Economics* 42(4): 891–907.

Dougherty, S., R. Herd, and T. Chalaux. 2010. "What Is Holding Back Productivity Growth in India?" *OECD Journal: Economic Studies* 2009(1): 1–22.

D'Souza, E. 2008. *Labor Market Institutions in India: Their Impact on Growth and Employment*. New Delhi: International Labor Organization, Subregional Office for South Asia.

Ghani, E., ed. 2010. *The Service Revolution in South Asia*. Oxford: Oxford University Press.

Goldar, B. N. 2004. "Indian Manufacturing: Productivity Trends in Pre- and Post-Reform Periods." *Economic and Political Weekly*: 5033–5043.

Goldar, Bishwanath and Arup Mitra. 2013. "Small versus large manufacturing units: how efficient are they?" *Journal of the Asia Pacific Economy*, Vol. 18, 4: 634–653.

Goldar, B. N., and A. Kumari. 2003. "Import Liberalization and Productivity Growth in Indian Manufacturing Industries in the 1990s." *The Developing Economies* XLI(4): 436–460.

Goldar, B. N., et al. 2014. "Estimates of Productivity Growth for Indian Economy." *KLEMS Project*.

Hasan, Rana and Lan Chen. 2003. "Trade and Workers: Evidence from the Philippines," *Economics Study Area Working Papers* 61, East-West Center, Economics Study Area.

Hasan, Rana, Devashish Mitra and Beyza P. Ural. 2006. "Trade Liberalization, Labor-Market Institutions, and Poverty Reduction: Evidence from Indian States", *India Policy Forum*, 3(1): 71–122.

Howitt, P. 2000. "Endogenous Growth and Cross-Country Income Differences." *American Economic Review* 90: 829–846.

Jovanovic, B. 1982. "Selection and the Evolution of Industry." *Econometrica* 50: 649–670.

Kaldor, N. 1966. *Causes of the Slow Rate of Economic Growth in the UK*. Cambridge: Cambridge University Press.

Kathuria, V., R. S. Raj, and N. K. Sen. 2010. "Organized Versus Unorganized Manufacturing Performance in the Post-Reform Period." *Economic and Political Weekly* 45: 55–64.

MckKinsey. 2002. How IT enables Productivity Growth? The US Experience across Three Sectors in the 1990S MckKinsey Global Institute, High Tech Practice, Business Technology Office, San Francisco.

Mitra, Arup. 2013. *Can Industry Be the Key to Pro-Poor Growth? An Exploratory Analysis for India*. New Delhi: International Labor Organization, DWT for South Asia and Country Office for India.

Mitra, Arup. 2016. "Productivity Growth in India: Determinants and Policy Initiatives Based on the Existing Literature." *UN-ESCAP Working Paper Series: Macroeconomic Policy and Financing for Development Division*, No. WP/16/08, UN-ESCAP.

Mitra, Arup, C. Sharma, and M. A. Véganzonès-Varoudakis. 2016. "Infrastructure, Information & Communication Technology and Firms' Productive Performance of the Indian Manufacturing." *Journal of Policy Modeling* 38(2): 353–371.

Murphy, K. M., A. Shleifer, and R. W. Vishny. 1989. "Industrialization and the Big Push." *Journal of Political Economy* 97(5): 1003–1026.

Planning Commission. 2012. *Improving the Productivity & Competitiveness of Industrial Clusters: A Holistic Strategy for India*. http://planningcommission.gov.in/reports/genrep/rep_tech2509.pdf\, accessed March 1, 2015.

Sharma, C. 2012. "R&D and Firm Performance: Evidence From the Indian Pharmaceutical Industry." *Journal of the Asia Pacific Economy* 17: 332–342.

Sharma, C., and R. K. Mishra. 2011. "Does Export and Productivity Growth Linkage Exist? Evidence From the Indian Manufacturing Industry." *International Review of Applied Economics* 25: 633–652.

Sharma, C., and R. K. Mishra. 2015. "International Trade and Performance of Firms: Unraveling Export, Import and Productivity Puzzle." *Quarterly Review of Economics and Finance* 57: 61–74.

Sharma, C., and S. Sehgal. 2010. "Impact of Infrastructure on Output, Productivity and Efficiency: Evidence From the Indian Manufacturing Industry." *Indian Growth and Development Review*: 100–121.

Tendulkar, S. D. 2000. "Employment Growth in Factory Manufacturing Sector During Pre and Post-Reform Periods." Paper Presented in the *Conference in Honour of K.L. Krishna*, Delhi School of Economics, New Delhi, December.

Tendulkar, S. D. 2004. "Organised Labor Market in India: Pre and Post Reform." Paper Presented at the *Conference on Anti Poverty and Social Policy in India*, Alwar, January 2–4.

Topalova, P., and A. Khandelwal. 2011. "Trade Liberalization and Firm Productivity: The Case of India." *Review of Economics and Statistics* 93: 995–1009.

Trivedi, P., A. Prakash, and D. Sinate. 2000. "Productivity in Major Manufacturing Industries in India: 1973–74 to 1997–98." In *Development Research Group Study*, 20. Mumbai: Department of Economic Analysis and Policy, Reserve Bank of India.

UNIDO. 2005. *Indian Manufacturing Industry: Technology Status and Prospects*. www.unido.org/fileadmin/media/documents/pdf/tcb_road map_to__qualitiy_vol1.pdf, accessed October 2011.

Van Biesebroeck, J. 2005. "Firm Size Matters: Growth and Productivity Growth in African Manufacturing." *Economic Development and Cultural Change* 53(3): 545–583.

Chapter 22

The challenges of "Make in India"

Does the investment climate matter for firm performance?

Rajesh Raj S.N. and Kunal Sen

Introduction

The investment climate – the institutional, policy, and regulatory environment in which firms operate – has been widely recognized as being a key determinant of firm performance. If the local government is highly bureaucratic and corrupt, then the returns on potential investments will be low and uncertain, and one would not expect much accumulation and growth in these environments (Dollar et al. 2005). Investment climate reforms promote private sector growth by reducing bureaucratic obstacles, costs, and time constraints to doing business and improving the efficiency of legal institutions (World Bank 2015). Investment climate reforms may be particularly beneficial for small firms, which face the highest costs of doing business relative to their sales (ibid.). In particular, transaction costs associated with regulations, bureaucracy, and weak institutions reflect resources diverted from production and, hence, may also have significant implications for firms' performance (Qureshi and Te Velde 2012, 2013).

The evidence on whether investment climate (IC) reforms lead to better firm performance is weak and contested (Aboal et al. 2012). For example, Bah and Fang (2015) use a model-based approach to show that businesses in Africa lose large shares of their sales due to government regulations, poor infrastructure, corruption, and crime, leading to lower output and productivity growth. On the other hand, Altenburg and von Drachenfels (2006) argue that IC reform is based on unrealistic assumptions and is not backed by sufficient empirical evidence. Moore and Schmitz (2008) argue that traditional IC reforms are undertaken with the assumption that there are impersonal arms-length relationships between state and business actors. In reality, in most low-income countries, synergistic state-business relations tend to be personalized and "hand-in-hand". They argue that reconstructing the relationship between investors and government, through interaction and experiential learning, rather than reforms of formal rules and regulations, is likely to yield higher returns in low-income countries, as was witnessed in China in the 1980s, where informal investment climate change preceded formal investment climate reform.

In the Indian context, the issue of investment climate reform has taken on particular relevance with the Indian government's "Make in India" initiative, which is a major national initiative designed to facilitate investment, foster innovation, enhance skill development, protect intellectual property, and build best-in-class manufacturing infrastructure (Government of India 2016). As the Economic Survey 2015–16 notes, "India's investment has been much below potential over the last few years" (Government of India 2015: 66). It is widely believed that India's very poor record in the ease of doing business – India ranks 130th out of 189 countries in the World Bank's *Doing Business Indicators*[1] – is a key factor behind India's weak investment and productivity performance in recent years (ibid.). However, there is little empirical evidence on whether the investment climate really matters for the performance of India's firms.[2] And neither is it clear which dimension of the investment climate matters most for firm performance (Carlin and Seabright 2008). This leaves policy makers in India in a dilemma: Is the investment climate all that important in kick-starting productivity in India? If it is, which part of the investment climate should they fix? Clear guidance to Indian policy makers on these questions can potentially improve the success of the "Make in India" initiative in India.

In this chapter, we use a recent rich firm-level database to look at the effect of the investment climate on firm performance in India. The data is the World Bank Enterprise Survey, which is an all-India firm-level dataset covering a broad range of business environment topics, such as access to finance, corruption, infrastructure, crime, competition, and performance measures. These surveys intend to provide information pertaining to measures of firm performance, firm structure as well as business perceptions on the major impediments to firm growth, and the business environment in general. Our data has several measures of the investment climate, which allows us to assess which specific feature of the investment climate matters for firm performance. Surprisingly, we find that conventional measures of ease of doing business, such as the amount of time firm management spend with government officials and the frequency of visits of tax inspectors, are not important in explaining firm productivity. Instead, we find that corruption has a clear and discernible negative effect on firm productivity. This suggests that the focus of Indian policy makers should be on reducing corruption rather than on improving the conventional measures of doing business.

The rest of the chapter has the following structure. First, we present the methodology and describe the data. We then present some stylized facts, followed by the results of the empirical analysis. Finally, we conclude.

Methodology and data

Methodology

We measure firm performance using labor productivity, which is defined as the ratio of real gross value added to total number of workers employed.

We test for the effect of investment climate variables on firm performance by running a regression of the following generic form:

$$p_{fi} = \beta_0 + \sum_{\gamma}\beta_{\gamma>1}IC_{fi} + \sum_{\delta}\beta_{\delta>1}FIRM_{fi} + \theta_i + e_{fi} \quad (22.1)$$

The dependent variable is p_{fi}, which stands for labor productivity of firm f in industry i. IC is our measure of investment climate environment that a firm faces in India. We use seven proxies to capture different aspects of investment climate environment: time spent on government regulations (*pertimregu*), percentage of total annual sales paid as informal payment (*salesgift*), percentage of contract value paid as gift to secure contacts (*pergiftcont*), number of meetings with the tax officials (*nvisittax*), whether informal payment was expected during these inspections (*gifttaxvisit*), and whether an informal payment was made or expected in connection with the application for import license (*giftimplic*) and operating license (*giftoplice*). We expect the coefficients of *salesgift*, *pergiftcont*, *gifttaxvisit*, *giftimplic* and *giftoplice* to have a negative effect on firm productivity. These variables tend to capture the extent of corruption at the firm level. We argue that the prevalence of corruption may negatively influence firm productivity, as it distorts resource allocation by increasing the returns to rent-seeking compared to those of productive activities (Baumol 1990). In the presence of corruptive practices, entrepreneurs may also allocate more time to obtaining valuable licenses and preferential market access than to improving productivity (Murphy et al. 1991). Besides estimating the influence of these 'bribe taxes' (De Rosa et al. 2015) on firm productivity, we also test the direct effects of 'time tax' on firm productivity.[3] In order to test the influence of 'time tax', we include two proxies, *pertimregu* and *nvisittax*, alternatively in the same specification. Consideration of both types of variables in the specification allows verifying the extent to which the time and the bribe tax are different phenomena, with different implications for firm productivity (De Rosa et al. 2015).[4] *Pertimregu* is used in our specification as a measure of doing business. There is enough evidence that business regulations measured as a higher share of management time spent dealing with regulations or inspections may hinder the growth of firms. As argued by Aterido et al. (2009), as the percentage of time that the firms spent on dealing with such regulations increase considerably with firm size, any small rise in enforcement can act as a strong deterrent to expand a firm. As there is an increasing focus at the government level on streamlining these regulations, the use of this variable would help us to understand how far these measures were useful in improving the growth and performance of firms.

As our dependent variable, labor productivity, varies substantially across industries owing to differences in capital intensity and in production processes, we have included in our regressions industry-fixed effects, which would control for such industry differences.

Data

The data used in the paper are drawn from the World Bank Enterprise Surveys (WBES) carried out worldwide in 2013–14. The main objective of these enterprise surveys is to gain an understanding of what firms experience in the private sector. The data are collected using stratified random sampling with replacement, based on face-to-face interviews and questionnaires from business owners and top managers of firms. By covering a broad range of business environment topics, such as access to finance, corruption, infrastructure, crime, competition, and performance measures, these surveys intend to provide information pertaining to measures of firm performance, firm structure as well as business perceptions on the major impediments to firm growth, and the business environment in general.

WBES on India

Our study relies on the WBES carried out by the World Bank in India between June 2013 and December 2014. The sample for India was constructed using a process of stratified random sampling, i.e., the elements in the population were first separated into non-overlapping groups or strata and then a simple random sample was selected from each stratum. The universe for the survey is the firms in the non-agricultural sector. The sampling frame for manufacturing establishments was from the Annual Survey of Industries, and for services sector establishments from the lists obtained through industry associations. The survey has used three levels of stratification namely, industry, firm size, and geographic region. Industry stratification was implemented by dividing the universe into 21 manufacturing industries and 7 services industries.[5] Based on firm size stratification, the firms were categorized into small (5 to 19 employees), medium (20 to 99 employees), and large (more than 99 employees).[6] Regional stratification was defined in 23 states.[7] In the end, a sample of 9,281 firms belonging to small, medium, and large categories across 27 industries and 23 states were identified and surveyed. Firms that operate in sectors subject to government price regulation and prudential supervision, such as banking, electric power, rail transport, water, and waste water, are not surveyed.

The WBES dataset provides four types of information that are relevant for our study. First, it includes information on the performance of the enterprise, including sales, materials, workers, and capital. This information also allows different measures of performance, such as productivity, to be computed and analyzed. Second, the dataset includes the responses of firms with respect to a host of variables that capture the investment climate environment in the country. The availability of this information would help us to address our main objective of analyzing the role of better investment climate provisions on firm performance. Third, it also includes measures of firm characteristics, such as the size and age of the enterprise, location of the enterprise, its ownership structure and innovative practices, and worker characteristics, such as human capital, education of the worker, managerial experience, and years of training. Fourth, the survey also contains information on infrastructure constraints that the firms face such as frequency of power outages, duration of power outages and so on. The availability of information on these characteristics helps us to control for their influence on firm performance thereby enabling us to capture the effect of investment climate variables on firm performance. The data have some weaknesses too, including (a) the small number of firms sampled in many states and for many industries, which led to dropping them from the analysis, (b) the inability to compute productivity growth (which would have been ideal as our dependent variable) due to lack of data on inputs for at least two time periods, and (c) numerous missing answers for some variables of interest (for example, capital and many investment climate variables).

Data cleaning

As mentioned before, the WBES for 2013–14 surveyed 9,281 Indian manufacturing firms in 23 states. We restrict our attention to major states, and smaller states with lesser observations were dropped. As a consequence, Arunachal Pradesh, Goa, Chhattisgarh, Himachal Pradesh, Jammu and Kashmir and Uttaranchal were excluded from our analysis. We also omitted recycling from the purview of the analysis, but retained all the three broader sectors, manufacturing, services, and construction, as the nature of deals may be quite different across these three broader industrial groups (Sen and Kar 2014). Firm-level data from developing countries usually contain missing values and outlier observations that may bias the estimated coefficients. This seems to be the case with our dataset, as well. Hence, we carefully cleaned the original dataset to handle those missing observations and outliers. We omitted firms which had not responded to one or more key questions and which had provided seemingly unrealistic information, such as missing, zero or negative sales; missing labor figures; missing capital stock values; and missing input figures. These elimination norms have reduced the number of firms in the dataset to 7,898 from 9,281 (about 15 percent of the firms were dropped). It is also important to note that sample size and its composition keep changing during the process of econometric estimations due to the non-availability of responses for our key variables capturing investment climate environment in the country. For instance, among the 7,898 firms in the dataset, only half of the firms (3,999 firms) responded to the question on the number of times they were visited by tax officials and only a quarter of firms (1,542 firms) returned an answer for the question on whether they faced any obstacle to obtain an operating license.

In order to make price corrections to the reported data on gross output, intermediate input, and gross fixed assets, suitable deflators have been constructed with the help of the official series on wholesale price indices. Data on wholesale price indices were obtained from the report *Index Number of Wholesale Prices in India*, published by the Office of the Economic Advisor, Ministry of Industry, Government of India. The construction of deflator for intermediate output requires that the price indices for various categories of items be combined using appropriate weights (representing their shares in the intermediate input cost). For this purpose, the weights for respective commodities have been taken from the Input-Output Transaction Table of India for 2007–08, prepared by the Central Statistical Organization (CSO).

Construction of variables

To address the main objective of the study, we need variables representing three broader categories: (a) firm performance, (b) investment climate environment, and (c) firm characteristics. The construction of variables belonging to the three categories are as discussed next.

Firm performance

We use labor productivity as a proxy for firm performance. Total number of full-time permanent and temporary workers engaged in establishments is taken as the measure of labor input. Firm sales are used to measure output. This is, then, deflated by the Index number of wholesale prices for relevant product groups, with 2004–05 prices as the base year. As the WPI is not available at the product level for construction and services sectors, we used implicit deflators of gross domestic product at 2004–05 prices for the respective sectors, i.e., Construction, Trade, Hotel, Transport and Communications and Finance, Insurance, Real Estate, and Business Services, to derive real output from retail sales for each product group under these broader industrial categories. (See Nagaraj 2009 for a discussion on the use of implicit GDP price deflator for services sectors.)

Investment climate measures

Our main objective of this chapter is to examine the relationship between different types of investment climate measures and economic performance at the firm level in India. In order to implement this, we need to construct variables that can represent the investment climate in the country. We turn to WBES dataset to identify specific questions that can be used to measure the investment climate. As explained, we identify seven such questions which we think can represent the nature and quality of institutions in the country. The investment climate variables, their construction, and the related questions from the WBES are presented in Table 22.1.

Firm characteristics

As control variables, we employ the usual set of firm characteristics used in the firm-level studies. These variables help us in controlling for the influence of firm-specific characteristics, thereby capturing the precise role of investment climate variables on firm performance. The firm-specific characteristics that we employ in this paper broadly control for the age, size, ownership, location, innovational activities, and education and training of workers of the firm. To be specific, the firm specific variables identified as controls in the study are *age, firmsize, ownership, locparkez, sizelocat, innovation, workeredn, perworksecdry, training, managexp,* and *Npoweroutage.* The variable *age* represents the age of the firm, and is defined as the number of years (plus one) elapsed since the year establishment began operations. We add one year to avoid ages of zero. The variable *firmsize* is a categorical ordered variable, and coded as *1* for small firms (5 to 19 workers), 2 for medium firms (20 to 99 workers), and 3 for large firms (100 or more workers). *Proprietorship* variable is derived from the question on a firm's current legal status and is constructed as a binary variable. The categories of a firm's legal status are sole proprietorship, limited partnership, partnership, shareholding company and others. In the construction of *proprietorship* variable, firms that reported proprietorship as their legal status take the value 1 and others 0. *Locparkez*, which stands for the location of the firm in the *export processing zone* or *other industrial park*, is a categorical variable ranging from 1 to 3 (1 = export processing zone, 2 = industrial park, 3 = others). *Sizelocat* is also a variable for location but represents the size of the locality (measured

Table 22.1 Construction of investment climate variables from the WBES

Sl. No.	Variable Name	Definition	Survey Question
1	Pertimregu	Percentage of time spent on dealing with government regulations (in terms of percentage)	In a typical week over the last year, what percentage of total senior management's time was spent on dealing with requirements imposed by government regulations? (Some examples of government regulations are taxes, customs, labor regulations, licensing and registration, including dealings with officials and completing forms.)
2	Nvisittax	Number of meetings with the tax officials	Over the last year, how many times was this establishment either inspected by tax officials or required to meet with them?
3	Gifttaxvisit	Binary variable taking the value 1 if gift or payment was expected, 0 otherwise	In any of these inspections or meetings was a gift or informal payment expected or requested?
4	Pergiftcont	Percentage of contract value paid as gift to secure contracts (in terms of percentage)	When establishments like this one do business with the government, what percent of the contract value would be typically paid in informal payments or gifts to secure the contract?
5	Salesgift	Percentage of total annual sales paid as informal payment (in terms of percentage)	It is said that establishments are sometimes required to make gifts or informal payments to public officials to "get things done" with regard to customs, taxes, licenses, regulations, services, etc. On average, what percentage of total annual sales, or estimated total annual value do establishments like this one pay in informal payments or gifts to public officials for this purpose?
6	Giftimplic	Binary variable taking the value 1 if gift or payment was expected, 0 otherwise	In reference to that application for an import license, was an informal gift or payment expected or requested?
7	Giftoplice	Binary variable taking the value 1 if gift or payment was expected, 0 otherwise	In reference to that application for an operating license, was an informal gift or payment expected or requested?

Source: Authors' construction.

in terms of the population size) where the firm is situated. This variable takes the value between 1 and 4–1 for less than 50,000 pop; 2 for 50,000 to 250,000; 3 for over 250,000 to 1 million; and 4 for over 1 million population. We have constructed an index for the presence of innovative activities in firms, and denote the variable as *innovation*. We have identified five specific questions, and these questions capture whether the firm has introduced improved products, improved methods, improved logistics and distribution, improved supporting activities and improved marketing methods during the last three years. We have constructed the index by assigning equal weights to all these five dimensions of innovational activities in firms. Thus, the value of the index ranges between 0 and 5, and a value of 0 indicates absence of any innovational activities in a firm. If the firm has introduced all types of innovation in the last three years, then the index takes the value 5. We also control for the influence of worker-level characteristics on firm performance. Our worker-specific control variables are average number of years of education of a typical permanent full-time production worker (*workeredn*), percentage of full-time permanent workers who completed secondary school (*perworksecdry*), whether the establishment has formal training programs for its permanent, full-time employees (*training*: yes = 1 and no = 0) and years of experience of top manager in the firm (*managexp*). Finally, we control for the influence of infrastructural constraints to firm performance, and include frequency of power outages (*Npoweroutage*) as a control variable. As electricity is an essential input, its shortage could significantly reduce output, thereby affecting productivity (Allcott et al. 2016). This is clearly evident when Indian firms testify that power outages result in losses equivalent to 6.6 percent in sales (Alam 2013).

Results

In this section, we assess how the differences in investment climate quality have translated into firm performance, as measured by real output per capita, which displayed considerable variation across the Indian states.[8] We perform this empirical exercise by estimating Equation 22.1, where we regress firm-level sales per worker (in logs) on various measures of investment climate constraints, as perceived by firm owners. As discussed before, we employ seven proxies to capture different aspects of investment climate environment namely, *pertimregu, salesgift, pergiftcont, nvisittax, gifttaxvisit, giftimplic,* and *giftoplice*. We do not include these variables together in the model but one at a time to avoid possible collinearity between them, thus estimate seven specifications of Equation 22.3. We report the results of these estimations in Table 22.2. All columns in the table report coefficient estimates with industry dummies to control for unobserved heterogeneity across industries.[9]

Among the variables representing investment climate quality, three variables are found to have a very large and significant impact on sales per capita, while other variables representing investment climate weaknesses do not seem to matter much for firm performance. The three variables that matter a lot for improving firm productivity, according to our analysis, are *salesgift*, *gifttaxvisit* and *giftoplice*. As expected, the coefficient of *salesgift* is negative and significant, suggesting that firm productivity deteriorates with rising share of informal payments to public officials in total sales (Table 22.2, Column 1). In other words, this suggests that a higher bribery level impedes the labor productivity of an average firm. The negative and significant coefficients of *gifttaxvisit* and *giftoplice* indicate that firms that bribe officials experience lower productivity than other firms. The size of the coefficient of *gifttaxvisit* suggests that a firm that pay bribes to evade taxes is on average around 32 percent less productive than a non-corrupt firm (Table 22.2, Column 5).[10] A firm that bribe officials to obtain operating license is on average 24 percent less productive than a firm that do not bribe, as is evident from the magnitude of the coefficient of *giftoplice* (Table 22.2, Column 7). Our results thus broadly emphasize the negative influence of 'bribe taxes' on firm performance. Our result of bribery as a burden on firm performance is consistent with some previous findings at both the micro (Fisman and Svensson 2007; Kochanova 2012; De Rosa et al. 2015) and macro level (Mauro 1995; Campos et al. 2010).

We also observe that the regression estimates on labor productivity are stronger and sounder than our estimates on output growth rates.[11] This possibly points to the effect of corruption on employment structure of firms, as argued by Kochanova (2012). Two possibilities are highlighted by Kochanova (2012): (a) in the presence of bribe taxes, firms are likely to employ a non-optimal (higher) number of workers due to misallocation of talent, and (b) having established a cordial relationship with firms, government officials do not let firms to sack their workers so as to keep the employment figures high in the region and hence more loyal voters.

Table 22.2 Regression results

Dependent Variable: Log of output per worker	(1)	(2)	(3)	(4)	(5)	(6)	(7)
Pertimregu	0.0003 (0.001)						
Salesgift		−0.029** (0.015)					
Pergiftcont			0.041 (0.026)				
Nvisittax				0.001 (0.004)			
Gifttaxvisit					−0.382*** (0.068)		
Giftimplic						0.221 (0.357)	
Giftoplice							−0.277*** (0.108)
Controls							
Age	−0.004*** (0.002)	−0.005*** (0.002)	−0.004 (0.003)	−0.004** (0.002)	−0.006*** (0.002)	−0.009 (0.009)	−0.009** (0.003)
Firm size	0.196** (0.029)	0.201** (0.032)	0.232*** (0.087)	0.266*** (0.036)	0.245*** (0.037)	0.008 (0.220)	0.149** (0.072)
Proprietorship	−0.418*** (0.041)	−0.456*** (0.045)	−0.672*** (0.118)	−0.500*** (0.053)	−0.516*** (0.054)	−0.054 (0.384)	−0.454*** (0.096)
Locparkez	−0.008 (0.046)	−0.065 (0.051)	−0.249** (0.121)	−0.116* (0.061)	0.102 (0.064)	0.036 (0.273)	−0.109 (0.094)
Sizelocat	−0.045*** (0.023)	−0.011 (0.026)	−0.020 (0.066)	−0.029 (0.030)	−0.030 (0.031)	0.101 (0.150)	0.172** (0.056)
Innovation	0.031*** (0.011)	0.028** (0.012)	−0.060* (0.031)	−0.021 (0.015)	−0.006 (0.016)	0.034 (0.088)	−0.031 (0.025)

Workeredn	0.029**	0.051***	0.104***	0.015	0.022	0.046	0.062**
	(0.012)	(0.014)	(0.040)	(0.016)	(0.018)	(0.064)	(0.032)
Perworksecdry	-0.0003	-0.0005	-0.001	-0.0004	-0.001	0.004	-0.005***
	(0.001)	(0.001)	(0.002)	(0.001)	(0.001)	(0.005)	(0.002)
Training	0.151***	0.093**	0.079	0.251***	0.304***	0.062	0.203**
	(0.043)	(0.047)	(0.124)	(0.054)	(0.057)	(0.261)	(0.098)
Managexp	0.004*	0.007***	0.014***	0.003	0.005	-0.016	0.010*
	(0.002)	(0.003)	(0.007)	(0.003)	(0.003)	(0.013)	(0.005)
Npoweroutage	0.0004	-0.001	-0.007***	0.0004	0.001	-0.001	0.002
	(0.001)	(0.001)	(0.003)	(0.001)	(0.001)	(0.009)	(0.002)
Industry dummies	YES	YES	YES	YES	YES	YES	YES
Constant	12.560***	12.356***	12.348***	12.698***	12.700***	13.318***	12.415***
	(0.158)	(0.180)	(0.425)	(0.204)	(0.215)	(1.284)	(0.365)
Number of Observations	3394	2777	549	2101	1952	119	827
R squared	0.16	0.17	0.27	0.20	0.22	0.26	0.18

Note: (a) The dependent variable is the log of firm-level output per worker. (b) Investment climate variables: *Pertimregu* is percentage of time spent on dealing with government regulations, *Nvisittax* is number of meetings with the tax officials, *Gifttaxvisit* is a binary variable for payment made during inspection by tax officials, *Pergiftcont* is percentage of contract value paid as gift to secure contracts, *Salesgift* is percentage of total annual sales paid as informal payment, *Giftoplic* is a binary variable for payment made to obtain an import license and *Giftoplice* is a binary variable for payment made to obtain an operating license. (c) Firm level controls: *Age* is age of the firm, *Firm size* is a categorical ordered variable taking value 1 for small firms, 2 for medium firms and 3 for large firms, *ownership* stands for firm's ownership and assigned codes 1 to 5 for sole proprietorship, limited partnership, partnership, shareholding company and others respectively, *Locparkez* is a binary variable for location for firm in the export processing zone or other industrial park, *Sizelocat* is a variable for size of the locality, measured using population size, *innovation* is an index for the presence of innovative activities in firms, *workeredn* is average number of years of education of a typical permanent full-time production worker, *perworksecdry* is percentage of full-time permanent workers who completed secondary school, *training* is a binary variable for formal training programs for its permanent, full-time employees, *mangexp* is years of experience of top manager in the firm and *Npoweroutage* is the number of power outages the firm experienced. *Industry* are industry dummies. (c) Robust standard errors are in parentheses. (d) * significant at 10 percent; ** significant at 5 percent; *** significant at 1 percent.

Source: Estimates based on WBES India, 2013–14.

On the other side, our results show that other measures of investment climate quality are not important in influencing firm performance. This is clearly evident from the insignificant coefficients of *pertimregu* and *nvisittax*.

Control variables

Barring some exceptions, our firm-specific control variables yield results on expected lines. Firm-level variables that have a positive and significant impact on firm productivity are size of the firm, innovative practices employed by the firm and attributes of workers employed by the firm, such as education, training, and experience. The finding that size has a positive effect on firm productivity is consistent with findings of previous studies (Pitt and Lee 1981; Little et al. 1987; Shanmugam and Bhaduri 2002; Batra and Tan 2003; Kim 2003; Margono and Sharma 2006; Backman 2012), and is ascribed to the economies of scale that large firms enjoy. In line with the existing evidence from other studies (Masso and Vahter 2008; Hall and Sena 2014; Raymond et al. 2015), our analysis also shows that innovation results in large productivity dividend for firms. Surprisingly, we find a negative relationship between age and firm productivity. Power (1998) too finds that productivity growth rates decrease with age, and attributes that fact to learning effects. The location of the firm and the size of the locality where the firms are located seem to have a negative influence on firm productivity, according to our study. As conjectured, our findings do confirm the positive role of worker-level characteristics, such as education, training and experience, in improving firm productivity. There is overwhelming evidence at the micro level, particularly at the firm-level, that education, training and experience enhance firm productivity. For instance, studies by Tan and Batra (1995), Dearden et al. (2000), Jones (2001), Tan and Lopez-Acevedo (2002), Takii (2003), Ilmakunnas et al. (2004) and Aw et al. (2006) confirm the positive role of human capital on firm's productivity. The negative and significant coefficient of *proprietorship* variable across all our estimations suggests that partnership firms tend to be more productive than single-owner (proprietary) enterprises, which is also consistent with the findings of previous studies (Raj 2011).

Conclusions

In this chapter, we study the effect of the investment climate on firm performance in India. This has become an important issue in the Indian context as it widely believed that India's lack of ease of doing business is an important constraint to India's economic growth. We use the recent World Bank Enterprise Survey for India to examine the role of the investment climate on firm productivity in India. We do not find evidence that the conventional measures of ease of doing business, such as the amount of time managers of firms spend with government officials or the frequency of visits of tax inspectors, matter in explaining firm productivity in India. Instead, the level of corruption has a clear negative effect on firm performance. The result that corruption matters much more than other investment climate variables suggests that the increasing focus of the government on streamlining the regulations pertaining to the ease of doing business is misplaced. The focus of the government needs to be redirected to address the corrupt practices at various levels rather than focusing just on the measures of doing business.

Appendix

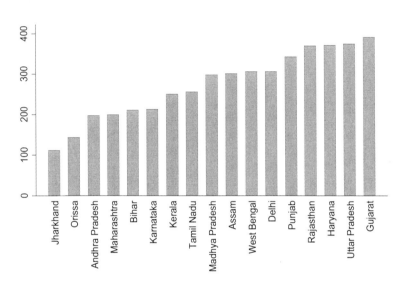

Figure 22.A.1 Median labor productivity: firms with 10–49 workers
Source: WBES India, 2013–14.

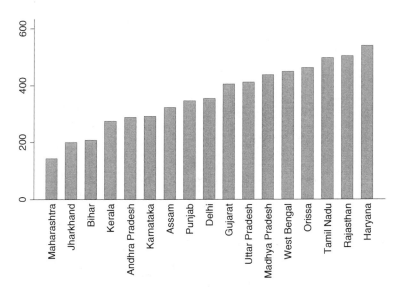

Figure 22.A.2 Median labor productivity: all firms
Source: WBES India, 2013–14.

Notes

1 See www.doingbusiness.org/data/exploreeconomies/india/, accessed 11 July 2016.
2 An early study on whether investment climate affect firm performance in developing countries, including India is Dollar et al. (2005). This study finds a positive effect in the case of India. More recently, Kathuria et al. (2013) look at the effect of state-business relations on firm performance.
3 See De Rosa et al., 2015 for a detailed exposition on the difference between 'bribe tax' and 'time tax'.
4 It needs to be stated here that the effect of bribes on productivity is likely to be underestimated due to selection bias, as firms that had to pay the largest bribes may have been driven out of business altogether and, therefore, they are omitted from analysis.
5 The 11 manufacturing industries are food products, tobacco, garments, textiles, wood products, chemicals, paper, plastics and rubber, non-metallic mineral products, basic metals, electronics, fabricated metal products, leather, machinery and equipment, precision instrument, publishing, printing and recorded media, transport machines, furniture, refined petroleum products, and recycling, and the seven services industries are construction, services of motor vehicles, wholesale, retail,

hotels and restaurants, transportation, storage, and communications and IT. See www.enterprisesurveys.org for further details, accessed 14 July 2016.
6 For the purpose of stratification, the number of employees is defined on the basis of reported permanent full-time workers (see www.enterprisesurveys.org for further details on the survey and its design), accessed on 14 July 2016.
7 Delhi was included as a state, while other union territories were excluded. Sikkim and Mizoram too were excluded from the purview of the survey. The remaining northeastern states of Arunachal Pradesh, Nagaland, Manipur, Tripura and Meghalaya (except Assam) were combined into one category for the purpose of regional stratification. See www.enterprisesurveys.org for further details, accessed 14 July 2016.
8 To conserve space, we do not discuss the estimates of labor productivity for Indian states in detail here. Figures 22.A1 and 22.A2 in Appendix I present these estimates.
9 Our regression estimates without industry dummies yielded similar results.
10 Calculated as exp (−0.382)−1.
11 Our estimates on sales are not reported here in order to conserve space. These estimates are available from authors upon request.

Bibliography

Aboal, D., N. Noya, and A. Rius. 2012. *The Evidence of the Impact on Investment Rates of Changes in the Enforcement of Contracts. A Systematic Review*. London: EPPI-Centre, Social Science Research Unit, Institute of Education, University of London.

Alam, M. M. 2013. "Coping With Blackouts: Power Outages and Firm Choices." Mimeo, Department of Economics, Yale University, New Haven.

Allcott, H., A. Collard-Wexler, and S. D. O'Connell. 2016. "How Do Electricity Shortages Affect Industry? Evidence From India." *American Economic Review* 106(3): 587–624.

Altenburg, T., and C. von Drachenfels. 2006. "The New Minimalist State Approach to Private Sector Development: A Critical Assessment." *Development Policy Review* 24(4): 387–411.

Aterido, R., M. Hallward-Driemeier, and C. Pages. 2009. "Big Constraints to Small Firms' Growth? Business Environment and Employment Growth Across Firms." *World Bank Policy Research Working Paper* 5032, World Bank, Washington, DC.

Aw, B. Y., M. J. Roberts, and T. Winston. 2006. "The Complementary Role of Exports and R&D Investments as Sources of Productivity Growth." *The World Economy* 30(1): 83–104.

Backman, M. 2012. "Human Capital in Firms and Regions: Impact on Firm Productivity." *Papers in Regional Science* 93(3): 557–575.

Bah, E., and L. Fang. 2015. "Impact of the Business Environment on Output and Productivity in Africa." *Journal of Development Economics* 114(C): 159–171.

Batra, G., and H. Tan. 2003. *SME Technical Efficiency and Its Correlates: Cross-National Evidence and Policy Implications*. Washington, DC: World Bank Institute.

Baumol, W. J. 1990. "Entrepreneurship: Productive, Unproductive, and Destructive." *The Journal of Political Economy* 98(5): 893–921.

Campos, N., R. Dimova, and A. Saleh. 2010. "Whither Corruption? A Quantitative Survey of the Literature on Corruption and Growth." *IZA Discussion Paper* No. 5334, Institute for the Study of Labor, Bonn.

Carlin, W., and P. Seabright. 2008. "Bring Me Sunshine: Which Part of the Business Climate Should Public Policy Try and Fix?" Paper presented at the *Annual Bank Conference on Development Economics 2008*, World Bank, Washington, DC.

De Rosa, D., N. Gooroochurn, and H. Goerg. 2015. "Corruption and Productivity: Firm-Level Evidence." *Journal of Economics and Statistics* 235(2): 115–138.

Dearden, L., H. Reed, and J. Van Reenen. 2000. "Who Gains When Workers Train? Training and Corporate Productivity in a Panel of British Industries." *Working Paper* W00/04, Institute for Fiscal Studies, London.

Dollar, D., M. Hallward-Driemier, and T. Mengistae. 2005. "Investment Climate and Firm Performance in Developing Countries." *Economic Development and Cultural Change* 54(1): 1–31.

Fisman, R., and J. Svensson. 2007. "Are Corruption and Taxation Really Harmful to Growth? Firm Level Evidence." *Journal of Development Economics* 83(1): 63–75.

Goldar, B. 2004. "Productivity Trends in Indian Manufacturing in the Pre- and Post-Reform Periods." *Working Paper* No. 137, ICRIER, New Delhi, India.

Goldar, B., and A. Kumari. 2003. "Import Liberalisation and Productivity Growth in Indian Manufacturing Industries in the 1990s." *The Developing Economies* 41(4): 436–460.

Government of India. 2015. The Investment Climate: Stalled Projects, Debt Overhang and the Equity Puzzle, Chapter 4, *Economic Survey* 2014-15, Ministry of Finance, Government of India, New Delhi.

Government of India. 2016. www.makeinindia.com/home, accessed July 10, 2016.

Hall, B. H., and V. Sena. 2014. "Appropriability Mechanisms, Innovation and Productivity: Evidence From UK." *NBER Working Paper* No. 20514, National Bureau of Economic Research, Cambridge, MA.

Ilmakunnas, P., M. Maliranta, and J. Vainionmaki. 2004. "The Roles of Employer and Employee Characteristics for Plant Productivity." *Journal of Productivity Analysis* 21(3): 249–276.

Jones, P. 2001. "Are Educated Workers Really More Productive?" *Journal of Development Economics* 64(1): 57–79.

Kathuria, V., R. Raj, and K. Sen. 2013. "State Business Relations and Productivity in Indian Industry." In K. Sen (ed.), *State-Business Relations and Economic Development in Africa and India*. London: Routledge.

Kim, S. 2003. "Identifying and Estimating Sources of Technical Inefficiency in Korean Manufacturing Industries." *Contemporary Economic Policy* 21(1): 132–144.

Kochanova, A. 2012. "The Impact of Bribery on Firm Performance: Evidence From Central and Eastern European Countries." *CERGE-EI Working Paper* 473, The Center for Economic Research and Graduate Education – Economics Institute, Prague.

Little, I. M. D., D. Mazumdar, and J. M. Page. 1987. *Small Manufacturing Enterprises: A Comparative Analysis of India and Other Economies*. Oxford: Oxford University Press.

Margono, H., and S. C. Sharma. 2006. "Efficiency and Productivity Analyses of Indonesian Manufacturing Industries." *Journal of Asian Economics* 17(6): 979–995.

Masso, J., and P. Vahter. 2008. "Technological Innovation and Productivity in Late-Transition Estonia: Econometric Evidence From Innovation Surveys." *European Journal of Development Research* 20(2): 240–261.

Mauro, P. 1995. "Corruption and Growth." *Quarterly Journal of Economics* 110(3): 681–712.

Moore, M., and H. Schmitz. 2008. "Idealism, Realism and the Investment Climate in Developing Countries." *Working Paper* No. 307, IDS, Sussex.

Murphy, K., A. Shleifer, and R. Vishny. 1991. "The Allocation of Talent: Implications for Growth." *Quarterly Journal of Economics* 106(2): 503–530.

Nagaraj, R. 2009. "Is Services Sector Output Overestimated? An Inquiry." *Economic and Political Weekly* 44(5): 40–45.

Pitt, M. M., and L. F. Lee. 1981. "The Measurement and Sources of Technical Inefficiency in the Indonesian Weaving Industry." *Journal of Development Economics* 9(1): 43–64.

Power, L. 1998. "The Missing Link: Technology, Investment and Productivity." *Review of Economics and Statistics* 80(2): 300–313.

Qureshi, M., and D. W. te Velde. 2012. "State-Business Relations, Investment Climate Reform and Firm Productivity in Sub-Saharan Africa." *Journal of International Development* 25(7): 912–935.

Qureshi, M., and D. W. te Velde. 2013. "State Business Relations and Firm Performance in Zambia." In Kunal Sen (Ed.), *State-Business Relations and Economic Development in Africa and India*. London: Routledge, 69–83.

Raj, R. S. N. 2011. "Technical Efficiency in the Informal Manufacturing Sector: Firm-Level Evidence From an Indian State." *Journal of South Asian Development* 6(2): 213–232.

Raymond, W., J. Mairesse, P. Mohnen, and F. Palm. 2015. "Dynamic Models of R&D, Innovation and Productivity: Panel Data Evidence for Dutch and French Manufacturing." *European Economic Review* 78(C): 285–306.

Sen, K., and S. Kar. 2014. "Boom and Bust? A Political Economy Reading of India's Growth Experience, 1993–2013." *Economic and Political Weekly* 49(50): 40–51.

Shanmugam, K., and S. Bhaduri. 2002. "Size, Age and Firm Growth in the Indian Manufacturing Sector." *Applied Economics Letters* 9(9): 607–613.

Takii, S. 2003. "Do Education Earnings Differentials Reflect Productivity? Evidence From Indonesian Manufacturing 1996." *Working Paper* 169, The European Institute of Japanese Studies, Stockholm.

Tan, H. W., and G. Batra. 1995. "Enterprise Training in Developing Countries: Overview of Incidence, Determinants, and Productivity Outcomes." *PSD Occasional Paper* No. 9, The World Bank, Washington, DC.

Tan, H., and G. Lopez-Acevedo. 2002. "Mexico: In-Firm Training for the Knowledge Economy." *World Bank Policy Research Working Paper* 2957, World Bank, Washington, DC.

World Bank. 2015. *Doing Business 2015: Going Beyond Efficiency*. Washington, DC: World Bank.

Index

Note: Page numbers in *italic* indicate a *figure* and page numbers in **bold** indicate a **table** on the corresponding page

'abenomics' period 200
Abramovitz, Moses 301
accumulated labor productivity growth **426–431**
Acemoglu, D. 185
aggregate capital 46
aggregate demand 188–192
aggregate labor productivity growth 315–318
aggregate production function (APF) approach 334
aggregate production possibility frontier (APPF) 18, 334, 336
aggregate productivity 46, 51
aggressive capital formation 224
Aghion, P. 186
agricultural areas growth 438
agricultural labor force 40
agriculture sector 406, 419, 544
Akkemik, K. Ali 287
Algeria 489
Altenburg, T. 627
Aly, H. Y. 506
American economic performance 4
Ando, Albert 200, 201, 211, 223
Ando, Koichi 201
annualization factor 86
Annual Survey of Industries (ASI) 367
Arab KLEMS dataset 489, 521–523; intermediate inputs 523; minimum list of variables 523–525; primary inputs 522–523
Arab League 489
Arab spring 22, 487, 494
Arab world 22; economies 487–528; employment elasticity *495*; growth and productivity in 506–525; growth dynamics in 489–490; KLEMS-based MFP estimates, data availability 511–521; KLEMS format, industrial productivity 499–506; macro aspects of growth 490–498; multifactor productivity (MFP) 487–528; productivity gains *495*; productivity in 487–528
Argentina 3, 7, 10, 13, 19, 20, 119, 177–179, 187; aggregate source of growth 444–452; ARKLEMS database 3.0 435–436; ARKLEMS+LAND growth 435–464; growth failure 435–464; growth profile 443–460; ICT investment boom 443; labor productivity growth, aggregate source 452; MFP slowdown, industry origin 452–460; productivity accounts 435–464; workpackages 436–442
Ariel Coremberg analyses 21

ARKLEMS database 3.0 435–436
ARKLEMS methodology 21
Arrow, K. J. 141, 185
Asia 3, 18; economies 1, 12, 81, 83, 108; sources of economic growth 94
Asia KLEMS manual 39, 236, 239
Asian Development Bank Institute 39
Asian financial crisis 1, 16, 105, 281, 283
Asian Productivity Organization (APO) 82
Asian Tigers 6
asset breakdown 156
asset-wise investment data 155
Atkinson, A. B. 178
Australia 38, 53, 187
average labor productivity (ALP) 280
Aw, Bee Yan 292, 640
Azariadis, C. 440, 452

Baba Saheb Ambedkar Hastshilp Vikas Yojana Scheme (AHVY) 622
Balakrishnan, P. 557, 558
Banga, R. 557, 559
Bangladesh 108
Barro, Robert J. 185, 186
Barro-Lee 143
Bartelsman, E. J. 615
Basu, S. 62, 441
Batra, G. 640
Baumol disease 460
Baumol effect 320, 321, 323
Becker, G. S. 186
Bems, Rudolfs 154
Benigno, Geanluca 224
Bernanke, Ben 441
Bhaduri, A. 183
Bleaney, M. F. 180
Blecker, R. A. 183
Bollard, A. 557, 558
Bolton, P. 186
Bosworth, Barry P. 460
Brasil Mais Produtivo 20, 399
Brazil 2, 3, 7, 10, 19, 20, 119; analytical references 399–401;
demographical bonus 421; economy 20, 401, 410, 411, 414; GDP growth rate 403, *404*; GFCF growth *405*; KLEMS methodology to 401; labor productivity 403, 409; micro–macro framework 400; productivity slowdown in 398–422; sectoral performance 406–409; shift-share analysis 409–420
Brazilian labor productivity growth 413–420
BRIC economies 20, 421
BRICS countries 7
Bruno, Michael 214, 223
Bureau of Economic Analysis (BEA) 42, 43, 163
Bureau of Labor Statistics (BLS) 42
Byrne, D. 63, 75, 163

Canada 38, 53, 187
capital accumulation 2
capital assets 60
capital compensation effect 164, 166
capital composition effect 170
capital deepening 70, 115, 148
capital formation 217
capital/income ratio 178, 179
capital inputs 82, 86, 438; constant quality index of 41; country-group growth of 90; country origins of 100; price differential factors, impact of *95*
capital-intensive methods 181
capitalist economy 186
capital-labor-energy-materials *see* KLEM
capital-labor (K/L) ratio 115
capital/output ratio 206; in Japan *209*
capital productivity 473–474; defined 473
capital quality: defined 308
capital quality index 388
capital reallocation effects 354
capital service price 472–473; defined 472

capital services 42, 63, 82,
  163, 164, 306–307, 437;
  constructing, new investment
  series 162–164; ICT, to GDP
  growth contribution 168;
  income share of 307; nominal
  rate of return 307; quantity of
  306; rental price of 306–307
capital shares 207, 211; in
  Japan 210
capital stocks 41, 163, 164,
  306, 437; constructing, new
  investment series 162–164
capital utilization 441
Caribbean 115; productivity and
  growth in 118–123
Caselli, Francesco 154
causality tests 15, 188–192
Central and East European
  socialist economies (CEEs) 17,
  314, 324
Cette, Gilbert 2
Chang, C. C. 231
Chemingui, M. A. 507
Chile 118
China 2, 3, 7, 15, 18, 63,
  65, 73, 98, 105, 177–180,
  526; CIP data, introduction
  339–340; economy 108, 340;
  growth accounting in 205;
  ICT-specific industry grouping
  340–342; industry origin of
  TFP, accounting 334–339;
  information and communication
  technology, accounting 331–356;
  productivity growth 331–356
China Industrial Productivity (CIP)
  data 39, 339–340
Chinese revolution 293
Cho, T. 178
Chowdhury, Samik 583
Christelis, Dimitris 201
Christian, M. S. 145, 147
Cimoli, Mario 38
CIP/China KLEMS industrial
  classification 357–358
Cobb-Douglas model 181
Colecchia, Alessandra 332
Colombia 115, 118, 133, 179

Commodity-Flow Method 14
commodity flow method
  (CFM) 157
commodity prices 435
competitive exchange rate
  461–462
Complementary Metal Oxide on
  Silicon (CMOS) plant 235
comprehensive industry level
  country datasets 4–6
Conference Board China Center
  for Economics and Business 63
Conference Board Total Economy
  Database (TED) 59, 62, 76, 83,
  155, 156, 367, 369
constant quality index: of capital
  inputs 41; of labor input 41
consumer price index (CPI) 340
contribution share from materials
  input (ConM) 272
contribution share of the services
  input (ConS) 272
Convergence Theory 399
Coremberg, Ariel 437,
  439–441, 444
Corrado, C. 63, 75, 163, 217
cost of capital 51
country aggregation 83–84
country origins: of capital input
  100; of labor input 101; of
  output growth 99; of TFP
  growth 102
Czech Republic 160

Das, Deb Kusum 160, 557,
  559, 583
data, definition 225
data and variables, India 564–568;
  capital 565–567; energy inputs
  567; labor 565; materials input
  567; output 565; services input
  567–568
De, P. K. 615
Dearden, L. 640
demographical bonus 20
De Negri, F. 410
Denison, Edward F. 335
Denison, E. F. 512
Denison effect 321, 323

Denmark 53
depreciation rates, assets 162
De Vries, G. J. 160
Diewert, W. Erwin 12, 81, 83, 410
Digital Planet Report on Global ICT spending 158
Dillman, B. 499
Dixit, A. K. 185
Doing Business Indicators 628
Domar, Evsey 46, 338
Domar weighting scheme 46, 442
Doms, M. 615
Dougherty, S. 617
Drazen, A. 452
Dumenil, G. 181
Dutt, A. K. 183

East Asia 7, 105; dataset 188–192; growth model 28, 277; Kaldor-Verdoorn law in 177–193
Economic Commission for Latin America and the Caribbean, in Santiago, Chile (ECLAC) 38, 123, 125
economic growth 14, 16, 23, 488
economic internationalization 233–234
economic liberalization 233–234
economic policy reforms 8
economic regimes 180–186
education categories 87
Egypt 10, 22, 487–490; growth and productivity in 507–511; macroeconomic profile of 498–499
electrical and optical equipment 271, 272
employment growth 63, 299
energy crisis 44
Epanechnikov function 612
Erumban, Abdul Azeez 160, 538
EU-9 dataset 188–192
EU (European Union) KLEMS 5, 10, 37, 38, 437, 438
EUKLEMS database 211
EU KLEMS project 38
Europe 2, 17, 41, 74, 187
European Commission 5

European debt crisis 1
Eurostat 84
'export expansion' stage 232
export-led industrialization effort 281

factor price differentials 87–90
factor price frontier 211–222
factor price PPPs: for capital 86–87; factor price differentials 87–90; for labor 87
factor reallocation effect 352–354
Feenstra, Robert C. 163
Fernald, J. G. 441
Fevereiro, J. 410, 411
financial crisis 74
financial sector reforms 74
Finland 53
firm characteristics 634–636
firm performance 627–641; construction of variables 633–636; control variables 640; data 630–633; methodology 629–630
firm structure 27
First Asia KLEMS Conference 39
fiscal crisis 37
Fixed Capital Formation 239
Fleck, Susan 43
foreign direct investment (FDI) 233, 556
Fornaro, Luca 224
Fox, Kevin J. 12, 81, 83
France 115, 179
Fraumeni, Barbara M. 143, 145, 147, 231, 236, 239, 354
Freitas, F. 410, 411
Fu, T. T. 231
Fukao, Kyoji 39, 201, 206, 223, 333

Galanis, G. 177, 179, 183, 187, 192
Galor, O. 186
Germany 2, 115, 160, 179
Ghate 583
Ghosh, Saibal 557, 559
global economic crisis 366
global economy: productivity in 58–78

global financial crisis (GFC) 1, 2, 12, 65, 81, 179, 201, 211, 223, 230, 236, 342
global growth accounting 154–172; *see also* growth accounting
global labor productivity growth 59; trends in and sources of 63–70
global recession 6, 7
Goldar, Bishwanath 19, 556–559, 618
Gollop, F. M.231, 236, 239, 354
goods and services tax (GST) 9–10
Granger, C. 181
Granger causality tests 180, 181, 188, **192**
Granger non-causality test *see* Granger causality tests
Great Recession 2, 44, 49, 50
Griliches, Zvi 86, 163, 185, 231, 236, 335, 512
Groningen Growth and Development Center 158
gross domestic product (GDP) 2, 18–20, 23, 25, 59, 60, 62, 63, 70, 73, 75, 84, 123, 143, 145, 155, 166, 183, 184, 230, 282, 284, 286, 287, 298, 363, 366, 368, 370, 373, 380, 389, 391, 399, 435, 437, 446
gross fixed capital formation (GFCF) 20, 155–156, 399, 400, 403, *405*, 420; disaggregation **128**
gross national income (GNI) 142
gross output growth: ICT-specific industry grouping 342–347
gross state domestic product (GSDP) 585
gross value-added (GVA) economy level 370, **371**, 372, 374, 380–383, 391, 504
growth accounting 12, 113, 114; in Japan *202*; in Korea *204*; modified method of 121–123; in Republic of China *205*; traditional method of 119–120; in United States *203*; *see also* global growth accounting

Growth and Modernity in World Economy 521
growth and productivity 14–22
Growth and Recession 49
growth predicting model 308–309

Hall, R. 558
Harberger, Arnold C. 313
Harmonized ICT deflation 305–306
Harper, Michael 42
Hashim, M. D. A.556, 557, 559
Hayashi, Fumio 200, 201
Hein, E. 187
Hindu rate of growth 363
Ho, Mun S. 44, 341, 351, 354
Hodrick-Prescott (HP) filter 65
Hong Kong 275, 277, 293, 302; TFPG 292–293
Hsieh, C. T.277, 293–297
Hsinchu Science-based Industrial Park (HSIP) 234–235
Huff, W. G. 293
Hulten, Charles 338, 499
human capital 3, 13, 140–141, 440; Barro-Lee 140; economic growth, contribution 145–151; Inclusive Wealth Report (IWR) 141; Jorgenson-Fraumeni (J-F) income approach 142; World Bank 140–141
human capital productivity 13, 14, 140–152; labor productivity *vs.* 142–145
human resource (HR) investment ratio 219, 220
human resources, investments 222

ICT-specific industry grouping 340–342, **357–358**; aggregate growth and growth source 347–351; aggregate TFP growth 351–352; gross output growth 342–347; total factor productivity index by *344*
Ilmakunnas, P. 640
'import substitution' stage 232
Inclusive Wealth Report (IWR) 141–142, 145
income inequality 179

Index 653

income per unit of capital 474–476
India 2, 3, 7, 18, 158, 178, 179, 187, 526; agricultural labor force 40; GDP growth 19; global economic order 7–10; globally competitive 8–9; growth story of 7–8; in new global order 22–27; per capita GDP 364, 365
India KLEMS database 388; KLEMS industries in 393
Indian economy: aggregate level real GVA and TFP growth 383–386; cross-country perspective 386–389; data sources 367; economy, manufacturing and market services 374–386; GDP and TFP growth 386–389; GDP growth at aggregate level 368–370; growth and structural changes 363–392; sectoral growth performance 370–372; since 1980 363–392; structural changes in 372–374; TFP growth estimates 378–383; TFP growth trends 374–386
Indian industry: capital services 540; co-variance/dynamic reallocation term 538; data and variables 539–540; decomposition of labor productivity 538; between effect 538; employment and labor composition 540; gross output 539; growth of labor productivity 541–544; growth sources, labor productivity 544–548; intermediate inputs 539–540; labor productivity, trends and behavior 540–544; labor productivity and sources 537; labor productivity dynamics 535–553; methodology and dataset 537–540; sectoral decomposition, productivity growth 548–551; static reallocation effect 538; structural change 536–537
Indian manufacturing sector: data 609; firm-level data 608–609; firm size, production function approach 616; kernel density estimators 611–612; policy initiatives and suggestions 616–623; preliminary regression results 612–614, **615**; size and productivity in 605–624; TFP growth, broad trends 605–608; total factor productivity, measuring 609–611
Indian organized manufacturing sector: coverage and the methodology, TFPG 590–591; data and variables 564–568; estimates of productivity 568–576; growth accounting approach 560–564; performance of selected states, MFG sector 591–596; productivity performance in 557–560; in selected states 585–590; state-level perspective, productivity growth 583–599; in total factor productivity 555–581
individual asset-wise capital compensations 164
Indonesia 98, 178, 179
Industrial Disputes Act 9
industrialized economy 3
industrial productivity, KLEMS format 499–506
Industrial Technology Research Institute (ITRI) 234
Industry codes **601, 602**
industry-level production 11, 53
industry-level productivity, of Taiwan 230–272
industry-level productivity growth 41
infinite accumulation, principle of 184
Infocomm Development Authority of Singapore (IDA) 278
information and communications technologies (ICTs) 11, 18, 58, 63, 72, 74, 115, 154; assets, investment 157–159; capital 63, 67, 115, 287, 288; CFM method 157; China 331–356; investment

127, 305; investment data sources **159**
innovation 53, 72; and profit-led growth 184–186
input–output tables 41, 43, 340
Institute National De la Statistique (INS) 508
Instituto de Pesquisas Econômicas Aplicadas (IPEA) 399
Instituto Tecnologico Autonomo de Mexico (ITAM) 38
intangible capital 141
intangible investment, service sector share *221*
intellectual property products 43
International Comparison Program (ICP) 84, 156
international productivity comparisons 53
International Standard Classification of Education (ISCED) 146, **147**; definitions **146**
Internet of Things 72
Investment Boom 44, 45, 49
investment climate 627–641; measures 634
investment patterns, shifting 154–172
investment price deflators 162, 164
investment-to-spending ratios 159, 160
Isaksson, A. 507
Italy 53, 115, 179
IT capital services 41
IT-producing industries 48

Japan 2, 3, 6, 7, 28, 38, 41, 67, 115, 177–180, 187, 188, 200, 333; capital, rate of return 200–224; capital/output ratio in *209*; capital share in *210*; economy 108, 223; growth accounting in *202*; intangibles, role 200–224
Japanese KLEMS (JIP) database 15, 200–224
Japan Industrial Productivity (JIP) database 39, 158
jobless growth 9, 49
jobless recovery 44, 51
Jones, P. 640
Jordan 487
Jorgenson, Dale W. 4, 5, 11, 18, 40–44, 51, 53, 86, 147, 154, 158–160, 163, 231, 236, 239, 279, 303, 331, 334, 335, 341, 347, 351, 354, 442, 499, 503, 512
Jorgenson-Fraumeni (J-F) income approach 142, 143, 145–147
Jorgensonian growth 338

Kaldor, N. 181
Kaldor-Verdoorn law 3, 15, 28, 177–193; empirical test results of **194**; empirical tests 186–192
Kalecki, M. 180
Kaleckian model 182
Kalita, Gunajit 559
Kathuria, V. 501
Kendrick arithmetic index 502, 560
Keynes, J. M. 180
Kim, Donald D. 44
Kim, J. I.275, 288
Kleinknecht, A. 187
KLEMS Conference 39, 40; *see also* World KLEMS Conference
KLEMS datasets 3, 5, 14, 16, 27, 28, 40
KLEMS framework 4–6, 10, 158, 501–503; capital input 504–505; emerging economies, productivity 505–506; gross output of industry 504; gross value-added 504; intermediate inputs 505; labor input 504; MFPG in 503
KLEMS methodology 21
KLEMS production function 6
Klenow, P. J. 141
knowledge-based assets 76
knowledge capital 219
knowledge economy 38
knowledge workers 51
Kochanova, A. 637
Korea 2, 3, 15, 28, 38, 177–180, 187, 188; growth accounting in *204*

Korean Industrial Productivity database 39
Krishna, Pravin 557–558
Krugman, Paul 26, 277, 297
Kumari, Anita 556, 557, 559

labor, PPP for 87
labor compensation 164, 304, 440
labor composition change 440
labor factor 119
labor income share 177, 303
labor inputs 46–47, 121, 134, 446, 449; constant quality index of 41; country origins of 101; price differential factors, impact of 95; quality in 110
labor-intensive exports 9
labor productivity 7, 21, 24, 461, 477–478; defined 142, 477; defining 61; growth 17, 60, 188–192; Kaldor-Verdoorn law and 177–193; rate of change in 142; total factor productivity 61
labor quality 13, 63, 133, 303–304
labor quality index 304, 376
labor quantity 63
labor reallocation effects 17, 354, 355
labor share, activities **423–426**
LA KLEMS database 38, 119, 127
LA KLEMS project 114
Landefeld, J. Steven 42
land markets 9
largest capital contribution 134
Latin America 3, 12, 436; economic growth and productivity 113–137; productivity gaps 114–118
Lau, L. J. 275, 288
Lavoie, M. 180, 182–183
Lehman Brothers 1
Levinsohn, J. 501
Levy, D. 181
Lewis, W. Arthur 301
liberalized economic policy 555
Libya 487, 489
"License-Permit" Raj 555
Lin, Y. M. 231
"Lisbon Agenda" 5
Lisbon and Barcelona Summit goal 5

local currency unit (LCU) 82, 83
Long Slump, 1973–1995 48, 51
Lopez-Acevedo, G. 640
low unemployment rates 20, 420
Lucas, Robert E. Jr. 440
Luh, Y. H. 231

macroeconomic policies 135
macroeconomic tripod 400
Maddison, Angus 63, 114, 122, 521
"Make in India" 627–641
Malmquist index 231
manufacturing sector 133
marginal costs 62
marginal productivity 164
marginal product of capital 207
Marglin, S. 183
market economy **218, 219**
market-oriented reforms 488
market services 319
Marquetti, A. 181, 187
Marx, K. 180
Mas, Matilde 38
material input 580
Mayerhauser, Nicole M. 43
McCombie, J. 187
McCulla, Stefanie H. 43
McKinsey 325
McKinsey Report 622
McMillan, M. S. 320, 322, 549
Measuring Capital 42
median labor productivity 642, 643
Mexico 3, 7, 10, 20, 38, 53, 177, 467–486; productivity determinants 470–480; TFP determinants 480–483; total factor contribution 468–470; total factor productivity 468–470
micro, small, and medium enterprises (MSMEs) 20, 621
microeconomic policies 135
Middle East and North African Economies (MENA) 490, 496, 510
mineral rents 439
mining industries 40

Ministry of Planning and International Cooperation (MPIC) 509
Mishra, R. K. 615
Mitra, Arup 616
Mitra, Devashish 557, 558
Miyagawa, Tsutomu 201, 211, 223
modified-GEAD method 410, 412
"modified" growth accounting 119
Moore, M. 627
Morocco 10, 22, 487–490; growth and productivity in 507–511; macroeconomic profile of 498–499
multifactor productivity (MFP) 21, 22, 143, 147, 148, 313, 314, 317, 439, 440, 442, 452; Arab world 487–528; computation, methods 500–501; data requirements 504–505; measuring 500
Murase, Hideaki 201

Naastepad, C. W. M. 187
Nagaraj, P. 615
National Accounts investment data 156
National Accounts Statistics (NAS) 367, 391
national income and product accounts (NIPAs) 42–44
National Institute of Statistics and Geography (INEGI) 21, 38, 467, 468
national manufacturing investment zones (NIMZs) 619
National Manufacturing Policy (NMP) 25, 619
National Science and Technology Project (NSTP) 234
national statistics institutes (NSI) 156
neoclassical theory 181
Netherlands 37, 53
New Economy boom economy 150
newly industrialized countries (NICs) 275, **276**; TFPG *vs.* Hong Kong **296**

New World Economic Order 29
Ng Wai Choong 287
non-ICT capital 63, 65, 115, 154
non-ICT investment/GDP ratio 165, 166, *167*
non-IT sector 45, 48
non observed economy (NOE) 439
North Africa 489
North American Industry Classification System (NAICS) 44, 45
Noughties, story of 555–581

OECD Human Capital Project 146
OECD Productivity Manual 41, 42
Olly, G. S. 501
O'Mahony, M. 332
Onaran, Ö. 177, 179, 183, 187, 192
Organisation for Economic Cooperation and Development (OECD) countries 2, 4, 40, 84, 141, 536; empirical results for 186–188
organizational investments 73
output growth: country origins **99**; defined 247

Pakes, A. 501
Pakistan 108
Parkinson, M. 441
Penn World Table (PWT) 83, 155, 157
per capita economic growth 363
per capita GDP 108, 169, 277, 297
per capita income 58, 59, 62
Peri, G. 75
perpetual inventory method (PIM) approach 162, 239, 306
personal income polarization 178
Petrin, A. 501
Philippines 109, 160
Piketty, T. 178, 180, 181, 184, 186
post and telecommunications 270, **271**
post-Kaleckian Model *182*
Postwar Recovery 48

Power, L. 640
price-differential factors 85
price index 290
price of labor service 476–477; defined 476
procyclical productivity 123–127
producer price index (PPI) matrix 340
production costs 21
production possibility frontier (PPF) model 279
productivity 10; by country 82–83; in country group 84–86; in global economy 58–78; understanding, growth accounting 60–63
productivity accounts, Argentina: economic growth 440; industry origins 441–442; utilization effects, adjustment 441
productivity and growth, in Caribbean 118–123; methodology 118–119
productivity determinants, Mexico 470–480; capital productivity 473–474; capital service price 472–473; income per unit of capital 474–476; labor productivity 477–478; price of labor service 476–477; unit labor cost 478–480
productivity determinants, sectoral aspects 127–133; investment by asset type 127–128; proximate determinants 128–133
productivity gains 338
productivity growth 50, 53, 439; in Asia 81–111
productivity–investment nexus 28
productivity losses 135
productivity measurement 10–14; framework for 40–44
productivity slowdown: in Brazil 398–422
profit-led growth 180–186; and innovation 184–186
profit rate 15

Programme for International Assessment of Adult Competencies (PIAAC) 141
Programme for International Student Assessment (PISA) 141
proprietorship variable 640
prototype industry-level production account 44–53
proximate determinants of growth: performance of 123–127
"proximate" factors of growth 121
purchasing power parities (PPPs) 12, 81–85, 109, 115; for capital 86–87; for capital inputs 88–89, 91; for labor 87; for labor inputs 88–89, 91
Pyo, Hak K. 177

quantitative restrictions (QRs) 365

rate of return, capital 207–211; in chemical industry *214*; in information service industry *216*; marginal 212, 213; movements in *208*; in retail industry *215*; in transportation equipment industry *215*; variances and relative standard deviations **214**
"real" GDP 83
reallocation effect 338, 339
real value-added growth rates 316
recession effect 70–72
regional economic growth 90
rental prices 164
Report on Employment-Unemployment Survey 388
research and development (R&D) 217, 219, 223, 224, 234–235
resource utilization efficiency 123, 136
Rocha, C. 410
Rodriguez-Clare, A. 141
Rodrik, Dani 320, 322, 363–364, 549
Rosenthal, Steven 44
Rowthorn, B. 183

Russia 2, 3, 7, 17, 28, 40, 158; aggregate labor productivity growth 315–318; capital intensity 324–326; convergence, in industries 324–326; economy *315*, 316, *317*, 319; labor productivity growth 318–324; labor reallocation in *321*; multifactor productivity 324–326; natural gas, catching up and informality 313–328; since 1995 313–328; structural change and informality 318–324

Sachs, Jeffery 214, 223
Sala-i-Martin, Xavier 185
Samuels, J. D. 44, 145, 148
Schmitz, H. 627
Schmookler, J. 185
Schreyer, Paul 41, 44, 63, 163, 332, 439
Schumpeter, J. A. 185
second law of capitalism 184
secular stagnation hypothesis 73
Shanghai capitalists 293
Shapiro, M. D. 441
Sharma, C. 615
shift-share analysis, Brazil 409–420; brief review 409–411; labor productivity growth 413–420; methodology 411–413
"shift-share" analysis 20
Singapore 3, 7, 17; business sector, vibrancy 292; data and growth accounting framework 278–281; economic growth 275–302; external markets, dependency 289–292; government policy 292; growth patterns 281–283; *vs*. Hong Kong *294*, *295*; interventionist policy 281; low TFPG in 289–292; measurement, insights and projection 275–302; output and labor productivity growth 283–288; productivity and output growth **299**; projecting, growth 2009–19 period 297–300; resilience 281; TFPG by Hsieh 293–297; TFPG in 288–297; *vs*. United States **297**; vulnerability 281
Singapore–US exchange rate 306
Sivasubramonian, S. 364
skill-biased technology change effect 450
Solow, Robert M. 4, 60, 185, 313, 512
Solow geometric index 502
Solow geometric Index 560
Solow residual 60, 62
South Africa 177–179, 187
Southeast Asia 98
South Korea 275, 333
Soviet Union 40, 277
Spain 115
Squeff, G. 410
Sri Lanka 370
Srivastava, Vivek 557, 558
Stehrer, Robert 38
Stiglitz, J. E. 185
Stiroh, Kevin J. 316, 334, 341, 351, 354
Stockhammer, E. 180, 182, 183
Storm, S. 187
Strassner, Erich H. 43
Strazicich, M. C. 506
Subramanian, Arvind 363–364
Sudan 489
Summers, Lawrence 200
Sweden 53
System of National Accounts (SNA) 154–155, 410
System of National Accounts, 2008 44
Szirmai, A. 410

Taiwan 3, 7, 16, 28, 275; cross-period comparisons 244–247; economic liberalization and internationalization 233–234; economic performance of 239–251; gross output growth, industry level 252–271; growth and productivity accounts 236–238; HSIP establishment 234–235; industrial development

233; industrial development strategies 232; industry-level productivity of 230–272; industry output growth, cross-period comparisons 257–271; industry output sources, sample period 252–257; industry structural change in 239–244; ITRI and NSTP 234; output growth, industry level 247; semiconductor industry promotion 235–236; Taiwan KLEMS database 238–239; tax incentives 235; TFP growth, industry level 247–251; value-added growth 244–247
Taiwan Economic Miracle 230
Taiwan KLEMS database 230–272
Taiwan Semiconductor Manufacturing Company (TSMC) 236
Takii, S. 640
Tan, H. W. 640
Tarassow, A. 187
Taylor, L. 180, 183
TCB database 512–517
Technical Change and Aggregate Production function 4
temporary shocks 126
Tequila Effect 468
terrorist attack, 9/11 283
TFP determinants, Mexico 480–483; primary sector 480–481; secondary sector 482–483; third sector 483
Thwaites, Gregory 201
Timmer, Marcel P. 5, 11, 37, 53, 326, 410, 503
Tinbergen, J. 4, 512
Toh, Mun Heng 287
Tornquist aggregation 438
Törnqvist index 63, 304, 335, 439, 440, 502, 522, 560
Total Contribution Factor (TCF) 467, 469
Total Economy Growth Accounting database 158
total factor productivity (TFP) 7, 11, 13, 19, 24, 25, 29, 65, 113, 118, 275–302; of Asian economy 81; Singapore 275–302; in Southeast Asia 109
total factor productivity growth (TFPG) 16, 25, 26, 28, 60, 62, 65, 67, 70, 85, 90, 275, 363, 584; country origins of **96–97**, *102*; defined 82; emerging markets, role of 73–74; measurement issues 74–75; pace of technology 72; policy and regulatory environment 74; recession effect 70–72; secular stagnation hypothesis 72–73; slowing trend in 70–75
trade liberalization 7, 556
"traditional" growth accounting 119
TRAD method 410
transition economies 53
Triplett, Jack E. 460
Trivedi, Pushpa 557, 558
Tsao, Y. 275, 288
Tunisia 10, 22, 487–490; growth and productivity in 507–511; macroeconomic profile of 498–499
Turkey 177

under-consumption theory 180
UNDESA research project 83
Unel, Bulent 557, 558
unemployment 70, 450
UNIDO industrial database 507, 517–518
UNIDO productivity database 517–521
United Kingdom 2, 53, 115, 177
United Microelectronic Corporation (UMC) 236
United Nations' *System of National Accounts 2008* 42
United States 2, 38, 41, 53, 67, 74, 86, 87, 154, 177–179, 187, 331, 469; constant-quality price deflators 163; growth accounting in *203*; investment-to-spending ratio 159; prototype industry-level

production account 44–53; *vs.* Singapore **297**
unit labor cost 478–480; defined 478
US economic growth 28, 53; sources of 52
US economy 41, 42, 45, 48
user-cost approach 336
US hedonic price index 306
utilization effect 446

value-added coefficient 442
value-added concept 336
Van Ark, Bart 332, 460
van Drachenfels, C. 627
Vergeer, R. 187
Virmani, M. A. 556–557, 559
Voskoboynikov, Ilya Borisovich 326
Vu, Khuong Minh 5, 154, 158–160

wage-led growth 179, 180–186; Kaldor-Verdoorn Law and 180–184
wage share 177, 178
Washington consensus 496
"weightless" economy 74
Weil, D. N. 186
well-developed market system 339
Western Sahara 489
Wholesale Price Index (WPI) 591
Wilson, Daniel J. 154
women: in household production 150
worker skills 60
working-age population 62
workpackages, Argentina 436–442; capital, produced 437–438; labor and human capital 439–440; natural capital 438–439; output and intermediate input accounts 436–437; productivity accounts 440–442
World Bank 84, 145, 627
World Bank Enterprise Surveys (WBES) 27, 630; data cleaning 632–633; on India 631–632
World Economic Outlook 1, 6
world economy growth 37–55
World Information Technology and Services Alliance (WITSA) 14, 158, 159, 171; ICT spending data 159–161; investment deriving from 159–161
World Input-Output Database (WIOD) 39, 40
World KLEMS Conference 38, 43, 44
World Trade Organization (WTO) 40, 73
Wright 583
Wu, Harry 63

Yemen 487
Young, A. 275, 277, 288

Zeira, J. 186